C# 10 and .NET 6 – Mod Cross-Platform Development

Sixth Edition

Build apps, websites, and services with ASP.NET Core 6, Blazor, and EF Core 6 using Visual Studio 2022 and Visual Studio Code

Mark J. Price

BIRMINGHAM—MUMBAI

C# 10 and .NET 6 – Modern Cross-Platform Development

Sixth Edition

Producer: Suman Sen

Acquisition Editor – Peer Reviews: Saby Dsilva

Project Editor: Amit Ramadas

Content Development Editor: Bhavesh Amin

Copy Editor: Safis Editing

Technical Editor: Aniket Shetty

Proofreader: Safis Editing

Indexer: Pratik Shirodkar

Presentation Designer: Pranit Padwal

First published: March 2016

Second edition: March 2017

Third edition: November 2017

Fourth edition: October 2019

Fifth edition: November 2020

Sixth edition: November 2021

Production reference: 1021121

Published by Packt Publishing Ltd.
Livery Place
35 Livery Street
Birmingham
B3 2PB, UK.

ISBN 978-1-80107-736-1

www.packt.com

Contributors

About the author

Mark J. Price is a Microsoft Specialist: Programming in C# and Architecting Microsoft Azure Solutions, with over 20 years' experience.

Microsoft
CERTIFIED
Solutions Developer

App Builder

Microsoft
Specialist

Programming in C#

Since 1993, he has passed more than 80 Microsoft programming exams and specializes in preparing others to pass them. Between 2001 and 2003, Mark was employed to write official courseware for Microsoft in Redmond, USA. His team wrote the first training courses for C# while it was still an early alpha version. While with Microsoft, he taught "train-the-trainer" classes to get other MCTs up to speed on C# and .NET. Currently, Mark creates and delivers training courses for Optimizely's Digital Experience Platform (DXP). Mark holds a BSc. Hons. Degree in computer science.

About the reviewers

Damir Arh has many years of experience with software development and maintenance; from complex enterprise software projects to modern consumer-oriented mobile applications. Although he has worked with a wide spectrum of different languages, his favorite language remains C#. In his drive toward better development processes, he is a proponent of test-driven development, continuous integration, and continuous deployment. He shares his knowledge by speaking at local user groups and conferences, blogging, and writing articles. He has received the prestigious Microsoft MVP award for developer technologies 10 times in a row. In his spare time, he's always on the move: hiking, geocaching, running, and rock climbing.

Geovanny Alzate Sandoval is a system engineer from Medellín, Colombia, and enjoys everything related to software development, new technologies, design patterns, and software architecture. He has 14+ years of experience working as a developer, technical leader, and software architect mostly with Microsoft technologies. He loves contributing to OSS, he has made contributions to Asp.Net Core SignalR, Polly, and Apollo Server to mention a few. He's also the co-author of Simmy, an OSS library for chaos engineering for .NET based on Polly. He's also a DDD lover and a cloud enthusiast. In addition, he's a .Net Foundation member and a co-organizer of MDE.NET community, which is a community for .NET developers in Medellín/Colombia. In recent years, he has been focused on building distributed and reliable systems using distributed architectures and cloud technologies. Last but not least, he strongly believes in teamwork, as he says: "I wouldn't be here if I wouldn't have learned that much from all the talented people I've worked with."

Geovanny currently works for Curbit, which is a US startup based in California, as Director of Engineering.

Table of Contents

Preface

There are programming books that are thousands of pages long that aim to be comprehensive references for the C# language, .NET libraries, app models like websites, services, and desktop, and mobile apps.

This book is different. It is concise and aims to be a brisk, fun read packed with practical hands-on walkthroughs of each subject. The breadth of the overarching narrative comes at the cost of some depth, but you will find many signposts to explore further if you wish.

This book is simultaneously a step-by-step guide to learning modern C# proven practices using cross-platform .NET and a brief introduction to the main types of practical applications that can be built with them. This book is best for beginners to C# and .NET, or programmers who have worked with C# in the past but feel left behind by the changes in the past few years.

If you already have experience with older versions of the C# language, then in the first section of *Chapter 2, Speaking C#*, you can review tables of the new language features and jump straight to them.

If you already have experience with older versions of the .NET libraries, then in the first section of *Chapter 7, Packaging and Distributing .NET Types*, you can review tables of the new library features and jump straight to them.

I will point out the cool corners and gotchas of C# and .NET, so you can impress colleagues and get productive fast. Rather than slowing down and boring some readers by explaining every little thing, I will assume that you are smart enough to Google an explanation for topics that are related but not necessary to include in a beginner-to-intermediate guide that has limited space in the printed book.

Where to find the code solutions

You can download solutions for the step-by-step guided tasks and exercises from the GitHub repository at the following link: `https://github.com/markjprice/cs10dotnet6`.

If you don't know how, then I provide instructions on how to do this at the end of *Chapter 1, Hello, C#! Welcome, .NET!*.

What this book covers

Chapter 1, Hello, C#! Welcome, .NET!, is about setting up your development environment and using either Visual Studio or Visual Studio Code to create the simplest application possible with C# and .NET. For simplified console apps, you will see the use of the top-level program feature introduced in C# 9. For learning how to write simple language constructs and library features, you will see the use of .NET Interactive Notebooks. You will also learn about some good places to look for help and ways to contact me to get help with an issue or give me feedback to improve the book and future editions through its GitHub repository.

Chapter 2, Speaking C#, introduces the versions of C# and has tables showing which versions introduced new features. I explain the grammar and vocabulary that you will use every day to write the source code for your applications. In particular, you will learn how to declare and work with variables of different types.

Chapter 3, Controlling Flow, Converting Types, and Handling Exceptions, covers using operators to perform simple actions on variables, including comparisons, writing code that makes decisions, pattern matching in C# 7 to C# 10, repeating a block of statements, and converting between types. It also covers writing code defensively to handle exceptions when they inevitably occur.

Chapter 4, Writing, Debugging, and Testing Functions, is about following the **Don't Repeat Yourself (DRY)** principle by writing reusable functions using both imperative and functional implementation styles. You will also learn how to use debugging tools to track down and remove bugs, monitoring your code while it executes to diagnose problems, and rigorously testing your code to remove bugs and ensure stability and reliability before it gets deployed into production.

Chapter 5, Building Your Own Types with Object-Oriented Programming, discusses all the different categories of members that a type can have, including fields to store data and methods to perform actions. You will use **object-oriented programming (OOP)** concepts, such as aggregation and encapsulation. You will learn about language features such as tuple syntax support and out variables, default literals, and inferred tuple names, as well as how to define and work with immutable types using the record keyword, init-only properties, and with expressions introduced in C# 9.

Chapter 6, Implementing Interfaces and Inheriting Classes, explains deriving new types from existing ones using OOP. You will learn how to define operators and local functions, delegates and events, how to implement interfaces about base and derived classes, how to override a member of a type, how to use polymorphism, how to create extension methods, how to cast between classes in an inheritance hierarchy, and about the big change in C# 8 with the introduction of nullable reference types.

Chapter 7, Packaging and Distributing .NET Types, introduces the versions of .NET and has tables showing which versions introduced new library features, and then presents .NET types that are compliant with .NET Standard and how they relate to C#. You will learn how to write and compile code on any of the supported operating systems: Windows, macOS, and Linux variants. You will learn how to package, deploy, and distribute your own apps and libraries.

Chapter 8, Working with Common .NET Types, discusses the types that allow your code to perform common practical tasks, such as manipulating numbers and text, dates and times, storing items in collections, working with the network and manipulating images, and implementing internationalization.

Chapter 9, Working with Files, Streams, and Serialization, covers interacting with the filesystem, reading and writing to files and streams, text encoding, and serialization formats like JSON and XML, including the improved functionality and performance of the System.Text.Json classes.

Chapter 10, Working with Data Using Entity Framework Core, explains reading and writing to relational databases, such as Microsoft SQL Server and SQLite, using the **object-relational mapping (ORM)** technology named **Entity Framework Core (EF Core)**. You will learn how to define entity models that map to existing tables in a database, as well as how to define Code First models that can create the tables and database at runtime.

Chapter 11, Querying and Manipulating Data Using LINQ, teaches you about **Language INtegrated Queries (LINQs)** — language extensions that add the ability to work with sequences of items and filter, sort, and project them into different outputs. You will learn about the special capabilities of **Parallel LINQ (PLINQ)** and LINQ to XML.

Chapter 12, Improving Performance and Scalability Using Multitasking, discusses allowing multiple actions to occur at the same time to improve performance, scalability, and user productivity. You will learn about the async Main feature and how to use types in the System.Diagnostics namespace to monitor your code to measure performance and efficiency.

Chapter 13, Introducing Practical Applications of C# and .NET, introduces you to the types of cross-platform applications that can be built using C# and .NET. You will also build an EF Core model to represent the Northwind database that will be used throughout the rest of the chapters in the book.

Chapter 14, Building Websites Using ASP.NET Core Razor Pages, is about learning the basics of building websites with a modern HTTP architecture on the server side using ASP.NET Core. You will learn how to implement the ASP.NET Core feature known as Razor Pages, which simplifies creating dynamic web pages for small websites, and about building the HTTP request and response pipeline.

Chapter 15, Building Websites Using the Model-View-Controller Pattern, is about learning how to build large, complex websites in a way that is easy to unit test and manage with teams of programmers using ASP.NET Core MVC. You will learn about startup configuration, authentication, routes, models, views, and controllers.

Chapter 16, Building and Consuming Web Services, explains building backend REST architecture web services using the ASP.NET Core Web API and how to properly consume them using factory-instantiated HTTP clients.

Chapter 17, Building User Interfaces Using Blazor, introduces how to build web user interface components using Blazor that can be executed either on the server side or inside the client-side web browser. You will see the differences between Blazor Server and Blazor WebAssembly and how to build components that are easier to switch between the two hosting models.

Three bonus online chapters complete this bumper edition. You can read the following chapters and the appendix at `https://static.packt-cdn.com/downloads/9781801077361_Bonus_Content.pdf`:

Chapter 18, Building and Consuming Specialized Services, introduces you to building services using gRPC, implementing real-time communications between server and client using SignalR, exposing an EF Core model using OData, and hosting functions in the cloud that respond to triggers using Azure Functions.

Chapter 19, Building Mobile and Desktop Apps Using .NET MAUI, introduces you to building cross-platform mobile and desktop apps for Android, iOS, macOS, and Windows. You will learn the basics of XAML, which can be used to define the user interface for a graphical app.

Chapter 20, Protecting Your Data and Applications, is about protecting your data from being viewed by malicious users using encryption, and from being manipulated or corrupted using hashing and signing. You will also learn about authentication and authorization to protect applications from unauthorized users.

Appendix, Answers to the Test Your Knowledge Questions, has the answers to the test questions at the end of each chapter.

What you need for this book

You can develop and deploy C# and .NET apps using Visual Studio Code on many platforms, including Windows, macOS, and many varieties of Linux.

An operating system that supports Visual Studio Code and an internet connection is all you need to complete all but one chapter.

If you prefer to use Visual Studio for Windows or macOS, or a third-party tool like JetBrains Rider, then you can.

You will need macOS to build the iOS app in *Chapter 19, Building Mobile and Desktop Apps Using .NET MAUI,* because you must have macOS and Xcode to compile iOS apps.

Downloading the color images of this book

We also provide you with a PDF file that has color images of the screenshots and diagrams used in this book. The color images will help you better understand the changes in the output.

You can download this file from `https://static.packt-cdn.com/downloads/9781801077361_ColorImages.pdf`.

Conventions

In this book, you will find a number of text styles that distinguish between different kinds of information. Here are some examples of these styles and an explanation of their meaning.

CodeInText: Indicates code words in text, database table names, folder names, filenames, file extensions, pathnames, dummy URLs, user input, and Twitter handles. For example; "The Controllers, Models, and Views folders contain ASP.NET Core classes and the .cshtml files for execution on the server."

A block of code is set as follows:

```
// storing items at index positions
names[0] = "Kate";
names[1] = "Jack";
names[2] = "Rebecca";
names[3] = "Tom";
```

When we wish to draw your attention to a particular part of a code block, the relevant lines or items are highlighted:

```
// storing items at index positions
names[0] = "Kate";
names[1] = "Jack";
names[2] = "Rebecca";
names[3] = "Tom";
```

Any command-line input or output is written as follows:

```
dotnet new console
```

Bold: Indicates a new **term**, an important **word**, or words that you see on the screen, for example, in menus or dialog boxes. For example: "Clicking on the **Next** button moves you to the next screen."

 Important notes and links to external sources of further reading appear in a box like this.

 Good Practice: Recommendations for how to program like an expert appear like this.

Get in touch

Feedback from our readers is always welcome.

General feedback: If you have questions about any aspect of this book, mention the book title in the subject of your message and email us at customercare@packtpub.com.

Errata: Although we have taken every care to ensure the accuracy of our content, mistakes do happen. If you have found a mistake in this book, we would be grateful if you would report this to us. Please visit, www.packtpub.com/support/errata, selecting your book, clicking on the Errata Submission Form link, and entering the details.

Piracy: If you come across any illegal copies of our works in any form on the internet, we would be grateful if you would provide us with the location address or website name. Please contact us at copyright@packt.com with a link to the material.

If you are interested in becoming an author: If there is a topic that you have expertise in and you are interested in either writing or contributing to a book, please visit authors.packtpub.com.

Share your thoughts

Once you've read *C# 10 and .NET 6 - Modern Cross-Platform Development, Sixth Edition*, we'd love to hear your thoughts! Scan the QR code below to go straight to the Amazon review page for this book and share your feedback.

https://packt.link/r/1801077363

Your review is important to us and the tech community and will help us make sure we're delivering excellent quality content.

01

Hello, C#! Welcome, .NET!

In this first chapter, the goals are setting up your development environment, understanding the similarities and differences between modern .NET, .NET Core, .NET Framework, Mono, Xamarin, and .NET Standard, creating the simplest application possible with C# 10 and .NET 6 using various code editors, and then discovering good places to look for help.

The GitHub repository for this book has solutions using full application projects for all code tasks and notebooks when possible:

https://github.com/markjprice/cs10dotnet6

Simply press the . (dot) key or change .com to .dev in the link above to change the GitHub repository into a live editor using Visual Studio Code for the Web, as shown in *Figure 1.1*:

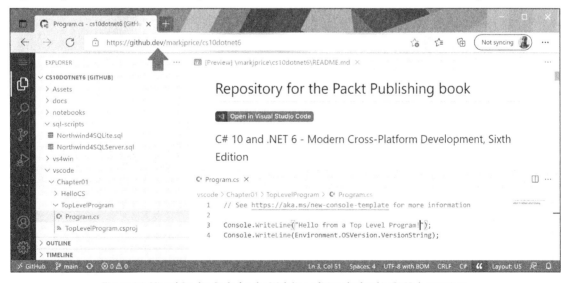

Figure 1.1: Visual Studio Code for the Web live editing the book's GitHub repository

---

This is great to run alongside your chosen code editor as you work through the book's coding tasks. You can compare your code to the solution code and easily copy and paste parts if needed.

Throughout this book, I use the term **modern .NET** to refer to .NET 6 and its predecessors like .NET 5 that come from .NET Core. I use the term **legacy .NET** to refer to .NET Framework, Mono, Xamarin, and .NET Standard. Modern .NET is a unification of those legacy platforms and standards.

After this first chapter, the book can be divided into three parts: first, the grammar and vocabulary of the C# language; second, the types available in .NET for building app features; and third, examples of common cross-platform apps you can build using C# and .NET.

Most people learn complex topics best by imitation and repetition rather than reading a detailed explanation of the theory; therefore, I will not overload you with detailed explanations of every step throughout this book. The idea is to get you to write some code and see it run.

You don't need to know all the nitty-gritty details immediately. That will be something that comes with time as you build your own apps and go beyond what any book can teach you.

In the words of Samuel Johnson, author of the English dictionary in 1755, I have committed "a few wild blunders, and risible absurdities, from which no work of such multiplicity is free." I take sole responsibility for these and hope you appreciate the challenge of my attempt to lash the wind by writing this book about rapidly evolving technologies like C# and .NET, and the apps that you can build with them.

This first chapter covers the following topics:

- Setting up your development environment
- Understanding .NET
- Building console apps using Visual Studio 2022
- Building console apps using Visual Studio Code
- Exploring code using .NET Interactive Notebooks
- Reviewing the folders and files for projects
- Making good use of the GitHub repository for this book
- Looking for help

Setting up your development environment

Before you start programming, you'll need a code editor for C#. Microsoft has a family of code editors and **Integrated Development Environments (IDEs)**, which include:

- Visual Studio 2022 for Windows
- Visual Studio 2022 for Mac

- Visual Studio Code for Windows, Mac, or Linux
- GitHub Codespaces

Third parties have created their own C# code editors, for example, JetBrains Rider.

Choosing the appropriate tool and application type for learning

What is the best tool and application type for learning C# and .NET?

When learning, the best tool is one that helps you write code and configuration but does not hide what is really happening. IDEs provide graphical user interfaces that are friendly to use, but what are they doing for you underneath? A more basic code editor that is closer to the action while providing help to write your code is better while you are learning.

Having said that, you can make the argument that the best tool is the one you are already familiar with or that you or your team will use as your daily development tool. For that reason, I want you to be free to choose any C# code editor or IDE to complete the coding tasks in this book, including Visual Studio Code, Visual Studio for Windows, Visual Studio for Mac, or even JetBrains Rider.

In the third edition of this book, I gave detailed step-by-step instructions for both Visual Studio for Windows and Visual Studio Code for all coding tasks. Unfortunately, that got messy and confusing quickly. In this sixth edition, I give detailed step-by-step instructions for how to create multiple projects in both Visual Studio 2022 for Windows and Visual Studio Code only in *Chapter 1*. After that, I give names of projects and general instructions that work with all tools so you can use whichever tool you prefer.

The best application type for learning the C# language constructs and many of the .NET libraries is one that does not distract with unnecessary application code. For example, there is no need to create an entire Windows desktop application or a website just to learn how to write a `switch` statement.

For that reason, I believe the best method for learning the C# and .NET topics in *Chapters 1* to *12* is to build console applications. Then, in *Chapter 13* to *19* onward, you will build websites, services, and graphical desktop and mobile apps.

Pros and cons of the .NET Interactive Notebooks extension

Another benefit of Visual Studio Code is the .NET Interactive Notebooks extension. This extension provides an easy and safe place to write simple code snippets. It enables you to create a single notebook file that mixes "cells" of Markdown (richly formatted text) and code using C# and other related languages, such as PowerShell, F#, and SQL (for databases).

However, .NET Interactive Notebooks does have some limitations:

- They cannot read input from the user, for example, you cannot use `ReadLine` or `ReadKey`.
- They cannot have arguments passed to them.
- They do not allow you to define your own namespaces.
- They do not have any debugging tools (but these are coming in the future).

Using Visual Studio Code for cross-platform development

The most modern and lightweight code editor to choose from, and the only one from Microsoft that is cross-platform, is Microsoft Visual Studio Code. It can run on all common operating systems, including Windows, macOS, and many varieties of Linux, including Red Hat Enterprise Linux (RHEL) and Ubuntu.

Visual Studio Code is a good choice for modern cross-platform development because it has an extensive and growing set of extensions to support many languages beyond C#.

Being cross-platform and lightweight, it can be installed on all platforms that your apps will be deployed to for quick bug fixes and so on. Choosing Visual Studio Code means a developer can use a cross-platform code editor to develop cross-platform apps.

Visual Studio Code has strong support for web development, although it currently has weak support for mobile and desktop development.

Visual Studio Code is supported on ARM processors so that you can develop on Apple Silicon computers and Raspberry Pi.

Visual Studio Code is by far the most popular integrated development environment, with over 70% of professional developers selecting it in the Stack Overflow 2021 survey.

Using GitHub Codespaces for development in the cloud

GitHub Codespaces is a fully configured development environment based on Visual Studio Code that can be spun up in an environment hosted in the cloud and accessed through any web browser. It supports Git repos, extensions, and a built-in command-line interface so you can edit, run, and test from any device.

Using Visual Studio for Mac for general development

Microsoft Visual Studio 2022 for Mac can create most types of applications, including console apps, websites, web services, desktop, and mobile apps.

To compile apps for Apple operating systems like iOS to run on devices like the iPhone and iPad, you must have Xcode, which only runs on macOS.

Using Visual Studio for Windows for general development

Microsoft Visual Studio 2022 for Windows can create most types of applications, including console apps, websites, web services, desktop, and mobile apps. Although you can use Visual Studio 2022 for Windows with its Xamarin extensions to write a cross-platform mobile app, you still need macOS and Xcode to compile it.

It only runs on Windows, version 7 SP1 or later. You must run it on Windows 10 or Windows 11 to create **Universal Windows Platform** (**UWP**) apps that are installed from the Microsoft Store and run in a sandbox to protect your computer.

What I used

To write and test the code for this book, I used the following hardware:

- HP Spectre (Intel) laptop
- Apple Silicon Mac mini (M1) desktop
- Raspberry Pi 400 (ARM v8) desktop

And I used the following software:

- Visual Studio Code on:
    - macOS on an Apple Silicon Mac mini (M1) desktop
    - Windows 10 on an HP Spectre (Intel) laptop
    - Ubuntu 64 on a Raspberry Pi 400
- Visual Studio 2022 for Windows on:
    - Windows 10 on an HP Spectre (Intel) laptop
- Visual Studio 2022 for Mac on:
    - macOS on an Apple Silicon Mac mini (M1) desktop

I hope that you have access to a variety of hardware and software too, because seeing the differences in platforms deepens your understanding of development challenges, although any one of the above combinations is enough to learn the fundamentals of C# and .NET and how to build practical apps and websites.

 More Information: You can learn how to write code with C# and .NET using a Raspberry Pi 400 with Ubuntu Desktop 64-bit by reading an extra article that I wrote at the following link: https://github.com/markjprice/ cs9dotnet5-extras/blob/main/raspberry-pi-ubuntu64/README.md.

Deploying cross-platform

Your choice of code editor and operating system for development does not limit where your code gets deployed.

.NET 6 supports the following platforms for deployment:

- **Windows**: Windows 7 SP1, or later. Windows 10 version 1607, or later, including Windows 11. Windows Server 2012 R2 SP1, or later. Nano Server version 1809, or later.
- **Mac**: macOS Mojave (version 10.14), or later.
- **Linux**: Alpine Linux 3.13, or later. CentOS 7, or later. Debian 10, or later. Fedora 32, or later. openSUSE 15, or later. Red Hat Enterprise Linux (RHEL) 7, or later. SUSE Enterprise Linux 12 SP2, or later. Ubuntu 16.04, 18.04, 20.04, or later.
- **Android**: API 21, or later.
- **iOS**: 10, or later.

Windows ARM64 support in .NET 5 and later means you can develop on, and deploy to, Windows ARM devices like Microsoft Surface Pro X. But developing on an Apple M1 Mac using Parallels and a Windows 10 ARM virtual machine is apparently twice as fast!

Downloading and installing Visual Studio 2022 for Windows

Many professional Microsoft developers use Visual Studio 2022 for Windows in their day-to-day development work. Even if you choose to use Visual Studio Code to complete the coding tasks in this book, you might want to familiarize yourself with Visual Studio 2022 for Windows too.

If you do not have a Windows computer, then you can skip this section and continue to the next section where you will download and install Visual Studio Code on macOS or Linux.

Since October 2014, Microsoft has made a professional quality edition of Visual Studio for Windows available to students, open source contributors, and individuals for free. It is called Community Edition. Any of the editions are suitable for this book. If you have not already installed it, let's do so now:

1. Download Microsoft Visual Studio 2022 version 17.0 or later for Windows from the following link: `https://visualstudio.microsoft.com/downloads/`.
2. Start the installer.
3. On the **Workloads** tab, select the following:
    - **ASP.NET and web development**
    - **Azure development**
    - **.NET desktop development**
    - **Desktop development with C++**

- **Universal Windows Platform development**
- **Mobile development with .NET**

4. On the **Individual components** tab, in the **Code tools** section, select the following:
   - **Class Designer**
   - **Git for Windows**
   - **PreEmptive Protection - Dotfuscator**

5. Click **Install** and wait for the installer to acquire the selected software and install it.

6. When the installation is complete, click **Launch**.

7. The first time that you run Visual Studio, you will be prompted to sign in. If you have a Microsoft account, you can use that account. If you don't, then register for a new one at the following link: `https://signup.live.com/`.

8. The first time that you run Visual Studio, you will be prompted to configure your environment. For **Development Settings**, choose **Visual C#**. For the color theme, I chose **Blue**, but you can choose whatever tickles your fancy.

9. If you want to customize your keyboard shortcuts, navigate to **Tools | Options...**, and then select the **Keyboard** section.

Microsoft Visual Studio for Windows keyboard shortcuts

In this book, I will avoid showing keyboard shortcuts since they are often customized. Where they are consistent across code editors and commonly used, I will try to show them. If you want to identify and customize your keyboard shortcuts, then you can, as shown at the following link: `https://docs.microsoft.com/en-us/visualstudio/ide/identifying-and-customizing-keyboard-shortcuts-in-visual-studio`.

Downloading and installing Visual Studio Code

Visual Studio Code has rapidly improved over the past couple of years and has pleasantly surprised Microsoft with its popularity. If you are brave and like to live on the bleeding edge, then there is an Insiders edition, which is a daily build of the next version.

Even if you plan to only use Visual Studio 2022 for Windows for development, I recommend that you download and install Visual Studio Code and try the coding tasks in this chapter using it, and then decide if you want to stick with just using Visual Studio 2022 for the rest of the book.

Let's now download and install Visual Studio Code, the .NET SDK, and the C# and .NET Interactive Notebooks extensions:

1. Download and install either the Stable build or the Insiders edition of Visual Studio Code from the following link: `https://code.visualstudio.com/`.

More Information: If you need more help installing Visual Studio Code, you can read the official setup guide at the following link: https://code.visualstudio.com/docs/setup/setup-overview.

2. Download and install the .NET SDKs for versions 3.1, 5.0, and 6.0 from the following link: https://www.microsoft.com/net/download.

 To fully learn how to control .NET SDKs, we need multiple versions installed. .NET Core 3.1, .NET 5.0, and .NET 6.0 are the three currently supported versions. You can safely install multiple ones side by side. You will learn how to target the one you want throughout this book.

3. To install the C# extension, you must first launch the Visual Studio Code application.

4. In Visual Studio Code, click the **Extensions** icon or navigate to **View | Extensions**.

5. C# is one of the most popular extensions available, so you should see it at the top of the list, or you can enter C# in the search box.

6. Click **Install** and wait for supporting packages to download and install.

7. Enter .NET Interactive in the search box to find the **.NET Interactive Notebooks** extension.

8. Click **Install** and wait for it to install.

Installing other extensions

In later chapters of this book, you will use more extensions. If you want to install them now, all the extensions that we will use are shown in the following table:

Extension name and identifier	Description
C# for Visual Studio Code (powered by OmniSharp) ms-dotnettools.csharp	C# editing support, including syntax highlighting, IntelliSense, Go to Definition, Find All References, debugging support for .NET, and support for csproj projects on Windows, macOS, and Linux.
.NET Interactive Notebooks ms-dotnettools.dotnet-interactive-vscode	This extension adds support for using .NET Interactive in a Visual Studio Code notebook. It has a dependency on the Jupyter extension (ms-toolsai.jupyter).
MSBuild project tools tinytoy.msbuild-project-tools	Provides IntelliSense for MSBuild project files, including autocomplete for <PackageReference> elements.
REST Client humao.rest-client	Send an HTTP request and view the response directly in Visual Studio Code.

ILSpy .NET Decompiler `icsharpcode.ilspy-vscode`	Decompile MSIL assemblies – support for modern .NET, .NET Framework, .NET Core, and .NET Standard.
Azure Functions for Visual Studio Code `ms-azuretools.vscode-azurefunctions`	Create, debug, manage, and deploy serverless apps directly from VS Code. It has dependencies on Azure Account (`ms-vscode.azure-account`) and Azure Resources (`ms-azuretools.vscode-azureresourcegroups`) extensions.
GitHub Repositories `github.remotehub`	Browse, search, edit, and commit to any remote GitHub repository directly from within Visual Studio Code.
SQL Server (mssql) for Visual Studio Code `ms-mssql.mssql`	For developing Microsoft SQL Server, Azure SQL Database, and SQL Data Warehouse everywhere with a rich set of functionalities.
Protobuf 3 support for Visual Studio Code `zxh404.vscode-proto3`	Syntax highlighting, syntax validation, code snippets, code completion, code formatting, brace matching, and line and block commenting.

Understanding Microsoft Visual Studio Code versions

Microsoft releases a new feature version of Visual Studio Code (almost) every month and bug fix versions more frequently. For example:

- Version 1.59, August 2021 feature release
- Version 1.59.1, August 2021 bug fix release

The version used in this book is 1.59, but the version of Microsoft Visual Studio Code is less important than the version of the C# for Visual Studio Code extension that you installed.

While the C# extension is not required, it provides IntelliSense as you type, code navigation, and debugging features, so it's something that's very handy to install and keep updated to support the latest C# language features.

Microsoft Visual Studio Code keyboard shortcuts

In this book, I will avoid showing keyboard shortcuts used for tasks like creating a new file since they are often different on different operating systems. The situations where I will show keyboard shortcuts are when you need to repeatedly press the key, for example, while debugging. These are also more likely to be consistent across operating systems.

If you want to customize your keyboard shortcuts for Visual Studio Code, then you can, as shown at the following link: `https://code.visualstudio.com/docs/getstarted/keybindings`.

I recommend that you download a PDF of keyboard shortcuts for your operating system from the following list:

- **Windows**: `https://code.visualstudio.com/shortcuts/keyboard-shortcuts-windows.pdf`

- **macOS**: https://code.visualstudio.com/shortcuts/keyboard-shortcuts-macos.pdf
- **Linux**: https://code.visualstudio.com/shortcuts/keyboard-shortcuts-linux.pdf

Understanding .NET

.NET 6, .NET Core, .NET Framework, and Xamarin are related and overlapping platforms for developers used to build applications and services. In this section, I'm going to introduce you to each of these .NET concepts.

Understanding .NET Framework

.NET Framework is a development platform that includes a **Common Language Runtime (CLR)**, which manages the execution of code, and a **Base Class Library (BCL)**, which provides a rich library of classes to build applications from.

Microsoft originally designed .NET Framework to have the possibility of being cross-platform, but Microsoft put their implementation effort into making it work best with Windows.

Since .NET Framework 4.5.2, it has been an official component of the Windows operating system. Components have the same support as their parent products, so 4.5.2 and later follow the life cycle policy of the Windows OS on which it is installed. .NET Framework is installed on over one billion computers, so it must change as little as possible. Even bug fixes can cause problems, so it is updated infrequently.

For .NET Framework 4.0 or later, all of the apps on a computer written for .NET Framework share the same version of the CLR and libraries stored in the **Global Assembly Cache (GAC)**, which can lead to issues if some of them need a specific version for compatibility.

 Good Practice: Practically speaking, .NET Framework is Windows-only and a legacy platform. Do not create new apps using it.

Understanding the Mono, Xamarin, and Unity projects

Third parties developed a .NET Framework implementation named the **Mono** project. Mono is cross-platform, but it fell well behind the official implementation of .NET Framework.

Mono has found a niche as the foundation of the **Xamarin** mobile platform as well as cross-platform game development platforms like **Unity**.

Microsoft purchased Xamarin in 2016 and now gives away what used to be an expensive Xamarin extension for free with Visual Studio. Microsoft renamed the Xamarin Studio development tool, which could only create mobile apps, to Visual Studio for Mac and gave it the ability to create other types of projects like console apps and web services. With Visual Studio 2022 for Mac, Microsoft has replaced parts of the Xamarin Studio editor with parts from Visual Studio 2022 for Windows to provide closer parity of experience and performance. Visual Studio 2022 for Mac was also rewritten to be a truly native macOS UI app to improve reliability and work with macOS's built-in assistive technologies.

Understanding .NET Core

Today, we live in a truly cross-platform world where modern mobile and cloud development have made Windows, as an operating system, much less important. Because of that, Microsoft has been working on an effort to decouple .NET from its close ties with Windows. While rewriting .NET Framework to be truly cross-platform, they've taken the opportunity to refactor and remove major parts that are no longer considered core.

This new product was branded .NET Core and includes a cross-platform implementation of the CLR known as CoreCLR and a streamlined BCL known as CoreFX.

Scott Hunter, Microsoft Partner Director Program Manager for .NET, has said that "Forty percent of our .NET Core customers are brand-new developers to the platform, which is what we want with .NET Core. We want to bring new people in."

.NET Core is fast-moving, and because it can be deployed side by side with an app, it can change frequently, knowing those changes will not affect other .NET Core apps on the same machine. Most improvements that Microsoft makes to .NET Core and modern .NET cannot be easily added to .NET Framework.

Understanding the journey to one .NET

At the Microsoft Build developer conference in May 2020, the .NET team announced that their plans for the unification of .NET had been delayed. They said that .NET 5 would be released on November 10, 2020, and it would unify all the various .NET platforms except mobile. It would not be until .NET 6 in November 2021 that mobile will also be supported by the unified .NET platform.

.NET Core has been renamed .NET and the major version number has skipped the number four to avoid confusion with .NET Framework 4.x. Microsoft plans on annual major version releases every November, rather like Apple does major version number releases of iOS every September.

The following table shows when the key versions of modern .NET were released, when future releases are planned, and which version is used by the various editions of this book:

Version	Released	Edition	Published
.NET Core RC1	November 2015	First	March 2016
.NET Core 1.0	June 2016		
.NET Core 1.1	November 2016		
.NET Core 1.0.4 and .NET Core 1.1.1	March 2017	Second	March 2017
.NET Core 2.0	August 2017		
.NET Core for UWP in Windows 10 Fall Creators Update	October 2017	Third	November 2017
.NET Core 2.1 (LTS)	May 2018		
.NET Core 2.2 (Current)	December 2018		
.NET Core 3.0 (Current)	September 2019	Fourth	October 2019
.NET Core 3.1 (LTS)	December 2019		
Blazor WebAssembly 3.2 (Current)	May 2020		
.NET 5.0 (Current)	November 2020	Fifth	November 2020
.NET 6.0 (LTS)	November 2021	Sixth	November 2021
.NET 7.0 (Current)	November 2022	Seventh	November 2022
.NET 8.0 (LTS)	November 2023	Eighth	November 2023

.NET Core 3.1 included Blazor Server for building web components. Microsoft had also planned to include Blazor WebAssembly in that release, but it was delayed. Blazor WebAssembly was later released as an optional add-on for .NET Core 3.1. I include it in the table above because it was versioned as 3.2 to exclude it from the LTS of .NET Core 3.1.

Understanding .NET support

.NET versions are either **Long Term Support (LTS)** or **Current**, as described in the following list:

- **LTS** releases are stable and require fewer updates over their lifetime. These are a good choice for applications that you do not intend to update frequently. LTS releases will be supported for 3 years after general availability, or 1 year after the next LTS release ships, whichever is longer.

- **Current** releases include features that may change based on feedback. These are a good choice for applications that you are actively developing because they provide access to the latest improvements. After a 6-month maintenance period, or 18 months after general availability, the previous minor version will no longer be supported.

Both receive critical fixes throughout their lifetime for security and reliability. You must stay up to date with the latest patches to get support. For example, if a system is running 1.0 and 1.0.1 has been released, 1.0.1 will need to be installed to get support.

To better understand your choices of Current and LTS releases, it is helpful to see it visually, with 3-year-long black bars for LTS releases, and variable-length gray bars for Current releases that end with cross-hatching for the 6 months after a new major or minor release that they retain support for, as shown in *Figure 1.2*:

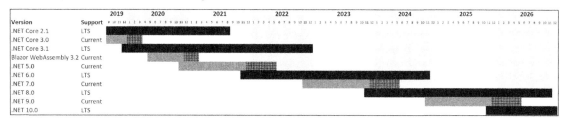

Figure 1.2: Support for various versions

For example, if you had created a project using .NET Core 3.0, then when Microsoft released .NET Core 3.1 in December 2019, you had to upgrade your project to .NET Core 3.1 by March 2020. (Before .NET 5, the maintenance period for Current releases was only three months.)

If you need long-term support from Microsoft, then choose .NET 6.0 today and stick with it until .NET 8.0, even once Microsoft releases .NET 7.0. This is because .NET 7.0 will be a current release and it will therefore lose support before .NET 6.0 does. Just remember that even with LTS releases you must upgrade to bug fix releases like 6.0.1.

All versions of .NET Core and modern .NET have reached their end of life except those shown in the following list:

- .NET 5.0 will reach end of life in May 2022.
- .NET Core 3.1 will reach end of life on December 3, 2022.
- .NET 6.0 will reach end of life in November 2024.

Understanding .NET Runtime and .NET SDK versions

.NET Runtime versioning follows semantic versioning, that is, a major increment indicates breaking changes, minor increments indicate new features, and patch increments indicate bug fixes.

.NET SDK versioning does not follow semantic versioning. The major and minor version numbers are tied to the runtime version it is matched with. The patch number follows a convention that indicates the major and minor versions of the SDK.

You can see an example of this in the following table:

Change	Runtime	SDK
Initial release	6.0.0	6.0.100
SDK bug fix	6.0.0	6.0.101
Runtime and SDK bug fix	6.0.1	6.0.102
SDK new feature	6.0.1	6.0.200

Removing old versions of .NET

.NET Runtime updates are compatible with a major version such as 6.x, and updated releases of the .NET SDK maintain the ability to build applications that target previous versions of the runtime, which enables the safe removal of older versions.

You can see which SDKs and runtimes are currently installed using the following commands:

- `dotnet --list-sdks`
- `dotnet --list-runtimes`

On Windows, use the **App & features** section to remove .NET SDKs. On macOS or Windows, use the `dotnet-core-uninstall` tool. This tool is not installed by default.

For example, while writing the fourth edition, I used the following command every month:

```
dotnet-core-uninstall remove --all-previews-but-latest --sdk
```

What is different about modern .NET?

Modern .NET is modularized compared to the legacy .NET Framework, which is monolithic. It is open source and Microsoft makes decisions about improvements and changes in the open. Microsoft has put particular effort into improving the performance of modern .NET.

It is smaller than the last version of .NET Framework due to the removal of legacy and non-cross-platform technologies. For example, workloads such as Windows Forms and **Windows Presentation Foundation (WPF)** can be used to build **graphical user interface (GUI)** applications, but they are tightly bound to the Windows ecosystem, so they are not included with .NET on macOS and Linux.

Windows development

One of the features of modern .NET is support for running old Windows Forms and WPF applications using the Windows Desktop Pack that is included with the Windows version of .NET Core 3.1 or later, which is why it is bigger than the SDKs for macOS and Linux. You can make some small changes to your legacy Windows app if necessary, and then rebuild it for .NET 6 to take advantage of new features and performance improvements.

Web development

ASP.NET Web Forms and Windows Communication Foundation (WCF) are old web application and service technologies that fewer developers are choosing to use for new development projects today, so they have also been removed from modern .NET. Instead, developers prefer to use ASP.NET MVC, ASP.NET Web API, SignalR, and gRPC. These technologies have been refactored and combined into a platform that runs on modern .NET, named ASP.NET Core. You'll learn about the technologies in *Chapter 14, Building Websites Using ASP.NET Core Razor Pages, Chapter 15, Building Websites Using the Model-View-Controller Pattern, Chapter 16, Building and Consuming Web Services*, and *Chapter 18, Building and Consuming Specialized Services*.

More Information: Some .NET Framework developers are upset that ASP.NET Web Forms, WCF, and Windows Workflow (WF) are missing from modern .NET and would like Microsoft to change their minds. There are open source projects to enable WCF and WF to migrate to modern .NET. You can read more at the following link: `https://devblogs.microsoft.com/dotnet/supporting-the-community-with-wf-and-wcf-oss-projects/`. There is an open source project for Blazor Web Forms components at the following link: `https://github.com/FritzAndFriends/BlazorWebFormsComponents`.

Database development

Entity Framework (EF) 6 is an object-relational mapping technology that is designed to work with data that is stored in relational databases such as Oracle and Microsoft SQL Server. It has gained baggage over the years, so the cross-platform API has been slimmed down, has been given support for non-relational databases like Microsoft Azure Cosmos DB, and has been renamed Entity Framework Core. You will learn about it in *Chapter 10, Working with Data Using Entity Framework Core*.

If you have existing apps that use the old EF, then version 6.3 is supported on .NET Core 3.0 or later.

Themes of modern .NET

Microsoft has created a website using Blazor that shows the major themes of modern .NET: `https://themesof.net/`.

Understanding .NET Standard

The situation with .NET in 2019 was that there were three forked .NET platforms controlled by Microsoft, as shown in the following list:

- **.NET Core**: For cross-platform and new apps
- **.NET Framework**: For legacy apps
- **Xamarin**: For mobile apps

Each had strengths and weaknesses because they were all designed for different scenarios. This led to the problem that a developer had to learn three platforms, each with annoying quirks and limitations.

Because of that, Microsoft defined .NET Standard – a specification for a set of APIs that all .NET platforms could implement to indicate what level of compatibility they have. For example, basic support is indicated by a platform being compliant with .NET Standard 1.4.

With .NET Standard 2.0 and later, Microsoft made all three platforms converge on a modern minimum standard, which made it much easier for developers to share code between any flavor of .NET.

For .NET Core 2.0 and later, this added most of the missing APIs that developers need to port old code written for .NET Framework to the cross-platform .NET Core. However, some APIs are implemented but throw an exception to indicate to a developer that they should not actually be used! This is usually due to differences in the operating system on which you run .NET. You'll learn how to handle these exceptions in *Chapter 2, Speaking C#*.

It is important to understand that .NET Standard is just a standard. You are not able to install .NET Standard in the same way that you cannot install HTML5. To use HTML5, you must install a web browser that implements the HTML5 standard.

To use .NET Standard, you must install a .NET platform that implements the .NET Standard specification. The last .NET Standard, version 2.1, is implemented by .NET Core 3.0, Mono, and Xamarin. Some features of C# 8.0 require .NET Standard 2.1. .NET Standard 2.1 is not implemented by .NET Framework 4.8, so we should treat .NET Framework as legacy.

With the release of .NET 6 in November 2021, the need for .NET Standard has reduced significantly because there is now a single .NET for all platforms, including mobile. .NET 6 has a single BCL and two CLRs: CoreCLR is optimized for server or desktop scenarios like websites and Windows desktop apps, and the Mono runtime is optimized for mobile and web browser apps that have limited resources.

Even now, apps and websites created for .NET Framework will need to be supported, so it is important to understand that you can create .NET Standard 2.0 class libraries that are backward compatible with legacy .NET platforms.

.NET platforms and tools used by the book editions

For the first edition of this book, which was written in March 2016, I focused on .NET Core functionality but used .NET Framework when important or useful features had not yet been implemented in .NET Core because that was before the final release of .NET Core 1.0. Visual Studio 2015 was used for most examples, with Visual Studio Code shown only briefly.

The second edition was (almost) completely purged of all .NET Framework code examples so that readers were able to focus on .NET Core examples that truly run cross-platform.

The third edition completed the switch. It was rewritten so that all of the code was pure .NET Core. But giving step-by-step instructions for both Visual Studio Code and Visual Studio 2017 for all tasks added complexity.

The fourth edition continued the trend by only showing coding examples using Visual Studio Code for all but the last two chapters. In *Chapter 20, Building Windows Desktop Apps*, it used Visual Studio running on Windows 10, and in *Chapter 21, Building Cross-Platform Mobile Apps*, it used Visual Studio for Mac.

In the fifth edition, *Chapter 20, Building Windows Desktop Apps*, was moved to *Appendix B* to make space for a new *Chapter 20, Building Web User Interfaces Using Blazor*. Blazor projects can be created using Visual Studio Code.

In this sixth edition, *Chapter 19, Building Mobile and Desktop Apps Using .NET MAUI*, was updated to show how mobile and desktop cross-platform apps can be created using Visual Studio 2022 and **.NET MAUI (Multi-platform App UI)**.

By the seventh edition and the release of .NET 7, Visual Studio Code will have an extension to support .NET MAUI. At that point, readers will be able to use Visual Studio Code for all examples in the book.

Understanding intermediate language

The C# compiler (named **Roslyn**) used by the dotnet CLI tool converts your C# source code into **intermediate language** (**IL**) code and stores the IL in an **assembly** (a DLL or EXE file). IL code statements are like assembly language instructions, which are executed by .NET's virtual machine, known as CoreCLR.

At runtime, CoreCLR loads the IL code from the assembly, the **just-in-time** (**JIT**) compiler compiles it into native CPU instructions, and then it is executed by the CPU on your machine.

The benefit of this two-step compilation process is that Microsoft can create CLRs for Linux and macOS, as well as for Windows. The same IL code runs everywhere because of the second compilation step, which generates code for the native operating system and CPU instruction set.

Regardless of which language the source code is written in, for example, C#, Visual Basic, or F#, all .NET applications use IL code for their instructions stored in an assembly. Microsoft and others provide disassembler tools that can open an assembly and reveal this IL code, such as the ILSpy .NET Decompiler extension.

Comparing .NET technologies

We can summarize and compare .NET technologies today, as shown in the following table:

Technology	Description	Host operating systems
Modern .NET	A modern feature set, full C# 8, 9, and 10 support, used to port existing apps or create new desktop, mobile, and web apps and services	Windows, macOS, Linux, Android, iOS

| .NET Framework | A legacy feature set, limited C# 8 support, no C# 9 or 10 support, used to maintain existing applications only | Windows only |
| Xamarin | Mobile and desktop apps only | Android, iOS, macOS |

Building console apps using Visual Studio 2022

The goal of this section is to showcase how to build a console app using Visual Studio 2022 for Windows.

If you do not have a Windows computer or you want to use Visual Studio Code, then you can skip this section since the code will be the same, just the tooling experience is different.

Managing multiple projects using Visual Studio 2022

Visual Studio 2022 has a concept named a **solution** that allows you to open and manage multiple projects simultaneously. We will use a solution to manage the two projects that you will create in this chapter.

Writing code using Visual Studio 2022

Let's get started writing code!

1. Start Visual Studio 2022.

2. In the Start window, click **Create a new project**.

3. In the **Create a new project** dialog, enter console in the **Search for templates** box, and select **Console Application**, making sure that you have chosen the C# project template rather than another language, such as F# or Visual Basic, as shown in *Figure 1.3*:

Figure 1.3: Selecting the Console Application project template

4. Click **Next**.

5. In the **Configure your new project** dialog, enter `HelloCS` for the project name, enter `C:\Code` for the location, and enter `Chapter01` for the solution name, as shown in *Figure 1.4*:

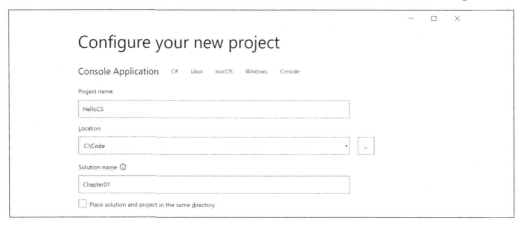

Figure 1.4: Configuring names and locations for your new project

6. Click **Next**.

 We are deliberately going to use the older project template for .NET 5.0 to see what a full console application looks like. In the next section, you will create a console application using .NET 6.0 and see what has changed.

7. In the **Additional information** dialog, in the **Target Framework** drop-down list, note the choices of Current and long-term support versions of .NET, and then select **.NET 5.0 (Current)** and click **Create**.

8. In **Solution Explorer**, double-click to open the file named `Program.cs`, and note that **Solution Explorer** shows the **HelloCS** project, as shown in *Figure 1.5*:

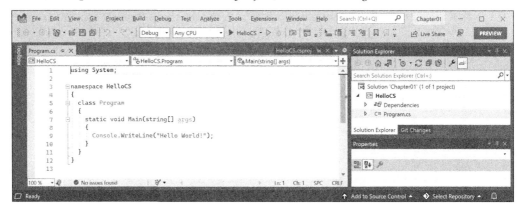

Figure 1.5: Editing Program.cs in Visual Studio 2022

9. In `Program.cs`, modify line 9 so that the text that is being written to the console says `Hello, C#!`

Compiling and running code using Visual Studio

The next task is to compile and run the code.

1. In Visual Studio, navigate to **Debug | Start Without Debugging**.
2. The output in the console window will show the result of running your application, as shown in *Figure 1.6*:

Figure 1.6: Running the console app on Windows

3. Press any key to close the console window and return to Visual Studio.
4. Select the **HelloCS** project and then, in the **Solution Explorer** toolbar, toggle on the **Show All Files** button, and note that the compiler-generated `bin` and `obj` folders are visible, as shown in *Figure 1.7*:

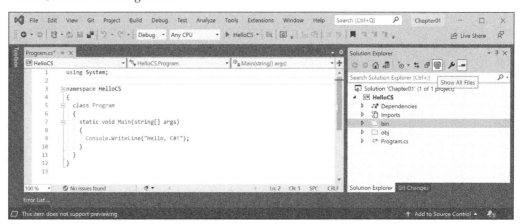

Figure 1.7: Showing the compiler-generated folders and files

Understanding the compiler-generated folders and files

Two compiler-generated folders were created, named obj and bin. You do not need to look inside these folders or understand their files yet. Just be aware that the compiler needs to create temporary folders and files to do its work. You could delete these folders and their files, and they can be recreated later. Developers often do this to "clean" a project. Visual Studio even has a command on the **Build** menu named **Clean Solution** that deletes some of these temporary files for you. The equivalent command with Visual Studio Code is dotnet clean.

- The obj folder contains one compiled *object* file for each source code file. These objects haven't been linked together into a final executable yet.

- The bin folder contains the *binary* executable for the application or class library. We will look at this in more detail in *Chapter 7, Packaging and Distributing .NET Types*.

Writing top-level programs

You might be thinking that was a lot of code just to output Hello, C#!.

Although the boilerplate code is written for you by the project template, is there a simpler way?

Well, in C# 9 or later, there is, and it is known as **top-level programs**.

Let's compare the console app created by the project template, as shown in the following code:

```
using System;

namespace HelloCS
{
  class Program
  {
    static void Main(string[] args)
    {
      Console.WriteLine("Hello World!");
    }
  }
}
```

To the new top-level program minimum console app, as shown in the following code:

```
using System;

Console.WriteLine("Hello World!");
```

That is a lot simpler, right? If you had to start with a blank file and write all the statements yourself, this is better. But how does it work?

During compilation, all the boilerplate code to define a namespace, the Program class, and its Main method, is generated and wrapped around the statements you write.

Key points to remember about top-level programs include the following list:

- Any using statements still must to go at the top of the file.
- There can be only one file like this in a project.

The using System; statement at the top of the file imports the System namespace. This enables the Console.WriteLine statement to work. You will learn more about namespaces in the next chapter.

Adding a second project using Visual Studio 2022

Let's add a second project to our solution to explore top-level programs:

1. In Visual Studio, navigate to **File | Add | New Project**.
2. In the **Add a new project** dialog, in **Recent project templates**, select **Console Application [C#]** and then click **Next**.
3. In the **Configure your new project** dialog, for the **Project name**, enter TopLevelProgram, leave the location as C:\Code\Chapter01, and then click **Next**.
4. In the **Additional information** dialog, select **.NET 6.0 (Long-term support)**, and then click **Create**.
5. In **Solution Explorer**, in the TopLevelProgram project, double-click Program.cs to open it.
6. In Program.cs, note the code consists of only a comment and a single statement because it uses the top-level program feature introduced in C# 9, as shown in the following code:

```
// See https://aka.ms/new-console-template for more information
Console.WriteLine("Hello, World!");
```

But when I introduced the concept of top-level programs earlier, we needed a using System; statement. Why don't we need that here?

Implicitly imported namespaces

The trick is that we do still need to import the System namespace, but it is now done for us using a feature introduced in C# 10. Let's see how:

1. In **Solution Explorer**, select the TopLevelProgram project and toggle on the **Show All Files** button, and note that the compiler-generated bin and obj folders are visible.
2. Expand the obj folder, expand the Debug folder, expand the net6.0 folder, and open the file named TopLevelProgram.GlobalUsings.g.cs.
3. Note that this file is automatically created by the compiler for projects that target .NET 6, and that it uses a feature introduced in C# 10 called **global imports** that imports some commonly used namespaces like System for use in all code files, as shown in the following code:

```
// <autogenerated />
global using global::System;
global using global::System.Collections.Generic;
global using global::System.IO;
global using global::System.Linq;
global using global::System.Net.Http;
global using global::System.Threading;
global using global::System.Threading.Tasks;
```

 I will explain more about this feature in the next chapter. For now, just note that a significant change between .NET 5 and .NET 6 is that many of the project templates, like the one for console applications, use new language features to hide what is really happening.

4. In the `TopLevelProgram` project, in `Program.cs`, modify the statement to output a different message and the version of the operating system, as shown in the following code:

```
Console.WriteLine("Hello from a Top Level Program!");
Console.WriteLine(Environment.OSVersion.VersionString);
```

5. In **Solution Explorer**, right-click the **Chapter01** solution, select **Set Startup Projects…**, set **Current selection**, and then click **OK**.

6. In **Solution Explorer**, click the **TopLevelProgram** project (or any file or folder within it), and note that Visual Studio indicates that **TopLevelProgram** is now the startup project by making the project name bold.

7. Navigate to **Debug | Start Without Debugging** to run the **TopLevelProgram** project, and note the result, as shown in *Figure 1.8*:

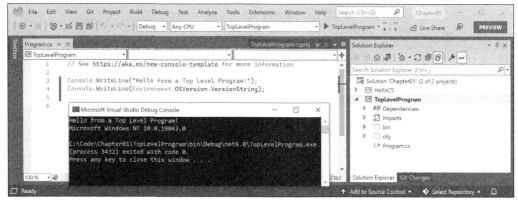

Figure 1.8: Running a top-level program in a Visual Studio solution with two projects on Windows

Building console apps using Visual Studio Code

The goal of this section is to showcase how to build a console app using Visual Studio Code.

If you never want to try Visual Studio Code or .NET Interactive Notebooks, then please feel free to skip this section and the next, and then continue with the *Reviewing the folders and files for projects* section.

Both the instructions and screenshots in this section are for Windows, but the same actions will work with Visual Studio Code on the macOS and Linux variants.

The main differences will be native command-line actions such as deleting a file: both the command and the path are likely to be different on Windows or macOS and Linux. Luckily, the dotnet command-line tool will be identical on all platforms.

Managing multiple projects using Visual Studio Code

Visual Studio Code has a concept named a **workspace** that allows you to open and manage multiple projects simultaneously. We will use a workspace to manage the two projects that you will create in this chapter.

Writing code using Visual Studio Code

Let's get started writing code!

1. Start Visual Studio Code.
2. Make sure that you do not have any open files, folders, or workspaces.
3. Navigate to **File** | **Save Workspace As...**.
4. In the dialog box, navigate to your user folder on macOS (mine is named markjprice), your Documents folder on Windows, or any directory or drive in which you want to save your projects.
5. Click the **New Folder** button and name the folder Code. (If you completed the section for Visual Studio 2022, then this folder will already exist.)
6. In the Code folder, create a new folder named Chapter01-vscode.
7. In the Chapter01-vscode folder, save the workspace as Chapter01.code-workspace.
8. Navigate to **File** | **Add Folder to Workspace...** or click the **Add Folder** button.

9. In the `Chapter01-vscode` folder, create a new folder named `HelloCS`.

10. Select the `HelloCS` folder and click the **Add** button.

11. Navigate to **View** | **Terminal**.

 We are deliberately going to use the older project template for .NET 5.0 to see what a full console application looks like. In the next section, you will create a console application using .NET 6.0 and see what has changed.

12. In **TERMINAL**, make sure that you are in the `HelloCS` folder, and then use the `dotnet` command-line tool to create a new console app that targets .NET 5.0, as shown in the following command:

```
dotnet new console -f net5.0
```

13. You will see that the `dotnet` command-line tool creates a new **Console Application** project for you in the current folder, and the **EXPLORER** window shows the two files created, `HelloCS.csproj` and `Program.cs`, and the `obj` folder, as shown in *Figure 1.9*:

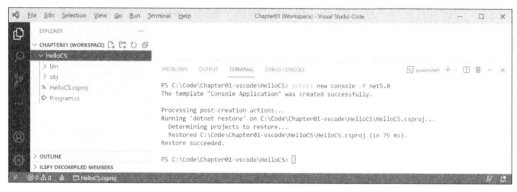

Figure 1.9: The EXPLORER window will show that two files and a folder have been created

14. In **EXPLORER**, click on the file named `Program.cs` to open it in the editor window. The first time that you do this, Visual Studio Code may have to download and install C# dependencies like OmniSharp, .NET Core Debugger, and Razor Language Server, if it did not do this when you installed the C# extension or if they need updating. Visual Studio Code will show progress in the **Output** window and eventually the message `Finished`, as shown in the following output:

```
Installing C# dependencies...
Platform: win32, x86_64

Downloading package 'OmniSharp for Windows (.NET 4.6 / x64)' (36150
KB)................... Done!
```

```
Validating download...
Integrity Check succeeded.
Installing package 'OmniSharp for Windows (.NET 4.6 / x64)'

Downloading package '.NET Core Debugger (Windows / x64)' (45048
KB)................... Done!
Validating download...
Integrity Check succeeded.
Installing package '.NET Core Debugger (Windows / x64)'

Downloading package 'Razor Language Server (Windows / x64)' (52344
KB)................... Done!
Installing package 'Razor Language Server (Windows / x64)'

Finished
```

 The preceding output is from Visual Studio Code on Windows. When run on macOS or Linux, the output will look slightly different, but the equivalent components for your operating system will be downloaded and installed.

15. Folders named `obj` and `bin` will have been created and when you see a notification saying that required assets are missing, click **Yes**, as shown in *Figure 1.10*:

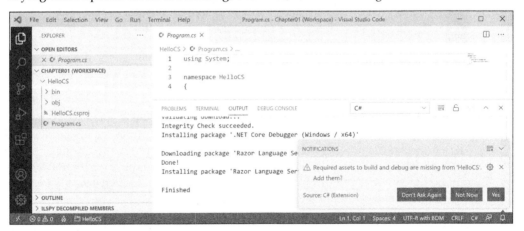

Figure 1.10: Warning message to add required build and debug assets

16. If the notification disappears before you can interact with it, then you can click the bell icon in the far-right corner of the status bar to show it again.

17. After a few seconds, another folder named .vscode will be created with some files that are used by Visual Studio Code to provide features like IntelliSense during debugging, which you will learn more about in *Chapter 4, Writing, Debugging, and Testing Functions.*

18. In Program.cs, modify line 9 so that the text that is being written to the console says Hello, C#!

 Good Practice: Navigate to **File | Auto Save**. This toggle will save the annoyance of remembering to save before rebuilding your application each time.

Compiling and running code using the dotnet CLI

The next task is to compile and run the code:

1. Navigate to **View | Terminal** and enter the following command:

```
dotnet run
```

2. The output in the **TERMINAL** window will show the result of running your application, as shown in *Figure 1.11*:

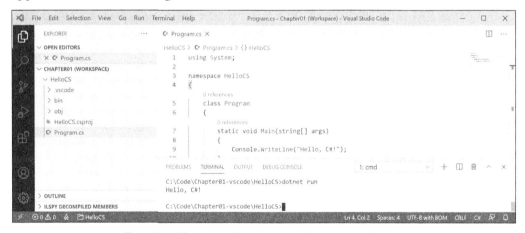

Figure 1.11: The output of running your first console application

Adding a second project using Visual Studio Code

Let's add a second project to our workspace to explore top-level programs:

1. In Visual Studio Code, navigate to **File | Add Folder to Workspace…**.

2. In the `Chapter01-vscode` folder, use the **New Folder** button to create a new folder named `TopLevelProgram`, select it, and click **Add**.

3. Navigate to **Terminal | New Terminal**, and in the drop-down list that appears, select **TopLevelProgram**. Alternatively, in **EXPLORER**, right-click the `TopLevelProgram` folder and then select **Open in Integrated Terminal**.

4. In **TERMINAL**, confirm that you are in the `TopLevelProgram` folder, and then enter the command to create a new console application, as shown in the following command:

```
dotnet new console
```

 Good Practice: When using workspaces, be careful when entering commands in **TERMINAL**. Be sure that you are in the correct folder before entering potentially destructive commands! That is why I got you to create a new terminal for `TopLevelProgram` before issuing the command to create a new console app.

5. Navigate to **View | Command Palette**.

6. Enter `omni`, and then, in the drop-down list that appears, select **OmniSharp: Select Project**.

7. In the drop-down list of two projects, select the **TopLevelProgram** project, and when prompted, click **Yes** to add required assets to debug.

 Good Practice: To enable debugging and other useful features, like code formatting and Go to Definition, you must tell OmniSharp which project you are actively working on in Visual Studio Code. You can quickly toggle active projects by clicking the project/folder to the right of the flame icon on the left side of the status bar.

8. In **EXPLORER**, in the `TopLevelProgram` folder, select `Program.cs`, and then change the existing statement to output a different message and also output the operating system version string, as shown in the following code:

```
Console.WriteLine("Hello from a Top Level Program!");
Console.WriteLine(Environment.OSVersion.VersionString);
```

9. In **TERMINAL**, enter the command to run a program, as shown in the following command:

```
dotnet run
```

10. Note the output in the **TERMINAL** window, as shown in *Figure 1.12*:

Figure 1.12: Running a top-level program in a Visual Studio Code workspace with two projects on Windows

If you were to run the program on macOS Big Sur, the environment operating system would be different, as shown in the following output:

```
Hello from a Top Level Program!
Unix 11.2.3
```

Managing multiple files using Visual Studio Code

If you have multiple files that you want to work with at the same time, then you can put them side by side as you edit them:

1. In **EXPLORER**, expand the two projects.

2. Open both Program.cs files from the two projects.

3. Click, hold, and drag the edit window tab for one of your open files to arrange them so that you can see both files at the same time.

Exploring code using .NET Interactive Notebooks

.NET Interactive Notebooks makes writing code even easier than top-level programs. It requires Visual Studio Code, so if you did not install it earlier, please install it now.

Creating a notebook

First, we need to create a notebook:

1. In Visual Studio Code, close any open workspaces or folders.
2. Navigate to **View | Command Palette**.
3. Type `.net inter`, and then select **.NET Interactive: Create new blank notebook**, as shown in *Figure 1.13*:

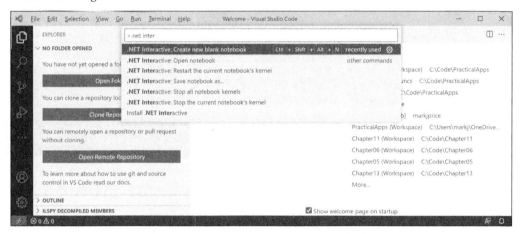

Figure 1.13: Creating a new blank .NET notebook

4. When prompted to select the file extension, choose **Create as '.dib'**.

> `.dib` is an experimental file format defined by Microsoft to avoid confusion and compatibility issues with the `.ipynb` format used by Python interactive notebooks. The file extension was historically only for Jupyter notebooks that can contain an interactive (I) mix of data, Python code (PY), and output in a notebook file (NB). With .NET Interactive Notebooks, the concept has expanded to allow a mix of C#, F#, SQL, HTML, JavaScript, Markdown, and other languages. `.dib` is polyglot, meaning it supports mixed languages. Conversion between the `.dib` and `.ipynb` file formats is supported.

5. Select **C#** for the default language for code cells in the notebook.
6. If a newer version of .NET Interactive is available, you might have to wait for it to uninstall the older version and install the newer one. Navigate to **View | Output** and select **.NET Interactive : diagnostics** in the drop-down list. Please be patient. It can take a few minutes for the notebook to appear because it has to start up a hosting environment for .NET. If nothing happens after a few minutes, then close Visual Studio Code and restart it.

7. Once the .NET Interactive Notebooks extension is downloaded and installed, the **OUTPUT** window diagnostics will show that a Kernel process has started (your process and port number will be different from the output below), as shown in the following output, which has been edited to save space:

```
Extension started for VS Code Stable.
...
Kernel process 12516 Port 59565 is using tunnel uri http://
localhost:59565/
```

Writing and running code in a notebook

Next, we can write code in the notebook cells:

1. The first cell should already be set to **C# (.NET Interactive)**, but if it is set to anything else, then click the language selector in the bottom-right corner of the code cell and then select **C# (.NET Interactive)** as the language mode for that cell, and note your other choices of language for a code cell, as shown in *Figure 1.14*:

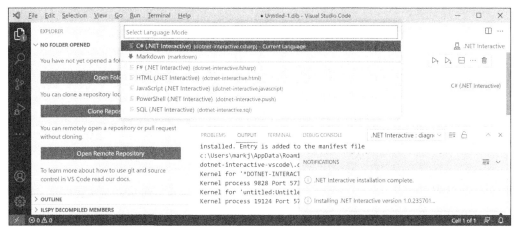

Figure 1.14: Changing the language for a code cell in a .NET Interactive notebook

2. Inside the **C# (.NET Interactive)** code cell, enter a statement to output a message to the console, and note that you do not need to end the statement with a semicolon, as you normally would in a full application, as shown in the following code:

```
Console.WriteLine("Hello, .NET Interactive!")
```

3. Click the **Execute Cell** button to the left of the code cell and note the output that appears in the gray box under the code cell, as shown in *Figure 1.15*:

Figure 1.15: Running code in a notebook and seeing the output below

Saving a notebook

Like any other file, we should save the notebook before continuing further:

1. Navigate to **File** | **Save As...**.
2. Change to the `Chapter01-vscode` folder and save the notebook as `Chapter01.dib`.
3. Close the `Chapter01.dib` editor tab.

Adding Markdown and special commands to a notebook

We can mix and match cells containing Markdown and code with special commands:

1. Navigate to **File** | **Open File...**, and select the `Chapter01.dib` file.
2. If you are prompted with `Do you trust the authors of these files?`, click **Open**.
3. Hover your mouse above the code block and click **+ Markup** to add a Markdown cell.
4. Type a heading level 1, as shown in the following Markdown:

    ```
    # Chapter 1 - Hello, C#! Welcome, .NET!
    Mixing *rich* **text** and code is cool!
    ```

5. Click the tick in the top-right corner of the cell to stop editing the cell and view the processed Markdown.

 If your cells are in the wrong order, then you can drag and drop to rearrange them.

6. Hover between the Markdown cell and the code cell and click **+ Code**.

7. Type a special command to output version information about .NET Interactive, as shown in the following code:

```
#!about
```

8. Click the **Execute Cell** button and note the output, as shown in *Figure 1.16*:

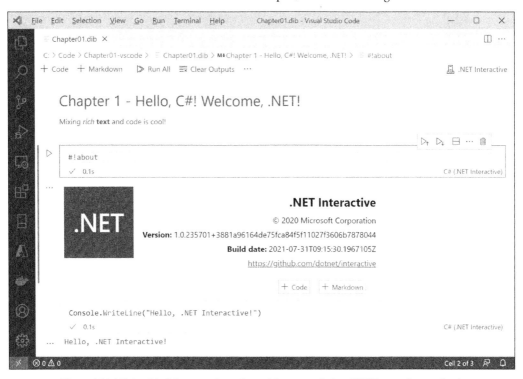

Figure 1.16: Mixing Markdown, code, and special commands in a .NET Interactive notebook

Executing code in multiple cells

When you have multiple code cells in a notebook, you must execute the preceding code cells before their context becomes available in subsequent code cells:

1. At the bottom of the notebook, add a new code cell, and then type a statement to declare a variable and assign an integer value, as shown in the following code:

```
int number = 8;
```

2. At the bottom of the notebook, add a new code cell, and then type a statement to output the number variable, as shown in the following code:

```
Console.WriteLine(number);
```

3. Note the second code cell does not know about the `number` variable because it was defined and assigned in another code cell, aka context, as shown in *Figure 1.17*:

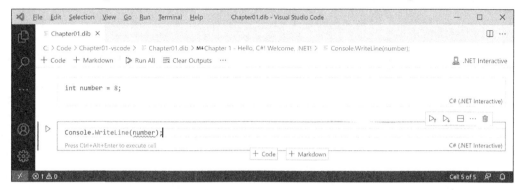

Figure 1.17: The number variable does not exist in the current cell or context

4. In the first cell, click the **Execute Cell** button to declare and assign a value to the variable, and then in the second cell, click the **Execute Cell** button to output the `number` variable, and note that this works. (Alternatively, in the first cell, you can click the **Execute Cell and Below** button.)

 Good Practice: If you have related code split between two cells, remember to execute the preceding cell before executing the subsequent cell. At the top of the notebook, there are the following buttons – **Clear Outputs** and **Run All**. These are very handy because you can click one and then the other to ensure that all code cells are executed properly, as long as they are in the correct order.

Using .NET Interactive Notebooks for the code in this book

Throughout the rest of the chapters, I will not give explicit instructions to use notebooks, but the GitHub repository for the book has solution notebooks when appropriate. I expect many readers will want to run my pre-created notebooks for language and library features covered in *Chapters 2* to *12*, which they want to see in action and learn about without having to write a complete application, even if it is just a console app:

```
https://github.com/markjprice/cs10dotnet6/tree/main/notebooks
```

Reviewing the folders and files for projects

In this chapter, you created two projects named `HelloCS` and `TopLevelProgram`.

Visual Studio Code uses a workspace file to manage multiple projects. Visual Studio 2022 uses a solution file to manage multiple projects. You also created a .NET Interactive notebook.

The result is a folder structure and files that will be repeated in subsequent chapters, although with more than just two projects, as shown in *Figure 1.18*:

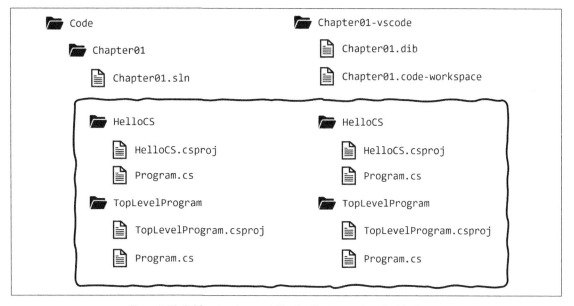

Figure 1.18: Folder structure and files for the two projects in this chapter

Understanding the common folders and files

Although `.code-workspace` and `.sln` files are different, the project folders and files such as `HelloCS` and `TopLevelProgram` are identical for Visual Studio 2022 and Visual Studio Code. This means that you can mix and match between both code editors if you like:

- In Visual Studio 2022, with a solution open, navigate to **File | Add Existing Project...** to add a project file created by another tool.
- In Visual Studio Code, with a workspace open, navigate to **File | Add Folder to Workspace...** to add a project folder created by another tool.

 Good Practice: Although the source code, like the `.csproj` and `.cs` files, is identical, the `bin` and `obj` folders that are automatically generated by the compiler could have mismatched file versions that give errors. If you want to open the same project in both Visual Studio 2022 and Visual Studio Code, delete the temporary `bin` and `obj` folders before opening the project in the other code editor. This is why I asked you to create a different folder for the Visual Studio Code solutions in this chapter.

Understanding the solution code on GitHub

The solution code in the GitHub repository for this book includes separate folders for Visual Studio Code, Visual Studio 2022, and .NET Interactive notebook files, as shown in the following list:

- Visual Studio 2022 solutions: `https://github.com/markjprice/cs10dotnet6/tree/main/vs4win`

- Visual Studio Code solutions: `https://github.com/markjprice/cs10dotnet6/tree/main/vscode`

- .NET Interactive Notebook solutions: `https://github.com/markjprice/cs10dotnet6/tree/main/notebooks`

 Good Practice: If you need to, return to this chapter to remind yourself how to create and manage multiple projects in the code editor of your choice. The GitHub repository has step-by-step instructions for four code editors (Visual Studio 2022 for Windows, Visual Studio Code, Visual Studio 2022 for Mac, and JetBrains Rider), along with additional screenshots: `https://github.com/markjprice/cs10dotnet6/blob/main/docs/code-editors/`.

Making good use of the GitHub repository for this book

Git is a commonly used source code management system. GitHub is a company, website, and desktop application that makes it easier to manage Git. Microsoft purchased GitHub in 2018, so it will continue to get closer integration with Microsoft tools.

I created a GitHub repository for this book, and I use it for the following:

- To store the solution code for the book that can be maintained after the print publication date.

- To provide extra materials that extend the book, like errata fixes, small improvements, lists of useful links, and longer articles that cannot fit in the printed book.

- To provide a place for readers to get in touch with me if they have issues with the book.

Raising issues with the book

If you get stuck following any of the instructions in this book, or if you spot a mistake in the text or the code in the solutions, please raise an issue in the GitHub repository:

1. Use your favorite browser to navigate to the following link: `https://github.com/markjprice/cs10dotnet6/issues`.

2. Click **New Issue**.

3. Enter as much detail as possible that will help me to diagnose the issue. For example:

   1. Your operating system, for example, Windows 11 64-bit, or macOS Big Sur version 11.2.3.

   2. Your hardware, for example, Intel, Apple Silicon, or ARM CPU.

   3. Your code editor, for example, Visual Studio 2022, Visual Studio Code, or something else, including the version number.

   4. As much of your code and configuration that you feel is relevant and necessary.

   5. Description of expected behavior and the behavior experienced.

   6. Screenshots (if possible).

Writing this book is a side hustle for me. I have a full-time job, so I mostly work on the book at weekends. This means that I cannot always respond immediately to issues. But I want all my readers to be successful with my book, so if I can help you (and others) without too much trouble, then I will gladly do so.

Giving me feedback

If you'd like to give me more general feedback about the book, then the GitHub repository `README.md` page has links to some surveys. You can provide the feedback anonymously, or if you would like a response from me, then you can supply an email address. I will only use this email address to answer your feedback.

I love to hear from my readers about what they like about my book, as well as suggestions for improvements and how they are working with C# and .NET, so don't be shy. Please get in touch!

Thank you in advance for your thoughtful and constructive feedback.

Downloading solution code from the GitHub repository

I use GitHub to store solutions to all the hands-on, step-by-step coding examples throughout chapters and the practical exercises that are featured at the end of each chapter. You will find the repository at the following link: `https://github.com/markjprice/cs10dotnet6`.

If you just want to download all the solution files without using Git, click the green **Code** button and then select **Download ZIP**, as shown in *Figure 1.19*:

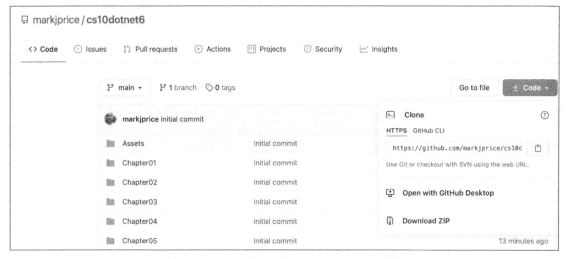

Figure 1.19: Downloading the repository as a ZIP file

I recommend that you add the preceding link to your favorite bookmarks because I also use the GitHub repository for this book for publishing errata (corrections) and other useful links.

Using Git with Visual Studio Code and the command line

Visual Studio Code has support for Git, but it will use your operating system's Git installation, so you must install Git 2.0 or later first before you get these features.

You can install Git from the following link: `https://git-scm.com/download`.

If you like to use a GUI, you can download GitHub Desktop from the following link: `https://desktop.github.com`.

Cloning the book solution code repository

Let's clone the book solution code repository. In the steps that follow, you will use the Visual Studio Code terminal, but you could enter the commands at any command prompt or terminal window:

1. Create a folder named `Repos-vscode` in your user or `Documents` folder, or wherever you want to store your Git repositories.
2. In Visual Studio Code, open the `Repos-vscode` folder.
3. Navigate to **View** | **Terminal**, and enter the following command:

```
git clone https://github.com/markjprice/cs10dotnet6.git
```

4. Note that cloning all the solutions for all of the chapters will take a minute or so, as shown in *Figure 1.20*:

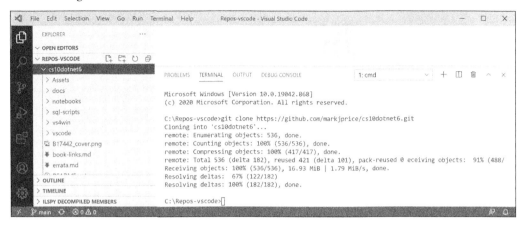

Figure 1.20: Cloning the book solution code using Visual Studio Code

Looking for help

This section is all about how to find quality information about programming on the web.

Reading Microsoft documentation

The definitive resource for getting help with Microsoft developer tools and platforms is Microsoft Docs, and you can find it at the following link: `https://docs.microsoft.com/`.

Getting help for the dotnet tool

At the command line, you can ask the `dotnet` tool for help with its commands:

1. To open the official documentation in a browser window for the `dotnet new` command, enter the following at the command line or in the Visual Studio Code terminal:

    ```
    dotnet help new
    ```

2. To get help output at the command line, use the `-h` or `--help` flag, as shown in the following command:

    ```
    dotnet new console -h
    ```

3. You will see the following partial output:

    ```
    Console Application (C#)
    Author: Microsoft
    Description: A project for creating a command-line application that can
    run on .NET Core on Windows, Linux and macOS
    ```

```
Options:
  -f|--framework. The target framework for the project.
                  net6.0          - Target net6.0
                  net5.0          - Target net5.0
                  netcoreapp3.1.  - Target netcoreapp3.1
                  netcoreapp3.0.  - Target netcoreapp3.0
              Default: net6.0


  --langVersion    Sets langVersion in the created project file text -
  Optional
```

Getting definitions of types and their members

One of the most useful features of a code editor is **Go To Definition**. It is available in Visual Studio Code and Visual Studio 2022. It will show what the public definition of the type or member looks like by reading the metadata in the compiled assembly.

Some tools, such as ILSpy .NET Decompiler, will even reverse-engineer from the metadata and IL code back into C# for you.

Let's see how to use the **Go To Definition** feature:

1. In Visual Studio 2022 or Visual Studio Code, open the solution/workspace named Chapter01.

2. In the HelloCS project, in Program.cs, in Main, enter the following statement to declare an integer variable named z:

    ```
    int z;
    ```

3. Click inside int and then right-click and choose **Go To Definition**.

4. In the code window that appears, you can see how the int data type is defined, as shown in *Figure 1.21*:

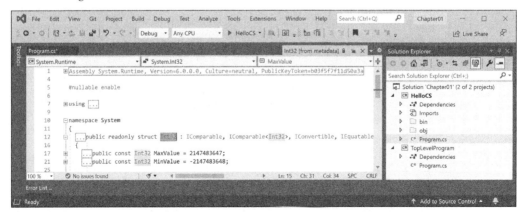

Figure 1.21: The int data type metadata

You can see that `int`:

- Is defined using the `struct` keyword
- Is in the `System.Runtime` assembly
- Is in the `System` namespace
- Is named `Int32`
- Is therefore an alias for the `System.Int32` type
- Implements interfaces such as `IComparable`
- Has constant values for its maximum and minimum values
- Has methods such as `Parse`

 Good Practice: When you try to use **Go To Definition** in Visual Studio Code, you will sometimes see an error saying **No definition found**. This is because the C# extension does not know about the current project. To fix this issue, navigate to **View | Command Palette**, enter omni, select **OmniSharp: Select Project**, and then select the project that you want to work with.

Right now, the **Go To Definition** feature is not that useful to you because you do not yet know what all of this information means.

By the end of the first part of this book, which consists of *Chapters 2* to *6*, and which teaches you about C#, you will know enough for this feature to become very handy.

5. In the code editor window, scroll down to find the `Parse` method with a single `string` parameter on line 106, and the comments that document it on lines 86 to 105, as shown in *Figure 1.22*:

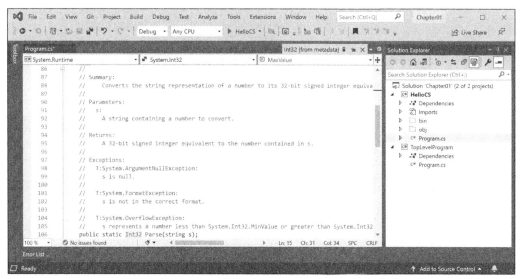

Figure 1.22: The comments for the Parse method with a string parameter

In the comments, you will see that Microsoft has documented the following:

- A summary that describes the method.

- Parameters like the `string` value that can be passed to the method.

- The return value of the method, including its data type.

- Three exceptions that might occur if you call this method, including `ArgumentNullException`, `FormatException`, and `OverflowException`. Now, we know that we could choose to wrap a call to this method in a `try` statement and which exceptions to catch.

Hopefully, you are getting impatient to learn what all this means!

Be patient for a little longer. You are almost at the end of this chapter, and in the next chapter, you will dive into the details of the C# language. But first, let's see where else you can look for help.

Looking for answers on Stack Overflow

Stack Overflow is the most popular third-party website for getting answers to difficult programming questions. It's so popular that search engines such as DuckDuckGo have a special way to write a query to search the site:

1. Start your favorite web browser.

2. Navigate to `DuckDuckGo.com`, enter the following query, and note the search results, which are also shown in *Figure 1.23*:

   ```
   !so securestring
   ```

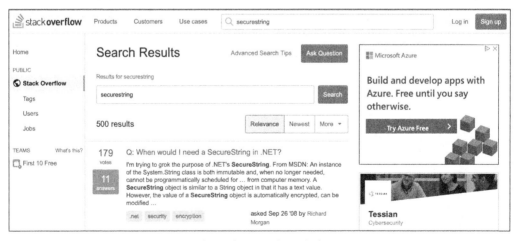

Figure 1.23: Stack Overflow search results for securestring

Searching for answers using Google

You can search Google with advanced search options to increase the likelihood of finding what you need:

1. Navigate to Google.

2. Search for information about `garbage collection` using a simple Google query, and note that you will probably see a lot of ads for garbage collection services in your local area before you see the Wikipedia definition of garbage collection in computer science.

3. Improve the search by restricting it to a useful site such as Stack Overflow, and by removing languages that we might not care about, such as C++, Rust, and Python, or by adding C# and .NET explicitly, as shown in the following search query:

```
garbage collection site:stackoverflow.com +C# -Java
```

Subscribing to the official .NET blog

To keep up to date with .NET, an excellent blog to subscribe to is the official .NET Blog, written by the .NET engineering teams, and you can find it at the following link: `https://devblogs.microsoft.com/dotnet/`.

Watching Scott Hanselman's videos

Scott Hanselman from Microsoft has an excellent YouTube channel about computer stuff they didn't teach you: `http://computerstufftheydidntteachyou.com/`.

I recommend it to everyone working with computers.

Practicing and exploring

Let's now test your knowledge and understanding by trying to answer some questions, getting some hands-on practice, and going into the topics covered throughout this chapter in greater detail.

Exercise 1.1 – Test your knowledge

Try to answer the following questions, remembering that although most answers can be found in this chapter, you should do some online research or code writing to answer others:

1. Is Visual Studio 2022 better than Visual Studio Code?

2. Is .NET 6 better than .NET Framework?

3. What is .NET Standard and why is it still important?

4. Why can a programmer use different languages, for example, C# and F#, to write applications that run on .NET?

5. What is the name of the entry point method of a .NET console application and how should it be declared?

6. What is a top-level program and how do you access any command-line arguments?

7. What do you type at the prompt to build and execute C# source code?

8. What are some benefits of using .NET Interactive Notebooks to write C# code?

9. Where would you look for help for a C# keyword?

10. Where would you look for solutions to common programming problems?

 Appendix, Answers to the Test Your Knowledge Questions, is available to download from a link in the README on the GitHub repository: https://github.com/markjprice/cs10dotnet6.

Exercise 1.2 – Practice C# anywhere

You don't need Visual Studio Code or even Visual Studio 2022 for Windows or Mac to write C#. You can go to .NET Fiddle – https://dotnetfiddle.net/ – and start coding online.

Exercise 1.3 – Explore topics

A book is a curated experience. I have tried to find the right balance of topics to include in the printed book. Other content that I have written can be found in the GitHub repository for this book.

I believe that this book covers all the fundamental knowledge and skills a C# and .NET developer should have or be aware of. Some longer examples are best included as links to Microsoft documentation or third-party article authors.

Use the links on the following page to learn more details about the topics covered in this chapter:

https://github.com/markjprice/cs10dotnet6/blob/main/book-links.md#chapter-1---hello-c-welcome-net

Summary

In this chapter, we:

- Set up your development environment.
- Discussed the similarities and differences between modern .NET, .NET Core, .NET Framework, Xamarin, and .NET Standard.
- Used Visual Studio Code with the .NET SDK and Visual Studio 2022 for Windows to create some simple console applications.
- Used .NET Interactive Notebooks to execute snippets of code for learning.
- Learned how to download the solution code for this book from a GitHub repository.
- And, most importantly, learned how to find help.

In the next chapter, you will learn how to "speak" C#.

02

Speaking C#

This chapter is all about the basics of the C# programming language. Over the course of this chapter, you'll learn how to write statements using the grammar of C#, as well as being introduced to some of the common vocabulary that you will use every day. In addition to this, by the end of the chapter, you'll feel confident in knowing how to temporarily store and work with information in your computer's memory.

This chapter covers the following topics:

- Introducing the C# language
- Understanding C# grammar and vocabulary
- Working with variables
- Exploring more about console applications

Introducing the C# language

This part of the book is about the C# language—the grammar and vocabulary that you will use every day to write the source code for your applications.

Programming languages have many similarities to human languages, except that in programming languages, you can make up your own words, just like Dr. Seuss!

In a book written by Dr. Seuss in 1950, *If I Ran the Zoo*, he states this:

> *"And then, just to show them, I'll sail to Ka-Troo And Bring Back an It-Kutch, a Preep, and a Proo, A Nerkle, a Nerd, and a Seersucker, too!"*

Understanding language versions and features

This part of the book covers the C# programming language and is written primarily for beginners, so it covers the fundamental topics that all developers need to know, from declaring variables to storing data to how to define your own custom data types.

This book covers features of the C# language from version 1.0 up to the latest version 10.0.

If you already have some familiarity with older versions of C# and are excited to find out about the new features in the most recent versions of C#, I have made it easier for you to jump around by listing language versions and their important new features below, along with the chapter number and topic title where you can learn about them.

C# 1.0

C# 1.0 was released in 2002 and included all the important features of a statically typed object-oriented modern language, as you will see throughout *Chapters 2 to 6*.

C# 2.0

C# 2.0 was released in 2005 and focused on enabling strong data typing using generics, to improve code performance and reduce type errors, including the topics listed in the following table:

Feature	Chapter	Topic
Nullable value types	6	Making a value type nullable
Generics	6	Making types more reusable with generics

C# 3.0

C# 3.0 was released in 2007 and focused on enabling declarative coding with **Language INtegrated Queries (LINQ)** and related features like anonymous types and lambda expressions, including the topics listed in the following table:

Feature	Chapter	Topic
Implicitly typed local variables	2	Inferring the type of a local variable
LINQ	11	All topics in *Chapter 11, Querying and Manipulating Data Using LINQ*

C# 4.0

C# 4.0 was released in 2010 and focused on improving interoperability with dynamic languages like F# and Python, including the topics listed in the following table:

Feature	Chapter	Topic
Dynamic types	2	Storing dynamic types
Named/optional arguments	5	Optional parameters and named arguments

C# 5.0

C# 5.0 was released in 2012 and focused on simplifying asynchronous operation support by automatically implementing complex state machines while writing what looks like synchronous statements, including the topics listed in the following table:

Feature	Chapter	Topic
Simplified asynchronous tasks	12	Understanding async and await

C# 6.0

C# 6.0 was released in 2015 and focused on minor refinements to the language, including the topics listed in the following table:

Feature	Chapter	Topic
static imports	2	Simplifying the usage of the console
Interpolated strings	2	Displaying output to the user
Expression bodied members	5	Defining read-only properties

C# 7.0

C# 7.0 was released in March 2017 and focused on adding functional language features like tuples and pattern matching, as well as minor refinements to the language, including the topics listed in the following table:

Feature	Chapter	Topic
Binary literals and digit separators	2	Storing whole numbers
Pattern matching	3	Pattern matching with the if statement
out variables	5	Controlling how parameters are passed
Tuples	5	Combining multiple values with tuples
Local functions	6	Defining local functions

C# 7.1

C# 7.1 was released in August 2017 and focused on minor refinements to the language, including the topics listed in the following table:

Feature	Chapter	Topic
Default literal expressions	5	Setting fields with default literal
Inferred tuple element names	5	Inferring tuple names
async Main	12	Improving responsiveness for console apps

C# 7.2

C# 7.2 was released in November 2017 and focused on minor refinements to the language, including the topics listed in the following table:

Feature	Chapter	Topic
Leading underscores in numeric literals	2	Storing whole numbers
Non-trailing named arguments	5	Optional parameters and named arguments
`private protected` access modifier	5	Understanding access modifiers
You can test `==` and `!=` with tuple types	5	Comparing tuples

C# 7.3

C# 7.3 was released in May 2018 and focused on performance-oriented safe code that improves `ref` variables, pointers, and `stackalloc`. These are advanced and rarely needed for most developers, so they are not covered in this book.

C# 8

C# 8 was released in September 2019 and focused on a major change to the language related to null handling, including the topics listed in the following table:

Feature	Chapter	Topic
Nullable reference types	6	Making a reference type nullable
Switch expressions	3	Simplifying `switch` statements with switch expressions
Default interface methods	6	Understanding default interface methods

C# 9

C# 9 was released in November 2020 and focused on record types, refinements to pattern matching, and minimal-code console apps, including the topics listed in the following table:

Feature	Chapter	Topic
Minimal-code console apps	1	Top-level programs
Target-typed new	2	Using target-typed new to instantiate objects
Enhanced pattern matching	5	Pattern matching with objects
Records	5	Working with records

C# 10

C# 10 was released in November 2021 and focused on features that minimize the amount of code needed in common scenarios, including the topics listed in the following table:

Feature	Chapter	Topic
Global namespace imports	2	Importing namespaces
Constant string literals	2	Formatting using interpolated strings
File-scoped namespaces	5	Simplifying namespace declarations
Required properties	5	Requiring properties to be set during instantiation
Record structs	6	Working with record struct types
Null parameter checks	6	Checking for null in method parameters

Understanding C# standards

Over the years, Microsoft has submitted a few versions of C# to standards bodies, as shown in the following table:

C# version	ECMA standard	ISO/IEC standard
1.0	ECMA-334:2003	ISO/IEC 23270:2003
2.0	ECMA-334:2006	ISO/IEC 23270:2006
5.0	ECMA-334:2017	ISO/IEC 23270:2018

The standard for C# 6 is still a draft and work on adding C# 7 features is progressing. Microsoft made C# open source in 2014.

There are currently three public GitHub repositories for making the work on C# and related technologies as open as possible, as shown in the following table:

Description	Link
C# language design	`https://github.com/dotnet/csharplang`
Compiler implementation	`https://github.com/dotnet/roslyn`
Standard to describe the language	`https://github.com/dotnet/csharpstandard`

Discovering your C# compiler versions

.NET language compilers for C# and Visual Basic, also known as Roslyn, along with a separate compiler for F#, are distributed as part of the .NET SDK. To use a specific version of C#, you must have at least that version of the .NET SDK installed, as shown in the following table:

.NET SDK	Roslyn compiler	Default C# language
1.0.4	2.0 - 2.2	7.0
1.1.4	2.3 - 2.4	7.1
2.1.2	2.6 - 2.7	7.2
2.1.200	2.8 - 2.10	7.3
3.0	3.0 - 3.4	8.0
5.0	3.8	9.0
6.0	3.9 - 3.10	10.0

When you create class libraries then you can choose to target .NET Standard as well as versions of modern .NET. They have default C# language versions, as shown in the following table:

.NET Standard	C#
2.0	7.3
2.1	8.0

How to output the SDK version

Let's see what .NET SDK and C# language compiler versions you have available:

1. On macOS, start **Terminal**. On Windows, start **Command Prompt**.

2. To determine which version of the .NET SDK you have available, enter the following command:

```
dotnet --version
```

3. Note the version at the time of writing is 6.0.100, indicating that it is the initial version of the SDK without any bug fixes or new features yet, as shown in the following output:

```
6.0.100
```

Enabling a specific language version compiler

Developer tools like Visual Studio and the dotnet command-line interface assume that you want to use the latest major version of a C# language compiler by default. Before C# 8.0 was released, C# 7.0 was the latest major version and was used by default. To use the improvements in a C# point release like 7.1, 7.2, or 7.3, you had to add a <LangVersion> configuration element to the project file, as shown in the following markup:

```
<LangVersion>7.3</LangVersion>
```

After the release of C# 10.0 with .NET 6.0, if Microsoft releases a C# 10.1 compiler and you want to use its new language features then you will have to add a configuration element to your project file, as shown in the following markup:

```
<LangVersion>10.1</LangVersion>
```

Potential values for the <LangVersion> are shown in the following table:

LangVersion	Description
7, 7.1, 7.2, 7.3 8, 9, 10	Entering a specific version number will use that compiler if it has been installed.
latestmajor	Uses the highest major number, for example, 7.0 in August 2019, 8.0 in October 2019, 9.0 in November 2020, 10.0 in November 2021.

latest	Uses the highest major and highest minor number, for example, 7.2 in 2017, 7.3 in 2018, 8 in 2019, perhaps 10.1 in early 2022.
preview	Uses the highest available preview version, for example, 10.0 in July 2021 with .NET 6.0 Preview 6 installed.

After creating a new project, you can edit the `.csproj` file and add the `<LangVersion>` element, as shown highlighted in the following markup:

```
<Project Sdk="Microsoft.NET.Sdk">

  <PropertyGroup>
    <OutputType>Exe</OutputType>
    <TargetFramework>net6.0</TargetFramework>
    <LangVersion>preview</LangVersion>
  </PropertyGroup>

</Project>
```

Your projects must target `net6.0` to use the full features of C# 10.

 Good Practice: If you are using Visual Studio Code and you have not done so already, install the Visual Studio Code extension named **MSBuild project tools**. This will give you IntelliSense while editing `.csproj` files, including making it easy to add the `<LangVersion>` element with appropriate values.

Understanding C# grammar and vocabulary

To learn simple C# language features, you can use .NET Interactive Notebooks, which remove the need to create an application of any kind.

To learn some other C# language features, you will need to create an application. The simplest type of application is a console application.

Let's start by looking at the basics of the grammar and vocabulary of C#. Throughout this chapter, you will create multiple console applications, with each one showing related features of the C# language.

Showing the compiler version

We will start by writing code that shows the compiler version:

1. If you've completed *Chapter 1, Hello, C#! Welcome, .NET!*, then you will already have a Code folder. If not, then you'll need to create it.

2. Use your preferred code editor to create a new console app, as defined in the following list:

   1. Project template: **Console Application [C#]** / `console`
   2. Workspace/solution file and folder: `Chapter02`
   3. Project file and folder: `Vocabulary`

    Good Practice: If you have forgotten how, or did not complete the previous chapter, then step-by-step instructions for creating a workspace/solution with multiple projects are given in *Chapter 1, Hello, C#! Welcome, .NET!*.

3. Open the `Program.cs` file, and at the top of the file, under the comment, add a statement to show the C# version as an error, as shown in the following code:

   ```
   #error version
   ```

4. Run the console application:

   1. In Visual Studio Code, in a terminal, enter the command `dotnet run`.
   2. In Visual Studio, navigate to **Debug | Start Without Debugging**. When prompted to continue and run the last successful build, click **No**.

5. Note the compiler version and language version appear as a compiler error message number `CS8304`, as shown in *Figure 2.1*:

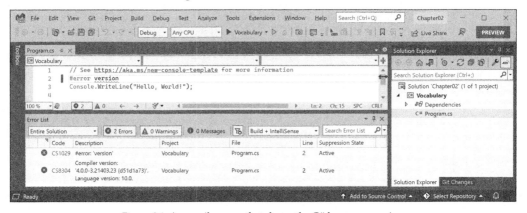

Figure 2.1: A compiler error that shows the C# language version

6. The error message in the Visual Studio Code **PROBLEMS** window or Visual Studio **Error List** window says `Compiler version: '4.0.0...'` with language version `10.0`.

7. Comment out the statement that causes the error, as shown in the following code:

   ```
   // #error version
   ```

8. Note that the compiler error messages disappear.

Understanding C# grammar

The grammar of C# includes statements and blocks. To document your code, you can use comments.

 Good Practice: Comments should not be the only way that you document your code. Choosing sensible names for variables and functions, writing unit tests, and creating actual documents are other ways to document your code.

Statements

In English, we indicate the end of a sentence with a full stop. A sentence can be composed of multiple words and phrases, with the order of words being part of the grammar. For example, in English, we say "the black cat."

The adjective, *black*, comes before the noun, *cat*. Whereas French grammar has a different order; the adjective comes after the noun: "le chat noir." What's important to take away from this is that the order matters.

C# indicates the end of a **statement** with a semicolon. A statement can be composed of multiple **variables** and **expressions**. For example, in the following statement, `totalPrice` is a variable and `subtotal + salesTax` is an expression:

```
var totalPrice = subtotal + salesTax;
```

The expression is made up of an operand named `subtotal`, an operator +, and another operand named `salesTax`. The order of operands and operators matters.

Comments

When writing your code, you're able to add comments to explain your code using a double slash, //. By inserting // the compiler will ignore everything after the // until the end of the line, as shown in the following code:

```
// sales tax must be added to the subtotal
var totalPrice = subtotal + salesTax;
```

To write a multiline comment, use /* at the beginning and */ at the end of the comment, as shown in the following code:

```
/*
This is a multi-line comment.
*/
```

Good Practice: Well-designed code, including function signatures with well-named parameters and class encapsulation, can be somewhat self-documenting. When you find yourself putting too many comments and explanations in your code, ask yourself: can I rewrite, aka refactor, this code to make it more understandable without long comments?

Your code editor has commands to make it easier to add and remove comment characters, as shown in the following list:

- **Visual Studio 2022 for Windows**: Navigate to **Edit | Advanced | Comment Selection** or **Uncomment Selection**
- **Visual Studio Code**: Navigate to **Edit | Toggle Line Comment** or **Toggle Block Comment**

Good Practice: You **comment** code by adding descriptive text above or after code statements. You **comment out** code by adding comment characters before or around statements to make them inactive. **Uncommenting** means removing the comment characters.

Blocks

In English, we indicate a new paragraph by starting a new line. C# indicates a **block** of code with the use of curly brackets, { }.

Blocks start with a declaration to indicate what is being defined. For example, a block can define the start and end of many language constructs including namespaces, classes, methods, or statements like `foreach`.

You will learn more about namespaces, classes, and methods later in this chapter and subsequent chapters but to briefly introduce some of those concepts now:

- A **namespace** contains types like classes to group them together.
- A **class** contains the members of an object including methods.
- A **method** contains statements that implement an action that an object can take.

Examples of statements and blocks

In the project template for console apps when targeting .NET 5.0, note that examples of the grammar of C# have been written for you by the project template. I've added some comments to the statements and blocks, as shown in the following code:

```
using System; // a semicolon indicates the end of a statement

namespace Basics
{ // an open brace indicates the start of a block
  class Program
  {
```

```
    static void Main(string[] args)
    {
      Console.WriteLine("Hello World!"); // a statement
    }
  }
} // a close brace indicates the end of a block
```

Understanding C# vocabulary

The C# vocabulary is made up of **keywords**, **symbol characters**, and **types**.

Some of the predefined, reserved keywords that you will see in this book include using, namespace, class, static, int, string, double, bool, if, switch, break, while, do, for, foreach, and, or, not, record, and init.

Some of the symbol characters that you will see include ", ', +, -, *, /, %, @, and $.

There are other contextual keywords that only have a special meaning in a specific context.

However, that still means that there are only about 100 actual C# keywords in the language.

Comparing programming languages to human languages

The English language has more than 250,000 distinct words, so how does C# get away with only having about 100 keywords? Moreover, why is C# so difficult to learn if it has only 0.0416% of the number of words in the English language?

One of the key differences between a human language and a programming language is that developers need to be able to define the new "words" with new meanings. Apart from the about 100 keywords in the C# language, this book will teach you about some of the hundreds of thousands of "words" that other developers have defined, but you will also learn how to define your own "words."

Programmers all over the world must learn English because most programming languages use English words such as namespace and class. There are programming languages that use other human languages, such as Arabic, but they are rare. If you are interested in learning more, this YouTube video shows a demonstration of an Arabic programming language: https://youtu.be/dk08cdwf6v8.

Changing the color scheme for C# syntax

By default, Visual Studio Code and Visual Studio show C# keywords in blue to make them easier to differentiate from other code. Both tools allow you to customize the color scheme:

1. In Visual Studio Code, navigate to **Code** | **Preferences** | **Color Theme** (it is on the **File** menu on Windows).

2. Select a color theme. For reference, I'll use the **Light+ (default light)** color theme so that the screenshots look good in a printed book.

3. In Visual Studio, navigate to **Tools | Options**.

4. In the **Options** dialog box, select **Fonts and Colors**, and then select the display items that you would like to customize.

Help for writing correct code

Plain text editors such as Notepad don't help you write correct English. Likewise, Notepad won't help you write correct C# either.

Microsoft Word can help you write English by highlighting spelling mistakes with red squiggles, with Word saying that "icecream" should be ice-cream or ice cream, and grammatical errors with blue squiggles, such as a sentence should have an uppercase first letter.

Similarly, Visual Studio Code's C# extension and Visual Studio help you write C# code by highlighting spelling mistakes, such as the method name should be WriteLine with an uppercase L, and grammatical errors, such as statements that must end with a semicolon.

The C# extension constantly watches what you type and gives you feedback by highlighting problems with colored squiggly lines, similar to that of Microsoft Word.

Let's see it in action:

1. In Program.cs, change the L in the WriteLine method to lowercase.

2. Delete the semicolon at the end of the statement.

3. In Visual Studio Code, navigate to **View | Problems**, or in Visual Studio navigate to **View | Error List**, and note that a red squiggle appears under the code mistakes and details are shown, as you can see in *Figure 2.2*:

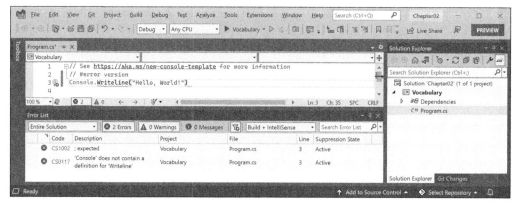

Figure 2.2: The Error List window showing two compile errors

4. Fix the two coding errors.

Importing namespaces

`System` is a namespace, which is like an address for a type. To refer to someone's location exactly, you might use `Oxford.HighStreet.BobSmith`, which tells us to look for a person named Bob Smith on the High Street in the city of Oxford.

`System.Console.WriteLine` tells the compiler to look for a method named `WriteLine` in a type named `Console` in a namespace named `System`. To simplify our code, the **Console Application** project template for every version of .NET before 6.0 added a statement at the top of the code file to tell the compiler to always look in the `System` namespace for types that haven't been prefixed with their namespace, as shown in the following code:

```
using System; // import the System namespace
```

We call this *importing the namespace*. The effect of importing a namespace is that all available types in that namespace will be available to your program without needing to enter the namespace prefix and will be seen in IntelliSense while you write code.

 .NET Interactive notebooks have most namespaces imported automatically.

Implicitly and globally importing namespaces

Traditionally, every `.cs` file that needs to import namespaces would have to start with `using` statements to import those namespaces. Namespaces like `System` and `System.Linq` are needed in almost all `.cs` files, so the first few lines of every `.cs` file often had at least a few `using` statements, as shown in the following code:

```
using System;
using System.Linq;
using System.Collections.Generic;
```

When creating websites and services using ASP.NET Core, there are often dozens of namespaces that each file would have to import.

C# 10 introduces some new features that simplify importing namespaces.

First, the `global using` statement means you only need to import a namespace in one `.cs` file and it will be available throughout all `.cs` files. You could put `global using` statements in the `Program.cs` file but I recommend creating a separate file for those statements named something like `GlobalUsings.cs` or `GlobalNamespaces.cs`, as shown in the following code:

```
global using System;
global using System.Linq;
global using System.Collections.Generic;
```

Good Practice: As developers get used to this new C# feature, I expect one naming convention for this file to become the standard.

Second, any projects that target .NET 6.0 and therefore use the C# 10 compiler generate a .cs file in the obj folder to implicitly globally import some common namespaces like System. The specific list of implicitly imported namespaces depends on which SDK you target, as shown in the following table:

SDK	Implicitly imported namespaces
Microsoft.NET.Sdk	System System.Collections.Generic System.IO System.Linq System.Net.Http System.Threading System.Threading.Tasks
Microsoft.NET.Sdk.Web	Same as Microsoft.NET.Sdk and: System.Net.Http.Json Microsoft.AspNetCore.Builder Microsoft.AspNetCore.Hosting Microsoft.AspNetCore.Http Microsoft.AspNetCore.Routing Microsoft.Extensions.Configuration Microsoft.Extensions.DependencyInjection Microsoft.Extensions.Hosting Microsoft.Extensions.Logging
Microsoft.NET.Sdk.Worker	Same as Microsoft.NET.Sdk and: Microsoft.Extensions.Configuration Microsoft.Extensions.DependencyInjection Microsoft.Extensions.Hosting Microsoft.Extensions.Logging

Let's see the current auto-generated implicit imports file:

1. In **Solution Explorer**, select the `Vocabulary` project, toggle on the **Show All Files** button, and note the compiler-generated `bin` and `obj` folders are visible.

2. Expand the `obj` folder, expand the `Debug` folder, expand the `net6.0` folder, and open the file named `Vocabulary.GlobalUsings.g.cs`.

3. Note this file is automatically created by the compiler for projects that target .NET 6.0, and that it imports some commonly used namespaces including `System.Threading`, as shown in the following code:

   ```
   // <autogenerated />
   global using global::System;
   global using global::System.Collections.Generic;
   global using global::System.IO;
   global using global::System.Linq;
   global using global::System.Net.Http;
   global using global::System.Threading;
   global using global::System.Threading.Tasks;
   ```

4. Close the `Vocabulary.GlobalUsings.g.cs` file.

5. In **Solution Explorer**, select the project, and then add additional entries to the project file to control which namespaces are implicitly imported, as shown highlighted in the following markup:

   ```
   <Project Sdk="Microsoft.NET.Sdk">

     <PropertyGroup>
       <OutputType>Exe</OutputType>
       <TargetFramework>net6.0</TargetFramework>
       <Nullable>enable</Nullable>
       <ImplicitUsings>enable</ImplicitUsings>
     </PropertyGroup>

     <ItemGroup>
       <Using Remove="System.Threading" />
       <Using Include="System.Numerics" />
     </ItemGroup>

   </Project>
   ```

6. Save the changes to the project file.

7. Expand the `obj` folder, expand the `Debug` folder, expand the `net6.0` folder, and open the file named `Vocabulary.GlobalUsings.g.cs`.

8. Note this file now imports `System.Numerics` instead of `System.Threading`, as shown highlighted in the following code:

   ```
   // <autogenerated />
   global using global::System;
   ```

```
global using global::System.Collections.Generic;
global using global::System.IO;
global using global::System.Linq;
global using global::System.Net.Http;
global using global::System.Threading.Tasks;
global using global::System.Numerics;
```

9. Close the `Vocabulary.GlobalUsings.g.cs` file.

You can disable the implicitly imported namespaces feature for all SDKs by removing an entry in the project file, as shown in the following markup:

```
<ImplicitUsings>enable</ImplicitUsings>
```

Verbs are methods

In English, verbs are doing or action words, like run and jump. In C#, doing or action words are called **methods**. There are hundreds of thousands of methods available to C#. In English, verbs change how they are written based on when in time the action happens. For example, Amir *was jumping* in the past, Beth *jumps* in the present, they *jumped* in the past, and Charlie *will jump* in the future.

In C#, methods such as `WriteLine` change how they are called or executed based on the specifics of the action. This is called overloading, which we'll cover in more detail in *Chapter 5, Building Your Own Types with Object-Oriented Programming*. But for now, consider the following example:

```
// outputs the current line terminator string
// by default, this is a carriage-return and line feed
Console.WriteLine();

// outputs the greeting and the current line terminator string
Console.WriteLine("Hello Ahmed");

// outputs a formatted number and date and the current line terminator string
Console.WriteLine("Temperature on {0:D} is {1}°C.",
  DateTime.Today, 23.4);
```

A different analogy is that some words are spelled the same but have different meanings depending on the context.

Nouns are types, variables, fields, and properties

In English, nouns are names that refer to things. For example, Fido is the name of a dog. The word "dog" tells us the type of thing that Fido is, and so in order for Fido to fetch a ball, we would use his name.

In C#, their equivalents are **types**, **variables**, **fields**, and **properties**. For example:

*   `Animal` and `Car` are types; they are nouns for categorizing things.
*   `Head` and `Engine` might be fields or properties; nouns that belong to `Animal` and `Car`.
*   `Fido` and `Bob` are variables; nouns for referring to a specific object.

There are tens of thousands of types available to C#, though have you noticed how I didn't say, "There are tens of thousands of types in C#?" The difference is subtle but important. The language of C# only has a few keywords for types, such as `string` and `int`, and strictly speaking, C# doesn't define any types. Keywords such as `string` that look like types are **aliases**, which represent types provided by the platform on which C# runs.

It's important to know that C# cannot exist alone; after all, it's a language that runs on variants of .NET. In theory, someone could write a compiler for C# that uses a different platform, with different underlying types. In practice, the platform for C# is .NET, which provides tens of thousands of types to C#, including `System.Int32`, which is the C# keyword alias `int` maps to, as well as many more complex types, such as `System.Xml.Linq.XDocument`.

It's worth taking note that the term **type** is often confused with **class**. Have you ever played the parlor game *Twenty Questions*, also known as *Animal, Vegetable, or Mineral*? In the game, everything can be categorized as an animal, vegetable, or mineral. In C#, every **type** can be categorized as a `class`, `struct`, `enum`, `interface`, or `delegate`. You will learn what these mean in *Chapter 6, Implementing Interfaces and Inheriting Classes*. As examples, the C# keyword `string` is a `class`, but `int` is a `struct`. So, it is best to use the term **type** to refer to both.

Revealing the extent of the C# vocabulary

We know that there are more than 100 keywords in C#, but how many types are there? Let's write some code to find out how many types (and their methods) are available to C# in our simple console application.

Don't worry exactly how this code works for now but know that it uses a technique called **reflection**:

1. We'll start by importing the `System.Reflection` namespace at the top of the `Program.cs` file, as shown in the following code:

    ```
    using System.Reflection;
    ```

2. Delete the statement that writes `Hello World!` and replace it with the following code:

    ```
    Assembly? assembly = Assembly.GetEntryAssembly();
    if (assembly == null) return;

    // Loop through the assemblies that this app references
    foreach (AssemblyName name in assembly.GetReferencedAssemblies())
    {
      // load the assembly so we can read its details
    ```

```csharp
Assembly a = Assembly.Load(name);

// declare a variable to count the number of methods
int methodCount = 0;

// loop through all the types in the assembly
foreach (TypeInfo t in a.DefinedTypes)
{
  // add up the counts of methods
  methodCount += t.GetMethods().Count();
}

// output the count of types and their methods
Console.WriteLine(
  "{0:N0} types with {1:N0} methods in {2} assembly.",
  arg0: a.DefinedTypes.Count(),
  arg1: methodCount, arg2: name.Name);
}
```

3. Run the code. You will see the actual number of types and methods that are available to you in the simplest application when running on your OS. The number of types and methods displayed will be different depending on the operating system that you are using, as shown in the following outputs:

```
// Output on Windows
0 types with 0 methods in System.Runtime assembly.
106 types with 1,126 methods in System.Linq assembly.
44 types with 645 methods in System.Console assembly.

// Output on macOS
0 types with 0 methods in System.Runtime assembly.
103 types with 1,094 methods in System.Linq assembly.
57 types with 701 methods in System.Console assembly.
```

 Why does the System.Runtime assembly contain zero types? This assembly is special because it contains only **type-forwarders** rather than actual types. A type-forwarder represents a type that has been implemented outside of .NET or for some other advanced reason.

4. Add statements to the top of the file after importing the namespace to declare some variables, as shown highlighted in the following code:

```csharp
using System.Reflection;

// declare some unused variables using types
// in additional assemblies
```

```
System.Data.DataSet ds;
HttpClient client;
```

By declaring variables that use types in other assemblies, those assemblies are loaded with our application, which allows our code to see all the types and methods in them. The compiler will warn you that you have unused variables but that won't stop your code from running.

5. Run the console application again and view the results, which should look similar to the following outputs:

```
// Output on Windows
0 types with 0 methods in System.Runtime assembly.
383 types with 6,854 methods in System.Data.Common assembly.
456 types with 4,590 methods in System.Net.Http assembly.
106 types with 1,126 methods in System.Linq assembly.
44 types with 645 methods in System.Console assembly.

// Output on macOS
0 types with 0 methods in System.Runtime assembly.
376 types with 6,763 methods in System.Data.Common assembly.
522 types with 5,141 methods in System.Net.Http assembly.
103 types with 1,094 methods in System.Linq assembly.
57 types with 701 methods in System.Console assembly.
```

Now, you have a better sense of why learning C# is a challenge, because there are so many types and methods to learn. Methods are only one category of a member that a type can have, and you and other programmers are constantly defining new types and members!

Working with variables

All applications process data. Data comes in, data is processed, and then data goes out.

Data usually comes into our program from files, databases, or user input, and it can be put temporarily into variables that will be stored in the memory of the running program. When the program ends, the data in memory is lost. Data is usually output to files and databases, or to the screen or a printer. When using variables, you should think about, firstly, how much space the variable takes in the memory, and, secondly, how fast it can be processed.

We control this by picking an appropriate type. You can think of simple common types such as int and double as being different-sized storage boxes, where a smaller box would take less memory but may not be as fast at being processed; for example, adding 16-bit numbers might not be processed as fast as adding 64-bit numbers on a 64-bit operating system. Some of these boxes may be stacked close by, and some may be thrown into a big heap further away.

Naming things and assigning values

There are naming conventions for things, and it is good practice to follow them, as shown in the following table:

Naming convention	Examples	Used for
Camel case	`cost, orderDetail, dateOfBirth`	Local variables, private fields
Title case aka Pascal case	`String, Int32, Cost, DateOfBirth, Run`	Types, non-private fields, and other members like methods

 Good Practice: Following a consistent set of naming conventions will enable your code to be easily understood by other developers (and yourself in the future!).

The following code block shows an example of declaring a named local variable and assigning a value to it with the = symbol. You should note that you can output the name of a variable using a keyword introduced in C# 6.0, nameof:

```
// let the heightInMetres variable become equal to the value 1.88
double heightInMetres = 1.88;
Console.WriteLine($"The variable {nameof(heightInMetres)} has the value
{heightInMetres}.");
```

The message in double quotes in the preceding code wraps onto a second line because the width of a printed page is too narrow. When entering a statement like this in your code editor, type it all in a single line.

Literal values

When you assign to a variable, you often, but not always, assign a **literal** value. But what is a literal value? A literal is a notation that represents a fixed value. Data types have different notations for their literal values, and over the next few sections, you will see examples of using literal notation to assign values to variables.

Storing text

For text, a single letter, such as an A, is stored as a char type.

 Good Practice: Actually, it can be more complicated than that. Egyptian Hieroglyph A002 (U+13001) needs two System.Char values (known as surrogate pairs) to represent it: \uD80C and \uDC01. Do not always assume one char equals one letter or you could introduce weird bugs into your code.

A char is assigned using single quotes around the literal value, or assigning the return value of a fictitious function call, as shown in the following code:

```
char letter = 'A'; // assigning literal characters
char digit = '1';
char symbol = '$';
char userChoice = GetSomeKeystroke(); // assigning from a fictitious function
```

For text, multiple letters, such as Bob, are stored as a string type and are assigned using double quotes around the literal value, or assigning the return value of a function call, as shown in the following code:

```
string firstName = "Bob"; // assigning literal strings
string lastName = "Smith";
string phoneNumber = "(215) 555-4256";

// assigning a string returned from a fictitious function
string address = GetAddressFromDatabase(id: 563);
```

Understanding verbatim strings

When storing text in a string variable, you can include escape sequences, which represent special characters like tabs and new lines using a backslash, as shown in the following code:

```
string fullNameWithTabSeparator = "Bob\tSmith";
```

But what if you are storing the path to a file on Windows, and one of the folder names starts with a T, as shown in the following code?

```
string filePath = "C:\televisions\sony\bravia.txt";
```

The compiler will convert the \t into a tab character and you will get errors!

You must prefix with the @ symbol to use a verbatim literal string, as shown in the following code:

```
string filePath = @"C:\televisions\sony\bravia.txt";
```

To summarize:

- **Literal string**: Characters enclosed in double-quote characters. They can use escape characters like \t for tab. To represent a backslash, use two: \\.

- **Verbatim string**: A literal string prefixed with @ to disable escape characters so that a backslash is a backslash. It also allows the string value to span multiple lines because the white space characters are treated as themselves instead of instructions to the compiler.

- **Interpolated string**: A literal string prefixed with $ to enable embedded formatted variables. You will learn more about this later in this chapter.

Storing numbers

Numbers are data that we want to perform an arithmetic calculation on, for example, multiplying. A telephone number is not a number. To decide whether a variable should be stored as a number or not, ask yourself whether you need to perform arithmetic operations on the number or whether the number includes non-digit characters such as parentheses or hyphens to format the number, such as (414) 555-1234. In this case, the number is a sequence of characters, so it should be stored as a string.

Numbers can be natural numbers, such as 42, used for counting (also called whole numbers); they can also be negative numbers, such as -42 (called integers); or, they can be real numbers, such as 3.9 (with a fractional part), which are called single- or double-precision floating-point numbers in computing.

Let's explore numbers:

1. Use your preferred code editor to add a new **Console Application** to the Chapter02 workspace/solution named Numbers:

    1. In Visual Studio Code, select Numbers as the active OmniSharp project. When you see the pop-up warning message saying that required assets are missing, click **Yes** to add them.

    2. In Visual Studio, set the startup project to the current selection.

2. In Program.cs, delete the existing code and then type statements to declare some number variables using various data types, as shown in the following code:

```
// unsigned integer means positive whole number or 0
uint naturalNumber = 23;

// integer means negative or positive whole number or 0
int integerNumber = -23;

// float means single-precision floating point
// F suffix makes it a float literal
float realNumber = 2.3F;

// double means double-precision floating point
double anotherRealNumber = 2.3; // double literal
```

Storing whole numbers

You might know that computers store everything as bits. The value of a bit is either 0 or 1. This is called a **binary number system**. Humans use a **decimal number system**.

The decimal number system, also known as Base 10, has 10 as its **base**, meaning there are ten digits, from 0 to 9. Although it is the number base most commonly used by human civilizations, other number base systems are popular in science, engineering, and computing. The binary number system, also known as Base 2, has two as its base, meaning there are two digits, 0 and 1.

The following table shows how computers store the decimal number 10. Take note of the bits with the value 1 in the 8 and 2 columns; 8 + 2 = 10:

128	64	32	16	8	4	2	1
0	0	0	0	1	0	1	0

So, 10 in decimal is 00001010 in binary.

Improving legibility by using digit separators

Two of the improvements seen in C# 7.0 and later are the use of the underscore character _ as a digit separator, and support for binary literals.

You can insert underscores anywhere into the digits of a number literal, including decimal, binary, or hexadecimal notation, to improve legibility.

For example, you could write the value for 1 million in decimal notation, that is, Base 10, as 1_000_000.

You can even use the 2/3 grouping common in India: 10_00_000.

Using binary notation

To use binary notation, that is, Base 2, using only 1s and 0s, start the number literal with 0b. To use hexadecimal notation, that is, Base 16, using 0 to 9 and A to F, start the number literal with 0x.

Exploring whole numbers

Let's enter some code to see some examples:

1. In Program.cs, type statements to declare some number variables using underscore separators, as shown in the following code:

```
// three variables that store the number 2 million
int decimalNotation = 2_000_000;
int binaryNotation = 0b_0001_1110_1000_0100_1000_0000;
int hexadecimalNotation = 0x_001E_8480;

// check the three variables have the same value
// both statements output true
Console.WriteLine($"{decimalNotation == binaryNotation}");
Console.WriteLine(
  $"{decimalNotation == hexadecimalNotation}");
```

2. Run the code and note the result is that all three numbers are the same, as shown in the following output:

```
True
True
```

Computers can always exactly represent integers using the int type or one of its sibling types, such as long and short.

Storing real numbers

Computers cannot always represent real, aka decimal or non-integer, numbers precisely. The float and double types store real numbers using single- and double-precision floating points.

Most programming languages implement the IEEE Standard for Floating-Point Arithmetic. IEEE 754 is a technical standard for floating-point arithmetic established in 1985 by the **Institute of Electrical and Electronics Engineers (IEEE)**.

The following table shows a simplification of how a computer represents the number 12.75 in binary notation. Note the bits with the value 1 in the 8, 4, ½, and ¼ columns.

$$8 + 4 + \frac{1}{2} + \frac{1}{4} = 12\frac{3}{4} = 12.75.$$

128	64	32	16	8	4	2	1	.	½	¼	1/8	1/16
0	0	0	0	1	1	0	0	.	1	1	0	0

So, 12.75 in decimal is 00001100.1100 in binary. As you can see, the number 12.75 can be exactly represented using bits. However, some numbers can't, something that we'll be exploring shortly.

Writing code to explore number sizes

C# has an operator named sizeof() that returns the number of bytes that a type uses in memory. Some types have members named MinValue and MaxValue, which return the minimum and maximum values that can be stored in a variable of that type. We are now going to use these features to create a console application to explore number types:

1. In Program.cs, type statements to show the size of three number data types, as shown in the following code:

```
Console.WriteLine($"int uses {sizeof(int)} bytes and can store numbers in
the range {int.MinValue:N0} to {int.MaxValue:N0}.");
Console.WriteLine($"double uses {sizeof(double)} bytes and can store
numbers in the range {double.MinValue:N0} to {double.MaxValue:N0}.");
Console.WriteLine($"decimal uses {sizeof(decimal)} bytes and can store
numbers in the range {decimal.MinValue:N0} to {decimal.MaxValue:N0}.");
```

The width of the printed pages in this book makes the string values (in double quotes) wrap over multiple lines. You must type them on a single line, or you will get compile errors.

2. Run the code and view the output, as shown in *Figure 2.3*:

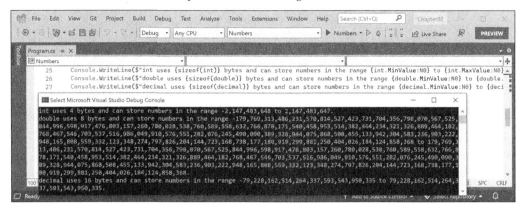

Figure 2.3: Size and range information for common number data types

An int variable uses four bytes of memory and can store positive or negative numbers up to about 2 billion. A double variable uses eight bytes of memory and can store much bigger values! A decimal variable uses 16 bytes of memory and can store big numbers, but not as big as a double type.

But you may be asking yourself, why might a double variable be able to store bigger numbers than a decimal variable, yet it's only using half the space in memory? Well, let's now find out!

Comparing double and decimal types

You will now write some code to compare double and decimal values. Although it isn't hard to follow, don't worry about understanding the syntax right now:

1. Type statements to declare two double variables, add them together and compare them to the expected result, and write the result to the console, as shown in the following code:

```
Console.WriteLine("Using doubles:");
double a = 0.1;
double b = 0.2;

if (a + b == 0.3)
{
  Console.WriteLine($"{a} + {b} equals {0.3}");
}
else
{
  Console.WriteLine($"{a} + {b} does NOT equal {0.3}");
}
```

2. Run the code and view the result, as shown in the following output:

```
Using doubles:
0.1 + 0.2 does NOT equal 0.3
```

In locales that use a comma for the decimal separator the result will look slightly different, as shown in the following output:

```
0,1 + 0,2 does NOT equal 0,3
```

The double type is not guaranteed to be accurate because some numbers like 0.1 literally cannot be represented as floating-point values.

As a rule of thumb, you should only use double when accuracy, especially when comparing the equality of two numbers, is not important. An example of this may be when you're measuring a person's height and you will only compare values using greater than or less than, but never equals.

The problem with the preceding code is illustrated by how the computer stores the number 0.1, or multiples of it. To represent 0.1 in binary, the computer stores 1 in the 1/16 column, 1 in the 1/32 column, 1 in the 1/256 column, 1 in the 1/512 column, and so on.

The number 0.1 in decimal is 0.00011001100110011... in binary, repeating forever:

4	2	1	.	½	¼	1/8	1/16	1/32	1/64	1/128	1/256	1/512	1/1024	1/2048
0	0	0	.	0	0	0	1	1	0	0	1	1	0	0

Good Practice: Never compare double values using ==. During the First Gulf War, an American Patriot missile battery used double values in its calculations. The inaccuracy caused it to fail to track and intercept an incoming Iraqi Scud missile, and 28 soldiers were killed; you can read about this at https://www.ima.umn.edu/~arnold/disasters/patriot.html.

1. Copy and paste the statements that you wrote before (that used the double variables).

2. Modify the statements to use decimal and rename the variables to c and d, as shown in the following code:

```
Console.WriteLine("Using decimals:");
decimal c = 0.1M; // M suffix means a decimal literal value
decimal d = 0.2M;

if (c + d == 0.3M)
{
  Console.WriteLine($"{c} + {d} equals {0.3M}");
}
else
{
```

```
        Console.WriteLine($"{c} + {d} does NOT equal {0.3M}");
    }
```

3. Run the code and view the result, as shown in the following output:

```
Using decimals:
0.1 + 0.2 equals 0.3
```

The `decimal` type is accurate because it stores the number as a large integer and shifts the decimal point. For example, `0.1` is stored as `1`, with a note to shift the decimal point one place to the left. `12.75` is stored as `1275`, with a note to shift the decimal point two places to the left.

 Good Practice: Use `int` for whole numbers. Use `double` for real numbers that will not be compared for equality to other values; it is okay to compare `double` values being less than or greater than, and so on. Use `decimal` for money, CAD drawings, general engineering, and wherever the accuracy of a real number is important.

The `double` type has some useful special values: `double.NaN` represents not-a-number (for example, the result of dividing by zero), `double.Epsilon` represents the smallest positive number that can be stored in a `double`, and `double.PositiveInfinity` and `double.NegativeInfinity` represent infinitely large positive and negative values.

Storing Booleans

Booleans can only contain one of the two literal values `true` or `false`, as shown in the following code:

```
bool happy = true;
bool sad = false;
```

They are most commonly used to branch and loop. You don't need to fully understand them yet, as they are covered more in *Chapter 3, Controlling Flow, Converting Types, and Handling Exceptions.*

Storing any type of object

There is a special type named `object` that can store any type of data, but its flexibility comes at the cost of messier code and possibly poor performance. Because of those two reasons, you should avoid it whenever possible. The following steps show how to use object types if you need to use them:

1. Use your preferred code editor to add a new **Console Application** to the `Chapter02` workspace/solution named `Variables`.

2. In Visual Studio Code, select `Variables` as the active OmniSharp project. When you see the pop-up warning message saying that required assets are missing, click **Yes** to add them.

3. In `Program.cs`, type statements to declare and use some variables using the `object` type, as shown in the following code:

```
object height = 1.88; // storing a double in an object
object name = "Amir"; // storing a string in an object
Console.WriteLine($"{name} is {height} metres tall.");

int length1 = name.Length; // gives compile error!
int length2 = ((string)name).Length; // tell compiler it is a string
Console.WriteLine($"{name} has {length2} characters.");
```

4. Run the code and note that the fourth statement cannot compile because the data type of the `name` variable is not known by the compiler, as shown in *Figure 2.4*:

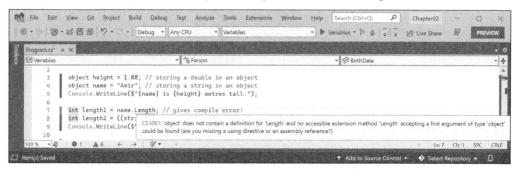

Figure 2.4: The object type does not have a Length property

5. Add comment double slashes to the beginning of the statement that cannot compile to "comment out" the statement to make it inactive.

6. Run the code again and note that the compiler can access the length of a `string` if the programmer explicitly tells the compiler that the `object` variable contains a `string` by prefixing with a cast expression like (`string`), as shown in the following output:

```
Amir is 1.88 metres tall.
Amir has 4 characters.
```

The `object` type has been available since the first version of C#, but C# 2.0 and later have a better alternative called **generics**, which we will cover in *Chapter 6, Implementing Interfaces and Inheriting Classes*, which will provide us with the flexibility we want, but without the performance overhead.

Storing dynamic types

There is another special type named `dynamic` that can also store any type of data, but even more than `object`, its flexibility comes at the cost of performance. The dynamic keyword was introduced in C# 4.0. However, unlike `object`, the value stored in the variable can have its members invoked without an explicit cast. Let's make use of a `dynamic` type:

1. Add statements to declare a dynamic variable and then assign a string literal value, and then an integer value, and then an array of integer values, as shown in the following code:

```
// storing a string in a dynamic object
// string has a Length property
dynamic something = "Ahmed";

// int does not have a Length property
// something = 12;

// an array of any type has a Length property
// something = new[] { 3, 5, 7 };
```

2. Add a statement to output the length of the dynamic variable, as shown in the following code:

```
// this compiles but would throw an exception at run-time
// if you later store a data type that does not have a
// property named Length
Console.WriteLine($"Length is {something.Length}");
```

3. Run the code and note it works because a string value does have a Length property, as shown in the following output:

```
Length is 5
```

4. Uncomment the statement that assigns an int value.

5. Run the code and note the runtime error because int does not have a Length property, as shown in the following output:

```
Unhandled exception. Microsoft.CSharp.RuntimeBinder.
RuntimeBinderException: 'int' does not contain a definition for 'Length'
```

6. Uncomment the statement that assigns the array.

7. Run the code and note the output because an array of three int values does have a Length property, as shown in the following output:

```
Length is 3
```

One limitation of dynamic is that code editors cannot show IntelliSense to help you write the code. This is because the compiler cannot check what the type is during build time. Instead, the CLR checks for the member at runtime and throws an exception if it is missing.

Exceptions are a way to indicate that something has gone wrong at runtime. You will learn more about them and how to handle them in *Chapter 3, Controlling Flow, Converting Types, and Handling Exceptions.*

Declaring local variables

Local variables are declared inside methods, and they only exist during the execution of that method, and once the method returns, the memory allocated to any local variables is released.

Strictly speaking, value types are released while reference types must wait for a garbage collection. You will learn about the difference between value types and reference types in *Chapter 6, Implementing Interfaces and Inheriting Classes*.

Specifying the type of a local variable

Let's explore local variables declared with specific types and using type inference:

1. Type statements to declare and assign values to some local variables using specific types, as shown in the following code:

```
int population = 66_000_000; // 66 million in UK
double weight = 1.88; // in kilograms
decimal price = 4.99M; // in pounds sterling
string fruit = "Apples"; // strings use double-quotes
char letter = 'Z'; // chars use single-quotes
bool happy = true; // Booleans have value of true or false
```

Depending on your code editor and color scheme, it will show green squiggles under each of the variable names and lighten their text color to warn you that the variable is assigned but its value is never used.

Inferring the type of a local variable

You can use the var keyword to declare local variables. The compiler will infer the type from the value that you assign after the assignment operator, =.

A literal number without a decimal point is inferred as an int variable, that is, unless you add a suffix, as described in the following list:

- L: infers long
- UL: infers ulong
- M: infers decimal
- D: infers double
- F: infers float

A literal number with a decimal point is inferred as double unless you add the M suffix, in which case, it infers a decimal variable, or the F suffix, in which case, it infers a float variable.

Double quotes indicate a `string` variable, single quotes indicate a `char` variable, and the `true` and `false` values infer a `bool` type:

1. Modify the previous statements to use var, as shown in the following code:

```
var population = 66_000_000; // 66 million in UK
var weight = 1.88; // in kilograms
var price = 4.99M; // in pounds sterling
var fruit = "Apples"; // strings use double-quotes
var letter = 'Z'; // chars use single-quotes
var happy = true; // Booleans have value of true or false
```

2. Hover your mouse over each of the var keywords and note that your code editor shows a tooltip with information about the type that has been inferred.

3. At the top of the class file, import the namespace for working with XML to enable us to declare some variables using types in that namespace, as shown in the following code:

```
using System.Xml;
```

 Good Practice: If you are using .NET Interactive Notebooks, then add using statements in a separate code cell above the code cell where you write the main code. Then click **Execute Cell** to ensure the namespaces are imported. They will then be available in subsequent code cells.

4. Under the previous statements, add statements to create some new objects, as shown in the following code:

```
// good use of var because it avoids the repeated type
// as shown in the more verbose second statement
var xml1 = new XmlDocument();
XmlDocument xml2 = new XmlDocument();

// bad use of var because we cannot tell the type, so we
// should use a specific type declaration as shown in
// the second statement
var file1 = File.CreateText("something1.txt");
StreamWriter file2 = File.CreateText("something2.txt");
```

 Good Practice: Although using var is convenient, some developers avoid using it, to make it easier for a code reader to understand the types in use. Personally, I use it only when the type is obvious. For example, in the preceding code statements, the first statement is just as clear as the second in stating what the type of the xml variables are, but it is shorter. However, the third statement isn't clear in showing the type of the `file` variable, so the fourth is better because it shows that the type is `StreamWriter`. If in doubt, spell it out!

Using target-typed new to instantiate objects

With C# 9, Microsoft introduced another syntax for instantiating objects known as **target-typed new**. When instantiating an object, you can specify the type first and then use new without repeating the type, as shown in the following code:

```
XmlDocument xml3 = new(); // target-typed new in C# 9 or later
```

If you have a type with a field or property that needs to be set, then the type can be inferred, as shown in the following code:

```
class Person
{
  public DateTime BirthDate;
}

Person kim = new();
kim.BirthDate = new(1967, 12, 26); // instead of: new DateTime(1967, 12, 26)
```

 Good Practice: Use target-typed new to instantiate objects unless you must use a pre-version 9 C# compiler. I have used target-typed new throughout the rest of this book. Please let me know if you spot any cases that I missed!

Getting and setting the default values for types

Most of the primitive types except string are **value types**, which means that they must have a value. You can determine the default value of a type by using the default() operator and passing the type as a parameter. You can assign the default value of a type by using the default keyword.

The string type is a **reference type**. This means that string variables contain the memory address of a value, not the value itself. A reference type variable can have a null value, which is a literal that indicates that the variable does not reference anything (yet). null is the default for all reference types.

You'll learn more about value types and reference types in *Chapter 6, Implementing Interfaces and Inheriting Classes*.

Let's explore default values:

1. Add statements to show the default values of an int, bool, DateTime, and string, as shown in the following code:

```
Console.WriteLine($"default(int) = {default(int)}");
Console.WriteLine($"default(bool) = {default(bool)}");
Console.WriteLine($"default(DateTime) = {default(DateTime)}");
Console.WriteLine($"default(string) = {default(string)}");
```

2. Run the code and view the result, noting that your output for the date and time might be formatted differently if you are not running it in the UK, and that `null` values output as an empty `string`, as shown in the following output:

```
default(int) = 0
default(bool) = False
default(DateTime) = 01/01/0001 00:00:00
default(string) =
```

3. Add statements to declare a number, assign a value, and then reset it to its default value, as shown in the following code:

```
int number = 13;
Console.WriteLine($"number has been set to: {number}");
number = default;
Console.WriteLine($"number has been reset to its default: {number}");
```

4. Run the code and view the result, as shown in the following output:

```
number has been set to: 13
number has been reset to its default: 0
```

Storing multiple values in an array

When you need to store multiple values of the same type, you can declare an **array**. For example, you may do this when you need to store four names in a `string` array.

The code that you will write next will allocate memory for an array for storing four `string` values. It will then store `string` values at index positions 0 to 3 (arrays usually have a lower bound of zero, so the index of the last item is one less than the length of the array).

> **Good Practice**: Do not assume that all arrays count from zero. The most common type of array in .NET is an **szArray**, a single-dimension zero-indexed array, and these use the normal [ ] syntax. But .NET also has **mdArray**, a multi-dimensional array, and they do not have to have a lower bound of zero. These are rarely used but you should know they exist.

Finally, it will loop through each item in the array using a `for` statement, something that we will cover in more detail in *Chapter 3, Controlling Flow, Converting Types, and Handling Exceptions*.

Let's look at how to use an array:

1. Type statements to declare and use an array of `string` values, as shown in the following code:

```
string[] names; // can reference any size array of strings

// allocating memory for four strings in an array
```

```
names = new string[4];

// storing items at index positions
names[0] = "Kate";
names[1] = "Jack";
names[2] = "Rebecca";
names[3] = "Tom";

// looping through the names
for (int i = 0; i < names.Length; i++)
{
  // output the item at index position i
  Console.WriteLine(names[i]);
}
```

2. Run the code and note the result, as shown in the following output:

```
Kate
Jack
Rebecca
Tom
```

Arrays are always of a fixed size at the time of memory allocation, so you need to decide how many items you want to store before instantiating them.

An alternative to defining the array in three steps as above is to use array initializer syntax, as shown in the following code:

```
string[] names2 = new[] { "Kate", "Jack", "Rebecca", "Tom" };
```

When you use the new[] syntax to allocate memory for the array, you must have at least one item in the curly braces so that the compiler can infer the data type.

Arrays are useful for temporarily storing multiple items, but collections are a more flexible option when adding and removing items dynamically. You don't need to worry about collections right now, as we will cover them in *Chapter 8, Working with Common .NET Types*.

Exploring more about console applications

We have already created and used basic console applications, but we're now at a stage where we should delve into them more deeply.

Console applications are text-based and are run at the command line. They typically perform simple tasks that need to be scripted, such as compiling a file or encrypting a section of a configuration file.

Equally, they can also have arguments passed to them to control their behavior.

An example of this would be to create a new console app using the F# language with a specified name instead of using the name of the current folder, as shown in the following command line:

```
dotnet new console -lang "F#" --name "ExploringConsole"
```

Displaying output to the user

The two most common tasks that a console application performs are writing and reading data. We have already been using the `WriteLine` method to output, but if we didn't want a carriage return at the end of the lines, we could have used the `Write` method.

Formatting using numbered positional arguments

One way of generating formatted strings is to use numbered positional arguments.

This feature is supported by methods like `Write` and `WriteLine`, and for methods that do not support the feature, the `string` parameter can be formatted using the `Format` method of `string`.

 The first few code examples in this section will work with a .NET Interactive notebook because they are about outputting to the console. Later in this section, you will learn about getting input via the console and sadly notebooks do not support this.

Let's begin formatting:

1. Use your preferred code editor to add a new **Console Application** to the `Chapter02` workspace/solution named `Formatting`.

2. In Visual Studio Code, select `Formatting` as the active OmniSharp project.

3. In `Program.cs`, type statements to declare some number variables and write them to the console, as shown in the following code:

```
int numberOfApples = 12;
decimal pricePerApple = 0.35M;

Console.WriteLine(
  format: "{0} apples costs {1:C}",
  arg0: numberOfApples,
  arg1: pricePerApple * numberOfApples);

string formatted = string.Format(
  format: "{0} apples costs {1:C}",
  arg0: numberOfApples,
  arg1: pricePerApple * numberOfApples);

//WriteToFile(formatted); // writes the string into a file
```

The `WriteToFile` method is a nonexistent method used to illustrate the idea.

Good Practice: Once you become more comfortable with formatting strings, you should stop naming the parameters, for example, stop using `format:`, `arg0:`, and `arg1:`. The preceding code uses a non-canonical style to show where the `0` and `1` came from while you are learning.

Formatting using interpolated strings

C# 6.0 and later have a handy feature named **interpolated strings**. A `string` prefixed with `$` can use curly braces around the name of a variable or expression to output the current value of that variable or expression at that position in the `string`, as the following shows:

1. Enter a statement at the bottom of the `Program.cs` file, as shown in the following code:

   ```
   Console.WriteLine($"{numberOfApples} apples costs {pricePerApple *
   numberOfApples:C}");
   ```

2. Run the code and view the result, as shown in the following partial output:

   ```
   12 apples costs £4.20
   ```

For short, formatted `string` values, an interpolated `string` can be easier for people to read. But for code examples in a book, where lines need to wrap over multiple lines, this can be tricky. For many of the code examples in this book, I will use numbered positional arguments.

Another reason to avoid interpolated strings is that they can't be read from resource files to be localized.

Before C# 10, string constants could only be combined by using concatenation, as shown in the following code:

```
private const string firstname = "Omar";
private const string lastname = "Rudberg";
private const string fullname = firstname + " " + lastname;
```

With C# 10, interpolated strings can now be used, as shown in the following code:

```
private const string fullname = "{firstname} {lastname}";
```

This only works for combining string constant values. It cannot work with other types like numbers that would require runtime data type conversions.

Understanding format strings

A variable or expression can be formatted using a format string after a comma or colon.

An `N0` format string means a number with a thousand separators and no decimal places, while a `C` format string means currency. The currency format will be determined by the current thread.

For instance, if you run this code on a PC in the UK, you'll get pounds sterling with commas as the thousand separators, but if you run this code on a PC in Germany, you will get euros with dots as the thousand separators.

The full syntax of a format item is:

```
{ index [, alignment ] [ : formatString ] }
```

Each format item can have an alignment, which is useful when outputting tables of values, some of which might need to be left- or right-aligned within a width of characters. Alignment values are integers. Positive integers mean right-aligned and negative integers mean left-aligned.

For example, to output a table of fruit and how many of each there are, we might want to left-align the names within a column of 10 characters and right-align the counts formatted as numbers with zero decimal places within a column of six characters:

1. At the bottom of `Program.cs`, enter the following statements:

```
string applesText = "Apples";
int applesCount = 1234;

string bananasText = "Bananas";
int bananasCount = 56789;

Console.WriteLine(
  format: "{0,-10} {1,6:N0}",
  arg0: "Name",
  arg1: "Count");

Console.WriteLine(
  format: "{0,-10} {1,6:N0}",
  arg0: applesText,
  arg1: applesCount);

Console.WriteLine(
  format: "{0,-10} {1,6:N0}",
  arg0: bananasText,
  arg1: bananasCount);
```

2. Run the code and note the effect of the alignment and number format, as shown in the following output:

```
Name          Count
Apples        1,234
Bananas      56,789
```

Getting text input from the user

We can get text input from the user using the ReadLine method. This method waits for the user to type some text, then as soon as the user presses *Enter*, whatever the user has typed is returned as a string value.

 Good Practice: If you are using a .NET Interactive notebook for this section, then note that it does not support reading input from the console using Console.ReadLine(). Instead, you must set literal values, as shown in the following code: string? firstName = "Gary";. This is often quicker to experiment with because you can simply change the literal string value and click the **Execute Cell** button instead of having to restart a console app each time you want to enter a different string value.

Let's get input from the user:

1. Type statements to ask the user for their name and age and then output what they entered, as shown in the following code:

    ```
    Console.Write("Type your first name and press ENTER: ");
    string? firstName = Console.ReadLine();

    Console.Write("Type your age and press ENTER: ");
    string? age = Console.ReadLine();

    Console.WriteLine(
      $"Hello {firstName}, you look good for {age}.");
    ```

2. Run the code, and then enter a name and age, as shown in the following output:

    ```
    Type your name and press ENTER: Gary
    Type your age and press ENTER: 34
    Hello Gary, you look good for 34.
    ```

 The question marks at the end of the string? data type declaration indicate that we acknowledge that a null (empty) value could be returned from the call to ReadLine. You will learn more about this in *Chapter 6, Implementing Interfaces and Inheriting Classes*.

Simplifying the usage of the console

In C# 6.0 and later, the using statement can be used not only to import a namespace but also to further simplify our code by importing a static class. Then, we won't need to enter the Console type name throughout our code. You can use your code editor's find and replace feature to remove the times we have previously written Console:

1. At the top of the `Program.cs` file, add a statement to **statically import** the `System.Console` class, as shown in the following code:

   ```
   using static System.Console;
   ```

2. Select the first `Console.` in your code, ensuring that you select the dot after the word `Console` too.

3. In Visual Studio, navigate to **Edit** | **Find and Replace** | **Quick Replace**, or in Visual Studio Code, navigate to **Edit** | **Replace**, and note that an overlay dialog appears ready for you to enter what you would like to replace **Console.** with, as shown in *Figure 2.5*:

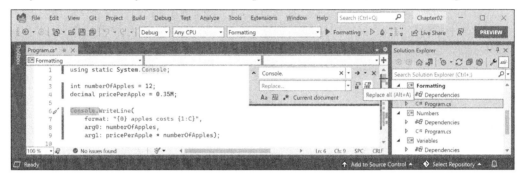

Figure 2.5: Using the Replace feature in Visual Studio to simplify your code

4. Leave the replace box empty, click on the **Replace all** button (the second of the two buttons to the right of the replace box), and then close the replace box by clicking on the cross in its top-right corner.

Getting key input from the user

We can get key input from the user using the `ReadKey` method. This method waits for the user to press a key or key combination that is then returned as a `ConsoleKeyInfo` value.

You will not be able to execute the call to the `ReadKey` method using a .NET Interactive notebook, but if you have created a console application, then let's explore reading key presses:

1. Type statements to ask the user to press any key combination and then output information about it, as shown in the following code:

   ```
   Write("Press any key combination: ");
   ConsoleKeyInfo key = ReadKey();
   WriteLine();
   WriteLine("Key: {0}, Char: {1}, Modifiers: {2}",
     arg0: key.Key,
     arg1: key.KeyChar,
     arg2: key.Modifiers);
   ```

2. Run the code, press the *K* key, and note the result, as shown in the following output:

```
Press any key combination: k
Key: K, Char: k, Modifiers: 0
```

3. Run the code, hold down *Shift* and press the *K* key, and note the result, as shown in the following output:

```
Press any key combination: K
Key: K, Char: K, Modifiers: Shift
```

4. Run the code, press the *F12* key, and note the result, as shown in the following output:

```
Press any key combination:
Key: F12, Char: , Modifiers: 0
```

 When running a console application in a terminal within Visual Studio Code, some keyboard combinations will be captured by the code editor or operating system before they can be processed by your app.

Passing arguments to a console app

You might have been wondering how to get any arguments that might be passed to a console application.

In every version of .NET prior to version 6.0, the console application project template made it obvious, as shown in the following code:

```
using System;

namespace Arguments
{
  class Program
  {
    static void Main(string[] args)
    {
      Console.WriteLine("Hello World!");
    }
  }
}
```

The string[] args arguments are declared and passed in the Main method of the Program class. They're an array used to pass arguments into a console application. But in top-level programs, as used by the console application project template in .NET 6.0 and later, the Program class and its Main method are hidden, along with the declaration of the args string array. The trick is that you must know it still exists.

Command-line arguments are separated by spaces. Other characters like hyphens and colons are treated as part of an argument value.

To include spaces in an argument value, enclose the argument value in single or double quotes.

Imagine that we want to be able to enter the names of some colors for the foreground and background, and the dimensions of the terminal window at the command line. We would be able to read the colors and numbers by reading them from the args array, which is always passed into the Main method aka the entry point of a console application:

1. Use your preferred code editor to add a new **Console Application** to the Chapter02 workspace/solution named Arguments. You will not be able to use a .NET Interactive notebook because you cannot pass arguments to a notebook.

2. In Visual Studio Code, select Arguments as the active OmniSharp project.

3. Add a statement to statically import the System.Console type and a statement to output the number of arguments passed to the application, as shown in the following code:

```
using static System.Console;

WriteLine($"There are {args.Length} arguments.");
```

 Good Practice: Remember to statically import the System.Console type in all future projects to simplify your code, as these instructions will not be repeated every time.

4. Run the code and view the result, as shown in the following output:

```
There are 0 arguments.
```

5. If you are using Visual Studio, then navigate to **Project | Arguments Properties**, select the **Debug** tab, and in the **Application arguments** box, enter some arguments, save the changes, and then run the console application, as shown in *Figure 2.6*:

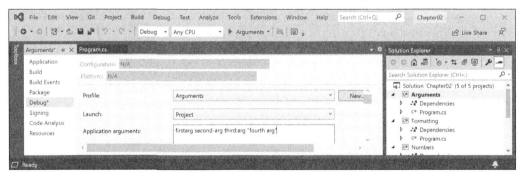

Figure 2.6: Entering application arguments in Visual Studio project properties

6. If you are using Visual Studio Code, then in a terminal, enter some arguments after the dotnet run command, as shown in the following command line:

```
dotnet run firstarg second-arg third:arg "fourth arg"
```

7. Note the result indicates four arguments, as shown in the following output:

```
There are 4 arguments.
```

8. To enumerate or iterate (that is, loop through) the values of those four arguments, add the following statements after outputting the length of the array:

```
foreach (string arg in args)
{
  WriteLine(arg);
}
```

9. Run the code again and note the result shows the details of the four arguments, as shown in the following output:

```
There are 4 arguments.
firstarg
second-arg
third:arg
fourth arg
```

Setting options with arguments

We will now use these arguments to allow the user to pick a color for the background, foreground, and cursor size of the output window. The cursor size can be an integer value from 1, meaning a line at the bottom of the cursor cell, up to 100, meaning a percentage of the height of the cursor cell.

The System namespace is already imported so that the compiler knows about the ConsoleColor and Enum types:

1. Add statements to warn the user if they do not enter three arguments and then parse those arguments and use them to set the color and dimensions of the console window, as shown in the following code:

```
if (args.Length < 3)
{
  WriteLine("You must specify two colors and cursor size, e.g.");
  WriteLine("dotnet run red yellow 50");
  return; // stop running
}

ForegroundColor = (ConsoleColor)Enum.Parse(
  enumType: typeof(ConsoleColor),
  value: args[0],
  ignoreCase: true);

BackgroundColor = (ConsoleColor)Enum.Parse(
  enumType: typeof(ConsoleColor),
```

```
    value: args[1],
    ignoreCase: true);

CursorSize = int.Parse(args[2]);
```

 Setting the `CursorSize` is only supported on Windows.

2. In Visual Studio, navigate to **Project | Arguments Properties**, and change the arguments to: red yellow 50, run the console app, and note the cursor is half the size and the colors have changed in the window, as shown in *Figure 2.7*:

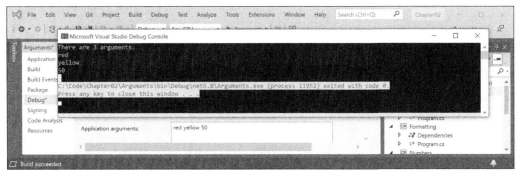

Figure 2.7: Setting colors and cursor size on Windows

3. In Visual Studio Code, run the code with arguments to set the foreground color to red, the background color to yellow, and the cursor size to 50%, as shown in the following command:

```
dotnet run red yellow 50
```

On macOS, you'll see an unhandled exception, as shown in *Figure 2.8*:

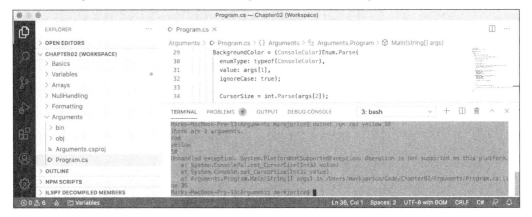

Figure 2.8: An unhandled exception on unsupported macOS

Although the compiler did not give an error or warning, at runtime some API calls may fail on some platforms. Although a console application running on Windows can change its cursor size, on macOS, it cannot, and complains if you try.

Handling platforms that do not support an API

So how do we solve this problem? We can solve this by using an exception handler. You will learn more details about the try-catch statement in *Chapter 3, Controlling Flow, Converting Types, and Handling Exceptions*, so for now, just enter the code:

1. Modify the code to wrap the lines that change the cursor size in a try statement, as shown in the following code:

```
try
{
  CursorSize = int.Parse(args[2]);
}
catch (PlatformNotSupportedException)
{
  WriteLine("The current platform does not support changing the size of
the cursor.");
}
```

2. If you were to run the code on macOS then you would see the exception is caught, and a friendlier message is shown to the user.

Another way to handle differences in operating systems is to use the OperatingSystem class in the System namespace, as shown in the following code:

```
if (OperatingSystem.IsWindows())
{
  // execute code that only works on Windows
}
else if (OperatingSystem.IsWindowsVersionAtLeast(major: 10))
{
  // execute code that only works on Windows 10 or later
}
else if (OperatingSystem.IsIOSVersionAtLeast(major: 14, minor: 5))
{
  // execute code that only works on iOS 14.5 or later
}
else if (OperatingSystem.IsBrowser())
{
  // execute code that only works in the browser with Blazor
}
```

The OperatingSystem class has equivalent methods for other common operating systems like Android, iOS, Linux, macOS, and even the browser, which is useful for Blazor web components.

A third way to handle different platforms is to use conditional compilation statements.

There are four preprocessor directives that control conditional compilation: #if, #elif, #else, and #endif.

You define symbols using #define, as shown in the following code:

```
#define MYSYMBOL
```

Many symbols are automatically defined for you, as shown in the following table:

Target Framework	Symbols
.NET Standard	NETSTANDARD2_0, NETSTANDARD2_1, and so on
Modern .NET	NET6_0, NET6_0_ANDROID, NET6_0_IOS, NET6_0_WINDOWS, and so on

You can then write statements that will compile only for the specified platforms, as shown in the following code:

```
#if NET6_0_ANDROID
// compile statements that only works on Android
#elif NET6_0_IOS
// compile statements that only works on iOS
#else
// compile statements that work everywhere else
#endif
```

Practicing and exploring

Test your knowledge and understanding by answering some questions, get some hands-on practice, and explore the topics covered in this chapter with deeper research.

Exercise 2.1 – Test your knowledge

To get the best answer to some of these questions, you will need to do your own research. I want you to "think outside the book" so I have deliberately not provided all the answers in the book.

I want to encourage you to get in to the good habit of looking for help elsewhere, following the principle of "teach a person to fish."

1. What statement can you type in a C# file to discover the compiler and language version?
2. What are the two types of comments in C#?

3. What is the difference between a verbatim string and an interpolated string?

4. Why should you be careful when using `float` and `double` values?

5. How can you determine how many bytes a type like `double` uses in memory?

6. When should you use the `var` keyword?

7. What is the newest way to create an instance of a class like `XmlDocument`?

8. Why should you be careful when using the `dynamic` type?

9. How do you right-align a format string?

10. What character separates arguments for a console application?

 Appendix, Answers to the Test Your Knowledge Questions is available to download from a link in the README on the GitHub repository: `https://github.com/markjprice/cs10dotnet6`.

Exercise 2.2 – Test your knowledge of number types

What type would you choose for the following "numbers"?

1. A person's telephone number

2. A person's height

3. A person's age

4. A person's salary

5. A book's ISBN

6. A book's price

7. A book's shipping weight

8. A country's population

9. The number of stars in the universe

10. The number of employees in each of the small or medium businesses in the United Kingdom (up to about 50,000 employees per business)

Exercise 2.3 – Practice number sizes and ranges

In the `Chapter02` solution/workspace, create a console application project named `Exercise02` that outputs the number of bytes in memory that each of the following number types uses and the minimum and maximum values they can have: `sbyte`, `byte`, `short`, `ushort`, `int`, `uint`, `long`, `ulong`, `float`, `double`, and `decimal`.

The result of running your console application should look something like *Figure 2.9*:

```
Microsoft Visual Studio Debug Console                                    —    □    ×
- - - - - - - - - - - - - - - - - - - - - - - - - - - - - - - - - - - - - - - - - - -
Type    Byte(s) of memory              Min                          Max
- - - - - - - - - - - - - - - - - - - - - - - - - - - - - - - - - - - - - - - - - - -
sbyte   1                             -128                          127
byte    1                                0                          255
short   2                           -32768                        32767
ushort  2                                0                        65535
int     4                      -2147483648                   2147483647
uint    4                                0                   4294967295
long    8             -9223372036854775808          9223372036854775807
ulong   8                                0         18446744073709551615
float   4                   -3.4028235E+38                3.4028235E+38
double  8          -1.7976931348623157E+308       1.7976931348623157E+308
decimal 16 -79228162514264337593543950335  79228162514264337593543950335
- - - - - - - - - - - - - - - - - - - - - - - - - - - - - - - - - - - - - - - - - - -
```

Figure 2.9: The result of outputting number type sizes

 Code solutions for all exercises are available to download or clone from the GitHub repository at the following link: https://github.com/markjprice/cs10dotnet6.

Exercise 2.4 – Explore topics

Use the links on the following page to learn more detail about the topics covered in this chapter:

https://github.com/markjprice/cs10dotnet6/blob/main/book-links.md#chapter-2---speaking-c

Summary

In this chapter, you learned how to:

- Declare variables with a specified or an inferred type.
- Use some of the built-in types for numbers, text, and Booleans.
- Choose between number types.
- Control output formatting in console apps.

In the next chapter, you will learn about operators, branching, looping, converting between types, and how to handle exceptions.

03

Controlling Flow, Converting Types, and Handling Exceptions

This chapter is all about writing code that performs simple operations on variables, makes decisions, performs pattern matching, repeats statements or blocks, converts variable or expression values from one type to another, handles exceptions, and checks for overflows in number variables.

This chapter covers the following topics:

- Operating on variables
- Understanding selection statements
- Understanding iteration statements
- Casting and converting between types
- Handling exceptions
- Checking for overflow

Operating on variables

Operators apply simple operations such as addition and multiplication to **operands** such as variables and literal values. They usually return a new value that is the result of the operation that can be assigned to a variable.

Most operators are binary, meaning that they work on two operands, as shown in the following pseudocode:

```
var resultOfOperation = firstOperand operator secondOperand;
```

Examples of binary operators include adding and multiplying, as shown in the following code:

```
int x = 5;
int y = 3;
int resultOfAdding = x + y;
int resultOfMultiplying = x * y;
```

Some operators are unary, meaning they work on a single operand, and can apply before or after the operand, as shown in the following pseudocode:

```
var resultOfOperation = onlyOperand operator;
var resultOfOperation2 = operator onlyOperand;
```

Examples of unary operators include incrementors and retrieving a type or its size in bytes, as shown in the following code:

```
int x = 5;
int postfixIncrement = x++;
int prefixIncrement = ++x;
Type theTypeOfAnInteger = typeof(int);
int howManyBytesInAnInteger = sizeof(int);
```

A ternary operator works on three operands, as shown in the following pseudocode:

```
var resultOfOperation = firstOperand firstOperator
  secondOperand secondOperator thirdOperand;
```

Exploring unary operators

Two common unary operators are used to increment, ++, and decrement, --, a number. Let us write some example code to show how they work:

1. If you've completed the previous chapters, then you will already have a Code folder. If not, then you'll need to create it.

2. Use your preferred coding tool to create a new console app, as defined in the following list:

    1. Project template: **Console Application** / console

    2. Workspace/solution file and folder: Chapter03

    3. Project file and folder: Operators

3. At the top of Program.cs, statically import System.Console.

4. In Program.cs, declare two integer variables named a and b, set a to 3, increment a while assigning the result to b, and then output their values, as shown in the following code:
    ```
    int a = 3;
    int b = a++;
    WriteLine($"a is {a}, b is {b}");
    ```

5. Before running the console application, ask yourself a question: what do you think the value of b will be when output? Once you've thought about that, run the code, and compare your prediction against the actual result, as shown in the following output:

```
a is 4, b is 3
```

The variable b has the value 3 because the ++ operator executes *after* the assignment; this is known as a **postfix operator**. If you need to increment *before* the assignment, then use the **prefix operator**.

6. Copy and paste the statements, and then modify them to rename the variables and use the prefix operator, as shown in the following code:

```
int c = 3;
int d = ++c; // increment c before assigning it
WriteLine($"c is {c}, d is {d}");
```

7. Rerun the code and note the result, as shown in the following output:

```
a is 4, b is 3
c is 4, d is 4
```

> **Good Practice**: Due to the confusion between prefix and postfix for the increment and decrement operators when combined with an assignment, the Swift programming language designers decided to drop support for this operator in version 3. My recommendation for usage in C# is to never combine the use of ++ and -- operators with an assignment operator, =. Perform the operations as separate statements.

Exploring binary arithmetic operators

Increment and decrement are unary arithmetic operators. Other arithmetic operators are usually binary and allow you to perform arithmetic operations on two numbers, as the following shows:

1. Add the statements to declare and assign values to two integer variables named e and f, and then apply the five common binary arithmetic operators to the two numbers, as shown in the following code:

```
int e = 11;
int f = 3;
WriteLine($"e is {e}, f is {f}");
WriteLine($"e + f = {e + f}");
WriteLine($"e - f = {e - f}");
WriteLine($"e * f = {e * f}");
WriteLine($"e / f = {e / f}");
WriteLine($"e % f = {e % f}");
```

2. Run the code and note the result, as shown in the following output:

```
e is 11, f is 3
e + f = 14
e - f = 8
e * f = 33
e / f = 3
e % f = 2
```

To understand the divide / and modulo % operators when applied to integers, you need to think back to primary school. Imagine you have eleven sweets and three friends.

How can you divide the sweets between your friends? You can give three sweets to each of your friends, and there will be two left over. Those two sweets are the **modulus**, also known as the **remainder** after dividing. If you have twelve sweets, then each friend gets four of them, and there are none left over, so the remainder would be 0.

3. Add statements to declare and assign a value to a `double` variable named g to show the difference between whole number and real number divisions, as shown in the following code:

```
double g = 11.0;
WriteLine($"g is {g:N1}, f is {f}");
WriteLine($"g / f = {g / f}");
```

4. Run the code and note the result, as shown in the following output:

```
g is 11.0, f is 3
g / f = 3.6666666666666665
```

If the first operand is a floating-point number, such as g with the value 11.0, then the divide operator returns a floating-point value, such as 3.6666666666665, rather than a whole number.

Assignment operators

You have already been using the most common assignment operator, =.

To make your code more concise, you can combine the assignment operator with other operators like arithmetic operators, as shown in the following code:

```
int p = 6;
p += 3; // equivalent to p = p + 3;
p -= 3; // equivalent to p = p - 3;
p *= 3; // equivalent to p = p * 3;
p /= 3; // equivalent to p = p / 3;
```

Exploring logical operators

Logical operators operate on Boolean values, so they return either `true` or `false`. Let's explore binary logical operators that operate on two Boolean values:

1. Use your preferred coding tool to add a new console app to the Chapter03 workspace/ solution named BooleanOperators.

   1. In Visual Studio Code, select BooleanOperators as the active OmniSharp project. When you see the pop-up warning message saying that required assets are missing, click **Yes** to add them.

   2. In Visual Studio, set the start up project for the solution to the current selection.

    Good Practice: Remember to statically import the System.Console type to simplify statements.

2. In Program.cs, add statements to declare two Boolean variables with values of true and false, and then output truth tables showing the results of applying AND, OR, and XOR (exclusive OR) logical operators, as shown in the following code:

```
bool a = true;
bool b = false;

WriteLine($"AND   | a     | b     ");
WriteLine($"a     | {a & a,-5} | {a & b,-5} ");
WriteLine($"b     | {b & a,-5} | {b & b,-5} ");
WriteLine();
WriteLine($"OR    | a     | b     ");
WriteLine($"a     | {a | a,-5} | {a | b,-5} ");
WriteLine($"b     | {b | a,-5} | {b | b,-5} ");
WriteLine();
WriteLine($"XOR   | a     | b     ");
WriteLine($"a     | {a ^ a,-5} | {a ^ b,-5} ");
WriteLine($"b     | {b ^ a,-5} | {b ^ b,-5} ");
```

3. Run the code and note the results, as shown in the following output:

```
AND   | a     | b
a     | True  | False
b     | False | False

OR    | a     | b
a     | True  | True
b     | True  | False

XOR   | a     | b
a     | False | True
b     | True  | False
```

For the AND & logical operator, both operands must be true for the result to be true. For the OR | logical operator, either operand can be true for the result to be true. For the XOR ^ logical operator, either operand can be true (but not both!) for the result to be true.

Exploring conditional logical operators

Conditional logical operators are like logical operators, but you use two symbols instead of one, for example, && instead of &, or || instead of |.

In *Chapter 4, Writing, Debugging, and Testing Functions,* you will learn about functions in more detail, but I need to introduce functions now to explain conditional logical operators, also known as short-circuiting Boolean operators.

A function executes statements and then returns a value. That value could be a Boolean value like true that is used in a Boolean operation. Let's make use of conditional logical operators:

1. At the bottom of Program.cs, write statements to declare a function that writes a message to the console and returns true, as shown in the following code:

   ```
   static bool DoStuff()
   {
     WriteLine("I am doing some stuff.");
     return true;
   }
   ```

    Good Practice: If you are using .NET Interactive Notebook, write the DoStuff function in a separate code cell and then execute it to make its context available to other code cells.

2. After the previous WriteLine statements, perform an AND & operation on the a and b variables and the result of calling the function, as shown in the following code:

   ```
   WriteLine();
   WriteLine($"a & DoStuff() = {a & DoStuff()}");
   WriteLine($"b & DoStuff() = {b & DoStuff()}");
   ```

3. Run the code, view the result, and note that the function was called twice, once for a and once for b, as shown in the following output:

   ```
   I am doing some stuff.
   a & DoStuff() = True
   I am doing some stuff.
   b & DoStuff() = False
   ```

4. Change the & operators into && operators, as shown in the following code:

   ```
   WriteLine($"a && DoStuff() - {a && DoStuff()}");
   WriteLine($"b && DoStuff() = {b && DoStuff()}");
   ```

5. Run the code, view the result, and note that the function does run when combined with the a variable. It does not run when combined with the b variable because the b variable is `false` so the result will be `false` anyway, so it does not need to execute the function, as shown in the following output:

```
I am doing some stuff.
a && DoStuff() = True
b && DoStuff() = False // DoStuff function was not executed!
```

> **Good Practice**: Now you can see why the conditional logical operators are described as being short-circuiting. They can make your apps more efficient, but they can also introduce subtle bugs in cases where you assume that the function would always be called. It is safest to avoid them when used in combination with functions that cause side effects.

Exploring bitwise and binary shift operators

Bitwise operators affect the bits in a number. Binary shift operators can perform some common arithmetic calculations much faster than traditional operators, for example, any multiplication by a factor of 2.

Let's explore bitwise and binary shift operators:

1. Use your preferred coding tool to add a new **Console Application** to the Chapter03 workspace/solution named BitwiseAndShiftOperators.

2. In Visual Studio Code, select BitwiseAndShiftOperators as the active OmniSharp project. When you see the pop-up warning message saying that required assets are missing, click **Yes** to add them.

3. In Program.cs, type statements to declare two integer variables with values 10 and 6, and then output the results of applying AND, OR, and XOR bitwise operators, as shown in the following code:

```
int a = 10; // 00001010
int b = 6;  // 00000110

WriteLine($"a = {a}");
WriteLine($"b = {b}");
WriteLine($"a & b = {a & b}"); // 2-bit column only
WriteLine($"a | b = {a | b}"); // 8, 4, and 2-bit columns
WriteLine($"a ^ b = {a ^ b}"); // 8 and 4-bit columns
```

4. Run the code and note the results, as shown in the following output:

```
a = 10
b = 6
a & b = 2
```

```
a | b = 14
a ^ b = 12
```

5. In `Program.cs`, add statements to output the results of applying the left-shift operator to move the bits of the variable a by three columns, multiplying a by 8, and right-shifting the bits of the variable b by one column, as shown in the following code:

```
// 01010000 left-shift a by three bit columns
WriteLine($"a << 3 = {a << 3}");

// multiply a by 8
WriteLine($"a * 8 = {a * 8}");

// 00000011 right-shift b by one bit column
WriteLine($"b >> 1 = {b >> 1}");
```

6. Run the code and note the results, as shown in the following output:

```
a << 3 = 80
a * 8 = 80
b >> 1 = 3
```

The 80 result is because the bits in it were shifted three columns to the left, so the 1-bits moved into the 64- and 16-bit columns and 64 + 16 = 80. This is the equivalent of multiplying by 8, but CPUs can perform a bit-shift faster. The 3 result is because the 1-bits in b were shifted one column into the 2- and 1-bit columns.

Good Practice: Remember that when operating on integer values, the & and | symbols are bitwise operators, and when operating on Boolean values like true and false, the & and | symbols are logical operators.

We can illustrate the operations by converting the integer values into binary strings of zeros and ones:

1. At the bottom of `Program.cs`, add a function to convert an integer value into a binary (Base2) string of up to eight zeros and ones, as shown in the following code:

```
static string ToBinaryString(int value)
{
  return Convert.ToString(value, toBase: 2).PadLeft(8, '0');
}
```

2. Above the function, add statements to output a, b, and the results of the various bitwise operators, as shown in the following code:

```
WriteLine();
WriteLine("Outputting integers as binary:");
```

```
WriteLine($"a =      {ToBinaryString(a)}");
WriteLine($"b =      {ToBinaryString(b)}");
WriteLine($"a & b = {ToBinaryString(a & b)}");
WriteLine($"a | b = {ToBinaryString(a | b)}");
WriteLine($"a ^ b = {ToBinaryString(a ^ b)}");
```

3. Run the code and note the results, as shown in the following output:

```
Outputting integers as binary:
a =      00001010
b =      00000110
a & b = 00000010
a | b = 00001110
a ^ b = 00001100
```

Miscellaneous operators

nameof and sizeof are convenient operators when working with types:

*   nameof returns the short name (without the namespace) of a variable, type, or member as a string value, which is useful when outputting exception messages.

*   sizeof returns the size in bytes of simple types, which is useful for determining the efficiency of data storage.

There are many other operators; for example, the dot between a variable and its members is called the **member access operator** and the round brackets at the end of a function or method name are called the **invocation operator**, as shown in the following code:

```
int age = 47;

// How many operators in the following statement?
char firstDigit = age.ToString()[0];

// There are four operators:
// = is the assignment operator
// . is the member access operator
// () is the invocation operator
// [] is the indexer access operator
```

Understanding selection statements

Every application needs to be able to select from choices and branch along different code paths. The two selection statements in C# are if and switch. You can use if for all your code, but switch can simplify your code in some common scenarios such as when there is a single variable that can have multiple values that each require different processing.

Branching with the if statement

The if statement determines which branch to follow by evaluating a Boolean expression. If the expression is true, then the block executes. The else block is optional, and it executes if the if expression is false. The if statement can be nested.

The if statement can be combined with other if statements as else if branches, as shown in the following code:

```
if (expression1)
{
  // runs if expression1 is true
}
else if (expression2)
{
  // runs if expression1 is false and expression2 if true
}
else if (expression3)
{
  // runs if expression1 and expression2 are false
  // and expression3 is true
}
else
{
  // runs if all expressions are false
}
```

Each if statement's Boolean expression is independent of the others and, unlike switch statements, does not need to reference a single value.

Let's write some code to explore selection statements like if:

1. Use your preferred coding tool to add a new **Console Application** to the Chapter03 workspace/solution named SelectionStatements.

2. In Visual Studio Code, select SelectionStatements as the active OmniSharp project.

3. In Program.cs, type statements to check if a password is at least eight characters, as shown in the following code:

```
string password = "ninja";

if (password.Length < 8)
{
  WriteLine("Your password is too short. Use at least 8 characters.");
}
else
{
  WriteLine("Your password is strong.");
}
```

4. Run the code and note the result, as shown in the following output:

```
Your password is too short. Use at least 8 characters.
```

Why you should always use braces with if statements

As there is only a single statement inside each block, the preceding code could be written without the curly braces, as shown in the following code:

```
if (password.Length < 8)
  WriteLine("Your password is too short. Use at least 8 characters.");
else
  WriteLine("Your password is strong.");
```

This style of `if` statement should be avoided because it can introduce serious bugs, for example, the infamous #gotofail bug in Apple's iPhone iOS operating system.

For 18 months after Apple's iOS 6 was released, in September 2012, it had a bug in its **Secure Sockets Layer** (**SSL**) encryption code, which meant that any user running Safari, the device's web browser, who tried to connect to secure websites, such as their bank, was not properly secure because an important check was being accidentally skipped.

Just because you can leave out the curly braces doesn't mean you should. Your code is not "more efficient" without them; instead, it is less maintainable and potentially more dangerous.

Pattern matching with the if statement

A feature introduced with C# 7.0 and later is pattern matching. The `if` statement can use the `is` keyword in combination with declaring a local variable to make your code safer:

1. Add statements so that if the value stored in the variable named o is an `int`, then the value is assigned to the local variable named i, which can then be used inside the `if` statement. This is safer than using the variable named o because we know for sure that i is an `int` variable and not something else, as shown in the following code:

```
// add and remove the "" to change the behavior
object o = "3";
int j = 4;

if (o is int i)
{
  WriteLine($"{i} x {j} = {i * j}");
}
else
{
  WriteLine("o is not an int so it cannot multiply!");
}
```

2. Run the code and view the results, as shown in the following output:

```
o is not an int so it cannot multiply!
```

3. Delete the double-quote characters around the "3" value so that the value stored in the variable named o is an int type instead of a string type.

4. Rerun the code to view the results, as shown in the following output:

```
3 x 4 = 12
```

Branching with the switch statement

The switch statement is different from the if statement because switch compares a single expression against a list of multiple possible case statements. Every case statement is related to the single expression. Every case section must end with:

- The break keyword (like case 1 in the following code)
- Or the goto case keywords (like case 2 in the following code)
- Or they should have no statements (like case 3 in the following code)
- Or the goto keyword that references a named label (like case 5 in the following code)
- Or the return keyword to leave the current function (not shown in the code)

Let's write some code to explore the switch statements:

1. Type statements for a switch statement. You should note that the penultimate statement is a label that can be jumped to, and the first statement generates a random number between 1 and 6 (the number 7 in the code is an exclusive upper bound). The switch statement branches are based on the value of this random number, as shown in the following code:

```
int number = (new Random()).Next(1, 7);
WriteLine($"My random number is {number}");

switch (number)
{
  case 1:
    WriteLine("One");
    break; // jumps to end of switch statement
  case 2:
    WriteLine("Two");
    goto case 1;
  case 3: // multiple case section
  case 4:
    WriteLine("Three or four");
    goto case 1;
  case 5:
    goto A_label;
```

```
    default:
      WriteLine("Default");
      break;
} // end of switch statement

WriteLine("After end of switch");
A_label:
WriteLine($"After A_label");
```

 Good Practice: You can use the goto keyword to jump to another case or a label. The goto keyword is frowned upon by most programmers but can be a good solution to code logic in some scenarios. However, you should use it sparingly.

2. Run the code multiple times to see what happens in various cases of random numbers, as shown in the following example output:

```
// first random run
My random number is 4
Three or four
One
After end of switch
After A_label

// second random run
My random number is 2
Two
One
After end of switch
After A_label

// third random run
My random number is 6
Default
After end of switch
After A_label

// fourth random run
My random number is 1
One
After end of switch
After A_label

// fifth random run
My random number is 5
After A_label
```

Pattern matching with the switch statement

Like the if statement, the switch statement supports pattern matching in C# 7.0 and later. The case values no longer need to be literal values; they can be patterns.

Let's see an example of pattern matching with the switch statement using a folder path. If you are using macOS, then swap the commented statement that sets the path variable and replace my username with your user folder name:

1. Add statements to declare a string path to a file, open it as either a read-only or writeable stream, and then show a message based on what type and capabilities the stream has, as shown in the following code:

```
// string path = "/Users/markjprice/Code/Chapter03";
string path = @"C:\Code\Chapter03";

Write("Press R for read-only or W for writeable: ");
ConsoleKeyInfo key = ReadKey();
WriteLine();

Stream? s;

if (key.Key == ConsoleKey.R)
{
  s =  File.Open(
    Path.Combine(path, "file.txt"),
    FileMode.OpenOrCreate,
    FileAccess.Read);
}
else
{
  s =  File.Open(
    Path.Combine(path, "file.txt"),
    FileMode.OpenOrCreate,
    FileAccess.Write);
}

string message;

switch (s)
{
  case FileStream writeableFile when s.CanWrite:
    message = "The stream is a file that I can write to.";
    break;
  case FileStream readOnlyFile:
    message = "The stream is a read-only file.";
    break;
```

```
      case MemoryStream ms:
        message = "The stream is a memory address.";
        break;
      default: // always evaluated last despite its current position
        message = "The stream is some other type.";
        break;
      case null:
        message = "The stream is null.";
        break;
    }

    WriteLine(message);
```

2. Run the code and note that the variable named s is declared as a Stream type so it could be any subtype of stream, such as a memory stream or file stream. In this code, the stream is created using the File.Open method, which returns a file stream and, depending on your key press, it will be writeable or read-only, so the result will be a message that describes the situation, as shown in the following output:

```
The stream is a file that I can write to.
```

In .NET, there are multiple subtypes of Stream, including FileStream and MemoryStream. In C# 7.0 and later, your code can more concisely branch, based on the subtype of stream, and declare and assign a local variable to safely use it. You will learn more about the System.IO namespace and the Stream type in *Chapter 9, Working with Files, Streams, and Serialization*.

Additionally, case statements can include a when keyword to perform more specific pattern matching. In the first case statement in the preceding code, s will only be a match if the stream is a FileStream and its CanWrite property is true.

Simplifying switch statements with switch expressions

In C# 8.0 or later, you can simplify switch statements using **switch expressions**.

Most switch statements are very simple, yet they require a lot of typing. switch expressions are designed to simplify the code you need to type while still expressing the same intent in scenarios where all cases return a value to set a single variable. switch expressions use a lambda, =>, to indicate a return value.

Let's implement the previous code that used a switch statement using a switch expression so that you can compare the two styles:

1. Type statements to set the message based on what type and capabilities the stream has, using a switch expression, as shown in the following code:

```
message = s switch
{
```

```
FileStream writeableFile when s.CanWrite
  => "The stream is a file that I can write to.",
FileStream readOnlyFile
  => "The stream is a read-only file.",
MemoryStream ms
  => "The stream is a memory address.",
null
  => "The stream is null.",

_
  => "The stream is some other type."
};

WriteLine(message);
```

The main differences are the removal of the case and break keywords. The underscore character _ is used to represent the default return value.

2. Run the code, and note the result is the same as before.

Understanding iteration statements

Iteration statements repeat a block of statements either while a condition is true or for each item in a collection. The choice of which statement to use is based on a combination of ease of understanding to solve the logic problem and personal preference.

Looping with the while statement

The while statement evaluates a Boolean expression and continues to loop while it is true. Let's explore iteration statements:

1. Use your preferred coding tool to add a new **Console Application** to the Chapter03 workspace/solution named IterationStatements.

2. In Visual Studio Code, select IterationStatements as the active OmniSharp project.

3. In Program.cs, type statements to define a while statement that loops while an integer variable has a value less than 10, as shown in the following code:

```
int x = 0;

while (x < 10)
{
  WriteLine(x);
  x++;
}
```

4. Run the code and view the results, which should be the numbers 0 to 9, as shown in the following output:

```
0
1
2
3
4
5
6
7
8
9
```

Looping with the do statement

The do statement is like `while`, except the Boolean expression is checked at the bottom of the block instead of the top, which means that the block always executes at least once, as the following shows:

1. Type statements to define a do loop, as shown in the following code:

```
string? password;

do
{
  Write("Enter your password: ");
  password = ReadLine();
}
while (password != "Pa$$w0rd");

WriteLine("Correct!");
```

2. Run the code, and note that you are prompted to enter your password repeatedly until you enter it correctly, as shown in the following output:

```
Enter your password: password
Enter your password: 12345678
Enter your password: ninja
Enter your password: correct horse battery staple
Enter your password: Pa$$w0rd
Correct!
```

3. As an optional challenge, add statements so that the user can only make ten attempts before an error message is displayed.

Looping with the for statement

The for statement is like while, except that it is more succinct. It combines:

- An **initializer expression**, which executes once at the start of the loop.
- A **conditional expression**, which executes on every iteration at the start of the loop to check whether the looping should continue.
- An **iterator expression**, which executes on every loop at the bottom of the statement.

The for statement is commonly used with an integer counter. Let's explore some code:

1. Type a for statement to output the numbers 1 to 10, as shown in the following code:

```
for (int y = 1; y <= 10; y++)
{
  WriteLine(y);
}
```

2. Run the code to view the result, which should be the numbers 1 to 10.

Looping with the foreach statement

The foreach statement is a bit different from the previous three iteration statements.

It is used to perform a block of statements on each item in a sequence, for example, an array or collection. Each item is usually read-only, and if the sequence structure is modified during iteration, for example, by adding or removing an item, then an exception will be thrown.

Try the following example:

1. Type statements to create an array of string variables and then output the length of each one, as shown in the following code:

```
string[] names = { "Adam", "Barry", "Charlie" };

foreach (string name in names)
{
  WriteLine($"{name} has {name.Length} characters.");
}
```

2. Run the code and view the results, as shown in the following output:

```
Adam has 4 characters.
Barry has 5 characters.
Charlie has 7 characters.
```

Understanding how foreach works internally

A creator of any type that represents multiple items, like an array or collection, should make sure that a programmer can use the `foreach` statement to enumerate through the type's items.

Technically, the `foreach` statement will work on any type that follows these rules:

1. The type must have a method named `GetEnumerator` that returns an object.
2. The returned object must have a property named `Current` and a method named `MoveNext`.
3. The `MoveNext` method must change the value of `Current` and return `true` if there are more items to enumerate through or return `false` if there are no more items.

There are interfaces named `IEnumerable` and `IEnumerable<T>` that formally define these rules, but technically the compiler does not require the type to implement these interfaces.

The compiler turns the `foreach` statement in the preceding example into something like the following pseudocode:

```
IEnumerator e = names.GetEnumerator();

while (e.MoveNext())
{
  string name = (string)e.Current; // Current is read-only!
  WriteLine($"{name} has {name.Length} characters.");
}
```

Due to the use of an iterator, the variable declared in a `foreach` statement cannot be used to modify the value of the current item.

Casting and converting between types

You will often need to convert values of variables between different types. For example, data input is often entered as text at the console, so it is initially stored in a variable of the `string` type, but it then needs to be converted into a date/time, or number, or some other data type, depending on how it should be stored and processed.

Sometimes you will need to convert between number types, like between an integer and a floating point, before performing calculations.

Converting is also known as **casting**, and it has two varieties: **implicit** and **explicit**. Implicit casting happens automatically, and it is safe, meaning that you will not lose any information.

Explicit casting must be performed manually because it may lose information, for example, the precision of a number. By explicitly casting, you are telling the C# compiler that you understand and accept the risk.

Casting numbers implicitly and explicitly

Implicitly casting an int variable into a double variable is safe because no information can be lost as the following shows:

1. Use your preferred coding tool to add a new **Console Application** to the Chapter03 workspace/solution named CastingConverting.

2. In Visual Studio Code, select CastingConverting as the active OmniSharp project.

3. In Program.cs, type statements to declare and assign an int variable and a double variable, and then implicitly cast the integer's value when assigning it to the double variable, as shown in the following code:

   ```
   int a = 10;
   double b = a; // an int can be safely cast into a double
   WriteLine(b);
   ```

4. Type statements to declare and assign a double variable and an int variable, and then implicitly cast the double value when assigning it to the int variable, as shown in the following code:

   ```
   double c = 9.8;
   int d = c; // compiler gives an error for this line
   WriteLine(d);
   ```

5. Run the code and note the error message, as shown in the following output:

   ```
   Error: (6,9): error CS0266: Cannot implicitly convert type 'double' to
   'int'. An explicit conversion exists (are you missing a cast?)
   ```

   This error message will also appear in the Visual Studio Error List or Visual Studio Code PROBLEMS window.

   You cannot implicitly cast a double variable into an int variable because it is potentially unsafe and could lose data, like the value after the decimal point. You must explicitly cast a double variable into an int variable using a pair of round brackets around the type you want to cast the double type into. The pair of round brackets is the **cast operator**. Even then, you must beware that the part after the decimal point will be trimmed off without warning because you have chosen to perform an explicit cast and therefore understand the consequences.

6. Modify the assignment statement for the d variable, as shown in the following code:

   ```
   int d = (int)c;
   WriteLine(d); // d is 9 losing the .8 part
   ```

7. Run the code to view the results, as shown in the following output:

   ```
   10
   9
   ```

We must perform a similar operation when converting values between larger integers and smaller integers. Again, beware that you might lose information because any value too big will have its bits copied and then be interpreted in ways that you might not expect!

8. Enter statements to declare and assign a long 64-bit variable to an int 32-bit variable, both using a small value that will work and a too-large value that will not, as shown in the following code:

```
long e = 10;
int f = (int)e;
WriteLine($"e is {e:N0} and f is {f:N0}");
e = long.MaxValue;
f = (int)e;
WriteLine($"e is {e:N0} and f is {f:N0}");
```

9. Run the code to view the results, as shown in the following output:

```
e is 10 and f is 10
e is 9,223,372,036,854,775,807 and f is -1
```

10. Modify the value of e to 5 billion, as shown in the following code:

```
e = 5_000_000_000;
```

11. Run the code to view the results, as shown in the following output:

```
e is 5,000,000,000 and f is 705,032,704
```

Converting with the System.Convert type

An alternative to using the cast operator is to use the System.Convert type. The System.Convert type can convert to and from all the C# number types, as well as Booleans, strings, and date and time values.

Let's write some code to see this in action:

1. At the top of Program.cs, statically import the System.Convert class, as shown in the following code:

```
using static System.Convert;
```

2. At the bottom of Program.cs, type statements to declare and assign a value to a double variable, convert it to an integer, and then write both values to the console, as shown in the following code:

```
double g = 9.8;
int h = ToInt32(g); // a method of System.Convert
WriteLine($"g is {g} and h is {h}");
```

3. Run the code and view the result, as shown in the following output:

```
g is 9.8 and h is 10
```

One difference between casting and converting is that converting rounds the `double` value 9.8 up to 10 instead of trimming the part after the decimal point.

Rounding numbers

You have now seen that the cast operator trims the decimal part of a real number and that the `System.Convert` methods round up or down. However, what is the rule for rounding?

Understanding the default rounding rules

In British primary schools for children aged 5 to 11, pupils are taught to round *up* if the decimal part is .5 or higher and round *down* if the decimal part is less.

Let's explore if C# follows the same primary school rule:

1. Type statements to declare and assign an array of `double` values, convert each of them to an integer, and then write the result to the console, as shown in the following code:

```
double[] doubles = new[]
  { 9.49, 9.5, 9.51, 10.49, 10.5, 10.51 };

foreach (double n in doubles)
{
  WriteLine($"ToInt32({n}) is {ToInt32(n)}");
}
```

2. Run the code and view the result, as shown in the following output:

```
ToInt32(9.49) is 9
ToInt32(9.5) is 10
ToInt32(9.51) is 10
ToInt32(10.49) is 10
ToInt32(10.5) is 10
ToInt32(10.51) is 11
```

We have shown that the rule for rounding in C# is subtly different from the primary school rule:

- It always rounds *down* if the decimal part is less than the midpoint .5.
- It always rounds *up* if the decimal part is more than the midpoint .5.
- It will round *up* if the decimal part is the midpoint .5 and the non-decimal part is *odd*, but it will round *down* if the non-decimal part is *even*.

This rule is known as **Banker's Rounding**, and it is preferred because it reduces bias by alternating when it rounds up or down. Sadly, other languages such as JavaScript use the primary school rule.

Taking control of rounding rules

You can take control of the rounding rules by using the Round method of the Math class:

1. Type statements to round each of the double values using the "away from zero" rounding rule, also known as rounding "up," and then write the result to the console, as shown in the following code:

```
foreach (double n in doubles)
{
  WriteLine(format:
    "Math.Round({0}, 0, MidpointRounding.AwayFromZero) is {1}",
    arg0: n,
    arg1: Math.Round(value: n, digits: 0,
          mode: MidpointRounding.AwayFromZero));
}
```

2. Run the code and view the result, as shown in the following output:

```
Math.Round(9.49, 0, MidpointRounding.AwayFromZero) is 9
Math.Round(9.5, 0, MidpointRounding.AwayFromZero) is 10
Math.Round(9.51, 0, MidpointRounding.AwayFromZero) is 10
Math.Round(10.49, 0, MidpointRounding.AwayFromZero) is 10
Math.Round(10.5, 0, MidpointRounding.AwayFromZero) is 11
Math.Round(10.51, 0, MidpointRounding.AwayFromZero) is 11
```

 Good Practice: For every programming language that you use, check its rounding rules. They may not work the way you expect!

Converting from any type to a string

The most common conversion is from any type into a string variable for outputting as human-readable text, so all types have a method named ToString that they inherit from the System. Object class.

The ToString method converts the current value of any variable into a textual representation. Some types can't be sensibly represented as text, so they return their namespace and type name instead.

Let's convert some types into a string:

1. Type statements to declare some variables, convert them to their string representation, and write them to the console, as shown in the following code:

```
int number = 12;
WriteLine(number.ToString());

bool boolean = true;
WriteLine(boolean.ToString());

DateTime now = DateTime.Now;
WriteLine(now.ToString());

object me = new();
WriteLine(me.ToString());
```

2. Run the code and view the result, as shown in the following output:

```
12
True
02/28/2021 17:33:54
System.Object
```

Converting from a binary object to a string

When you have a binary object like an image or video that you want to either store or transmit, you sometimes do not want to send the raw bits because you do not know how those bits could be misinterpreted, for example, by the network protocol transmitting them or another operating system that is reading the store binary object.

The safest thing to do is to convert the binary object into a string of safe characters. Programmers call this **Base64** encoding.

The Convert type has a pair of methods, ToBase64String and FromBase64String, that perform this conversion for you. Let's see them in action:

1. Type statements to create an array of bytes randomly populated with byte values, write each byte nicely formatted to the console, and then write the same bytes converted to Base64 to the console, as shown in the following code:

```
// allocate array of 128 bytes
byte[] binaryObject = new byte[128];

// populate array with random bytes
(new Random()).NextBytes(binaryObject);

WriteLine("Binary Object as bytes:");

for(int index = 0; index < binaryObject.Length; index++)
```

```
{
  Write($"{binaryObject[index]:X} ");
}
WriteLine();

// convert to Base64 string and output as text
string encoded = ToBase64String(binaryObject);

WriteLine($"Binary Object as Base64: {encoded}");
```

By default, an int value would output assuming decimal notation, that is, base10. You can use format codes such as :X to format the value using hexadecimal notation.

2. Run the code and view the result, as shown in the following output:

```
Binary Object as bytes:
B3 4D 55 DE 2D E BB CF BE 4D E6 53 C3 C2 9B 67 3 45 F9 E5 20 61 7E 4F 7A
81 EC 49 F0 49 1D 8E D4 F7 DB 54 AF A0 81 5 B8 BE CE F8 36 90 7A D4 36 42
4 75 81 1B AB 51 CE 5 63 AC 22 72 DE 74 2F 57 7F CB E7 47 B7 62 C3 F4 2D
61 93 85 18 EA 6 17 12 AE 44 A8 D B8 4C 89 85 A9 3C D5 E2 46 E0 59 C9 DF
10 AF ED EF 8AA1 B1 8D EE 4A BE 48 EC 79 A5 A 5F 2F 30 87 4A C7 7F 5D C1 D
26 EE
Binary Object as Base64: s01V3i0Ou8++TeZTw8KbZwNF +eUgYX5PeoHsSfBJHY7U99tU
r6CBBbi+zvg2kHrUNkIEdYEbq1HOBWOsInLedC9Xf8vnR7diw/QtYZOFGOoGFxKuRKgNuEyJha
k81eJG4FnJ3xCv7e+KobGN7kq+SO x5pQpfLzCHSsd/XcENJu4=
```

Parsing from strings to numbers or dates and times

The second most common conversion is from strings to numbers or date and time values.

The opposite of ToString is Parse. Only a few types have a Parse method, including all the number types and DateTime.

Let's see Parse in action:

1. Type statements to parse an integer and a date and time value from strings and then write the result to the console, as shown in the following code:

```
int age = int.Parse("27");
DateTime birthday = DateTime.Parse("4 July 1980");

WriteLine($"I was born {age} years ago.");
WriteLine($"My birthday is {birthday}.");
WriteLine($"My birthday is {birthday:D}.");
```

2. Run the code and view the result, as shown in the following output:

```
I was born 27 years ago.
My birthday is 04/07/1980 00:00:00.
My birthday is 04 July 1980.
```

By default, a date and time value outputs with the short date and time format. You can use format codes such as D to output only the date part using the long date format.

 Good Practice: Use the standard date and time format specifiers, as shown at the following link: `https://docs.microsoft.com/en-us/dotnet/standard/base-types/standard-date-and-time-format-strings#table-of-format-specifiers`

Errors using Parse

One problem with the Parse method is that it gives errors if the string cannot be converted.

1. Type a statement to attempt to parse a string containing letters into an integer variable, as shown in the following code:

   ```
   int count = int.Parse("abc");
   ```

2. Run the code and view the result, as shown in the following output:

   ```
   Unhandled Exception: System.FormatException: Input string was not in a
   correct format.
   ```

As well as the preceding exception message, you will see a stack trace. I have not included stack traces in this book because they take up too much space.

Avoiding exceptions using the TryParse method

To avoid errors, you can use the TryParse method instead. TryParse attempts to convert the input string and returns true if it can convert it and false if it cannot.

The out keyword is required to allow the TryParse method to set the count variable when the conversion works.

Let's see TryParse in action:

1. Replace the int count declaration with statements to use the TryParse method and ask the user to input a count for a number of eggs, as shown in the following code:

   ```
   Write("How many eggs are there? ");
   string? input = ReadLine(); // or use "12" in notebook

   if (int.TryParse(input, out int count))
   {
     WriteLine($"There are {count} eggs.");
   }
   else
   {
     WriteLine("I could not parse the input.");
   }
   ```

2. Run the code, enter 12, and view the result, as shown in the following output:

```
How many eggs are there? 12
There are 12 eggs.
```

3. Run the code, enter `twelve` (or change the `string` value to `"twelve"` in a notebook), and view the result, as shown in the following output:

```
How many eggs are there? twelve
I could not parse the input.
```

You can also use methods of the `System.Convert` type to convert `string` values into other types; however, like the `Parse` method, it gives an error if it cannot convert.

Handling exceptions

You've seen several scenarios where errors have occurred when converting types. Some languages return error codes when something goes wrong. .NET uses exceptions that are richer and designed only for failure reporting compared to return values that have multiple uses. When this happens, we say a *runtime exception has been thrown*.

When an exception is thrown, the thread is suspended and if the calling code has defined a `try-catch` statement, then it is given a chance to handle the exception. If the current method does not handle it, then its calling method is given a chance, and so on up the call stack.

As you have seen, the default behavior of a console application or a .NET Interactive notebook is to output a message about the exception, including a stack trace, and then stop running the code. The application is terminated. This is better than allowing the code to continue executing in a potentially corrupt state. Your code should only catch and handle exceptions that it understands and can properly fix.

 Good Practice: Avoid writing code that will throw an exception whenever possible, perhaps by performing `if` statement checks. Sometimes you can't, and sometimes it is best to allow the exception to be caught by a higher-level component that is calling your code. You will learn how to do this in *Chapter 4, Writing, Debugging, and Testing Functions*.

Wrapping error-prone code in a try block

When you know that a statement can cause an error, you should wrap that statement in a `try` block. For example, parsing from text to a number can cause an error. Any statements in the `catch` block will be executed only if an exception is thrown by a statement in the `try` block.

We don't have to do anything inside the catch block. Let's see this in action:

1. Use your preferred coding tool to add a new **Console Application** to the Chapter03 workspace/solution named HandlingExceptions.

2. In Visual Studio Code, select HandlingExceptions as the active OmniSharp project.

3. Type statements to prompt the user to enter their age and then write their age to the console, as shown in the following code:

```
WriteLine("Before parsing");
Write("What is your age? ");
string? input = ReadLine(); // or use "49" in a notebook

try
{
  int age = int.Parse(input);
  WriteLine($"You are {age} years old.");
}
catch
{
}
WriteLine("After parsing");
```

 You will see the following compiler message: Warning CS8604 Possible null reference argument for parameter 's' in 'int int. Parse(string s)'. By default in new .NET 6 projects, Microsoft has enabled nullable reference types so you will see many more compiler warnings like this. In production code, you should add code to check for null and handle that possibility appropriately. In this book, I will not include these null checks because the code samples are not designed to be production quality and null checks everywhere will clutter the code and use up valuable pages. In this case, it is impossible for input to be null because the user must press *Enter* for ReadLine to return and that will return an empty string. You will see hundreds of more examples of potentially null variables throughout the code samples in this book. Those warnings are safe to ignore for the book code examples. You only need similar warnings when you write your own production code. You will see more about null handling in *Chapter 6, Implementing Interfaces and Inheriting Classes*.

This code includes two messages to indicate *before* parsing and *after* parsing to make clearer the flow through the code. These will be especially useful as the example code grows more complex.

4. Run the code, enter 49, and view the result, as shown in the following output:

```
Before parsing
What is your age? 49
You are 49 years old.
After parsing
```

5. Run the code, enter `Kermit`, and view the result, as shown in the following output:

```
Before parsing
What is your age? Kermit
After parsing
```

When the code was executed, the error exception was caught and the default message and stack trace were not output, and the console application continued running. This is better than the default behavior, but it might be useful to see the type of error that occurred.

 Good Practice: You should never use an empty `catch` statement like this in production code because it "swallows" exceptions and hides potential problems. You should at least log the exception if you cannot or do not want to handle it properly, or rethrow it so that higher-level code can decide instead. You will learn about logging in *Chapter 4, Writing, Debugging, and Testing Functions*.

Catching all exceptions

To get information about any type of exception that might occur, you can declare a variable of type `System.Exception` to the `catch` block:

1. Add an exception variable declaration to the `catch` block and use it to write information about the exception to the console, as shown in the following code:

```
catch (Exception ex)
{
  WriteLine($"{ex.GetType()} says {ex.Message}");
}
```

2. Run the code, enter `Kermit` again, and view the result, as shown in the following output:

```
Before parsing
What is your age? Kermit
System.FormatException says Input string was not in a correct format.
After parsing
```

Catching specific exceptions

Now that we know which specific type of exception occurred, we can improve our code by catching just that type of exception and customizing the message that we display to the user:

1. Leave the existing `catch` block, and above it, add a new `catch` block for the format exception type, as shown in the following highlighted code:

```
catch (FormatException)
{
  WriteLine("The age you entered is not a valid number format.");
```

```
}
catch (Exception ex)
{
  WriteLine($"{ex.GetType()} says {ex.Message}");
}
```

2. Run the code, enter `Kermit` again, and view the result, as shown in the following output:

```
Before parsing
What is your age? Kermit
The age you entered is not a valid number format.
After parsing
```

The reason we want to leave the more general catch below is that there might be other types of exceptions that can occur.

3. Run the code, enter `9876543210`, and view the result, as shown in the following output:

```
Before parsing
What is your age? 9876543210
System.OverflowException says Value was either too large or too small for
an Int32.
After parsing
```

Let's add another `catch` block for this type of exception.

4. Leave the existing `catch` blocks, and add a new `catch` block for the overflow exception type, as shown in the following highlighted code:

```
catch (OverflowException)
{
  WriteLine("Your age is a valid number format but it is either too big or
small.");
}
catch (FormatException)
{
  WriteLine("The age you entered is not a valid number format.");
}
```

5. Run the code, enter `9876543210`, and view the result, as shown in the following output:

```
Before parsing
What is your age? 9876543210
Your age is a valid number format but it is either too big or small.
After parsing
```

The order in which you catch exceptions is important. The correct order is related to the inheritance hierarchy of the exception types. You will learn about inheritance in *Chapter 5, Building Your Own Types with Object-Oriented Programming*. However, don't worry too much about this—the compiler will give you build errors if you get exceptions in the wrong order anyway.

Good Practice: Avoid over-catching exceptions. They should often be allowed to propagate up the call stack to be handled at a level where more information is known about the circumstances that could change the logic of how they should be handled. You will learn about this in *Chapter 4, Writing, Debugging, and Testing Functions*.

Catching with filters

You can also add filters to a catch statement using the when keyword, as shown in the following code:

```
Write("Enter an amount: ");
string? amount = ReadLine();
try
{
  decimal amountValue = decimal.Parse(amount);
}
catch (FormatException) when (amount.Contains("$"))
{
  WriteLine("Amounts cannot use the dollar sign!");
}
catch (FormatException)
{
  WriteLine("Amounts must only contain digits!");
}
```

Checking for overflow

Earlier, we saw that when casting between number types, it was possible to lose information, for example, when casting from a long variable to an int variable. If the value stored in a type is too big, it will overflow.

Throwing overflow exceptions with the checked statement

The checked statement tells .NET to throw an exception when an overflow happens instead of allowing it to happen silently, which is done by default for performance reasons.

We will set the initial value of an int variable to its maximum value minus one. Then, we will increment it several times, outputting its value each time. Once it gets above its maximum value, it overflows to its minimum value and continues incrementing from there. Let's see this in action:

1. Use your preferred coding tool to add a new **Console Application** to the Chapter03 workspace/solution named CheckingForOverflow.

2. In Visual Studio Code, select `CheckingForOverflow` as the active OmniSharp project.

3. In `Program.cs`, type statements to declare and assign an integer to one less than its maximum possible value, and then increment it and write its value to the console three times, as shown in the following code:

```
int x = int.MaxValue - 1;
WriteLine($"Initial value: {x}");
x++;
WriteLine($"After incrementing: {x}");
x++;
WriteLine($"After incrementing: {x}");
x++;
WriteLine($"After incrementing: {x}");
```

4. Run the code and view the result that shows the value overflowing silently and wrapping around to large negative values, as shown in the following output:

```
Initial value: 2147483646
After incrementing: 2147483647
After incrementing: -2147483648
After incrementing: -2147483647
```

5. Now, let's get the compiler to warn us about the overflow by wrapping the statements using a `checked` statement block, as shown highlighted in the following code:

```
checked
{
    int x = int.MaxValue - 1;
    WriteLine($"Initial value: {x}");
    x++;
    WriteLine($"After incrementing: {x}");
    x++;
    WriteLine($"After incrementing: {x}");
    x++;
    WriteLine($"After incrementing: {x}");
}
```

6. Run the code and view the result that shows the overflow being checked and causing an exception to be thrown, as shown in the following output:

```
Initial value: 2147483646
After incrementing: 2147483647
Unhandled Exception: System.OverflowException: Arithmetic operation
resulted in an overflow.
```

7. Just like any other exception, we should wrap these statements in a try statement block and display a nicer error message for the user, as shown in the following code:

```
try
{
  // previous code goes here
}
catch (OverflowException)
{
  WriteLine("The code overflowed but I caught the exception.");
}
```

8. Run the code and view the result, as shown in the following output:

```
Initial value: 2147483646
After incrementing: 2147483647
The code overflowed but I caught the exception.
```

Disabling compiler overflow checks with the unchecked statement

The previous section was about the default overflow behavior at *runtime* and how to use the checked statement to change that behavior. This section is about *compile time* overflow behavior and how to use the unchecked statement to change that behavior.

A related keyword is unchecked. This keyword switches off overflow checks performed by the compiler within a block of code. Let's see how to do this:

1. Type the following statement at the end of the previous statements. The compiler will not compile this statement because it knows it would overflow:

```
int y = int.MaxValue + 1;
```

2. Hover your mouse pointer over the error, and note a compile-time check is shown as an error message, as shown in *Figure 3.1*:

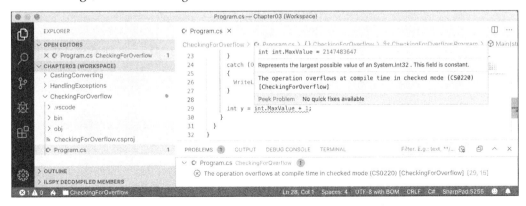

Figure 3.1: A compile-time check in the PROBLEMS window

3. To disable compile-time checks, wrap the statement in an unchecked block, write the value of y to the console, decrement it, and repeat, as shown in the following code:

```
unchecked
{
  int y = int.MaxValue + 1;
  WriteLine($"Initial value: {y}");
  y--;
  WriteLine($"After decrementing: {y}");
  y--;
  WriteLine($"After decrementing: {y}");
}
```

4. Run the code and view the results, as shown in the following output:

```
Initial value: -2147483648
After decrementing: 2147483647
After decrementing: 2147483646
```

Of course, it would be rare that you would want to explicitly switch off a check like this because it allows an overflow to occur. But perhaps you can think of a scenario where you might want that behavior.

Practicing and exploring

Test your knowledge and understanding by answering some questions, get some hands-on practice, and explore with deeper research into this chapter's topics.

Exercise 3.1 – Test your knowledge

Answer the following questions:

1. What happens when you divide an int variable by 0?
2. What happens when you divide a double variable by 0?
3. What happens when you overflow an int variable, that is, set it to a value beyond its range?
4. What is the difference between x = y++; and x = ++y;?
5. What is the difference between break, continue, and return when used inside a loop statement?
6. What are the three parts of a for statement and which of them are required?
7. What is the difference between the = and == operators?

8. Does the following statement compile?

    ```
    for ( ; true; ) ;
    ```

9. What does the underscore _ represent in a `switch` expression?

10. What interface must an object implement to be enumerated over by using the `foreach` statement?

Exercise 3.2 – Explore loops and overflow

What will happen if this code executes?

```
int max = 500;
for (byte i = 0; i < max; i++)
{
  WriteLine(i);
}
```

Create a console application in `Chapter03` named `Exercise02` and enter the preceding code. Run the console application and view the output. What happens?

What code could you add (don't change any of the preceding code) to warn us about the problem?

Exercise 3.3 – Practice loops and operators

FizzBuzz is a group word game for children to teach them about division. Players take turns to count incrementally, replacing any number divisible by three with the word *fizz*, any number divisible by five with the word *buzz*, and any number divisible by both with *fizzbuzz*.

Create a console application in `Chapter03` named `Exercise03` that outputs a simulated FizzBuzz game counting up to 100. The output should look something like *Figure 3.2*:

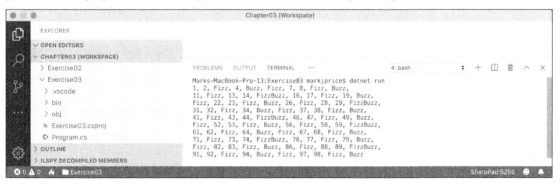

Figure 3.2: A simulated FizzBuzz game output

Exercise 3.4 – Practice exception handling

Create a console application in `Chapter03` named `Exercise04` that asks the user for two numbers in the range 0-255 and then divides the first number by the second:

```
Enter a number between 0 and 255: 100
Enter another number between 0 and 255: 8
100 divided by 8 is 12
```

Write exception handlers to catch any thrown errors, as shown in the following output:

```
Enter a number between 0 and 255: apples
Enter another number between 0 and 255: bananas
FormatException: Input string was not in a correct format.
```

Exercise 3.5 – Test your knowledge of operators

What are the values of x and y after the following statements execute?

1. Increment and addition operators:

    ```
    x = 3;
    y = 2 + ++x;
    ```

2. Binary shift operators:

    ```
    x = 3 << 2;
    y = 10 >> 1;
    ```

3. Bitwise operators:

    ```
    x = 10 & 8;
    y = 10 | 7;
    ```

Exercise 3.6 – Explore topics

Use the links on the following page to learn about the topics covered in this chapter in more detail:

```
https://github.com/markjprice/cs10dotnet6/blob/main/book-links.md#chapter-3---
controlling-flow-and-converting-types
```

Summary

In this chapter, you experimented with some operators, learned how to branch and loop, how to convert between types, and how to catch exceptions.

You are now ready to learn how to reuse blocks of code by defining functions, how to pass values into them and get values back, and how to track down bugs in your code and squash them!

04

Writing, Debugging, and Testing Functions

This chapter is about writing functions to reuse code, debugging logic errors during development, logging exceptions during runtime, unit testing your code to remove bugs, and ensuring stability and reliability.

This chapter covers the following topics:

- Writing functions
- Debugging during development
- Logging during runtime
- Unit testing
- Throwing and catching exceptions in functions

Writing functions

A fundamental principle of programming is **Don't Repeat Yourself (DRY)**.

While programming, if you find yourself writing the same statements over and over again, then turn those statements into a function. Functions are like tiny programs that complete one small task. For example, you might write a function to calculate sales tax and then reuse that function in many places in a financial application.

Like programs, functions usually have inputs and outputs. They are sometimes described as black boxes, where you feed some raw materials in one end, and a manufactured item emerges at the other. Once created, you don't need to think about how they work.

Times table example

Let's say that you want to help your child learn their times tables, so you want to make it easy to generate a times table for a number, such as the 12 times table:

```
1 x 12 = 12
2 x 12 = 24
...
12 x 12 = 144
```

You previously learned about the for statement earlier in this book, so you know that it can be used to generate repeated lines of output when there is a regular pattern, such as the 12 times table, as shown in the following code:

```
for (int row = 1; row <= 12; row++)
{
    Console.WriteLine($"{row} x 12 = {row * 12}");
}
```

However, instead of outputting the 12 times table, we want to make this more flexible, so it could output the times table for any number. We can do this by creating a function.

Writing a times table function

Let's explore functions by creating one to output any times table for numbers 0 to 255 multiplied by 1 to 12:

1. Use your preferred coding tool to create a new console app, as defined in the following list:
   1. Project template: **Console Application** / console
   2. Workspace/solution file and folder: Chapter04
   3. Project file and folder: WritingFunctions

2. Statically import System.Console.

3. In Program.cs, write statements to define a function named TimesTable, as shown in the following code:

```
static void TimesTable(byte number)
{
    WriteLine($"This is the {number} times table:");

    for (int row = 1; row <= 12; row++)
    {
        WriteLine($"{row} x {number} = {row * number}");
    }
    WriteLine();
}
```

In the preceding code, note the following:

- TimesTable must have a byte value passed to it as a parameter named number.

- TimesTable is a static method because it will be called by the static method Main.

- TimesTable does not return a value to the caller, so it is declared with the void keyword before its name.

- TimesTable uses a for statement to output the times table for the number passed to it.

4. After the statement that statically imports the Console class and before the TimesTable function, call the function and pass in a byte value for the number parameter, for example, 6, as shown highlighted in the following code:

```
using static System.Console;

TimesTable(6);
```

 Good Practice: If a function has one or more parameters where just passing the values may not provide enough meaning, then you can optionally specify the name of the parameter as well as its value, as shown in the following code: TimesTable(number: 6).

5. Run the code and then view the result, as shown in the following output:

```
This is the 6 times table:
1 x 6 = 6
2 x 6 = 12
3 x 6 = 18
4 x 6 = 24
5 x 6 = 30
6 x 6 = 36
7 x 6 = 42
8 x 6 = 48
9 x 6 = 54
10 x 6 = 60
11 x 6 = 66
12 x 6 = 72
```

6. Change the number passed into the TimesTable function to other byte values between 0 and 255 and confirm that the output times tables are correct.

7. Note that if you try to pass a non-byte number, for example, an int or double or string, an error is returned, as shown in the following output:

```
Error: (1,12): error CS1503: Argument 1: cannot convert from 'int' to
'byte'
```

Writing a function that returns a value

The previous function performed actions (looping and writing to the console), but it did not return a value. Let's say that you need to calculate sales or value-added tax (VAT). In Europe, VAT rates can range from 8% in Switzerland to 27% in Hungary. In the United States, state sales taxes can range from 0% in Oregon to 8.25% in California.

 Tax rates change all the time, and they vary based on many factors. You do not need to contact me to tell me that the tax rate in Virginia is 6%. Thank you.

Let's implement a function to calculate taxes in various regions around the world:

1. Add a function named `CalculateTax`, as shown in the following code:

```
static decimal CalculateTax(
  decimal amount, string twoLetterRegionCode)
{
  decimal rate = 0.0M;

  switch (twoLetterRegionCode)
  {
    case "CH": // Switzerland
      rate = 0.08M;
      break;
    case "DK": // Denmark
    case "NO": // Norway
      rate = 0.25M;
      break;
    case "GB": // United Kingdom
    case "FR": // France
      rate = 0.2M;
      break;
    case "HU": // Hungary
      rate = 0.27M;
      break;
    case "OR": // Oregon
    case "AK": // Alaska
    case "MT": // Montana
      rate = 0.0M;
      break;
    case "ND": // North Dakota
    case "WI": // Wisconsin
    case "ME": // Maine
```

```
case "VA": // Virginia
  rate = 0.05M;
  break;
case "CA": // California
  rate = 0.0825M;
  break;
default: // most US states
  rate = 0.06M;
  break;
}

return amount * rate;
}
```

In the preceding code, note the following:

- CalculateTax has two inputs: a parameter named amount that will be the amount of money spent, and a parameter named twoLetterRegionCode that will be the region the amount is spent in.

- CalculateTax will perform a calculation using a switch statement and then return the sales tax or VAT owed on the amount as a decimal value; so, before the name of the function, we have declared the data type of the return value to be decimal.

2. Comment out the TimesTable method call and call the CalculateTax method, passing values for the amount such as 149 and a valid region code such as FR, as shown in the following code:

```
// TimesTable(6);

decimal taxToPay = CalculateTax(amount: 149, twoLetterRegionCode: "FR");
WriteLine($"You must pay {taxToPay} in tax.");
```

3. Run the code and view the result, as shown in the following output:

```
You must pay 29.8 in tax.
```

> We could format the taxToPay output as currency by using {taxToPay:C} but it will use your local culture to decide how to format the currency symbol and decimals. For example, for me in the UK, I would see £29.80.

Can you think of any problems with the CalculateTax function as written? What would happen if the user enters a code such as fr or UK? How could you rewrite the function to improve it? Would using a switch *expression* instead of a switch *statement* be clearer?

Converting numbers from cardinal to ordinal

Numbers that are used to count are called **cardinal** numbers, for example, 1, 2, and 3, whereas numbers used to order are **ordinal** numbers, for example, 1st, 2nd, and 3rd. Let's create a function to convert cardinals to ordinals:

1. Write a function named `CardinalToOrdinal` that converts a cardinal `int` value into an ordinal `string` value; for example, it converts 1 into 1st, 2 into 2nd, and so on, as shown in the following code:

    ```
    static string CardinalToOrdinal(int number)
    {
      switch (number)
      {
        case 11: // special cases for 11th to 13th
        case 12:
        case 13:
          return $"{number}th";
        default:
          int lastDigit = number % 10;

          string suffix = lastDigit switch
          {
            1 => "st",
            2 => "nd",
            3 => "rd",
            _ => "th"
          };
          return $"{number}{suffix}";
      }
    }
    ```

    From the preceding code, note the following:

    *   `CardinalToOrdinal` has one input: a parameter of the `int` type named `number`, and one output: a return value of the `string` type.

    *   A `switch` *statement* is used to handle the special cases of 11, 12, and 13.

    *   A `switch` *expression* then handles all other cases: if the last digit is 1, then use `st` as the suffix; if the last digit is 2, then use `nd` as the suffix; if the last digit is 3, then use `rd` as the suffix; and if the last digit is anything else, then use `th` as the suffix.

2. Write a function named `RunCardinalToOrdinal` that uses a `for` statement to loop from 1 to 40, calling the `CardinalToOrdinal` function for each number and writing the returned `string` to the console, separated by a space character, as shown in the following code:

```
static void RunCardinalToOrdinal()
{
  for (int number = 1; number <= 40; number++)
  {
    Write($"{CardinalToOrdinal(number)} ");
  }
  WriteLine();
}
```

3. Comment out the `CalculateTax` statements, and call the `RunCardinalToOrdinal` method, as shown in the following code:

```
// TimesTable(6);

// decimal taxToPay = CalculateTax(amount: 149, twoLetterRegionCode: "FR");
// WriteLine($"You must pay {taxToPay} in tax.");

RunCardinalToOrdinal();
```

4. Run the code and view the results, as shown in the following output:

```
1st 2nd 3rd 4th 5th 6th 7th 8th 9th 10th 11th 12th 13th 14th 15th 16th
17th 18th 19th 20th 21st 22nd 23rd 24th 25th 26th 27th 28th 29th 30th 31st
32nd 33rd 34th 35th 36th 37th 38th 39th 40th
```

Calculating factorials with recursion

The factorial of 5 is 120, because factorials are calculated by multiplying the starting number by one less than itself, and then by one less again, and so on, until the number is reduced to 1. An example can be seen here: 5 x 4 x 3 x 2 x 1 = 120.

Factorials are written like this: 5!, where the exclamation mark is read as bang, so 5! = 120, that is, *five bang equals one hundred and twenty*. Bang is a good name for factorials because they increase in size very rapidly, just like an explosion.

We will write a function named `Factorial`; this will calculate the factorial for an `int` passed to it as a parameter. We will use a clever technique called **recursion**, which means a function that calls itself within its implementation, either directly or indirectly:

1. Add a function named `Factorial`, and a function to call it, as shown in the following code:

```
static int Factorial(int number)
{
  if (number < 1)
  {
```

```
        return 0;
    }
    else if (number == 1)
    {
        return 1;
    }
    else
    {
        return number * Factorial(number - 1);
    }
}
```

As before, there are several noteworthy elements of the preceding code, including the following:

- If the input parameter number is zero or negative, Factorial returns 0.

- If the input parameter number is 1, Factorial returns 1, and therefore stops calling itself.

- If the input parameter number is larger than one, which it will be in all other cases, Factorial multiplies the number by the result of calling itself and passing one less than number. This makes the function recursive.

 More Information: Recursion is clever, but it can lead to problems, such as a stack overflow due to too many function calls because memory is used to store data on every function call, and it eventually uses too much. Iteration is a more practical, if less succinct, solution in languages such as C#. You can read more about this at the following link: https://en.wikipedia.org/wiki/ Recursion_(computer_ science)#Recursion_versus_iteration.

2. Add a function named RunFactorial that uses a for statement to output the factorials of numbers from 1 to 14, calls the Factorial function inside its loop, and then outputs the result, formatted using the code N0, which means number format uses thousand separators with zero decimal places, as shown in the following code:

```
static void RunFactorial()
{
    for (int i = 1; i < 15; i++)
    {
        WriteLine($"{i}! = {Factorial(i):N0}");
    }
}
```

3. Comment out the RunCardinalToOrdinal method call and call the RunFactorial method.

4. Run the code and view the results, as shown in the following output:

```
1! = 1
2! = 2
3! = 6
4! = 24
5! = 120
6! = 720
7! = 5,040
8! = 40,320
9! = 362,880
10! = 3,628,800
11! = 39,916,800
12! = 479,001,600
13! = 1,932,053,504
14! = 1,278,945,280
```

It is not immediately obvious in the previous output, but factorials of 13 and higher overflow the int type because they are so big. 12! is 479,001,600, which is about half a billion. The maximum positive value that can be stored in an int variable is about two billion. 13! is 6,227,020,800, which is about six billion and when stored in a 32-bit integer it overflows silently without showing any problems.

Do you remember what we can do to be notified of a numeric overflow?

What should you do to get notified when an overflow happens? Of course, we could solve the problem for 13! and 14! by using a long (64-bit integer) instead of an int (32-bit integer), but we will quickly hit the overflow limit again.

The point of this section is to understand that numbers can overflow and how to show that rather than ignore it, not specifically how to calculate factorials higher than 12!.

1. Modify the Factorial function to check for overflows, as shown highlighted in the following code:

```
checked // for overflow
{
    return number * Factorial(number - 1);
}
```

2. Modify the RunFactorial function to handle overflow exceptions when calling the Factorial function, as shown highlighted in the following code:

```
try
{
    WriteLine($"{i}! = {Factorial(i):N0}");
}
```

```
catch (System.OverflowException)
{
  WriteLine($"{i}! is too big for a 32-bit integer.");
}
```

3. Run the code and view the results, as shown in the following output:

```
 1! = 1
 2! = 2
 3! = 6
 4! = 24
 5! = 120
 6! = 720
 7! = 5,040
 8! = 40,320
 9! = 362,880
10! = 3,628,800
11! = 39,916,800
12! = 479,001,600
13! is too big for a 32-bit integer.
14! is too big for a 32-bit integer.
```

Documenting functions with XML comments

By default, when calling a function such as CardinalToOrdinal, code editors will show a tooltip with basic information, as shown in *Figure 4.1*:

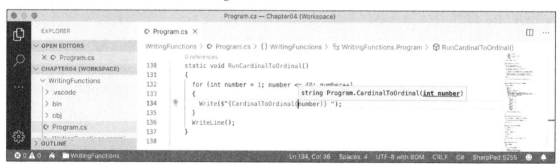

Figure 4.1: A tooltip showing the default simple method signature

Let's improve the tooltip by adding extra information:

1. If you are using Visual Studio Code with the C# extension, you should navigate to **View | Command Palette | Preferences: Open Settings (UI)**, and then search for formatOnType and make sure that is enabled. C# XML documentation comments are a built-in feature of Visual Studio 2022.

2. On the line above the CardinalToOrdinal function, type three forward slashes ///, and note that they are expanded into an XML comment that recognizes that the function has a single parameter named number.

3. Enter suitable information for the XML documentation comment for a summary and to describe the input parameter and the return value for the `CardinalToOrdinal` function, as shown in the following code:

```
/// <summary>
/// Pass a 32-bit integer and it will be converted into its ordinal
equivalent.
/// </summary>
/// <param name="number">Number is a cardinal value e.g. 1, 2, 3, and so
on.</param>
/// <returns>Number as an ordinal value e.g. 1st, 2nd, 3rd, and so on.
</returns>
```

4. Now, when calling the function, you will see more details, as shown in *Figure 4.2*:

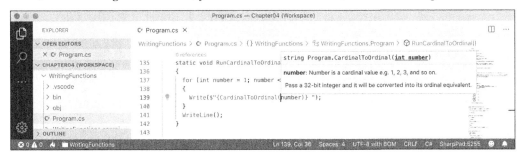

Figure 4.2: A tooltip showing the more detailed method signature

At the time of writing the sixth edition, C# XML documentation comments do not work in .NET Interactive notebooks.

 Good Practice: Add XML documentation comments to all your functions.

Using lambdas in function implementations

F# is Microsoft's strongly typed functional-first programming language that, like C#, compiles to IL to be executed by .NET. Functional languages evolved from lambda calculus; a computational system based only on functions. The code looks more like mathematical functions than steps in a recipe.

Some of the important attributes of functional languages are defined in the following list:

- **Modularity**: The same benefit of defining functions in C# applies to functional languages. Break up a large complex code base into smaller pieces.

- **Immutability**: Variables in the C# sense do not exist. Any data value inside a function cannot change. Instead, a new data value can be created from an existing one. This reduces bugs.

- **Maintainability**: Code is cleaner and clearer (for mathematically inclined programmers!).

Since C# 6, Microsoft has worked to add features to the language to support a more functional approach. For example, adding **tuples** and **pattern matching** in C# 7, **non-null reference types** in C# 8, and improving pattern matching and adding records, that is, **immutable objects** in C# 9.

In C# 6, Microsoft added support for **expression-bodied function members**. We will look at an example of this now.

The **Fibonacci sequence** of numbers always starts with 0 and 1. Then the rest of the sequence is generated using the rule of adding together the previous two numbers, as shown in the following sequence of numbers:

```
0 1 1 2 3 5 8 13 21 34 55 ...
```

The next term in the sequence would be 34 + 55, which is 89.

We will use the Fibonacci sequence to illustrate the difference between an imperative and declarative function implementation:

1. Add a function named `FibImperative` that will be written in an imperative style, as shown in the following code:

```
static int FibImperative(int term)
{
  if (term == 1)
  {
    return 0;
  }
  else if (term == 2)
  {
    return 1;
  }
  else
  {
    return FibImperative(term - 1) + FibImperative(term - 2);
  }
}
```

2. Add a function named `RunFibImperative` that calls `FibImperative` inside a for statement that loops from 1 to 30, as shown in the following code:

```
static void RunFibImperative()
{
  for (int i = 1; i <= 30; i++)
  {
    WriteLine("The {0} term of the Fibonacci sequence is {1:N0}.",
      arg0: CardinalToOrdinal(i),
      arg1: FibImperative(term: i));
```

}

}

3. Comment out the other method calls and call the RunFibImperative method.

4. Run the code and view the results, as shown in the following output:

```
The 1st term of the Fibonacci sequence is 0.
The 2nd term of the Fibonacci sequence is 1.
The 3rd term of the Fibonacci sequence is 1.
The 4th term of the Fibonacci sequence is 2.
The 5th term of the Fibonacci sequence is 3.
The 6th term of the Fibonacci sequence is 5.
The 7th term of the Fibonacci sequence is 8.
The 8th term of the Fibonacci sequence is 13.
The 9th term of the Fibonacci sequence is 21.
The 10th term of the Fibonacci sequence is 34.
The 11th term of the Fibonacci sequence is 55.
The 12th term of the Fibonacci sequence is 89.
The 13th term of the Fibonacci sequence is 144.
The 14th term of the Fibonacci sequence is 233.
The 15th term of the Fibonacci sequence is 377.
The 16th term of the Fibonacci sequence is 610.
The 17th term of the Fibonacci sequence is 987.
The 18th term of the Fibonacci sequence is 1,597.
The 19th term of the Fibonacci sequence is 2,584.
The 20th term of the Fibonacci sequence is 4,181.
The 21st term of the Fibonacci sequence is 6,765.
The 22nd term of the Fibonacci sequence is 10,946.
The 23rd term of the Fibonacci sequence is 17,711.
The 24th term of the Fibonacci sequence is 28,657.
The 25th term of the Fibonacci sequence is 46,368.
The 26th term of the Fibonacci sequence is 75,025.
The 27th term of the Fibonacci sequence is 121,393.
The 28th term of the Fibonacci sequence is 196,418.
The 29th term of the Fibonacci sequence is 317,811.
The 30th term of the Fibonacci sequence is 514,229.
```

5. Add a function named FibFunctional written in a declarative style, as shown in the following code:

```
static int FibFunctional(int term) =>
  term switch
  {
    1 => 0,
    2 => 1,
    _ => FibFunctional(term - 1) + FibFunctional(term - 2)
  };
```

6. Add a function to call it inside a `for` statement that loops from 1 to 30, as shown in the following code:

```
static void RunFibFunctional()
{
  for (int i = 1; i <= 30; i++)
  {
    WriteLine("The {0} term of the Fibonacci sequence is {1:N0}.",
      arg0: CardinalToOrdinal(i),
      arg1: FibFunctional(term: i));
  }
}
```

7. Comment out the `RunFibImperative` method call, and call the `RunFibFunctional` method.

8. Run the code and view the results (which will be the same as before).

Debugging during development

In this section, you will learn how to debug problems at development time. You must use a code editor that has debugging tools such as Visual Studio or Visual Studio Code. At the time of writing, you cannot use .NET Interactive Notebooks to debug code, but this is expected to be added in the future.

More Information: Some people find it tricky setting up the OmniSharp debugger for Visual Studio Code. I have included instructions for the most common issues, but if you still have trouble, try reading the information at the following link: https://github.com/OmniSharp/omnisharp-vscode/blob/master/debugger.md

Creating code with a deliberate bug

Let's explore debugging by creating a console app with a deliberate bug that we will then use the debugger tools in your code editor to track down and fix:

1. Use your preferred coding tool to add a new **Console Application** to the `Chapter04` workspace/solution named `Debugging`.

2. In Visual Studio Code, select `Debugging` as the active OmniSharp project. When you see the pop-up warning message saying that required assets are missing, click **Yes** to add them.

3. In Visual Studio, set the startup project for the solution to the current selection.

4. In `Program.cs`, add a function with a deliberate bug, as shown in the following code:

```
static double Add(double a, double b)
{
  return a * b; // deliberate bug!
}
```

5. Below the Add function, write statements to declare and set some variables and then add them together using the buggy function, as shown in the following code:

```
double a = 4.5;
double b = 2.5;
double answer = Add(a, b);
WriteLine($"{a} + {b} = {answer}");

WriteLine("Press ENTER to end the app.");
ReadLine(); // wait for user to press ENTER
```

6. Run the console application and view the result, as shown in the following partial output:

```
4.5 + 2.5 = 11.25
```

But wait, there's a bug! 4.5 added to 2.5 should be 7, not 11.25!

We will use the debugging tools to hunt for and squash the bug.

Setting a breakpoint and start debugging

Breakpoints allow us to mark a line of code that we want to pause at to inspect the program state and find bugs.

Using Visual Studio 2022

Let's set a breakpoint and then start debugging using Visual Studio 2022:

1. Click in the statement that declares the variable named a.

2. Navigate to **Debug** | **Toggle Breakpoint** or press *F9*. A red circle will then appear in the margin bar on the left-hand side and the statement will be highlighted in red to indicate that a breakpoint has been set, as shown in *Figure 4.3*:

Figure 4.3: Toggling breakpoints using Visual Studio 2022

Breakpoints can be toggled off with the same action. You can also left-click in the margin to toggle a breakpoint on and off, or right-click a breakpoint to see more options, such as delete, disable, or edit conditions or actions for an existing breakpoint.

3. Navigate to **Debug** | **Start Debugging** or press *F5*. Visual Studio starts the console application and then pauses when it hits the breakpoint. This is known as break mode. Extra windows titled **Locals** (showing current values of local variables), **Watch 1** (showing any watch expressions you have defined), **Call Stack**, **Exception Settings**, and **Immediate Window** appear. The **Debugging** toolbar appears. The line that will be executed next is highlighted in yellow, and a yellow arrow points at the line from the margin bar, as shown in *Figure 4.4*:

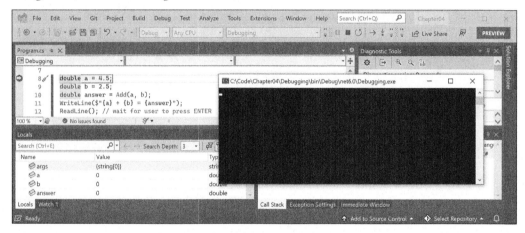

Figure 4.4: Break mode in Visual Studio 2022

If you do not want to see how to use Visual Studio Code to start debugging then you can skip the next section and continue to the section titled *Navigating with the debugging toolbar*.

Using Visual Studio Code

Let's set a breakpoint and then start debugging using Visual Studio Code:

1. Click in the statement that declares the variable named a.

2. Navigate to **Run** | **Toggle Breakpoint** or press *F9*. A red circle will appear in the margin bar on the left-hand side to indicate that a breakpoint has been set, as shown in *Figure 4.5*:

Figure 4.5: Toggling breakpoints using Visual Studio Code

Breakpoints can be toggled off with the same action. You can also left-click in the margin to toggle a breakpoint on and off, or right-click to see more options, such as remove, edit, or disable an existing breakpoint; or adding a breakpoint, conditional breakpoint, or logpoint when a breakpoint does not yet exist.

> Logpoints, also known as tracepoints, indicate that you want to record some information without having to actually stop executing the code at that point.

3. Navigate to **View | Run**, or in the left navigation bar you can click the **Run and Debug** icon (the triangle "play" button and "bug"), as shown in *Figure 4.5*.

4. At the top of the **DEBUG** window, click on the dropdown to the right of the **Start Debugging** button (green triangular "play" button), and select **.NET Core Launch (console) (Debugging)**, as shown in *Figure 4.6*:

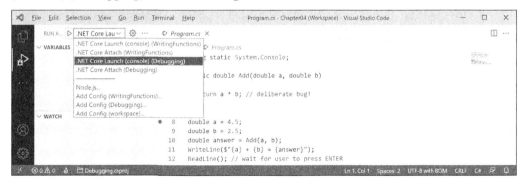

Figure 4.6: Selecting the project to debug using Visual Studio Code

Good Practice: If you do not see a choice in the dropdown list for the **Debugging** project, it is because that project does not have the assets needed to debug. Those assets are stored in the `.vscode` folder. To create the `.vscode` folder for a project, navigate to **View | Command Palette**, select **OmniSharp: Select Project**, and then select the **Debugging** project. After a few seconds, when prompted, **Required assets to build and debug are missing from 'Debugging'. Add them?**, click **Yes** to add the missing assets.

5. At the top of the **DEBUG** window, click the **Start Debugging** button (green triangular "play" button), or navigate to **Run | Start Debugging**, or press *F5*. Visual Studio Code starts the console application and then pauses when it hits the breakpoint. This is known as break mode. The line that will be executed next is highlighted in yellow, and a yellow block points at the line from the margin bar, as shown in *Figure 4.7*:

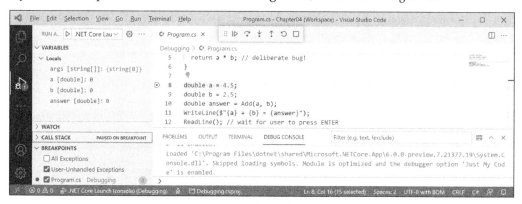

Figure 4.7: Break mode in Visual Studio Code

Navigating with the debugging toolbar

Visual Studio Code shows a floating toolbar with buttons to make it easy to access debugging features. Visual Studio 2022 has one button in its **Standard** toolbar to start or continue debugging and a separate **Debugging** toolbar for the rest of the tools.

Both are shown in *Figure 4.8* and as described in the following list:

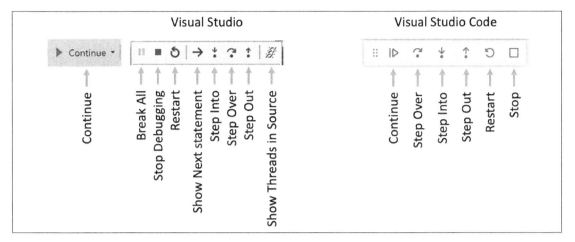

Figure 4.8: Debugging toolbars in Visual Studio 2022 and Visual Studio Code

- **Continue**/*F5*: This button will continue running the program from the current position until it ends or hits another breakpoint.
- **Step Over**/*F10*, **Step Into**/*F11*, and **Step Out**/*Shift + F11* (blue arrows over dots): These buttons step through the code statements in various ways, as you will see in a moment.
- **Restart**/*Ctrl* or *Cmd + Shift + F5* (circular arrow): This button will stop and then immediately restart the program with the debugger attached again.
- **Stop**/*Shift + F5* (red square): This button will stop the debugging session.

Debugging windows

While debugging, both Visual Studio Code and Visual Studio show extra windows that allow you to monitor useful information, such as variables, while you step through your code.

The most useful windows are described in the following list:

- **VARIABLES**, including **Locals**, which shows the name, value, and type for any local variables automatically. Keep an eye on this window while you step through your code.
- **WATCH**, or **Watch 1**, which shows the value of variables and expressions that you manually enter.
- **CALL STACK**, which shows the stack of function calls.
- **BREAKPOINTS**, which shows all your breakpoints and allows finer control over them.

When in break mode, there is also a useful window at the bottom of the edit area:

- **DEBUG CONSOLE** or **Immediate Window** enables live interaction with your code. You can interrogate the program state, for example, by entering the name of a variable. For example, you can ask a question such as, "What is 1+2?" by typing 1+2 and pressing *Enter*, as shown in *Figure 4.9*:

Figure 4.9: Interrogating the program state

Stepping through code

Let's explore some ways to step through the code using either Visual Studio or Visual Studio Code:

1. Navigate to **Run/Debug | Step Into**, or click on the **Step Into** button in the toolbar, or press *F11*. The yellow highlight steps forward one line.

2. Navigate to **Run/Debug | Step Over**, or click on the **Step Over** button in the toolbar, or press *F10*. The yellow highlight steps forward one line. At the moment, you can see that there is no difference between using **Step Into** or **Step Over**.

3. You should now be on the line that calls the Add method, as shown in *Figure 4.10*:

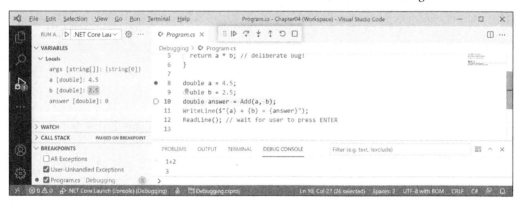

Figure 4.10: Stepping into and over code

The difference between **Step Into** and **Step Over** can be seen when you are about to execute a method call:

- If you click on **Step Into**, the debugger steps *into* the method so that you can step through every line in that method.

- If you click on **Step Over**, the whole method is executed in one go; it does not skip over the method without executing it.

4. Click on **Step Into** to step inside the method.

5. Hover your mouse pointer over the a or b parameters in the code editing window and note that a tooltip appears showing their current value.

6. Select the expression a * b, right-click the expression, and select **Add to Watch** or **Add Watch**. The expression is added to the **WATCH** window, showing that this operator is multiplying a by b to give the result 11.25.

7. In the **WATCH** or **Watch 1** window, right-click the expression and choose **Remove Expression** or **Delete Watch**.

8. Fix the bug by changing * to + in the Add function.

9. Stop debugging, recompile, and restart debugging by clicking the circular arrow **Restart** button or pressing *Ctrl* or *Cmd + Shift + F5*.

10. Step over the function, take a minute to note how it now calculates correctly, and click the **Continue** button or press **F5**.

11. With Visual Studio Code, note that when writing to the console during debugging, the output appears in the **DEBUG CONSOLE** window instead of the **TERMINAL** window, as shown in *Figure 4.11*:

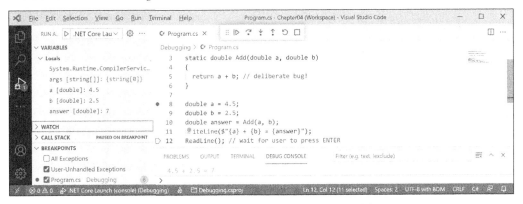

Figure 4.11: Writing to the DEBUG CONSOLE during debugging

Customizing breakpoints

It is easy to make more complex breakpoints:

1. If you are still debugging, click the **Stop** button in the debugging toolbar, or navigate to **Run/Debug | Stop Debugging**, or press *Shift + F5*.

2. Navigate to **Run | Remove All Breakpoints** or **Debug | Delete All Breakpoints**.

3. Click on the WriteLine statement that outputs the answer.

4. Set a breakpoint by pressing *F9* or navigating to **Run/Debug | Toggle Breakpoint**.

5. In Visual Studio Code, right-click the breakpoint and choose **Edit Breakpoint...**, and then enter an expression, such as the answer variable must be greater than 9, and note the expression must evaluate to true for the breakpoint to activate, as shown in *Figure 4.12*:

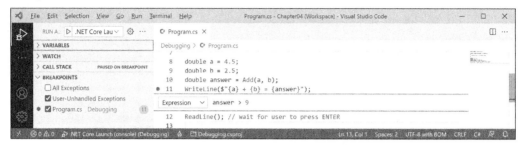

Figure 4.12: Customizing a breakpoint with an expression using Visual Studio Code

6. In Visual Studio, right-click the breakpoint and choose **Conditions...**, and then enter an expression, such as the answer variable must be greater than 9, and note the expression must evaluate to true for the breakpoint to activate.

7. Start debugging and note the breakpoint is not hit.

8. Stop debugging.

9. Edit the breakpoint or its conditions and change its expression to less than 9.

10. Start debugging and note the breakpoint is hit.

11. Stop debugging.

12. Edit the breakpoint or its conditions, (in Visual Studio click **Add condition**) and select **Hit Count**, then enter a number such as 3, meaning that you would have to hit the breakpoint three times before it activates, as shown in *Figure 4.13*:

Figure 4.13: Customizing a breakpoint with an expression and hot count using Visual Studio 2022

13. Hover your mouse over the breakpoint's red circle to see a summary, as shown in
    Figure 4.14:

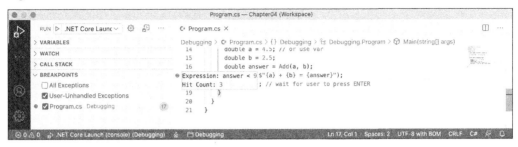

Figure 4.14: A summary of a customized breakpoint in Visual Studio Code

You have now fixed a bug using some debugging tools and seen some advanced possibilities
for setting breakpoints.

Logging during development and runtime

Once you believe that all the bugs have been removed from your code, you would then compile
a release version and deploy the application, so that people can use it. But no code is ever bug
free, and during runtime unexpected errors can occur.

End users are notoriously bad at remembering, admitting to, and then accurately describing
what they were doing when an error occurred, so you should not rely on them accurately
providing useful information to reproduce the problem to understand what caused the
problem and then fix it. Instead, you can **instrument your code**, which means logging events
of interest.

 Good Practice: Add code throughout your application to log what is
happening, and especially when exceptions occur, so that you can review the
logs and use them to trace the issue and fix the problem. Although we will see
logging again in *Chapter 10, Working with Data Using Entity Framework Core*,
and in *Chapter 15, Building Websites Using the Model-View-Controller Pattern*,
logging is a huge topic, so we can only cover the basics in this book.

Understanding logging options

.NET includes some built-in ways to instrument your code by adding logging capabilities. We
will cover the basics in this book. But logging is an area where third parties have created a rich
ecosystem of powerful solutions that extend what Microsoft provides. I cannot make specific
recommendations because the best logging framework depends on your needs. But I include
some common ones in the following list:

- Apache log4net
- NLog
- Serilog

Instrumenting with Debug and Trace

There are two types that can be used to add simple logging to your code: Debug and Trace.

Before we delve into them in more detail, let's look at a quick overview of each one:

- The Debug class is used to add logging that gets written only during development.
- The Trace class is used to add logging that gets written during both development and runtime.

You have seen the use of the Console type and its WriteLine method write out to the console window. There is also a pair of types named Debug and Trace that have more flexibility in where they write out to.

The Debug and Trace classes write to any trace listener. A trace listener is a type that can be configured to write output anywhere you like when the WriteLine method is called. There are several trace listeners provided by .NET, including one that outputs to the console, and you can even make your own by inheriting from the TraceListener type.

Writing to the default trace listener

One trace listener, the DefaultTraceListener class, is configured automatically and writes to Visual Studio Code's **DEBUG CONSOLE** window or Visual Studio's **Debug** window. You can configure other trace listeners using code.

Let's see trace listeners in action:

1. Use your preferred coding tool to add a new **Console Application** to the Chapter04 workspace/solution named Instrumenting.

2. In Visual Studio Code, select Instrumenting as the active OmniSharp project. When you see the pop-up warning message saying that required assets are missing, click **Yes** to add them.

3. In Program.cs, import the System.Diagnostics namespace.

4. Write a message from the Debug and Trace classes, as shown in the following code:

```
Debug.WriteLine("Debug says, I am watching!");
Trace.WriteLine("Trace says, I am watching!");
```

5. In Visual Studio, navigate to **View | Output** and make sure **Show output from: Debug** is selected.

6. Start debugging the Instrumenting console application, and note that **DEBUG CONSOLE** in Visual Studio Code or the **Output** window in Visual Studio 2022 shows the two messages, mixed with other debugging information, such as loaded assembly DLLs, as shown in *Figures 4.15* and *4.16*:

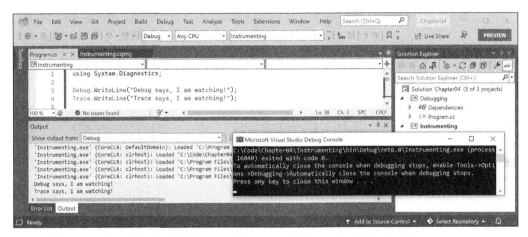

Figure 4.15: Visual Studio Code DEBUG CONSOLE shows the two messages in blue

Figure 4.16: Visual Studio 2022 Output window shows Debug output including the two messages

Configuring trace listeners

Now, we will configure another trace listener that will write to a text file:

1. Before the Debug and Trace calls to WriteLine, add a statement to create a new text file on the desktop and pass it into a new trace listener that knows how to write to a text file, and enable automatic flushing for its buffer, as shown highlighted in the following code:

```csharp
// write to a text file in the project folder
Trace.Listeners.Add(new TextWriterTraceListener(
  File.CreateText(Path.Combine(Environment.GetFolderPath(
    Environment.SpecialFolder.DesktopDirectory), "log.txt"))));

// text writer is buffered, so this option calls
// Flush() on all listeners after writing
Trace.AutoFlush = true;

Debug.WriteLine("Debug says, I am watching!");
Trace.WriteLine("Trace says, I am watching!");
```

> **Good Practice:** Any type that represents a file usually implements a buffer to improve performance. Instead of writing immediately to the file, data is written to an in-memory buffer and only once the buffer is full will it be written in one chunk to the file. This behavior can be confusing while debugging because we do not immediately see the results! Enabling `AutoFlush` means it calls the `Flush` method automatically after every write.

2. In Visual Studio Code, run the release configuration of the console app by entering the following command in the **TERMINAL** window for the `Instrumenting` project and note that nothing will appear to have happened:

```
dotnet run --configuration Release
```

3. In Visual Studio 2022, in the standard toolbar, select **Release** in the **Solution Configurations** dropdown list, as shown in *Figure 4.17*:

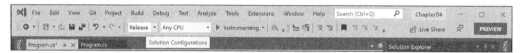

Figure 4.17: Selecting the Release configuration in Visual Studio

4. In Visual Studio 2022, run the release configuration of the console app by navigating to **Debug | Start Without Debugging**.

5. On your desktop, open the file named `log.txt` and note that it contains the message `Trace says, I am watching!`.

6. In Visual Studio Code, run the debug configuration of the console app by entering the following command in the **TERMINAL** window for the `Instrumenting` project:

```
dotnet run --configuration Debug
```

7. In Visual Studio, in the standard toolbar, select **Debug** in the **Solution Configurations** dropdown list and then run the console app by navigating to **Debug | Start Debugging**.

8. On your desktop, open the file named `log.txt` and note that it contains both the message, `Debug says, I am watching!` and `Trace says, I am watching!`.

> **Good Practice:** When running with the `Debug` configuration, both `Debug` and `Trace` are active and will write to any trace listeners. When running with the `Release` configuration, only `Trace` will write to any trace listeners. You can therefore use `Debug.WriteLine` calls liberally throughout your code, knowing they will be stripped out automatically when you build the release version of your application and will therefore not affect performance.

Switching trace levels

The Trace.WriteLine calls are left in your code even after release. So, it would be great to have fine control over when they are output. This is something we can do with a **trace switch**.

The value of a trace switch can be set using a number or a word. For example, the number 3 can be replaced with the word Info, as shown in the following table:

Number	Word	Description
0	Off	This will output nothing.
1	Error	This will output only errors.
2	Warning	This will output errors and warnings.
3	Info	This will output errors, warnings, and information.
4	Verbose	This will output all levels.

Let's explore using trace switches. First, we will add some NuGet packages to our project to enable loading configuration settings from a JSON appsettings file.

Adding packages to a project in Visual Studio Code

Visual Studio Code does not have a mechanism to add NuGet packages to a project, so we will use the command-line tool:

1. Navigate to the **TERMINAL** window for the Instrumenting project.
2. Enter the following command:
   ```
   dotnet add package Microsoft.Extensions.Configuration
   ```
3. Enter the following command:
   ```
   dotnet add package Microsoft.Extensions.Configuration.Binder
   ```
4. Enter the following command:
   ```
   dotnet add package Microsoft.Extensions.Configuration.Json
   ```
5. Enter the following command:
   ```
   dotnet add package Microsoft.Extensions.Configuration.FileExtensions
   ```

> dotnet add package adds a reference to a NuGet package to your project file. It will be downloaded during the build process. dotnet add reference adds a project-to-project reference to your project file. The referenced project will be compiled if needed during the build process.

Adding packages to a project in Visual Studio 2022

Visual Studio has a graphical user interface for adding packages.

1. In **Solution Explorer**, right-click the **Instrumenting** project and select **Manage NuGet Packages**.

2. Select the **Browse** tab.

3. In the search box, enter `Microsoft.Extensions.Configuration`.

4. Select each of these NuGet packages and click the **Install** button, as shown in *Figure 4.18*:

    1. `Microsoft.Extensions.Configuration`

    2. `Microsoft.Extensions.Configuration.Binder`

    3. `Microsoft.Extensions.Configuration.Json`

    4. `Microsoft.Extensions.Configuration.FileExtensions`

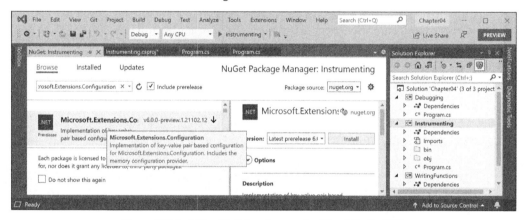

Figure 4.18: Installing NuGet packages using Visual Studio 2022

 Good Practice: There are also packages for loading configuration from XML files, INI files, environment variables, and the command line. Use the most appropriate technique for setting configuration in your projects.

Reviewing project packages

After adding the NuGet packages, we can see the references in the project file:

1. Open `Instrumenting.csproj` (double-click the **Instrumenting** project in Visual Studio's **Solution Explorer**) and note the `<ItemGroup>` section with the added NuGet packages, as shown highlighted in the following markup:

    ```
    <Project Sdk="Microsoft.NET.Sdk">

      <PropertyGroup>
    ```

```
    <OutputType>Exe</OutputType>
    <TargetFramework>net6.0</TargetFramework>
    <Nullable>enable</Nullable>
    <ImplicitUsings>enable</ImplicitUsings>
  </PropertyGroup>

  <ItemGroup>
    <PackageReference
      Include="Microsoft.Extensions.Configuration"
      Version="6.0.0" />
    <PackageReference
      Include="Microsoft.Extensions.Configuration.Binder"
      Version="6.0.0" />
    <PackageReference
      Include="Microsoft.Extensions.Configuration.FileExtensions"
      Version="6.0.0" />
    <PackageReference
      Include="Microsoft.Extensions.Configuration.Json"
      Version="6.0.0" />
  </ItemGroup>

</Project>
```

2. Add a file named appsettings.json to the Instrumenting project folder.

3. Modify appsettings.json to define a setting named PacktSwitch with a Level value, as shown in the following code:

```
{
  "PacktSwitch": {
    "Level": "Info"
  }
}
```

4. In Visual Studio 2022, in **Solution Explorer**, right-click appsettings.json, select **Properties**, and then in the **Properties** window, change **Copy to Output Directory** to **Copy if newer**. This is necessary because unlike Visual Studio Code, which runs the console app in the project folder, Visual Studio runs the console app in Instrumenting\bin\Debug\net6.0 or Instrumenting\bin\Release\net6.0.

5. At the top of Program.cs, import the Microsoft.Extensions.Configuration namespace.

6. Add some statements to the end of Program.cs to create a configuration builder that looks in the current folder for a file named appsettings.json, build the configuration, create a trace switch, set its level by binding to the configuration, and then output the four trace switch levels, as shown in the following code:

```
ConfigurationBuilder builder = new();

builder.SetBasePath(Directory.GetCurrentDirectory())
```

```
    .AddJsonFile("appsettings.json",
      optional: true, reloadOnChange: true);

IConfigurationRoot configuration = builder.Build();

TraceSwitch ts = new(
  displayName: "PacktSwitch",
  description: "This switch is set via a JSON config.");

configuration.GetSection("PacktSwitch").Bind(ts);

Trace.WriteLineIf(ts.TraceError, "Trace error");
Trace.WriteLineIf(ts.TraceWarning, "Trace warning");
Trace.WriteLineIf(ts.TraceInfo, "Trace information");
Trace.WriteLineIf(ts.TraceVerbose, "Trace verbose");
```

7. Set a breakpoint on the `Bind` statement.

8. Start debugging the `Instrumenting` console app. In the **VARIABLES** or **Locals** window, expand the `ts` variable expression, and note that its `Level` is `Off` and its `TraceError`, `TraceWarning`, and so on are all `false`, as shown in *Figure 4.19*:

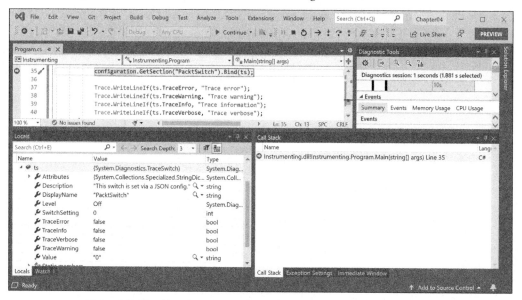

Figure 4.19: Watching the trace switch variable properties in Visual Studio 2022

9. Step into the call to the `Bind` method by clicking the **Step Into** or **Step Over** buttons or pressing *F11* or *F10*, and note the `ts` variable watch expression updates to the `Info` level.

10. Step into or over the four calls to `Trace.WriteLineIf` and note that all levels up to `Info` are written to the **DEBUG CONSOLE** or **Output - Debug** window, but not `Verbose`, as shown in *Figure 4.20*:

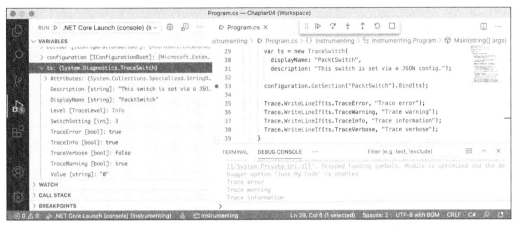

Figure 4.20: Different trace levels shown in the DEBUG CONSOLE in Visual Studio Code

11. Stop debugging.

12. Modify `appsettings.json` to set a level of 2, which means warning, as shown in the following JSON file:

```
{
    "PacktSwitch": {
        "Level": "2"
    }
}
```

13. Save the changes.

14. In Visual Studio Code, run the console application by entering the following command in the **TERMINAL** window for the `Instrumenting` project:

```
dotnet run --configuration Release
```

15. In Visual Studio, in the standard toolbar, select **Release** in the **Solution Configurations** dropdown list and then run the console app by navigating to **Debug | Start Without Debugging**.

16. Open the file named `log.txt` and note that this time, only trace error and warning levels are the output of the four potential trace levels, as shown in the following text file:

```
Trace says, I am watching!
Trace error
Trace warning
```

If no argument is passed, the default trace switch level is `Off` (0), so none of the switch levels are output.

Unit testing

Fixing bugs in code is expensive. The earlier that a bug is discovered in the development process, the less expensive it will be to fix.

Unit testing is a good way to find bugs early in the development process. Some developers even follow the principle that programmers should create unit tests before they write code, and this is called **Test-Driven Development (TDD)**.

Microsoft has a proprietary unit testing framework known as **MS Test**. There is also a framework named **NUnit**. However, we will use the free and open-source third-party framework **xUnit.net**. xUnit was created by the same team that built NUnit but they fixed the mistakes they felt they made previously. xUnit is more extensible and has better community support.

Understanding types of testing

Unit testing is just one of many types of testing, as described in the following table:

Type of testing	Description
Unit	Tests the smallest unit of code, typically a method or function. Unit testing is performed on a unit of code isolated from its dependencies by mocking them if needed. Each unit should have multiple tests: some with typical inputs and expected outputs, some with extreme input values to test boundaries, and some with deliberately wrong inputs to test exception handling.
Integration	Tests if the smaller units and larger components work together as a single piece of software. Sometimes involves integrating with external components that you do not have source code for.
System	Tests the whole system environment in which your software will run.
Performance	Tests the performance of your software; for example, your code must return a web page full of data to a visitor in under 20 milliseconds.
Load	Tests how many requests your software can handle simultaneously while maintaining required performance, for example, 10,000 concurrent visitors to a website.
User Acceptance	Tests if users can happily complete their work using your software.

Creating a class library that needs testing

First, we will create a function that needs testing. We will create it in a class library project. A class library is a package of code that can be distributed and referenced by other .NET applications:

1. Use your preferred coding tool to add a new **Class Library** to the Chapter04 workspace/solution named CalculatorLib. The dotnet new template is named classlib.

2. Rename the file named Class1.cs to Calculator.cs.

3. Modify the file to define a `Calculator` class (with a deliberate bug!), as shown in the following code:

```
namespace Packt
{
  public class Calculator
  {
    public double Add(double a, double b)
    {
      return a * b;
    }
  }
}
```

4. Compile your class library project:

    1. In Visual Studio 2022, navigate to **Build | Build CalculatorLib**.

    2. In Visual Studio Code, in **TERMINAL**, enter the command `dotnet build`.

5. Use your preferred coding tool to add a new **xUnit Test Project [C#]** to the `Chapter04` workspace/solution named `CalculatorLibUnitTests`. The `dotnet new` template is named `xunit`.

6. If you are using Visual Studio, in **Solution Explorer**, select the `CalculatorLibUnitTests` project, navigate to **Project | Add Project Reference…**, check the box to select the `CalculatorLib` project, and then click **OK**.

7. If you are using Visual Studio Code, use the `dotnet add reference` command or click on the file named `CalculatorLibUnitTests.csproj`, and modify the configuration to add an item group with a project reference to the `CalculatorLib` project, as shown highlighted in the following markup:

```
<Project Sdk="Microsoft.NET.Sdk">

  <PropertyGroup>
    <TargetFramework>net6.0</TargetFramework>
    <Nullable>enable</Nullable>

    <IsPackable>false</IsPackable>
  </PropertyGroup>

  <ItemGroup>
    <PackageReference Include="Microsoft.NET.Test.Sdk" Version="16.10.0" />
    <PackageReference Include="xunit" Version="2.4.1" />
    <PackageReference Include="xunit.runner.visualstudio" Version="2.4.3">
      <IncludeAssets>runtime; build; native; contentfiles;
        analyzers; buildtransitive</IncludeAssets>
      <PrivateAssets>all</PrivateAssets>
    </PackageReference>
    <PackageReference Include="coverlet.collector" Version="3.0.2">
```

```
        <IncludeAssets>runtime; build; native; contentfiles;
          analyzers; buildtransitive</IncludeAssets>
        <PrivateAssets>all</PrivateAssets>
      </PackageReference>
    </ItemGroup>

    <ItemGroup>
      <ProjectReference
        Include="..\CalculatorLib\CalculatorLib.csproj" />
    </ItemGroup>
  </Project>
```

8. Build the CalculatorLibUnitTests project.

Writing unit tests

A well-written unit test will have three parts:

- **Arrange**: This part will declare and instantiate variables for input and output.

- **Act**: This part will execute the unit that you are testing. In our case, that means calling the method that we want to test.

- **Assert**: This part will make one or more assertions about the output. An assertion is a belief that, if not true, indicates a failed test. For example, when adding 2 and 2, we would expect the result to be 4.

Now, we will write some unit tests for the Calculator class:

1. Rename the file UnitTest1.cs to CalculatorUnitTests.cs and then open it.

2. In Visual Studio Code, rename the class to CalculatorUnitTests. (Visual Studio prompts you to rename the class when you rename the file.)

3. Import the Packt namespace.

4. Modify the CalculatorUnitTests class to have two test methods for adding 2 and 2, and adding 2 and 3, as shown in the following code:

```
using Packt;
using Xunit;

namespace CalculatorLibUnitTests
{
  public class CalculatorUnitTests
  {
```

```
[Fact]
public void TestAdding2And2()
{
  // arrange
  double a = 2;
  double b = 2;
  double expected = 4;
  Calculator calc = new();

  // act
  double actual = calc.Add(a, b);

  // assert
  Assert.Equal(expected, actual);
}

[Fact]
public void TestAdding2And3()
{
  // arrange
  double a = 2;
  double b = 3;
  double expected = 5;
  Calculator calc = new();

  // act
  double actual = calc.Add(a, b);

  // assert
  Assert.Equal(expected, actual);
  }
 }
}
```

Running unit tests using Visual Studio Code

Now we are ready to run the unit tests and see the results:

1. In the `CalculatorLibUnitTest` project's **TERMINAL** window, run the tests, as shown in the following command:

```
dotnet test
```

2. Note that the results indicate that two tests ran, one test passed, and one test failed, as shown in *Figure 4.21*:

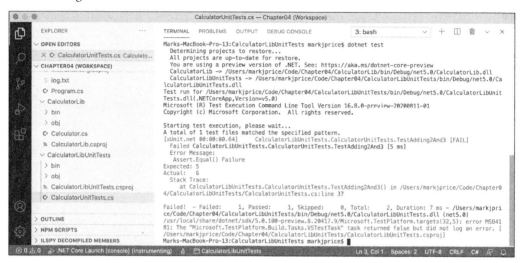

Figure 4.21: The unit test results in Visual Studio Code's TERMINAL

Running unit tests using Visual Studio

Now we are ready to run the unit tests and see the results:

1. Navigate to **Test | Run All Tests**.
2. In **Test Explorer**, note that the results indicate that two tests ran, one test passed, and one test failed, as shown in *Figure 4.22*:

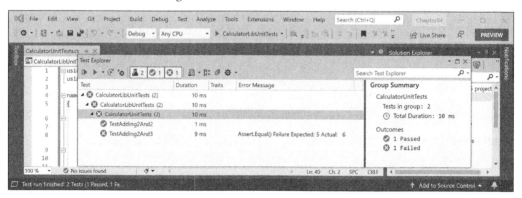

Figure 4.22: The unit test results in Visual Studio 2022's Test Explorer

Fix the bug

Now you can fix the bug:

1. Fix the bug in the Add method.
2. Run the unit tests again to see that the bug has now been fixed and both tests pass.

Throwing and catching exceptions in functions

In *Chapter 3, Controlling Flow, Converting Types, and Handling Exceptions*, you were introduced to exceptions and how to use a `try-catch` statement to handle them. But you should only catch and handle an exception if you have enough information to mitigate the issue. If you do not, then you should allow the exception to pass up through the call stack to a higher level.

Understanding usage errors and execution errors

Usage errors are when a programmer misuses a function, typically by passing invalid values as parameters. They could be avoided by that programmer changing their code to pass valid values. When some programmers first learn C# and .NET, they sometimes think exceptions can always be avoided because they assume all errors are usage errors. Usage errors should all be fixed before production runtime.

Execution errors are when something happens at runtime that cannot be fixed by writing "better" code. Execution errors can be split into **program errors** and **system errors**. If you attempt to access a network resource but the network is down, you need to be able to handle that system error by logging an exception, and possibly backing off for a time and trying again. But some system errors, such as running out of memory, simply cannot be handled. If you attempt to open a file that does not exist, you might be able to catch that error and handle it programmatically by creating a new file. Program errors can be programmatically fixed by writing smart code. System errors often cannot be fixed programmatically.

Commonly thrown exceptions in functions

Very rarely should you define new types of exceptions to indicate usage errors. .NET already defines many that you should use.

When defining your own functions with parameters, your code should check the parameter values and throw exceptions if they have values that will prevent your function from properly functioning.

For example, if a parameter should not be `null`, throw `ArgumentNullException`. For other problems, throw `ArgumentException`, `NotSupportedException`, or `InvalidOperationException`. For any exception, include a message that describes the problem for whoever will have to read it (typically a developer audience for class libraries and functions, or end users if it is at the highest level of a GUI app), as shown in the following code:

```
static void Withdraw(string accountName, decimal amount)
{
  if (accountName is null)
  {
    throw new ArgumentNullException(paramName: nameof(accountName));
  }

  if (amount < 0)
```

```
  {
    throw new ArgumentException(
      message: $"{nameof(amount)} cannot be less than zero.");
  }

  // process parameters
}
```

 Good Practice: If a function cannot successfully perform its operation, you should consider that a function failure and report it by throwing an exception.

You should never need to write a try-catch statement to catch these usage type errors. You want the application to terminate. These exceptions should cause the programmer who is calling the function to fix their code to prevent the problem. They should be fixed before production deployment. That does not mean that your code does not need to throw usage error type exceptions. You should — to force other programmers to call your functions correctly!

Understanding the call stack

The entry point for a .NET console application is the Main method of the Program class, regardless of if you have explicitly defined this class and method or if it was created for you by the top-level program feature.

The Main method will call other methods, that call other methods, and so on, and these methods could be in the current project or in referenced projects and NuGet packages, as shown in *Figure 4.23*:

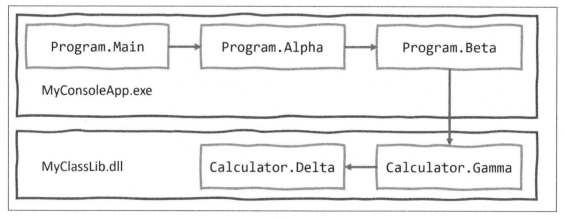

Figure 4.23: A chain of method calls that create a call stack

Let's create a similar chain of methods to explore where we could catch and handle exceptions:

1. Use your preferred coding tool to add a new **Class Library** to the Chapter04 workspace/solution named CallStackExceptionHandlingLib.

2. Rename the Class1.cs file to Calculator.cs.

3. Open Calculator.cs and modify its contents, as shown in the following code:

```
using static System.Console;

namespace Packt;

public class Calculator
{
  public static void Gamma() // public so it can be called from outside
  {
    WriteLine("In Gamma");
    Delta();
  }

  private static void Delta() // private so it can only be called internally
  {
    WriteLine("In Delta");
    File.OpenText("bad file path");
  }
}
```

4. Use your preferred coding tool to add a new **Console Application** to the Chapter04 workspace/solution named CallStackExceptionHandling.

5. In Visual Studio Code, select CallStackExceptionHandling as the active OmniSharp project. When you see the pop-up warning message saying that required assets are missing, click **Yes** to add them.

6. In the CallStackExceptionHandling project, add a reference to the CallStackExceptionHandlingLib project.

7. In Program.cs, add statements to define two methods and chain calls to them, and the methods in the class library, as shown in the following code:

```
using Packt;

using static System.Console;

WriteLine("In Main");
Alpha();

static void Alpha()
{
  WriteLine("In Alpha");
  Beta();
}
```

```
static void Beta()
{
  WriteLine("In Beta");
  Calculator.Gamma();
}
```

8. Run the console app, and note the results, as shown in the following partial output:

```
In Main
In Alpha
In Beta
In Gamma
In Delta
Unhandled exception. System.IO.FileNotFoundException: Could not find file
'C:\Code\Chapter04\CallStackExceptionHandling\bin\Debug\net6.0\bad file
path'.
   at Microsoft.Win32.SafeHandles.SafeFileHandle.CreateFile(...
   at Microsoft.Win32.SafeHandles.SafeFileHandle.Open(...
   at System.IO.Strategies.OSFileStreamStrategy..ctor(...
   at System.IO.Strategies.FileStreamHelpers.ChooseStrategyCore(...
   at System.IO.Strategies.FileStreamHelpers.ChooseStrategy(...
   at System.IO.StreamReader.ValidateArgsAndOpenPath(...
   at System.IO.File.OpenText(String path) in ...
   at Packt.Calculator.Delta() in C:\Code\Chapter04\
CallStackExceptionHandlingLib\Calculator.cs:line 16
   at Packt.Calculator.Gamma() in C:\Code\Chapter04\
CallStackExceptionHandlingLib\Calculator.cs:line 10
   at <Program>$.<<Main>$>g__Beta|0_1() in C:\Code\Chapter04\
CallStackExceptionHandling\Program.cs:line 16
   at <Program>$.<<Main>$>g__Alpha|0_0() in C:\Code\Chapter04\
CallStackExceptionHandling\Program.cs:line 10
   at <Program>$.<Main>$(String[] args) in C:\Code\Chapter04\
CallStackExceptionHandling\Program.cs:line 5
```

Note the following:

- The call stack is upside-down. Starting from the bottom, you see:
  - The first call is to the Main entry point function in the auto-generated Program class. This is where arguments are passed in as a string array.
  - The second call is to the Alpha function.
  - The third call is to the Beta function.
  - The fourth call is to the Gamma function.
  - The fifth call is to the Delta function. This function attempts to open a file by passing a bad file path. This causes an exception to be thrown. Any function with a try-catch statement could catch this exception. If they do not, it is automatically passed up the call stack until it reaches the top, where .NET outputs the exception (and the details of this call stack).

Where to catch exceptions

Programmers can decide if they want to catch an exception near the failure point, or centralized higher up the call stack. This allows your code to be simplified and standardized. You might know that calling an exception could throw one or more types of exception, but you do not need to handle any of them at the current point in the call stack.

Rethrowing exceptions

Sometimes you want to catch an exception, log it, and then rethrow it. There are three ways to rethrow an exception inside a `catch` block, as shown in the following list:

1. To throw the caught exception with its original call stack, call `throw`.

2. To throw the caught exception as if it was thrown at the current level in the call stack, call `throw` with the caught exception, for example, `throw ex`. This is usually poor practice because you have lost some potentially useful information for debugging.

3. To wrap the caught exception in another exception that can include more information in a message that might help the caller understand the problem, throw a new exception and pass the caught exception as the `innerException` parameter.

If an error could occur when we call the `Gamma` function then we could catch the exception and then perform one of the three techniques of rethrowing an exception, as shown in the following code:

```
try
{
  Gamma();
}
catch (IOException ex)
{
  LogException(ex);

  // throw the caught exception as if it happened here
  // this will lose the original call stack
  throw ex;

  // rethrow the caught exception and retain its original call stack
  throw;

  // throw a new exception with the caught exception nested within it
  throw new InvalidOperationException(
    message: "Calculation had invalid values. See inner exception for why.",
    innerException: ex);
}
```

Let's see this in action with our call stack example:

1. In the `CallStackExceptionHandling` project, in `Program.cs`, in the `Beta` function, add a `try-catch` statement around the call to the `Gamma` function, as shown highlighted in the following code:

```
static void Beta()
{
  WriteLine("In Beta");

  try
  {
    Calculator.Gamma();
  }
  catch (Exception ex)
  {
    WriteLine($"Caught this: {ex.Message}");
    throw ex;
  }
}
```

2. Note the green squiggle under the `ex` to warn you that you will lose call stack information.

3. Run the console app and note the output excludes some details of the call stack, as shown in the following output:

```
Caught this: Could not find file 'C:\Code\Chapter04\
CallStackExceptionHandling\bin\Debug\net6.0\bad file path'.
Unhandled exception. System.IO.FileNotFoundException: Could not find file
'C:\Code\Chapter04\CallStackExceptionHandling\bin\Debug\net6.0\bad file
path'.
File name: 'C:\Code\Chapter04\CallStackExceptionHandling\bin\Debug\net6.0\
bad file path'
   at <Program>$.<<Main>$>g__Beta|0_1() in C:\Code\Chapter04\
CallStackExceptionHandling\Program.cs:line 25
   at <Program>$.<<Main>$>g__Alpha|0_0() in C:\Code\Chapter04\
CallStackExceptionHandling\Program.cs:line 11
   at <Program>$.<Main>$(String[] args) in C:\Code\Chapter04\
CallStackExceptionHandling\Program.cs:line 6
```

4. Delete the `ex` when rethrowing.

5. Run the console app and note the output includes all the details of the call stack.

Implementing the tester-doer pattern

The **tester-doer pattern** can avoid some thrown exceptions (but not eliminate them completely). This pattern uses pairs of functions: one to perform a test, the other to perform an action that would fail if the test is not passed.

.NET implements this pattern itself. For example, before adding an item to a collection by calling the Add method, you can test to see if it is read-only, which would cause Add to fail and therefore throw an exception.

For example, before withdrawing money from a bank account, you might test that the account is not overdrawn, as shown in the following code:

```
if (!bankAccount.IsOverdrawn())
{
  bankAccount.Withdraw(amount);
}
```

Problems with the tester-doer pattern

The tester-doer pattern can add performance overhead, so you can also implement the **try pattern**, which in effect combines the test and do parts into a single function, as we saw with TryParse.

Another problem with the tester-doer pattern occurs when you are using multiple threads. In this scenario, one thread could call the test function and it returns okay. But then another thread executes that changes the state. Then the original thread continues executing assuming everything is fine, but it is not fine. This is called a race condition. We will see how we could handle it in *Chapter 12, Improving Performance and Scalability Using Multitasking*.

If you implement your own try pattern function and it fails, remember to set the out parameter to the default value of its type and then return false, as shown in the following code:

```
static bool TryParse(string? input, out Person value)
{
  if (someFailure)
  {
    value = default(Person);
    return false;
  }

  // successfully parsed the string into a Person
  value = new Person() { ... };
  return true;
}
```

Practicing and exploring

Test your knowledge and understanding by answering some questions, get some hands-on practice, and explore with deeper research into the topics covered in this chapter.

Exercise 4.1 – Test your knowledge

Answer the following questions. If you get stuck, try Googling the answers if necessary, while remembering that if you get totally stuck, the answers are in the Appendix:

1. What does the C# keyword void mean?
2. What are some differences between imperative and functional programming styles?
3. In Visual Studio Code or Visual Studio, what is the difference between pressing *F5*, *Ctrl* or *Cmd + F5*, *Shift + F5*, and *Ctrl* or *Cmd + Shift + F5*?
4. Where does the Trace.WriteLine method write its output to?
5. What are the five trace levels?
6. What is the difference between the Debug and Trace classes?
7. When writing a unit test, what are the three "A"s?
8. When writing a unit test using xUnit, what attribute must you decorate the test methods with?
9. What dotnet command executes xUnit tests?
10. What statement should you use to rethrow a caught exception named ex without losing the stack trace?

Exercise 4.2 – Practice writing functions with debugging and unit testing

Prime factors are the combination of the smallest prime numbers that, when multiplied together, will produce the original number. Consider the following example:

- Prime factors of 4 are: 2 x 2
- Prime factors of 7 are: 7
- Prime factors of 30 are: 5 x 3 x 2
- Prime factors of 40 are: 5 x 2 x 2 x 2
- Prime factors of 50 are: 5 x 5 x 2

Create a workspace/solution named PrimeFactors to contain three projects: a class library with a method named PrimeFactors that, when passed an int variable as a parameter, returns a string showing its prime factors; a unit tests project; and a console application to use it.

To keep it simple, you can assume that the largest number entered will be 1,000.

Use the debugging tools and write unit tests to ensure that your function works correctly with multiple inputs and returns the correct output.

Exercise 4.3 – Explore topics

Use the links on the following page to learn more detail about the topics covered in this chapter:

```
https://github.com/markjprice/cs10dotnet6/blob/main/book-links.md#chapter-4---
writing-debugging-and-testing-functions
```

Summary

In this chapter, you learned how to write reusable functions with input parameters and return values, in both an imperative and functional style, and then how to use the Visual Studio and Visual Studio Code debugging and diagnostic features to fix any bugs in them. Finally, you learned how to throw and catch exceptions in functions and understand the call stack.

In the next chapter, you will learn how to build your own types using object-oriented programming techniques.

05

Building Your Own Types with Object-Oriented Programming

This chapter is about making your own types using **object-oriented programming (OOP)**. You will learn about all the different categories of members that a type can have, including fields to store data and methods to perform actions. You will use OOP concepts such as aggregation and encapsulation. You will also learn about language features such as tuple syntax support, out variables, inferred tuple names, and default literals.

This chapter will cover the following topics:

- Talking about OOP
- Building class libraries
- Storing data with fields
- Writing and calling methods
- Controlling access with properties and indexers
- Pattern matching with objects
- Working with records

Talking about OOP

An object in the real world is a thing, such as a car or a person, whereas an object in programming often represents something in the real world, such as a product or bank account, but this can also be something more abstract.

In C#, we use the class (mostly) or struct (sometimes) C# keywords to define a type of object. You will learn about the difference between classes and structs in *Chapter 6, Implementing Interfaces and Inheriting Classes*. You can think of a type as being a blueprint or template for an object.

The concepts of OOP are briefly described here:

- **Encapsulation** is the combination of the data and actions that are related to an object. For example, a BankAccount type might have data, such as Balance and AccountName, as well as actions, such as Deposit and Withdraw. When encapsulating, you often want to control what can access those actions and the data, for example, restricting how the internal state of an object can be accessed or modified from the outside.

- **Composition** is about what an object is made of. For example, a Car is composed of different parts, such as four Wheel objects, several Seat objects, and an Engine.

- **Aggregation** is about what can be combined with an object. For example, a Person is not part of a Car object, but they could sit in the driver's Seat and then become the car's Driver—two separate objects that are aggregated together to form a new component.

- **Inheritance** is about reusing code by having a **subclass** derive from a **base** or **superclass**. All functionality in the base class is inherited by and becomes available in the **derived** class. For example, the base or super Exception class has some members that have the same implementation across all exceptions, and the sub or derived SqlException class inherits those members and has extra members only relevant to when a SQL database exception occurs, like a property for the database connection.

- **Abstraction** is about capturing the core idea of an object and ignoring the details or specifics. C# has the abstract keyword that formalizes this concept. If a class is not explicitly **abstract**, then it can be described as being **concrete**. Base or superclasses are often abstract, for example, the superclass Stream is abstract, and its subclasses, like FileStream and MemoryStream, are concrete. Only concrete classes can be used to create objects; abstract classes can only be used as the base for other classes because they are missing some implementation. Abstraction is a tricky balance. If you make a class more abstract, more classes will be able to inherit from it, but at the same time, there will be less functionality to share.

- **Polymorphism** is about allowing a derived class to override an inherited action to provide custom behavior.

Building class libraries

Class library assemblies group types together into easily deployable units (DLL files). Apart from when you learned about unit testing, you have only created console applications or .NET Interactive notebooks to contain your code. To make the code that you write reusable across multiple projects, you should put it in class library assemblies, just like Microsoft does.

Creating a class library

The first task is to create a reusable .NET class library:

1. Use your preferred coding tool to create a new class library, as defined in the following list:

   1. Project template: **Class Library** / classlib

2. Workspace/solution file and folder: `Chapter05`

3. Project file and folder: `PacktLibrary`

2. Open the `PacktLibrary.csproj` file, and note that by default class libraries target .NET 6 and therefore can only work with other .NET 6-compatible assemblies, as shown in the following markup:

```
<Project Sdk="Microsoft.NET.Sdk">

  <PropertyGroup>
    <TargetFramework>net6.0</TargetFramework>
    <Nullable>enable</Nullable>
    <ImplicitUsings>enable</ImplicitUsings>
  </PropertyGroup>

</Project>
```

3. Modify the framework to target .NET Standard 2.0 and remove the entries that enable nullable and implicit usings, as shown highlighted in the following markup:

```
<Project Sdk="Microsoft.NET.Sdk">

  <PropertyGroup>
    <TargetFramework>netstandard2.0</TargetFramework>
  </PropertyGroup>

</Project>
```

4. Save and close the file.

5. Delete the file named `Class1.cs`.

6. Compile the project so that other projects can reference it later:

   1. In Visual Studio Code, enter the following command: `dotnet build`.

   2. In Visual Studio, navigate to **Build** | **Build PacktLibrary**.

 Good Practice: To use the latest C# language and .NET platform features, put types in a .NET 6 class library. To support legacy .NET platforms like .NET Core, .NET Framework, and Xamarin, put types that you might reuse in a .NET Standard 2.0 class library.

Defining a class in a namespace

The next task is to define a class that will represent a person:

1. Add a new class file named `Person.cs`.

2. Statically import `System.Console`.

3. Set the namespace to `Packt.Shared`.

Good Practice: We're doing this because it is important to put your classes in a logically named namespace. A better namespace name would be domain-specific, for example, System.Numerics for types related to advanced numbers. In this case, the types we will create are Person, BankAccount, and WondersOfTheWorld and they do not have a typical domain so we will use the more generic Packt.Shared.

Your class file should now look like the following code:

```
using System;
using static System.Console;

namespace Packt.Shared
{
  public class Person
  {
  }
}
```

Note that the C# keyword public is applied before class. This keyword is an **access modifier**, and it allows for any other code to access this class.

If you do not explicitly apply the public keyword, then it will only be accessible within the assembly that defined it. This is because the implicit access modifier for a class is internal. We need this class to be accessible outside the assembly, so we must make sure it is public.

Simplifying namespace declarations

To simplify your code if you are targeting .NET 6.0 and therefore using C# 10 or later, you can end a namespace declaration with a semi-colon and remove the braces, as shown in the following code:

```
using System;

namespace Packt.Shared; // the class in this file is in this namespace

public class Person
{
}
```

This is known as a file-scoped namespace declaration. You can only have one file-scoped namespace per file. We will use this in a class library that targets .NET 6.0 later in this chapter.

Good Practice: Put each type that you create in its own file so that you can use file-scoped namespace declarations.

Understanding members

This type does not yet have any members encapsulated within it. We will create some over the following pages. Members can be fields, methods, or specialized versions of both. You'll find a description of them here:

- **Fields** are used to store data. There are also three specialized categories of field, as shown in the following bullets:
    - **Constant**: The data never changes. The compiler literally copies the data into any code that reads it.
    - **Read-only**: The data cannot change after the class is instantiated, but the data can be calculated or loaded from an external source at the time of instantiation.
    - **Event**: The data references one or more methods that you want to execute when something happens, such as clicking on a button or responding to a request from some other code. Events will be covered in *Chapter 6, Implementing Interfaces and Inheriting Classes*.

- **Methods** are used to execute statements. You saw some examples when you learned about functions in *Chapter 4, Writing, Debugging, and Testing Functions*. There are also four specialized categories of method:
    - **Constructor**: The statements execute when you use the new keyword to allocate memory to instantiate a class.
    - **Property**: The statements execute when you get or set data. The data is commonly stored in a field but could be stored externally or calculated at runtime. Properties are the preferred way to encapsulate fields unless the memory address of the field needs to be exposed.
    - **Indexer**: The statements execute when you get or set data using "array" syntax [].
    - **Operator**: The statements execute when you use an operator like + and / on operands of your type.

Instantiating a class

In this section, we will make an instance of the Person class.

Referencing an assembly

Before we can instantiate a class, we need to reference the assembly that contains it from another project. We will use the class in a console app:

1. Use your preferred coding tool to add a new console app to the Chapter05 workspace/ solution named PeopleApp.

2. If you are using Visual Studio Code:

    1. Select PeopleApp as the active OmniSharp project. When you see the pop-up warning message saying that required assets are missing, click **Yes** to add them.

    2. Edit PeopleApp.csproj to add a project reference to PacktLibrary, as shown highlighted in the following markup:

```xml
<Project Sdk="Microsoft.NET.Sdk">

  <PropertyGroup>
    <OutputType>Exe</OutputType>
    <TargetFramework>net6.0</TargetFramework>
    <Nullable>enable</Nullable>
    <ImplicitUsings>enable</ImplicitUsings>
  </PropertyGroup>

  <ItemGroup>
    <ProjectReference Include="../PacktLibrary/PacktLibrary.csproj" />
  </ItemGroup>

</Project>
```

    3. In a terminal, enter a command to compile the PeopleApp project and its dependency PacktLibrary project, as shown in the following command:

```
dotnet build
```

3. If you are using Visual Studio:

    1. Set the startup project for the solution to the current selection.

    2. In **Solution Explorer**, select the PeopleApp project, navigate to **Project | Add Project Reference...**, check the box to select the PacktLibrary project, and then click **OK**.

    3. Navigate to **Build | Build PeopleApp**.

Importing a namespace to use a type

Now, we are ready to write statements to work with the Person class:

1. In the PeopleApp project/folder, open Program.cs.

2. At the top of the `Program.cs` file, delete the comment, and add statements to import the namespace for our `Person` class and statically import the `Console` class, as shown in the following code:

```
using Packt.Shared;
using static System.Console;
```

3. In `Program.cs`, add statements to:

   - Create an instance of the `Person` type.

   - Output the instance using a textual description of itself.

The `new` keyword allocates memory for the object and initializes any internal data. We could use `var` in place of the `Person` class name, but then we would need to specify `Person` after the `new` keyword, as shown in the following code:

```
// var bob = new Person(); // C# 1.0 or later
Person bob = new(); // C# 9.0 or later
WriteLine(bob.ToString());
```

You might be wondering, "Why does the `bob` variable have a method named `ToString`? The `Person` class is empty!" Don't worry, we're about to find out!

4. Run the code and view the result, as shown in the following output:

```
Packt.Shared.Person
```

Understanding objects

Although our `Person` class did not explicitly choose to inherit from a type, all types ultimately inherit directly or indirectly from a special type named `System.Object`.

The implementation of the `ToString` method in the `System.Object` type simply outputs the full namespace and type name.

Back in the original `Person` class, we could have explicitly told the compiler that `Person` inherits from the `System.Object` type, as shown in the following code:

```
public class Person : System.Object
```

When class B inherits from class A, we say that A is the base or superclass and B is the derived or subclass. In this case, `System.Object` is the base or superclass and `Person` is the derived or subclass.

You can also use the C# alias keyword `object`, as shown in the following code:

```
public class Person : object
```

Inheriting from System.Object

Let's make our class explicitly inherit from `object` and then review what members all objects have:

1. Modify your `Person` class to explicitly inherit from `object`.
2. Click inside the `object` keyword and press *F12*, or right-click on the `object` keyword and choose **Go to Definition**.

You will see the Microsoft-defined `System.Object` type and its members. This is something you don't need to understand the details of yet, but notice that it has a method named `ToString`, as shown in *Figure 5.1*:

```
[metadata] Object.cs — Chapter05 (Workspace)

C# [metadata] Object.cs ×

 1    #region Assembly netstandard, Version=2.0.0.0, Culture=neutral, PublicKeyToken=cc7b13ffcd2ddd51
 2    // netstandard.dll
 3    #endregion
 4
 5    namespace System
 6    {
 7      public class Object
 8      {
 9        public Object();
10
11        ~Object();
12
13        public static bool Equals(Object objA, Object objB);
14        public static bool ReferenceEquals(Object objA, Object objB);
15        public virtual bool Equals(Object obj);
16        public virtual int GetHashCode();
17        public Type GetType();
18        public virtual string ToString();
19        protected Object MemberwiseClone();
20      }
21    }

⊗ 0 ⚠ 0    PeopleApp                                      Ln 7, Col 16    Spaces: 2    C#    SharpPad:5255
```

Figure 5.1: System.Object class definition

 Good Practice: Assume other programmers know that if inheritance is not specified, the class will inherit from `System.Object`.

Storing data within fields

In this section, we will be defining a selection of fields in the class to store information about a person.

Defining fields

Let's say that we have decided that a person is composed of a name and a date of birth. We will encapsulate these two values inside a person, and the values will be visible outside it.

Inside the `Person` class, write statements to declare two public fields for storing a person's name and date of birth, as shown in the following code:

```
public class Person : object
{
  // fields
  public string Name;
  public DateTime DateOfBirth;
}
```

You can use any type for a field, including arrays and collections such as lists and dictionaries. These would be used if you needed to store multiple values in one named field. In this example, a person only has one name and one date of birth.

Understanding access modifiers

Part of encapsulation is choosing how visible the members are.

Note that, as we did with the class, we explicitly applied the `public` keyword to these fields. If we hadn't, then they would be implicitly `private` to the class, which means they are accessible only inside the class.

There are four access modifier keywords, and two combinations of access modifier keywords that you can apply to a class member, like a field or method, as shown in the following table:

Access Modifier	Description
private	Member is accessible inside the type only. This is the default.
internal	Member is accessible inside the type and any type in the same assembly.
protected	Member is accessible inside the type and any type that inherits from the type.
public	Member is accessible everywhere.
internal protected	Member is accessible inside the type, any type in the same assembly, and any type that inherits from the type. Equivalent to a fictional access modifier named `internal_or_protected`.
private protected	Member is accessible inside the type and any type that inherits from the type and is in the same assembly. Equivalent to a fictional access modifier named `internal_and_protected`. This combination is only available with C# 7.2 or later.

 Good Practice: Explicitly apply one of the access modifiers to all type members, even if you want to use the implicit access modifier for members, which is `private`. Additionally, fields should usually be `private` or `protected`, and you should then create `public` properties to get or set the field values. This is because it controls access. You will do this later in the chapter.

Setting and outputting field values

Now we will use those fields in your code:

1. At the top of `Program.cs`, make sure the `System` namespace is imported. We need to do this to use the `DateTime` type.

2. After instantiating `bob`, add statements to set his name and date of birth, and then output those fields formatted nicely, as shown in the following code:

    ```
    bob.Name = "Bob Smith";
    bob.DateOfBirth = new DateTime(1965, 12, 22); // C# 1.0 or later

    WriteLine(format: "{0} was born on {1:dddd, d MMMM yyyy}",
      arg0: bob.Name,
      arg1: bob.DateOfBirth);
    ```

    We could have used string interpolation too, but for long strings it will wrap over multiple lines, which can be harder to read in a printed book. In the code examples in this book, remember that {0} is a placeholder for arg0, and so on.

3. Run the code and view the result, as shown in the following output:

    ```
    Bob Smith was born on Wednesday, 22 December 1965
    ```

    Your output may look different based on your locale, that is, language and culture.

    The format code for `arg1` is made of several parts. `dddd` means the name of the day of the week. `d` means the number of the day of the month. `MMMM` means the name of the month. Lowercase `m` is used for minutes in time values. `yyyy` means the full number of the year. `yy` would mean the two-digit year.

    You can also initialize fields using a shorthand **object initializer** syntax using curly braces. Let's see how.

4. Add statements underneath the existing code to create another new person named Alice. Note the different format code for the date of birth when writing her to the console, as shown in the following code:

    ```
    Person alice = new()
    {
      Name = "Alice Jones",
      DateOfBirth = new(1998, 3, 7) // C# 9.0 or later
    };

    WriteLine(format: "{0} was born on {1:dd MMM yy}",
      arg0: alice.Name,
      arg1: alice.DateOfBirth);
    ```

5. Run the code and view the result, as shown in the following output:

    ```
    Alice Jones was born on 07 Mar 98
    ```

Storing a value using an enum type

Sometimes, a value needs to be one of a limited set of options. For example, there are seven ancient wonders of the world, and a person may have one favorite. At other times, a value needs to be a combination of a limited set of options. For example, a person may have a bucket list of ancient world wonders they want to visit. We are able to store this data by defining an enum type.

An enum type is a very efficient way of storing one or more choices because, internally, it uses integer values in combination with a lookup table of string descriptions:

1. Add a new file to the PacktLibrary project named WondersOfTheAncientWorld.cs.

2. Modify the WondersOfTheAncientWorld.cs file, as shown in the following code:

```
namespace Packt.Shared
{
  public enum WondersOfTheAncientWorld
  {
    GreatPyramidOfGiza,
    HangingGardensOfBabylon,
    StatueOfZeusAtOlympia,
    TempleOfArtemisAtEphesus,
    MausoleumAtHalicarnassus,
    ColossusOfRhodes,
    LighthouseOfAlexandria
  }
}
```

 Good Practice: If you use are writing code in a .NET Interactive notebook, then the code cell containing the enum must be above the code cell defining the Person class.

3. In the Person class, add the following statement to your list of fields:

```
public WondersOfTheAncientWorld FavoriteAncientWonder;
```

4. In Program.cs, add the following statements:

```
bob.FavoriteAncientWonder = WondersOfTheAncientWorld.
StatueOfZeusAtOlympia;

WriteLine(
  format: "{0}'s favorite wonder is {1}. Its integer is {2}.",
  arg0: bob.Name,
  arg1: bob.FavoriteAncientWonder,
  arg2: (int)bob.FavoriteAncientWonder);
```

5. Run the code and view the result, as shown in the following output:

```
Bob Smith's favorite wonder is StatueOfZeusAtOlympia. Its integer is 2.
```

The enum value is internally stored as an int for efficiency. The int values are automatically assigned starting at 0, so the third world wonder in our enum has a value of 2. You can assign int values that are not listed in the enum. They will output as the int value instead of a name since a match will not be found.

Storing multiple values using an enum type

For the bucket list, we could create an array or collection of instances of the enum, and collections will be explained later in this chapter, but there is a better way. We can combine multiple choices into a single value using enum **flags**:

1. Modify the enum by decorating it with the [System.Flags] attribute, and explicitly set a byte value for each wonder that represents different bit columns, as shown highlighted in the following code:

```
namespace Packt.Shared
{
    [System.Flags]
    public enum WondersOfTheAncientWorld : byte
    {
        None                      = 0b_0000_0000, // i.e. 0
        GreatPyramidOfGiza        = 0b_0000_0001, // i.e. 1
        HangingGardensOfBabylon   = 0b_0000_0010, // i.e. 2
        StatueOfZeusAtOlympia     = 0b_0000_0100, // i.e. 4
        TempleOfArtemisAtEphesus  = 0b_0000_1000, // i.e. 8
        MausoleumAtHalicarnassus  = 0b_0001_0000, // i.e. 16
        ColossusOfRhodes          = 0b_0010_0000, // i.e. 32
        LighthouseOfAlexandria    = 0b_0100_0000  // i.e. 64
    }
}
```

We are assigning explicit values for each choice that would not overlap when looking at the bits stored in memory. We should also decorate the enum type with the System. Flags attribute so that when the value is returned it can automatically match with multiple values as a comma-separated string instead of returning an int value.

Normally, an enum type uses an int variable internally, but since we don't need values that big, we can reduce memory requirements by 75%, that is, 1 byte per value instead of 4 bytes, by telling it to use a byte variable.

If we want to indicate that our bucket list includes the *Hanging Gardens of Babylon* and the *Mausoleum at Halicarnassus* ancient world wonders, then we would want the 16 and 2 bits set to 1. In other words, we would store the value 18:

64	32	16	8	4	2	1
0	0	1	0	0	1	0

2. In the `Person` class, add the following statement to your list of fields, as shown in the following code:

```
public WondersOfTheAncientWorld BucketList;
```

3. In `Program.cs`, add statements to set the bucket list using the | operator (bitwise logical OR) to combine the enum values. We could also set the value using the number 18 cast into the enum type, as shown in the comment, but we shouldn't because that would make the code harder to understand, as shown in the following code:

```
bob.BucketList =
  WondersOfTheAncientWorld.HangingGardensOfBabylon
  | WondersOfTheAncientWorld.MausoleumAtHalicarnassus;

// bob.BucketList = (WondersOfTheAncientWorld)18;

WriteLine($"{bob.Name}'s bucket list is {bob.BucketList}");
```

4. Run the code and view the result, as shown in the following output:

```
Bob Smith's bucket list is HangingGardensOfBabylon,
MausoleumAtHalicarnassus
```

Good Practice: Use the enum values to store combinations of discrete options. Derive an enum type from byte if there are up to eight options, from ushort if there are up to 16 options, from uint if there are up to 32 options, and from ulong if there are up to 64 options.

Storing multiple values using collections

Let's now add a field to store a person's children. This is an example of aggregation because children are instances of a class that is related to the current person but are not part of the person itself. We will use a generic `List<T>` collection type that can store an ordered collection of any type. You will learn more about collections in *Chapter 8, Working with Common .NET Types*. For now, just follow along:

1. In `Person.cs`, import the `System.Collections.Generic` namespace, as shown in the following code:

```
using System.Collections.Generic; // List<T>
```

2. Declare a new field in the `Person` class, as shown in the following code:

```
public List<Person> Children = new List<Person>();
```

List<Person> is read aloud as "list of Person," for example, "the type of the property named Children is a list of Person instances." We explicitly changed the class library to target .NET Standard 2.0 (that uses the C# 7 compiler), so we cannot use target-typed new to initialize the Children field. If we had left it targeting .NET 6.0, then we could use target-typed new, as shown in the following code:

```
public List<Person> Children = new();
```

We must ensure the collection is initialized to a new instance of a list of Person before we can add items to it, otherwise, the field will be null and it will throw runtime exceptions when we try to use any of its members like Add.

Understanding generic collections

The angle brackets in the List<T> type is a feature of C# called **generics** that was introduced in 2005 with C# 2.0. It's a fancy term for making a collection **strongly typed**, that is, the compiler knows specifically what type of object can be stored in the collection. Generics improve the performance and correctness of your code.

Strongly typed has a different meaning to **statically typed**. The old System.Collection types are statically typed to contain weakly typed System.Object items. The newer System. Collection.Generic types are statically typed to contain strongly typed <T> instances.

Ironically, the term *generics* means we can use a more specific static type!

1. In Program.cs, add statements to add two children for Bob and then show how many children he has and what their names are, as shown in the following code:

```
bob.Children.Add(new Person { Name = "Alfred" }); // C# 3.0 and later
bob.Children.Add(new() { Name = "Zoe" }); // C# 9.0 and later

WriteLine(
  $"{bob.Name} has {bob.Children.Count} children:");

for (int childIndex = 0; childIndex < bob.Children.Count; childIndex++)
{
  WriteLine($"  {bob.Children[childIndex].Name}");
}
```

We could also use a foreach statement to enumerate over the collection. As an extra challenge, change the for statement to output the same information using foreach.

2. Run the code and view the result, as shown in the following output:

```
Bob Smith has 2 children:
  Alfred
  Zoe
```

Making a field static

The fields that we have created so far have all been **instance** members, meaning that a different value of each field exists for each instance of the class that is created. The `alice` and `bob` variables have different `Name` values.

Sometimes, you want to define a field that only has one value that is shared across all instances.

These are called **static** *members* because fields are not the only members that can be static. Let's see what can be achieved using `static` fields:

1. In the `PacktLibrary` project, add a new class file named `BankAccount.cs`.

2. Modify the class to give it three fields, two instance fields and one static field, as shown in the following code:

    ```
    namespace Packt.Shared
    {
      public class BankAccount
      {
        public string AccountName; // instance member
        public decimal Balance; // instance member
        public static decimal InterestRate; // shared member
      }
    }
    ```

    Each instance of `BankAccount` will have its own `AccountName` and `Balance` values, but all instances will share a single `InterestRate` value.

3. In `Program.cs`, add statements to set the shared interest rate and then create two instances of the `BankAccount` type, as shown in the following code:

    ```
    BankAccount.InterestRate = 0.012M; // store a shared value

    BankAccount jonesAccount = new(); // C# 9.0 and Later
    jonesAccount.AccountName = "Mrs. Jones";
    jonesAccount.Balance = 2400;

    WriteLine(format: "{0} earned {1:C} interest.",
      arg0: jonesAccount.AccountName,
      arg1: jonesAccount.Balance * BankAccount.InterestRate);

    BankAccount gerrierAccount = new();
    gerrierAccount.AccountName = "Ms. Gerrier";
    gerrierAccount.Balance = 98;

    WriteLine(format: "{0} earned {1:C} interest.",
      arg0: gerrierAccount.AccountName,
      arg1: gerrierAccount.Balance * BankAccount.InterestRate);
    ```

:C is a format code that tells .NET to use the currency format for the numbers. In *Chapter 8, Working with Common .NET Types,* you will learn how to control the culture that determines the currency symbol. For now, it will use the default for your operating system installation. I live in London, UK, hence my output shows British Pounds (£).

4. Run the code and view the additional output:

```
Mrs. Jones earned £28.80 interest.
Ms. Gerrier earned £1.18 interest.
```

 Fields are not the only members that can be static. Constructors, methods, properties, and other members can also be static.

Making a field constant

If the value of a field will never ever change, you can use the const keyword and assign a literal value at compile time:

1. In Person.cs, add the following code:

    ```
    // constants
    public const string Species = "Homo Sapien";
    ```

2. To get the value of a constant field, you must write the name of the class, not the name of an instance of the class. In Program.cs, add a statement to write Bob's name and species to the console, as shown in the following code:

    ```
    WriteLine($"{bob.Name} is a {Person.Species}");
    ```

3. Run the code and view the result, as shown in the following output:

    ```
    Bob Smith is a Homo Sapien
    ```

Examples of const fields in Microsoft types include System.Int32.MaxValue and System.Math.PI because neither value will ever change, as you can see in *Figure 5.2*:

```
● ● ●                              [metadata] Math.cs — Chapter05 (Workspace)
C• [metadata] Math.cs ×                                                                    ⊓ ···
     1   #region Assembly System.Runtime, Version=5.0.0.0, Culture=neutral, PublicKeyToken=b03f5f7f11d50a3a
     2   // System.Runtime.dll
     3   #endregion
     4
     5
     6   namespace System
     7   {
     8       //
     9       // Summary:
    10       //     Provides constants and static methods for trigonometric, logarithmic, and other
    11       //     common mathematical functions.
    12       public static class Math
    13       {
    14           //
    15           // Summary:
    16           //     Represents the natural logarithmic base, specified by the constant, e.
    17           public const double E = 2.7182818284590451;
    18           //
    19           // Summary:
    20           //     Represents the ratio of the circumference of a circle to its diameter, specified
    21           //     by the constant, π.
    22           public const double PI = 3.1415926535897931;
    23           public const double Tau = 6.2831853071795862;
⊗ 3 ⚠ 0   ⌂   ⊡ PeopleApp                                              Ln 12, Col 23   Spaces: 2   C#  ⌀  ⌁
```

Figure 5.2: Examples of constants

> **Good Practice**: Constants are not always the best choice for two important reasons: the value must be known at compile time, and it must be expressible as a literal string, Boolean, or number value. Every reference to the const field is replaced with the literal value at compile time, which will, therefore, not be reflected if the value changes in a future version and you do not recompile any assemblies that reference it to get the new value.

Making a field read-only

Often a better choice for fields that should not change is to mark them as read-only:

1. In Person.cs, add a statement to declare an instance read-only field to store a person's home planet, as shown in the following code:

    ```
    // read-only fields
    public readonly string HomePlanet = "Earth";
    ```

2. In Program.cs, add a statement to write Bob's name and home planet to the console, as shown in the following code:

    ```
    WriteLine($"{bob.Name} was born on {bob.HomePlanet}");
    ```

3. Run the code and view the result, as shown in the following output:

    ```
    Bob Smith was born on Earth
    ```

> **Good Practice**: Use read-only fields over constant fields for two important reasons: the value can be calculated or loaded at runtime and can be expressed using any executable statement. So, a read-only field can be set using a constructor or a field assignment. Every reference to the field is a live reference, so any future changes will be correctly reflected by the calling code.

You can also declare `static readonly` fields whose values will be shared across all instances of the type.

Initializing fields with constructors

Fields often need to be initialized at runtime. You do this in a constructor that will be called when you make an instance of the class using the `new` keyword. Constructors execute before any fields are set by the code that is using the type.

1. In `Person.cs`, add statements after the existing read-only `HomePlanet` field to define a second read-only field and then set the `Name` and `Instantiated` fields in a constructor, as shown highlighted in the following code:

```
// read-only fields
public readonly string HomePlanet = "Earth";
public readonly DateTime Instantiated;

// constructors
public Person()
{
    // set default values for fields
    // including read-only fields
    Name = "Unknown";
    Instantiated = DateTime.Now;
}
```

2. In `Program.cs`, add statements to instantiate a new person and then output its initial field values, as shown in the following code:

```
Person blankPerson = new();

WriteLine(format:
    "{0} of {1} was created at {2:hh:mm:ss} on a {2:dddd}.",
    arg0: blankPerson.Name,
    arg1: blankPerson.HomePlanet,
    arg2: blankPerson.Instantiated);
```

3. Run the code and view the result, as shown in the following output:

```
Unknown of Earth was created at 11:58:12 on a Sunday
```

Defining multiple constructors

You can have multiple constructors in a type. This is especially useful to encourage developers to set initial values for fields:

1. In `Person.cs`, add statements to define a second constructor that allows a developer to set initial values for the person's name and home planet, as shown in the following code:

    ```
    public Person(string initialName, string homePlanet)
    {
      Name = initialName;
      HomePlanet = homePlanet;
      Instantiated = DateTime.Now;
    }
    ```

2. In `Program.cs`, add statements to create another person using the constructor with two parameters, as shown in the following code:

    ```
    Person gunny = new(initialName: "Gunny", homePlanet: "Mars");

    WriteLine(format:
      "{0} of {1} was created at {2:hh:mm:ss} on a {2:dddd}.",
      arg0: gunny.Name,
      arg1: gunny.HomePlanet,
      arg2: gunny.Instantiated);
    ```

3. Run the code and view the result:

    ```
    Gunny of Mars was created at 11:59:25 on a Sunday
    ```

Constructors are a special category of method. Let's look at methods in more detail.

Writing and calling methods

Methods are members of a type that execute a block of statements. They are functions that belong to a type.

Returning values from methods

Methods can return a single value or return nothing:

*   A method that performs some actions but does not return a value indicates this with the void type before the name of the method.
*   A method that performs some actions and returns a value indicates this with the type of the return value before the name of the method.

For example, in the next task, you will create two methods:

- WriteToConsole: This will perform an action (writing some text to the console), but it will return nothing from the method, indicated by the void keyword.

- GetOrigin: This will return a text value, indicated by the string keyword.

Let's write the code:

1. In Person.cs, add statements to define the two methods that I described earlier, as shown in the following code:

   ```
   // methods
   public void WriteToConsole()
   {
     WriteLine($"{Name} was born on a {DateOfBirth:dddd}.");
   }

   public string GetOrigin()
   {
     return $"{Name} was born on {HomePlanet}.";
   }
   ```

2. In Program.cs, add statements to call the two methods, as shown in the following code:

   ```
   bob.WriteToConsole();
   WriteLine(bob.GetOrigin());
   ```

3. Run the code and view the result, as shown in the following output:

   ```
   Bob Smith was born on a Wednesday.
   Bob Smith was born on Earth.
   ```

Combining multiple returned values using tuples

Each method can only return a single value that has a single type. That type could be a simple type, such as string in the previous example, a complex type, such as Person, or a collection type, such as List<Person>.

Imagine that we want to define a method named GetTheData that needs to return both a string value and an int value. We could define a new class named TextAndNumber with a string field and an int field, and return an instance of that complex type, as shown in the following code:

```
public class TextAndNumber
{
  public string Text;
  public int Number;
}
```

```
public class LifeTheUniverseAndEverything
{
  public TextAndNumber GetTheData()
  {
    return new TextAndNumber
    {
      Text = "What's the meaning of life?",
      Number = 42
    };
  }
}
```

But defining a class just to combine two values together is unnecessary, because in modern versions of C# we can use **tuples**. Tuples are an efficient way to combine two or more values into a single unit. I pronounce them as tuh-ples but I have heard other developers pronounce them as too-ples. To-may-toe, to-mah-toe, po-tay-toe, po-tah-toe, I guess.

Tuples have been a part of some languages such as F# since their first version, but .NET only added support for them with .NET 4.0 in 2010 using the System.Tuple type.

Language support for tuples

It was only with C# 7.0 in 2017 that C# added language syntax support for tuples using the parentheses characters () and at the same time, .NET added a new System.ValueTuple type that is more efficient in some common scenarios than the old .NET 4.0 System.Tuple type. The C# tuple syntax uses the more efficient one.

Let's explore tuples:

1. In Person.cs, add statements to define a method that returns a tuple that combines a string and int, as shown in the following code:

    ```
    public (string, int) GetFruit()
    {
      return ("Apples", 5);
    }
    ```

2. In Program.cs, add statements to call the GetFruit method and then output the tuple's fields automatically named Item1 and Item2, as shown in the following code:

    ```
    (string, int) fruit = bob.GetFruit();

    WriteLine($"{fruit.Item1}, {fruit.Item2} there are.");
    ```

3. Run the code and view the result, as shown in the following output:

    ```
    Apples, 5 there are.
    ```

Naming the fields of a tuple

To access the fields of a tuple, the default names are Item1, Item2, and so on.

You can explicitly specify the field names:

1. In Person.cs, add statements to define a method that returns a tuple with named fields, as shown in the following code:

```
public (string Name, int Number) GetNamedFruit()
{
  return (Name: "Apples", Number: 5);
}
```

2. In Program.cs, add statements to call the method and output the tuple's named fields, as shown in the following code:

```
var fruitNamed = bob.GetNamedFruit();

WriteLine($"There are {fruitNamed.Number} {fruitNamed.Name}.");
```

3. Run the code and view the result, as shown in the following output:

```
There are 5 Apples.
```

Inferring tuple names

If you are constructing a tuple from another object, you can use a feature introduced in C# 7.1 called **tuple name inference**.

In Program.cs, create two tuples, made of a string and int value each, as shown in the following code:

```
var thing1 = ("Neville", 4);
WriteLine($"{thing1.Item1} has {thing1.Item2} children.");

var thing2 = (bob.Name, bob.Children.Count);
WriteLine($"{thing2.Name} has {thing2.Count} children.");
```

In C# 7.0, both things would use the Item1 and Item2 naming schemes. In C# 7.1 and later, thing2 can infer the names Name and Count.

Deconstructing tuples

You can also deconstruct tuples into separate variables. The deconstructing declaration has the same syntax as named field tuples, but without a named variable for the tuple, as shown in the following code:

```
// store return value in a tuple variable with two fields
(string TheName, int TheNumber) tupleWithNamedFields = bob.GetNamedFruit();
// tupleWithNamedFields.TheName
// tupleWithNamedFields.TheNumber

// deconstruct return value into two separate variables
(string name, int number) = GetNamedFruit();
// name
// number
```

This has the effect of splitting the tuple into its parts and assigning those parts to new variables.

1. In `Program.cs`, add statements to deconstruct the tuple returned from the `GetFruit` method, as shown in the following code:

   ```
   (string fruitName, int fruitNumber) = bob.GetFruit();

   WriteLine($"Deconstructed: {fruitName}, {fruitNumber}");
   ```

2. Run the code and view the result, as shown in the following output:

   ```
   Deconstructed: Apples, 5
   ```

Deconstructing types

Tuples are not the only type that can be deconstructed. Any type can have special methods named `Deconstruct` that break down the object into parts. Let's implement some for the `Person` class:

1. In `Person.cs`, add two `Deconstruct` methods with out parameters defined for the parts we want to deconstruct into, as shown in the following code:

   ```
   // deconstructors
   public void Deconstruct(out string name, out DateTime dob)
   {
     name = Name;
     dob = DateOfBirth;
   }

   public void Deconstruct(out string name,
     out DateTime dob, out WondersOfTheAncientWorld fav)
   {
     name = Name;
     dob = DateOfBirth;
     fav = FavoriteAncientWonder;
   }
   ```

2. In `Program.cs`, add statements to deconstruct bob, as shown in the following code:

```
// Deconstructing a Person

var (name1, dob1) = bob;
WriteLine($"Deconstructed: {name1}, {dob1}");

var (name2, dob2, fav2) = bob;
WriteLine($"Deconstructed: {name2}, {dob2}, {fav2}");
```

3. Run the code and view the result, as shown in the following output:

```
Deconstructed: Bob Smith, 22/12/1965 00:00:00
Deconstructed: Bob Smith, 22/12/1965 00:00:00, StatueOfZeusAtOlympia
B
```

Defining and passing parameters to methods

Methods can have parameters passed to them to change their behavior. Parameters are defined a bit like variable declarations but inside the parentheses of the method, as you saw earlier in this chapter with constructors. Let's see more examples:

1. In `Person.cs`, add statements to define two methods, the first without parameters and the second with one parameter, as shown in the following code:

```
public string SayHello()
{
  return $"{Name} says 'Hello!'";
}

public string SayHelloTo(string name)
{
  return $"{Name} says 'Hello {name}!'";
}
```

2. In `Program.cs`, add statements to call the two methods and write the return value to the console, as shown in the following code:

```
WriteLine(bob.SayHello());
WriteLine(bob.SayHelloTo("Emily"));
```

3. Run the code and view the result:

```
Bob Smith says 'Hello!'
Bob Smith says 'Hello Emily!'
```

When typing a statement that calls a method, IntelliSense shows a tooltip with the name and type of any parameters, and the return type of the method, as shown in *Figure 5.3*:

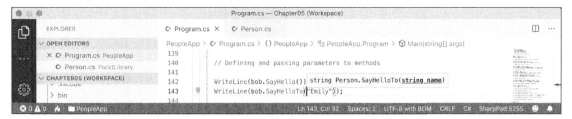

Figure 5.3: An IntelliSense tooltip for a method with no overloads

Overloading methods

Instead of having two different method names, we could give both methods the same name. This is allowed because the methods each have a different signature.

A **method signature** is a list of parameter types that can be passed when calling the method. Overloaded methods cannot differ only in the return type.

1. In `Person.cs`, change the name of the `SayHelloTo` method to `SayHello`.
2. In `Program.cs`, change the method call to use the `SayHello` method, and note that the quick info for the method tells you that it has one additional overload, 1/2, as well as 2/2, as shown in *Figure 5.4*:

Figure 5.4: An IntelliSense tooltip for an overloaded method

 Good Practice: Use overloaded methods to simplify your class by making it appear to have fewer methods.

Passing optional and named parameters

Another way to simplify methods is to make parameters optional. You make a parameter optional by assigning a default value inside the method parameter list. Optional parameters must always come last in the list of parameters.

We will now create a method with three optional parameters:

1. In `Person.cs`, add statements to define the method, as shown in the following code:

    ```
    public string OptionalParameters(
      string command  = "Run!",
      double number = 0.0,
      bool active = true)
    {
      return string.Format(
        format: "command is {0}, number is {1}, active is {2}",
        arg0: command,
        arg1: number,
        arg2: active);
    }
    ```

2. In `Program.cs`, add a statement to call the method and write its return value to the console, as shown in the following code:

    ```
    WriteLine(bob.OptionalParameters());
    ```

3. Watch IntelliSense appear as you type the code. You will see a tooltip, showing the three optional parameters with their default values, as shown in *Figure 5.5*:

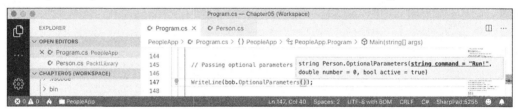

Figure 5.5: IntelliSense showing optional parameters as you type code

4. Run the code and view the result, as shown in the following output:

    ```
    command is Run!, number is 0, active is True
    ```

5. In `Program.cs`, add a statement to pass a `string` value for the `command` parameter and a `double` value for the `number` parameter, as shown in the following code:

    ```
    WriteLine(bob.OptionalParameters("Jump!", 98.5));
    ```

6. Run the code and see the result, as shown in the following output:

    ```
    command is Jump!, number is 98.5, active is True
    ```

The default values for the `command` and `number` parameters have been replaced, but the default for `active` is still `true`.

Naming parameter values when calling methods

Optional parameters are often combined with naming parameters when you call the method, because naming a parameter allows the values to be passed in a different order than how they were declared.

1. In `Program.cs`, add a statement to pass a `string` value for the `command` parameter and a `double` value for the `number` parameter but using named parameters, so that the order they are passed through can be swapped around, as shown in the following code:

    ```
    WriteLine(bob.OptionalParameters(
        number: 52.7, command: "Hide!"));
    ```

2. Run the code and view the result, as shown in the following output:

    ```
    command is Hide!, number is 52.7, active is True
    ```

    You can even use named parameters to skip over optional parameters.

3. In `Program.cs`, add a statement to pass a `string` value for the `command` parameter using positional order, skip the `number` parameter, and use the named `active` parameter, as shown in the following code:

    ```
    WriteLine(bob.OptionalParameters("Poke!", active: false));
    ```

4. Run the code and view the result, as shown in the following output:

    ```
    command is Poke!, number is 0, active is False
    ```

Controlling how parameters are passed

When a parameter is passed into a method, it can be passed in one of three ways:

*   By **value** (this is the default): Think of these as being *in-only*.
*   By **reference** as a `ref` parameter: Think of these as being *in-and-out*.
*   As an `out` parameter: Think of these as being *out-only*.

Let's see some examples of passing parameters in and out:

1. In `Person.cs`, add statements to define a method with three parameters, one in parameter, one `ref` parameter, and one `out` parameter, as shown in the following method:

    ```
    public void PassingParameters(int x, ref int y, out int z)
    {
        // out parameters cannot have a default
        // AND must be initialized inside the method
        z = 99;
    ```

```
// increment each parameter
x++;
y++;
z++;
}
```

2. In `Program.cs`, add statements to declare some `int` variables and pass them into the method, as shown in the following code:

```
int a = 10;
int b = 20;
int c = 30;

WriteLine($"Before: a = {a}, b = {b}, c = {c}");
bob.PassingParameters(a, ref b, out c);
WriteLine($"After: a = {a}, b = {b}, c = {c}");
```

3. Run the code and view the result, as shown in the following output:

```
Before: a = 10, b = 20, c = 30
After: a = 10, b = 21, c = 100
```

- When passing a variable as a parameter by default, its current value gets passed, not the variable itself. Therefore, x has a copy of the value of the a variable. The a variable retains its original value of 10.

- When passing a variable as a `ref` parameter, a reference to the variable gets passed into the method. Therefore, y is a reference to b. The b variable gets incremented when the y parameter gets incremented.

- When passing a variable as an `out` parameter, a reference to the variable gets passed into the method. Therefore, z is a reference to c. The value of the c variable gets replaced by whatever code executes inside the method. We could simplify the code in the `Main` method by not assigning the value 30 to the c variable since it will always be replaced anyway.

Simplified out parameters

In C# 7.0 and later, we can simplify code that uses the out variables.

In `Program.cs`, add statements to declare some more variables including an out parameter named f declared inline, as shown in the following code:

```
int d = 10;
int e = 20;

WriteLine($"Before: d = {d}, e = {e}, f doesn't exist yet!");
```

```
// simplified C# 7.0 or later syntax for the out parameter
bob.PassingParameters(d, ref e, out int f);
WriteLine($"After: d = {d}, e = {e}, f = {f}");
```

Understanding ref returns

In C# 7.0 or later, the ref keyword is not just for passing parameters into a method; it can also be applied to the return value. This allows an external variable to reference an internal variable and modify its value after the method call. This might be useful in advanced scenarios, for example, passing around placeholders into big data structures, but it's beyond the scope of this book.

Splitting classes using partial

When working on large projects with multiple team members, or when working with especially large and complex class implementations, it is useful to be able to split the definition of a class across multiple files. You do this using the partial keyword.

Imagine we want to add statements to the Person class that are automatically generated by a tool like an object-relational mapper that reads schema information from a database. If the class is defined as partial, then we can split the class into an autogenerated code file and a manually edited code file.

Let's write some code that simulates this example:

1. In Person.cs, add the partial keyword, as shown highlighted in the following code:

   ```
   namespace Packt.Shared
   {
     public partial class Person
     {
   ```

2. In the PacktLibrary project/folder, add a new class file named PersonAutoGen.cs.

3. Add statements to the new file, as shown in the following code:

   ```
   namespace Packt.Shared
   {
     public partial class Person
     {
     }
   }
   ```

The rest of the code we write for this chapter will be written in the PersonAutoGen.cs file.

Controlling access with properties and indexers

Earlier, you created a method named GetOrigin that returned a string containing the name and origin of the person. Languages such as Java do this a lot. C# has a better way: properties.

A property is simply a method (or a pair of methods) that acts and looks like a field when you want to get or set a value, thereby simplifying the syntax.

Defining read-only properties

A readonly property only has a get implementation.

1. In PersonAutoGen.cs, in the Person class, add statements to define three properties:

    1. The first property will perform the same role as the GetOrigin method using the property syntax that works with all versions of C# (although, it uses the string interpolation syntax from C# 6 and later).

    2. The second property will return a greeting message using the lambda expression body => syntax from C# 6 and later.

    3. The third property will calculate the person's age.

    Here's the code:

    ```
    // a property defined using C# 1 - 5 syntax
    public string Origin
    {
      get
      {
        return $"{Name} was born on {HomePlanet}";
      }
    }


    // two properties defined using C# 6+ lambda expression body syntax
    public string Greeting => $"{Name} says 'Hello!'";

    public int Age => System.DateTime.Today.Year - DateOfBirth.Year;
    ```

    > **Good Practice**: This isn't the best way to calculate someone's age, but we aren't learning how to calculate an age from a date of birth. If you need to do that properly, read the discussion at the following link: https://stackoverflow.com/questions/9/how-do-i-calculate-someones-age-in-c

2. In `Program.cs`, add the statements to get the properties, as shown in the following code:

```
Person sam = new()
{
  Name = "Sam",
  DateOfBirth = new(1972, 1, 27)
};

WriteLine(sam.Origin);
WriteLine(sam.Greeting);
WriteLine(sam.Age);
```

3. Run the code and view the result, as shown in the following output:

```
Sam was born on Earth
Sam says 'Hello!'
49
```

The output shows 49 because I ran the console application on August 15, 2021 when Sam was 49 years old.

Defining settable properties

To create a settable property, you must use the older syntax and provide a pair of methods—not just a get part, but also a set part:

1. In `PersonAutoGen.cs`, add statements to define a `string` property that has both a get and set method (also known as a getter and setter), as shown in the following code:

```
public string FavoriteIceCream { get; set; } // auto-syntax
```

Although you have not manually created a field to store the person's favorite ice cream, it is there, automatically created by the compiler for you.

Sometimes, you need more control over what happens when a property is set. In this scenario, you must use a more detailed syntax and manually create a `private` field to store the value for the property.

2. In `PersonAutoGen.cs`, add statements to define a `string` field and `string` property that has both a get and set, as shown in the following code:

```
private string favoritePrimaryColor;

public string FavoritePrimaryColor
{
  get
  {
    return favoritePrimaryColor;
  }
```

```
    set
    {
      switch (value.ToLower())
      {
        case "red":
        case "green":
        case "blue":
          favoritePrimaryColor = value;
          break;
        default:
          throw new System.ArgumentException(
            $"{value} is not a primary color. " +
            "Choose from: red, green, blue.");
      }
    }
  }
}
```

 Good Practice: Avoid adding too much code to your getters and setters. This could indicate a problem with your design. Consider adding private methods that you then call in setters and getters to simplify your implementations.

3. In `Program.cs`, add statements to set Sam's favorite ice cream and color, and then write them out, as shown in the following code:

```
sam.FavoriteIceCream = "Chocolate Fudge";

WriteLine($"Sam's favorite ice-cream flavor is {sam.FavoriteIceCream}.");

sam.FavoritePrimaryColor = "Red";

WriteLine($"Sam's favorite primary color is {sam.FavoritePrimaryColor}.");
```

4. Run the code and view the result, as shown in the following output:

```
Sam's favorite ice-cream flavor is Chocolate Fudge.
Sam's favorite primary color is Red.
```

If you try to set the color to any value other than red, green, or blue, then the code will throw an exception. The calling code could then use a `try` statement to display the error message.

 Good Practice: Use properties instead of fields when you want to validate what value can be stored when you want to data bind in XAML, which we will cover in *Chapter 19, Building Mobile and Desktop Apps Using .NET MAUI*, and when you want to read and write to a field without using a method pair like `GetAge` and `SetAge`.

Requiring properties to be set during instantiation

C# 10 introduces the `required` modifier. If you use it on a property, the compiler will ensure that you set the property to a value when you instantiate it, as shown in the following code:

```
public class Book
{
  public required string Isbn { get; set; }
  public string Title { get; set; }
}
```

If you attempt to instantiate a `Book` without setting the `Isbn` property you will see a compiler error, as shown in the following code:

```
Book novel = new();
```

> The `required` keyword might not make it into the final release version of .NET 6 so treat this section as theoretical.

Defining indexers

Indexers allow the calling code to use the array syntax to access a property. For example, the `string` type defines an **indexer** so that the calling code can access individual characters in the string.

We will define an indexer to simplify access to the children of a person:

1. In `PersonAutoGen.cs`, add statements to define an indexer to get and set a child using the index of the child, as shown in the following code:

    ```
    // indexers
    public Person this[int index]
    {
      get
      {
        return Children[index]; // pass on to the List<T> indexer
      }
      set
      {
        Children[index] = value;
      }
    }
    ```

    You can overload indexers so that different types can be used for their parameters. For example, as well as passing an `int` value, you could also pass a `string` value.

2. In `Program.cs`, add statements to add two children to `Sam`, and then access the first and second child using the longer `Children` field and the shorter indexer syntax, as shown in the following code:

```
sam.Children.Add(new() { Name = "Charlie" });
sam.Children.Add(new() { Name = "Ella" });

WriteLine($"Sam's first child is {sam.Children[0].Name}");
WriteLine($"Sam's second child is {sam.Children[1].Name}");

WriteLine($"Sam's first child is {sam[0].Name}");
WriteLine($"Sam's second child is {sam[1].Name}");
```

3. Run the code and view the result, as shown in the following output:

```
Sam's first child is Charlie
Sam's second child is Ella
Sam's first child is Charlie
Sam's second child is Ella
```

Pattern matching with objects

In *Chapter 3, Controlling Flow, Converting Types, and Handling Exceptions*, you were introduced to basic pattern matching. In this section, we will explore pattern matching in more detail.

Creating and referencing a .NET 6 class library

The enhanced pattern matching features are only available in modern .NET class libraries that support C# 9 or later.

1. Use your preferred coding tool to add a new class library named `PacktLibraryModern` to the workspace/solution named `Chapter05`.

2. In the `PeopleApp` project, add a reference to the `PacktLibraryModern` class library, as shown highlighted in the following markup:

```
<Project Sdk="Microsoft.NET.Sdk">

  <PropertyGroup>
    <OutputType>Exe</OutputType>
    <TargetFramework>net6.0</TargetFramework>
    <Nullable>enable</Nullable>
    <ImplicitUsings>enable</ImplicitUsings>
  </PropertyGroup>

  <ItemGroup>
    <ProjectReference Include="../PacktLibrary/PacktLibrary.csproj" />
```

```
<ProjectReference
  Include="../PacktLibraryModern/PacktLibraryModern.csproj" />
</ItemGroup>
</Project>
```

3. Build the `PeopleApp` project.

Defining flight passengers

In this example, we will define some classes that represent various types of passengers on a flight and then we will use a switch expression with pattern matching to determine the cost of their flight.

1. In the `PacktLibraryModern` project/folder, rename the file `Class1.cs` to `FlightPatterns.cs`.

2. In `FlightPatterns.cs`, add statements to define three types of passengers with different properties, as shown in the following code:

```
namespace Packt.Shared; // C# 10 file-scoped namespace

public class BusinessClassPassenger
{
  public override string ToString()
  {
    return $"Business Class";
  }
}

public class FirstClassPassenger
{
  public int AirMiles { get; set; }

  public override string ToString()
  {
    return $"First Class with {AirMiles:N0} air miles";
  }
}

public class CoachClassPassenger
{
  public double CarryOnKG { get; set; }

  public override string ToString()
  {
    return $"Coach Class with {CarryOnKG:N2} KG carry on";
  }
}
```

3. In Program.cs, add statements to define an object array containing five passengers of various types and property values, and then enumerate them, outputting the cost of their flight, as shown in the following code:

```
object[] passengers = {
  new FirstClassPassenger { AirMiles = 1_419 },
  new FirstClassPassenger { AirMiles = 16_562 },
  new BusinessClassPassenger(),
  new CoachClassPassenger { CarryOnKG = 25.7 },
  new CoachClassPassenger { CarryOnKG = 0 },
};

foreach (object passenger in passengers)
{
  decimal flightCost = passenger switch
  {
    FirstClassPassenger p when p.AirMiles > 35000 => 1500M,
    FirstClassPassenger p when p.AirMiles > 15000 => 1750M,
    FirstClassPassenger _                         => 2000M,
    BusinessClassPassenger _                      => 1000M,
    CoachClassPassenger p when p.CarryOnKG < 10.0 => 500M,
    CoachClassPassenger _                         => 650M,
    _                                             => 800M
  };

  WriteLine($"Flight costs {flightCost:C} for {passenger}");
}
```

While reviewing the preceding code, note the following:

- To pattern match on the properties of an object, you must name a local variable that can then be used in an expression like p.
- To pattern match on a type only, you can use _ to discard the local variable.
- The switch expression also uses _ to represent its default branch.

4. Run the code and view the result, as shown in the following output:

```
Flight costs £2,000.00 for First Class with 1,419 air miles
Flight costs £1,750.00 for First Class with 16,562 air miles
Flight costs £1,000.00 for Business Class
Flight costs £650.00 for Coach Class with 25.70 KG carry on
Flight costs £500.00 for Coach Class with 0.00 KG carry on
```

Enhancements to pattern matching in C# 9 or later

The previous examples worked with C# 8. Now we will look at some enhancements in C# 9 and later. First, you no longer need to use the underscore to discard when doing type matching:

1. In `Program.cs`, comment out the C# 8 syntax and add C# 9 and later syntax to modify the branches for first-class passengers to use a nested switch expression and the new support for conditionals like >, as shown in the following code:

```
decimal flightCost = passenger switch
{
  /* C# 8 syntax
  FirstClassPassenger p when p.AirMiles > 35000 => 1500M,
  FirstClassPassenger p when p.AirMiles > 15000 => 1750M,
  FirstClassPassenger                           => 2000M, */

  // C# 9 or later syntax
  FirstClassPassenger p => p.AirMiles switch
  {
    > 35000 => 1500M,
    > 15000 => 1750M,
    _       => 2000M
  },

  BusinessClassPassenger                        => 1000M,
  CoachClassPassenger p when p.CarryOnKG < 10.0 => 500M,
  CoachClassPassenger                           => 650M,
  _                                             => 800M
};
```

2. Run the code to view the results, and note they are the same as before.

You could also use the relational pattern in combination with the property pattern to avoid the nested switch expression, as shown in the following code:

```
FirstClassPassenger { AirMiles: > 35000 } => 1500,
FirstClassPassenger { AirMiles: > 15000 } => 1750M,
FirstClassPassenger => 2000M,
```

Working with records

Before we dive into the new records language feature of C# 9 and later, let us see some other related new features.

Init-only properties

You have used object initialization syntax to instantiate objects and set initial properties throughout this chapter. Those properties can also be changed after instantiation.

Sometimes you want to treat properties like `readonly` fields so they can be set during instantiation but not after. The new `init` keyword enables this. It can be used in place of the `set` keyword:

1. In the `PacktLibraryModern` project/folder, add a new file named `Records.cs`.

2. In `Records.cs`, define an immutable person class, as shown in the following code:

```
namespace Packt.Shared; // C# 10 file-scoped namespace

public class ImmutablePerson
{
  public string? FirstName { get; init; }
  public string? LastName { get; init; }
}
```

3. In `Program.cs`, add statements to instantiate a new immutable person and then try to change one of its properties, as shown in the following code:

```
ImmutablePerson jeff = new()
{
  FirstName = "Jeff",
  LastName = "Winger"
};

jeff.FirstName = "Geoff";
```

4. Compile the console app and note the compile error, as shown in the following output:

```
Program.cs(254,7): error CS8852: Init-only property or indexer
'ImmutablePerson.FirstName' can only be assigned in an object initializer,
or on 'this' or 'base' in an instance constructor or an 'init' accessor.
[/Users/markjprice/Code/Chapter05/PeopleApp/PeopleApp.csproj]
```

5. Comment out the attempt to set the `FirstName` property after instantiation.

Understanding records

Init-only properties provide some immutability to C#. You can take the concept further by using **records**. These are defined by using the `record` keyword instead of the `class` keyword. That can make the whole object immutable, and it acts like a value when compared. We will discuss equality and comparisons of classes, records, and value types in more detail in *Chapter 6, Implementing Interfaces and Inheriting Classes*.

Records should not have any state (properties and fields) that changes after instantiation. Instead, the idea is that you create new records from existing ones with any changed state. This is called non-destructive mutation. To do this, C# 9 introduced the `with` keyword:

1. In `Records.cs`, add a record named `ImmutableVehicle`, as shown in the following code:

    ```
    public record ImmutableVehicle
    {
      public int Wheels { get; init; }
      public string? Color { get; init; }
      public string? Brand { get; init; }
    }
    ```

2. In `Program.cs`, add statements to create a car and then a mutated copy of it, as shown in the following code:

    ```
    ImmutableVehicle car = new()
    {
      Brand = "Mazda MX-5 RF",
      Color = "Soul Red Crystal Metallic",
      Wheels = 4
    };

    ImmutableVehicle repaintedCar = car
      with { Color = "Polymetal Grey Metallic" };

    WriteLine($"Original car color was {car.Color}.");
    WriteLine($"New car color is {repaintedCar.Color}.");
    ```

3. Run the code to view the results, and note the change to the car color in the mutated copy, as shown in the following output:

    ```
    Original car color was Soul Red Crystal Metallic.
    New car color is Polymetal Grey Metallic.
    ```

Positional data members in records

The syntax for defining a record can be greatly simplified using positional data members.

Simplifying data members in records

Instead of using object initialization syntax with curly braces, sometimes you might prefer to provide a constructor with positional parameters as you saw earlier in this chapter. You can also combine this with a deconstructor for splitting the object into individual parts, as shown in the following code:

```
public record ImmutableAnimal
{
  public string Name { get; init; }
  public string Species { get; init; }
```

```
  public ImmutableAnimal(string name, string species)
  {
    Name = name;
    Species = species;
  }

  public void Deconstruct(out string name, out string species)
  {
    name = Name;
    species = Species;
  }
}
```

The properties, constructor, and deconstructor can be generated for you:

1. In Records.cs, add statements to define another record using simplified syntax known as positional records, as shown in the following code:

   ```
   // simpler way to define a record
   // auto-generates the properties, constructor, and deconstructor
   public record ImmutableAnimal(string Name, string Species);
   ```

2. In Program.cs, add statements to construct and deconstruct immutable animals, as shown in the following code:

   ```
   ImmutableAnimal oscar = new("Oscar", "Labrador");
   var (who, what) = oscar; // calls Deconstruct method
   WriteLine($"{who} is a {what}.");
   ```

3. Run the application and view the results, as shown in the following output:

   ```
   Oscar is a Labrador.
   ```

 You will see records again when we look at C# 10 support for creating struct records in *Chapter 6, Implementing Interfaces and Inheriting Classes*.

Practicing and exploring

Test your knowledge and understanding by answering some questions, get some hands-on practice, and explore this chapter's topics with deeper research.

Exercise 5.1 – Test your knowledge

Answer the following questions:

1. What are the six combinations of access modifier keywords and what do they do?
2. What is the difference between the `static`, `const`, and `readonly` keywords when applied to a type member?
3. What does a constructor do?
4. Why should you apply the `[Flags]` attribute to an `enum` type when you want to store combined values?
5. Why is the `partial` keyword useful?
6. What is a tuple?
7. What does the `record` keyword do?
8. What does overloading mean?
9. What is the difference between a field and a property?
10. How do you make a method parameter optional?

Exercise 5.2 – Explore topics

Use the links on the following page to learn more detail about the topics covered in this chapter:

https://github.com/markjprice/cs10dotnet6/blob/main/book-links.md#chapter-5---building-your-own-types-with-object-oriented-programming

Summary

In this chapter, you learned about making your own types using OOP. You learned about some of the different categories of members that a type can have, including fields to store data and methods to perform actions, and you used OOP concepts, such as aggregation and encapsulation. You saw examples of how to use modern C# features like relational and property pattern matching enhancements, init-only properties, and records.

In the next chapter, you will take these concepts further by defining delegates and events, implementing interfaces, and inheriting from existing classes.

06

Implementing Interfaces and Inheriting Classes

This chapter is about deriving new types from existing ones using **object-oriented programming** (**OOP**). You will learn about defining operators and local functions for performing simple actions and delegates and events for exchanging messages between types. You will implement interfaces for common functionality. You will learn about generics and the difference between reference and value types. You will create a derived class to inherit from a base class to reuse functionality, override an inherited type member, and use polymorphism. Finally, you will learn how to create extension methods and how to cast between classes in an inheritance hierarchy.

This chapter covers the following topics:

- Setting up a class library and console application
- More about methods
- Raising and handling events
- Making types safely reusable with generics
- Implementing interfaces
- Managing memory with reference and value types
- Working with null values
- Inheriting from classes
- Casting within inheritance hierarchies
- Inheriting and extending .NET types
- Using an analyzer to write better code

Setting up a class library and console application

We will start by defining a workspace/solution with two projects like the one created in *Chapter 5, Building Your Own Types with Object-Oriented Programming*. Even if you completed all the exercises in that chapter, follow the instructions below because we will use C# 10 features in the class library, so it needs to target .NET 6.0 rather than .NET Standard 2.0:

1. Use your preferred coding tool to create a new workspace/solution named Chapter06.
2. Add a class library project, as defined in the following list:
    1. Project template: **Class Library** / classlib
    2. Workspace/solution file and folder: Chapter06
    3. Project file and folder: PacktLibrary
3. Add a console app project, as defined in the following list:
    1. Project template: **Console Application** / console
    2. Workspace/solution file and folder: Chapter06
    3. Project file and folder: PeopleApp
4. In the PacktLibrary project, rename the file named Class1.cs to Person.cs.
5. Modify the Person.cs file contents, as shown in the following code:

```
using static System.Console;

namespace Packt.Shared;

public class Person : object
{
  // fields
  public string? Name;     // ? allows null
  public DateTime DateOfBirth;
  public List<Person> Children = new(); // C# 9 or later

  // methods
  public void WriteToConsole()
  {
    WriteLine($"{Name} was born on a {DateOfBirth:dddd}.");
  }
}
```

6. In the PeopleApp project, add a project reference to PacktLibrary, as shown highlighted in the following markup:

```
<Project Sdk="Microsoft.NET.Sdk">

  <PropertyGroup>
    <OutputType>Exe</OutputType>
    <TargetFramework>net6.0</TargetFramework>
    <Nullable>enable</Nullable>
    <ImplicitUsings>enable</ImplicitUsings>
  </PropertyGroup>

  <ItemGroup>
    <ProjectReference
      Include="..\PacktLibrary\PacktLibrary.csproj" />
  </ItemGroup>

</Project>
```

7. Build the `PeopleApp` project and note the output indicating that both projects have been built successfully.

More about methods

We might want two instances of `Person` to be able to procreate. We can implement this by writing methods. Instance methods are actions that an object does to itself; static methods are actions the type does.

Which you choose depends on what makes the most sense for the action.

 Good Practice: Having both static and instance methods to perform similar actions often makes sense. For example, `string` has both a `Compare` static method and a `CompareTo` instance method. This puts the choice of how to use the functionality in the hands of the programmers using your type, giving them more flexibility.

Implementing functionality using methods

Let's start by implementing some functionality by using both static and instance methods:

1. Add one instance method and one static method to the `Person` class that will allow two `Person` objects to procreate, as shown in the following code:

```
// static method to "multiply"
public static Person Procreate(Person p1, Person p2)
{
```

```
      Person baby = new()
      {
        Name = $"Baby of {p1.Name} and {p2.Name}"
      };

      p1.Children.Add(baby);
      p2.Children.Add(baby);

      return baby;
    }

    // instance method to "multiply"
    public Person ProcreateWith(Person partner)
    {
      return Procreate(this, partner);
    }
```

Note the following:

- In the static method named Procreate, the Person objects to procreate are passed as parameters named p1 and p2.

- A new Person class named baby is created with a name composed of a combination of the two people who have procreated. This could be changed later by setting the returned baby variable's Name property.

- The baby object is added to the Children collection of both parents and then returned. Classes are reference types, meaning a reference to the baby object stored in memory is added, not a clone of the baby object. You will learn the difference between reference types and value types later in this chapter.

- In the instance method named ProcreateWith, the Person object to procreate with is passed as a parameter named partner, and it, along with this, is passed to the static Procreate method to reuse the method implementation. this is a keyword that references the current instance of the class.

 Good Practice: A method that creates a new object, or modifies an existing object, should return a reference to that object so that the caller can access the results.

2. In the PeopleApp project, at the top of the Program.cs file, delete the comment and import the namespace for our Person class and statically import the Console type, as shown in the following code:

```
using Packt.Shared;
using static System.Console;
```

3. In `Program.cs`, create three people and have them procreate with each other, noting that to add a double-quote character into a `string`, you must prefix it with a backslash character like this, \", as shown in the following code:

```
Person harry = new() { Name = "Harry" };
Person mary = new() { Name = "Mary" };
Person jill = new() { Name = "Jill" };

// call instance method
Person baby1 = mary.ProcreateWith(harry);
baby1.Name = "Gary";

// call static method
Person baby2 = Person.Procreate(harry, jill);

WriteLine($"{harry.Name} has {harry.Children.Count} children.");
WriteLine($"{mary.Name} has {mary.Children.Count} children.");
WriteLine($"{jill.Name} has {jill.Children.Count} children.");
WriteLine(
    format: "{0}'s first child is named \"{1}\".",
    arg0: harry.Name,
    arg1: harry.Children[0].Name);
```

4. Run the code and view the result, as shown in the following output:

```
Harry has 2 children.
Mary has 1 children.
Jill has 1 children.
Harry's first child is named "Gary".
```

Implementing functionality using operators

The `System.String` class has a `static` method named `Concat` that concatenates two string values and returns the result, as shown in the following code:

```
string s1 = "Hello ";
string s2 = "World!";
string s3 = string.Concat(s1, s2);
WriteLine(s3); // Hello World!
```

Calling a method like `Concat` works, but it might be more natural for a programmer to use the + symbol operator to "add" two `string` values together, as shown in the following code:

```
string s3 = s1 + s2;
```

A well-known biblical phrase is *Go forth and multiply,* meaning to procreate. Let's write code so that the * (multiply) symbol will allow two `Person` objects to procreate.

We do this by defining a static operator for the * symbol. The syntax is rather like a method, because in effect, an operator *is* a method, but uses a symbol instead of a method name, which makes the syntax more concise.

1. In `Person.cs`, create a static operator for the * symbol, as shown in the following code:

```
// operator to "multiply"
public static Person operator *(Person p1, Person p2)
{
  return Person.Procreate(p1, p2);
}
```

 Good Practice: Unlike methods, operators do not appear in IntelliSense lists for a type. For every operator that you define, make a method as well, because it may not be obvious to a programmer that the operator is available. The implementation of the operator can then call the method, reusing the code you have written. A second reason for providing a method is that operators are not supported by every language compiler; for example, although arithmetic operators like * are supported by Visual Basic and F#, there is no requirement that other languages support all operators supported by C#.

2. In `Program.cs`, after calling the `Procreate` method and before the statements that write to the console, use the * operator to make another baby, as shown highlighted in the following code:

```
// call static method
Person baby2 = Person.Procreate(harry, jill);

// call an operator
Person baby3 = harry * mary;
```

3. Run the code and view the result, as shown in the following output:

```
Harry has 3 children.
Mary has 2 children.
Jill has 1 children.
Harry's first child is named "Gary".
```

Implementing functionality using local functions

A language feature introduced in C# 7.0 is the ability to define a **local function**.

Local functions are the method equivalent of local variables. In other words, they are methods that are only accessible from within the containing method in which they have been defined. In other languages, they are sometimes called **nested** or **inner functions**.

Local functions can be defined anywhere inside a method: the top, the bottom, or even somewhere in the middle!

We will use a local function to implement a factorial calculation:

1. In Person.cs, add statements to define a Factorial function that uses a local function inside itself to calculate the result, as shown in the following code:

```
// method with a local function
public static int Factorial(int number)
{
  if (number < 0)
  {
    throw new ArgumentException(
      $"{nameof(number)} cannot be less than zero.");
  }
  return localFactorial(number);

  int localFactorial(int localNumber) // local function
  {
    if (localNumber < 1) return 1;
    return localNumber * localFactorial(localNumber - 1);
  }
}
```

2. In Program.cs, add a statement to call the Factorial function and write the return value to the console, as shown in the following code:

```
WriteLine($"5! is {Person.Factorial(5)}");
```

3. Run the code and view the result, as shown in the following output:

```
5! is 120
```

Raising and handling events

Methods are often described as *actions that an object can perform, either on itself or on related objects*. For example, List<T> can add an item to itself or clear itself, and File can create or delete a file in the filesystem.

Events are often described as *actions that happen to an object*. For example, in a user interface, Button has a Click event, a click being something that happens to a button, and FileSystemWatcher listens to the filesystem for change notifications and raises events like Created and Deleted that are triggered when a directory or file changes.

Another way of thinking of events is that they provide a way of exchanging messages between two objects.

Events are built on **delegates**, so let's start by having a look at what delegates are and how they work.

Calling methods using delegates

You have already seen the most common way to call or execute a method: use the . operator to access the method using its name. For example, `Console.WriteLine` tells the `Console` type to access its `WriteLine` method.

The other way to call or execute a method is to use a delegate. If you have used languages that support **function pointers**, then think of a delegate as being a **type-safe method pointer**.

In other words, a delegate contains the memory address of a method that matches the same signature as the delegate so that it can be called safely with the correct parameter types.

For example, imagine there is a method in the `Person` class that must have a `string` type passed as its only parameter, and it returns an `int` type, as shown in the following code:

```
public int MethodIWantToCall(string input)
{
  return input.Length; // it doesn't matter what the method does
}
```

I can call this method on an instance of `Person` named p1 like this:

```
int answer = p1.MethodIWantToCall("Frog");
```

Alternatively, I can define a delegate with a matching signature to call the method indirectly. Note that the names of the parameters do not have to match. Only the types of parameters and return values must match, as shown in the following code:

```
delegate int DelegateWithMatchingSignature(string s);
```

Now, I can create an instance of the delegate, point it at the method, and finally, call the delegate (which calls the method), as shown in the following code:

```
// create a delegate instance that points to the method
DelegateWithMatchingSignature d = new(p1.MethodIWantToCall);

// call the delegate, which calls the method
int answer2 = d("Frog");
```

You are probably thinking, "What's the point of that?" Well, it provides flexibility.

For example, we could use delegates to create a queue of methods that need to be called in order. Queuing actions that need to be performed is common in services to provide improved scalability.

Another example is to allow multiple actions to perform in parallel. Delegates have built-in support for asynchronous operations that run on a different thread, and that can provide improved responsiveness. You will learn how to do this in *Chapter 12, Improving Performance and Scalability Using Multitasking*.

The most important example is that delegates allow us to implement events for sending messages between different objects that do not need to know about each other. Events are an example of loose coupling between components because the components do not need to know about each other, they just need to know the event signature.

Delegates and events are two of the most confusing features of C# and can take a few attempts to understand, so don't worry if you feel lost!

Defining and handling delegates

Microsoft has two predefined delegates for use as events. Their signatures are simple, yet flexible, as shown in the following code:

```
public delegate void EventHandler(
  object? sender, EventArgs e);

public delegate void EventHandler<TEventArgs>(
  object? sender, TEventArgs e);
```

 Good Practice: When you want to define an event in your own types, you should use one of these two predefined delegates.

Let's explore delegates and events:

1. Add statements to the Person class and note the following points, as shown in the following code:

    *   It defines an EventHandler delegate field named Shout.
    *   It defines an int field to store AngerLevel.
    *   It defines a method named Poke.
    *   Each time a person is poked, their AngerLevel increments. Once their AngerLevel reaches three, they raise the Shout event, but only if there is at least one event delegate pointing at a method defined somewhere else in the code; that is, it is not null:

    ```
    // delegate field
    public EventHandler? Shout;
    ```

```csharp
// data field
public int AngerLevel;

// method
public void Poke()
{
  AngerLevel++;

  if (AngerLevel >= 3)
  {
    // if something is listening...
    if (Shout != null)
    {
      // ...then call the delegate
      Shout(this, EventArgs.Empty);
    }
  }
}
```

Checking whether an object is not `null` before calling one of its methods is very common. C# 6.0 and later allows null checks to be simplified inline using a ? symbol before the . operator, as shown in the following code:

```csharp
Shout?.Invoke(this, EventArgs.Empty);
```

2. At the bottom of `Program.cs`, add a method with a matching signature that gets a reference to the `Person` object from the `sender` parameter and outputs some information about them, as shown in the following code:

```csharp
static void Harry_Shout(object? sender, EventArgs e)
{
  if (sender is null) return;
  Person p = (Person)sender;
  WriteLine($"{p.Name} is this angry: {p.AngerLevel}.");
}
```

Microsoft's convention for method names that handle events is `ObjectName_EventName`.

3. In `Program.cs`, add a statement to assign the method to the delegate field, as shown in the following code:

```csharp
harry.Shout = Harry_Shout;
```

4. Add statements to call the `Poke` method four times, after assigning the method to the `Shout` event, as shown highlighted in the following code:

```csharp
harry.Shout = Harry_Shout;
harry.Poke();
harry.Poke();
harry.Poke();
harry.Poke();
```

5. Run the code and view the result, and note that Harry says nothing the first two times he is poked, and only gets angry enough to shout once he's been poked at least three times, as shown in the following output:

```
Harry is this angry: 3.
Harry is this angry: 4.
```

Defining and handling events

You've now seen how delegates implement the most important functionality of events: the ability to define a signature for a method that can be implemented by a completely different piece of code, and then call that method and any others that are hooked up to the delegate field.

But what about events? There is less to them than you might think.

When assigning a method to a delegate field, you should not use the simple assignment operator as we did in the preceding example.

Delegates are multicast, meaning that you can assign multiple delegates to a single delegate field. Instead of the = assignment, we could have used the += operator so we could add more methods to the same delegate field. When the delegate is called, all the assigned methods are called, although you have no control over the order in which they are called.

If the Shout delegate field was already referencing one or more methods, by assigning a method, it would replace all the others. With delegates that are used for events, we usually want to make sure that a programmer only ever uses either the += operator or the -= operator to assign and remove methods:

1. To enforce this, in Person.cs, add the event keyword to the delegate field declaration, as shown highlighted in the following code:

   ```
   public event EventHandler? Shout;
   ```

2. Build the PeopleApp project and note the compiler error message, as shown in the following output:

   ```
   Program.cs(41,13): error CS0079: The event 'Person.Shout' can only appear
   on the left hand side of += or -=
   ```

   This is (almost) all that the event keyword does! If you will never have more than one method assigned to a delegate field, then technically you do not need "events," but it is still good practice to indicate your meaning and that you expect a delegate field to be used as an event.

3. Modify the method assignment to use +=, as shown in the following code:

   ```
   harry.Shout += Harry_Shout;
   ```

4. Run the code and note that it has the same behavior as before.

Making types safely reusable with generics

In 2005, with C# 2.0 and .NET Framework 2.0, Microsoft introduced a feature named **generics**, which enables your types to be more safely reusable and more efficient. It does this by allowing a programmer to pass types as parameters, similar to how you can pass objects as parameters.

Working with non-generic types

First, let's look at an example of working with a non-generic type so that you can understand the problem that generics are designed to solve, such as weakly typed parameters and values, and performance problems caused by using System.Object.

System.Collections.Hashtable can be used to store multiple values each with a unique key that can later be used to quickly look up its value. Both the key and value can be any object because they are declared as System.Object. Although this provides flexibility when storing value types like integers, it is slow, and bugs are easier to introduce because no type checks are made when adding items.

Let's write some code:

1. In Program.cs, create an instance of the non-generic collection, System.Collections. Hashtable, and then add four items to it, as shown in the following code:

```
// non-generic lookup collection
System.Collections.Hashtable lookupObject = new();

lookupObject.Add(key: 1, value: "Alpha");
lookupObject.Add(key: 2, value: "Beta");
lookupObject.Add(key: 3, value: "Gamma");
lookupObject.Add(key: harry, value: "Delta");
```

2. Add statements to define a key with the value of 2 and use it to look up its value in the hash table, as shown in the following code:

```
int key = 2; // Lookup the value that has 2 as its key
WriteLine(format: "Key {0} has value: {1}",
    arg0: key,
    arg1: lookupObject[key]);
```

3. Add statements to use the harry object to look up its value, as shown in the following code:

```
// Lookup the value that has harry as its key
WriteLine(format: "Key {0} has value: {1}",
    arg0: harry,
    arg1: lookupObject[harry]);
```

4. Run the code and note that it works, as shown in the following output:

```
Key 2 has value: Beta
Key Packt.Shared.Person has value: Delta
```

Although the code works, there is potential for mistakes because literally any type can be used for the key or value. If another developer used your lookup object and expected all the items to be a certain type, they might cast them to that type and get exceptions because some values might be a different type. A lookup object with lots of items would also give poor performance.

 Good Practice: Avoid types in the System.Collections namespace.

Working with generic types

System.Collections.Generic.Dictionary<TKey, TValue> can be used to store multiple values each with a unique key that can later be used to quickly look up its value. Both the key and value can be any object, but you must tell the compiler what the types of the key and value will be when you first instantiate the collection. You do this by specifying types for the **generic parameters** in angle brackets <>, TKey, and TValue.

 Good Practice: When a generic type has one definable type, it should be named T, for example, List<T>, where T is the type stored in the list. When a generic type has multiple definable types, they should use T as a name prefix and have a sensible name, for example, Dictionary<TKey, TValue>.

This provides flexibility, it is faster, and bugs are easier to avoid because type checks are made when adding items.

Let's write some code to solve the problem by using generics:

1. In Program.cs, create an instance of the generic lookup collection Dictionary<TKey, TValue> and then add four items to it, as shown in the following code:

```
// generic lookup collection
Dictionary<int, string> lookupIntString = new();

lookupIntString.Add(key: 1, value: "Alpha");
lookupIntString.Add(key: 2, value: "Beta");
lookupIntString.Add(key: 3, value: "Gamma");
lookupIntString.Add(key: harry, value: "Delta");
```

2. Note the compile error when using harry as a key, as shown in the following output:

```
/Users/markjprice/Code/Chapter06/PeopleApp/Program.cs(98,32): error
CS1503: Argument 1: cannot convert from 'Packt.Shared.Person' to 'int' [/
Users/markjprice/Code/Chapter06/PeopleApp/PeopleApp.csproj]
```

3. Replace harry with 4.

4. Add statements to set the key to 3 and use it to look up its value in the dictionary, as shown in the following code:

```
key = 3;
WriteLine(format: "Key {0} has value: {1}",
    arg0: key,
    arg1: lookupIntString[key]);
```

5. Run the code and note that it works, as shown in the following output:

```
Key 3 has value: Gamma
```

Implementing interfaces

Interfaces are a way of connecting different types to make new things. Think of them like the studs on top of LEGO™ bricks, which allow them to "stick" together, or electrical standards for plugs and sockets.

If a type implements an interface, then it is making a promise to the rest of .NET that it supports specific functionality. This is why they are sometimes described as being contracts.

Common interfaces

Here are some common interfaces that your types might need to implement:

Interface	Method(s)	Description
IComparable	CompareTo(other)	This defines a comparison method that a type implements to order or sort its instances.
IComparer	Compare(first, second)	This defines a comparison method that a secondary type implements to order or sort instances of a primary type.
IDisposable	Dispose()	This defines a disposal method to release unmanaged resources more efficiently than waiting for a finalizer (see the *Releasing unmanaged resources* section later in this chapter for more details.
IFormattable	ToString(format, culture)	This defines a culture-aware method to format the value of an object into a string representation.
IFormatter	Serialize(stream, object) Deserialize(stream)	This defines methods to convert an object to and from a stream of bytes for storage or transfer.
IFormatProvider	GetFormat(type)	This defines a method to format inputs based on a language and region.

Comparing objects when sorting

One of the most common interfaces that you will want to implement is `IComparable`. It has one method named `CompareTo`. It has two variations, one that works with a nullable `object` type and one that works with a nullable generic type `T`, as shown in the following code:

```
namespace System
{
  public interface IComparable
  {
    int CompareTo(object? obj);
  }

  public interface IComparable<in T>
  {
    int CompareTo(T? other);
  }
}
```

For example, the `string` type implements `IComparable` by returning -1 if the `string` is less than the `string` being compared to or 1 if it is greater. The `int` type implements `IComparable` by returning -1 if the `int` is less than the `int` being compared to or 1 if it is greater.

If a type implements one of the `IComparable` interfaces, then arrays and collections can sort it.

Before we implement the `IComparable` interface and its `CompareTo` method for the `Person` class, let's see what happens when we try to sort an array of `Person` instances:

1. In `Program.cs`, add statements that create an array of `Person` instances and write the items to the console, and then attempt to sort the array and write the items to the console again, as shown in the following code:

    ```
    Person[] people =
    {
      new() { Name = "Simon" },
      new() { Name = "Jenny" },
      new() { Name = "Adam" },
      new() { Name = "Richard" }
    };

    WriteLine("Initial list of people:");
    foreach (Person p in people)
    {
      WriteLine($"  {p.Name}");
    }

    WriteLine("Use Person's IComparable implementation to sort:");
    Array.Sort(people);
    ```

```
foreach (Person p in people)
{
  WriteLine($"  {p.Name}");
}
```

2. Run the code and an exception will be thrown. As the message explains, to fix the problem, our type must implement IComparable, as shown in the following output:

```
Unhandled Exception: System.InvalidOperationException: Failed to compare
two elements in the array. ---> System.ArgumentException: At least one
object must implement IComparable.
```

3. In Person.cs, after inheriting from object, add a comma and enter IComparable<Person>, as shown in the following code:

```
public class Person : object, IComparable<Person>
```

Your code editor will draw a red squiggle under the new code to warn you that you have not yet implemented the method you have promised to. Your code editor can write the skeleton implementation for you if you click on the light bulb and choose the **Implement interface** option.

4. Scroll down to the bottom of the Person class to find the method that was written for you and delete the statement that throws the NotImplementedException error, as shown highlighted in the following code:

```
public int CompareTo(Person? other)
{
  throw new NotImplementedException();
}
```

5. Add a statement to call the CompareTo method of the Name field, which uses the string type's implementation of CompareTo and return the result, as shown highlighted in the following code:

```
public int CompareTo(Person? other)
{
  if (Name is null) return 0;
  return Name.CompareTo(other?.Name);
}
```

We have chosen to compare two Person instances by comparing their Name fields. Person instances will, therefore, be sorted alphabetically by their name. For simplicity, I have not added null checks throughout these examples.

6. Run the code and note that this time it works as it should, as shown in the following output:

```
Initial list of people:
  Simon
  Jenny
```

```
    Adam
    Richard
Use Person's IComparable implementation to sort:
    Adam
    Jenny
    Richard
    Simon
```

 Good Practice: If anyone will want to sort an array or collection of instances of your type, then implement the IComparable interface.

Comparing objects using a separate class

Sometimes, you won't have access to the source code for a type, and it might not implement the IComparable interface. Luckily, there is another way to sort instances of a type. You can create a separate type that implements a slightly different interface, named IComparer:

1. In the PacktLibrary project, add a new class file named PersonComparer.cs containing a class that implements the IComparer interface that will compare two people, that is, two Person instances. Implement it by comparing the length of their Name field, or if the names are the same length, then by comparing the names alphabetically, as shown in the following code:

```
namespace Packt.Shared;

public class PersonComparer : IComparer<Person>
{
  public int Compare(Person? x, Person? y)
  {
    if (x is null || y is null)
    {
      return 0;
    }
    // Compare the Name Lengths...
    int result = x.Name.Length.CompareTo(y.Name.Length);

    // ...if they are equal...
    if (result == 0)
    {
      // ...then compare by the Names...
      return x.Name.CompareTo(y.Name);
    }
```

```
      else // result will be -1 or 1
      {
        // ...otherwise compare by the lengths.
        return result;
      }
    }
  }
}
```

2. In `Program.cs`, add statements to sort the array using this alternative implementation, as shown in the following code:

```
WriteLine("Use PersonComparer's IComparer implementation to sort:");
Array.Sort(people, new PersonComparer());
foreach (Person p in people)
{
  WriteLine($"  {p.Name}");
}
```

3. Run the code and view the result, as shown in the following output:

```
Use PersonComparer's IComparer implementation to sort:
  Adam
  Jenny
  Simon
  Richard
```

This time, when we sort the `people` array, we explicitly ask the sorting algorithm to use the `PersonComparer` type instead, so that the people are sorted with the shortest names first, like Adam, and the longest names last, like Richard; and when the lengths of two or more names are equal, to sort them alphabetically, like Jenny and Simon.

Implicit and explicit interface implementations

Interfaces can be implemented implicitly and explicitly. Implicit implementations are simpler and more common. Explicit implementations are only necessary if a type must have multiple methods with the same name and signature.

For example, both `IGamePlayer` and `IKeyHolder` might have a method called `Lose` with the same parameters because both a game and a key can be lost. In a type that must implement both interfaces, only one implementation of `Lose` can be the implicit method. If both interfaces can share the same implementation, that works, but if not then the other `Lose` method will have to be implemented differently and called explicitly, as shown in the following code:

```
public interface IGamePlayer
{
  void Lose();
}
```

```
public interface IKeyHolder
{
  void Lose();
}

public class Person : IGamePlayer, IKeyHolder
{
  public void Lose() // implicit implementation
  {
    // implement losing a key
  }

  void IGamePlayer.Lose() // explicit implementation
  {
    // implement losing a game
  }
}

// calling implicit and explicit implementations of Lose
Person p = new();
p.Lose(); // calls implicit implementation of losing a key

((IGamePlayer)p).Lose(); // calls explicit implementation of losing a game

IGamePlayer player = p as IGamePlayer;
player.Lose(); // calls explicit implementation of losing a game
```

Defining interfaces with default implementations

A language feature introduced in C# 8.0 is **default implementations** for an interface. Let's see it in action:

1. In the PacktLibrary project, add a new file named IPlayable.cs.

2. Modify the statements to define a public IPlayable interface with two methods to Play and Pause, as shown in the following code:

   ```
   namespace Packt.Shared;

   public interface IPlayable
   {
     void Play();
     void Pause();
   }
   ```

3. In the `PacktLibrary` project, add a new class file named `DvdPlayer.cs`.

4. Modify the statements in the file to implement the `IPlayable` interface, as shown in the following code:

```
using static System.Console;

namespace Packt.Shared;

public class DvdPlayer : IPlayable
{
  public void Pause()
  {
    WriteLine("DVD player is pausing.");
  }

  public void Play()
  {
    WriteLine("DVD player is playing.");
  }
}
```

This is useful, but what if we decide to add a third method named `Stop`? Before C# 8.0, this would be impossible once at least one type implements the original interface. One of the main points of an interface is that it is a fixed contract.

C# 8.0 allows an interface to add new members after release as long as they have a default implementation. C# purists do not like the idea, but for practical reasons, such as avoiding breaking changes or having to define a whole new interface, it is useful, and other languages such as Java and Swift enable similar techniques.

Support for default interface implementations requires some fundamental changes to the underlying platform, so they are only supported with C# if the target framework is .NET 5.0 or later, .NET Core 3.0 or later, or .NET Standard 2.1. They are therefore not supported by .NET Framework.

5. Modify the `IPlayable` interface to add a `Stop` method with a default implementation, as shown highlighted in the following code:

```
using static System.Console;

namespace Packt.Shared;

public interface IPlayable
{
  void Play();
  void Pause();

  void Stop() // default interface implementation
  {
```

```
        WriteLine("Default implementation of Stop.");
    }
}
```

6. Build the PeopleApp project and note that the projects compile successfully despite the DvdPlayer class not implementing Stop. In the future, we could override the default implementation of Stop by implementing it in the DvdPlayer class.

Managing memory with reference and value types

I have mentioned reference types a couple of times. Let's look at them in more detail.

There are two categories of memory: **stack** memory and **heap** memory. With modern operating systems, the stack and heap can be anywhere in physical or virtual memory.

Stack memory is faster to work with (because it is managed directly by the CPU and because it uses a last-in, first-out mechanism, it is more likely to have the data in its L1 or L2 cache) but limited in size, while heap memory is slower but much more plentiful.

For example, in a macOS terminal, I can enter the command ulimit -a to discover that the stack size is limited to 8,192 KB and that other memory is "unlimited." This limited amount of stack memory is why it is so easy to fill it up and get a "stack overflow."

Defining reference and value types

There are three C# keywords that you can use to define object types: class, record, and struct. All can have the same members, such as fields and methods. One difference between them is how memory is allocated.

When you define a type using record or class, you are defining a **reference type**. This means that the memory for the object itself is allocated on the heap, and only the memory address of the object (and a little overhead) is stored on the stack.

When you define a type using record struct or struct, you are defining a **value type**. This means that the memory for the object itself is allocated on the stack.

If a struct uses field types that are not of the struct type, then those fields will be stored on the heap, meaning the data for that object is stored in both the stack and the heap!

These are the most common struct types:

- **Number** System **types**: byte, sbyte, short, ushort, int, uint, long, ulong, float, double, and decimal
- **Other** System **types**: char, DateTime, and bool
- System.Drawing **types**: Color, Point, and Rectangle

Almost all the other types are class types, including string.

Apart from the difference in terms of where in memory the data for a type is stored, the other major difference is that you cannot inherit from a struct.

How reference and value types are stored in memory

Imagine that you have a console app that declares some variables, as shown in the following code:

```
int number1 = 49;
long number2 = 12;
System.Drawing.Point location = new(x: 4, y: 5);
Person kevin = new() { Name = "Kevin",
  DateOfBirth = new(year: 1988, month: 9, day: 23) };
Person sally;
```

Let's review what memory is allocated on the stack and heap when these statements execute, as shown in *Figure 6.1* and as described in the following list:

- The number1 variable is a value type (also known as struct) so it is allocated on the stack and it uses 4 bytes of memory since it is a 32-bit integer. Its value, 49, is stored directly in the variable.

- The number2 variable is also a value type so it is also allocated on the stack, and it uses 8 bytes since it is a 64-bit integer.

- The location variable is also a value type so it is allocated on the stack and it uses 8 bytes since it is made up of two 32-bit integers, x and y.

- The kevin variable is a reference type (also known as class) so 8 bytes for a 64-bit memory address (assuming a 64-bit operating system) is allocated on the stack and enough bytes on the heap to store an instance of a Person.

- The sally variable is a reference type so 8 bytes for a 64-bit memory address is allocated on the stack. It is currently null, meaning no memory has yet been allocated for it on the heap.

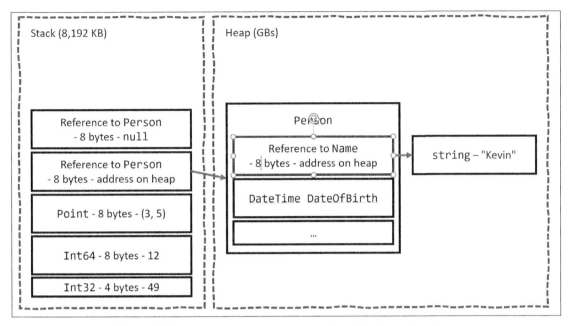

Figure 6.1: How value and reference types are allocated in the stack and heap

All the allocated memory for a reference type is stored on the heap. If a value type such as DateTime is used for a field of a reference type like Person, then the DateTime value is stored on the heap.

If a value type has a field that is a reference type, then that part of the value type is stored on the heap. Point is a value type that consists of two fields, both of which are themselves value types, so the entire object can be allocated on the stack. If the Point value type had a field that was a reference type, like string, then the string bytes would be stored on the heap.

Equality of types

It is common to compare two variables using the == and != operators. The behavior of these two operators is different for reference types and value types.

When you check the equality of two value type variables, .NET literally compares the values of those two variables on the stack and returns true if they are equal, as shown in the following code:

```
int a = 3;
int b = 3;
WriteLine($"a == b: {(a == b)}"); // true
```

When you check the equality of two reference type variables, .NET compares the memory addresses of those two variables and returns `true` if they are equal, as shown in the following code:

```
Person a = new() { Name = "Kevin" };
Person b = new() { Name = "Kevin" };
WriteLine($"a == b: {(a == b)}"); // false
```

This is because they are not the same object. If both variables literally point to the same object on the heap, then they would be equal, as shown in the following code:

```
Person a = new() { Name = "Kevin" };
Person b = a;
WriteLine($"a == b: {(a == b)}"); // true
```

The one exception to this behavior is the `string` type. It is a reference type, but the equality operators have been overridden to make them behave as if they were value types, as shown in the following code:

```
string a = "Kevin";
string b = "Kevin";
WriteLine($"a == b: {(a == b)}"); // true
```

You can do something similar with your classes to make the equality operators return `true` even if they are not the same object (same memory address on the heap) but instead if their fields have the same values, but that is beyond the scope of this book. Alternatively, use a `record class` because one of their benefits is that they implement this behavior for you.

Defining struct types

Let's explore defining your own value types:

1. In the `PacktLibrary` project, add a file named `DisplacementVector.cs`.

2. Modify the file, as shown in the following code, and note the following:
   - The type is declared using `struct` instead of `class`.
   - It has two `int` fields, named `X` and `Y`.
   - It has a constructor for setting initial values for `X` and `Y`.
   - It has an operator for adding two instances together that returns a new instance of the type with `X` added to `X`, and `Y` added to `Y`.

   ```
   namespace Packt.Shared;

   public struct DisplacementVector
   {
     public int X;
   ```

```
    public int Y;

    public DisplacementVector(int initialX, int initialY)
    {
      X = initialX;
      Y = initialY;
    }

    public static DisplacementVector operator +(
      DisplacementVector vector1,
      DisplacementVector vector2)
    {
      return new(
        vector1.X + vector2.X,
        vector1.Y + vector2.Y);
    }
  }
```

3. In `Program.cs`, add statements to create two new instances of `DisplacementVector`, add them together, and output the result, as shown in the following code:

```
DisplacementVector dv1 = new(3, 5);
DisplacementVector dv2 = new(-2, 7);
DisplacementVector dv3 = dv1 + dv2;

WriteLine($"({dv1.X}, {dv1.Y}) + ({dv2.X}, {dv2.Y}) = ({dv3.X},
{dv3.Y})");
```

4. Run the code and view the result, as shown in the following output:

```
(3, 5) + (-2, 7) = (1, 12)
```

Good Practice: If the total bytes used by all the fields in your type is 16 bytes or less, your type only uses value types for its fields, and you will never want to derive from your type, then Microsoft recommends that you use `struct`. If your type uses more than 16 bytes of stack memory, if it uses reference types for its fields, or if you might want to inherit from it, then use `class`.

Working with record struct types

C# 10 introduced the ability to use the `record` keyword with `struct` types as well as with class types.

We could define the `DisplacementVector` type, as shown in the following code:

```
public record struct DisplacementVector(int X, int Y);
```

With this change, Microsoft recommends explicitly specifying class if you want to define a record class even though the class keyword is optional, as shown in the following code:

```
public record class ImmutableAnimal(string Name);
```

Releasing unmanaged resources

In the previous chapter, we saw that constructors can be used to initialize fields and that a type may have multiple constructors. Imagine that a constructor allocates an unmanaged resource; that is, anything that is not controlled by .NET, such as a file or mutex under the control of the operating system. The unmanaged resource must be manually released because .NET cannot do it for us using its automatic garbage collection feature.

Garbage collection is an advanced topic, so for this topic, I will show some code examples, but you do not need to write the code yourself.

Each type can have a single **finalizer** that will be called by the .NET runtime when the resources need to be released. A finalizer has the same name as a constructor; that is, the type name, but it is prefixed with a tilde, ~.

Do not confuse a finalizer (also known as a **destructor**) with a Deconstruct method. A destructor releases resources; that is, it destroys an object in memory. A Deconstruct method returns an object split up into its constituent parts and uses the C# deconstruction syntax, for example, when working with tuples:

```
public class Animal
{
  public Animal() // constructor
  {
    // allocate any unmanaged resources
  }

  ~Animal() // Finalizer aka destructor
  {
    // deallocate any unmanaged resources
  }
}
```

The preceding code example is the minimum you should do when working with unmanaged resources. But the problem with only providing a finalizer is that the .NET garbage collector requires two garbage collections to completely release the allocated resources for this type.

Though optional, it is recommended to also provide a method to allow a developer who uses your type to explicitly release resources so that the garbage collector can release managed parts of an unmanaged resource, such as a file, immediately and deterministically, and then release the managed memory part of the object in a single garbage collection instead of two rounds of garbage collection.

There is a standard mechanism for doing this by implementing the IDisposable interface, as shown in the following example:

```
public class Animal : IDisposable
{
  public Animal()
  {
    // allocate unmanaged resource
  }

  ~Animal() // Finalizer
  {
    Dispose(false);
  }

  bool disposed = false; // have resources been released?

  public void Dispose()
  {
    Dispose(true);

    // tell garbage collector it does not need to call the finalizer
    GC.SuppressFinalize(this);
  }

  protected virtual void Dispose(bool disposing)
  {
    if (disposed) return;

    // deallocate the *unmanaged* resource
    // ...

    if (disposing)
    {
      // deallocate any other *managed* resources
      // ...
    }
    disposed = true;
  }
}
```

There are two Dispose methods, one public and one protected:

- The public void Dispose method will be called by a developer using your type. When called, both unmanaged and managed resources need to be deallocated.

- The protected virtual void Dispose method with a bool parameter is used internally to implement the deallocation of resources. It needs to check the disposing parameter and disposed field because if the finalizer thread has already run and it called the ~Animal method, then only unmanaged resources need to be deallocated.

The call to GC.SuppressFinalize(this) is what notifies the garbage collector that it no longer needs to run the finalizer, and removes the need for a second garbage collection.

Ensuring that Dispose is called

When someone uses a type that implements IDisposable, they can ensure that the public Dispose method is called with the using statement, as shown in the following code:

```
using (Animal a = new())
{
  // code that uses the Animal instance
}
```

The compiler converts your code into something like the following, which guarantees that even if an exception occurs, the Dispose method will still be called:

```
Animal a = new();
try
{
  // code that uses the Animal instance
}
finally
{
  if (a != null) a.Dispose();
}
```

You will see practical examples of releasing unmanaged resources with IDisposable, using statements, and try...finally blocks in *Chapter 9, Working with Files, Streams, and Serialization*.

Working with null values

You have seen how to store primitive values like numbers in struct variables. But what if a variable does not yet have a value? How can we indicate that? C# has the concept of a null value, which can be used to indicate that a variable has not been set.

Making a value type nullable

By default, value types like int and DateTime must always have a value, hence their name. Sometimes, for example, when reading values stored in a database that allows empty, missing, or null values, it is convenient to allow a value type to be null. We call this a **nullable value type**.

You can enable this by adding a question mark as a suffix to the type when declaring a variable.

Let's see an example:

1. Use your preferred coding tool to add a new **Console Application** to the Chapter06 workspace/solution named NullHandling. This section requires a full application with a project file, so you will not be able to use a .NET Interactive notebook.

2. In Visual Studio Code, select NullHandling as the active OmniSharp project. In Visual Studio, set NullHandling as the startup project.

3. In Program.cs, type statements to declare and assign values, including null, to int variables, as shown in the following code:

```
int thisCannotBeNull   = 4;
thisCannotBeNull = null; // compile error!

int? thisCouldBeNull = null;
WriteLine(thisCouldBeNull);
WriteLine(thisCouldBeNull.GetValueOrDefault());

thisCouldBeNull = 7;
WriteLine(thisCouldBeNull);
WriteLine(thisCouldBeNull.GetValueOrDefault());
```

4. Comment out the statement that gives a compile error.

5. Run the code and view the result, as shown in the following output:

```
0
7
7
```

The first line is blank because it is outputting the null value!

Understanding nullable reference types

The use of the null value is so common, in so many languages, that many experienced programmers never question the need for its existence. But there are many scenarios where we could write better, simpler code if a variable is not allowed to have a null value.

The most significant change to the language in C# 8 was the introduction of nullable and non-nullable reference types. "But wait!", you are probably thinking, "Reference types are already nullable!"

And you would be right, but in C# 8 and later, reference types can be configured to no longer allow the null value by setting a file- or project-level option to enable this useful new feature. Since this is a big change for C#, Microsoft decided to make the feature opt-in.

It will take multiple years for this new C# language feature to make an impact since thousands of existing library packages and apps will expect the old behavior. Even Microsoft did not have time to fully implement this new feature in all the main .NET packages until .NET 6.

During the transition, you can choose between several approaches for your own projects:

- **Default**: No changes are needed. Non-nullable reference types are not supported.
- **Opt-in project, opt-out files**: Enable the feature at the project level and, for any files that need to remain compatible with old behavior, opt out. This is the approach Microsoft is using internally while it updates its own packages to use this new feature.
- **Opt-in files**: Only enable the feature for individual files.

Enabling nullable and non-nullable reference types

To enable the feature at the project level, add the following to your project file:

```
<PropertyGroup>
  ...
  <Nullable>enable</Nullable>
</PropertyGroup>
```

This is now done by default in project templates that target .NET 6.0.

To disable the feature at the file level, add the following to the top of a code file:

```
#nullable disable
```

To enable the feature at the file level, add the following to the top of a code file:

```
#nullable enable
```

Declaring non-nullable variables and parameters

If you enable nullable reference types and you want a reference type to be assigned the null value, then you will have to use the same syntax as making a value type nullable, that is, adding a ? symbol after the type declaration.

So, how do nullable reference types work? Let's look at an example. When storing information about an address, you might want to force a value for the street, city, and region, but the building can be left blank, that is, null:

1. In `NullHandling.csproj`, in `Program.cs`, at the bottom of the file, add statements to declare an `Address` class with four fields, as shown in the following code:

```
class Address
{
  public string? Building;
  public string Street;
  public string City;
  public string Region;
}
```

2. After a few seconds, note the warnings about non-nullable fields, like `Street` not being initialized, as shown in *Figure 6.2*:

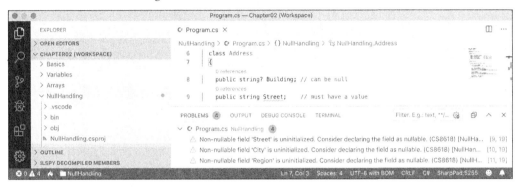

Figure 6.2: Warning messages about non-nullable fields in the PROBLEMS window

3. Assign the empty `string` value to each of the three fields that are non-nullable, as shown in the following code:

```
public string Street = string.Empty;
public string City = string.Empty;
public string Region = string.Empty;
```

4. In `Program.cs`, at the top of the file, statically import `Console` and then add statements to instantiate an `Address` and set its properties, as shown in the following code:

```
Address address = new();
address.Building = null;
address.Street = null;
address.City = "London";
address.Region = null;
```

5. Note the warnings, as shown in *Figure 6.3*:

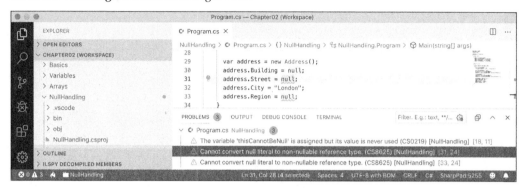

Figure 6.3: Warning message about assigning null to a non-nullable field

So, this is why the new language feature is named nullable reference types. Starting with C# 8.0, unadorned reference types can become non-nullable, and the same syntax is used to make a reference type nullable as is used for value types.

Checking for null

Checking whether a nullable reference type or nullable value type variable currently contains null is important because if you do not, a NullReferenceException can be thrown, which results in an error. You should check for a null value before using a nullable variable, as shown in the following code:

```
// check that the variable is not null before using it
if (thisCouldBeNull != null)
{
  // access a member of thisCouldBeNull
  int length = thisCouldBeNull.Length; // could throw exception
  ...
}
```

C# 7 introduced is combined with the ! (not) operator as an alternative to !=, as shown in the following code:

```
if (!(thisCouldBeNull is null))
{
```

C# 9 introduced is not as an even clearer alternative, as shown in the following code:

```
if (thisCouldBeNull is not null)
{
```

If you are trying to use a member of a variable that might be null, use the null-conditional operator ?., as shown in the following code:

```
string authorName = null;

// the following throws a NullReferenceException
int x = authorName.Length;

// instead of throwing an exception, null is assigned to y
int? y = authorName?.Length;
```

Sometimes you want to either assign a variable to a result or use an alternative value, such as 3, if the variable is null. You do this using the null-coalescing operator, ??, as shown in the following code:

```
// result will be 3 if authorName?.Length is null
int result = authorName?.Length ?? 3;
Console.WriteLine(result);
```

Good Practice: Even if you enable nullable reference types, you should still check non-nullable parameters for null and throw an ArgumentNullException.

Checking for null in method parameters

When defining methods with parameters, it is good practice to check for null values.

In earlier versions of C#, you would have to write if statements to check for null parameter values and then throw an ArgumentNullException for any parameter that is null, as shown in the following code:

```
public void Hire(Person manager, Person employee)
{
  if (manager == null)
  {
    throw new ArgumentNullException(nameof(manager));
  }
  if (employee == null)
  {
    throw new ArgumentNullException(nameof(employee));
  }
  ...
}
```

C# 11 might introduce a new !! suffix that does this for you, as shown in the following code:

```
public void Hire(Person manager!!, Person employee!!)
{
  ...
}
```

The `if` statement and throwing of the exception are done for you.

Inheriting from classes

The `Person` type we created earlier derived (inherited) from `object`, the alias for `System.Object`. Now, we will create a subclass that inherits from `Person`:

1. In the `PacktLibrary` project, add a new class file named `Employee.cs`.

2. Modify its contents to define a class named `Employee` that derives from `Person`, as shown in the following code:

```
using System;

namespace Packt.Shared;

public class Employee : Person
{
}
```

3. In `Program.cs`, add statements to create an instance of the `Employee` class, as shown in the following code:

```
Employee john = new()
{
  Name = "John Jones",
  DateOfBirth = new(year: 1990, month: 7, day: 28)
};
john.WriteToConsole();
```

4. Run the code and view the result, as shown in the following output:

```
John Jones was born on a Saturday.
```

Note that the `Employee` class has inherited all the members of `Person`.

Extending classes to add functionality

Now, we will add some employee-specific members to extend the class.

1. In `Employee.cs`, add statements to define two properties for an employee code and the date they were hired, as shown in the following code:

```
public string? EmployeeCode { get; set; }
public DateTime HireDate { get; set; }
```

2. In `Program.cs`, add statements to set John's employee code and hire date, as shown in the following code:

```
john.EmployeeCode = "JJ001";
john.HireDate = new(year: 2014, month: 11, day: 23);
WriteLine($"{john.Name} was hired on {john.HireDate:dd/MM/yy}");
```

3. Run the code and view the result, as shown in the following output:

```
John Jones was hired on 23/11/14
```

Hiding members

So far, the `WriteToConsole` method is inherited from `Person`, and it only outputs the employee's name and date of birth. We might want to change what this method does for an employee:

1. In `Employee.cs`, add statements to redefine the `WriteToConsole` method, as shown highlighted in the following code:

```
using static System.Console;

namespace Packt.Shared;

public class Employee : Person
{
  public string? EmployeeCode { get; set; }
  public DateTime HireDate { get; set; }

  public void WriteToConsole()
  {
    WriteLine(format:
      "{0} was born on {1:dd/MM/yy} and hired on {2:dd/MM/yy}",
      arg0: Name,
      arg1: DateOfBirth,
      arg2: HireDate);
  }
}
```

2. Run the code and view the result, as shown in the following output:

```
John Jones was born on 28/07/90 and hired on 01/01/01
John Jones was hired on 23/11/14
```

Your coding tool warns you that your method now hides the method from Person by drawing a squiggle under the method name, the **PROBLEMS/Error List** window includes more details, and the compiler will output the warning when you build and run the console application, as shown in *Figure 6.4*:

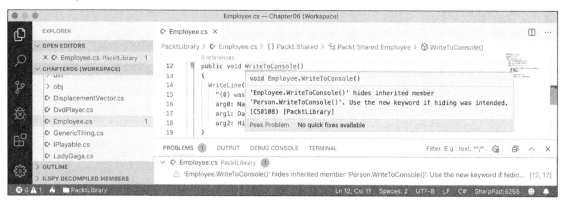

Figure 6.4: Hidden method warning

As the warning describes, you can hide this message by applying the new keyword to the method, to indicate that you are deliberately replacing the old method, as shown highlighted in the following code:

```
public new void WriteToConsole()
```

Overriding members

Rather than hiding a method, it is usually better to **override** it. You can only override if the base class chooses to allow overriding, by applying the virtual keyword to any methods that should allow overriding.

Let's see an example:

1. In Program.cs, add a statement to write the value of the john variable to the console using its string representation, as shown in the following code:

   ```
   WriteLine(john.ToString());
   ```

2. Run the code and note that the ToString method is inherited from System.Object, so the implementation returns the namespace and type name, as shown in the following output:

   ```
   Packt.Shared.Employee
   ```

3. In Person.cs, override this behavior by adding a ToString method to output the name of the person as well as the type name, as shown in the following code:

   ```
   // overridden methods
   public override string ToString()
   {
   ```

```
        return $"{Name} is a {base.ToString()}";
    }
```

The base keyword allows a subclass to access members of its superclass; that is, the **base class** that it inherits or derives from.

4. Run the code and view the result. Now, when the ToString method is called, it outputs the person's name, as well as returning the base class's implementation of ToString, as shown in the following output:

```
John Jones is a Packt.Shared.Employee
```

 Good Practice: Many real-world APIs, for example, Microsoft's Entity Framework Core, Castle's DynamicProxy, and Episerver's content models, require the properties that you define in your classes to be marked as virtual so that they can be overridden. Carefully decide which of your method and property members should be marked as virtual.

Inheriting from abstract classes

Earlier in this chapter, you learned about interfaces that can define a set of members that a type must have to meet a basic level of functionality. These are very useful, but their main limitation is that until C# 8 they could not provide any implementation of their own.

This is a particular problem if you still need to create class libraries that will work with .NET Framework and other platforms that do not support .NET Standard 2.1.

In those earlier platforms, you could use abstract classes as a sort of halfway house between a pure interface and a fully implemented class.

When a class is marked as abstract, this means that it cannot be instantiated because you are indicating that the class is not complete. It needs more implementation before it can be instantiated.

For example, the System.IO.Stream class is abstract because it implements common functionality that all streams would need but is not complete, so you cannot instantiate it using new Stream().

Let's compare the two types of interface and two types of class, as shown in the following code:

```
public interface INoImplementation // C# 1.0 and later
{
  void Alpha(); // must be implemented by derived type
}

public interface ISomeImplementation // C# 8.0 and later
{
  void Alpha(); // must be implemented by derived type
```

```
  void Beta()
  {
    // default implementation; can be overridden
  }
}

public abstract class PartiallyImplemented // C# 1.0 and later
{
  public abstract void Gamma(); // must be implemented by derived type

  public virtual void Delta() // can be overridden
  {
    // implementation
  }
}

public class FullyImplemented : PartiallyImplemented, ISomeImplementation
{
  public void Alpha()
  {
    // implementation
  }

  public override void Gamma()
  {
    // implementation
  }
}

// you can only instantiate the fully implemented class
FullyImplemented a = new();

// all the other types give compile errors
PartiallyImplemented b = new(); // compile error!
ISomeImplementation c = new(); // compile error!
INoImplementation d = new(); // compile error!
```

Preventing inheritance and overriding

You can prevent another developer from inheriting from your class by applying the sealed keyword to its definition. No one can inherit from Scrooge McDuck, as shown in the following code:

```
public sealed class ScroogeMcDuck
{
}
```

An example of sealed in .NET is the string class. Microsoft has implemented some extreme optimizations inside the string class that could be negatively affected by your inheritance, so Microsoft prevents that.

You can prevent someone from further overriding a virtual method in your class by applying the sealed keyword to the method. No one can change the way Lady Gaga sings, as shown in the following code:

```
using static System.Console;

namespace Packt.Shared;

public class Singer
{
  // virtual allows this method to be overridden
  public virtual void Sing()
  {
    WriteLine("Singing...");
  }
}

public class LadyGaga : Singer
{
  // sealed prevents overriding the method in subclasses
  public sealed override void Sing()
  {
    WriteLine("Singing with style...");
  }
}
```

You can only seal an overridden method.

Understanding polymorphism

You have now seen two ways to change the behavior of an inherited method. We can *hide* it using the new keyword (known as **non-polymorphic inheritance**), or we can *override* it (known as **polymorphic inheritance**).

Both ways can access members of the base or superclass by using the base keyword, so what is the difference?

It all depends on the type of variable holding a reference to the object. For example, a variable of the Person type can hold a reference to a Person class, or any type that derives from Person.

Let's see how this could affect your code:

1. In `Employee.cs`, add statements to override the `ToString` method so it writes the employee's name and code to the console, as shown in the following code:

    ```
    public override string ToString()
    {
      return $"{Name}'s code is {EmployeeCode}";
    }
    ```

2. In `Program.cs`, write statements to create a new employee named Alice, store it in a variable of type `Person`, and call both variables' `WriteToConsole` and `ToString` methods, as shown in the following code:

    ```
    Employee aliceInEmployee = new()
      { Name = "Alice", EmployeeCode = "AA123" };

    Person aliceInPerson = aliceInEmployee;
    aliceInEmployee.WriteToConsole();
    aliceInPerson.WriteToConsole();
    WriteLine(aliceInEmployee.ToString());
    WriteLine(aliceInPerson.ToString());
    ```

3. Run the code and view the result, as shown in the following output:

    ```
    Alice was born on 01/01/01 and hired on 01/01/01
    Alice was born on a Monday
    Alice's code is AA123
    Alice's code is AA123
    ```

When a method is hidden with `new`, the compiler is not smart enough to know that the object is an `Employee`, so it calls the `WriteToConsole` method in `Person`.

When a method is overridden with `virtual` and `override`, the compiler is smart enough to know that although the variable is declared as a `Person` class, the object itself is an `Employee` class and, therefore, the `Employee` implementation of `ToString` is called.

The member modifiers and the effect they have are summarized in the following table:

Variable type	Member modifier	Method executed	In class
Person		WriteToConsole	Person
Employee	new	WriteToConsole	Employee
Person	virtual	ToString	Employee
Employee	override	ToString	Employee

In my opinion, polymorphism is academic to most programmers. If you get the concept, that's cool; but, if not, I suggest that you don't worry about it. Some people like to make others feel inferior by saying understanding polymorphism is important for all C# programmers to learn, but IMHO it's not.

You can have a successful career with C# and never need to be able to explain polymorphism, just as a racing car driver doesn't need to be able to explain the engineering behind fuel injection.

> **Good Practice**: You should use `virtual` and `override` rather than `new` to change the implementation of an inherited method whenever possible.

Casting within inheritance hierarchies

Casting between types is subtly different from converting between types. Casting is between similar types, like between a 16-bit integer and a 32-bit integer, or between a superclass and one of its subclasses. Converting is between dissimilar types, such as between text and a number.

Implicit casting

In the previous example, you saw how an instance of a derived type can be stored in a variable of its base type (or its base's base type, and so on). When we do this, it is called **implicit casting**.

Explicit casting

Going the other way is an explicit cast, and you must use parentheses around the type you want to cast into as a prefix to do it:

1. In `Program.cs`, add a statement to assign the `aliceInPerson` variable to a new `Employee` variable, as shown in the following code:

   ```
   Employee explicitAlice = aliceInPerson;
   ```

2. Your coding tool displays a red squiggle and a compile error, as shown in *Figure 6.5*:

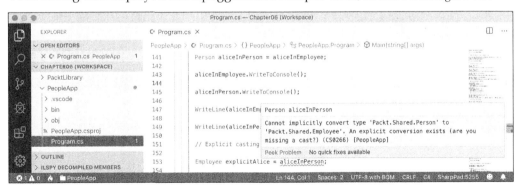

Figure 6.5: A missing explicit cast compile error

3. Change the statement to prefix the assigned variable named with a cast to the `Employee` type, as shown in the following code:

   ```
   Employee explicitAlice = (Employee)aliceInPerson;
   ```

Avoiding casting exceptions

The compiler is now happy; but, because aliceInPerson might be a different derived type, like Student instead of Employee, we need to be careful. In a real application with more complex code, the current value of this variable could have been set to a Student instance, and then this statement would throw an InvalidCastException error.

We can handle this by writing a try statement, but there is a better way. We can check the type of an object using the is keyword:

1. Wrap the explicit cast statement in an if statement, as shown highlighted in the following code:

```
if (aliceInPerson is Employee)
{
  WriteLine($"{nameof(aliceInPerson)} IS an Employee");
  Employee explicitAlice = (Employee)aliceInPerson;
  // safely do something with explicitAlice
}
```

2. Run the code and view the result, as shown in the following output:

```
aliceInPerson IS an Employee
```

You can simplify the code further using a declaration pattern and this will avoid needing to perform an explicit cast, as shown in the following code:

```
if (aliceInPerson is Employee explicitAlice)
{
  WriteLine($"{nameof(aliceInPerson)} IS an Employee");
  // safely do something with explicitAlice
}
```

Alternatively, you can use the as keyword to cast. Instead of throwing an exception, the as keyword returns null if the type cannot be cast.

3. In Main, add the statements to cast Alice using the as keyword and then check whether the return value is not null, as shown in the following code:

```
Employee? aliceAsEmployee = aliceInPerson as Employee; // could be null

if (aliceAsEmployee != null)
{
  WriteLine($"{nameof(aliceInPerson)} AS an Employee");
  // safely do something with aliceAsEmployee
}
```

Since accessing a member of a null variable will throw a NullReferenceException error, you should always check for null before using the result.

4. Run the code and view the result, as shown in the following output:

```
aliceInPerson AS an Employee
```

What if you want to execute a block of statements when Alice is not an employee?

In the past, you would have had to use the ! (not) operator, as shown in the following code:

```
if (!(aliceInPerson is Employee))
```

With C# 9 and later, you can use the not keyword, as shown in the following code:

```
if (aliceInPerson is not Employee)
```

 Good Practice: Use the is and as keywords to avoid throwing exceptions when casting between derived types. If you don't do this, you must write try-catch statements for InvalidCastException.

Inheriting and extending .NET types

.NET has prebuilt class libraries containing hundreds of thousands of types. Rather than creating your own completely new types, you can often get a head start by deriving from one of Microsoft's types to inherit some or all of its behavior and then overriding or extending it.

Inheriting exceptions

As an example of inheritance, we will derive a new type of exception:

1. In the PacktLibrary project, add a new class file named PersonException.cs.

2. Modify the contents of the file to define a class named PersonException with three constructors, as shown in the following code:

```
namespace Packt.Shared;

public class PersonException : Exception
{
  public PersonException() : base() { }

  public PersonException(string message) : base(message) { }

  public PersonException(string message, Exception innerException)
    : base(message, innerException) { }
}
```

Unlike ordinary methods, constructors are not inherited, so we must explicitly declare and explicitly call the base constructor implementations in `System.Exception` to make them available to programmers who might want to use those constructors with our custom exception.

3. In `Person.cs`, add statements to define a method that throws an exception if a date/time parameter is earlier than a person's date of birth, as shown in the following code:

```
public void TimeTravel(DateTime when)
{
  if (when <= DateOfBirth)
  {
    throw new PersonException("If you travel back in time to a date
earlier than your own birth, then the universe will explode!");
  }
  else
  {
    WriteLine($"Welcome to {when:yyyy}!");
  }
}
```

4. In `Program.cs`, add statements to test what happens when employee John Jones tries to time travel too far back, as shown in the following code:

```
try
{
  john.TimeTravel(when: new(1999, 12, 31));
  john.TimeTravel(when: new(1950, 12, 25));
}
catch (PersonException ex)
{
  WriteLine(ex.Message);
}
```

5. Run the code and view the result, as shown in the following output:

```
Welcome to 1999!
If you travel back in time to a date earlier than your own birth, then the
universe will explode!
```

Good Practice: When defining your own exceptions, give them the same three constructors that explicitly call the built-in ones.

Extending types when you can't inherit

Earlier, we saw how the `sealed` modifier can be used to prevent inheritance.

Microsoft has applied the `sealed` keyword to the `System.String` class so that no one can inherit and potentially break the behavior of strings.

Can we still add new methods to strings? Yes, if we use a language feature named **extension methods**, which was introduced with C# 3.0.

Using static methods to reuse functionality

Since the first version of C#, we've been able to create `static` methods to reuse functionality, such as the ability to validate that a `string` contains an email address. The implementation will use a regular expression that you will learn more about in *Chapter 8, Working with Common .NET Types*.

Let's write some code:

1. In the `PacktLibrary` project, add a new class named `StringExtensions`, as shown in the following code, and note the following:

    *   The class imports a namespace for handling regular expressions.

    *   The `IsValidEmail` method is `static` and it uses the `Regex` type to check for matches against a simple email pattern that looks for valid characters before and after the @ symbol.

    ```
    using System.Text.RegularExpressions;

    namespace Packt.Shared;

    public class StringExtensions
    {
      public static bool IsValidEmail(string input)
      {
        // use simple regular expression to check
        // that the input string is a valid email
        return Regex.IsMatch(input,
          @"[a-zA-Z0-9\.-_]+@[a-zA-Z0-9\.-_]+");
      }
    }
    ```

2. In `Program.cs`, add statements to validate two examples of email addresses, as shown in the following code:

    ```
    string email1 = "pamela@test.com";
    string email2 = "ian&test.com";
    ```

```
WriteLine("{0} is a valid e-mail address: {1}",
  arg0: email1,
  arg1: StringExtensions.IsValidEmail(email1));

WriteLine("{0} is a valid e-mail address: {1}",
  arg0: email2,
  arg1: StringExtensions.IsValidEmail(email2));
```

3. Run the code and view the result, as shown in the following output:

```
pamela@test.com is a valid e-mail address: True
ian&test.com is a valid e-mail address: False
```

This works, but extension methods can reduce the amount of code we must type and simplify the usage of this function.

Using extension methods to reuse functionality

It is easy to make static methods into extension methods:

1. In StringExtensions.cs, add the static modifier before the class, and add the this modifier before the string type, as highlighted in the following code:

```
public static class StringExtensions
{
  public static bool IsValidEmail(this string input)
  {
```

These two changes tell the compiler that it should treat the method as one that extends the string type.

2. In Program.cs, add statements to use the extension method for string values that need to be checked for valid email addresses, as shown in the following code:

```
WriteLine("{0} is a valid e-mail address: {1}",
  arg0: email1,
  arg1: email1.IsValidEmail());

WriteLine("{0} is a valid e-mail address: {1}",
  arg0: email2,
  arg1: email2.IsValidEmail());
```

Note the subtle simplification in the syntax for calling the IsValidEmail method. The older, longer syntax still works too.

3. The IsValidEmail extension method now appears to be a method just like all the actual instance methods of the string type, such as IsNormalized and Insert, as shown in *Figure 6.6*:

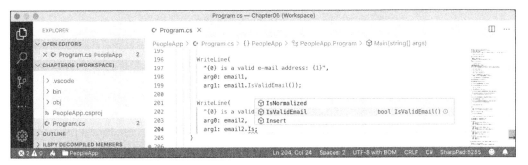

Figure 6.6: Extension methods appear in IntelliSense alongside instance methods

4. Run the code and view the result, which will be the same as before.

> **Good Practice**: Extension methods cannot replace or override existing instance methods. You cannot, for example, redefine the `Insert` method. The extension method will appear as an overload in IntelliSense, but an instance method will be called in preference to an extension method with the same name and signature.

Although extension methods might not seem to give a big benefit, in *Chapter 11, Querying and Manipulating Data Using LINQ*, you will see some extremely powerful uses of extension methods.

Using an analyzer to write better code

.NET analyzers find potential issues and suggest fixes for them. **StyleCop** is a commonly used analyzer for helping you write better C# code.

Let's see it in action, advising how to improve the code in the project template for a console app when targeting .NET 5.0 so that the console app already has a `Program` class with a `Main` method:

1. Use your preferred code editor to add a console app project, as defined in the following list:

    1. Project template: **Console Application** / `console -f net5.0`
    2. Workspace/solution file and folder: `Chapter06`
    3. Project file and folder: `CodeAnalyzing`
    4. Target framework: **.NET 5.0 (Current)**

2. In the `CodeAnalyzing` project, add a package reference for `StyleCop.Analyzers`.

3. Add a JSON file to your project named `stylecop.json` for controlling StyleCop settings.

4. Modify its contents, as shown in the following markup:

```
{
  "$schema": "https://raw.githubusercontent.com/DotNetAnalyzers/
StyleCopAnalyzers/master/StyleCop.Analyzers/StyleCop.Analyzers/Settings/
stylecop.schema.json",
  "settings": {
  }
}
```

 The $schema entry enables IntelliSense while editing the stylecop.json file in your code editor.

5. Edit the project file, change the target framework to net6.0, add entries to configure the file named stylecop.json to not be included in published deployments, and to enable it as an additional file for processing during development, as shown highlighted in the following markup:

```
<Project Sdk="Microsoft.NET.Sdk">

  <PropertyGroup>
    <OutputType>Exe</OutputType>
    <TargetFramework>net6.0</TargetFramework>
  </PropertyGroup>

  <ItemGroup>
    <None Remove="stylecop.json" />
  </ItemGroup>

  <ItemGroup>
    <AdditionalFiles Include="stylecop.json" />
  </ItemGroup>

  <ItemGroup>
    <PackageReference Include="StyleCop.Analyzers" Version="1.2.0-*">
      <PrivateAssets>all</PrivateAssets>
      <IncludeAssets>runtime; build; native; contentfiles; analyzers</
IncludeAssets>
    </PackageReference>
  </ItemGroup>

</Project>
```

6. Build your project.

7. You will see warnings for everything it thinks is wrong, as shown in *Figure 6.7*:

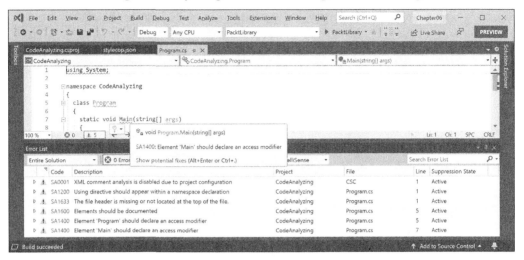

Figure 6.7: StyleCop code analyzer warnings

8. For example, it wants `using` directives to be put within the namespace declaration, as shown in the following output:

```
C:\Code\Chapter06\CodeAnalyzing\Program.cs(1,1): warning SA1200: Using
directive should appear within a namespace declaration [C:\Code\Chapter06\
CodeAnalyzing\CodeAnalyzing.csproj]
```

Suppressing warnings

To suppress a warning, you have several options, including adding code and setting configuration.

To suppress using an attribute, as shown in the following code:

```
[assembly:SuppressMessage("StyleCop.CSharp.OrderingRules", "SA1200:UsingDirectiv
esMustBePlacedWithinNamespace", Justification = "Reviewed.")]
```

To suppress using a directive, as shown in the following code:

```
#pragma warning disable SA1200 // UsingDirectivesMustBePlacedWithinNamespace
using System;
#pragma warning restore SA1200 // UsingDirectivesMustBePlacedWithinNamespace
```

Let's suppress the warning by modifying the `stylecop.json` file:

1. In `stylecop.json`, add a configuration option to set `using` statements to be allowable outside a namespace, as shown highlighted in the following markup:

```
{
  "$schema": "https://raw.githubusercontent.com/DotNetAnalyzers/
StyleCopAnalyzers/master/StyleCop.Analyzers/StyleCop.Analyzers/Settings/
stylecop.schema.json",
  "settings": {
    "orderingRules": {
      "usingDirectivesPlacement": "outsideNamespace"
    }
  }
}
```

2. Build the project and note that warning SA1200 has disappeared.

3. In `stylecop.json`, set the using directives placement to `preserve`, which allows `using` statements both inside and outside a namespace, as shown in the following markup:

```
"orderingRules": {
  "usingDirectivesPlacement": "preserve"
}
```

Fixing the code

Now, let's fix all the other warnings:

1. In `CodeAnalyzing.csproj`, add an element to automatically generate an XML file for documentation, as shown highlighted in the following markup:

```
<Project Sdk="Microsoft.NET.Sdk">

  <PropertyGroup>
    <OutputType>Exe</OutputType>
    <TargetFramework>net6.0</TargetFramework>
    <GenerateDocumentationFile>true</GenerateDocumentationFile>
  </PropertyGroup>
```

2. In `stylecop.json`, add a configuration option to provide values for documentation for the company name and copyright text, as shown highlighted in the following markup:

```
{
  "$schema": "https://raw.githubusercontent.com/DotNetAnalyzers/
StyleCopAnalyzers/master/StyleCop.Analyzers/StyleCop.Analyzers/Settings/
stylecop.schema.json",
  "settings": {
```

```
    "orderingRules": {
      "usingDirectivesPlacement": "preserve"
    },
    "documentationRules": {
      "companyName": "Packt",
      "copyrightText": "Copyright (c) Packt. All rights reserved."
    }
  }
}
```

3. In `Program.cs`, add comments for a file header with company and copyright text, move the `using System;` declaration inside the namespace, and set explicit access modifiers and XML comments for the class and method, as shown in the following code:

```csharp
// <copyright file="Program.cs" company="Packt">
// Copyright (c) Packt. All rights reserved.
// </copyright>

namespace CodeAnalyzing
{
  using System;

  /// <summary>
  /// The main class for this console app.
  /// </summary>
  public class Program
  {
    /// <summary>
    /// The main entry point for this console app.
    /// </summary>
    /// <param name="args">A string array of arguments passed to the
console app.</param>
    public static void Main(string[] args)
    {
      Console.WriteLine("Hello World!");
    }
  }
}
```

4. Build the project.

5. Expand the `bin/Debug/net6.0` folder and note the autogenerated file named `CodeAnalyzing.xml`, as shown in the following markup:

```xml
<?xml version="1.0"?>
<doc>
    <assembly>
```

```
                        <name>CodeAnalyzing</name>
                </assembly>
                <members>
                        <member name="T:CodeAnalyzing.Program">
                                <summary>
                                The main class for this console app.
                                </summary>
                        </member>
                        <member name="M:CodeAnalyzing.Program.Main(System.String[])">
                                <summary>
                                The main entry point for this console app.
                                </summary>
                                <param name="args">A string array of arguments passed to the
        console app.</param>
                        </member>
                </members>
        </doc>
```

Understanding common StyleCop recommendations

Inside a code file, you should order the contents, as shown in the following list:

1. External alias directives
2. Using directives
3. Namespaces
4. Delegates
5. Enums
6. Interfaces
7. Structs
8. Classes

Within a class, record, struct, or interface, you should order the contents, as shown in the following list:

1. Fields
2. Constructors
3. Destructors (finalizers)
4. Delegates
5. Events
6. Enums
7. Interfaces
8. Properties
9. Indexers
10. Methods

11. Structs

12. Nested classes and records

 Good Practice: You can learn about all the StyleCop rules at the following link: `https://github.com/DotNetAnalyzers/StyleCopAnalyzers/blob/master/DOCUMENTATION.md`.

Practicing and exploring

Test your knowledge and understanding by answering some questions. Get some hands-on practice and explore this chapter's topics with more in-depth research.

Exercise 6.1 – Test your knowledge

Answer the following questions:

1. What is a delegate?
2. What is an event?
3. How are a base class and a derived class related, and how can the derived class access the base class?
4. What is the difference between `is` and `as` operators?
5. Which keyword is used to prevent a class from being derived from or a method from being further overridden?
6. Which keyword is used to prevent a class from being instantiated with the `new` keyword?
7. Which keyword is used to allow a member to be overridden?
8. What's the difference between a destructor and a deconstruct method?
9. What are the signatures of the constructors that all exceptions should have?
10. What is an extension method, and how do you define one?

Exercise 6.2 – Practice creating an inheritance hierarchy

Explore inheritance hierarchies by following these steps:

1. Add a new console application named `Exercise02` to your `Chapter06` solution/workspace.
2. Create a class named `Shape` with properties named `Height`, `Width`, and `Area`.

3. Add three classes that derive from it — Rectangle, Square, and Circle — with any additional members you feel are appropriate and that override and implement the Area property correctly.

4. In Main, add statements to create one instance of each shape, as shown in the following code:

```
Rectangle r = new(height: 3, width: 4.5);
WriteLine($"Rectangle H: {r.Height}, W: {r.Width}, Area: {r.Area}");

Square s = new(5);
WriteLine($"Square H: {s.Height}, W: {s.Width}, Area: {s.Area}");

Circle c = new(radius: 2.5);
WriteLine($"Circle H: {c.Height}, W: {c.Width}, Area: {c.Area}");
```

5. Run the console application and ensure that the result looks like the following output:

```
Rectangle H: 3, W: 4.5, Area: 13.5
Square H: 5, W: 5, Area: 25
Circle H: 5, W: 5, Area: 19.6349540849362
```

Exercise 6.3 – Explore topics

Use the links on the following page to learn more about the topics covered in this chapter:

https://github.com/markjprice/cs10dotnet6/blob/main/book-links.md#chapter-6---
implementing-interfaces-and-inheriting-classes

Summary

In this chapter, you learned about local functions and operators, delegates and events, implementing interfaces, generics, and deriving types using inheritance and OOP. You also learned about base and derived classes, and how to override a type member, use polymorphism, and cast between types.

In the next chapter, you will learn how .NET is packaged and deployed, and, in subsequent chapters, the types that it provides you with to implement common functionality such as file handling, database access, encryption, and multitasking.

07
Packaging and Distributing .NET Types

This chapter is about how C# keywords are related to .NET types, and about the relationship between namespaces and assemblies. You'll also become familiar with how to package and publish your .NET apps and libraries for cross-platform use, how to use legacy .NET Framework libraries in .NET libraries, and the possibility of porting legacy .NET Framework code bases to modern .NET.

This chapter covers the following topics:

- The road to .NET 6
- Understanding .NET components
- Publishing your applications for deployment
- Decompiling .NET assemblies
- Packaging your libraries for NuGet distribution
- Porting from .NET Framework to modern .NET
- Working with preview features

The road to .NET 6

This part of the book is about the functionality in the **Base Class Library** (**BCL**) APIs provided by .NET and how to reuse functionality across all the different .NET platforms using .NET Standard.

First, we will review the route to this point and why it is important to understand the past.

.NET Core 2.0 and later's support for a minimum of .NET Standard 2.0 is important because it provides many of the APIs that were missing from the first version of .NET Core. The 15 years' worth of libraries and applications that .NET Framework developers had available to them that are relevant for modern development have now been migrated to .NET and can run cross-platform on macOS and Linux variants, as well as on Windows.

.NET Standard 2.1 added about 3,000 new APIs. Some of those APIs need runtime changes that would break backward compatibility, so .NET Framework 4.8 only implements .NET Standard 2.0. .NET Core 3.0, Xamarin, Mono, and Unity implement .NET Standard 2.1.

.NET 6 removes the need for .NET Standard if all your projects can use .NET 6. Since you might still need to create class libraries for legacy .NET Framework projects or legacy Xamarin mobile apps, there is still a need to create .NET Standard 2.0 and 2.1 class libraries. In March 2021, I surveyed professional developers, and half still needed to create .NET Standard 2.0 compliant class libraries.

Now that .NET 6 has been released with preview support for mobile and desktop apps built using .NET MAUI, the need for .NET Standard has been further reduced.

To summarize the progress that .NET has made over the past five years, I have compared the major .NET Core and modern .NET versions with the equivalent .NET Framework versions in the following list:

- **.NET Core 1.x**: much smaller API compared to .NET Framework 4.6.1, which was the current version in March 2016.

- **.NET Core 2.x**: reached API parity with .NET Framework 4.7.1 for modern APIs because they both implement .NET Standard 2.0.

- **.NET Core 3.x**: larger API compared to .NET Framework for modern APIs because. NET Framework 4.8 does not implement .NET Standard 2.1.

- **.NET 5**: even larger API compared to .NET Framework 4.8 for modern APIs, with much-improved performance.

- **.NET 6**: final unification with the support for mobile apps in .NET MAUI, expected by May 2022.

.NET Core 1.0

.NET Core 1.0 was released in June 2016 and focused on implementing an API suitable for building modern cross-platform apps, including web and cloud applications and services for Linux using ASP.NET Core.

.NET Core 1.1

.NET Core 1.1 was released in November 2016 and focused on fixing bugs, increasing the number of Linux distributions supported, supporting .NET Standard 1.6, and improving performance, especially with ASP.NET Core for web apps and services.

.NET Core 2.0

.NET Core 2.0 was released in August 2017 and focused on implementing .NET Standard 2.0, the ability to reference .NET Framework libraries, and more performance improvements.

The third edition of this book was published in November 2017, so it covered up to .NET Core 2.0 and .NET Core for **Universal Windows Platform (UWP)** apps.

.NET Core 2.1

.NET Core 2.1 was released in May 2018 and focused on an extendable tooling system, adding new types like Span<T>, new APIs for cryptography and compression, a Windows Compatibility Pack with an additional 20,000 APIs to help port old Windows applications, Entity Framework Core value conversions, LINQ GroupBy conversions, data seeding, query types, and even more performance improvements, including the topics listed in the following table:

Feature	Chapter	Topic
Spans	8	Working with spans, indexes, and ranges
Brotli compression	9	Compressing with the Brotli algorithm
Cryptography	20	What's new in cryptography?
EF Core Lazy loading	10	Enabling lazy loading
EF Core Data seeding	10	Understanding data seeding

.NET Core 2.2

.NET Core 2.2 was released in December 2018 and focused on diagnostic improvements for the runtime, optional tiered compilation, and adding new features to ASP.NET Core and Entity Framework Core like spatial data support using types from the **NetTopologySuite (NTS)** library, query tags, and collections of owned entities.

.NET Core 3.0

.NET Core 3.0 was released in September 2019 and focused on adding support for building Windows desktop applications using Windows Forms (2001), **Windows Presentation Foundation (WPF; 2006)**, and Entity Framework 6.3, side-by-side and app-local deployments, a fast JSON reader, serial port access and other pinout access for **Internet of Things (IoT)** solutions, and tiered compilation by default, including the topics listed in the following table:

Feature	Chapter	Topic
Embedding .NET in-app	7	Publishing your applications for deployment
Index and Range	8	Working with spans, indexes, and ranges
System.Text.Json	9	High-performance JSON processing
Async streams	12	Working with async streams

The fourth edition of this book was published in October 2019, so it covered some of the new APIs added in later versions up to .NET Core 3.0.

.NET Core 3.1

.NET Core 3.1 was released in December 2019 and focused on bug fixes and refinements so that it could be a **Long Term Support (LTS)** release, not losing support until December 2022.

.NET 5.0

.NET 5.0 was released in November 2020 and focused on unifying the various .NET platforms except mobile, refining the platform, and improving performance, including the topics listed in the following table:

Feature	Chapter	Topic
Half type	8	Working with numbers
Regular expression performance improvements	8	Regular expression performance improvements
System.Text.Json improvements	9	High-performance JSON processing
EF Core generated SQL	10	Getting the generated SQL
EF Core Filtered Include	10	Filtering included entities
EF Core Scaffold-DbContext now singularizes using Humanizer	10	Scaffolding models using an existing database

.NET 6.0

.NET 6.0 was released in November 2021 and focused on unifying with the mobile platform, adding more features to EF Core for data management, and improving performance, including the topics listed in the following table:

Feature	Chapter	Topic
Check .NET SDK status	7	Checking your .NET SDKs for updates
Support for Apple Silicon	7	Creating a console application to publish
Link trim mode as default	7	Reducing the size of apps using app trimming
DateOnly and TimeOnly	8	Specifying date and time values
EnsureCapacity for List<T>	8	Improving performance by ensuring the capacity of a collection
EF Core configure conventions	10	Configuring preconvention models
New LINQ methods	11	Building LINQ expressions with the Enumerable class

Improving performance from .NET Core 2.0 to .NET 5

Microsoft has made significant improvements to performance in the past few years. You can read a detailed blog post at the following link: `https://devblogs.microsoft.com/dotnet/performance-improvements-in-net-5/`.

Checking your .NET SDKs for updates

With .NET 6, Microsoft added a command to check the versions of .NET SDKs and runtimes that you have installed and warn you if any need updating. For example, you enter the following command:

```
dotnet sdk check
```

You will then see results, including the status of available updates, as shown in the following partial output:

```
.NET SDKs:
Version                           Status
------------------------------------------------------------------------------
3.1.412                           Up to date.
5.0.202                           Patch 5.0.206 is available.
...
```

Understanding .NET components

.NET is made up of several pieces, which are shown in the following list:

- **Language compilers**: These turn your source code written with languages such as C#, F#, and Visual Basic into **intermediate language (IL)** code stored in assemblies. With C# 6.0 and later, Microsoft switched to an open-source rewritten compiler known as Roslyn that is also used by Visual Basic.

- **Common Language Runtime (CoreCLR)**: This runtime loads assemblies, compiles the IL code stored in them into native code instructions for your computer's CPU, and executes the code within an environment that manages resources such as threads and memory.

- **Base Class Libraries (BCL or CoreFX)**: These are prebuilt assemblies of types packaged and distributed using NuGet for performing common tasks when building applications. You can use them to quickly build anything you want, rather like combining LEGO™ pieces. .NET Core 2.0 implemented .NET Standard 2.0, which is a superset of all previous versions of .NET Standard, and lifted .NET Core up to parity with .NET Framework and Xamarin. .NET Core 3.0 implemented .NET Standard 2.1, which added new capabilities and enables performance improvements beyond those available in .NET Framework. .NET 6 implements a unified BCL across all types of apps, including mobile.

Understanding assemblies, NuGet packages, and namespaces

An **assembly** is where a type is stored in the filesystem. Assemblies are a mechanism for deploying code. For example, the System.Data.dll assembly contains types for managing data. To use types in other assemblies, they must be referenced. Assemblies can be static (pre-created) or dynamic (generated at runtime). Dynamic assemblies are an advanced feature that we will not cover in this book. Assemblies can be compiled into a single file as a DLL (class library) or an EXE (console app).

Assemblies are distributed as **NuGet packages**, which are files downloadable from public online feeds and can contain multiple assemblies and other resources. You will also hear about **project SDKs**, **workloads**, and **platforms**, which are combinations of NuGet packages.

Microsoft's NuGet feed is found here: https://www.nuget.org/.

What is a namespace?

A namespace is the address of a type. Namespaces are a mechanism to uniquely identify a type by requiring a full address rather than just a short name. In the real world, *Bob of 34 Sycamore Street* is different from *Bob of 12 Willow Drive*.

In .NET, the IActionFilter interface of the System.Web.Mvc namespace is different from the IActionFilter interface of the System.Web.Http.Filters namespace.

Understanding dependent assemblies

If an assembly is compiled as a class library and provides types for other assemblies to use, then it has the file extension .dll (**dynamic link library**), and it cannot be executed standalone.

Likewise, if an assembly is compiled as an application, then it has the file extension .exe (**executable**) and can be executed standalone. Before .NET Core 3.0, console apps were compiled to .dll files and had to be executed by the dotnet run command or a host executable.

Any assembly can reference one or more class library assemblies as dependencies, but you cannot have circular references. So, assembly *B* cannot reference assembly *A* if assembly *A* already references assembly *B*. The compiler will warn you if you attempt to add a dependency reference that would cause a circular reference. Circular references are often a warning sign of poor code design. If you are sure that you need a circular reference, then use an interface to solve it.

Understanding the Microsoft .NET project SDKs

By default, console applications have a dependency reference on the Microsoft .NET project SDK. This platform contains thousands of types in NuGet packages that almost all applications would need, such as the System.Int32 and System.String types.

When using .NET, you reference the dependency assemblies, NuGet packages, and platforms that your application needs in a project file.

Let's explore the relationship between assemblies and namespaces:

1. Use your preferred code editor to create a new solution/workspace named Chapter07.
2. Add a console app project, as defined in the following list:
    1. Project template: **Console Application** / console
    2. Workspace/solution file and folder: Chapter07
    3. Project file and folder: AssembliesAndNamespaces
3. Open AssembliesAndNamespaces.csproj and note that it is a typical project file for a .NET 6 application, as shown in the following markup:

```
<Project Sdk="Microsoft.NET.Sdk">

  <PropertyGroup>
    <OutputType>Exe</OutputType>
    <TargetFramework>net6.0</TargetFramework>
    <Nullable>enable</Nullable>
    <ImplicitUsings>enable</ImplicitUsings>
  </PropertyGroup>

</Project>
```

Understanding namespaces and types in assemblies

Many common .NET types are in the System.Runtime.dll assembly. There is not always a one-to-one mapping between assemblies and namespaces. A single assembly can contain many namespaces and a namespace can be defined in many assemblies. You can see the relationship between some assemblies and the namespaces that they supply types for, as shown in the following table:

Assembly	Example namespaces	Example types
System.Runtime.dll	System, System.Collections, System.Collections.Generic	Int32, String, IEnumerable<T>
System.Console.dll	System	Console
System.Threading.dll	System.Threading	Interlocked, Monitor, Mutex
System.Xml.XDocument.dll	System.Xml.Linq	XDocument, XElement, XNode

Understanding NuGet packages

.NET is split into a set of packages, distributed using a Microsoft-supported package management technology named NuGet. Each of these packages represents a single assembly of the same name. For example, the System.Collections package contains the System.Collections.dll assembly.

The following are the benefits of packages:

- Packages can be easily distributed on public feeds.
- Packages can be reused.
- Packages can ship on their own schedule.
- Packages can be tested independently of other packages.
- Packages can support different OSes and CPUs by including multiple versions of the same assembly built for different OSes and CPUs.
- Packages can have dependencies specific to only one library.
- Apps are smaller because unreferenced packages aren't part of the distribution. The following table lists some of the more important packages and their important types:

Package	Important types
System.Runtime	Object, String, Int32, Array
System.Collections	List<T>, Dictionary<TKey, TValue>
System.Net.Http	HttpClient, HttpResponseMessage
System.IO.FileSystem	File, Directory
System.Reflection	Assembly, TypeInfo, MethodInfo

Understanding frameworks

There is a two-way relationship between frameworks and packages. Packages define the APIs, while frameworks group packages. A framework without any packages would not define any APIs.

.NET packages each support a set of frameworks. For example, the System.IO.FileSystem package version 4.3.0 supports the following frameworks:

- .NET Standard, version 1.3 or later.
- .NET Framework, version 4.6 or later.
- Six Mono and Xamarin platforms (for example, Xamarin.iOS 1.0).

> **More Information**: You can read the details at the following link: https://www.nuget.org/packages/System.IO.FileSystem/.

Importing a namespace to use a type

Let's explore how namespaces are related to assemblies and types:

1. In the AssembliesAndNamespaces project, in Program.cs, enter the following code:

   ```
   XDocument doc = new();
   ```

2. Build the project and note the compiler error message, as shown in the following output:

   ```
   The type or namespace name 'XDocument' could not be found (are you missing
   a using directive or an assembly reference?)
   ```

   The XDocument type is not recognized because we have not told the compiler what the namespace of the type is. Although this project already has a reference to the assembly that contains the type, we also need to either prefix the type name with its namespace or import the namespace.

3. Click inside the XDocument class name. Your code editor displays a light bulb, showing that it recognizes the type and can automatically fix the problem for you.

4. Click the light bulb, and select using System.Xml.Linq; from the menu.

This will *import the namespace* by adding a using statement to the top of the file. Once a namespace is imported at the top of a code file, then all the types within the namespace are available for use in that code file by just typing their name without the type name needing to be fully qualified by prefixing it with its namespace.

Sometimes I like to add a comment with a type name after importing a namespace to remind me why I need to import that namespace, as shown in the following code:

```
using System.Xml.Linq; // XDocument
```

Relating C# keywords to .NET types

One of the common questions I get from new C# programmers is, "What is the difference between string with a lowercase s and String with an uppercase S?"

The short answer is easy: none. The long answer is that all C# type keywords like string or int are aliases for a .NET type in a class library assembly.

When you use the string keyword, the compiler recognizes it as a System.String type. When you use the int type, the compiler recognizes it as a System.Int32 type.

Let's see this in action with some code:

1. In Program.cs, declare two variables to hold string values, one using lowercase string and one using uppercase String, as shown in the following code:

   ```
   string s1 = "Hello";
   String s2 = "World";
   ```

```
WriteLine($"{s1} {s2}");
```

2. Run the code, and note that at the moment, they both work equally well, and literally mean the same thing.

3. In `AssembliesAndNamespaces.csproj`, add entries to prevent the `System` namespace from being globally imported, as shown in the following markup:

```
<ItemGroup>
  <Using Remove="System" />
</ItemGroup>
```

4. In `Program.cs` note the compiler error message, as shown in the following output:

```
The type or namespace name 'String' could not be found (are you missing a
using directive or an assembly reference?)
```

5. At the top of `Program.cs`, import the `System` namespace with a `using` statement that will fix the error, as shown in the following code:

```
using System; // String
```

 Good Practice: When you have a choice, use the C# keyword instead of the actual type because the keywords do not need the namespace imported.

Mapping C# aliases to .NET types

The following table shows the 18 C# type keywords along with their actual .NET types:

Keyword	.NET type	Keyword	.NET type
string	System.String	char	System.Char
sbyte	System.SByte	byte	System.Byte
short	System.Int16	ushort	System.UInt16
int	System.Int32	uint	System.UInt32
long	System.Int64	ulong	System.UInt64
nint	System.IntPtr	nuint	System.UIntPtr
float	System.Single	double	System.Double
decimal	System.Decimal	bool	System.Boolean
object	System.Object	dynamic	System.Dynamic.DynamicObject

Other .NET programming language compilers can do the same thing. For example, the Visual Basic .NET language has a type named `Integer` that is its alias for `System.Int32`.

Understanding native-sized integers

C# 9 introduced `nint` and `nuint` keyword alias for **native-sized integers**, meaning that the storage size for the integer value is platform specific. They store a 32-bit integer in a 32-bit process and `sizeof()` returns 4 bytes; they store a 64-bit integer in a 64-bit process and `sizeof()` returns 8 bytes. The aliases represent pointers to the integer value in memory, which is why their .NET names are `IntPtr` and `UIntPtr`. The actual storage type will be either `System.Int32` or `System.Int64` depending on the process.

In a 64-bit process, the following code:

```
WriteLine($"int.MaxValue = {int.MaxValue:N0}");
WriteLine($"nint.MaxValue = {nint.MaxValue:N0}");
```

produces this output:

```
int.MaxValue = 2,147,483,647
nint.MaxValue = 9,223,372,036,854,775,807
```

Revealing the location of a type

Code editors provide built-in documentation for .NET types. Let's explore:

1. Right-click inside `XDocument` and choose **Go to Definition**.
2. Navigate to the top of the code file and note the assembly filename is `System.Xml. XDocument.dll`, but the class is in the `System.Xml.Linq` namespace, as shown in *Figure 7.1*:

Figure 7.1: Assembly and namespace that contains the XDocument type

3. Close the **XDocument [from metadata]** tab.
4. Right-click inside `string` or `String` and choose **Go to Definition**.
5. Navigate to the top of the code file and note the assembly filename is `System.Runtime. dll` but the class is in the `System` namespace.

Actually, your code editor is technically lying to you. If you remember when we wrote code in *Chapter 2*, *Speaking C#*, when we revealed the extent of the C# vocabulary, we discovered that the `System.Runtime.dll` assembly contains zero types.

What it does contain are type-forwarders. These are special types that appear to exist in an assembly but actually are implemented elsewhere. In this case, they are implemented deep inside the .NET runtime using highly optimized code.

Sharing code with legacy platforms using .NET Standard

Before .NET Standard, there were **Portable Class Libraries (PCLs)**. With PCLs, you could create a library of code and explicitly specify which platforms you want the library to support, such as Xamarin, Silverlight, and Windows 8. Your library could then use the intersection of APIs that are supported by the specified platforms.

Microsoft realized that this is unsustainable, so they created .NET Standard – a single API that all future .NET platforms would support. There are older versions of .NET Standard, but .NET Standard 2.0 was an attempt to unify all important recent .NET platforms. .NET Standard 2.1 was released in late 2019 but only .NET Core 3.0 and that year's version of Xamarin support its new features. For the rest of this book, I will use the term .NET Standard to mean .NET Standard 2.0.

.NET Standard is similar to HTML5 in that they are both standards that a platform should support. Just as Google's Chrome browser and Microsoft's Edge browser implement the HTML5 standard, .NET Core, .NET Framework, and Xamarin all implement .NET Standard. If you want to create a library of types that will work across variants of legacy .NET, you can do so most easily with .NET Standard.

> **Good Practice**: Since many of the API additions in .NET Standard 2.1 required runtime changes, and .NET Framework is Microsoft's legacy platform that needs to remain as unchanging as possible, .NET Framework 4.8 remained on .NET Standard 2.0 rather than implementing .NET Standard 2.1. If you need to support .NET Framework customers, then you should create class libraries on .NET Standard 2.0 even though it is not the latest and does not support all the recent language and BCL new features.

Your choice of which .NET Standard version to target comes down to a balance between maximizing platform support and available functionality. A lower version supports more platforms but has a smaller set of APIs. A higher version supports fewer platforms but has a larger set of APIs. Generally, you should choose the lowest version that supports all the APIs that you need.

Understanding defaults for class libraries with different SDKs

When using the dotnet SDK tool to create a class library it might be useful to know which target framework will be used by default, as shown in the following table:

SDK	Default target framework for new class libraries
.NET Core 3.1	`netstandard2.0`
.NET 5	`net5.0`
.NET 6	`net6.0`

Of course, just because a class library targets a specific version of .NET by default does not mean you cannot change it after creating a class library project using the default template.

You can manually set the target framework to a value that supports the projects that need to reference that library, as shown in the following table:

Class library target framework	Can be used by projects that target
`netstandard2.0`	.NET Framework 4.6.1 or later, .NET Core 2.0 or later, .NET 5.0 or later, Mono 5.4 or later, Xamarin.Android 8.0 or later, Xamarin.iOS 10.14 or later
`netstandard2.1`	.NET Core 3.0 or later, .NET 5.0 or later, Mono 6.4 or later, Xamarin.Android 10.0 or later, Xamarin.iOS 12.16 or later
`net5.0`	.NET 5.0 or later
`net6.0`	.NET 6.0 or later

 Good Practice: Always check the target framework of a class library and then manually change it to something more appropriate if necessary. Make a conscious decision about what it should be rather than accept the default.

Creating a .NET Standard 2.0 class library

We will create a class library using .NET Standard 2.0 so that it can be used across all important .NET legacy platforms and cross-platform on Windows, macOS, and Linux operating systems, while also having access to a wide set of .NET APIs:

1. Use your preferred code editor to add a new class library named SharedLibrary to the Chapter07 solution/workspace.

2. If you use Visual Studio 2022, when prompted for the **Target Framework**, select **.NET Standard 2.0**, and then set the startup project for the solution to the current selection.

3. If you use Visual Studio Code, include a switch to target .NET Standard 2.0, as shown in the following command:

```
dotnet new classlib -f netstandard2.0
```

4. If you use Visual Studio Code, select SharedLibrary as the active OmniSharp project.

Good Practice: If you need to create types that use new features in .NET 6.0, as well as types that only use .NET Standard 2.0 features, then you can create two separate class libraries: one targeting .NET Standard 2.0 and one targeting .NET 6.0. You will see this in action in *Chapter 10, Working with Data Using Entity Framework Core*.

An alternative to manually creating two class libraries is to create one that supports multi-targeting. If you would like me to add a section about multi-targeting to the next edition, please let me know. You can read about multi-targeting here: `https://docs.microsoft.com/en-us/dotnet/standard/library-guidance/cross-platform-targeting#multi-targeting`.

Controlling the .NET SDK

By default, executing `dotnet` commands uses the most recent installed .NET SDK. There may be times when you want to control which SDK is used.

For example, one reader of the fourth edition wanted their experience to match the book steps that use the .NET Core 3.1 SDK. But they had installed the .NET 5.0 SDK as well and that was being used by default. As described in the previous section, the behavior when creating new class libraries changed to target .NET 5.0 instead of .NET Standard 2.0, and that confused the reader.

You can control the .NET SDK used by default by using a `global.json` file. The `dotnet` command searches the current folder and ancestor folders for a `global.json` file.

1. Create a subdirectory/folder in the `Chapter07` folder named `ControlSDK`.

2. On Windows, start **Command Prompt** or **Windows Terminal**. On macOS, start **Terminal**. If you are using Visual Studio Code, then you can use the integrated terminal.

3. In the `ControlSDK` folder, at the command prompt or terminal, enter a command to create a `global.json` file that forces the use of the latest .NET Core 3.1 SDK, as shown in the following command:

```
dotnet new globaljson --sdk-version 3.1.412
```

4. Open the `global.json` file and review its contents, as shown in the following markup:

```
{
  "sdk": {
    "version": "3.1.412"
  }
}
```

You can discover the version numbers of the latest .NET SDKs in the table at the following link: `https://dotnet.microsoft.com/download/visual-studio-sdks`

5. In the `ControlSDK` folder, at the command prompt or terminal, enter a command to create a class library project, as shown in the following command:

```
dotnet new classlib
```

6. If you do not have the .NET Core 3.1 SDK installed then you will see an error, as shown in the following output:

```
Could not execute because the application was not found or a compatible
.NET SDK is not installed.
```

7. If you do have the .NET Core 3.1 SDK installed, then a class library project will be created that targets .NET Standard 2.0 by default.

You do not need to complete the above steps, but if you want to try and do not already have .NET Core 3.1 SDK installed then you can install it from the following link:

```
https://dotnet.microsoft.com/download/dotnet/3.1
```

Publishing your code for deployment

If you write a novel and you want other people to read it, you must publish it.

Most developers write code for other developers to use in their own code, or for users to run as an app. To do so, you must publish your code as packaged class libraries or executable applications.

There are three ways to publish and deploy a .NET application. They are:

1. **Framework-dependent deployment (FDD).**
2. **Framework-dependent executables (FDEs).**
3. Self-contained.

If you choose to deploy your application and its package dependencies, but not .NET itself, then you rely on .NET already being on the target computer. This works well for web applications deployed to a server because .NET and lots of other web applications are likely already on the server.

Framework-dependent deployment (FDD) means you deploy a DLL that must be executed by the `dotnet` command-line tool. **Framework-dependent executables (FDE)** means you deploy an EXE that can be run directly from the command line. Both require .NET to be already installed on the system.

Sometimes, you want to be able to give someone a USB stick containing your application and know that it can execute on their computer. You want to perform a self-contained deployment. While the size of the deployment files will be larger, you'll know that it will work.

Creating a console application to publish

Let's explore how to publish a console application:

1. Use your preferred code editor to add a new console app named `DotNetEverywhere` to the `Chapter07` solution/workspace.

2. In Visual Studio Code, select `DotNetEverywhere` as the active OmniSharp project. When you see the pop-up warning message saying that required assets are missing, click **Yes** to add them.

3. In `Program.cs`, delete the comment and statically import the `Console` class.

4. In `Program.cs`, add a statement to output a message saying the console app can run everywhere and some information about the operating system, as shown in the following code:

```
WriteLine("I can run everywhere!");

WriteLine($"OS Version is {Environment.OSVersion}.");

if (OperatingSystem.IsMacOS())
{
  WriteLine("I am macOS.");
}
else if (OperatingSystem.IsWindowsVersionAtLeast(major: 10))
{
  WriteLine("I am Windows 10 or 11.");
}
else
{
  WriteLine("I am some other mysterious OS.");
}

WriteLine("Press ENTER to stop me.");
ReadLine();
```

5. Open `DotNetEverywhere.csproj` and add the runtime identifiers to target three operating systems inside the `<PropertyGroup>` element, as shown highlighted in the following markup:

```
<Project Sdk="Microsoft.NET.Sdk">

  <PropertyGroup>
    <OutputType>Exe</OutputType>
    <TargetFramework>net6.0</TargetFramework>
    <Nullable>enable</Nullable>
    <ImplicitUsings>enable</ImplicitUsings>
    <RuntimeIdentifiers>
      win10-x64;osx-x64;osx.11.0-arm64;linux-x64;linux-arm64
    </RuntimeIdentifiers>
  </PropertyGroup>

</Project>
```

- The `win10-x64` RID value means Windows 10 or Windows Server 2016 64-bit. You could also use the `win10-arm64` RID value to deploy to a Microsoft Surface Pro X.

- The `osx-x64` RID value means macOS Sierra 10.12 or later. You can also specify version-specific RID values like `osx.10.15-x64` (Catalina), `osx.11.0-x64` (Big Sur on Intel), or `osx.11.0-arm64` (Big Sur on Apple Silicon).

- The `linux-x64` RID value means most desktop distributions of Linux like Ubuntu, CentOS, Debian, or Fedora. Use `linux-arm` for Raspbian or Raspberry Pi OS 32-bit. Use `linux-arm64` for a Raspberry Pi running Ubuntu 64-bit.

Understanding dotnet commands

When you install the .NET SDK, it includes a **command-line interface (CLI)** named `dotnet`.

Creating new projects

The .NET CLI has commands that work on the current folder to create a new project using templates:

1. On Windows, start **Command Prompt** or **Windows Terminal**. On macOS, start **Terminal**. If you are using Visual Studio Code, then you can use the integrated terminal.

2. Enter the `dotnet new --list` or `dotnet new -l` command to list your currently installed templates, as shown in *Figure 7.2*:

Figure 7.2: A list of installed dotnet new project templates

 Most `dotnet` command-line switches have a long and a short version. For example, `--list` or `-l`. The short ones are quicker to type but more likely to be misinterpreted by you or other humans. Sometimes more typing is clearer.

Getting information about .NET and its environment

It is useful to see what .NET SDKs and runtimes are currently installed, alongside information about the operating system, as shown in the following command:

```
dotnet --info
```

Note the results, as shown in the following partial output:

```
.NET SDK (reflecting any global.json):
 Version:   6.0.100
 Commit:    22d70b47bc

Runtime Environment:
 OS Name:      Windows
 OS Version:   10.0.19043
 OS Platform: Windows
 RID:          win10-x64
 Base Path:    C:\Program Files\dotnet\sdk\6.0.100\

Host (useful for support):
  Version: 6.0.0
  Commit:  91ba01788d

.NET SDKs installed:
  3.1.412 [C:\Program Files\dotnet\sdk]
  5.0.400 [C:\Program Files\dotnet\sdk]
  6.0.100 [C:\Program Files\dotnet\sdk]

.NET runtimes installed:
  Microsoft.AspNetCore.All 2.1.29 [...\dotnet\shared\Microsoft.AspNetCore.All]
...
```

Managing projects

The .NET CLI has the following commands that work on the project in the current folder, to manage the project:

- `dotnet restore`: This downloads dependencies for the project.
- `dotnet build`: This builds, aka compiles, the project.
- `dotnet test`: This builds and then runs unit tests for the project.
- `dotnet run`: This builds and then runs the project.
- `dotnet pack`: This creates a NuGet package for the project.
- `dotnet publish`: This builds and then publishes the project, either with dependencies or as a self-contained application.
- `dotnet add`: This adds a reference to a package or class library to the project.
- `dotnet remove`: This removes a reference to a package or class library from the project.
- `dotnet list`: This lists the package or class library references for the project.

Publishing a self-contained app

Now that you have seen some example dotnet tool commands, we can publish our cross-platform console app:

1. At the command line, make sure that you are in the DotNetEverywhere folder.

2. Enter a command to build and publish the release version of the console application for Windows 10, as shown in the following command:

```
dotnet publish -c Release -r win10-x64
```

3. Note the build engine restores any needed packages, compiles the project source code into an assembly DLL, and creates a publish folder, as shown in the following output:

```
Microsoft (R) Build Engine version 17.0.0+073022eb4 for .NET
Copyright (C) Microsoft Corporation. All rights reserved.

  Determining projects to restore...
  Restored C:\Code\Chapter07\DotNetEverywhere\DotNetEverywhere.csproj (in
46.89 sec).
  DotNetEverywhere -> C:\Code\Chapter07\DotNetEverywhere\bin\Release\
net6.0\win10-x64\DotNetEverywhere.dll
  DotNetEverywhere -> C:\Code\Chapter07\DotNetEverywhere\bin\Release\
net6.0\win10-x64\publish\
```

4. Enter the commands to build and publish the release versions for macOS and Linux variants, as shown in the following commands:

```
dotnet publish -c Release -r osx-x64
dotnet publish -c Release -r osx.11.0-arm64
dotnet publish -c Release -r linux-x64
dotnet publish -c Release -r linux-arm64
```

 Good Practice: You could automate these commands by using a scripting language like PowerShell and execute it on any operating system using the cross-platform PowerShell Core. Just create a file with the extension .ps1 with the five commands on it. Then execute the file. Learn more about PowerShell at the following link: https://github.com/markjprice/cs10dotnet6/tree/main/docs/powershell

5. Open a macOS **Finder** window or Windows **File Explorer**, navigate to DotNetEverywhere\bin\Release\net6.0, and note the output folders for the various operating systems.

6. In the win10-x64 folder, select the publish folder, note all the supporting assemblies like Microsoft.CSharp.dll.

7. Select the DotNetEverywhere executable file, and note it is 161 KB, as shown in *Figure 7.3*:

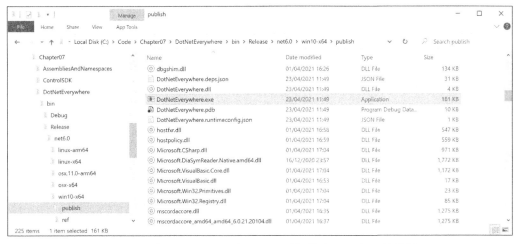

Figure 7.3: The DotNetEverywhere executable file for Windows 10 64-bit

8. If you are on Windows, then double-click to execute the program and note the result, as shown in the following output:

```
I can run everywhere!
OS Version is Microsoft Windows NT 10.0.19042.0.
I am Windows 10.
Press ENTER to stop me.
```

9. Note that the total size of the publish folder and all its files is 64.8 MB.

10. In the osx.11.0-arm64 folder, select the publish folder, note all the supporting assemblies, and then select the DotNetEverywhere executable file, and note the executable is 126 KB, and the publish folder is 71.8 MB.

If you copy any of those publish folders to the appropriate operating system, the console application will run; this is because it is a self-contained deployable .NET application. For example, on macOS with Intel, as shown in the following output:

```
I can run everywhere!
OS Version is Unix 11.2.3
I am macOS.
Press ENTER to stop me.
```

This example used a console app, but you could just as easily create an ASP.NET Core website or web service, or a Windows Forms or WPF app. Of course, you can only deploy Windows desktop apps to Windows computers, not Linux or macOS.

Publishing a single-file app

To publish as a "single" file, you can specify flags when publishing. With .NET 5, single-file apps were primarily focused on Linux because there are limitations in both Windows and macOS that mean true single-file publishing is not technically possible. With .NET 6, you can now create proper single-file apps on Windows.

If you can assume that .NET 6 is already installed on the computer on which you want to run your app, then you can use the extra flags when you publish your app for release to say that it does not need to be self-contained and that you want to publish it as a single file (if possible), as shown in the following command (that must be entered on a single line):

```
dotnet publish -r win10-x64 -c Release --self-contained=false
/p:PublishSingleFile=true
```

This will generate two files: DotNetEverywhere.exe and DotNetEverywhere.pdb. The .exe is the executable. The .pdb file is a **program debug database** file that stores debugging information.

 There is no .exe file extension for published applications on macOS, so if you use osx-x64 in the command above, the filename will not have an extension.

If you prefer the .pdb file to be embedded in the .exe file, then add a <DebugType> element to the <PropertyGroup> element in your .csproj file and set it to embedded, as shown highlighted in the following markup:

```
<PropertyGroup>

  <OutputType>Exe</OutputType>
  <TargetFramework>net6.0</TargetFramework>
  <Nullable>enable</Nullable>
  <ImplicitUsings>enable</ImplicitUsings>
  <RuntimeIdentifiers>
    win10-x64;osx-x64;osx.11.0-arm64;linux-x64;linux-arm64
  </RuntimeIdentifiers>
  <DebugType>embedded</DebugType>

</PropertyGroup>
```

If you cannot assume that .NET 6 is already installed on a computer, then although Linux also only generates the two files, expect the following additional files for Windows: coreclr.dll, clrjit.dll, clrcompression.dll, and mscordaccore.dll.

Let's see an example for Windows:

1. At the command line, enter the command to build the release version of the console application for Windows 10, as shown in the following command:

   ```
   dotnet publish -c Release -r win10-x64 /p:PublishSingleFile=true
   ```

2. Navigate to the DotNetEverywhere\bin\Release\net6.0\win10-x64\publish folder, select the DotNetEverywhere executable file, and note the executable is now 58.3 MB, and there is also a .pdb file that is 10 KB. The sizes on your system will vary.

Reducing the size of apps using app trimming

One of the problems with deploying a .NET app as a self-contained app is that the .NET libraries take up a lot of space. One of the biggest needs for reduced size is Blazor WebAssembly components because all the .NET libraries need to be downloaded to the browser.

Luckily, you can reduce this size by not packaging unused assemblies with your deployments. Introduced with .NET Core 3.0, the app trimming system can identify the assemblies needed by your code and remove those that are not needed.

With .NET 5, the trimming went further by removing individual types, and even members like methods from within an assembly if they are not used. For example, with a Hello World console app, the System.Console.dll assembly is trimmed from 61.5 KB to 31.5 KB. For .NET 5, this is an experimental feature so it is disabled by default.

With .NET 6, Microsoft added annotations to their libraries to indicate how they can be safely trimmed so the trimming of types and members was made the default. This is known as **link trim mode**.

The catch is how well the trimming identifies unused assemblies, types, and members. If your code is dynamic, perhaps using reflection, then it might not work correctly, so Microsoft also allows manual control.

Enabling assembly-level trimming

There are two ways to enable assembly-level trimming.

The first way is to add an element in the project file, as shown in the following markup:

```
<PublishTrimmed>true</PublishTrimmed>
```

The second way is to add a flag when publishing, as shown highlighted in the following command:

```
dotnet publish ... -p:PublishTrimmed=True
```

Enabling type-level and member-level trimming

There are two ways to enable type-level and member-level trimming.

The first way is to add two elements in the project file, as shown in the following markup:

```
<PublishTrimmed>true</PublishTrimmed>
<TrimMode>Link</TrimMode>
```

The second way is to add two flags when publishing, as shown highlighted in the following command:

```
dotnet publish ... -p:PublishTrimmed=True -p:TrimMode=Link
```

For .NET 6, link trim mode is the default, so you only need to specify the switch if you want to set an alternative trim mode like `copyused`, which means assembly-level trimming.

Decompiling .NET assemblies

One of the best ways to learn how to code for .NET is to see how professionals do it.

 Good Practice: You could decompile someone else's assemblies for non-learning purposes like copying their code for use in your own production library or application, but remember that you are viewing their intellectual property, so please respect that.

Decompiling using the ILSpy extension for Visual Studio 2022

For learning purposes, you can decompile any .NET assembly with a tool like ILSpy.

1. In Visual Studio 2022 for Windows, navigate to **Extensions** | **Manage Extensions**.
2. In the search box, enter `ilspy`.
3. For the **ILSpy** extension, click **Download**.
4. Click **Close**.
5. Close Visual Studio to allow the extension to install.
6. Restart Visual Studio and reopen the `Chapter07` solution.
7. In **Solution Explorer**, right-click the **DotNetEverywhere** project and select **Open output in ILSpy**.
8. Navigate to **File** | **Open...**.
9. Navigate to the following folder:

    `Code/Chapter07/DotNetEverywhere/bin/Release/net6.0/linux-x64`

10. Select the `System.IO.FileSystem.dll` assembly and click **Open**.
11. In the **Assemblies** tree, expand the **System.IO.FileSystem** assembly, expand the **System.IO** namespace, select the **Directory** class, and wait for it to decompile.
12. In the `Directory` class, click the **[+]** to expand the `GetParent` method, as shown in *Figure 7.4*:

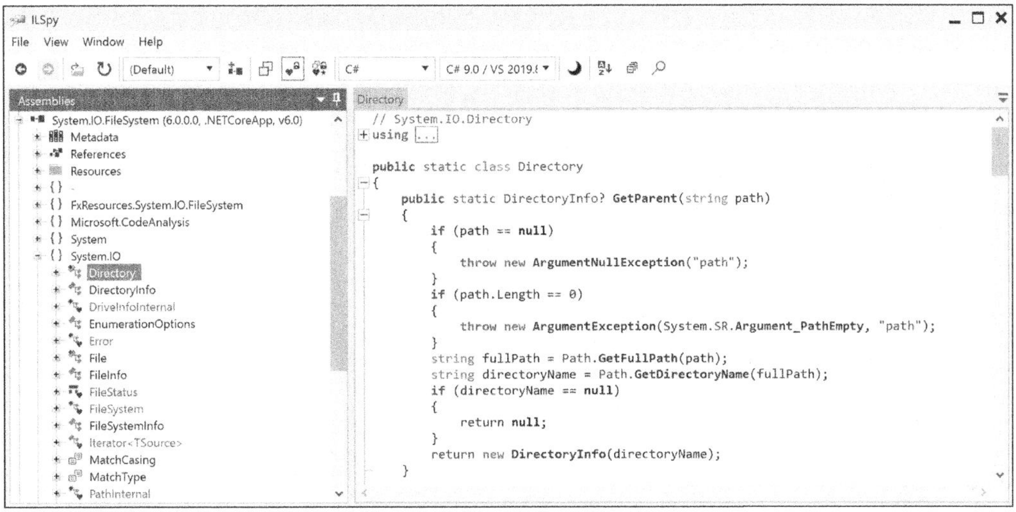

Figure 7.4: Decompiled GetParent method of Directory class on Windows

13. Note the good practice of checking the path parameter and throwing an ArgumentNullException if it is null or an ArgumentException if it is zero length.

14. Close ILSpy.

Decompiling using the ILSpy extension for Visual Studio Code

A similar capability is available cross-platform as an extension for Visual Studio Code.

1. If you have not already installed the **ILSpy .NET Decompiler** extension for Visual Studio Code, then search for it and install it now.

2. On macOS or Linux the extension has a dependency on Mono so you will also need to install Mono from the following link: https://www.mono-project.com/download/stable/.

3. In Visual Studio Code, navigate to **View** | **Command Palette...**.

4. Type ilspy and then select **ILSpy: Decompile IL Assembly (pick file)**.

5. Navigate to the following folder:

```
Code/Chapter07/DotNetEverywhere/bin/Release/net6.0/linux-x64
```

6. Select the `System.IO.FileSystem.dll` assembly and click **Select assembly**. Nothing will appear to happen, but you can confirm that ILSpy is working by viewing the **Output** window, selecting **ilspy-vscode** in the dropdown list, and seeing the processing, as shown in *Figure 7.5*:

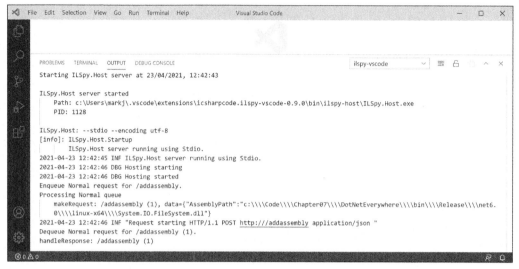

Figure 7.5: ILSpy extension output when selecting an assembly to decompile

7. In **EXPLORER**, expand **ILSPY DECOMPILED MEMBERS**, select the assembly, close the **Output** window, and note the two edit windows that open showing assembly attributes using C# code and external DLL and assembly references using IL code, as shown in *Figure 7.6*:

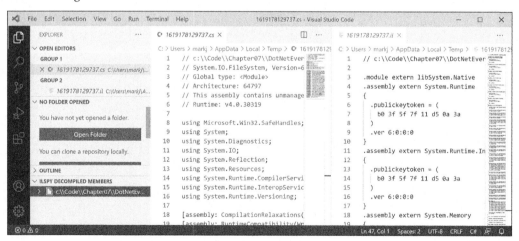

Figure 7.6: Expanding ILSPY DECOMPILED MEMBERS

8. In the IL code on the right side, note the reference to the `System.Runtime` assembly, including the version number, as shown in the following code:

```
.module extern libSystem.Native
.assembly extern System.Runtime
{
  .publickeytoken = (
    b0 3f 5f 7f 11 d5 0a 3a
  )
  .ver 6:0:0:0
}
```

`.module extern libSystem.Native` means this assembly makes function calls to Linux system APIs as you would expect from code that interacts with the filesystem. If we had decompiled the Windows equivalent of this assembly, it would use `.module extern kernel32.dll` instead, which is a Win32 API.

9. In **EXPLORER**, in **ILSPY DECOMPILED MEMBERS**, expand the assembly, expand the **System.IO** namespace, select **Directory**, and note the two edit windows that open showing the decompiled `Directory` class using C# code on the left and IL code on the right, as shown in *Figure 7.7*:

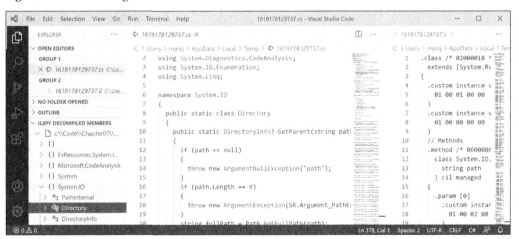

Figure 7.7: The decompiled Directory class in C# and IL code

10. Compare the C# source code for the `GetParent` method, shown in the following code:

```
public static DirectoryInfo? GetParent(string path)
{
  if (path == null)
  {
    throw new ArgumentNullException("path");
  }
  if (path.Length == 0)
  {
    throw new ArgumentException(SR.Argument_PathEmpty, "path");
  }
  string fullPath = Path.GetFullPath(path);
```

```
    string directoryName = Path.GetDirectoryName(fullPath);
    if (directoryName == null)
    {
      return null;
    }
    return new DirectoryInfo(directoryName);
  }
```

11. With the equivalent IL source code of the GetParent method, as shown in the following code:

```
.method /* 06000067 */ public hidebysig static
  class System.IO.DirectoryInfo GetParent (
    string path
  ) cil managed
{
  .param [0]
    .custom instance void System.Runtime.CompilerServices
    .NullableAttribute::.ctor(uint8) = (
      01 00 02 00 00
    )
  // Method begins at RVA 0x62d4
  // Code size 64 (0x40)
  .maxstack 2
  .locals /* 1100000E */ (
    [0] string,
    [1] string
  )

  IL_0000: ldarg.0
  IL_0001: brtrue.s IL_000e

  IL_0003: ldstr "path" /* 700005CB */
  IL_0008: newobj instance void [System.Runtime]
    System.ArgumentNullException::.ctor(string) /* 0A000035 */
  IL_000d: throw

  IL_000e: ldarg.0
  IL_000f: callvirt instance int32 [System.Runtime]
    System.String::get_Length() /* 0A000022 */
  IL_0014: brtrue.s IL_0026
  IL_0016: call string System.SR::get_Argument_PathEmpty() /* 0600004C */
  IL_001b: ldstr "path" /* 700005CB */
  IL_0020: newobj instance void [System.Runtime]
    System.ArgumentException::.ctor(string, string) /* 0A000036 */
  IL_0025: throw IL_0026: ldarg.0
```

```
IL_0027: call string [System.Runtime.Extensions]
  System.IO.Path::GetFullPath(string) /* 0A000037 */
IL_002c: stloc.0 IL_002d: ldloc.0
IL_002e: call string [System.Runtime.Extensions]
  System.IO.Path::GetDirectoryName(string) /* 0A000038 */
IL_0033: stloc.1
IL_0034: ldloc.1
IL_0035: brtrue.s IL_0039 IL_0037: ldnull
IL_0038: ret IL_0039: ldloc.1
IL_003a: newobj instance void
  System.IO.DirectoryInfo::.ctor(string) /* 06000097 */
IL_003f: ret
} // end of method Directory::GetParent
```

> **Good Practice**: The IL code edit windows are not especially useful unless you get very advanced with C# and .NET development when knowing how the C# compiler translates your source code into IL code can be important. The much more useful edit windows contain the equivalent C# source code written by Microsoft experts. You can learn a lot of good practices from seeing how professionals implement types. For example, the GetParent method shows how to check arguments for null and other argument exceptions.

12. Close the edit windows without saving changes.

13. In **EXPLORER**, in **ILSPY DECOMPILED MEMBERS**, right-click the assembly and choose **Unload Assembly**.

No, you cannot technically prevent decompilation

I sometimes get asked if there is a way to protect compiled code to prevent decompilation. The quick answer is no, and if you think about it, you'll see why this has to be the case. You can make it harder using obfuscation tools like **Dotfuscator**, but ultimately you cannot completely prevent it.

All compiled applications contain instructions to the platform, operating system, and hardware on which it runs. Those instructions have to be functionally the same as the original source code but are just harder for a human to read. Those instructions must be readable to execute your code; they therefore must be readable to be decompiled. If you protect your code from decompilation using some custom technique, then you would also prevent your code from running!

Virtual machines simulate hardware and so can capture all interaction between your running application and the software and hardware that it thinks it is running on.

If you could protect your code, then you would also prevent attaching to it with a debugger and stepping through it. If the compiled application has a pdb file, then you can attach a debugger and step through the statements line-by-line. Even without the pdb file, you can still attach a debugger and get some idea of how the code works.

This is true for all programming languages. Not just .NET languages like C#, Visual Basic, and F#, but also C, C++, Delphi, assembly language: all can be attached to for debugging or to be disassembled or decompiled. Some tools used by professionals are shown in the following table:

Type	Product	Description
Virtual Machine	VMware	Professionals like malware analysts always run software inside a VM.
Debugger	SoftICE	Runs underneath the operating system usually in a VM.
Debugger	WinDbg	Useful for understanding Windows internals because it knows more about Windows data structures than other debuggers.
Disassembler	IDA Pro	Used by professional malware analysts.
Decompiler	HexRays	Decompiles C apps. Plugin for IDA Pro.
Decompiler	DeDe	Decompiles Delphi apps.
Decompiler	dotPeek	.NET decompiler from JetBrains.

 Good Practice: Debugging, disassembling, and decompiling someone else's software is likely against its license agreement and illegal in many jurisdictions. Instead of trying to protect your intellectual property with a technical solution, the law is sometimes your only recourse.

Packaging your libraries for NuGet distribution

Before we learn how to create and package our own libraries, we will review how a project can use an existing package.

Referencing a NuGet package

Let's say that you want to add a package created by a third-party developer, for example, Newtonsoft.Json, a popular package for working with the JavaScript Object Notation (JSON) serialization format:

1. In the AssembliesAndNamespaces project, add a reference to the Newtonsoft.Json NuGet package, either using the GUI for Visual Studio 2022 or the dotnet add package command for Visual Studio Code.

2. Open the AssembliesAndNamespaces.csproj file and note that a package reference has been added, as shown in the following markup:

```
<ItemGroup>
  <PackageReference Include="newtonsoft.json" Version="13.0.1" />
</ItemGroup>
```

If you have a more recent version of the newtonsoft.json package, then it has been updated since this chapter was written.

Fixing dependencies

To consistently restore packages and write reliable code, it's important that you **fix dependencies**. Fixing dependencies means you are using the same family of packages released for a specific version of .NET, for example, SQLite for .NET 6.0, as shown highlighted in the following markup:

```
<Project Sdk="Microsoft.NET.Sdk">

  <PropertyGroup>
    <OutputType>Exe</OutputType>
    <TargetFramework>net6.0</TargetFramework>
  </PropertyGroup>

  <ItemGroup>
    <PackageReference
      Include="Microsoft.EntityFrameworkCore.Sqlite"
      Version="6.0.0" />
  </ItemGroup>

</Project>
```

To fix dependencies, every package should have a single version with no additional qualifiers. Additional qualifiers include betas (beta1), release candidates (rc4), and wildcards (*).

Wildcards allow future versions to be automatically referenced and used because they always represent the most recent release. But wildcards are therefore dangerous because they could result in the use of future incompatible packages that break your code.

This can be worth the risk while writing a book where new preview versions are released every month and you do not want to keep updating the package references, as I did during 2021, and as shown in the following markup:

```
<PackageReference
  Include="Microsoft.EntityFrameworkCore.Sqlite"
  Version="6.0.0-preview.*" />
```

If you use the dotnet add package command, or Visual Studio's **Manage NuGet Packages**, then it will by default use the latest specific version of a package. But if you copy and paste configuration from a blog article or manually add a reference yourself, you might include wildcard qualifiers.

The following dependencies are examples of NuGet package references that are *not* fixed and therefore should be avoided unless you know the implications:

```
<PackageReference Include="System.Net.Http" Version="4.1.0-*" />
<PackageReference Include="Newtonsoft.Json" Version="12.0.3-beta1" />
```

 Good Practice: Microsoft guarantees that if you fixed your dependencies to what ships with a specific version of .NET, for example, 6.0.0, those packages will all work together. Almost always fix your dependencies.

Packaging a library for NuGet

Now, let's package the SharedLibrary project that you created earlier:

1. In the SharedLibrary project, rename the Class1.cs file to StringExtensions.cs.

2. Modify its contents to provide some useful extension methods for validating various text values using regular expressions, as shown in the following code:

```
using System.Text.RegularExpressions;

namespace Packt.Shared
{
  public static class StringExtensions
  {
    public static bool IsValidXmlTag(this string input)
    {
      return Regex.IsMatch(input,
        @"^<([a-z]+)([^<]+)*(?:>(.*)<\/\1>|\s+\/>)$");
    }

    public static bool IsValidPassword(this string input)
    {
      // minimum of eight valid characters
      return Regex.IsMatch(input, "^[a-zA-Z0-9_-]{8,}$");
    }

    public static bool IsValidHex(this string input)
    {
      // three or six valid hex number characters
      return Regex.IsMatch(input,
        "^#?([a-fA-F0-9]{3}|[a-fA-F0-9]{6})$");
    }
  }
}
```

You will learn how to write regular expressions in *Chapter 8, Working with Common .NET Types.*

3. In `SharedLibrary.csproj`, modify its contents, as shown highlighted in the following markup, and note the following:

    *   `PackageId` must be globally unique, so you must use a different value if you want to publish this NuGet package to the `https://www.nuget.org/` public feed for others to reference and download.

    *   `PackageLicenseExpression` must be a value from the following link: `https://spdx.org/licenses/` or you could specify a custom license.

    *   All the other elements are self-explanatory:

```xml
<Project Sdk="Microsoft.NET.Sdk">

  <PropertyGroup>
    <TargetFramework>netstandard2.0</TargetFramework>

    <GeneratePackageOnBuild>true</GeneratePackageOnBuild>
    <PackageId>Packt.CSdotnet.SharedLibrary</PackageId>
    <PackageVersion>6.0.0.0</PackageVersion>
    <Title>C# 10 and .NET 6 Shared Library</Title>
    <Authors>Mark J Price</Authors>
    <PackageLicenseExpression>
      MS-PL
    </PackageLicenseExpression>
    <PackageProjectUrl>
      https://github.com/markjprice/cs10dotnet6
    </PackageProjectUrl>
    <PackageIcon>packt-csdotnet-sharedlibrary.png</PackageIcon>
    <PackageRequireLicenseAcceptance>true</PackageRequireLicenseAcceptance>
    <PackageReleaseNotes>
      Example shared library packaged for NuGet.
    </PackageReleaseNotes>
    <Description>
      Three extension methods to validate a string value.
    </Description>
    <Copyright>
      Copyright © 2016-2021 Packt Publishing Limited
    </Copyright>
    <PackageTags>string extensions packt csharp dotnet</PackageTags>

  </PropertyGroup>

  <ItemGroup>
    <None Include="packt-csdotnet-sharedlibrary.png">
```

```
        <Pack>True</Pack>
        <PackagePath></PackagePath>
      </None>
    </ItemGroup>

  </Project>
```

> **Good Practice**: Configuration property values that are
> true or false values cannot have any whitespace so the
> `<PackageRequireLicenseAcceptance>` entry cannot have a
> carriage return and indentation as shown in the preceding markup.

4. Download the icon file and save it in the `SharedLibrary` folder from the following link: `https://github.com/markjprice/cs10dotnet6/blob/main/vs4win/Chapter07/SharedLibrary/packt-csdotnet-sharedlibrary.png`.

5. Build the release assembly:

    1. In Visual Studio, select **Release** in the toolbar, and then navigate to **Build | Build SharedLibrary**.

    2. In Visual Studio Code, in **Terminal**, enter `dotnet build -c Release`

6. If we had not set `<GeneratePackageOnBuild>` to true in the project file, then we would have to create a NuGet package manually using the following additional steps:

    1. In Visual Studio, navigate to **Build | Pack SharedLibrary**.

    2. In Visual Studio Code, in **Terminal**, enter `dotnet pack -c Release`.

Publishing a package to a public NuGet feed

If you want everyone to be able to download and use your NuGet package, then you must upload it to a public NuGet feed like Microsoft's:

1. Start your favorite browser and navigate to the following link: `https://www.nuget.org/packages/manage/upload`.

2. You will need to sign in with a Microsoft account at `https://www.nuget.org/` if you want to upload a NuGet package for other developers to reference as a dependency package.

3. Click on **Browse...** and select the `.nupkg` file that was created by generating the NuGet package. The folder path should be `Code\Chapter07\SharedLibrary\bin\Release` and the file is named `Packt.CSdotnet.SharedLibrary.6.0.0.nupkg`.

4. Verify that the information you entered in the `SharedLibrary.csproj` file has been correctly filled in, and then click **Submit**.

5. Wait a few seconds, and you will see a success message showing that your package has been uploaded, as shown in *Figure 7.8*:

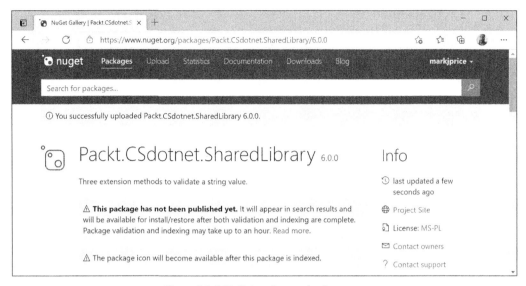

Figure 7.8: A NuGet package upload message

 Good Practice: If you get an error, then review the project file for mistakes, or read more information about the PackageReference format at https:// docs.microsoft.com/en-us/nuget/reference/msbuild-targets.

Publishing a package to a private NuGet feed

Organizations can host their own private NuGet feeds. This can be a handy way for many developer teams to share work. You can read more at the following link:

https://docs.microsoft.com/en-us/nuget/hosting-packages/overview

Exploring NuGet packages with a tool

A handy tool named **NuGet Package Explorer** for opening and reviewing more details about a NuGet package was created by Uno Platform. As well as being a website, it can be installed as a cross-platform app. Let's see what it can do:

1. Start your favorite browser and navigate to the following link: https://nuget.info.
2. In the search box, enter Packt.CSdotnet.SharedLibrary.
3. Select the package **v6.0.0** published by **Mark J Price** and then click the **Open** button.
4. In the **Contents** section, expand the **lib** folder and the **netstandard2.0** folder.

5. Select **SharedLibrary.dll**, and note the details, as shown in *Figure 7.9*:

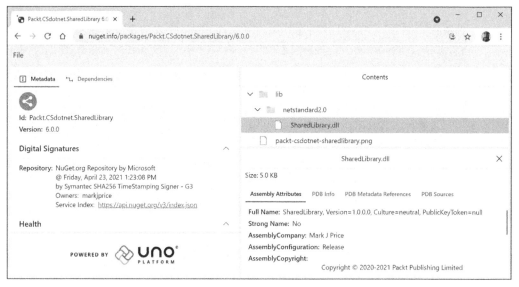

Figure 7.9: Exploring my package using NuGet Package Explorer from Uno Platform

6. If you want to use this tool locally in the future, click the install button in your browser.

7. Close your browser.

 Not all browsers support installing web apps like this. I recommend Chrome for testing and development.

Testing your class library package

You will now test your uploaded package by referencing it in the AssembliesAndNamespaces project:

1. In the AssembliesAndNamespaces project, add a reference to your (or my) package, as shown highlighted in the following markup:

```
<ItemGroup>
  <PackageReference Include="newtonsoft.json" Version="13.0.1" />
  <PackageReference Include="packt.csdotnet.sharedlibrary"
    Version="6.0.0" />
</ItemGroup>
```

2. Build the console app.

3. In Program.cs, import the Packt.Shared namespace.

4. In `Program.cs`, prompt the user to enter some `string` values, and then validate them using the extension methods in the package, as shown in the following code:

```
Write("Enter a color value in hex: ");
string? hex = ReadLine(); // or "00ffc8"
WriteLine("Is {0} a valid color value? {1}",
  arg0: hex, arg1: hex.IsValidHex());

Write("Enter a XML element: ");
string? xmlTag = ReadLine(); // or "<h1 class=\"<\" />"
WriteLine("Is {0} a valid XML element? {1}",
  arg0: xmlTag, arg1: xmlTag.IsValidXmlTag());

Write("Enter a password: ");
string? password = ReadLine(); // or "secretsauce"
WriteLine("Is {0} a valid password? {1}",
  arg0: password, arg1: password.IsValidPassword());
```

5. Run the code, enter some values as prompted, and view the results, as shown in the following output:

```
Enter a color value in hex: 00ffc8
Is 00ffc8 a valid color value? True
Enter an XML element: <h1 class="<" />
Is <h1 class="<" /> a valid XML element? False
Enter a password: secretsauce
Is secretsauce a valid password? True
```

Porting from .NET Framework to modern .NET

If you are an existing .NET Framework developer, then you may have existing applications that you think you should port to modern .NET. But you should carefully consider if porting is the right choice for your code, because sometimes, the best choice is not to port.

For example, you might have a complex website project that runs on .NET Framework 4.8 but is only visited by a small number of users. If it works and handles the visitor traffic on minimal hardware, then potentially spending months porting it to .NET 6 could be a waste of time. But if the website currently requires many expensive Windows servers, then the cost of porting could eventually pay off if you can migrate to fewer, less costly Linux servers.

Could you port?

Modern .NET has great support for the following types of applications on Windows, macOS, and Linux so they are good candidates for porting:

- **ASP.NET Core MVC** websites.
- **ASP.NET Core Web API** web services (REST/HTTP).

- **ASP.NET Core SignalR** services.
- **Console application** command-line interfaces.

Modern .NET has decent support for the following types of applications on Windows, so they are potential candidates for porting:

- **Windows Forms** applications.
- **Windows Presentation Foundation (WPF)** applications.

Modern .NET has good support for the following types of applications on cross-platform desktop and mobile devices:

- **Xamarin** apps for mobile iOS and Android.
- **.NET MAUI** for desktop Windows and macOS, or mobile iOS and Android.

Modern .NET does not support the following types of legacy Microsoft projects:

- **ASP.NET Web Forms** websites. These might be best reimplemented using **ASP.NET Core Razor Pages** or **Blazor**.
- **Windows Communication Foundation (WCF)** services (but there is an open-source project named **CoreWCF** that you might be able to use depending on requirements). WCF services might be better reimplemented using **ASP.NET Core gRPC** services.
- **Silverlight** applications. These might be best reimplemented using **.NET MAUI**.

Silverlight and ASP.NET Web Forms applications will never be able to be ported to modern .NET, but existing Windows Forms and WPF applications could be ported to .NET on Windows in order to benefit from the new APIs and faster performance.

Legacy ASP.NET MVC web applications and ASP.NET Web API web services currently on .NET Framework could be ported to modern .NET and then be hosted on Windows, Linux, or macOS.

Should you port?

Even if you *could* port, *should* you? What benefits do you gain? Some common benefits include the following:

- **Deployment to Linux, Docker, or Kubernetes for websites and web services**: These OSes are lightweight and cost-effective as website and web service platforms, especially when compared to the more costly Windows Server.
- **Removal of dependency on IIS and System.Web.dll**: Even if you continue to deploy to Windows Server, ASP.NET Core can be hosted on lightweight, higher-performance Kestrel (or other) web servers.
- **Command-line tools**: Tools that developers and administrators use to automate their tasks are often built as console applications. The ability to run a single tool cross-platform is very useful.

Differences between .NET Framework and modern .NET

There are three key differences, as shown in the following table:

Modern .NET	.NET Framework
Distributed as NuGet packages, so each application can be deployed with its own app-local copy of the version of .NET that it needs.	Distributed as a system-wide, shared set of assemblies (literally, in the Global Assembly Cache (GAC)).
Split into small, layered components, so a minimal deployment can be performed.	Single, monolithic deployment.
Removes older technologies, such as ASP.NET Web Forms, and non-cross-platform features, such as AppDomains, .NET Remoting, and binary serialization.	As well as some similar technologies to those in modern .NET like ASP.NET Core MVC, it also retains some older technologies, such as ASP.NET Web Forms.

Understanding the .NET Portability Analyzer

Microsoft has a useful tool that you can run against your existing applications to generate a report for porting. You can watch a demonstration of the tool at the following link: `https://channel9.msdn.com/Blogs/Seth-Juarez/A-Brief-Look-at-the-NET-Portability-Analyzer`.

Understanding the .NET Upgrade Assistant

Microsoft's latest tool for upgrading legacy projects to modern .NET is the .NET Upgrade Assistant.

For my day job, I work for a company named Optimizely. We have an enterprise-scale Digital Experience Platform (DXP) based on .NET Framework comprising a Content Management System (CMS) and for building digital commerce websites. Microsoft needed a challenging migration project to design and test the .NET Upgrade Assistant with, so we worked with them to build a great tool.

Currently, it supports the following .NET Framework project types and more will be added later:

- ASP.NET MVC
- Windows Forms
- WPF
- Console Application
- Class Library

It is installed as a global `dotnet` tool, as shown in the following command:

```
dotnet tool install -g upgrade-assistant
```

You can read more about this tool and how to use it at the following link:

`https://docs.microsoft.com/en-us/dotnet/core/porting/upgrade-assistant-overview`

Using non-.NET Standard libraries

Most existing NuGet packages can be used with modern .NET, even if they are not compiled for .NET Standard or a modern version like .NET 6. If you find a package that does not officially support .NET Standard, as shown on its `nuget.org` web page, you do not have to give up. You should try it and see if it works.

For example, there is a package of custom collections for handling matrices created by Dialect Software LLC, documented at the following link:

`https://www.nuget.org/packages/DialectSoftware.Collections.Matrix/`

This package was last updated in 2013, which was long before .NET Core or .NET 6 existed, so this package was built for .NET Framework. As long as an assembly package like this only uses APIs available in .NET Standard, it can be used in a modern .NET project.

Let's try using it and see if it works:

1. In the `AssembliesAndNamespaces` project, add a package reference for Dialect Software's package, as shown in the following markup:

   ```
   <PackageReference
     Include="dialectsoftware.collections.matrix"
     Version="1.0.0" />
   ```

2. Build the `AssembliesAndNamespaces` project to restore packages.

3. In `Program.cs`, add statements to import the `DialectSoftware.Collections` and `DialectSoftware.Collections.Generics` namespaces.

4. Add statements to create instances of `Axis` and `Matrix<T>`, populate them with values, and output them, as shown in the following code:

   ```
   Axis x = new("x", 0, 10, 1);
   Axis y = new("y", 0, 4, 1);

   Matrix<long> matrix = new(new[] { x, y });

   for (int i = 0; i < matrix.Axes[0].Points.Length; i++)
   {
     matrix.Axes[0].Points[i].Label = "x" + i.ToString();
   }

   for (int i = 0; i < matrix.Axes[1].Points.Length; i++)
   {
   ```

```
    matrix.Axes[1].Points[i].Label = "y" + i.ToString();
}

foreach (long[] c in matrix)
{
  matrix[c] = c[0] + c[1];
}

foreach (long[] c in matrix)
{
  WriteLine("{0},{1} ({2},{3}) = {4}",
    matrix.Axes[0].Points[c[0]].Label,
    matrix.Axes[1].Points[c[1]].Label,
    c[0], c[1], matrix[c]);
}
```

5. Run the code, noting the warning message and the results, as shown in the following output:

```
warning NU1701: Package 'DialectSoftware.Collections.Matrix
1.0.0' was restored using '.NETFramework,Version=v4.6.1,
.NETFramework,Version=v4.6.2, .NETFramework,Version=v4.7,
.NETFramework,Version=v4.7.1, .NETFramework,Version=v4.7.2,
.NETFramework,Version=v4.8' instead of the project target framework
'net6.0'. This package may not be fully compatible with your project.
x0,y0 (0,0) = 0
x0,y1 (0,1) = 1
x0,y2 (0,2) = 2
x0,y3 (0,3) = 3
...
```

Even though this package was created before .NET 6 existed, and the compiler and runtime have no way of knowing if it will work and therefore show warnings, because it happens to only call .NET Standard-compatible APIs, it works.

Working with preview features

It is a challenge for Microsoft to deliver some new features that have cross-cutting effects across many parts of .NET like the runtime, language compilers, and API libraries. It is the classic chicken and egg problem. What do you do first?

From a practical perspective, it means that although Microsoft might have completed the majority of the work needed for a feature, the whole thing might not be ready until very late in their now annual cycle of .NET releases, too late for proper testing in "the wild."

So, from .NET 6 onward, Microsoft will include preview features in **general availability (GA)** releases. Developers can opt into these preview features and provide Microsoft with feedback. In a later GA release, they can be enabled for everyone.

 Good Practice: Preview features are not supported in production code. Preview features are likely to have breaking changes before the final release. Enable preview features at your own risk.

Requiring preview features

The [RequiresPreviewFeatures] attribute is used to indicate assemblies, types, or members that use and therefore require warnings about preview features. A code analyzer then scans for this assembly and generates warnings if needed. If your code does not use any preview features, you will not see any warnings. If you use any preview features, then your code should warn consumers of your code that you use preview features.

Enabling preview features

Let's look at an example of a preview feature available in .NET 6, the ability to define an interface with a static abstract method:

1. Use your preferred code editor to add a new console app named UsingPreviewFeatures to the Chapter07 solution/workspace.

2. In Visual Studio Code, select UsingPreviewFeatures as the active OmniSharp project. When you see the pop-up warning message saying that required assets are missing, click **Yes** to add them.

3. In the project file, add an element to enable preview features and an element to enable preview language features, as shown highlighted in the following markup:

```
<Project Sdk="Microsoft.NET.Sdk">

  <PropertyGroup>
    <OutputType>Exe</OutputType>
    <TargetFramework>net6.0</TargetFramework>
    <Nullable>enable</Nullable>
    <ImplicitUsings>enable</ImplicitUsings>
    <EnablePreviewFeatures>true</EnablePreviewFeatures>
    <LangVersion>preview</LangVersion>
  </PropertyGroup>

</Project>
```

4. In Program.cs, delete the comment and statically import the Console class.

5. Add statements to define an interface with a static abstract method, a class that implements it, and then call the method in the top-level program, as shown in the following code:

```
using static System.Console;

Doer.DoSomething();

public interface IWithStaticAbstract
{
  static abstract void DoSomething();
}

public class Doer : IWithStaticAbstract
{
  public static void DoSomething()
  {
    WriteLine("I am an implementation of a static abstract method.");
  }
}
```

6. Run the console app and note that it outputs correctly.

Generic mathematics

Why has Microsoft added the ability to define static abstract methods? What are they useful for?

For a long time, developers have asked Microsoft for the ability to use operators like * on generic types. This would enable a developer to define mathematical methods to perform operations like adding, averaging, and so on to any generic type rather than having to create dozens of overloaded methods for all the numeric types they want to support. Support for static abstract methods in interfaces is a foundational feature that would enable generic mathematics.

If you are interested, you can read more about this at the following link:

https://devblogs.microsoft.com/dotnet/preview-features-in-net-6-generic-math/

Practicing and exploring

Test your knowledge and understanding by answering some questions, getting some hands-on practice, and exploring with deeper research into topics of this chapter.

Exercise 7.1 – Test your knowledge

Answer the following questions:

1. What is the difference between a namespace and an assembly?
2. How do you reference another project in a `.csproj` file?
3. What is the benefit of a tool like ILSpy?
4. Which .NET type does the C# `float` alias represent?
5. When porting an application from .NET Framework to .NET 6, what tool should you run before porting, and what tool could you run to perform much of the porting work?
6. What is the difference between framework-dependent and self-contained deployments of .NET applications?
7. What is a RID?
8. What is the difference between the `dotnet pack` and `dotnet publish` commands?
9. What types of applications written for the .NET Framework can be ported to modern .NET?
10. Can you use packages written for .NET Framework with modern .NET?

Exercise 7.2 – Explore topics

Use the links on the following page to learn more detail about the topics covered in this chapter:

```
https://github.com/markjprice/cs10dotnet6/blob/main/book-links.md#chapter-7---
understanding-and-packaging-net-types
```

Exercise 7.3 – Explore PowerShell

PowerShell is Microsoft's scripting language for automating tasks on every operating system. Microsoft recommends Visual Studio Code with the PowerShell extension for writing PowerShell scripts.

Since PowerShell is its own extensive language there is not space in this book to cover it. Instead, I have created some supplementary pages on the books GitHub repository to introduce you to some key concepts and show some examples:

```
https://github.com/markjprice/cs10dotnet6/tree/main/docs/powershell
```

Summary

In this chapter, we reviewed the journey to .NET 6, we explored the relationship between assemblies and namespaces, we saw options for publishing an app for distribution to multiple operating systems, packaged and distributed a class library, and we discussed options for porting existing .NET Framework code bases.

In the next chapter, you will learn about some common Base Class Library types that are included with modern .NET.

08

Working with Common .NET Types

This chapter is about some common types that are included with .NET. These include types for manipulating numbers, text, collections, network access, reflection, and attributes; improving working with spans, indexes, and ranges; manipulating images; and internationalization.

This chapter covers the following topics:

- Working with numbers
- Working with text
- Working with dates and times
- Pattern matching with regular expressions
- Storing multiple objects in collections
- Working with spans, indexes, and ranges
- Working with network resources
- Working with reflection and attributes
- Working with images
- Internationalizing your code

Working with numbers

One of the most common types of data is numbers. The most common types in .NET for working with numbers are shown in the following table:

Namespace	Example type(s)	Description
System	SByte, Int16, Int32, Int64	Integers; that is, zero and positive and negative whole numbers
System	Byte, UInt16, UInt32, UInt64	Cardinals; that is, zero and positive whole numbers
System	Half, Single, Double	Reals; that is, floating-point numbers
System	Decimal	Accurate reals; that is, for use in science, engineering, or financial scenarios
System.Numerics	BigInteger, Complex, Quaternion	Arbitrarily large integers, complex numbers, and quaternion numbers

.NET has had the 32-bit float and 64-bit double types since .NET Framework 1.0. The IEEE 754 specification also defines a 16-bit floating point standard. Machine learning and other algorithms would benefit from this smaller, lower-precision number type so Microsoft introduced the System.Half type with .NET 5 and later.

Currently, the C# language does not define a half alias so you must use the .NET type System. Half. This might change in the future.

Working with big integers

The largest whole number that can be stored in .NET types that have a C# alias is about eighteen and a half quintillion, stored in an unsigned long integer. But what if you need to store numbers larger than that?

Let's explore numerics:

1.   Use your preferred code editor to create a new solution/workspace named Chapter08.

2.   Add a console app project, as defined in the following list:

    1.   Project template: **Console Application** / console

    2.   Workspace/solution file and folder: Chapter08

    3.   Project file and folder: WorkingWithNumbers

3.   In Program.cs, delete the existing statements and add a statement to import System. Numerics, as shown in the following code:

    ```
    using System.Numerics;
    ```

4.   Add statements to output the maximum value of the ulong type, and a number with 30 digits using BigInteger, as shown in the following code:

```
WriteLine("Working with large integers:");
WriteLine("---------------------------------");

ulong big = ulong.MaxValue;
WriteLine($"{big,40:N0}");

BigInteger bigger =
  BigInteger.Parse("123456789012345678901234567890");

WriteLine($"{bigger,40:N0}");
```

The `40` in the format code means right-align 40 characters, so both numbers are lined up to the right-hand edge. The `N0` means use thousand separators and zero decimal places.

5. Run the code and view the result, as shown in the following output:

```
Working with large integers:
----------------------------------------
             18,446,744,073,709,551,615
 123,456,789,012,345,678,901,234,567,890
```

Working with complex numbers

A complex number can be expressed as $a + bi$, where a and b are real numbers, and i is an imaginary unit, where $i^2 = -1$. If the real part a is zero, it is a pure imaginary number. If the imaginary part b is zero, it is a real number.

Complex numbers have practical applications in many **STEM (science, technology, engineering, and mathematics)** fields of study. Additionally, they are added by separately adding the real and imaginary parts of the summands; consider this:

```
(a + bi) + (c + di) = (a + c) + (b + d)i
```

Let's explore complex numbers:

1. In `Program.cs`, add statements to add two complex numbers, as shown in the following code:

```
WriteLine("Working with complex numbers:");
Complex c1 = new(real: 4, imaginary: 2);
Complex c2 = new(real: 3, imaginary: 7);
Complex c3 = c1 + c2;

// output using default ToString implementation
WriteLine($"{c1} added to {c2} is {c3}");

// output using custom format
```

```
WriteLine("{0} + {1}i added to {2} + {3}i is {4} + {5}i",
    c1.Real, c1.Imaginary,
    c2.Real, c2.Imaginary,
    c3.Real, c3.Imaginary);
```

2. Run the code and view the result, as shown in the following output:

```
Working with complex numbers:
(4, 2) added to (3, 7) is (7, 9)
4 + 2i added to 3 + 7i is 7 + 9i
```

Understanding quaternions

Quaternions are a number system that extends complex numbers. They form a four-dimensional associative normed division algebra over the real numbers, and therefore also a domain.

Huh? Yes, I know. I don't understand that either. Don't worry; we're not going to write any code using them! Suffice to say, they are good at describing spatial rotations, so video game engines use them, as do many computer simulations and flight control systems.

Working with text

One of the other most common types of data for variables is text. The most common types in .NET for working with text are shown in the following table:

Namespace	Type	Description
System	Char	Storage for a single text character
System	String	Storage for multiple text characters
System.Text	StringBuilder	Efficiently manipulates strings
System.Text.RegularExpressions	Regex	Efficiently pattern-matches strings

Getting the length of a string

Let's explore some common tasks when working with text; for example, sometimes you need to find out the length of a piece of text stored in a string variable:

1. Use your preferred code editor to add a new console app named WorkingWithText to the Chapter08 solution/workspace:

    1. In Visual Studio, set the startup project for the solution to the current selection.

    2. In Visual Studio Code, select WorkingWithText as the active OmniSharp project.

2. In the `WorkingWithText` project, in `Program.cs`, add statements to define a variable to store the name of the city London, and then write its name and length to the console, as shown in the following code:

```
string city = "London";
WriteLine($"{city} is {city.Length} characters long.");
```

3. Run the code and view the result, as shown in the following output:

```
London is 6 characters long.
```

Getting the characters of a string

The `string` class uses an array of `char` internally to store the text. It also has an indexer, which means that we can use the array syntax to read its characters. Array indexes start at zero, so the third character will be at index 2.

Let's see this in action:

1. Add a statement to write the characters at the first and third positions in the `string` variable, as shown in the following code:

```
WriteLine($"First char is {city[0]} and third is {city[2]}.");
```

2. Run the code and view the result, as shown in the following output:

```
First char is L and third is n.
```

Splitting a string

Sometimes, you need to split some text wherever there is a character, such as a comma:

1. Add statements to define a single `string` variable containing comma-separated city names, then use the `Split` method and specify that you want to treat commas as the separator, and then enumerate the returned array of `string` values, as shown in the following code:

```
string cities = "Paris,Tehran,Chennai,Sydney,New York,Medellín";

string[] citiesArray = cities.Split(',');

WriteLine($"There are {citiesArray.Length} items in the array.");
foreach (string item in citiesArray)
{
  WriteLine(item);
}
```

2. Run the code and view the result, as shown in the following output:

```
There are 6 items in the array.
Paris
Tehran
Chennai
Sydney
New York
Medellín
```

Later in this chapter, you will learn how to handle more complex scenarios.

Getting part of a string

Sometimes, you need to get part of some text. The IndexOf method has nine overloads that return the index position of a specified char or string within a string. The Substring method has two overloads, as shown in the following list:

- Substring(startIndex, length): returns a substring starting at startIndex and containing the next length characters.

- Substring(startIndex): returns a substring starting at startIndex and containing all characters up to the end of the string.

Let's explore a simple example:

1. Add statements to store a person's full name in a string variable with a space character between the first and last name, find the position of the space, and then extract the first name and last name as two parts so that they can be recombined in a different order, as shown in the following code:

```
string fullName = "Alan Jones";
int indexOfTheSpace = fullName.IndexOf(' ');

string firstName = fullName.Substring(
  startIndex: 0, length: indexOfTheSpace);

string lastName = fullName.Substring(
  startIndex: indexOfTheSpace + 1);

WriteLine($"Original: {fullName}");
WriteLine($"Swapped: {lastName}, {firstName}");
```

2. Run the code and view the result, as shown in the following output:

```
Original: Alan Jones
Swapped: Jones, Alan
```

If the format of the initial full name was different, for example, "LastName, FirstName", then the code would need to be different. As an optional exercise, try writing some statements that would change the input "Jones, Alan" into "Alan Jones".

Checking a string for content

Sometimes, you need to check whether a piece of text starts or ends with some characters or contains some characters. You can achieve this with methods named StartsWith, EndsWith, and Contains:

1. Add statements to store a string value and then check if it starts with or contains a couple of different string values, as shown in the following code:

```
string company = "Microsoft";
bool startsWithM = company.StartsWith("M");
bool containsN = company.Contains("N");
WriteLine($"Text: {company}");
WriteLine($"Starts with M: {startsWithM}, contains an N: {containsN}");
```

2. Run the code and view the result, as shown in the following output:

```
Text: Microsoft
Starts with M: True, contains an N: False
```

Joining, formatting, and other string members

There are many other string members, as shown in the following table:

Member	Description
Trim, TrimStart, TrimEnd	These methods trim whitespace characters such as space, tab, and carriage return from the beginning and/or end.
ToUpper, ToLower	These convert all the characters into uppercase or lowercase.
Insert, Remove	These methods insert or remove some text.
Replace	This replaces some text with other text.
string.Empty	This can be used instead of allocating memory each time you use a literal string value using an empty pair of double quotes ("").
string.Concat	This concatenates two string variables. The + operator does the equivalent when used between string operands.
string.Join	This concatenates one or more string variables with a character in between each one.
string.IsNullOrEmpty	This checks whether a string variable is null or empty.
string. IsNullOrWhitespace	This checks whether a string variable is null or whitespace; that is, a mix of any number of horizontal and vertical spacing characters, for example, tab, space, carriage return, line feed, and so on.
string.Format	An alternative method to string interpolation for outputting formatted string values, which uses positioned instead of named parameters.

Some of the preceding methods are static methods. This means that the method can only be called from the type, not from a variable instance. In the preceding table, I indicated the static methods by prefixing them with string., as in string.Format.

Let's explore some of these methods:

1. Add statements to take an array of string values and combine them back together into a single string variable with separators using the `Join` method, as shown in the following code:

    ```
    string recombined = string.Join(" => ", citiesArray);
    WriteLine(recombined);
    ```

2. Run the code and view the result, as shown in the following output:

    ```
    Paris => Tehran => Chennai => Sydney => New York => Medellín
    ```

3. Add statements to use positioned parameters and interpolated string formatting syntax to output the same three variables twice, as shown in the following code:

    ```
    string fruit = "Apples";
    decimal price =  0.39M;
    DateTime when = DateTime.Today;

    WriteLine($"Interpolated:  {fruit} cost {price:C} on {when:dddd}.");

    WriteLine(string.Format("string.Format: {0} cost {1:C} on {2:dddd}.",
        arg0: fruit, arg1: price, arg2: when));
    ```

4. Run the code and view the result, as shown in the following output:

    ```
    Interpolated:  Apples cost £0.39 on Thursday.
    string.Format: Apples cost £0.39 on Thursday.
    ```

Note that we could have simplified the second statement because `WriteLine` supports the same format codes as `string.Format`, as shown in the following code:

```
WriteLine("WriteLine: {0} cost {1:C} on {2:dddd}.",
  arg0: fruit, arg1: price, arg2: when);
```

Building strings efficiently

You can concatenate two strings to make a new `string` using the `String.Concat` method or simply by using the + operator. But both of these choices are bad practice because .NET must create a completely new `string` in memory.

This might not be noticeable if you are only adding two `string` values, but if you concatenate inside a loop with many iterations, it can have a significant negative impact on performance and memory use. In *Chapter 12, Improving Performance and Scalability Using Multitasking*, you will learn how to concatenate `string` variables efficiently using the `StringBuilder` type.

Working with dates and times

After numbers and text, the next most popular types of data to work with are dates and times. The two main types are as follows:

- `DateTime`: represents a combined date and time value for a fixed point in time.
- `TimeSpan`: represents a duration of time.

These two types are often used together. For example, if you subtract one `DateTime` value from another, the result is a `TimeSpan`. If you add a `TimeSpan` to a `DateTime` then the result is a `DateTime` value.

Specifying date and time values

A common way to create a date and time value is to specify individual values for the date and time components like day and hour, as described in the following table:

Date/time parameter	Value range
year	1 to 9999
month	1 to 12
day	1 to the number of days in that month
hour	0 to 23
minute	0 to 59
second	0 to 59

An alternative is to provide the value as a `string` to be parsed, but this can be misinterpreted depending on the default culture of the thread. For example, in the UK, dates are specified as day/month/year, compared to the US, where dates are specified as month/day/year.

Let's see what you might want to do with dates and times:

1. Use your preferred code editor to add a new console app named `WorkingWithTime` to the `Chapter08` solution/workspace.

2. In Visual Studio Code, select `WorkingWithTime` as the active OmniSharp project.

3. In `Program.cs`, delete the existing statements and then add statements to initialize some special date/time values, as shown in the following code:

```
WriteLine("Earliest date/time value is: {0}",
  arg0: DateTime.MinValue);

WriteLine("UNIX epoch date/time value is: {0}",
  arg0: DateTime.UnixEpoch);

WriteLine("Date/time value Now is: {0}",
```

```
    arg0: DateTime.Now);

  WriteLine("Date/time value Today is: {0}",
    arg0: DateTime.Today);
```

4. Run the code and note the results, as shown in the following output:

```
Earliest date/time value is: 01/01/0001 00:00:00
UNIX epoch date/time value is: 01/01/1970 00:00:00
Date/time value Now is: 23/04/2021 14:14:54
Date/time value Today is: 23/04/2021 00:00:00
```

5. Add statements to define Christmas Day in 2021 (if this is in the past then use a future year) and display it in various ways, as shown in the following code:

```
DateTime christmas = new(year: 2021, month: 12, day: 25);

WriteLine("Christmas: {0}",
  arg0: christmas); // default format

WriteLine("Christmas: {0:dddd, dd MMMM yyyy}",
  arg0: christmas); // custom format

WriteLine("Christmas is in month {0} of the year.",
  arg0: christmas.Month);

WriteLine("Christmas is day {0} of the year.",
  arg0: christmas.DayOfYear);

WriteLine("Christmas {0} is on a {1}.",
  arg0: christmas.Year,
  arg1: christmas.DayOfWeek);
```

6. Run the code and note the results, as shown in the following output:

```
Christmas: 25/12/2021 00:00:00
Christmas: Saturday, 25 December 2021
Christmas is in month 12 of the year.
Christmas is day 359 of the year.
Christmas 2021 is on a Saturday.
```

7. Add statements to perform addition and subtraction with Christmas, as shown in the following code:

```
DateTime beforeXmas = christmas.Subtract(TimeSpan.FromDays(12));
DateTime afterXmas = christmas.AddDays(12);

WriteLine("12 days before Christmas is: {0}",
```

```
    arg0: beforeXmas);

WriteLine("12 days after Christmas is: {0}",
    arg0: afterXmas);

TimeSpan untilChristmas = christmas - DateTime.Now;

WriteLine("There are {0} days and {1} hours until Christmas.",
    arg0: untilChristmas.Days,
    arg1: untilChristmas.Hours);

WriteLine("There are {0:N0} hours until Christmas.",
    arg0: untilChristmas.TotalHours);
```

8. Run the code and note the results, as shown in the following output:

```
12 days before Christmas is: 13/12/2021 00:00:00
12 days after Christmas is: 06/01/2022 00:00:00
There are 245 days and 9 hours until Christmas.
There are 5,890 hours until Christmas.
```

9. Add statements to define the time on Christmas Day that your children might wake up to open presents, and display it in various ways, as shown in the following code:

```
DateTime kidsWakeUp = new(
    year: 2021, month: 12, day: 25,
    hour: 6, minute: 30, second: 0);

WriteLine("Kids wake up on Christmas: {0}",
    arg0: kidsWakeUp);

WriteLine("The kids woke me up at {0}",
    arg0: kidsWakeUp.ToShortTimeString());
```

10. Run the code and note the results, as shown in the following output:

```
Kids wake up on Christmas: 25/12/2021 06:30:00
The kids woke me up at 06:30
```

Globalization with dates and times

The current culture controls how dates and times are parsed:

1. At the top of `Program.cs`, import the `System.Globalization` namespace.

2. Add statements to show the current culture that is used to display date and time values, and then parse United States Independence Day and display it in various ways, as shown in the following code:

```
WriteLine("Current culture is: {0}",
  arg0: CultureInfo.CurrentCulture.Name);

string textDate = "4 July 2021";
DateTime independenceDay = DateTime.Parse(textDate);

WriteLine("Text: {0}, DateTime: {1:d MMMM}",
  arg0: textDate,
  arg1: independenceDay);

textDate = "7/4/2021";
independenceDay = DateTime.Parse(textDate);

WriteLine("Text: {0}, DateTime: {1:d MMMM}",
  arg0: textDate,
  arg1: independenceDay);

independenceDay = DateTime.Parse(textDate,
  provider: CultureInfo.GetCultureInfo("en-US"));

WriteLine("Text: {0}, DateTime: {1:d MMMM}",
  arg0: textDate,
  arg1: independenceDay);
```

3. Run the code and note the results, as shown in the following output:

```
Current culture is: en-GB
Text: 4 July 2021, DateTime: 4 July
Text: 7/4/2021, DateTime: 7 April
Text: 7/4/2021, DateTime: 4 July
```

On my computer, the current culture is British English. If a date is given as 4 July 2021, then it is correctly parsed regardless of whether the current culture is British or American. But if the date is given as 7/4/2021, then it is wrongly parsed as 7 April. You can override the current culture by specifying the correct culture as a provider when parsing, as shown in the third example above.

4. Add statements to loop from the year 2020 to 2025, displaying if the year is a leap year and how many days there are in February, and then show if Christmas and Independence Day are during daylight saving time, as shown in the following code:

```
for (int year = 2020; year < 2026; year++)
{
  Write($"{year} is a leap year: {DateTime.IsLeapYear(year)}. ");
  WriteLine("There are {0} days in February {1}.",
    arg0: DateTime.DaysInMonth(year: year, month: 2), arg1: year);
```

```
    }

    WriteLine("Is Christmas daylight saving time? {0}",
      arg0: christmas.IsDaylightSavingTime());

    WriteLine("Is July 4th daylight saving time? {0}",
      arg0: independenceDay.IsDaylightSavingTime());
```

5. Run the code and note the results, as shown in the following output:

```
2020 is a leap year: True. There are 29 days in February 2020.
2021 is a leap year: False. There are 28 days in February 2021.
2022 is a leap year: False. There are 28 days in February 2022.
2023 is a leap year: False. There are 28 days in February 2023.
2024 is a leap year: True. There are 29 days in February 2024.
2025 is a leap year: False. There are 28 days in February 2025.
Is Christmas daylight saving time? False
Is July 4th daylight saving time? True
```

Working with only a date or a time

.NET 6 introduces some new types for working with only a date value or only a time value named DateOnly and TimeOnly. These are better than using a DateTime value with a zero time to store a date-only value because it is type-safe and avoids misuse. DateOnly also maps better to database column types, for example, a date column in SQL Server. TimeOnly is good for setting alarms and scheduling regular meetings or events, and it maps to a time column in SQL Server.

Let's use them to plan a party for the Queen of England:

1. Add statements to define the Queen's birthday, and a time for her party to start, and then combine the two values to make a calendar entry so we don't miss her party, as shown in the following code:

```
DateOnly queensBirthday = new(year: 2022, month: 4, day: 21);
WriteLine($"The Queen's next birthday is on {queensBirthday}.");

TimeOnly partyStarts = new(hour: 20, minute: 30);
WriteLine($"The Queen's party starts at {partyStarts}.");

DateTime calendarEntry = queensBirthday.ToDateTime(partyStarts);
WriteLine($"Add to your calendar: {calendarEntry}.");
```

2. Run the code and note the results, as shown in the following output:

```
The Queen's next birthday is on 21/04/2022.
The Queen's party starts at 20:30.
Add to your calendar: 21/04/2022 20:30:00.
```

Pattern matching with regular expressions

Regular expressions are useful for validating input from the user. They are very powerful and can get very complicated. Almost all programming languages have support for regular expressions and use a common set of special characters to define them.

Let's try out some example regular expressions:

1. Use your preferred code editor to add a new console app named
   WorkingWithRegularExpressions to the Chapter08 solution/workspace.

2. In Visual Studio Code, select WorkingWithRegularExpressions as the active OmniSharp project.

3. In Program.cs, import the following namespace:

   ```
   using System.Text.RegularExpressions;
   ```

Checking for digits entered as text

We will start by implementing the common example of validating number input:

1. Add statements to prompt the user to enter their age and then check that it is valid using a regular expression that looks for a digit character, as shown in the following code:

   ```
   Write("Enter your age: ");
   string? input = ReadLine();

   Regex ageChecker = new(@"\d");

   if (ageChecker.IsMatch(input))
   {
     WriteLine("Thank you!");
   }
   else
   {
     WriteLine($"This is not a valid age: {input}");
   }
   ```

   Note the following about the code:

   - The @ character switches off the ability to use escape characters in the string. Escape characters are prefixed with a backslash. For example, \t means a tab and \n means a new line. When writing regular expressions, we need to disable this feature. To paraphrase the television show The West Wing, "Let backslash be backslash."

- Once escape characters are disabled with @, then they can be interpreted by a regular expression. For example, \d means digit. You will learn more regular expressions that are prefixed with a backslash later in this topic.

2. Run the code, enter a whole number such as 34 for the age, and view the result, as shown in the following output:

```
Enter your age: 34
Thank you!
```

3. Run the code again, enter carrots, and view the result, as shown in the following output:

```
Enter your age: carrots
This is not a valid age: carrots
```

4. Run the code again, enter bob30smith, and view the result, as shown in the following output:

```
Enter your age: bob30smith
Thank you!
```

The regular expression we used is \d, which means *one digit*. However, it does not specify what can be entered before and after that one digit. This regular expression could be described in English as "Enter any characters you want as long as you enter at least one digit character."

In regular expressions, you indicate the start of some input with the caret ^ symbol and the end of some input with the dollar $ symbol. Let's use these symbols to indicate that we expect nothing else between the start and end of the input except for a digit.

5. Change the regular expression to ^\d$, as shown highlighted in the following code:

```
Regex ageChecker = new(@"^\d$");
```

6. Run the code again and note that it rejects any input except a single digit. We want to allow one or more digits. To do this, we add a + after the \d expression to modify the meaning to one or more.

7. Change the regular expression, as shown highlighted in the following code:

```
Regex ageChecker = new(@"^\d+$");
```

8. Run the code again and note the regular expression only allows zero or positive whole numbers of any length.

Regular expression performance improvements

The .NET types for working with regular expressions are used throughout the .NET platform and many of the apps built with it. As such, they have a significant impact on performance, but until now, they have not received much optimization attention from Microsoft.

With .NET 5 and later, the `System.Text.RegularExpressions` namespace has rewritten internals to squeeze out maximum performance. Common regular expression benchmarks using methods like `IsMatch` are now five times faster. And the best thing is, you do not have to change your code to get the benefits!

Understanding the syntax of a regular expression

Here are some common regular expression symbols that you can use in regular expressions:

Symbol	Meaning	Symbol	Meaning
`^`	Start of input	`$`	End of input
`\d`	A single digit	`\D`	A single NON-digit
`\s`	Whitespace	`\S`	NON-whitespace
`\w`	Word characters	`\W`	NON-word characters
`[A-Za-z0-9]`	Range(s) of characters	`\^`	^ (caret) character
`[aeiou]`	Set of characters	`[^aeiou]`	NOT in a set of characters
`.`	Any single character	`\.`	. (dot) character

In addition, here are some regular expression quantifiers that affect the previous symbols in a regular expression:

Symbol	Meaning	Symbol	Meaning
`+`	One or more	`?`	One or none
`{3}`	Exactly three	`{3,5}`	Three to five
`{3,}`	At least three	`{,3}`	Up to three

Examples of regular expressions

Here are some examples of regular expressions with a description of their meaning:

Expression	Meaning
`\d`	A single digit somewhere in the input
`a`	The character *a* somewhere in the input
`Bob`	The word *Bob* somewhere in the input
`^Bob`	The word *Bob* at the start of the input
`Bob$`	The word *Bob* at the end of the input
`^\d{2}$`	Exactly two digits
`^[0-9]{2}$`	Exactly two digits
`^[A-Z]{4,}$`	At least four uppercase English letters in the ASCII character set only
`^[A-Za-z]{4,}$`	At least four upper or lowercase English letters in the ASCII character set only
`^[A-Z]{2}\d{3}$`	Two uppercase English letters in the ASCII character set and three digits only

`^[A-Za-z\` `u00c0-\u017e]+$`	At least one uppercase or lowercase English letter in the ASCII character set or European letters in the Unicode character set, as shown in the following list: ÀÁÂÃÄÅÆÇÈÉÊËÌÍÎÏÐÑÒÓÔÕÖ×ØÙÚÛÜÝ Þßàáâãäåæçèéêëìíîïðñòóôõö÷øùúûüýþÿıŒœŠšŸ Žž
`^d.g$`	The letter *d*, then any character, and then the letter *g*, so it would match both *dig* and *dog* or any single character between the *d* and *g*
`^d\.g$`	The letter *d*, then a dot (.), and then the letter *g*, so it would match *d.g* only

Good Practice: Use regular expressions to validate input from the user. The same regular expressions can be reused in other languages such as JavaScript and Python.

Splitting a complex comma-separated string

Earlier in this chapter, you learned how to split a simple comma-separated string variable. But what about the following example of film titles?

```
"Monsters, Inc.","I, Tonya","Lock, Stock and Two Smoking Barrels"
```

The `string` value uses double quotes around each film title. We can use these to identify whether we need to split on a comma (or not). The `Split` method is not powerful enough, so we can use a regular expression instead.

Good Practice: You can read a fuller explanation in the Stack Overflow article that inspired this task at the following link: `https://stackoverflow.com/questions/18144431/regex-to-split-a-csv`

To include double quotes inside a `string` value, we prefix them with a backslash:

1. Add statements to store a complex comma-separated `string` variable, and then split it in a dumb way using the `Split` method, as shown in the following code:

```
string films = "\"Monsters, Inc.\",\"I, Tonya\",\"Lock, Stock and Two
Smoking Barrels\"";

WriteLine($"Films to split: {films}");

string[] filmsDumb = films.Split(',');

WriteLine("Splitting with string.Split method:");
```

```
foreach (string film in filmsDumb)
{
  WriteLine(film);
}
```

2. Add statements to define a regular expression to split and write the film titles in a smart way, as shown in the following code:

```
WriteLine();

Regex csv = new(
  "(?:^|,)(?=[^\"]|(\")?)\"?((?(1)[^\"]*|[^,\"]*))\"?(?=,|$)");

MatchCollection filmsSmart = csv.Matches(films);

WriteLine("Splitting with regular expression:");
foreach (Match film in filmsSmart)
{
  WriteLine(film.Groups[2].Value);
}
```

3. Run the code and view the result, as shown in the following output:

```
Splitting with string.Split method:
"Monsters
 Inc."
"I
 Tonya"
"Lock
 Stock and Two Smoking Barrels"

Splitting with regular expression:
Monsters, Inc.
I, Tonya
Lock, Stock and Two Smoking Barrels
```

Storing multiple objects in collections

Another of the most common types of data is collections. If you need to store multiple values in a variable, then you can use a collection.

A collection is a data structure in memory that can manage multiple items in different ways, although all collections have some shared functionality.

The most common types in .NET for working with collections are shown in the following table:

Namespace	Example type(s)	Description
System .Collections	IEnumerable, IEnumerable<T>	Interfaces and base classes used by collections.
System .Collections .Generic	List<T>, Dictionary<T>, Queue<T>, Stack<T>	Introduced in C# 2.0 with .NET Framework 2.0. These collections allow you to specify the type you want to store using a generic type parameter (which is safer, faster, and more efficient).
System .Collections .Concurrent	BlockingCollection, ConcurrentDictionary, ConcurrentQueue	These collections are safe to use in multithreaded scenarios.
System .Collections .Immutable	ImmutableArray, ImmutableDictionary, ImmutableList, ImmutableQueue	Designed for scenarios where the contents of the original collection will never change, although they can create modified collections as a new instance.

Common features of all collections

All collections implement the ICollection interface; this means that they must have a Count property to tell you how many objects are in them, as shown in the following code:

```
namespace System.Collections
{
  public interface ICollection : IEnumerable
  {
    int Count { get; }
    bool IsSynchronized { get; }
    object SyncRoot { get; }
    void CopyTo(Array array, int index);
  }
}
```

For example, if we had a collection named passengers, we could do this:

```
int howMany = passengers.Count;
```

All collections implement the IEnumerable interface, which means that they can be iterated using the foreach statement. They must have a GetEnumerator method that returns an object that implements IEnumerator; this means that the returned object must have MoveNext and Reset methods for navigating through the collection and a Current property containing the current item in the collection, as shown in the following code:

```
namespace System.Collections
{
  public interface IEnumerable
  {
```

```
      IEnumerator GetEnumerator();
  }
}

namespace System.Collections
{
  public interface IEnumerator
  {
    object Current { get; }
    bool MoveNext();
    void Reset();
  }
}
```

For example, to perform an action on each object in the passengers collection, we could write the following code:

```
foreach (Passenger p in passengers)
{
  // perform an action on each passenger
}
```

As well as object-based collection interfaces, there are also generic interfaces and classes, where the generic type defines the type stored in the collection, as shown in the following code:

```
namespace System.Collections.Generic
{
  public interface ICollection<T> : IEnumerable<T>, IEnumerable
  {
    int Count { get; }
    bool IsReadOnly { get; }
    void Add(T item);
    void Clear();
    bool Contains(T item);
    void CopyTo(T[] array, int index);
    bool Remove(T item);
  }
}
```

Improving performance by ensuring the capacity of a collection

Since .NET 1.1, types like StringBuilder have had a method named EnsureCapacity that can presize its internal storage array to the expected final size of the string. This improves performance because it does not have to repeatedly increment the size of the array as more characters are appended.

Since .NET Core 2.1, types like `Dictionary<T>` and `HashSet<T>` have also had `EnsureCapacity`.

In .NET 6 and later, collections like `List<T>`, `Queue<T>`, and `Stack<T>` now have an `EnsureCapacity` method too, as shown in the following code:

```
List<string> names = new();
names.EnsureCapacity(10_000);
// load ten thousand names into the list
```

Understanding collection choices

There are several different choices of collection that you can use for different purposes: lists, dictionaries, stacks, queues, sets, and many other more specialized collections.

Lists

Lists, that is, a type that implements `IList<T>`, are **ordered collections**, as shown in the following code:

```
namespace System.Collections.Generic
{
  [DefaultMember("Item")] // aka this indexer
  public interface IList<T> : ICollection<T>, IEnumerable<T>, IEnumerable
  {
    T this[int index] { get; set; }
    int IndexOf(T item);
    void Insert(int index, T item);
    void RemoveAt(int index);
  }
}
```

`IList<T>` derives from `ICollection<T>` so it has a `Count` property, and an `Add` method to put an item at the end of the collection, as well as an `Insert` method to put an item in the list at a specified position, and `RemoveAt` to remove an item at a specified position.

Lists are a good choice when you want to manually control the order of items in a collection. Each item in a list has a unique index (or position) that is automatically assigned. Items can be any type defined by `T` and items can be duplicated. Indexes are `int` types and start from 0, so the first item in a list is at index 0, as shown in the following table:

Index	Item
0	London
1	Paris
2	London
3	Sydney

If a new item (for example, Santiago) is inserted between London and Sydney, then the index of Sydney is automatically incremented. Therefore, you must be aware that an item's index can change after inserting or removing items, as shown in the following table:

Index	Item
0	London
1	Paris
2	London
3	Santiago
4	Sydney

Dictionaries

Dictionaries are a good choice when each **value** (or object) has a unique sub value (or a made-up value) that can be used as a **key** to quickly find a value in the collection later. The key must be unique. For example, if you are storing a list of people, you could choose to use a government-issued identity number as the key.

Think of the key as being like an index entry in a real-world dictionary. It allows you to quickly find the definition of a word because the words (for example, keys) are kept sorted, and if we know we're looking for the definition of *manatee*, we would jump to the middle of the dictionary to start looking, because the letter *M* is in the middle of the alphabet.

Dictionaries in programming are similarly smart when looking something up. They must implement the interface IDictionary<TKey, TValue>, as shown in the following code:

```
namespace System.Collections.Generic
{
  [DefaultMember("Item")] // aka this indexer
  public interface IDictionary<TKey, TValue>
    : ICollection<KeyValuePair<TKey, TValue>>,
      IEnumerable<KeyValuePair<TKey, TValue>>, IEnumerable
  {
    TValue this[TKey key] { get; set; }
    ICollection<TKey> Keys { get; }
    ICollection<TValue> Values { get; }
    void Add(TKey key, TValue value);
    bool ContainsKey(TKey key);
    bool Remove(TKey key);
    bool TryGetValue(TKey key, [MaybeNullWhen(false)] out TValue value);
  }
}
```

Items in a dictionary are instances of the struct, aka the value type KeyValuePair<TKey, TValue>, where TKey is the type of the key and TValue is the type of the value, as shown in the following code:

```
namespace System.Collections.Generic
{
  public readonly struct KeyValuePair<TKey, TValue>
  {
    public KeyValuePair(TKey key, TValue value);
    public TKey Key { get; }
    public TValue Value { get; }
    [EditorBrowsable(EditorBrowsableState.Never)]
    public void Deconstruct(out TKey key, out TValue value);
    public override string ToString();
  }
}
```

An example `Dictionary<string, Person>` uses a `string` as the key and a `Person` instance as the value. `Dictionary<string, string>` uses `string` values for both, as shown in the following table:

Key	Value
BSA	Bob Smith
MW	Max Williams
BSB	Bob Smith
AM	Amir Mohammed

Stacks

Stacks are a good choice when you want to implement **last-in, first-out (LIFO)** behavior. With a stack, you can only directly access or remove the one item at the top of the stack, although you can enumerate to read through the whole stack of items. You cannot, for example, directly access the second item in a stack.

For example, word processors use a stack to remember the sequence of actions you have recently performed, and then when you press *Ctrl* + *Z*, it will undo the last action in the stack, and then the next-to-last action, and so on.

Queues

Queues are a good choice when you want to implement the **first-in, first-out (FIFO)** behavior. With a queue, you can only directly access or remove the one item at the front of the queue, although you can enumerate to read through the whole queue of items. You cannot, for example, directly access the second item in a queue.

For example, background processes use a queue to process work items in the order that they arrive, just like people standing in line at the post office.

.NET 6 introduces the `PriorityQueue`, where each item in the queue has a priority value assigned as well as their position in the queue.

Sets

Sets are a good choice when you want to perform set operations between two collections. For example, you may have two collections of city names, and you want to know which names appear in both sets (known as the *intersect* between the sets). Items in a set must be unique.

Collection methods summary

Each collection has a different set of methods for adding and removing items, as shown in the following table:

Collection	Add methods	Remove methods	Description
List	Add, Insert	Remove, RemoveAt	Lists are ordered so items have an integer index position. Add will add a new item at the end of the list. Insert will add a new item at the index position specified.
Dictionary	Add	Remove	Dictionaries are not ordered so items do not have integer index positions. You can check if a key has been used by calling the ContainsKey method.
Stack	Push	Pop	Stacks always add a new item at the top of the stack using the Push method. The first item is at the bottom. Items are always removed from the top of the stack using the Pop method. Call the Peek method to see this value without removing it.
Queue	Enqueue	Dequeue	Queues always add a new item at the end of the queue using the Enqueue method. The first item is at the front of the queue. Items are always removed from the front of the queue using the Dequeue method. Call the Peek method to see this value without removing it.

Working with lists

Let's explore lists:

1. Use your preferred code editor to add a new console app named WorkingWithCollections to the Chapter08 solution/workspace.

2. In Visual Studio Code, select WorkingWithCollections as the active OmniSharp project.

3. In Program.cs, delete the existing statements and then define a function to output a collection of string values with a title, as shown in the following code:

```
static void Output(string title, IEnumerable<string> collection)
{
  WriteLine(title);
  foreach (string item in collection)
```

```
  {
    WriteLine($"  {item}");
  }
}
```

4. Define a static method named `WorkingWithLists` to illustrate some of the common ways of defining and working with lists, as shown in the following code:

```
static void WorkingWithLists()
{
  // Simple syntax for creating a list and adding three items
  List<string> cities = new();
  cities.Add("London");
  cities.Add("Paris");
  cities.Add("Milan");

  /* Alternative syntax that is converted by the compiler into
     the three Add method calls above
  List<string> cities = new()
    { "London", "Paris", "Milan" };
  */

  /* Alternative syntax that passes an
     array of string values to AddRange method
  List<string> cities = new();
  cities.AddRange(new[] { "London", "Paris", "Milan" });
  */

  Output("Initial list", cities);

  WriteLine($"The first city is {cities[0]}.");
  WriteLine($"The last city is {cities[cities.Count - 1]}.");

  cities.Insert(0, "Sydney");

  Output("After inserting Sydney at index 0", cities);

  cities.RemoveAt(1);
  cities.Remove("Milan");

  Output("After removing two cities", cities);
}
```

5. At the top of `Program.cs`, after the namespace imports, call the `WorkingWithLists` method, as shown in the following code:

```
WorkingWithLists();
```

6. Run the code and view the result, as shown in the following output:

```
Initial list
  London
  Paris
  Milan
The first city is London.
The last city is Milan.
After inserting Sydney at index 0
  Sydney
  London
  Paris
  Milan
After removing two cities
  Sydney
  Paris
```

Working with dictionaries

Let's explore dictionaries:

1. In `Program.cs`, define a static method named `WorkingWithDictionaries` to illustrate some of the common ways of working with dictionaries, for example, looking up word definitions, as shown in the following code:

```
static void WorkingWithDictionaries()
{
  Dictionary<string, string> keywords = new();

  // add using named parameters
  keywords.Add(key: "int", value: "32-bit integer data type");

  // add using positional parameters
  keywords.Add("long", "64-bit integer data type");
  keywords.Add("float", "Single precision floating point number");

  /* Alternative syntax; compiler converts this to calls to Add method
  Dictionary<string, string> keywords = new()
  {
    { "int", "32-bit integer data type" },
    { "long", "64-bit integer data type" },
```

```
    { "float", "Single precision floating point number" },
  }; */

  /* Alternative syntax; compiler converts this to calls to Add method
  Dictionary<string, string> keywords = new()
  {
    ["int"] = "32-bit integer data type",
    ["long"] = "64-bit integer data type",
    ["float"] = "Single precision floating point number", // last comma is
optional
  }; */

  Output("Dictionary keys:", keywords.Keys);
  Output("Dictionary values:", keywords.Values);

  WriteLine("Keywords and their definitions");
  foreach (KeyValuePair<string, string> item in keywords)
  {
    WriteLine($"  {item.Key}: {item.Value}");
  }

  // lookup a value using a key
  string key = "long";
  WriteLine($"The definition of {key} is {keywords[key]}");
}
```

2. At the top of `Program.cs`, comment out the previous method call and then call the `WorkingWithDictionaries` method, as shown in the following code:

```
// WorkingWithLists();
WorkingWithDictionaries();
```

3. Run the code and view the result, as shown in the following output:

```
Dictionary keys:
  int
  long
  float
Dictionary values:
  32-bit integer data type
  64-bit integer data type
  Single precision floating point number
Keywords and their definitions
  int: 32-bit integer data type
  long: 64-bit integer data type
  float: Single precision floating point number
The definition of long is 64-bit integer data type
```

Working with queues

Let's explore queues:

1. In `Program.cs`, define a static method named `WorkingWithQueues` to illustrate some of the common ways of working with queues, for example, handling customers in a queue for coffee, as shown in the following code:

    ```
    static void WorkingWithQueues()
    {
      Queue<string> coffee = new();

      coffee.Enqueue("Damir"); // front of queue
      coffee.Enqueue("Andrea");
      coffee.Enqueue("Ronald");
      coffee.Enqueue("Amin");
      coffee.Enqueue("Irina"); // back of queue

      Output("Initial queue from front to back", coffee);

      // server handles next person in queue
      string served = coffee.Dequeue();
      WriteLine($"Served: {served}.");

      // server handles next person in queue
      served = coffee.Dequeue();
      WriteLine($"Served: {served}.");

      Output("Current queue from front to back", coffee);

      WriteLine($"{coffee.Peek()} is next in line.");

      Output("Current queue from front to back", coffee);
    }
    ```

2. At the top of `Program.cs`, comment out the previous method calls and call the `WorkingWithQueues` method.

3. Run the code and view the result, as shown in the following output:

    ```
    Initial queue from front to back
      Damir
      Andrea
      Ronald
      Amin
      Irina
    Served: Damir.
    Served: Andrea.
    ```

```
Current queue from front to back
  Ronald
  Amin
  Irina
Ronald is next in line.
Current queue from front to back
  Ronald
  Amin
  Irina
```

4. Define a static method named `OutputPQ`, as shown in the following code:

```
static void OutputPQ<TElement, TPriority>(string title,
  IEnumerable<(TElement Element, TPriority Priority)> collection)
{
  WriteLine(title);
  foreach ((TElement, TPriority) item in collection)
  {
    WriteLine($"  {item.Item1}: {item.Item2}");
  }
}
```

Note that the `OutputPQ` method is generic. You can specify the two types used in the tuples that are passed in as `collection`.

5. Define a static method named `WorkingWithPriorityQueues`, as shown in the following code:

```
static void WorkingWithPriorityQueues()
{
  PriorityQueue<string, int> vaccine = new();

  // add some people
  // 1 = high priority people in their 70s or poor health
  // 2 = medium priority e.g. middle aged
  // 3 = low priority e.g. teens and twenties
  vaccine.Enqueue("Pamela", 1);  // my mum (70s)
  vaccine.Enqueue("Rebecca", 3); // my niece (teens)
  vaccine.Enqueue("Juliet", 2);  // my sister (40s)
  vaccine.Enqueue("Ian", 1);     // my dad (70s)

  OutputPQ("Current queue for vaccination:", vaccine.UnorderedItems);

  WriteLine($"{vaccine.Dequeue()} has been vaccinated.");
  WriteLine($"{vaccine.Dequeue()} has been vaccinated.");

  OutputPQ("Current queue for vaccination:", vaccine.UnorderedItems);
```

```
            WriteLine($"{vaccine.Dequeue()} has been vaccinated.");

            vaccine.Enqueue("Mark", 2); // me (40s)
            WriteLine($"{vaccine.Peek()} will be next to be vaccinated.");

            OutputPQ("Current queue for vaccination:", vaccine.UnorderedItems);
        }
```

6. At the top of `Program.cs`, comment out the previous method calls and call the `WorkingWithPriorityQueues` method.

7. Run the code and view the result, as shown in the following output:

```
Current queue for vaccination:
   Pamela: 1
   Rebecca: 3
   Juliet: 2
   Ian: 1
Pamela has been vaccinated.
Ian has been vaccinated.
Current queue for vaccination:
   Juliet: 2
   Rebecca: 3
Juliet has been vaccinated.
Mark will be next to be vaccinated.
Current queue for vaccination:
   Mark: 2
   Rebecca: 3
```

Sorting collections

A `List<T>` class can be sorted by manually calling its `Sort` method (but remember that the indexes of each item will change). Manually sorting a list of `string` values or other built-in types will work without extra effort on your part, but if you create a collection of your own type, then that type must implement an interface named `IComparable`. You learned how to do this in *Chapter 6, Implementing Interfaces and Inheriting Classes*.

A `Stack<T>` or `Queue<T>` collection cannot be sorted because you wouldn't usually want that functionality; for example, you would probably never sort a queue of guests checking into a hotel. But sometimes, you might want to sort a dictionary or a set.

Sometimes it would be useful to have an automatically sorted collection, that is, one that maintains the items in a sorted order as you add and remove them.

There are multiple auto-sorting collections to choose from. The differences between these sorted collections are often subtle but can have an impact on the memory requirements and performance of your application, so it is worth putting effort into picking the most appropriate option for your requirements.

Some common auto-sorting collections are shown in the following table:

Collection	Description
SortedDictionary<TKey, TValue>	This represents a collection of key/value pairs that are sorted by key.
SortedList<TKey, TValue>	This represents a collection of key/value pairs that are sorted by key.
SortedSet<T>	This represents a collection of unique objects that are maintained in a sorted order.

More specialized collections

There are a few other collections for special situations.

Working with a compact array of bit values

The System.Collections.BitArray collection manages a compact array of bit values, which are represented as Booleans, where true indicates that the bit is on (value is 1) and false indicates the bit is off (value is 0).

Working with efficient lists

The System.Collections.Generics.LinkedList<T> collection represents a doubly linked list where every item has a reference to its previous and next items. They provide better performance compared to List<T> for scenarios where you will frequently insert and remove items from the middle of the list. In a LinkedList<T> the items do not have to be rearranged in memory.

Using immutable collections

Sometimes you need to make a collection immutable, meaning that its members cannot change; that is, you cannot add or remove them.

If you import the System.Collections.Immutable namespace, then any collection that implements IEnumerable<T> is given six extension methods to convert it into an immutable list, dictionary, hash set, and so on.

Let's see a simple example:

1. In the WorkingWithCollections project, in Program.cs, import the System.Collections. Immutable namespace.

2. In the WorkingWithLists method, add statements to the end of the method to convert the cities list into an immutable list and then add a new city to it, as shown in the following code:

```
ImmutableList<string> immutableCities = cities.ToImmutableList();
ImmutableList<string> newList = immutableCities.Add("Rio");
```

```
Output("Immutable list of cities:", immutableCities);
Output("New list of cities:", newList);
```

3. At the top of `Program.cs`, comment the previous method calls and uncomment the call to the `WorkingWithLists` method.

4. Run the code, view the result, and note that the immutable list of cities does not get modified when you call the `Add` method on it; instead, it returns a new list with the newly added city, as shown in the following output:

```
Immutable list of cities:
  Sydney
  Paris
New list of cities:
  Sydney
  Paris
  Rio
```

> **Good Practice**: To improve performance, many applications store a shared copy of commonly accessed objects in a central cache. To safely allow multiple threads to work with those objects knowing they won't change, you should make them immutable or use a concurrent collection type that you can read about at the following link: https://docs.microsoft.com/en-us/dotnet/api/system.collections.concurrent

Good practice with collections

Let's say you need to create a method to process a collection. For maximum flexibility, you could declare the input parameter to be `IEnumerable<T>` and make the method generic, as shown in the following code:

```
void ProcessCollection<T>(IEnumerable<T> collection)
{
  // process the items in the collection,
  // perhaps using a foreach statement
}
```

I could pass an array, a list, a queue, a stack, or anything else that implements `IEnumerable<T>` into this method and it will process the items. However, the flexibility to pass any collection to this method comes at a performance cost.

One of the performance problems with `IEnumerable<T>` is also one of its benefits: deferred execution, also known as lazy loading. Types that implement this interface do not have to implement deferred execution, but many do.

But the worst performance problem with IEnumerable<T> is that the iteration has to allocate an object on the heap. To avoid this memory allocation, you should define your method using a concrete type, as shown highlighted in the following code:

```
void ProcessCollection<T>(List<T> collection)
{
  // process the items in the collection,
  // perhaps using a foreach statement
}
```

This will use the List<T>.Enumerator GetEnumerator() method that returns a struct instead of the IEnumerator<T> GetEnumerator() method that returns a reference type. Your code will be two to three times faster and require less memory. As with all recommendations related to performance, you should confirm the benefit by running performance tests on your actual code in a product environment. You will learn how to do this in *Chapter 12, Improving Performance and Scalability Using Multitasking*.

Working with spans, indexes, and ranges

One of Microsoft's goals with .NET Core 2.1 was to improve performance and resource usage. A key .NET feature that enables this is the Span<T> type.

Using memory efficiently using spans

When manipulating arrays, you will often create new copies of subsets of existing ones so that you can process just the subset. This is not efficient because duplicate objects must be created in memory.

If you need to work with a subset of an array, use a **span** because it is like a window into the original array. This is more efficient in terms of memory usage and improves performance. Spans only work with arrays, not collections, because the memory must be contiguous.

Before we look at spans in more detail, we need to understand some related objects: indexes and ranges.

Identifying positions with the Index type

C# 8.0 introduced two features for identifying an item's index within an array and a range of items using two indexes.

You learned in the previous topic that objects in a list can be accessed by passing an integer into their indexer, as shown in the following code:

```
int index = 3;
Person p = people[index]; // fourth person in array
char letter = name[index]; // fourth letter in name
```

The `Index` value type is a more formal way of identifying a position, and supports counting from the end, as shown in the following code:

```
// two ways to define the same index, 3 in from the start
Index i1 = new(value: 3); // counts from the start
Index i2 = 3; // using implicit int conversion operator

// two ways to define the same index, 5 in from the end
Index i3 = new(value: 5, fromEnd: true);
Index i4 = ^5; // using the caret operator
```

Identifying ranges with the Range type

The `Range` value type uses `Index` values to indicate the start and end of its range, using its constructor, C# syntax, or its static methods, as shown in the following code:

```
Range r1 = new(start: new Index(3), end: new Index(7));
Range r2 = new(start: 3, end: 7); // using implicit int conversion
Range r3 = 3..7; // using C# 8.0 or later syntax
Range r4 = Range.StartAt(3); // from index 3 to last index
Range r5 = 3..; // from index 3 to last index
Range r6 = Range.EndAt(3); // from index 0 to index 3
Range r7 = ..3; // from index 0 to index 3
```

Extension methods have been added to `string` values (that internally use an array of `char`), `int` arrays, and spans to make ranges easier to work with. These extension methods accept a range as a parameter and return a `Span<T>`. This makes them very memory efficient.

Using indexes, ranges, and spans

Let's explore using indexes and ranges to return spans:

1. Use your preferred code editor to add a new console app named `WorkingWithRanges` to the `Chapter08` solution/workspace.
2. In Visual Studio Code, select `WorkingWithRanges` as the active OmniSharp project.
3. In `Program.cs`, type statements to compare using the `string` type's `Substring` method using ranges to extract parts of someone's name, as shown in the following code:

```
string name = "Samantha Jones";

// Using Substring

int lengthOfFirst = name.IndexOf(' ');
int lengthOfLast = name.Length - lengthOfFirst - 1;

string firstName = name.Substring(
  startIndex: 0,
  length: lengthOfFirst);
```

```
string lastName = name.Substring(
  startIndex: name.Length - lengthOfLast,
  length: lengthOfLast);

WriteLine($"First name: {firstName}, Last name: {lastName}");

// Using spans

ReadOnlySpan<char> nameAsSpan = name.AsSpan();
ReadOnlySpan<char> firstNameSpan = nameAsSpan[0..lengthOfFirst];
ReadOnlySpan<char> lastNameSpan = nameAsSpan[^lengthOfLast..^0];

WriteLine("First name: {0}, Last name: {1}",
  arg0: firstNameSpan.ToString(),
  arg1: lastNameSpan.ToString());
```

4. Run the code and view the result, as shown in the following output:

```
First name: Samantha, Last name: Jones
First name: Samantha, Last name: Jones
```

Working with network resources

Sometimes you will need to work with network resources. The most common types in .NET for working with network resources are shown in the following table:

Namespace	Example type(s)	Description
System.Net	Dns, Uri, Cookie, WebClient, IPAddress	These are for working with DNS servers, URIs, IP addresses, and so on.
System.Net	FtpStatusCode, FtpWebRequest, FtpWebResponse	These are for working with FTP servers.
System.Net	HttpStatusCode, HttpWebRequest, HttpWebResponse	These are for working with HTTP servers; that is, websites and services. Types from System.Net.Http are easier to use.
System.Net.Http	HttpClient, HttpMethod, HttpRequestMessage, HttpResponseMessage	These are for working with HTTP servers; that is, websites and services. You will learn how to use these in *Chapter 16, Building and Consuming Web Services*.
System.Net.Mail	Attachment, MailAddress, MailMessage, SmtpClient	These are for working with SMTP servers; that is, sending email messages.
System.Net .NetworkInformation	IPStatus, NetworkChange, Ping, TcpStatistics	These are for working with low-level network protocols.

Working with URIs, DNS, and IP addresses

Let's explore some common types for working with network resources:

1. Use your preferred code editor to add a new console app named WorkingWithNetworkResources to the Chapter08 solution/workspace.

2. In Visual Studio Code, select WorkingWithNetworkResources as the active OmniSharp project.

3. At the top of Program.cs, import the namespace for working with the network, as shown in the following code:

   ```
   using System.Net; // IPHostEntry, Dns, IPAddress
   ```

4. Type statements to prompt the user to enter a website address, and then use the Uri type to break it down into its parts, including the scheme (HTTP, FTP, and so on), port number, and host, as shown in the following code:

   ```
   Write("Enter a valid web address: ");
   string? url = ReadLine();

   if (string.IsNullOrWhiteSpace(url))
   {
     url = "https://stackoverflow.com/search?q=securestring";
   }

   Uri uri = new(url);

   WriteLine($"URL: {url}");
   WriteLine($"Scheme: {uri.Scheme}");
   WriteLine($"Port: {uri.Port}");
   WriteLine($"Host: {uri.Host}");
   WriteLine($"Path: {uri.AbsolutePath}");
   WriteLine($"Query: {uri.Query}");
   ```

   For convenience, the code also allows the user to press *ENTER* to use an example URL.

5. Run the code, enter a valid website address or press *ENTER*, and view the result, as shown in the following output:

   ```
   Enter a valid web address:
   URL: https://stackoverflow.com/search?q=securestring
   Scheme: https
   Port: 443
   Host: stackoverflow.com
   Path: /search
   Query: ?q=securestring
   ```

6. Add statements to get the IP address for the entered website, as shown in the following code:

```
IPHostEntry entry = Dns.GetHostEntry(uri.Host);
WriteLine($"{entry.HostName} has the following IP addresses:");
foreach (IPAddress address in entry.AddressList)
{
  WriteLine($"  {address} ({address.AddressFamily})");
}
```

7. Run the code, enter a valid website address or press *ENTER*, and view the result, as shown in the following output:

```
stackoverflow.com has the following IP addresses:
  151.101.193.69 (InterNetwork)
  151.101.129.69 (InterNetwork)
  151.101.1.69 (InterNetwork)
  151.101.65.69 (InterNetwork)
```

Pinging a server

Now you will add code to ping a web server to check its health:

1. Import the namespace to get more information about networks, as shown in the following code:

```
using System.Net.NetworkInformation; // Ping, PingReply, IPStatus
```

2. Add statements to ping the entered website, as shown in the following code:

```
try
{
  Ping ping = new();
  WriteLine("Pinging server. Please wait...");
  PingReply reply = ping.Send(uri.Host);

  WriteLine($"{uri.Host} was pinged and replied: {reply.Status}.");
  if (reply.Status == IPStatus.Success)
  {
    WriteLine("Reply from {0} took {1:N0}ms",
      arg0: reply.Address,
      arg1: reply.RoundtripTime);
  }
}
catch (Exception ex)
{
  WriteLine($"{ex.GetType().ToString()} says {ex.Message}");
}
```

3. Run the code, press *ENTER*, and view the result, as shown in the following output on macOS:

```
Pinging server. Please wait...
stackoverflow.com was pinged and replied: Success.
Reply from 151.101.193.69 took 18ms took 136ms
```

4. Run the code again but this time enter `http://google.com`, as shown in the following output:

```
Enter a valid web address: http://google.com
URL: http://google.com
Scheme: http
Port: 80
Host: google.com
Path: /
Query:
google.com has the following IP addresses:
   2a00:1450:4009:807::200e (InterNetworkV6)
   216.58.204.238 (InterNetwork)
Pinging server. Please wait...
google.com was pinged and replied: Success.
Reply from 2a00:1450:4009:807::200e took 24ms
```

Working with reflection and attributes

Reflection is a programming feature that allows code to understand and manipulate itself. An assembly is made up of up to four parts:

- **Assembly metadata and manifest**: Name, assembly, and file version, referenced assemblies, and so on.
- **Type metadata**: Information about the types, their members, and so on.
- **IL code**: Implementation of methods, properties, constructors, and so on.
- **Embedded resources** (optional): Images, strings, JavaScript, and so on.

The metadata comprises items of information about your code. The metadata is generated automatically from your code (for example, information about the types and members) or applied to your code using attributes.

Attributes can be applied at multiple levels: to assemblies, to types, and to their members, as shown in the following code:

```
// an assembly-level attribute
[assembly: AssemblyTitle("Working with Reflection")]

// a type-level attribute
```

```
[Serializable]
public class Person
{
  // a member-level attribute
  [Obsolete("Deprecated: use Run instead.")]
  public void Walk()
  {
...
```

Attribute-based programming is used a lot in app models like ASP.NET Core to enable features like routing, security, and caching.

Versioning of assemblies

Version numbers in .NET are a combination of three numbers, with two optional additions. If you follow the rules of semantic versioning, the three numbers denote the following:

- **Major**: Breaking changes.
- **Minor**: Non-breaking changes, including new features, and often bug fixes.
- **Patch**: Non-breaking bug fixes.

> **Good Practice**: When updating a NuGet package that you already use in a project, to be safe you should specify an optional flag to make sure that you only upgrade to the highest minor to avoid breaking changes, or to the highest patch if you are extra cautious and only want to receive bug fixes, as shown in the following commands: `Update-Package Newtonsoft.Json -ToHighestMinor` or `Update-Package Newtonsoft.Json -ToHighestPatch`.

Optionally, a version can include these:

- **Prerelease**: Unsupported preview releases.
- **Build number**: Nightly builds.

> **Good Practice**: Follow the rules of semantic versioning, as described at the following link: `http://semver.org`

Reading assembly metadata

Let's explore working with attributes:

1. Use your preferred code editor to add a new console app named `WorkingWithReflection` to the `Chapter08` solution/workspace.

2. In Visual Studio Code, select WorkingWithReflection as the active OmniSharp project.

3. At the top of Program.cs, import the namespace for reflection, as shown in the following code:

```
using System.Reflection; // Assembly
```

4. Add statements to get the console app's assembly, output its name and location, and get all assembly-level attributes and output their types, as shown in the following code:

```
WriteLine("Assembly metadata:");
Assembly? assembly = Assembly.GetEntryAssembly();
if (assembly is null)
{
  WriteLine("Failed to get entry assembly.");
  return;
}

WriteLine($"  Full name: {assembly.FullName}");
WriteLine($"  Location: {assembly.Location}");

IEnumerable<Attribute> attributes = assembly.GetCustomAttributes();

WriteLine($"  Assembly-level attributes:");
foreach (Attribute a in attributes)
{
  WriteLine($"    {a.GetType()}");
}
```

5. Run the code and view the result, as shown in the following output:

```
Assembly metadata:
  Full name: WorkingWithReflection, Version=1.0.0.0, Culture=neutral,
PublicKeyToken=null
  Location: /Users/markjprice/Code/Chapter08/WorkingWithReflection/bin/
Debug/net6.0/WorkingWithReflection.dll
  Assembly-level attributes:
    System.Runtime.CompilerServices.CompilationRelaxationsAttribute
    System.Runtime.CompilerServices.RuntimeCompatibilityAttribute
    System.Diagnostics.DebuggableAttribute
    System.Runtime.Versioning.TargetFrameworkAttribute
    System.Reflection.AssemblyCompanyAttribute
    System.Reflection.AssemblyConfigurationAttribute
    System.Reflection.AssemblyFileVersionAttribute
    System.Reflection.AssemblyInformationalVersionAttribute
    System.Reflection.AssemblyProductAttribute
    System.Reflection.AssemblyTitleAttribute
```

Note that because the full name of an assembly must uniquely identify the assembly, it is a combination of the following:

- **Name**, for example, `WorkingWithReflection`
- **Version**, for example, `1.0.0.0`
- **Culture**, for example, `neutral`
- **Public key token**, although this can be `null`

Now that we know some of the attributes decorating the assembly, we can ask for them specifically.

6. Add statements to get the `AssemblyInformationalVersionAttribute` and `AssemblyCompanyAttribute` classes and then output their values, as shown in the following code:

```
AssemblyInformationalVersionAttribute? version = assembly
  .GetCustomAttribute<AssemblyInformationalVersionAttribute>();

WriteLine($"  Version: {version?.InformationalVersion}");

AssemblyCompanyAttribute? company = assembly
  .GetCustomAttribute<AssemblyCompanyAttribute>();

WriteLine($"  Company: {company?.Company}");
```

7. Run the code and view the result, as shown in the following output:

```
Version: 1.0.0
Company: WorkingWithReflection
```

Hmmm, unless you set the version, it defaults to 1.0.0, and unless you set the company, it defaults to the name of the assembly. Let's explicitly set this information. The legacy .NET Framework way to set these values was to add attributes in the C# source code file, as shown in the following code:

```
[assembly: AssemblyCompany("Packt Publishing")]
[assembly: AssemblyInformationalVersion("1.3.0")]
```

The Roslyn compiler used by .NET sets these attributes automatically, so we can't use the old way. Instead, they must be set in the project file.

8. Edit the `WorkingWithReflection.csproj` project file to add elements for version and company, as shown highlighted in the following markup:

```
<Project Sdk="Microsoft.NET.Sdk">

  <PropertyGroup>
    <OutputType>Exe</OutputType>
    <TargetFramework>net6.0</TargetFramework>
```

```
<Nullable>enable</Nullable>
<ImplicitUsings>enable</ImplicitUsings>
<Version>6.3.12</Version>
<Company>Packt Publishing</Company>
</PropertyGroup>

</Project>
```

9. Run the code and view the result, as shown in the following output:

```
Version: 6.3.12
Company: Packt Publishing
```

Creating custom attributes

You can define your own attributes by inheriting from the Attribute class:

1. Add a class file to your project named CoderAttribute.cs.

2. Define an attribute class that can decorate either classes or methods with two properties to store the name of a coder and the date they last modified some code, as shown in the following code:

```
namespace Packt.Shared;

[AttributeUsage(AttributeTargets.Class | AttributeTargets.Method,
  AllowMultiple = true)]
public class CoderAttribute : Attribute
{
  public string Coder { get; set; }
  public DateTime LastModified { get; set; }

  public CoderAttribute(string coder, string lastModified)
  {
    Coder = coder;
    LastModified = DateTime.Parse(lastModified);
  }
}
```

3. In Program.cs, import some namespaces, as shown in the following code:

```
using System.Runtime.CompilerServices; // CompilerGeneratedAttribute
using Packt.Shared; // CoderAttribute
```

4. At the bottom of Program.cs, add a class with a method, and decorate the method with the Coder attribute with data about two coders, as shown in the following code:

```
class Animal
{
  [Coder("Mark Price", "22 August 2021")]
  [Coder("Johnni Rasmussen", "13 September 2021")]
  public void Speak()
  {
    WriteLine("Woof...");
  }
}
```

5. In `Program.cs`, above the `Animal` class, add code to get the types, enumerate their members, read any `Coder` attributes on those members, and output the information, as shown in the following code:

```
WriteLine();
WriteLine($"* Types:");
Type[] types = assembly.GetTypes();

foreach (Type type in types)
{
  WriteLine();
  WriteLine($"Type: {type.FullName}");
  MemberInfo[] members = type.GetMembers();

  foreach (MemberInfo member in members)
  {
    WriteLine("{0}: {1} ({2})",
      arg0: member.MemberType,
      arg1: member.Name,
      arg2: member.DeclaringType?.Name);

    IOrderedEnumerable<CoderAttribute> coders =
      member.GetCustomAttributes<CoderAttribute>()
      .OrderByDescending(c => c.LastModified);

    foreach (CoderAttribute coder in coders)
    {
      WriteLine("-> Modified by {0} on {1}",
        coder.Coder, coder.LastModified.ToShortDateString());
    }
  }
}
```

6. Run the code and view the result, as shown in the following partial output:

```
* Types:
...
```

```
Type: Animal
Method: Speak (Animal)
-> Modified by Johnni Rasmussen on 13/09/2021
-> Modified by Mark Price on 22/08/2021
Method: GetType (Object)
Method: ToString (Object)
Method: Equals (Object)
Method: GetHashCode (Object)
Constructor: .ctor (Program)
...
Type: <Program>$+<>c
Method: GetType (Object)
Method: ToString (Object)
Method: Equals (Object)
Method: GetHashCode (Object)
Constructor: .ctor (<>c)
Field: <>9 (<>c)
Field: <>9__0_0 (<>c)
```

What is the `<Program>$+<>c` type?

It is a compiler-generated **display class**. `<>` indicates compiler-generated and `c` indicates a display class. They are undocumented implementation details of the compiler and could change at any time. You can ignore them, so as an optional challenge, add statements to your console application to filter compiler-generated types by skipping types decorated with `CompilerGeneratedAttribute`.

Doing more with reflection

This is just a taster of what can be achieved with reflection. We only used reflection to read metadata from our code. Reflection can also do the following:

- **Dynamically load assemblies that are not currently referenced**: https://docs. microsoft.com/en-us/dotnet/standard/assembly/unloadability

- **Dynamically execute code**: https://docs.microsoft.com/en-us/dotnet/api/system. reflection.methodbase.invoke

- **Dynamically generate new code and assemblies**: https://docs.microsoft.com/en-us/ dotnet/api/system.reflection.emit.assemblybuilder

Working with images

ImageSharp is a third-party cross-platform 2D graphics library. When .NET Core 1.0 was in development, there was negative feedback from the community about the missing `System. Drawing` namespace for working with 2D images.

The **ImageSharp** project was started to fill that gap for modern .NET applications.

In their official documentation for System.Drawing, Microsoft says, "The System.Drawing namespace is not recommended for new development due to not being supported within a Windows or ASP.NET service, and it is not cross-platform. ImageSharp and SkiaSharp are recommended as alternatives."

Let us see what can be achieved with ImageSharp:

1. Use your preferred code editor to add a new console app named WorkingWithImages to the Chapter08 solution/workspace.

2. In Visual Studio Code, select WorkingWithImages as the active OmniSharp project.

3. Create an images folder and download the nine images from the following link: https://github.com/markjprice/cs10dotnet6/tree/master/Assets/Categories

4. Add a package reference for SixLabors.ImageSharp, as shown in the following markup:

```
<ItemGroup>
  <PackageReference Include="SixLabors.ImageSharp" Version="1.0.3" />
</ItemGroup>
```

5. Build the WorkingWithImages project.

6. At the top of Program.cs, import some namespaces for working with images, as shown in the following code:

```
using SixLabors.ImageSharp;
using SixLabors.ImageSharp.Processing;
```

7. In Program.cs, enter statements to convert all the files in the images folder into grayscale thumbnails at one-tenth size, as shown in the following code:

```
string imagesFolder = Path.Combine(
  Environment.CurrentDirectory, "images");

IEnumerable<string> images =
  Directory.EnumerateFiles(imagesFolder);

foreach (string imagePath in images)
{
  string thumbnailPath = Path.Combine(
    Environment.CurrentDirectory, "images",
    Path.GetFileNameWithoutExtension(imagePath)
    + "-thumbnail" + Path.GetExtension(imagePath));

  using (Image image = Image.Load(imagePath))
  {
```

```
        image.Mutate(x => x.Resize(image.Width / 10, image.Height / 10));
        image.Mutate(x => x.Grayscale());
        image.Save(thumbnailPath);
      }
    }
    WriteLine("Image processing complete. View the images folder.");
```

8. Run the code.

9. In the filesystem, open the images folder and note the much-smaller-in-bytes grayscale thumbnails, as shown in *Figure 8.1*:

Figure 8.1: Images after processing

ImageSharp also has NuGet packages for programmatically drawing images and working with images on the web, as shown in the following list:

- `SixLabors.ImageSharp.Drawing`
- `SixLabors.ImageSharp.Web`

Internationalizing your code

Internationalization is the process of enabling your code to run correctly all over the world. It has two parts: **globalization** and **localization**.

Globalization is about writing your code to accommodate multiple languages and region combinations. The combination of a language and a region is known as a culture. It is important for your code to know both the language and region because, for example, the date and currency formats are different in Quebec and Paris, despite them both using the French language.

There are **International Organization for Standardization (ISO)** codes for all culture combinations. For example, in the code da-DK, da indicates the Danish language and DK indicates the Denmark region, and in the code fr-CA, fr indicates the French language and CA indicates the Canada region.

ISO is not an acronym. ISO is a reference to the Greek word *isos* (which means equal).

Localization is about customizing the user interface to support a language, for example, changing the label of a button to be Close (en) or Fermer (fr). Since localization is more about the language, it doesn't always need to know about the region, although ironically enough, standardization (en-US) and standardisation (en-GB) suggest otherwise.

Detecting and changing the current culture

Internationalization is a huge topic on which several thousand-page books have been written. In this section, you will get a brief introduction to the basics using the CultureInfo type in the System.Globalization namespace.

Let's write some code:

1. Use your preferred code editor to add a new console app named Internationalization to the Chapter08 solution/workspace.

2. In Visual Studio Code, select Internationalization as the active OmniSharp project.

3. At the top of Program.cs, import the namespace for using globalization types, as shown in the following code:

   ```
   using System.Globalization; // CultureInfo
   ```

4. Add statements to get the current globalization and localization cultures and output some information about them, and then prompt the user to enter a new culture code and show how that affects the formatting of common values such as dates and currency, as shown in the following code:

   ```
   CultureInfo globalization = CultureInfo.CurrentCulture;
   CultureInfo localization = CultureInfo.CurrentUICulture;

   WriteLine("The current globalization culture is {0}: {1}",
     globalization.Name, globalization.DisplayName);

   WriteLine("The current localization culture is {0}: {1}",
     localization.Name, localization.DisplayName);

   WriteLine();

   WriteLine("en-US: English (United States)");
   WriteLine("da-DK: Danish (Denmark)");
   WriteLine("fr-CA: French (Canada)");

   Write("Enter an ISO culture code: ");
   string? newCulture = ReadLine();

   if (!string.IsNullOrEmpty(newCulture))
   ```

```
  {
    CultureInfo ci = new(newCulture);

    // change the current cultures
    CultureInfo.CurrentCulture = ci;
    CultureInfo.CurrentUICulture = ci;
  }
  WriteLine();

  Write("Enter your name: ");
  string? name = ReadLine();

  Write("Enter your date of birth: ");
  string? dob = ReadLine();

  Write("Enter your salary: ");
  string? salary = ReadLine();

  DateTime date = DateTime.Parse(dob);
  int minutes = (int)DateTime.Today.Subtract(date).TotalMinutes;
  decimal earns = decimal.Parse(salary);

  WriteLine(
    "{0} was born on a {1:dddd}, is {2:N0} minutes old, and earns {3:C}",
    name, date, minutes, earns);
```

When you run an application, it automatically sets its thread to use the culture of the operating system. I am running my code in London, UK, so the thread is set to English (United Kingdom).

The code prompts the user to enter an alternative ISO code. This allows your applications to replace the default culture at runtime.

The application then uses standard format codes to output the day of the week using format code dddd; the number of minutes with thousand separators using format code N0; and the salary with the currency symbol. These adapt automatically, based on the thread's culture.

5. Run the code and enter en-GB for the ISO code and then enter some sample data including a date in a format valid for British English, as shown in the following output:

```
Enter an ISO culture code: en-GB
Enter your name: Alice
Enter your date of birth: 30/3/1967
Enter your salary: 23500
Alice was born on a Thursday, is 25,469,280 minutes old, and earns
£23,500.00
```

If you enter en-US instead of en-GB, then you must enter the date using month/day/year.

6. Rerun the code and try a different culture, such as Danish in Denmark, as shown in the following output:

```
Enter an ISO culture code: da-DK
Enter your name: Mikkel
Enter your date of birth: 12/3/1980
Enter your salary: 340000
Mikkel was born on a onsdag, is 18.656.640 minutes old, and earns
340.000,00 kr.
```

In this example, only the date and salary are globalized into Danish. The rest of the text is hardcoded as English. This book does not currently include how to translate text from one language to another. If you would like me to include that in the next edition, please let me know.

Good Practice: Consider whether your application needs to be internationalized and plan for that before you start coding! Write down all the pieces of text in the user interface that will need to be localized. Think about all the data that will need to be globalized (date formats, number formats, and sorting text behavior).

Practicing and exploring

Test your knowledge and understanding by answering some questions, get some hands-on practice, and explore with deeper research into the topics in this chapter.

Exercise 8.1 – Test your knowledge

Use the web to answer the following questions:

1. What is the maximum number of characters that can be stored in a string variable?
2. When and why should you use a SecureString type?
3. When is it appropriate to use a StringBuilder class?
4. When should you use a LinkedList<T> class?
5. When should you use a SortedDictionary<T> class rather than a SortedList<T> class?

6. What is the ISO culture code for Welsh?

7. What is the difference between localization, globalization, and internationalization?

8. In a regular expression, what does $ mean?

9. In a regular expression, how can you represent digits?

10. Why should you *not* use the official standard for email addresses to create a regular expression to validate a user's email address?

Exercise 8.2 – Practice regular expressions

In the Chapter08 solution/workspace, create a console application named Exercise02 that prompts the user to enter a regular expression and then prompts the user to enter some input and compare the two for a match until the user presses *Esc*, as shown in the following output:

```
The default regular expression checks for at least one digit.
Enter a regular expression (or press ENTER to use the default): ^[a-z]+$
Enter some input: apples
apples matches ^[a-z]+$? True
Press ESC to end or any key to try again.
Enter a regular expression (or press ENTER to use the default): ^[a-z]+$
Enter some input: abc123xyz
abc123xyz matches ^[a-z]+$? False
Press ESC to end or any key to try again.
```

Exercise 8.3 – Practice writing extension methods

In the Chapter08 solution/workspace, create a class library named Exercise03 that defines extension methods that extend number types such as BigInteger and int with a method named ToWords that returns a string describing the number; for example, 18,000,000 would be eighteen million, and 18,456,002,032,011,000,007 would be eighteen quintillion, four hundred and fifty-six quadrillion, two trillion, thirty-two billion, eleven million, and seven.

You can read more about names for large numbers at the following link: https:// en.wikipedia.org/wiki/Names_of_large_numbers

Exercise 8.4 – Explore topics

Use the links on the following page to learn more detail about the topics covered in this chapter:

https://github.com/markjprice/cs10dotnet6/blob/main/book-links.md#chapter-8---working-with-common-net-types

Summary

In this chapter, you explored some choices for types to store and manipulate numbers, dates and times, and text including regular expressions, and which collections to use for storing multiple items; worked with indexes, ranges, and spans; used some network resources; reflected on code and attributes; manipulated images using a Microsoft-recommended third-party library; and learned how to internationalize your code.

In the next chapter, we will manage files and streams, encode and decode text, and perform serialization.

09

Working with Files, Streams, and Serialization

This chapter is about reading and writing to files and streams, text encoding, and serialization.

We will cover the following topics:

- Managing the filesystem
- Reading and writing with streams
- Encoding and decoding text
- Serializing object graphs
- Controlling JSON processing

Managing the filesystem

Your applications will often need to perform input and output operations with files and directories in different environments. The System and System.IO namespaces contain classes for this purpose.

Handling cross-platform environments and filesystems

Let's explore how to handle cross-platform environments like the differences between Windows and Linux or macOS. Paths are different for Windows, macOS, and Linux, so we will start by exploring how .NET handles this:

1. Use your preferred code editor to create a new solution/workspace named Chapter09.

2. Add a console app project, as defined in the following list:

    1. Project template: **Console Application**/`console`

    2. Workspace/solution file and folder: `Chapter09`

    3. Project file and folder: `WorkingWithFileSystems`

3. In `Program.cs`, add statements to statically import the `System.Console`, `System. IO.Directory`, `System.Environment`, and `System.IO.Path` types, as shown in the following code:

```
using static System.Console;
using static System.IO.Directory;
using static System.IO.Path;
using static System.Environment;
```

4. In `Program.cs`, create a static `OutputFileSystemInfo` method, and write statements in it to do the following:

- Output the path and directory separation characters.

- Output the path of the current directory.

- Output some special paths for system files, temporary files, and documents.

```
static void OutputFileSystemInfo()
{
  WriteLine("{0,-33} {1}", arg0: "Path.PathSeparator",
    arg1: PathSeparator);
  WriteLine("{0,-33} {1}", arg0: "Path.DirectorySeparatorChar",
    arg1: DirectorySeparatorChar);
  WriteLine("{0,-33} {1}", arg0: "Directory.GetCurrentDirectory()",
    arg1: GetCurrentDirectory());
  WriteLine("{0,-33} {1}", arg0: "Environment.CurrentDirectory",
    arg1: CurrentDirectory);
  WriteLine("{0,-33} {1}", arg0: "Environment.SystemDirectory",
    arg1: SystemDirectory);
  WriteLine("{0,-33} {1}", arg0: "Path.GetTempPath()",
    arg1: GetTempPath());

  WriteLine("GetFolderPath(SpecialFolder");
  WriteLine("{0,-33} {1}", arg0: " .System)",
    arg1: GetFolderPath(SpecialFolder.System));
  WriteLine("{0,-33} {1}", arg0: " .ApplicationData)",
    arg1: GetFolderPath(SpecialFolder.ApplicationData));
  WriteLine("{0,-33} {1}", arg0: " .MyDocuments)",
    arg1: GetFolderPath(SpecialFolder.MyDocuments));
  WriteLine("{0,-33} {1}", arg0: " .Personal)",
    arg1: GetFolderPath(SpecialFolder.Personal));
}
```

The `Environment` type has many other useful members that we did not use in this code, including the `GetEnvironmentVariables` method and the `OSVersion` and `ProcessorCount` properties.

5. In `Program.cs`, above the function, call the `OutputFileSystemInfo` method, as shown in the following code:

    ```
    OutputFileSystemInfo();
    ```

6. Run the code and view the result, as shown in *Figure 9.1*:

```
Microsoft Visual Studio Debug Console                                        —   □   ×
Path.PathSeparator                      ;
Path.DirectorySeparatorChar             \
Directory.GetCurrentDirectory()         C:\Code\Chapter09\WorkingWithFileSystems\bin\Debug\net6.0
Environment.CurrentDirectory            C:\Code\Chapter09\WorkingWithFileSystems\bin\Debug\net6.0
Environment.SystemDirectory             C:\WINDOWS\system32
Path.GetTempPath()                      C:\Users\markj\AppData\Local\Temp\
GetFolderPath(SpecialFolder
  .System)                              C:\WINDOWS\system32
  .ApplicationData)                     C:\Users\markj\AppData\Roaming
  .MyDocuments)                         \\Mac\Home\Documents
  .Personal)                            \\Mac\Home\Documents
```

Figure 9.1: Running your application to show filesystem information on Windows

When running the console app using `dotnet run` with Visual Studio Code, the `CurrentDirectory` will be the project folder, not a folder inside `bin`.

Good Practice: Windows uses a backslash \ for the directory separator character. macOS and Linux use a forward slash / for the directory separator character. Do not assume what character is used in your code when combining paths.

Managing drives

To manage drives, use the `DriveInfo` type, which has a static method that returns information about all the drives connected to your computer. Each drive has a drive type.

Let's explore drives:

1. Create a `WorkWithDrives` method, and write statements to get all the drives and output their name, type, size, available free space, and format, but only if the drive is ready, as shown in the following code:

    ```
    static void WorkWithDrives()
    {
    ```

```csharp
    WriteLine("{0,-30} | {1,-10} | {2,-7} | {3,18} | {4,18}",
      "NAME", "TYPE", "FORMAT", "SIZE (BYTES)", "FREE SPACE");

    foreach (DriveInfo drive in DriveInfo.GetDrives())
    {
      if (drive.IsReady)
      {
        WriteLine(
          "{0,-30} | {1,-10} | {2,-7} | {3,18:N0} | {4,18:N0}",
          drive.Name, drive.DriveType, drive.DriveFormat,
          drive.TotalSize, drive.AvailableFreeSpace);
      }
      else
      {
        WriteLine("{0,-30} | {1,-10}", drive.Name, drive.DriveType);
      }
    }
  }
}
```

> **Good Practice**: Check that a drive is ready before reading properties such as TotalSize or you will see an exception thrown with removable drives.

2. In `Program.cs`, comment out the previous method call and add a call to `WorkWithDrives`, as shown highlighted in the following code:

```csharp
// OutputFileSystemInfo();
WorkWithDrives();
```

3. Run the code and view the result, as shown in *Figure 9.2*:

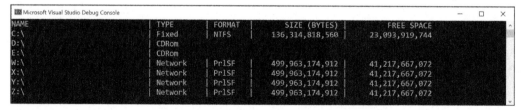

Figure 9.2: Showing drive information on Windows

Managing directories

To manage directories, use the `Directory`, `Path`, and `Environment` static classes. These types include many members for working with the filesystem.

When constructing custom paths, you must be careful to write your code so that it makes no assumptions about the platform, for example, what to use for the directory separator character:

1. Create a `WorkWithDirectories` method, and write statements to do the following:

   - Define a custom path under the user's home directory by creating an array of strings for the directory names, and then properly combining them with the `Path` type's `Combine` method.

   - Check for the existence of the custom directory path using the `Exists` method of the `Directory` class.

   - Create and then delete the directory, including files and subdirectories within it, using the `CreateDirectory` and `Delete` methods of the `Directory` class:

```
static void WorkWithDirectories()
{
  // define a directory path for a new folder
  // starting in the user's folder
  string newFolder = Combine(
    GetFolderPath(SpecialFolder.Personal),
    "Code", "Chapter09", "NewFolder");

  WriteLine($"Working with: {newFolder}");

  // check if it exists
  WriteLine($"Does it exist? {Exists(newFolder)}");

  // create directory
  WriteLine("Creating it...");
  CreateDirectory(newFolder);
  WriteLine($"Does it exist? {Exists(newFolder)}");
  Write("Confirm the directory exists, and then press ENTER: ");
  ReadLine();

  // delete directory
  WriteLine("Deleting it...");
  Delete(newFolder, recursive: true);
  WriteLine($"Does it exist? {Exists(newFolder)}");
}
```

2. In `Program.cs`, comment out the previous method call, and add a call to `WorkWithDirectories`.

3. Run the code and view the result, and use your favorite file management tool to confirm that the directory has been created before pressing *Enter* to delete it, as shown in the following output:

```
Working with: /Users/markjprice/Code/Chapter09/NewFolder Does it exist?
False
```

```
Creating it...
Does it exist? True
Confirm the directory exists, and then press ENTER:
Deleting it...
Does it exist? False
```

Managing files

When working with files, you could statically import the file type, just as we did for the directory type, but, for the next example, we will not, because it has some of the same methods as the directory type and they would conflict. The file type has a short enough name not to matter in this case. The steps are as follows:

1. Create a WorkWithFiles method, and write statements to do the following:

    1. Check for the existence of a file.

    2. Create a text file.

    3. Write a line of text to the file.

    4. Close the file to release system resources and file locks (this would normally be done inside a try-finally statement block to ensure that the file is closed even if an exception occurs when writing to it).

    5. Copy the file to a backup.

    6. Delete the original file.

    7. Read the backup file's contents and then close it:

```
static void WorkWithFiles()
{
  // define a directory path to output files
  // starting in the user's folder
  string dir = Combine(
    GetFolderPath(SpecialFolder.Personal),
    "Code", "Chapter09", "OutputFiles");

  CreateDirectory(dir);

  // define file paths
  string textFile = Combine(dir, "Dummy.txt");
  string backupFile = Combine(dir, "Dummy.bak");
  WriteLine($"Working with: {textFile}");

  // check if a file exists
  WriteLine($"Does it exist? {File.Exists(textFile)}");

  // create a new text file and write a line to it
  StreamWriter textWriter = File.CreateText(textFile);
```

```
textWriter.WriteLine("Hello, C#!");
textWriter.Close(); // close file and release resources
WriteLine($"Does it exist? {File.Exists(textFile)}");

// copy the file, and overwrite if it already exists
File.Copy(sourceFileName: textFile,
  destFileName: backupFile, overwrite: true);
WriteLine(
  $"Does {backupFile} exist? {File.Exists(backupFile)}");
Write("Confirm the files exist, and then press ENTER: ");
ReadLine();

// delete file
File.Delete(textFile);
WriteLine($"Does it exist? {File.Exists(textFile)}");

// read from the text file backup
WriteLine($"Reading contents of {backupFile}:");
StreamReader textReader = File.OpenText(backupFile);
WriteLine(textReader.ReadToEnd());
textReader.Close();
}
```

2. In `Program.cs`, comment out the previous method call, and add a call to `WorkWithFiles`.

3. Run the code and view the result, as shown in the following output:

```
Working with: /Users/markjprice/Code/Chapter09/OutputFiles/Dummy.txt
Does it exist? False
Does it exist? True
Does /Users/markjprice/Code/Chapter09/OutputFiles/Dummy.bak exist? True
Confirm the files exist, and then press ENTER:
Does it exist? False
Reading contents of /Users/markjprice/Code/Chapter09/OutputFiles/Dummy.
bak:
Hello, C#!
```

Managing paths

Sometimes, you need to work with parts of a path; for example, you might want to extract just the folder name, the filename, or the extension. Sometimes, you need to generate temporary folders and filenames. You can do this with static methods of the `Path` class:

1. Add the following statements to the end of the `WorkWithFiles` method:

```
// Managing paths
WriteLine($"Folder Name: {GetDirectoryName(textFile)}");
WriteLine($"File Name: {GetFileName(textFile)}");
```

```
WriteLine("File Name without Extension: {0}",
  GetFileNameWithoutExtension(textFile));
WriteLine($"File Extension: {GetExtension(textFile)}");
WriteLine($"Random File Name: {GetRandomFileName()}");
WriteLine($"Temporary File Name: {GetTempFileName()}");
```

2. Run the code and view the result, as shown in the following output:

```
Folder Name: /Users/markjprice/Code/Chapter09/OutputFiles
File Name: Dummy.txt
File Name without Extension: Dummy
File Extension: .txt
Random File Name: u45w1zki.co3
Temporary File Name:
/var/folders/tz/xx0y_wld5sx0nv0fjtq4tnpc0000gn/T/tmpyqrepP.tmp
```

GetTempFileName creates a zero-byte file and returns its name, ready for you to use. GetRandomFileName just returns a filename; it doesn't create the file.

Getting file information

To get more information about a file or directory, for example, its size or when it was last accessed, you can create an instance of the FileInfo or DirectoryInfo class.

FileInfo and DirectoryInfo both inherit from FileSystemInfo, so they both have members such as LastAccessTime and Delete, as well as extra members specific to themselves, as shown in the following table:

Class	Members
FileSystemInfo	Fields: FullPath, OriginalPath
	Properties: Attributes, CreationTime, CreationTimeUtc, Exists, Extension, FullName, LastAccessTime, LastAccessTimeUtc, LastWriteTime, LastWriteTimeUtc, Name
	Methods: Delete, GetObjectData, Refresh
DirectoryInfo	Properties: Parent, Root
	Methods: Create, CreateSubdirectory, EnumerateDirectories, EnumerateFiles, EnumerateFileSystemInfos, GetAccessControl, GetDirectories, GetFiles, GetFileSystemInfos, MoveTo, SetAccessControl
FileInfo	Properties: Directory, DirectoryName, IsReadOnly, Length
	Methods: AppendText, CopyTo, Create, CreateText, Decrypt, Encrypt, GetAccessControl, MoveTo, Open, OpenRead, OpenText, OpenWrite, Replace, SetAccessControl

Let's write some code that uses a FileInfo instance for efficiently performing multiple actions on a file:

1. Add statements to the end of the WorkWithFiles method to create an instance of FileInfo for the backup file and write information about it to the console, as shown in the following code:

```
FileInfo info = new(backupFile);
WriteLine($"{backupFile}:");
WriteLine($"Contains {info.Length} bytes");
WriteLine($"Last accessed {info.LastAccessTime}");
WriteLine($"Has readonly set to {info.IsReadOnly}");
```

2. Run the code and view the result, as shown in the following output:

```
/Users/markjprice/Code/Chapter09/OutputFiles/Dummy.bak:
Contains 11 bytes
Last accessed 26/10/2021 09:08:26
Has readonly set to False
```

The number of bytes might be different on your operating system because operating systems can use different line endings.

Controlling how you work with files

When working with files, you often need to control how they are opened. The File.Open method has overloads to specify additional options using enum values.

The enum types are as follows:

- FileMode: This controls what you want to do with the file, like CreateNew, OpenOrCreate, or Truncate.
- FileAccess: This controls what level of access you need, like ReadWrite.
- FileShare: This controls locks on the file to allow other processes the specified level of access, like Read.

You might want to open a file and read from it, and allow other processes to read it too, as shown in the following code:

```
FileStream file = File.Open(pathToFile,
  FileMode.Open, FileAccess.Read, FileShare.Read);
```

There is also an enum for attributes of a file as follows:

- FileAttributes: This is to check a FileSystemInfo-derived types' Attributes property for values like Archive and Encrypted.

You could check a file or directory's attributes, as shown in the following code:

```
FileInfo info = new(backupFile);
WriteLine("Is the backup file compressed? {0}",
    info.Attributes.HasFlag(FileAttributes.Compressed));
```

Reading and writing with streams

A **stream** is a sequence of bytes that can be read from and written to. Although files can be processed rather like arrays, with random access provided by knowing the position of a byte within the file, it can be useful to process files as a stream in which the bytes can be accessed in sequential order.

Streams can also be used to process terminal input and output and networking resources such as sockets and ports that do not provide random access and cannot seek (that is, move) to a position. You can write code to process some arbitrary bytes without knowing or caring where it comes from. Your code simply reads or writes to a stream, and another piece of code handles where the bytes are actually stored.

Understanding abstract and concrete streams

There is an abstract class named Stream that represents any type of stream. Remember that an abstract class cannot be instantiated using new; they can only be inherited.

There are many concrete classes that inherit from this base class, including FileStream, MemoryStream, BufferedStream, GZipStream, and SslStream, so they all work the same way. All streams implement IDisposable, so they have a Dispose method to release unmanaged resources.

Some of the common members of the Stream class are described in the following table:

Member	Description
CanRead, CanWrite	These properties determine if you can read from and write to the stream.
Length, Position	These properties determine the total number of bytes and the current position within the stream. These properties may throw an exception for some types of streams.
Dispose	This method closes the stream and releases its resources.
Flush	If the stream has a buffer, then this method writes the bytes in the buffer to the stream and the buffer is cleared.
CanSeek	This property determines if the Seek method can be used.
Seek	This method moves the current position to the one specified in its parameter.
Read, ReadAsync	These methods read a specified number of bytes from the stream into a byte array and advance the position.
ReadByte	This method reads the next byte from the stream and advances the position.
Write, WriteAsync	These methods write the contents of a byte array into the stream.
WriteByte	This method writes a byte to the stream.

Understanding storage streams

Some storage streams that represent a location where the bytes will be stored are described in the following table:

Namespace	Class	Description
System.IO	FileStream	Bytes stored in the filesystem.
System.IO	MemoryStream	Bytes stored in memory in the current process.
System.Net.Sockets	NetworkStream	Bytes stored at a network location.

FileStream has been re-written in .NET 6 to have much higher performance and reliability on Windows.

Understanding function streams

Some function streams that cannot exist on their own, but can only be "plugged onto" other streams to add functionality, are described in the following table:

Namespace	Class	Description
System.Security.Cryptography	CryptoStream	This encrypts and decrypts the stream.
System.IO.Compression	GZipStream, DeflateStream	These compress and decompress the stream.
System.Net.Security	AuthenticatedStream	This sends credentials across the stream.

Understanding stream helpers

Although there will be occasions where you need to work with streams at a low level, most often, you can plug helper classes into the chain to make things easier. All the helper types for streams implement IDisposable, so they have a Dispose method to release unmanaged resources.

Some helper classes to handle common scenarios are described in the following table:

Namespace	Class	Description
System.IO	StreamReader	This reads from the underlying stream as plain text.
System.IO	StreamWriter	This writes to the underlying stream as plain text.
System.IO	BinaryReader	This reads from streams as .NET types. For example, the ReadDecimal method reads the next 16 bytes from the underlying stream as a decimal value and the ReadInt32 method reads the next 4 bytes as an int value.
System.IO	BinaryWriter	This writes to streams as .NET types. For example, the Write method with a decimal parameter writes 16 bytes to the underlying stream and the Write method with an int parameter writes 4 bytes.

System.Xml	XmlReader	This reads from the underlying stream using XML format.
System.Xml	XmlWriter	This writes to the underlying stream using XML format.

Writing to text streams

Let's type some code to write text to a stream:

1. Use your preferred code editor to add a new console app named WorkingWithStreams to the Chapter09 solution/workspace:

    1. In Visual Studio, set the startup project for the solution to the current selection.

    2. In Visual Studio Code, select WorkingWithStreams as the active OmniSharp project.

2. In the WorkingWithStreams project, in Program.cs, import the System.Xml namespace and statically import the System.Console, System.Environment, and System.IO.Path types.

3. At the bottom of Program.cs, define a static class named Viper with a static array of string values named Callsigns, as shown in the following code:

    ```
    static class Viper
    {
      // define an array of Viper pilot call signs
      public static string[] Callsigns = new[]
      {
        "Husker", "Starbuck", "Apollo", "Boomer",
        "Bulldog", "Athena", "Helo", "Racetrack"
      };
    }
    ```

4. Above the Viper class, define a WorkWithText method that enumerates the Viper call signs, writing each one on its own line in a single text file, as shown in the following code:

    ```
    static void WorkWithText()
    {
      // define a file to write to
      string textFile = Combine(CurrentDirectory, "streams.txt");

      // create a text file and return a helper writer
      StreamWriter text = File.CreateText(textFile);

      // enumerate the strings, writing each one
      // to the stream on a separate line
      foreach (string item in Viper.Callsigns)
      {
        text.WriteLine(item);
    ```

```
  }
  text.Close(); // release resources

  // output the contents of the file
  WriteLine("{0} contains {1:N0} bytes.",
    arg0: textFile,
    arg1: new FileInfo(textFile).Length);

  WriteLine(File.ReadAllText(textFile));
}
```

5. Below the namespace imports, call the `WorkWithText` method.

6. Run the code and view the result, as shown in the following output:

```
/Users/markjprice/Code/Chapter09/WorkingWithStreams/streams.txt contains
60 bytes.
Husker
Starbuck
Apollo
Boomer
Bulldog
Athena
Helo
Racetrack
```

7. Open the file that was created and check that it contains the list of call signs.

Writing to XML streams

There are two ways to write an XML element, as follows:

*   `WriteStartElement` and `WriteEndElement`: Use this pair when an element might have child elements.

*   `WriteElementString`: Use this when an element does not have children.

Now, let's try storing the Viper pilot call signs array of `string` values in an XML file:

1. Create a `WorkWithXml` method that enumerates the call signs, writing each one as an element in a single XML file, as shown in the following code:

```
static void WorkWithXml()
{
  // define a file to write to
  string xmlFile = Combine(CurrentDirectory, "streams.xml");

  // create a file stream
  FileStream xmlFileStream = File.Create(xmlFile);
```

```csharp
  // wrap the file stream in an XML writer helper
  // and automatically indent nested elements
  XmlWriter xml = XmlWriter.Create(xmlFileStream,
    new XmlWriterSettings { Indent = true });

  // write the XML declaration
  xml.WriteStartDocument();

  // write a root element
  xml.WriteStartElement("callsigns");

  // enumerate the strings writing each one to the stream
  foreach (string item in Viper.Callsigns)
  {
    xml.WriteElementString("callsign", item);
  }

  // write the close root element
  xml.WriteEndElement();

  // close helper and stream
  xml.Close();
  xmlFileStream.Close();

  // output all the contents of the file
  WriteLine("{0} contains {1:N0} bytes.",
    arg0: xmlFile,
    arg1: new FileInfo(xmlFile).Length);

  WriteLine(File.ReadAllText(xmlFile));
}
```

2. In `Program.cs`, comment out the previous method call, and add a call to the `WorkWithXml` method.

3. Run the code and view the result, as shown in the following output:

```
/Users/markjprice/Code/Chapter09/WorkingWithStreams/streams.xml contains
310 bytes.
<?xml version="1.0" encoding="utf-8"?>
<callsigns>
  <callsign>Husker</callsign>
  <callsign>Starbuck</callsign>
  <callsign>Apollo</callsign>
  <callsign>Boomer</callsign>
  <callsign>Bulldog</callsign>
```

```
<callsign>Athena</callsign>
<callsign>Helo</callsign>
<callsign>Racetrack</callsign>
</callsigns>
```

Disposing of file resources

When you open a file to read or write to it, you are using resources outside of .NET. These are called **unmanaged resources** and must be disposed of when you are done working with them. To deterministically control when they are disposed of, we can call the `Dispose` method inside of a `finally` block.

Let's improve our previous code that works with XML to properly dispose of its unmanaged resources:

1. Modify the `WorkWithXml` method, as shown highlighted in the following code:

```
static void WorkWithXml()
{
  FileStream? xmlFileStream = null;
  XmlWriter? xml = null;

  try
  {
    // define a file to write to
    string xmlFile = Combine(CurrentDirectory, "streams.xml");

    // create a file stream
    xmlFileStream = File.Create(xmlFile);

    // wrap the file stream in an XML writer helper
    // and automatically indent nested elements
    xml = XmlWriter.Create(xmlFileStream,
      new XmlWriterSettings { Indent = true });

    // write the XML declaration
    xml.WriteStartDocument();

    // write a root element
    xml.WriteStartElement("callsigns");

    // enumerate the strings writing each one to the stream
    foreach (string item in Viper.Callsigns)
    {
      xml.WriteElementString("callsign", item);
    }
```

```
      // write the close root element
      xml.WriteEndElement();

      // close helper and stream
      xml.Close();
      xmlFileStream.Close();

      // output all the contents of the file
      WriteLine($"{0} contains {1:N0} bytes.",
        arg0: xmlFile,
        arg1: new FileInfo(xmlFile).Length);

      WriteLine(File.ReadAllText(xmlFile));
    }
    catch (Exception ex)
    {
      // if the path doesn't exist the exception will be caught
      WriteLine($"{ex.GetType()} says {ex.Message}");
    }
    finally
    {
      if (xml != null)
      {
        xml.Dispose();
        WriteLine("The XML writer's unmanaged resources have been
disposed.");
        if (xmlFileStream != null)
        {
          xmlFileStream.Dispose();
          WriteLine("The file stream's unmanaged resources have been
disposed.");
        }
      }
    }
}
```

You could also go back and modify the other methods you previously created but I will leave that as an optional exercise for you.

2. Run the code and view the result, as shown in the following output:

```
The XML writer's unmanaged resources have been disposed.
The file stream's unmanaged resources have been disposed.
```

Good Practice: Before calling the Dispose method, check that the object is not null.

Simplifying disposal by using the using statement

You can simplify the code that needs to check for a null object and then call its Dispose method by using the using statement. Generally, I would recommend using using rather than manually calling Dispose unless you need a greater level of control.

Confusingly, there are two uses for the using keyword: importing a namespace and generating a finally statement that calls Dispose on an object that implements IDisposable.

The compiler changes a using statement block into a try-finally statement without a catch statement. You can use nested try statements; so, if you do want to catch any exceptions, you can, as shown in the following code example:

```
using (FileStream file2 = File.OpenWrite(
  Path.Combine(path, "file2.txt")))
{
  using (StreamWriter writer2 = new StreamWriter(file2))
  {
    try
    {
      writer2.WriteLine("Welcome, .NET!");
    }
    catch(Exception ex)
    {
      WriteLine($"{ex.GetType()} says {ex.Message}");
    }
  } // automatically calls Dispose if the object is not null
} // automatically calls Dispose if the object is not null
```

You can even simplify the code further by not explicitly specifying the braces and indentation for the using statements, as shown in the following code:

```
using FileStream file2 = File.OpenWrite(
  Path.Combine(path, "file2.txt"));

using StreamWriter writer2 = new(file2);

try
{
  writer2.WriteLine("Welcome, .NET!");
}
```

```
catch(Exception ex)
{
  WriteLine($"{ex.GetType()} says {ex.Message}");
}
```

Compressing streams

XML is relatively verbose, so it takes up more space in bytes than plain text. Let's see how we can squeeze the XML using a common compression algorithm known as GZIP:

1. At the top of `Program.cs`, import the namespace for working with compression, as shown in the following code:

   ```
   using System.IO.Compression; // BrotliStream, GZipStream, CompressionMode
   ```

2. Add a `WorkWithCompression` method, which uses instances of `GZipStream` to create a compressed file containing the same XML elements as before and then decompresses it while reading it and outputting to the console, as shown in the following code:

   ```
   static void WorkWithCompression()
   {
     string fileExt = "gzip";

     // compress the XML output
     string filePath = Combine(
       CurrentDirectory, $"streams.{fileExt}");

     FileStream file = File.Create(filePath);

     Stream compressor = new GZipStream(file, CompressionMode.Compress);

     using (compressor)
     {
       using (XmlWriter xml = XmlWriter.Create(compressor))
       {
         xml.WriteStartDocument();
         xml.WriteStartElement("callsigns");

         foreach (string item in Viper.Callsigns)
         {
           xml.WriteElementString("callsign", item);
         }

         // the normal call to WriteEndElement is not necessary
   ```

```
        // because when the XmlWriter disposes, it will
        // automatically end any elements of any depth
      }
    } // also closes the underlying stream

    // output all the contents of the compressed file
    WriteLine("{0} contains {1:N0} bytes.",
      filePath, new FileInfo(filePath).Length);

    WriteLine($"The compressed contents:");
    WriteLine(File.ReadAllText(filePath));

    // read a compressed file
    WriteLine("Reading the compressed XML file:");
    file = File.Open(filePath, FileMode.Open);

    Stream decompressor = new GZipStream(file,
      CompressionMode.Decompress);

    using (decompressor)
    {
      using (XmlReader reader = XmlReader.Create(decompressor))
      {
        while (reader.Read()) // read the next XML node
        {
          // check if we are on an element node named callsign
          if ((reader.NodeType == XmlNodeType.Element)
            && (reader.Name == "callsign"))
          {
            reader.Read(); // move to the text inside element
            WriteLine($"{reader.Value}"); // read its value
          }
        }
      }
    }
  }
```

3. In `Program.cs`, leave the call to `WorkWithXml`, and add a call to `WorkWithCompression`, as shown highlighted in the following code:

```
// WorkWithText();
WorkWithXml();
WorkWithCompression();
```

4. Run the code and compare the sizes of the XML file and the compressed XML file. It is less than half the size of the same XML without compression, as shown in the following edited output:

```
/Users/markjprice/Code/Chapter09/WorkingWithStreams/streams.xml contains
310 bytes.
/Users/markjprice/Code/Chapter09/WorkingWithStreams/streams.gzip contains
150 bytes.
```

Compressing with the Brotli algorithm

In .NET Core 2.1, Microsoft introduced an implementation of the Brotli compression algorithm. In performance, Brotli is like the algorithm used in DEFLATE and GZIP, but the output is about 20% denser. The steps are as follows:

1. Modify the WorkWithCompression method to have an optional parameter to indicate if Brotli should be used and to use Brotli by default, as shown highlighted in the following code:

```
static void WorkWithCompression(bool useBrotli = true)
{
  string fileExt = useBrotli ? "brotli" : "gzip";

  // compress the XML output
  string filePath = Combine(
    CurrentDirectory, $"streams.{fileExt}");

  FileStream file = File.Create(filePath);

  Stream compressor;

  if (useBrotli)
  {
    compressor = new BrotliStream(file, CompressionMode.Compress);
  }
  else
  {
    compressor = new GZipStream(file, CompressionMode.Compress);
  }

  using (compressor)
  {
    using (XmlWriter xml = XmlWriter.Create(compressor))
    {
      xml.WriteStartDocument();
      xml.WriteStartElement("callsigns");
      foreach (string item in Viper.Callsigns)
```

```
      {
        xml.WriteElementString("callsign", item);
      }
    }
  } // also closes the underlying stream

  // output all the contents of the compressed file
  WriteLine("{0} contains {1:N0} bytes.",
    filePath, new FileInfo(filePath).Length);

  WriteLine($"The compressed contents:");
  WriteLine(File.ReadAllText(filePath));

  // read a compressed file
  WriteLine("Reading the compressed XML file:");
  file = File.Open(filePath, FileMode.Open);

  Stream decompressor;
  if (useBrotli)
  {
    decompressor = new BrotliStream(
      file, CompressionMode.Decompress);
  }
  else
  {
    decompressor = new GZipStream(
      file, CompressionMode.Decompress);
  }

  using (decompressor)
  {
    using (XmlReader reader = XmlReader.Create(decompressor))
    {
      while (reader.Read())
      {
        // check if we are on an element node named callsign
        if ((reader.NodeType == XmlNodeType.Element)
          && (reader.Name == "callsign"))
        {
          reader.Read(); // move to the text inside element
          WriteLine($"{reader.Value}"); // read its value
        }
      }
    }
  }
}
```

2. Near the top of `Program.cs`, call `WorkWithCompression` twice, once with the default using Brotli and once with GZIP, as shown in the following code:

    ```
    WorkWithCompression();
    WorkWithCompression(useBrotli: false);
    ```

3. Run the code and compare the sizes of the two compressed XML files. Brotli is more than 21% denser, as shown in the following edited output:

    ```
    /Users/markjprice/Code/Chapter09/WorkingWithStreams/streams.brotli
    contains 118 bytes.
    /Users/markjprice/Code/Chapter09/WorkingWithStreams/streams.gzip contains
    150 bytes.
    ```

Encoding and decoding text

Text characters can be represented in different ways. For example, the alphabet can be encoded using Morse code into a series of dots and dashes for transmission over a telegraph line.

In a similar way, text inside a computer is stored as bits (ones and zeros) representing a code point within a code space. Most code points represent a single character, but they can also have other meanings like formatting.

For example, ASCII has a code space with 128 code points. .NET uses a standard called **Unicode** to encode text internally. Unicode has more than one million code points.

Sometimes, you will need to move text outside .NET for use by systems that do not use Unicode or use a variation of Unicode, so it is important to learn how to convert between encodings.

The following table lists some alternative text encodings commonly used by computers:

Encoding	Description
ASCII	This encodes a limited range of characters using the lower seven bits of a byte.
UTF-8	This represents each Unicode code point as a sequence of one to four bytes.
UTF-7	This is designed to be more efficient over 7-bit channels than UTF-8 but it has security and robustness issues, so UTF-8 is recommended over UTF-7.
UTF-16	This represents each Unicode code point as a sequence of one or two 16-bit integers.
UTF-32	This represents each Unicode code point as a 32-bit integer and is therefore a fixed-length encoding unlike the other Unicode encodings, which are all variable-length encodings.
ANSI/ISO encodings	This provides support for a variety of code pages that are used to support a specific language or group of languages.

Good Practice: In most cases today, UTF-8 is a good default, which is why it is literally the default encoding, that is, `Encoding.Default`.

Encoding strings as byte arrays

Let's explore text encodings:

1. Use your preferred code editor to add a new console app named `WorkingWithEncodings` to the `Chapter09` solution/workspace.

2. In Visual Studio Code, select `WorkingWithEncodings` as the active OmniSharp project.

3. In `Program.cs`, import the `System.Text` namespace and statically import the `Console` class.

4. Add statements to encode a `string` using an encoding chosen by the user, loop through each byte, and then decode it back into a `string` and output it, as shown in the following code:

```
WriteLine("Encodings");
WriteLine("[1] ASCII");
WriteLine("[2] UTF-7");
WriteLine("[3] UTF-8");
WriteLine("[4] UTF-16 (Unicode)");
WriteLine("[5] UTF-32");
WriteLine("[any other key] Default");

// choose an encoding
Write("Press a number to choose an encoding: ");
ConsoleKey number = ReadKey(intercept: false).Key;
WriteLine();
WriteLine();

Encoding encoder = number switch
{
  ConsoleKey.D1 => Encoding.ASCII,
  ConsoleKey.D2 => Encoding.UTF7,
  ConsoleKey.D3 => Encoding.UTF8,
  ConsoleKey.D4 => Encoding.Unicode,
  ConsoleKey.D5 => Encoding.UTF32,
  _             => Encoding.Default
};

// define a string to encode
string message = "Café cost: £4.39";
```

```
// encode the string into a byte array
byte[] encoded = encoder.GetBytes(message);

// check how many bytes the encoding needed
WriteLine("{0} uses {1:N0} bytes.",
  encoder.GetType().Name, encoded.Length);
WriteLine();

// enumerate each byte
WriteLine($"BYTE HEX CHAR");
foreach (byte b in encoded)
{
  WriteLine($"{b,4} {b.ToString("X"),4} {(char)b,5}");
}

// decode the byte array back into a string and display it
string decoded = encoder.GetString(encoded);
WriteLine(decoded);
```

5. Run the code and note the warning to avoid using `Encoding.UTF7` because it is insecure. Of course, if you need to generate text using that encoding for compatibility with another system, it needs to remain an option in .NET.

6. Press *1* to choose ASCII and note that when outputting the bytes, the pound sign (£) and accented e (é) cannot be represented in ASCII, so it uses a question mark instead.

```
BYTE  HEX  CHAR
  67   43     C
  97   61     a
 102   66     f
  63   3F     ?
  32   20
 111   6F     o
 115   73     s
 116   74     t
  58   3A     :
  32   20
  63   3F     ?
  52   34     4
  46   2E     .
  51   33     3
  57   39     9
Caf? cost: ?4.39
```

7. Rerun the code and press 3 to choose UTF-8 and note that UTF-8 requires two extra bytes for the two characters that need 2 bytes each (18 bytes instead of 16 bytes total) but it can encode and decode the é and £ characters.

```
UTF8EncodingSealed uses 18 bytes.

BYTE   HEX   CHAR
  67    43     C
  97    61     a
 102    66     f
 195    C3     Ã
 169    A9     ©
  32    20
 111    6F     o
 115    73     s
 116    74     t
  58    3A     :
  32    20
 194    C2     Â
 163    A3     £
  52    34     4
  46    2E     .
  51    33     3
  57    39     9
Café cost: £4.39
```

8. Rerun the code and press 4 to choose Unicode (UTF-16) and note that UTF-16 requires two bytes for every character, so 32 bytes in total, and it can encode and decode the é and £ characters. This encoding is used internally by .NET to store char and string values.

Encoding and decoding text in files

When using stream helper classes, such as StreamReader and StreamWriter, you can specify the encoding you want to use. As you write to the helper, the text will automatically be encoded, and as you read from the helper, the bytes will be automatically decoded.

To specify an encoding, pass the encoding as a second parameter to the helper type's constructor, as shown in the following code:

```
StreamReader reader = new(stream, Encoding.UTF8);
StreamWriter writer = new(stream, Encoding.UTF8);
```

Good Practice: Often, you won't have the choice of which encoding to use, because you will be generating a file for use by another system. However, if you do, pick one that uses the least number of bytes, but can store every character you need.

Serializing object graphs

Serialization is the process of converting a live object into a sequence of bytes using a specified format. **Deserialization** is the reverse process. You would do this to save the current state of a live object so that you can recreate it in the future. For example, saving the current state of a game so that you can continue at the same place tomorrow. Serialized objects are usually stored in a file or database.

There are dozens of formats you can specify, but the two most common ones are **eXtensible Markup Language (XML)** and **JavaScript Object Notation (JSON)**.

> **Good Practice**: JSON is more compact and is best for web and mobile applications. XML is more verbose but is better supported in more legacy systems. Use JSON to minimize the size of serialized object graphs. JSON is also a good choice when sending object graphs to web applications and mobile applications because JSON is the native serialization format for JavaScript and mobile apps often make calls over limited bandwidth, so the number of bytes is important.

.NET has multiple classes that will serialize to and from XML and JSON. We will start by looking at `XmlSerializer` and `JsonSerializer`.

Serializing as XML

Let's start by looking at XML, probably the world's most used serialization format (for now). To show a typical example, we will define a custom class to store information about a person and then create an object graph using a list of `Person` instances with nesting:

1. Use your preferred code editor to add a new console app named `WorkingWithSerialization` to the `Chapter09` solution/workspace.

2. In Visual Studio Code, select `WorkingWithSerialization` as the active OmniSharp project.

3. Add a class named `Person` with a `Salary` property that is `protected`, meaning it is only accessible to itself and derived classes. To populate the salary, the class has a constructor with a single parameter to set the initial salary, as shown in the following code:

```
namespace Packt.Shared;

public class Person
{
  public Person(decimal initialSalary)
  {
    Salary = initialSalary;
  }
```

```
    public string? FirstName { get; set; }
    public string? LastName { get; set; }
    public DateTime DateOfBirth { get; set; }
    public HashSet<Person>? Children { get; set; }
    protected decimal Salary { get; set; }
}
```

4. In `Program.cs`, import namespaces for working with XML serialization and statically import the `Console`, `Environment`, and `Path` classes, as shown in the following code:

```
using System.Xml.Serialization; // XmlSerializer
using Packt.Shared; // Person

using static System.Console;
using static System.Environment;
using static System.IO.Path;
```

5. Add statements to create an object graph of `Person` instances, as shown in the following code:

```
// create an object graph
List<Person> people = new()
{
  new(30000M)
  {
    FirstName = "Alice",
    LastName = "Smith",
    DateOfBirth = new(1974, 3, 14)
  },
  new(40000M)
  {
    FirstName = "Bob",
    LastName = "Jones",
    DateOfBirth = new(1969, 11, 23)
  },
  new(20000M)
  {
    FirstName = "Charlie",
    LastName = "Cox",
    DateOfBirth = new(1984, 5, 4),
    Children = new()
    {
      new(0M)
      {
        FirstName = "Sally",
        LastName = "Cox",
```

```
        DateOfBirth = new(2000, 7, 12)
      }
    }
  }
};

// create object that will format a List of Persons as XML
XmlSerializer xs = new(people.GetType());

// create a file to write to
string path = Combine(CurrentDirectory, "people.xml");

using (FileStream stream = File.Create(path))
{
  // serialize the object graph to the stream
  xs.Serialize(stream, people);
}

WriteLine("Written {0:N0} bytes of XML to {1}",
  arg0: new FileInfo(path).Length,
  arg1: path);
WriteLine();

// Display the serialized object graph
WriteLine(File.ReadAllText(path));
```

6. Run the code, view the result, and note that an exception is thrown, as shown in the following output:

```
Unhandled Exception: System.InvalidOperationException: Packt.Shared.Person
cannot be serialized because it does not have a parameterless constructor.
```

7. In `Person`, add a statement to define a parameterless constructor, as shown in the following code:

```
public Person() { }
```

The constructor does not need to do anything, but it must exist so that the `XmlSerializer` can call it to instantiate new `Person` instances during the deserialization process.

8. Rerun the code and view the result, and note that the object graph is serialized as XML elements like `<FirstName>Bob</FirstName>` and that the `Salary` property is not included because it is not a `public` property, as shown in the following output:

```
Written 752 bytes of XML to
/Users/markjprice/Code/Chapter09/WorkingWithSerialization/people.xml
<?xml version="1.0"?>
```

```xml
<ArrayOfPerson xmlns:xsi="http://www.w3.org/2001/XMLSchema-instance"
xmlns:xsd="http://www.w3.org/2001/XMLSchema">
  <Person>
    <FirstName>Alice</FirstName>
    <LastName>Smith</LastName>
    <DateOfBirth>1974-03-14T00:00:00</DateOfBirth>
  </Person>
  <Person>
    <FirstName>Bob</FirstName>
    <LastName>Jones</LastName>
    <DateOfBirth>1969-11-23T00:00:00</DateOfBirth>
  </Person>
  <Person>
    <FirstName>Charlie</FirstName>
    <LastName>Cox</LastName>
    <DateOfBirth>1984-05-04T00:00:00</DateOfBirth>
    <Children>
      <Person>
        <FirstName>Sally</FirstName>
        <LastName>Cox</LastName>
        <DateOfBirth>2000-07-12T00:00:00</DateOfBirth>
      </Person>
    </Children>
  </Person>
</ArrayOfPerson>
```

Generating compact XML

We could make the XML more compact using attributes instead of elements for some fields:

1. In `Person`, import the `System.Xml.Serialization` namespace so that you can decorate some properties with the `[XmlAttribute]` attribute.

2. Decorate the first name, last name, and date of birth properties with the `[XmlAttribute]` attribute, and set a short name for each property, as shown highlighted in the following code:

    ```csharp
    [XmlAttribute("fname")]
    public string FirstName { get; set; }

    [XmlAttribute("lname")]
    public string LastName { get; set; }

    [XmlAttribute("dob")]
    public DateTime DateOfBirth { get; set; }
    ```

3. Run the code and note that the size of the file has been reduced from 752 to 462 bytes, a space-saving of more than a third, by outputting property values as XML attributes, as shown in the following output:

```
Written 462 bytes of XML to /Users/markjprice/Code/Chapter09/
WorkingWithSerialization/people.xml
<?xml version="1.0"?>
<ArrayOfPerson xmlns:xsi="http://www.w3.org/2001/XMLSchema-instance"
xmlns:xsd="http://www.w3.org/2001/XMLSchema">
  <Person fname="Alice" lname="Smith" dob="1974-03-14T00:00:00" />
  <Person fname="Bob" lname="Jones" dob="1969-11-23T00:00:00" />
  <Person fname="Charlie" lname="Cox" dob="1984-05-04T00:00:00">
    <Children>
      <Person fname="Sally" lname="Cox" dob="2000-07-12T00:00:00" />
    </Children>
  </Person>
</ArrayOfPerson>
```

Deserializing XML files

Now let's try deserializing the XML file back into live objects in memory:

1. Add statements to open the XML file and then deserialize it, as shown in the following code:

```
using (FileStream xmlLoad = File.Open(path, FileMode.Open))
{
  // deserialize and cast the object graph into a List of Person
  List<Person>? loadedPeople =
    xs.Deserialize(xmlLoad) as List<Person>;

  if (loadedPeople is not null)
  {
    foreach (Person p in loadedPeople)
    {
      WriteLine("{0} has {1} children.",
        p.LastName, p.Children?.Count ?? 0);
    }
  }
}
```

2. Run the code and note that the people are loaded successfully from the XML file and then enumerated, as shown in the following output:

```
Smith has 0 children.
Jones has 0 children.
Cox has 1 children.
```

There are many other attributes that can be used to control the XML generated.

If you don't use any annotations, XmlSerializer performs a case-insensitive match using the property name when deserializing.

 Good Practice: When using XmlSerializer, remember that only the public fields and properties are included, and the type must have a parameterless constructor. You can customize the output with attributes.

Serializing with JSON

One of the most popular .NET libraries for working with the JSON serialization format is Newtonsoft.Json, known as Json.NET. It is mature and powerful. Let's see it in action:

1. In the WorkingWithSerialization project, add a package reference for the latest version of Newtonsoft.Json, as shown in the following markup:

```
<ItemGroup>
  <PackageReference Include="Newtonsoft.Json"
    Version="13.0.1" />
</ItemGroup>
```

2. Build the WorkingWithSerialization project to restore packages.

3. In Program.cs, add statements to create a text file and then serialize the people into the file as JSON, as shown in the following code:

```
// create a file to write to
string jsonPath = Combine(CurrentDirectory, "people.json");

using (StreamWriter jsonStream = File.CreateText(jsonPath))
{
  // create an object that will format as JSON
  Newtonsoft.Json.JsonSerializer jss = new();

  // serialize the object graph into a string
  jss.Serialize(jsonStream, people);
}
WriteLine();
WriteLine("Written {0:N0} bytes of JSON to: {1}",
  arg0: new FileInfo(jsonPath).Length,
  arg1: jsonPath);

// Display the serialized object graph
WriteLine(File.ReadAllText(jsonPath));
```

4. Run the code and note that JSON requires less than half the number of bytes compared to XML with elements. It's even smaller than the XML file, which uses attributes, as shown in the following output:

```
Written 366 bytes of JSON to: /Users/markjprice/Code/Chapter09/
WorkingWithSerialization/people.json [{"FirstName":"Alice","LastName":"Smi
th","DateOfBirth":"1974-03-
14T00:00:00","Children":null},{"FirstName":"Bob","LastName":"Jones","Date
OfBirth":"1969-11-23T00:00:00","Children":null},{"FirstName":"Charlie","L
astName":"Cox","DateOfBirth":"1984-05-04T00:00:00","Children":[{"FirstNam
e":"Sally","LastName":"Cox","DateOfBirth":"2000-07-12T00:00:00","Children
":null}]}]
```

High-performance JSON processing

.NET Core 3.0 introduced a new namespace for working with JSON, System.Text.Json, which is optimized for performance by leveraging APIs like Span<T>.

Also, older libraries like Json.NET are implemented by reading UTF-16. It would be more performant to read and write JSON documents using UTF-8 because most network protocols, including HTTP, use UTF-8 and you can avoid transcoding UTF-8 to and from Json.NET's Unicode string values.

With the new API, Microsoft achieved between 1.3x and 5x improvement, depending on the scenario.

The original author of Json.NET, James Newton-King, joined Microsoft and has been working with them to develop their new JSON types. As he says in a comment discussing the new JSON APIs, "Json.NET isn't going away," as shown in *Figure 9.3*:

Figure 9.3: A comment by the original author of Json.NET

Let's see how to use the new JSON APIs to deserialize a JSON file:

1. In the WorkingWithSerialization project, in Program.cs, import the new JSON class for performing serialization using an alias to avoid conflicting names with the Json.NET one we used before, as shown in the following code:

```
using NewJson = System.Text.Json.JsonSerializer;
```

2. Add statements to open the JSON file, deserialize it, and output the names and counts of the children of the people, as shown in the following code:

```
using (FileStream jsonLoad = File.Open(jsonPath, FileMode.Open))
{
  // deserialize object graph into a List of Person
  List<Person>? loadedPeople =
    await NewJson.DeserializeAsync(utf8Json: jsonLoad,
      returnType: typeof(List<Person>)) as List<Person>;

  if (loadedPeople is not null)
  {
    foreach (Person p in loadedPeople)
    {
      WriteLine("{0} has {1} children.",
        p.LastName, p.Children?.Count ?? 0);
    }
  }
}
```

3. Run the code and view the result, as shown in the following output:

```
Smith has 0 children.
Jones has 0 children.
Cox has 1 children.
```

 Good Practice: Choose Json.NET for developer productivity and a large feature set or System.Text.Json for performance.

Controlling JSON processing

There are many options for taking control of how JSON is processed, as shown in the following list:

- Including and excluding fields.
- Setting a casing policy.
- Selecting a case-sensitivity policy.
- Choosing between compact and prettified whitespace.

Let's see some in action:

1. Use your preferred code editor to add a new console app named WorkingWithJson to the Chapter09 solution/workspace.

2. In Visual Studio Code, select `WorkingWithJson` as the active OmniSharp project.

3. In the `WorkingWithJson` project, in `Program.cs`, delete the existing code, import the two main namespaces for working with JSON, and then statically import the `System.Console`, `System.Environment`, and `System.IO.Path` types, as shown in the following code:

```
using System.Text.Json; // JsonSerializer
using System.Text.Json.Serialization; // [JsonInclude]

using static System.Console;
using static System.Environment;
using static System.IO.Path;
```

4. At the bottom of `Program.cs`, define a class named `Book`, as shown in the following code:

```
public class Book
{
  // constructor to set non-nullable property
  public Book(string title)
  {
    Title = title;
  }

  // properties

  public string Title { get; set; }
  public string? Author { get; set; }

  // fields

  [JsonInclude] // include this field
  public DateOnly PublishDate;

  [JsonInclude] // include this field
  public DateTimeOffset Created;

  public ushort Pages;
}
```

5. Above the `Book` class, add statements to create an instance of the `Book` class and serialize it to JSON, as shown in the following code:

```
Book csharp10 = new(title:
  "C# 10 and .NET 6 - Modern Cross-platform Development")
{
  Author = "Mark J Price",
  PublishDate = new(year: 2021, month: 11, day: 9),
  Pages = 823,
```

```
    Created = DateTimeOffset.UtcNow,
};

JsonSerializerOptions options = new()
{
  IncludeFields = true, // includes all fields
  PropertyNameCaseInsensitive = true,
  WriteIndented = true,
  PropertyNamingPolicy = JsonNamingPolicy.CamelCase,
};

string filePath = Combine(CurrentDirectory, "book.json");

using (Stream fileStream = File.Create(filePath))
{
  JsonSerializer.Serialize<Book>(
    utf8Json: fileStream, value: csharp10, options);
}

WriteLine("Written {0:N0} bytes of JSON to {1}",
  arg0: new FileInfo(filePath).Length,
  arg1: filePath);

WriteLine();

// Display the serialized object graph
WriteLine(File.ReadAllText(filePath));
```

6. Run the code and view the result, as shown in the following output:

```
Written 315 bytes of JSON to C:\Code\Chapter09\WorkingWithJson\bin\Debug\
net6.0\book.json

{
  "title": "C# 10 and .NET 6 - Modern Cross-platform Development",
  "author": "Mark J Price",
  "publishDate": {
    "year": 2021,
    "month": 11,
    "day": 9,
    "dayOfWeek": 2,
    "dayOfYear": 313,
    "dayNumber": 738102
  },
  "created": "2021-08-20T08:07:02.3191648+00:00",
  "pages": 823
}
```

Note the following:

- The JSON file is 315 bytes.

- The member names use camelCasing, for example, `publishDate`. This is best for subsequent processing in a browser with JavaScript.

- All fields are included due to the options set, including `pages`.

- JSON is prettified for easier human legibility.

- `DateTimeOffset` values are stored as a single standard string format.

- `DateOnly` values are stored as an object with sub-properties for date parts like `year` and `month`.

7. In `Program.cs`, when setting the `JsonSerializerOptions`, comment out the setting of casing policy, write indented, and include fields.

8. Run the code and view the result, as shown in the following output:

```
Written 230 bytes of JSON to C:\Code\Chapter09\WorkingWithJson\bin\Debug\
net6.0\book.json

{"Title":"C# 10 and .NET 6 - Modern Cross-platform
Development","Author":"Mark J Price","PublishDate":{"Year":2021,"Month
":11,"Day":9,"DayOfWeek":2,"DayOfYear":313,"DayNumber":738102},"Creat
ed":"2021-08-20T08:12:31.6852484+00:00"}
```

Note the following:

- The JSON file is 230 bytes, a more than 25% reduction.

- The member names use normal casing, for example, `PublishDate`.

- The `Pages` field is missing. The other fields are included due to the `[JsonInclude]` attribute on `PublishDate` and `Created` field.

- JSON is compact with minimal whitespace to save bandwidth for transmission or storage.

New JSON extension methods for working with HTTP responses

In .NET 5, Microsoft added refinements to the types in the `System.Text.Json` namespace like extension methods for `HttpResponse`, which you will see in *Chapter 16, Building and Consuming Web Services*.

Migrating from Newtonsoft to new JSON

If you have existing code that uses the Newtonsoft Json.NET library and you want to migrate to the new `System.Text.Json` namespace, then Microsoft has specific documentation for that, which you will find at the following link:

https://docs.microsoft.com/en-us/dotnet/standard/serialization/system-text-json-migrate-from-newtonsoft-how-to

Practicing and exploring

Test your knowledge and understanding by answering some questions, get some hands-on practice, and explore this chapter's topics with more in-depth research.

Exercise 9.1 – Test your knowledge

Answer the following questions:

1. What is the difference between using the `File` class and the `FileInfo` class?
2. What is the difference between the `ReadByte` method and the `Read` method of a stream?
3. When would you use the `StringReader`, `TextReader`, and `StreamReader` classes?
4. What does the `DeflateStream` type do?
5. How many bytes per character does UTF-8 encoding use?
6. What is an object graph?
7. What is the best serialization format to choose for minimizing space requirements?
8. What is the best serialization format to choose for cross-platform compatibility?
9. Why is it bad to use a `string` value like `"\Code\Chapter01"` to represent a path, and what should you do instead?
10. Where can you find information about NuGet packages and their dependencies?

Exercise 9.2 – Practice serializing as XML

In the `Chapter09` solution/workspace, create a console application named `Exercise02` that creates a list of shapes, uses serialization to save it to the filesystem using XML, and then deserializes it back:

```
// create a list of Shapes to serialize
List<Shape> listOfShapes = new()
{
  new Circle { Colour = "Red", Radius = 2.5 },
  new Rectangle { Colour = "Blue", Height = 20.0, Width = 10.0 },
  new Circle { Colour = "Green", Radius = 8.0 },
  new Circle { Colour = "Purple", Radius = 12.3 },
  new Rectangle { Colour = "Blue", Height = 45.0, Width = 18.0 }
};
```

Shapes should have a read-only property named `Area` so that when you deserialize, you can output a list of shapes, including their areas, as shown here:

```
List<Shape> loadedShapesXml =
  serializerXml.Deserialize(fileXml) as List<Shape>;

foreach (Shape item in loadedShapesXml)
{
  WriteLine("{0} is {1} and has an area of {2:N2}",
    item.GetType().Name, item.Colour, item.Area);
}
```

This is what your output should look like when you run your console application:

```
Loading shapes from XML:
Circle is Red and has an area of 19.63
Rectangle is Blue and has an area of 200.00
Circle is Green and has an area of 201.06
Circle is Purple and has an area of 475.29
Rectangle is Blue and has an area of 810.00
```

Exercise 9.3 – Explore topics

Use the links on the following page to learn more detail about the topics covered in this chapter:

https://github.com/markjprice/cs10dotnet6/blob/main/book-links.md#chapter-9---
working-with-files-streams-and-serialization

Summary

In this chapter, you learned how to read from and write to text files and XML files, how to compress and decompress files, how to encode and decode text, and how to serialize an object into JSON and XML (and deserialize it back again).

In the next chapter, you will learn how to work with databases using Entity Framework Core.

10

Working with Data Using Entity Framework Core

This chapter is about reading and writing to data stores, such as Microsoft SQL Server, SQLite, and Azure Cosmos DB, by using the object-to-data store mapping technology named **Entity Framework Core (EF Core)**.

This chapter will cover the following topics:

- Understanding modern databases
- Setting up EF Core
- Defining EF Core models
- Querying EF Core models
- Loading patterns with EF Core
- Manipulating data with EF Core
- Working with transactions
- Code First EF Core models

Understanding modern databases

Two of the most common places to store data are in a **Relational Database Management System (RDBMS)** such as Microsoft SQL Server, PostgreSQL, MySQL, and SQLite, or in a **NoSQL** database such as Microsoft Azure Cosmos DB, Redis, MongoDB, and Apache Cassandra.

Understanding legacy Entity Framework

Entity Framework (EF) was first released as part of .NET Framework 3.5 with Service Pack 1 back in late 2008. Since then, Entity Framework has evolved, as Microsoft has observed how programmers use an **object-relational mapping (ORM)** tool in the real world.

ORMs use a mapping definition to associate columns in tables to properties in classes. Then, a programmer can interact with objects of different types in a way that they are familiar with, instead of having to deal with knowing how to store the values in a relational table or another structure provided by a NoSQL data store.

The version of EF included with .NET Framework is **Entity Framework 6 (EF6)**. It is mature, stable, and supports an EDMX (XML file) way of defining the model as well as complex inheritance models, and a few other advanced features.

EF 6.3 and later have been extracted from .NET Framework as a separate package so it can be supported on .NET Core 3.0 and later. This enables existing projects like web applications and services to be ported and run cross-platform. However, EF6 should be considered a legacy technology because it has some limitations when running cross-platform and no new features will be added to it.

Using the legacy Entity Framework 6.3 or later

To use the legacy Entity Framework in a .NET Core 3.0 or later project, you must add a package reference to it in your project file, as shown in the following markup:

```
<PackageReference Include="EntityFramework" Version="6.4.4" />
```

Good Practice: Only use legacy EF6 if you have to, for example, when migrating a WPF app that uses it. This book is about modern cross-platform development so, in the rest of this chapter, I will only cover the modern Entity Framework Core. You will not need to reference the legacy EF6 package as shown above in the projects for this chapter.

Understanding Entity Framework Core

The truly cross-platform version, **EF Core**, is different from the legacy Entity Framework. Although EF Core has a similar name, you should be aware of how it varies from EF6. The latest EF Core is version 6.0 to match .NET 6.0.

EF Core 5 and later only support .NET 5 and later. EF Core 3.0 and later only run on platforms that support .NET Standard 2.1, meaning .NET Core 3.0 and later. It does not support .NET Standard 2.0 platforms like .NET Framework 4.8.

As well as traditional RDBMSs, EF Core supports modern cloud-based, nonrelational, schemaless data stores, such as Microsoft Azure Cosmos DB and MongoDB, sometimes with third-party providers.

EF Core has so many improvements that this chapter cannot cover them all. I will focus on the fundamentals that all .NET developers should know and some of the cooler new features.

There are two approaches to working with EF Core:

1. **Database First**: A database already exists, so you build a model that matches its structure and features.
2. **Code First**: No database exists, so you build a model and then use EF Core to create a database that matches its structure and features.

We will start by using EF Core with an existing database.

Creating a console app for working with EF Core

First, we will create a console app project for this chapter:

1. Use your preferred code editor to create a new solution/workspace named Chapter10.
2. Add a console app project, as defined in the following list:
   1. Project template: **Console Application** / console
   2. Workspace/solution file and folder: Chapter10
   3. Project file and folder: WorkingWithEFCore

Using a sample relational database

To learn how to manage an RDBMS using .NET, it would be useful to have a sample one so that you can practice on one that has a medium complexity and a decent amount of sample records. Microsoft offers several sample databases, most of which are too complex for our needs, so instead, we will use a database that was first created in the early 1990s known as **Northwind**.

Let's take a minute to look at a diagram of the Northwind database. You can use the following diagram to refer to as we write code and queries throughout this book:

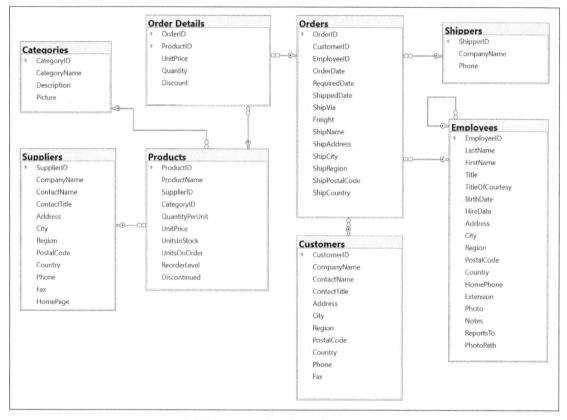

Figure 10.1: The Northwind database tables and relationships

You will write code to work with the `Categories` and `Products` tables later in this chapter and other tables in later chapters. But before we do, note that:

- Each category has a unique identifier, name, description, and picture.
- Each product has a unique identifier, name, unit price, units in stock, and other fields.
- Each product is associated with a category by storing the category's unique identifier.
- The relationship between `Categories` and `Products` is one-to-many, meaning each category can have zero or more products.

Using Microsoft SQL Server for Windows

Microsoft offers various editions of its popular and capable SQL Server product for Windows, Linux, and Docker containers. We will use a free version that can run standalone, known as SQL Server Developer Edition. You can also use the Express edition or the free SQL Server LocalDB edition that can be installed with Visual Studio for Windows.

If you do not have a Windows computer or you want to use a cross-platform database system, then you can skip ahead to the topic *Using SQLite*.

Downloading and installing SQL Server

You can download SQL Server editions from the following link:

`https://www.microsoft.com/en-us/sql-server/sql-server-downloads`

1. Download the **Developer** edition.
2. Run the installer.
3. Select the **Custom** installation type.
4. Select a folder for the installation files and then click **Install**.
5. Wait for the 1.5 GB of installer files to download.
6. In **SQL Server Installation Center**, click **Installation**, and then click **New SQL Server stand-alone installation or add features to an existing installation**.
7. Select **Developer** as the free edition and then click **Next**.
8. Accept the license terms and then click **Next**.
9. Review the install rules, fix any issues, and then click **Next**.
10. In **Feature Selection**, select **Database Engine Services**, and then click **Next**.
11. In **Instance Configuration**, select **Default instance**, and then click **Next**. If you already have a default instance configured, then you could create a named instance, perhaps called `cs10dotnet6`.
12. In **Server Configuration**, note the **SQL Server Database Engine** is configured to start automatically. Set the **SQL Server Browser** to start automatically, and then click **Next**.
13. In **Database Engine Configuration**, on the **Server Configuration** tab, set **Authentication Mode** to **Mixed**, set the **sa** account password to a strong password, click **Add Current User**, and then click **Next**.
14. In **Ready to Install**, review the actions that will be taken, and then click **Install**.
15. In **Complete**, note the successful actions taken, and then click **Close**.
16. In **SQL Server Installation Center**, in **Installation**, click **Install SQL Server Management Tools**.
17. In the browser window, click to download the latest version of SSMS.
18. Run the installer and click **Install**.
19. When the installer has finished, click **Restart** if needed or **Close**.

Creating the Northwind sample database for SQL Server

Now we can run a database script to create the Northwind sample database:

1. If you have not previously downloaded or cloned the GitHub repository for this book, then do so now using the following link: `https://github.com/markjprice/cs10dotnet6/`.

2. Copy the script to create the Northwind database for SQL Server from the following path in your local Git repository: `/sql-scripts/Northwind4SQLServer.sql` into the `WorkingWithEFCore` folder.

3. Start **SQL Server Management Studio**.

4. In the **Connect to Server** dialog, for **Server name**, enter . (a dot) meaning the local computer name, and then click **Connect**.

> If you had to create a named instance, like `cs10dotnet6`, then enter `.\cs10dotnet6`

5. Navigate to **File** | **Open** | **File....**

6. Browse to select the `Northwind4SQLServer.sql` file and then click **Open**.

7. In the toolbar, click **Execute**, and note the **the Command(s) completed successfully** message.

8. In **Object Explorer**, expand the **Northwind** database, and then expand **Tables**.

9. Right-click **Products**, click **Select Top 1000 Rows**, and note the returned results, as shown in *Figure 10.2*:

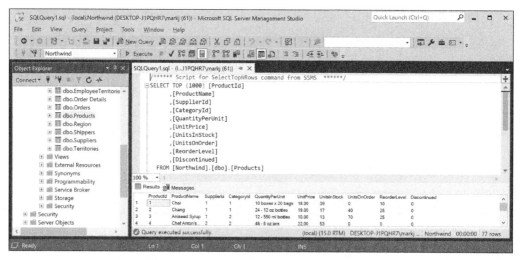

Figure 10.2: The Products table in SQL Server Management Studio

10. In the **Object Explorer** toolbar, click the **Disconnect** button.

11. Exit SQL Server Management Studio.

Managing the Northwind sample database with Server Explorer

We did not have to use SQL Server Management Studio to execute the database script. We can also use tools in Visual Studio including the **SQL Server Object Explorer** and **Server Explorer**:

1. In Visual Studio, choose **View | Server Explorer**.

2. In the **Server Explorer** window, right-click **Data Connections** and choose **Add Connection...**.

3. If you see the **Choose Data Source** dialog, as shown in *Figure 10.3*, select **Microsoft SQL Server** and then click **Continue**:

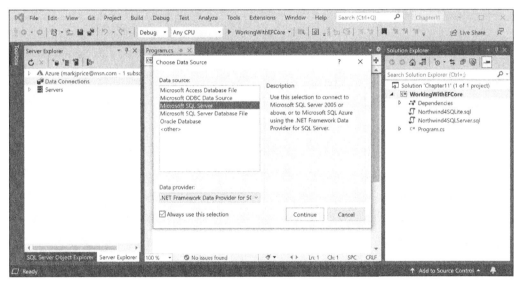

Figure 10.3: Choosing SQL Server as the data source

4. In the **Add Connection** dialog, enter the server name as `.`, enter the database name as Northwind, and then click **OK**.

5. In **Server Explorer**, expand the data connection and its tables. You should see 13 tables, including the **Categories** and **Products** tables.

6. Right-click the **Products** table, choose **Show Table Data**, and note the 77 rows of products are returned.

7. To see the details of the **Products** table columns and types, right-click **Products** and choose **Open Table Definition**, or double-click the table in **Server Explorer**.

Using SQLite

SQLite is a small, cross-platform, self-contained RDBMS that is available in the public domain. It's the most common RDBMS for mobile platforms such as iOS (iPhone and iPad) and Android. Even if you use Windows and set up SQL Server in the previous section, you might want to set up SQLite too. The code that we write will work with both and it can be interesting to see the subtle differences.

Setting up SQLite for macOS

SQLite is included in macOS in the /usr/bin/ directory as a command-line application named sqlite3.

Setting up SQLite for Windows

On Windows, we need to add the folder for SQLite to the system path so it will be found when we enter commands at a command prompt or terminal:

1. Start your favorite browser and navigate to the following link: https://www.sqlite.org/download.html.
2. Scroll down the page to the **Precompiled Binaries for Windows** section.
3. Click **sqlite-tools-win32-x86-3360000.zip**. Note the file might have a higher version number after this book is published.
4. Extract the ZIP file into a folder named C:\Sqlite\.
5. Navigate to **Windows Settings**.
6. Search for environment and choose **Edit the system environment variables**. On non-English versions of Windows, please search for the equivalent word in your local language to find the setting.
7. Click the **Environment Variables** button.
8. In **System variables**, select **Path** in the list, and then click **Edit...**.
9. Click **New**, enter C:\Sqlite, and press *Enter*.
10. Click **OK**.
11. Click **OK**.
12. Click **OK**.
13. Close **Windows Settings**.

Setting up SQLite for other OSes

SQLite can be downloaded and installed for other OSes from the following link: https://www.sqlite.org/download.html.

Creating the Northwind sample database for SQLite

Now we can create the Northwind sample database for SQLite using an SQL script:

1. If you have not previously cloned the GitHub repository for this book, then do so now using the following link: `https://github.com/markjprice/cs10dotnet6/`.

2. Copy the script to create the Northwind database for SQLite from the following path in your local Git repository: `/sql-scripts/Northwind4SQLite.sql` into the `WorkingWithEFCore` folder.

3. Start a command line in the `WorkingWithEFCore` folder:

   1. On Windows, start **File Explorer**, right-click the `WorkingWithEFCore` folder, and select **New Command Prompt at Folder** or **Open in Windows Terminal**.

   2. On macOS, start **Finder**, right-click the `WorkingWithEFCore` folder, and select **New Terminal at Folder**.

4. Enter the command to execute the SQL script using SQLite and create the `Northwind.db` database, as shown in the following command:

   ```
   sqlite3 Northwind.db -init Northwind4SQLite.sql
   ```

5. Be patient because this command might take a while to create the database structure. Eventually, you will see the SQLite command prompt, as shown in the following output:

   ```
   -- Loading resources from Northwind4SQLite.sql
   SQLite version 3.36.0 2021-08-24 15:20:15
   Enter ".help" for usage hints.
   sqlite>
   ```

6. Press *Ctrl* + *C* on Windows or *Ctrl* + *D* on macOS to exit SQLite command mode.

7. Leave your terminal or command prompt window open because you will use it again soon.

Managing the Northwind sample database with SQLiteStudio

You can use a cross-platform graphical database manager named **SQLiteStudio** to easily manage SQLite databases:

1. Navigate to the following link, `https://sqlitestudio.pl`, and download and extract the application to your preferred location.

2. Start **SQLiteStudio**.

3. On the **Database** menu, choose **Add a database**.

4. In the **Database** dialog, in the **File** section, click on the yellow folder button to browse for an existing database file on the local computer, select the Northwind.db file in the WorkingWithEFCore folder, and then click **OK**.

5. Right-click on the **Northwind** database and choose **Connect to the database**. You will see the 10 tables that were created by the script. (The script for SQLite is simpler than the one for SQL Server; it does not create as many tables or other database objects.)

6. Right-click on the **Products** table and choose **Edit the table**.

7. In the table editor window, note the structure of the Products table, including column names, data types, keys, and constraints, as shown in *Figure 10.4*:

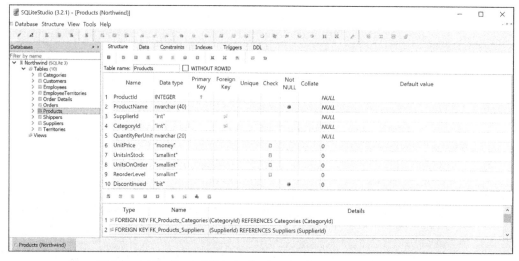

Figure 10.4: The table editor in SQLiteStudio showing the structure of the Products table

8. In the table editor window, click the **Data** tab, and you will see 77 products, as shown in *Figure 10.5*:

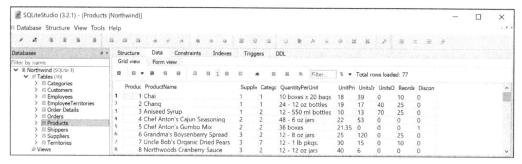

Figure 10.5: The Data tab showing the rows in the Products table

9. In the **Database** window, right-click **Northwind** and select **Disconnect from the database**.

10. Exit SQLiteStudio.

Setting up EF Core

Before we dive into the practicalities of managing data using EF Core, let's briefly talk about choosing between EF Core data providers.

Choosing an EF Core database provider

To manage data in a specific database, we need classes that know how to efficiently talk to that database.

EF Core database providers are sets of classes that are optimized for a specific data store. There is even a provider for storing the data in the memory of the current process, which can be useful for high-performance unit testing since it avoids hitting an external system.

They are distributed as NuGet packages, as shown in the following table:

To manage this data store	Install this NuGet package
Microsoft SQL Server 2012 or later	`Microsoft.EntityFrameworkCore.SqlServer`
SQLite 3.7 or later	`Microsoft.EntityFrameworkCore.SQLite`
MySQL	`MySQL.Data.EntityFrameworkCore`
In-memory	`Microsoft.EntityFrameworkCore.InMemory`
Azure Cosmos DB SQL API	`Microsoft.EntityFrameworkCore.Cosmos`
Oracle DB 11.2	`Oracle.EntityFrameworkCore`

You can install as many EF Core database providers in the same project as you need. Each package includes the shared types as well as provider-specific types.

Connecting to a database

To connect to an SQLite database, we just need to know the database filename, set using the parameter `Filename`.

To connect to an SQL Server database, we need to know multiple pieces of information, as shown in the following list:

- The name of the server (and the instance if it has one).
- The name of the database.
- Security information, such as username and password, or if we should pass the currently logged-on user's credentials automatically.

We specify this information in a **connection string**.

For backward compatibility, there are multiple possible keywords we can use in an SQL Server connection string for the various parameters, as shown in the following list:

- `Data Source` or `server` or `addr`: These keywords are the name of the server (and an optional instance). You can use a dot `.` to mean the local server.

- `Initial Catalog` or `database`: These keywords are the name of the database.

- `Integrated Security` or `trusted_connection`: These keywords are set to `true` or `SSPI` to pass the thread's current user credentials.

- `MultipleActiveResultSets`: This keyword is set to `true` to enable a single connection to be used to work with multiple tables simultaneously to improve efficiency. It is used for lazy loading rows from related tables.

As described in the list above, when you write code to connect to an SQL Server database, you need to know its server name. The server name depends on the edition and version of SQL Server that you will connect to, as shown in the following table:

SQL Server edition	Server name \ Instance name
LocalDB 2012	`(localdb)\v11.0`
LocalDB 2016 or later	`(localdb)\mssqllocaldb`
Express	`.\sqlexpress`
Full/Developer (default instance)	`.`
Full/Developer (named instance)	`.\cs10dotnet6`

 Good Practice: Use a dot `.` as shorthand for the local computer name. Remember that server names for SQL Server are made of two parts: the name of the computer and the name of an SQL Server instance. You provide instance names during custom installation.

Defining the Northwind database context class

The `Northwind` class will be used to represent the database. To use EF Core, the class must inherit from `DbContext`. This class understands how to communicate with databases and dynamically generate SQL statements to query and manipulate data.

Your `DbContext`-derived class should have an overridden method named `OnConfiguring`, which will set the database connection string.

To make it easy for you to try SQLite and SQL Server, we will create a project that supports both, with a `string` field to control which is used at runtime:

1. In the `WorkingWithEFCore` project, add package references to the EF Core data provider for both SQL Server and SQLite, as shown in the following markup:

```
<ItemGroup>
  <PackageReference
    Include="Microsoft.EntityFrameworkCore.Sqlite"
```

```
      Version="6.0.0" />
    <PackageReference
      Include="Microsoft.EntityFrameworkCore.SqlServer"
      Version="6.0.0" />
  </ItemGroup>
```

2. Build the project to restore packages.

3. Add a class file named `ProjectConstants.cs`.

4. In `ProjectConstants.cs`, define a class with a public string constant to store the database provider name that you want to use, as shown in the following code:

```
namespace Packt.Shared;

public class ProjectConstants
{
  public const string DatabaseProvider = "SQLite"; // or "SQLServer"
}
```

5. In `Program.cs`, import the `Packt.Shared` namespace and output the database provider, as shown in the following code:

```
WriteLine($"Using {ProjectConstants.DatabaseProvider} database
provider.");
```

6. Add a class file named `Northwind.cs`.

7. In `Northwind.cs`, define a class named `Northwind`, import the main namespace for EF Core, make the class inherit from `DbContext`, and in an `OnConfiguring` method, check the provider field to either use SQLite or SQL Server, as shown in the following code:

```
using Microsoft.EntityFrameworkCore; // DbContext, DbContextOptionsBuilder

using static System.Console;

namespace Packt.Shared;

// this manages the connection to the database
public class Northwind : DbContext
{
  protected override void OnConfiguring(
    DbContextOptionsBuilder optionsBuilder)
  {
    if (ProjectConstants.DatabaseProvider == "SQLite")
    {
      string path = Path.Combine(
        Environment.CurrentDirectory, "Northwind.db");

      WriteLine($"Using {path} database file.");
```

```
          optionsBuilder.UseSqlite($"Filename={path}");
        }
        else
        {
          string connection = "Data Source=.;" +
            "Initial Catalog=Northwind;" +
            "Integrated Security=true;" +
            "MultipleActiveResultSets=true;";

          optionsBuilder.UseSqlServer(connection);
        }
      }
    }
```

If you are using Visual Studio for Windows, then the compiled application executes in the WorkingWithEFCore\bin\Debug\net6.0 folder so it will not find the database file.

8. In **Solution Explorer**, right-click the Northwind.db file and select **Properties**.

9. In **Properties**, set **Copy to Output Directory** to **Copy always**.

10. Open WorkingWithEFCore.csproj and note the new elements, as shown in the following markup:

```
<ItemGroup>
  <None Update="Northwind.db">
    <CopyToOutputDirectory>Always</CopyToOutputDirectory>
  </None>
</ItemGroup>
```

If you are using Visual Studio Code, then the compiled application executes in the WorkingWithEFCore folder so it will find the database file without it being copied.

11. Run the console application and note the output showing which database provider you chose to use.

Defining EF Core models

EF Core uses a combination of **conventions**, **annotation attributes**, and **Fluent API** statements to build an entity model at runtime so that any actions performed on the classes can later be automatically translated into actions performed on the actual database. An entity class represents the structure of a table and an instance of the class represents a row in that table.

First, we will review the three ways to define a model, with code examples, and then we will create some classes that implement those techniques.

Using EF Core conventions to define the model

The code we will write will use the following conventions:

- The name of a table is assumed to match the name of a DbSet<T> property in the DbContext class, for example, Products.

- The names of the columns are assumed to match the names of properties in the entity model class, for example, ProductId.

- The string .NET type is assumed to be a nvarchar type in the database.

- The int .NET type is assumed to be an int type in the database.

- The primary key is assumed to be a property that is named Id or ID, or when the entity model class is named Product, then the property can be named ProductId or ProductID. If this property is an integer type or the Guid type, then it is also assumed to be an IDENTITY column (a column type that automatically assigns a value when inserting).

 Good Practice: There are many other conventions that you should know, and you can even define your own, but that is beyond the scope of this book. You can read about them at the following link: https://docs.microsoft.com/en-us/ef/core/modeling/

Using EF Core annotation attributes to define the model

Conventions often aren't enough to completely map the classes to the database objects. A simple way of adding more smarts to your model is to apply annotation attributes.

Some common attributes are shown in the following table:

Attribute	Description
[Required]	Ensures the value is not null.
[StringLength(50)]	Ensures the value is up to 50 characters in length.
[RegularExpression(expression)]	Ensures the value matches the specified regular expression.
[Column(TypeName = "money", Name = "UnitPrice")]	Specifies the column type and column name used in the table.

For example, in the database, the maximum length of a product name is 40, and the value cannot be null, as shown highlighted in the following **Data Definition Language (DDL)** code that defines how to create a table named Products with its columns, data types, keys, and other constraints:

```
CREATE TABLE Products (
    ProductId      INTEGER        PRIMARY KEY,
    ProductName    NVARCHAR (40) NOT NULL,
    SupplierId     "INT",
```

```
    CategoryId      "INT",
    QuantityPerUnit NVARCHAR (20),
    UnitPrice       "MONEY"      CONSTRAINT DF_Products_UnitPrice DEFAULT (0),
    UnitsInStock    "SMALLINT"   CONSTRAINT DF_Products_UnitsInStock DEFAULT (0),
    UnitsOnOrder    "SMALLINT"   CONSTRAINT DF_Products_UnitsOnOrder DEFAULT (0),
    ReorderLevel    "SMALLINT"   CONSTRAINT DF_Products_ReorderLevel DEFAULT (0),
    Discontinued    "BIT"        NOT NULL
                                 CONSTRAINT DF_Products_Discontinued DEFAULT (0),
    CONSTRAINT FK_Products_Categories FOREIGN KEY (
        CategoryId
    )
    REFERENCES Categories (CategoryId),
    CONSTRAINT FK_Products_Suppliers FOREIGN KEY (
        SupplierId
    )
    REFERENCES Suppliers (SupplierId),
    CONSTRAINT CK_Products_UnitPrice CHECK (UnitPrice >= 0),
    CONSTRAINT CK_ReorderLevel CHECK (ReorderLevel >= 0),
    CONSTRAINT CK_UnitsInStock CHECK (UnitsInStock >= 0),
    CONSTRAINT CK_UnitsOnOrder CHECK (UnitsOnOrder >= 0)
);
```

In a `Product` class, we could apply attributes to specify this, as shown in the following code:

```
[Required]
[StringLength(40)]
public string ProductName { get; set; }
```

When there isn't an obvious map between .NET types and database types, an attribute can be used.

For example, in the database, the column type of `UnitPrice` for the `Products` table is money. .NET does not have a money type, so it should use decimal instead, as shown in the following code:

```
[Column(TypeName = "money")]
public decimal? UnitPrice { get; set; }
```

Another example is for the `Categories` table, as shown in the following DDL code:

```
CREATE TABLE Categories (
    CategoryId   INTEGER       PRIMARY KEY,
    CategoryName NVARCHAR (15) NOT NULL,
    Description  "NTEXT",
    Picture      "IMAGE"
);
```

The Description column can be longer than the maximum 8,000 characters that can be stored in a nvarchar variable, so it needs to map to ntext instead, as shown in the following code:

```
[Column(TypeName = "ntext")]
public string Description { get; set; }
```

Using the EF Core Fluent API to define the model

The last way that the model can be defined is by using the Fluent API. This API can be used instead of attributes, as well as being used in addition to them. For example, to define the ProductName property, instead of decorating the property with two attributes, an equivalent Fluent API statement could be written in the OnModelCreating method of the database context class, as shown in the following code:

```
modelBuilder.Entity<Product>()
  .Property(product => product.ProductName)
  .IsRequired()
  .HasMaxLength(40);
```

This keeps the entity model class simpler.

Understanding data seeding with the Fluent API

Another benefit of the Fluent API is to provide initial data to populate a database. EF Core automatically works out what insert, update, or delete operations must be executed.

For example, if we wanted to make sure that a new database has at least one row in the Product table, then we would call the HasData method, as shown in the following code:

```
modelBuilder.Entity<Product>()
  .HasData(new Product
  {
    ProductId = 1,
    ProductName = "Chai",
    UnitPrice = 8.99M
  });
```

Our model will map to an existing database that is already populated with data so we will not need to use this technique in our code.

Building an EF Core model for the Northwind tables

Now that you've learned about ways to define an EF Core model, let's build a model to represent two tables in the Northwind database.

The two entity classes will refer to each other, so to avoid compiler errors, we will create the classes without any members first:

1. In the `WorkingWithEFCore` project, add two class files named `Category.cs` and `Product.cs`.

2. In `Category.cs`, define a class named `Category`, as shown in the following code:

    ```
    namespace Packt.Shared;

    public class Category
    {
    }
    ```

3. In `Product.cs`, define a class named `Product`, as shown in the following code:

    ```
    namespace Packt.Shared;

    public class Product
    {
    }
    ```

Defining the Category and Product entity classes

The `Category` class, also known as an entity model, will be used to represent a row in the `Categories` table. This table has four columns, as shown in the following DDL:

```
CREATE TABLE Categories (
    CategoryId   INTEGER         PRIMARY KEY,
    CategoryName NVARCHAR (15) NOT NULL,
    Description  "NTEXT",
    Picture      "IMAGE"
);
```

We will use conventions to define:

*   Three of the four properties (we will not map the `Picture` column).
*   The primary key.
*   The one-to-many relationship to the `Products` table.

To map the `Description` column to the correct database type, we will need to decorate the `string` property with the `Column` attribute.

Later in this chapter, we will use the Fluent API to define that `CategoryName` cannot be null and is limited to a maximum of 15 characters.

Let's go:

1. Modify the `Category` entity model class, as shown in the following code:

    ```
    using System.ComponentModel.DataAnnotations.Schema; // [Column]

    namespace Packt.Shared;
    ```

```
public class Category
{
  // these properties map to columns in the database
  public int CategoryId { get; set; }
  public string? CategoryName { get; set; }

  [Column(TypeName = "ntext")]
  public string? Description { get; set; }

  // defines a navigation property for related rows
  public virtual ICollection<Product> Products { get; set; }

  public Category()
  {
    // to enable developers to add products to a Category we must
    // initialize the navigation property to an empty collection
    Products = new HashSet<Product>();
  }
}
```

The Product class will be used to represent a row in the Products table, which has ten columns.

You do not need to include all columns from a table as properties of a class. We will only map six properties: ProductId, ProductName, UnitPrice, UnitsInStock, Discontinued, and CategoryId.

Columns that are not mapped to properties cannot be read or set using the class instances. If you use the class to create a new object, then the new row in the table will have NULL or some other default value for the unmapped column values in that row. You must make sure that those missing columns are optional or have default values set by the database or an exception will be thrown at runtime. In this scenario, the rows already have data values and I have decided that I do not need to read those values in this application.

We can rename a column by defining a property with a different name, like Cost, and then decorating the property with the [Column] attribute and specifying its column name, like UnitPrice.

The final property, CategoryId, is associated with a Category property that will be used to map each product to its parent category.

2. Modify the Product class, as shown in the following code:

```
using System.ComponentModel.DataAnnotations; // [Required], [StringLength]
using System.ComponentModel.DataAnnotations.Schema; // [Column]

namespace Packt.Shared;
```

```
public class Product
{
    public int ProductId { get; set; } // primary key

    [Required]
    [StringLength(40)]
    public string ProductName { get; set; } = null!;

    [Column("UnitPrice", TypeName = "money")]
    public decimal? Cost { get; set; } // property name != column name

    [Column("UnitsInStock")]
    public short? Stock { get; set; }

    public bool Discontinued { get; set; }

    // these two define the foreign key relationship
    // to the Categories table
    public int CategoryId { get; set; }
    public virtual Category Category { get; set; } = null!;
}
```

The two properties that relate the two entities, `Category.Products` and `Product.Category`, are both marked as `virtual`. This allows EF Core to inherit and override the properties to provide extra features, such as lazy loading.

Adding tables to the Northwind database context class

Inside your `DbContext`-derived class, you must define at least one property of the `DbSet<T>` type. These properties represent the tables. To tell EF Core what columns each table has, the `DbSet<T>` properties use generics to specify a class that represents a row in the table. That entity model class has properties that represent its columns.

The `DbContext`-derived class can optionally have an overridden method named `OnModelCreating`. This is where you can write Fluent API statements as an alternative to decorating your entity classes with attributes.

Let's write some code:

1. Modify the `Northwind` class to add statements to define two properties for the two tables and an `OnModelCreating` method, as shown highlighted in the following code:

    ```
    public class Northwind : DbContext
    {
        // these properties map to tables in the database
    ```

```
public DbSet<Category>? Categories { get; set; }
public DbSet<Product>? Products { get; set; }

protected override void OnConfiguring(
  DbContextOptionsBuilder optionsBuilder)
{
  ...
}

protected override void OnModelCreating(
  ModelBuilder modelBuilder)
{
  // example of using Fluent API instead of attributes
  // to limit the length of a category name to 15
  modelBuilder.Entity<Category>()
    .Property(category => category.CategoryName)
    .IsRequired() // NOT NULL
    .HasMaxLength(15);

  if (ProjectConstants.DatabaseProvider == "SQLite")
  {
    // added to "fix" the lack of decimal support in SQLite
    modelBuilder.Entity<Product>()
      .Property(product => product.Cost)
      .HasConversion<double>();
  }
}
}
```

 In EF Core 3.0 and later, the decimal type is not supported by the SQLite database provider for sorting and other operations. We can fix this by telling the model that decimal values can be converted to double values when using the SQLite database provider. This does not actually perform any conversion at runtime.

Now that you have seen some examples of defining an entity model manually, let's see a tool that can do some of the work for you.

Setting up the dotnet-ef tool

.NET has a command-line tool named dotnet. It can be extended with capabilities useful for working with EF Core. It can perform design-time tasks like creating and applying migrations from an older model to a newer model and generating code for a model from an existing database.

The dotnet ef command-line tool is not automatically installed. You have to install this package as either a **global** or **local tool**. If you have already installed an older version of the tool, then you should uninstall any existing version:

1. At a command prompt or terminal, check if you have already installed dotnet-ef as a global tool, as shown in the following command:

   ```
   dotnet tool list --global
   ```

2. Check in the list if an older version of the tool has been installed, like the one for .NET Core 3.1, as shown in the following output:

   ```
   Package Id        Version      Commands
   -----------------------------------------
   dotnet-ef         3.1.0        dotnet-ef
   ```

3. If an old version is already installed, then uninstall the tool, as shown in the following command:

   ```
   dotnet tool uninstall --global dotnet-ef
   ```

4. Install the latest version, as shown in the following command:

   ```
   dotnet tool install --global dotnet-ef --version 6.0.0
   ```

5. If necessary, follow any OS-specific instructions to add the dotnet tools directory to your PATH environment variable as described in the output of installing the dotnet-ef tool.

Scaffolding models using an existing database

Scaffolding is the process of using a tool to create classes that represent the model of an existing database using reverse engineering. A good scaffolding tool allows you to extend the automatically generated classes and then regenerate those classes without losing your extended classes.

If you know that you will never regenerate the classes using the tool, then feel free to change the code for the automatically generated classes as much as you want. The code generated by the tool is just the best approximation.

 Good Practice: Do not be afraid to overrule a tool when you know better.

Let's see if the tool generates the same model as we did manually:

1. Add the Microsoft.EntityFrameworkCore.Design package to the WorkingWithEFCore project.

2. At a command prompt or terminal in the WorkingWithEFCore folder, generate a model for the Categories and Products tables in a new folder named AutoGenModels, as shown in the following command:

```
dotnet ef dbcontext scaffold "Filename=Northwind.db" Microsoft.
EntityFrameworkCore.Sqlite --table Categories --table Products --output-
dir AutoGenModels --namespace WorkingWithEFCore.AutoGen --data-annotations
--context Northwind
```

Note the following:

- The command action: dbcontext scaffold
- The connection string: "Filename=Northwind.db"
- The database provider: Microsoft.EntityFrameworkCore.Sqlite
- The tables to generate models for: --table Categories --table Products
- The output folder: --output-dir AutoGenModels
- The namespace: --namespace WorkingWithEFCore.AutoGen
- To use data annotations as well as the Fluent API: --data-annotations
- To rename the context from [database_name]Context: --context Northwind

For SQL Server, change the database provider and connection string, as shown in the following command:

```
dotnet ef dbcontext scaffold "Data Source=.;Initial
Catalog=Northwind;Integrated Security=true;" Microsoft.
EntityFrameworkCore.SqlServer --table Categories
--table Products --output-dir AutoGenModels --namespace
WorkingWithEFCore.AutoGen --data-annotations --context
Northwind
```

3. Note the build messages and warnings, as shown in the following output:

```
Build started...
Build succeeded.
To protect potentially sensitive information in your connection string,
you should move it out of source code. You can avoid scaffolding the
connection string by using the Name= syntax to read it from configuration
- see https://go.microsoft.com/fwlink/?linkid=2131148. For more
guidance on storing connection strings, see http://go.microsoft.com/
fwlink/?LinkId=723263.
Skipping foreign key with identity '0' on table 'Products' since principal
table 'Suppliers' was not found in the model. This usually happens when
the principal table was not included in the selection set.
```

4. Open the AutoGenModels folder and note the three class files that were automatically generated: Category.cs, Northwind.cs, and Product.cs.

5. Open Category.cs and note the differences compared to the one you created manually, as shown in the following code:

```
using System;
using System.Collections.Generic;
using System.ComponentModel.DataAnnotations;
using System.ComponentModel.DataAnnotations.Schema;
using Microsoft.EntityFrameworkCore;

namespace WorkingWithEFCore.AutoGen
{
  [Index(nameof(CategoryName), Name = "CategoryName")]
  public partial class Category
  {
    public Category()
    {
      Products = new HashSet<Product>();
    }

    [Key]
    public long CategoryId { get; set; }

    [Required]
    [Column(TypeName = "nvarchar (15)")] // SQLite
    [StringLength(15)] // SQL Server
    public string CategoryName { get; set; }

    [Column(TypeName = "ntext")]
    public string? Description { get; set; }

    [Column(TypeName = "image")]
    public byte[]? Picture { get; set; }

    [InverseProperty(nameof(Product.Category))]
    public virtual ICollection<Product> Products { get; set; }
  }
}
```

Note the following:

- It decorates the entity class with the [Index] attribute that was introduced in EF Core 5.0. This indicates properties that should have an index. In earlier versions, only the Fluent API was supported for defining indexes. Since we are working with an existing database, this is not needed. But if we want to recreate a new empty database from our code then this information will be needed.

- The table name in the database is Categories but the dotnet-ef tool uses the **Humanizer** third-party library to automatically singularize the class name to Category, which is a more natural name when creating a single entity.

- The entity class is declared using the `partial` keyword so that you can create a matching `partial` class for adding additional code. This allows you to rerun the tool and regenerate the entity class without losing that extra code.

- The `CategoryId` property is decorated with the `[Key]` attribute to indicate that it is the primary key for this entity. The data type for this property is `int` for SQL Server and `long` for SQLite.

- The `Products` property uses the `[InverseProperty]` attribute to define the foreign key relationship to the `Category` property on the `Product` entity class.

6. Open `Product.cs` and note the differences compared to the one you created manually.

7. Open `Northwind.cs` and note the differences compared to the one you created manually, as shown in the following edited-for-space code:

```
using Microsoft.EntityFrameworkCore;

namespace WorkingWithEFCore.AutoGen
{
  public partial class Northwind : DbContext
  {
    public Northwind()
    {
    }

    public Northwind(DbContextOptions<Northwind> options)
      : base(options)
    {
    }

    public virtual DbSet<Category> Categories { get; set; } = null!;
    public virtual DbSet<Product> Products { get; set; } = null!;

    protected override void OnConfiguring(
      DbContextOptionsBuilder optionsBuilder)
    {
      if (!optionsBuilder.IsConfigured)
      {
#warning To protect potentially sensitive information in your connection
string, you should move it out of source code. You can avoid scaffolding
the connection string by using the Name= syntax to read it from
configuration - see https://go.microsoft.com/fwlink/?linkid=2131148. For
more guidance on storing connection strings, see http://go.microsoft.com/
fwlink/?LinkId=723263.
        optionsBuilder.UseSqlite("Filename=Northwind.db");
      }
    }
```

```
    protected override void OnModelCreating(ModelBuilder modelBuilder)
    {
      modelBuilder.Entity<Category>(entity =>
      {
        ...
      });

      modelBuilder.Entity<Product>(entity =>
      {
        ...
      });

      OnModelCreatingPartial(modelBuilder);
    }

    partial void OnModelCreatingPartial(ModelBuilder modelBuilder);
  }
}
```

Note the following:

- The `Northwind` data context class is `partial` to allow you to extend it and regenerate it in the future.

- It has two constructors: a default parameter-less one and one that allows options to be passed in. This is useful in apps where you want to specify the connection string at runtime.

- The two `DbSet<T>` properties that represent the `Categories` and `Products` tables are set to the `null`-forgiving value to prevent static compiler analysis warnings at compile time. It has no effect at runtime.

- In the `OnConfiguring` method, if options have not been specified in the constructor, then it defaults to using a connection string that looks for the database file in the current folder. It has a compiler warning to remind you that you should not hardcode security information in this connection string.

- In the `OnModelCreating` method, the Fluent API is used to configure the two entity classes, and then a partial method named `OnModelCreatingPartial` is invoked. This allows you to implement that partial method in your own partial `Northwind` class to add your own Fluent API configuration that will not be lost if you regenerate the model classes.

8. Close the automatically generated class files.

Configuring preconvention models

Along with support for the `DateOnly` and `TimeOnly` types for use with the SQLite database provider, one of the new features introduced with EF Core 6 is configuring preconvention models.

As models become more complex, relying on conventions to discover entity types and their properties and successfully map them to tables and columns becomes harder. It would be useful if you could configure the conventions themselves before they are used to analyze and build a model.

For example, you might want to define a convention to say that all `string` properties should have a maximum length of 50 characters as a default, or any property types that implement a custom interface should not be mapped, as shown in the following code:

```
protected override void ConfigureConventions(
  ModelConfigurationBuilder configurationBuilder)
{
  configurationBuilder.Properties<string>().HaveMaxLength(50);
  configurationBuilder.IgnoreAny<IDoNotMap>();
}
```

In the rest of this chapter, we will use the classes that you manually created.

Querying EF Core models

Now that we have a model that maps to the Northwind database and two of its tables, we can write some simple LINQ queries to fetch data. You will learn much more about writing LINQ queries in *Chapter 11, Querying and Manipulating Data Using LINQ*.

For now, just write the code and view the results:

1. At the top of `Program.cs`, import the main EF Core namespace to enable the use of the `Include` extension method to prefetch from a related table:

   ```
   using Microsoft.EntityFrameworkCore; // Include extension method
   ```

2. At the bottom of `Program.cs`, define a `QueryingCategories` method, and add statements to do these tasks, as shown in the following code:

   - Create an instance of the `Northwind` class that will manage the database. Database context instances are designed for short lifetimes in a unit of work. They should be disposed of as soon as possible so we will wrap it in a `using` statement. In *Chapter 14, Building Websites Using ASP.NET Core Razor Pages*, you will learn how to get a database context using dependency injection.

   - Create a query for all categories that include their related products.

   - Enumerate through the categories, outputting the name and number of products for each one:

   ```
   static void QueryingCategories()
   {
     using (Northwind db = new())
     {
       WriteLine("Categories and how many products they have:");
   ```

```
        // a query to get all categories and their related products
        IQueryable<Category>? categories = db.Categories?
          .Include(c => c.Products);

        if (categories is null)
        {
          WriteLine("No categories found.");
          return;
        }

        // execute query and enumerate results
        foreach (Category c in categories)
        {
          WriteLine($"{c.CategoryName} has {c.Products.Count} products.");
        }
      }
    }
```

3. At the top of `Program.cs`, after outputting the database provider name, call the `QueryingCategories` method, as shown highlighted in the following code:

    ```
    WriteLine($"Using {ProjectConstants.DatabaseProvider} database provider.");
    QueryingCategories();
    ```

4. Run the code and view the result (if run with Visual Studio 2022 for Windows using the SQLite database provider), as shown in the following output:

    ```
    Using SQLite database provider.
    Categories and how many products they have:
    Using C:\Code\Chapter10\WorkingWithEFCore\bin\Debug\net6.0\Northwind.db
    database file.
    Beverages has 12 products.
    Condiments has 12 products.
    Confections has 13 products.
    Dairy Products has 10 products.
    Grains/Cereals has 7 products.
    Meat/Poultry has 6 products.
    Produce has 5 products.
    Seafood has 12 products.
    ```

 If you run with Visual Studio Code using the SQLite database provider, then the path will be the `WorkingWithEFCore` folder. If you run using the SQL Server database provider, then there is no database file path output.

Warning! If you see the following exception when using SQLite with Visual Studio 2022, the most likely problem is that the Northwind.db file is not being copied to the output directory. Make sure **Copy to Output Directory** is set to **Copy always**:

```
Unhandled exception. Microsoft.Data.Sqlite.SqliteException
(0x80004005): SQLite Error 1: 'no such table: Categories'.
```

Filtering included entities

EF Core 5.0 introduced **filtered includes**, which means you can specify a lambda expression in the Include method call to filter which entities are returned in the results:

1. At the bottom of Program.cs, define a FilteredIncludes method, and add statements to do these tasks, as shown in the following code:

    - Create an instance of the Northwind class that will manage the database.

    - Prompt the user to enter a minimum value for units in stock.

    - Create a query for categories that have products with that minimum number of units in stock.

    - Enumerate through the categories and products, outputting the name and units in stock for each one:

    ```
    static void FilteredIncludes()
    {
      using (Northwind db = new())
      {
        Write("Enter a minimum for units in stock: ");
        string unitsInStock = ReadLine() ?? "10";
        int stock = int.Parse(unitsInStock);

        IQueryable<Category>? categories = db.Categories?
          .Include(c => c.Products.Where(p => p.Stock >= stock));

        if (categories is null)
        {
          WriteLine("No categories found.");
          return;
        }

        foreach (Category c in categories)
        {
          WriteLine($"{c.CategoryName} has {c.Products.Count} products with a
    minimum of {stock} units in stock.");

          foreach(Product p in c.Products)
          {
    ```

```
                WriteLine($"  {p.ProductName} has {p.Stock} units in stock.");
            }
        }
    }
}
```

2. In `Program.cs`, comment out the `QueryingCategories` method and invoke the `FilteredIncludes` method, as shown highlighted in the following code:

    ```
    WriteLine($"Using {ProjectConstants.DatabaseProvider} database provider.");
    // QueryingCategories();
    FilteredIncludes();
    ```

3. Run the code, enter a minimum for units in stock like 100, and view the result, as shown in the following output:

```
Enter a minimum for units in stock: 100
Beverages has 2 products with a minimum of 100 units in stock.
  Sasquatch Ale has 111 units in stock.
  Rhönbräu Klosterbier has 125 units in stock.
Condiments has 2 products with a minimum of 100 units in stock.
  Grandma's Boysenberry Spread has 120 units in stock.
  Sirop d'érable has 113 units in stock.
Confections has 0 products with a minimum of 100 units in stock.
Dairy Products has 1 products with a minimum of 100 units in stock.
  Geitost has 112 units in stock.
Grains/Cereals has 1 products with a minimum of 100 units in stock.
  Gustaf's Knäckebröd has 104 units in stock.
Meat/Poultry has 1 products with a minimum of 100 units in stock.
  Pâté chinois has 115 units in stock.
Produce has 0 products with a minimum of 100 units in stock.
Seafood has 3 products with a minimum of 100 units in stock.
  Inlagd Sill has 112 units in stock.
  Boston Crab Meat has 123 units in stock.
  Röd Kaviar has 101 units in stock.
```

Unicode characters in the Windows console

There is a limitation with the console provided by Microsoft on versions of Windows before the Windows 10 Fall Creators Update. By default, the console cannot display Unicode characters, for example, in the name Rhönbräu.

If you have this issue, then you can temporarily change the code page (also known as the character set) in a console to Unicode UTF-8 by entering the following command at the prompt before running the app:

```
chcp 65001
```

Filtering and sorting products

Let's explore a more complex query that will filter and sort data:

1. At the bottom of `Program.cs`, define a `QueryingProducts` method, and add statements to do the following, as shown in the following code:

    *   Create an instance of the `Northwind` class that will manage the database.
    *   Prompt the user for a price for products. Unlike the previous code example, we will loop until the input is a valid price.
    *   Create a query for products that cost more than the price using LINQ.
    *   Loop through the results, outputting the Id, name, cost (formatted in US dollars), and the number of units in stock:

```
static void QueryingProducts()
{
  using (Northwind db = new())
  {
    WriteLine("Products that cost more than a price, highest at top.");
    string? input;
    decimal price;

    do
    {
      Write("Enter a product price: ");
      input = ReadLine();
    } while (!decimal.TryParse(input, out price));

    IQueryable<Product>? products = db.Products?
      .Where(product => product.Cost > price)
      .OrderByDescending(product => product.Cost);

    if (products is null)
    {
      WriteLine("No products found.");
      return;
    }

    foreach (Product p in products)
    {
      WriteLine(
        "{0}: {1} costs {2:$#,##0.00} and has {3} in stock.",
        p.ProductId, p.ProductName, p.Cost, p.Stock);
    }
  }
}
```

2. In `Program.cs`, comment out the previous method, and call the `QueryingProducts` method

3. Run the code, enter 50 when prompted to enter a product price, and view the result, as shown in the following output:

```
Products that cost more than a price, highest at top.
Enter a product price: 50
38: Côte de Blaye costs $263.50 and has 17 in stock.
29: Thüringer Rostbratwurst costs $123.79 and has 0 in stock.
9: Mishi Kobe Niku costs $97.00 and has 29 in stock.
20: Sir Rodney's Marmalade costs $81.00 and has 40 in stock.
18: Carnarvon Tigers costs $62.50 and has 42 in stock.
59: Raclette Courdavault costs $55.00 and has 79 in stock.
51: Manjimup Dried Apples costs $53.00 and has 20 in stock.
```

Getting the generated SQL

You might be wondering how well written the SQL statements are that are generated from the C# queries we write. EF Core 5.0 introduced a quick and easy way to see the SQL generated:

1. In the `FilteredIncludes` method, before using the `foreach` statement to enumerate the query, add a statement to output the generated SQL, as shown highlighted in the following code:

```
WriteLine($"ToQueryString: {categories.ToQueryString()}");

foreach (Category c in categories)
```

2. In `Program.cs`, comment out the call to the `QueryingProducts` method and uncomment the call to the `FilteredIncludes` method.

3. Run the code, enter a minimum for units in stock like 99, and view the result (when run with SQLite), as shown in the following output:

```
Enter a minimum for units in stock: 99
Using SQLite database provider.
ToQueryString: .param set @_stock_0 99

SELECT "c"."CategoryId", "c"."CategoryName", "c"."Description",
"t"."ProductId", "t"."CategoryId", "t"."UnitPrice", "t"."Discontinued",
"t"."ProductName", "t"."UnitsInStock"
FROM "Categories" AS "c"
LEFT JOIN (
    SELECT "p"."ProductId", "p"."CategoryId", "p"."UnitPrice",
"p"."Discontinued", "p"."ProductName", "p"."UnitsInStock"
    FROM "Products" AS "p"
    WHERE ("p"."UnitsInStock" >= @_stock_0)
) AS "t" ON "c"."CategoryId" = "t"."CategoryId"
```

```
ORDER BY "c"."CategoryId", "t"."ProductId"
Beverages has 2 products with a minimum of 99 units in stock.
  Sasquatch Ale has 111 units in stock.
  Rhönbräu Klosterbier has 125 units in stock.
...
```

Note the SQL parameter named @_stock_0 has been set to a minimum stock value of 99.

For SQL Server, the SQL generated is slightly different, for example, it uses square brackets instead of double-quotes around object names, as shown in the following output:

```
Enter a minimum for units in stock: 99
Using SqlServer database provider.
ToQueryString: DECLARE @__stock_0 smallint = CAST(99 AS smallint);

SELECT [c].[CategoryId], [c].[CategoryName], [c].[Description], [t].[ProductId],
[t].[CategoryId], [t].[UnitPrice], [t].[Discontinued], [t].[ProductName], [t].
[UnitsInStock]
FROM [Categories] AS [c]
LEFT JOIN (
    SELECT [p].[ProductId], [p].[CategoryId], [p].[UnitPrice], [p].
[Discontinued], [p].[ProductName], [p].[UnitsInStock]
    FROM [Products] AS [p]
    WHERE [p].[UnitsInStock] >= @__stock_0
) AS [t] ON [c].[CategoryId] = [t].[CategoryId]
ORDER BY [c].[CategoryId], [t].[ProductId]
```

Logging EF Core using a custom logging provider

To monitor the interaction between EF Core and the database, we can enable logging. This requires the following two tasks:

- The registering of a **logging provider**.
- The implementation of a **logger**.

Let's see an example of this in action:

1. Add a file to your project named ConsoleLogger.cs.

2. Modify the file to define two classes, one to implement ILoggerProvider and one to implement ILogger, as shown in the following code, and note the following:

   - ConsoleLoggerProvider returns an instance of ConsoleLogger. It does not need any unmanaged resources, so the Dispose method does not do anything, but it must exist.

   - ConsoleLogger is disabled for log levels None, Trace, and Information. It is enabled for all other log levels.

- ConsoleLogger implements its Log method by writing to Console:

```
using Microsoft.Extensions.Logging; // ILoggerProvider, ILogger, LogLevel

using static System.Console;

namespace Packt.Shared;

public class ConsoleLoggerProvider : ILoggerProvider
{
  public ILogger CreateLogger(string categoryName)
  {
    // we could have different logger implementations for
    // different categoryName values but we only have one
    return new ConsoleLogger();
  }

  // if your logger uses unmanaged resources,
  // then you can release them here
  public void Dispose() { }
}

public class ConsoleLogger : ILogger
{
  // if your logger uses unmanaged resources, you can
  // return the class that implements IDisposable here
  public IDisposable BeginScope<TState>(TState state)
  {
    return null;
  }

  public bool IsEnabled(LogLevel logLevel)
  {
    // to avoid overlogging, you can filter on the log level
    switch(logLevel)
    {
      case LogLevel.Trace:
      case LogLevel.Information:
      case LogLevel.None:
        return false;
      case LogLevel.Debug:
      case LogLevel.Warning:
      case LogLevel.Error:
      case LogLevel.Critical:
      default:
        return true;
```

```
    };
  }

  public void Log<TState>(LogLevel logLevel,
    EventId eventId, TState state, Exception? exception,
    Func<TState, Exception, string> formatter)
  {
    // log the level and event identifier
    Write($"Level: {logLevel}, Event Id: {eventId.Id}");

    // only output the state or exception if it exists
    if (state != null)
    {
      Write($", State: {state}");
    }

    if (exception != null)
    {
      Write($", Exception: {exception.Message}");
    }
    WriteLine();
  }
}
```

3. At the top of `Program.cs`, add statements to import the namespaces needed for logging, as shown in the following code:

```
using Microsoft.EntityFrameworkCore.Infrastructure;
using Microsoft.Extensions.DependencyInjection;
using Microsoft.Extensions.Logging;
```

4. We already used the `ToQueryString` method to get the SQL for `FilteredIncludes` so we do not need to add logging to that method. To both the `QueryingCategories` and `QueryingProducts` methods, add statements immediately inside the using block for the Northwind database context to get the logging factory and register your custom console logger, as shown highlighted in the following code:

```
using (Northwind db = new())
{
  ILoggerFactory loggerFactory = db.GetService<ILoggerFactory>();
  loggerFactory.AddProvider(new ConsoleLoggerProvider());
```

5. At the top of `Program.cs`, comment out the call to the `FilteredIncludes` method and uncomment the call to the `QueryingProducts` method.

6. Run the code and view the logs, which are partially shown in the following output:

```
...
Level: Debug, Event Id: 20000, State: Opening connection to database
'main' on server '/Users/markjprice/Code/Chapter10/WorkingWithEFCore/
Northwind.db'.
Level: Debug, Event Id: 20001, State: Opened connection to database 'main'
on server '/Users/markjprice/Code/Chapter10/WorkingWithEFCore/Northwind.
db'.
Level: Debug, Event Id: 20100, State: Executing DbCommand [Parameters=[@__
price_0='?'], CommandType='Text', CommandTimeout='30']
SELECT "p"."ProductId", "p"."CategoryId", "p"."UnitPrice",
"p"."Discontinued", "p"."ProductName", "p"."UnitsInStock"
FROM "Products" AS "p"
WHERE "p"."UnitPrice" > @__price_0
ORDER BY "product"."UnitPrice" DESC
...
```

 Your logs might vary from those shown above based on your chosen database provider and code editor, and future improvements to EF Core. For now, note that different events like opening a connection or executing a command have different event ids.

Filtering logs by provider-specific values

The event id values and what they mean will be specific to the .NET data provider. If we want to know how the LINQ query has been translated into SQL statements and is executing, then the event Id to output has an Id value of 20100:

1. Modify the Log method in ConsoleLogger to only output events with an Id of 20100, as highlighted in the following code:

```
public void Log<TState>(LogLevel logLevel, EventId eventId,
  TState state, Exception? exception,
  Func<TState, Exception, string> formatter)
{
  if (eventId.Id == 20100)
  {
    // log the level and event identifier
    Write("Level: {0}, Event Id: {1}, Event: {2}",
      logLevel, eventId.Id, eventId.Name);

    // only output the state or exception if it exists
    if (state != null)
    {
      Write($", State: {state}");
    }
```

```
    if (exception != null)
    {
      Write($", Exception: {exception.Message}");
    }
    WriteLine();
  }
}
```

2. In `Program.cs`, uncomment the `QueryingCategories` method and comment out the other methods so that we can monitor the SQL statements that are generated when joining two tables.

3. Run the code, and note the following SQL statements that were logged, as shown in the following output that has been edited for space:

```
Using SQLServer database provider.
Categories and how many products they have:
Level: Debug, Event Id: 20100, State: Executing DbCommand [Parameters=[],
CommandType='Text', CommandTimeout='30']
SELECT [c].[CategoryId], [c].[CategoryName], [c].[Description], [p].
[ProductId], [p].[CategoryId], [p].[UnitPrice], [p].[Discontinued], [p].
[ProductName], [p].[UnitsInStock]
FROM [Categories] AS [c]
LEFT JOIN [Products] AS [p] ON [c].[CategoryId] = [p].[CategoryId]
ORDER BY [c].[CategoryId], [p].[ProductId]
Beverages has 12 products.
Condiments has 12 products.
Confections has 13 products.
Dairy Products has 10 products.
Grains/Cereals has 7 products.
Meat/Poultry has 6 products.
Produce has 5 products.
Seafood has 12 products.
```

Logging with query tags

When logging LINQ queries, it can be tricky to correlate log messages in complex scenarios. EF Core 2.2 introduced the query tags feature to help by allowing you to add SQL comments to the log.

You can annotate a LINQ query using the `TagWith` method, as shown in the following code:

```
IQueryable<Product>? products = db.Products?
  .TagWith("Products filtered by price and sorted.")
  .Where(product => product.Cost > price)
  .OrderByDescending(product => product.Cost);
```

This will add an SQL comment to the log, as shown in the following output:

```
-- Products filtered by price and sorted.
```

Pattern matching with Like

EF Core supports common SQL statements including `Like` for pattern matching:

1. At the bottom of `Program.cs`, add a method named `QueryingWithLike`, as shown in the following code, and note:

   - We have enabled logging.

   - We prompt the user to enter part of a product name and then use the `EF.Functions.Like` method to search anywhere in the `ProductName` property.

   - For each matching product, we output its name, stock, and if it is discontinued:

```
static void QueryingWithLike()
{
  using (Northwind db = new())
  {
    ILoggerFactory loggerFactory = db.GetService<ILoggerFactory>();
    loggerFactory.AddProvider(new ConsoleLoggerProvider());

    Write("Enter part of a product name: ");
    string? input = ReadLine();

    IQueryable<Product>? products = db.Products?
      .Where(p => EF.Functions.Like(p.ProductName, $"%{input}%"));

    if (products is null)
    {
      WriteLine("No products found.");
      return;
    }

    foreach (Product p in products)
    {
      WriteLine("{0} has {1} units in stock. Discontinued? {2}",
        p.ProductName, p.Stock, p.Discontinued);
    }
  }
}
```

2. In `Program.cs`, comment out the existing methods, and call `QueryingWithLike`.

3. Run the code, enter a partial product name such as che, and view the result, as shown in the following output:

```
Using SQLServer database provider.
Enter part of a product name: che
Level: Debug, Event Id: 20100, State: Executing DbCommand [Parameters=[@__
Format_1='?' (Size = 40)], CommandType='Text', CommandTimeout='30']
SELECT "p"."ProductId", "p"."CategoryId", "p"."UnitPrice",
"p"."Discontinued", "p"."ProductName", "p"."UnitsInStock" FROM "Products"
AS "p"
WHERE "p"."ProductName" LIKE @__Format_1
Chef Anton's Cajun Seasoning has 53 units in stock. Discontinued? False
Chef Anton's Gumbo Mix has 0 units in stock. Discontinued? True
Queso Manchego La Pastora has 86 units in stock. Discontinued? False
Gumbär Gummibärchen has 15 units in stock. Discontinued? False
```

 EF Core 6.0 introduces another useful function, EF.Functions.Random, that maps to a database function returning a pseudo-random number between 0 and 1 exclusive. For example, you could multiply the random number by the count of rows in a table to select one random row from that table.

Defining global filters

Northwind products can be discontinued, so it might be useful to ensure that discontinued products are never returned in results, even if the programmer does not use Where to filter them out in their queries:

1. In Northwind.cs, modify the OnModelCreating method to add a global filter to remove discontinued products, as shown highlighted in the following code:

```
protected override void OnModelCreating(ModelBuilder modelBuilder)
{
    ...

    // global filter to remove discontinued products
    modelBuilder.Entity<Product>()
        .HasQueryFilter(p => !p.Discontinued);
}
```

2. Run the code, enter the partial product name che, view the result, and note that **Chef Anton's Gumbo Mix** is now missing, because the SQL statement generated includes a filter for the Discontinued column, as shown highlighted in the following output:

```
SELECT "p"."ProductId", "p"."CategoryId", "p"."UnitPrice",
"p"."Discontinued", "p"."ProductName", "p"."UnitsInStock"
```

```
FROM "Products" AS "p"
WHERE ("p"."Discontinued" = 0) AND "p"."ProductName" LIKE @__Format_1
Chef Anton's Cajun Seasoning has 53 units in stock. Discontinued? False
Queso Manchego La Pastora has 86 units in stock. Discontinued? False
Gumbär Gummibärchen has 15 units in stock. Discontinued? False
```

Loading patterns with EF Core

There are three loading patterns that are commonly used with EF Core:

- **Eager loading**: Load data early.
- **Lazy loading**: Load data automatically just before it is needed.
- **Explicit loading**: Load data manually.

In this section, we're going to introduce each of them.

Eager loading entities

In the QueryingCategories method, the code currently uses the Categories property to loop through each category, outputting the category name and the number of products in that category.

This works because when we wrote the query, we enabled eager loading by calling the Include method for the related products.

Let's see what happens if we do not call Include:

1. Modify the query to comment out the Include method call, as shown in the following code:

   ```
   IQueryable<Category>? categories =
     db.Categories; //.Include(c => c.Products);
   ```

2. In Program.cs, comment out all methods except QueryingCategories.

3. Run the code and view the result, as shown in the following partial output:

   ```
   Beverages has 0 products.
   Condiments has 0 products.
   Confections has 0 products.
   Dairy Products has 0 products.
   Grains/Cereals has 0 products.
   Meat/Poultry has 0 products.
   Produce has 0 products.
   Seafood has 0 products.
   ```

Each item in `foreach` is an instance of the `Category` class, which has a property named `Products`, that is, the list of products in that category. Since the original query is only selected from the `Categories` table, this property is empty for each category.

Enabling lazy loading

Lazy loading was introduced in EF Core 2.1, and it can automatically load missing related data. To enable lazy loading, developers must:

- Reference a NuGet package for proxies.
- Configure lazy loading to use a proxy.

Let's see this in action:

1. In the `WorkingWithEFCore` project, add a package reference for EF Core proxies, as shown in the following markup:

```
<PackageReference
  Include="Microsoft.EntityFrameworkCore.Proxies"
  Version="6.0.0" />
```

2. Build the project to restore packages.

3. Open `Northwind.cs`, and call an extension method to use lazy loading proxies at the top of the `OnConfiguring` method, as shown highlighted in the following code:

```
protected override void OnConfiguring(
  DbContextOptionsBuilder optionsBuilder)
{
  optionsBuilder.UseLazyLoadingProxies();
```

Now, every time the loop enumerates, and an attempt is made to read the `Products` property, the lazy loading proxy will check if they are loaded. If not, it will load them for us "lazily" by executing a `SELECT` statement to load just that set of products for the current category, and then the correct count will be returned to the output.

4. Run the code and note that the product counts are now correct. But you will see that the problem with lazy loading is that multiple round trips to the database server are required to eventually fetch all the data, as shown in the following partial output:

```
Categories and how many products they have:
Level: Debug, Event Id: 20100, State: Executing DbCommand [Parameters=[],
CommandType='Text', CommandTimeout='30']
SELECT "c"."CategoryId", "c"."CategoryName", "c"."Description" FROM
"Categories" AS "c"
Level: Debug, Event Id: 20100, State: Executing DbCommand [Parameters=[@
p_0='?'], CommandType='Text', CommandTimeout='30']
SELECT "p"."ProductId", "p"."CategoryId", "p"."UnitPrice",
"p"."Discontinued", "p"."ProductName", "p"."UnitsInStock"
```

```
FROM "Products" AS "p"
WHERE ("p"."Discontinued" = 0) AND ("p"."CategoryId" = @ p_0)
Beverages has 11 products.
Level: Debug, Event ID: 20100, State: Executing DbCommand [Parameters=[@
p_0='?'], CommandType='Text', CommandTimeout='30']
SELECT "p"."ProductId", "p"."CategoryId", "p"."UnitPrice",
"p"."Discontinued", "p"."ProductName", "p"."UnitsInStock"
FROM "Products" AS "p"
WHERE ("p"."Discontinued" = 0) AND ("p"."CategoryId" = @ p_0)
Condiments has 11 products.
```

Explicit loading entities

Another type of loading is explicit loading. It works in a similar way to lazy loading, with the difference being that you are in control of exactly what related data is loaded and when:

1. At the top of `Program.cs`, import the change tracking namespace to enable us to use the `CollectionEntry` class to manually load related entities, as shown in the following code:

   ```
   using Microsoft.EntityFrameworkCore.ChangeTracking; // CollectionEntry
   ```

2. In the `QueryingCategories` method, modify the statements to disable lazy loading and then prompt the user as to whether they want to enable eager loading and explicit loading, as shown in the following code:

   ```
   IQueryable<Category>? categories;
     // = db.Categories;
     // .Include(c => c.Products);

   db.ChangeTracker.LazyLoadingEnabled = false;

   Write("Enable eager loading? (Y/N): ");
   bool eagerloading = (ReadKey().Key == ConsoleKey.Y);
   bool explicitloading = false;
   WriteLine();

   if (eagerloading)
   {
     categories = db.Categories?.Include(c => c.Products);
   }
   else
   {
     categories = db.Categories;

     Write("Enable explicit loading? (Y/N): ");
     explicitloading = (ReadKey().Key == ConsoleKey.Y);
     WriteLine();
   }
   ```

3. In the `foreach` loop, before the `WriteLine` method call, add statements to check if explicit loading is enabled, and if so, prompt the user as to whether they want to explicitly load each individual category, as shown in the following code:

```
if (explicitloading)
{
  Write($"Explicitly load products for {c.CategoryName}? (Y/N): ");
  ConsoleKeyInfo key = ReadKey();
  WriteLine();
  if (key.Key == ConsoleKey.Y)
  {
    CollectionEntry<Category, Product> products =
      db.Entry(c).Collection(c2 => c2.Products);
    if (!products.IsLoaded) products.Load();
  }
}
WriteLine($"{c.CategoryName} has {c.Products.Count} products.");
```

4. Run the code:

   1. Press N to disable eager loading.

   2. Then press Y to enable explicit loading.

   3. For each category, press Y or N to load its products as you wish.

 I chose to load products for only two of the eight categories, Beverages and Seafood, as shown in the following output that has been edited for space:

```
Categories and how many products they have:
Enable eager loading? (Y/N): n
Enable explicit loading? (Y/N): y
Level: Debug, Event Id: 20100, State: Executing DbCommand [Parameters=[],
CommandType='Text', CommandTimeout='30']
SELECT "c"."CategoryId", "c"."CategoryName", "c"."Description" FROM
"Categories" AS "c"
Explicitly load products for Beverages? (Y/N): y
Level: Debug, Event Id: 20100, State: Executing DbCommand [Parameters=[@
p_0='?'], CommandType='Text', CommandTimeout='30']
SELECT "p"."ProductId", "p"."CategoryId", "p"."UnitPrice",
"p"."Discontinued", "p"."ProductName", "p"."UnitsInStock"
FROM "Products" AS "p"
WHERE ("p"."Discontinued" = 0) AND ("p"."CategoryId" = @ p_0)
Beverages has 11 products.
Explicitly load products for Condiments? (Y/N): n
Condiments has 0 products.
```

```
Explicitly load products for Confections? (Y/N): n
Confections has 0 products.
Explicitly load products for Dairy Products? (Y/N): n
Dairy Products has 0 products.
Explicitly load products for Grains/Cereals? (Y/N): n
Grains/Cereals has 0 products.
Explicitly load products for Meat/Poultry? (Y/N): n
Meat/Poultry has 0 products.
Explicitly load products for Produce? (Y/N): n
Produce has 0 products.
Explicitly load products for Seafood? (Y/N): y
Level: Debug, Event ID: 20100, State: Executing DbCommand [Parameters=[@
p_0='?'], CommandType='Text', CommandTimeout='30']
SELECT "p"."ProductId", "p"."CategoryId", "p"."UnitPrice",
"p"."Discontinued", "p"."ProductName", "p"."UnitsInStock"
FROM "Products" AS "p"
WHERE ("p"."Discontinued" = 0) AND ("p"."CategoryId" = @ p_0)
Seafood has 12 products.
```

Good Practice: Carefully consider which loading pattern is best for your code. Lazy loading could literally make you a lazy database developer! Read more about loading patterns at the following link: `https://docs.microsoft.com/en-us/ef/core/querying/related-data`

Manipulating data with EF Core

Inserting, updating, and deleting entities using EF Core is an easy task to accomplish.

DbContext maintains change tracking automatically, so the local entities can have multiple changes tracked, including adding new entities, modifying existing entities, and removing entities. When you are ready to send those changes to the underlying database, call the SaveChanges method. The number of entities successfully changed will be returned.

Inserting entities

Let's start by looking at how to add a new row to a table:

1. In Program.cs, create a new method named AddProduct, as shown in the following code:

```
static bool AddProduct(
  int categoryId, string productName, decimal? price)
{
  using (Northwind db = new())
  {
    Product p = new()
```

```
    {
      CategoryId = categoryId,
      ProductName = productName,
      Cost = price
    };

    // mark product as added in change tracking
    db.Products.Add(p);

    // save tracked change to database
    int affected = db.SaveChanges();
    return (affected == 1);
  }
}
```

2. In `Program.cs`, create a new method named `ListProducts` that outputs the Id, name, cost, stock, and discontinued properties of each product sorted with the costliest first, as shown in the following code:

```
static void ListProducts()
{
  using (Northwind db = new())
  {
    WriteLine("{0,-3} {1,-35} {2,8} {3,5} {4}",
      "Id", "Product Name", "Cost", "Stock", "Disc.");

    foreach (Product p in db.Products
      .OrderByDescending(product => product.Cost))
    {
      WriteLine("{0:000} {1,-35} {2,8:$#,##0.00} {3,5} {4}",
        p.ProductId, p.ProductName, p.Cost, p.Stock, p.Discontinued);
    }
  }
}
```

Remember that `1,-35` means left-align argument 1 within a 35-character-wide column and `3,5` means right-align argument 3 within a 5-character-wide column.

3. In `Program.cs`, comment out previous method calls, and then call `AddProduct` and `ListProducts`, as shown in the following code:

```
// QueryingCategories();
// FilteredIncludes();
// QueryingProducts();
// QueryingWithLike();

if (AddProduct(categoryId: 6,
  productName: "Bob's Burgers", price: 500M))
```

```
    {
        WriteLine("Add product successful.");
    }

    ListProducts();
```

4. Run the code, view the result, and note the new product has been added, as shown in the following partial output:

```
Add product successful.
Id  Product Name              Cost Stock Disc.
078 Bob's Burgers          $500.00       False
038 Côte de Blaye          $263.50    17 False
020 Sir Rodney's Marmalade $81.00     40 False
...
```

Updating entities

Now, let's modify an existing row in a table:

1. In `Program.cs`, add a method to increase the price of the first product with a name that begins with a specified value (we'll use Bob in our example) by a specified amount like $20, as shown in the following code:

```
static bool IncreaseProductPrice(
    string productNameStartsWith, decimal amount)
{
    using (Northwind db = new())
    {
        // get first product whose name starts with name
        Product updateProduct = db.Products.First(
            p => p.ProductName.StartsWith(productNameStartsWith));

        updateProduct.Cost += amount;

        int affected = db.SaveChanges();
        return (affected == 1);
    }
}
```

2. In `Program.cs`, comment out the whole `if` block that calls `AddProduct`, and add a call to `IncreaseProductPrice` before the call to list products, as shown highlighted in the following code:

```
/*
if (AddProduct(categoryId: 6,
    productName: "Bob's Burgers", price: 500M))
{
```

```
    WriteLine("Add product successful.");
  }
  */

  if (IncreaseProductPrice(
    productNameStartsWith: "Bob", amount: 20M))
  {
    WriteLine("Update product price successful.");
  }

  ListProducts();
```

3. Run the code, view the result, and note that the existing entity for Bob's Burgers has increased in price by $20, as shown in the following partial output:

```
Update product price successful.
Id  Product Name              Cost Stock Disc.
078 Bob's Burgers            $520.00       False
038 Côte de Blaye            $263.50    17 False
020 Sir Rodney's Marmalade   $81.00     40 False
...
```

Deleting entities

You can remove individual entities with the Remove method. RemoveRange is more efficient when you want to delete multiple entities.

Now let's see how to delete rows from a table:

1. At the bottom of Program.cs, add a method to delete all products with a name that begins with a specified value (Bob in our example), as shown in the following code:

```
static int DeleteProducts(string productNameStartsWith)
{
  using (Northwind db = new())
  {
    IQueryable<Product>? products = db.Products?.Where(
      p => p.ProductName.StartsWith(productNameStartsWith));

    if (products is null)
    {
      WriteLine("No products found to delete.");
      return 0;
    }
    else
    {
      db.Products.RemoveRange(products);
```

```
    }

    int affected = db.SaveChanges();
    return affected;
    }
}
```

2. In `Program.cs`, comment out the whole `if` statement block that calls `IncreaseProductPrice`, and add a call to `DeleteProducts`, as shown in the following code:

   ```
   int deleted = DeleteProducts(productNameStartsWith: "Bob");
   WriteLine($"{deleted} product(s) were deleted.");
   ```

3. Run the code and view the result, as shown in the following output:

   ```
   1 product(s) were deleted.
   ```

If multiple product names started with Bob, then they are all deleted. As an optional challenge, modify the statements to add three new products that start with Bob and then delete them.

Pooling database contexts

The `DbContext` class is disposable and is designed following the single-unit-of-work principle. In the previous code examples, we created all the `DbContext`-derived Northwind instances in a `using` block so that `Dispose` is properly called at the end of each unit of work.

A feature of ASP.NET Core that is related to EF Core is that it makes your code more efficient by pooling database contexts when building websites and services. This allows you to create and dispose of as many `DbContext`-derived objects as you want, knowing that your code is still as efficient as possible.

Working with transactions

Every time you call the `SaveChanges` method, an **implicit transaction** is started so that if something goes wrong, it will automatically roll back all the changes. If the multiple changes within the transaction succeed, then the transaction and all changes are committed.

Transactions maintain the integrity of your database by applying locks to prevent reads and writes while a sequence of changes is occurring.

Transactions are **ACID**, which is an acronym explained in the following list:

- **A is for atomic.** Either all the operations in the transaction commit, or none of them do.
- **C is for consistent.** The state of the database before and after a transaction is consistent. This is dependent on your code logic; for example, when transferring money between bank accounts, it is up to your business logic to ensure that if you debit $100 in one account, you credit $100 in the other account.

- **I is for isolated**. During a transaction, changes are hidden from other processes. There are multiple isolation levels that you can pick from (refer to the following table). The stronger the level, the better the integrity of the data. However, more locks must be applied, which will negatively affect other processes. Snapshot is a special case because it creates multiple copies of rows to avoid locks, but this will increase the size of your database while transactions occur.

- **D is for durable**. If a failure occurs during a transaction, it can be recovered. This is often implemented as a two-phase commit and transaction logs. Once the transaction is committed it is guaranteed to endure even if there are subsequent errors. The opposite of durable is volatile.

Controlling transactions using isolation levels

A developer can control transactions by setting an **isolation level**, as described in the following table:

Isolation level	Lock(s)	Integrity problems allowed
ReadUncommitted	None	Dirty reads, nonrepeatable reads, and phantom data
ReadCommitted	When editing, it applies read lock(s) to block other users from reading the record(s) until the transaction ends	Nonrepeatable reads and phantom data
RepeatableRead	When reading, it applies edit lock(s) to block other users from editing the record(s) until the transaction ends	Phantom data
Serializable	Applies key-range locks to prevent any action that would affect the results, including inserts and deletes	None
Snapshot	None	None

Defining an explicit transaction

You can control explicit transactions using the Database property of the database context:

1. In Program.cs, import the EF Core storage namespace to use the IDbContextTransaction interface, as shown in the following code:

   ```
   using Microsoft.EntityFrameworkCore.Storage; // IDbContextTransaction
   ```

2. In the DeleteProducts method, after the instantiation of the db variable, add statements to start an explicit transaction and output its isolation level. At the bottom of the method, commit the transaction, and close the brace, as shown highlighted in the following code:

   ```
   static int DeleteProducts(string name)
   {
   ```

```
using (Northwind db = new())
{
  using (IDbContextTransaction t = db.Database.BeginTransaction())
  {
    WriteLine("Transaction isolation level: {0}",
      arg0: t.GetDbTransaction().IsolationLevel);

    IQueryable<Product>? products = db.Products?.Where(
      p => p.ProductName.StartsWith(name));

    if (products is null)
    {
      WriteLine("No products found to delete.");
      return 0;
    }
    else
    {
      db.Products.RemoveRange(products);
    }

    int affected = db.SaveChanges();
    t.Commit();
    return affected;
  }
}
}
```

3. Run the code and view the result using SQL Server, as shown in the following output:

```
Transaction isolation level: ReadCommitted
```

4. Run the code and view the result using SQLite, as shown in the following output:

```
Transaction isolation level: Serializable
```

Code First EF Core models

Sometimes you will not have an existing database. Instead, you define the EF Core model as Code First, and then EF Core can generate a matching database using create and drop APIs.

 Good Practice: The create and drop APIs should only be used during development. Once you release the app, you do not want it to delete a production database!

For example, we might need to create an application for managing students and courses for an academy. One student can sign up to attend multiple courses. One course can be attended by multiple students. This is an example of a many-to-many relationship between students and courses.

Let's model this example:

1. Use your preferred code editor to add a new console app named CoursesAndStudents to the Chapter10 solution/workspace.

2. In Visual Studio, set the startup project for the solution to the current selection.

3. In Visual Studio Code, select CoursesAndStudents as the active OmniSharp project.

4. In the CoursesAndStudents project, add package references for the following packages:

   - Microsoft.EntityFrameworkCore.Sqlite
   - Microsoft.EntityFrameworkCore.SqlServer
   - Microsoft.EntityFrameworkCore.Design

5. Build the CoursesAndStudents project to restore packages.

6. Add classes named Academy.cs, Student.cs, and Course.cs.

7. Modify Student.cs, and note that it is a POCO (plain old CLR object) with no attributes decorating the class, as shown in the following code:

   ```
   namespace CoursesAndStudents;

   public class Student
   {
     public int StudentId { get; set; }
     public string? FirstName { get; set; }
     public string? LastName { get; set; }

     public ICollection<Course>? Courses { get; set; }
   }
   ```

8. Modify Course.cs, and note that we have decorated the Title property with some attributes to provide more information to the model, as shown in the following code:

   ```
   using System.ComponentModel.DataAnnotations;

   namespace CoursesAndStudents;

   public class Course
   {
     public int CourseId { get; set; }
   ```

```
[Required]
[StringLength(60)]
public string? Title { get; set; }

public ICollection<Student>? Students { get; set; }
}
```

9. Modify Academy.cs, as shown in the following code:

```
using Microsoft.EntityFrameworkCore;

using static System.Console;

namespace CoursesAndStudents;

public class Academy : DbContext
{
  public DbSet<Student>? Students { get; set; }
  public DbSet<Course>? Courses { get; set; }

  protected override void OnConfiguring(
    DbContextOptionsBuilder optionsBuilder)
  {
    string path = Path.Combine(
      Environment.CurrentDirectory, "Academy.db");

    WriteLine($"Using {path} database file.");

    optionsBuilder.UseSqlite($"Filename={path}");

    // optionsBuilder.UseSqlServer(@"Data Source=.;Initial
Catalog=Academy;Integrated Security=true;MultipleActiveResultSets=true;");
  }

  protected override void OnModelCreating(ModelBuilder modelBuilder)
  {
    // Fluent API validation rules

    modelBuilder.Entity<Student>()
        .Property(s => s.LastName).HasMaxLength(30).IsRequired();

    // populate database with sample data

    Student alice = new() { StudentId = 1,
      FirstName = "Alice", LastName = "Jones" };
```

```
Student bob = new() { StudentId = 2,
  FirstName = "Bob", LastName = "Smith" };

Student cecilia = new() { StudentId = 3,
  FirstName = "Cecilia", LastName = "Ramirez" };

Course csharp = new()
{
  CourseId = 1,
  Title = "C# 10 and .NET 6",
};

Course webdev = new()
{
  CourseId = 2,
  Title = "Web Development",
};

Course python = new()
{
  CourseId = 3,
  Title = "Python for Beginners",
};

modelBuilder.Entity<Student>()
  .HasData(alice, bob, cecilia);

modelBuilder.Entity<Course>()
  .HasData(csharp, webdev, python);

modelBuilder.Entity<Course>()
  .HasMany(c => c.Students)
  .WithMany(s => s.Courses)
  .UsingEntity(e => e.HasData(
    // all students signed up for C# course
    new { CoursesCourseId = 1, StudentsStudentId = 1 },
    new { CoursesCourseId = 1, StudentsStudentId = 2 },
    new { CoursesCourseId = 1, StudentsStudentId = 3 },
    // only Bob signed up for Web Dev
    new { CoursesCourseId = 2, StudentsStudentId = 2 },
    // only Cecilia signed up for Python
    new { CoursesCourseId = 3, StudentsStudentId = 3 }
  ));
  }
}
```

Good Practice: Use an anonymous type to supply data for the intermediate table in a many-to-many relationship. The property names follow the naming convention `NavigationPropertyNamePropertyName`, for example, `Courses` is the navigation property name and `CourseId` is the property name so `CoursesCourseId` will be the property name of the anonymous type.

10. In `Program.cs`, at the top of the file, import the namespace for EF Core and working with tasks, and statically import `Console`, as shown in the following code:

```
using Microsoft.EntityFrameworkCore; // for GenerateCreateScript()
using CoursesAndStudents; // Academy

using static System.Console;
```

11. In `Program.cs`, add statements to create an instance of the `Academy` database context and use it to delete the database if it exists, create the database from the model and output the SQL script it uses, and then enumerate the students and their courses, as shown in the following code:

```
using (Academy a = new())
{
    bool deleted = await a.Database.EnsureDeletedAsync();
    WriteLine($"Database deleted: {deleted}");

    bool created = await a.Database.EnsureCreatedAsync();
    WriteLine($"Database created: {created}");

    WriteLine("SQL script used to create database:");
    WriteLine(a.Database.GenerateCreateScript());

    foreach (Student s in a.Students.Include(s => s.Courses))
    {
        WriteLine("{0} {1} attends the following {2} courses:",
            s.FirstName, s.LastName, s.Courses.Count);

        foreach (Course c in s.Courses)
        {
            WriteLine($"  {c.Title}");
        }
    }
}
```

12. Run the code, and note that the first time you run the code it will not need to delete the database because it does not exist yet, as shown in the following output:

```
Using C:\Code\Chapter10\CoursesAndStudents\bin\Debug\net6.0\Academy.db
database file.
```

```
Database deleted: False
Database created: True
SQL script used to create database:
CREATE TABLE "Courses" (
    "CourseId" INTEGER NOT NULL CONSTRAINT "PK_Courses" PRIMARY KEY
AUTOINCREMENT,
    "Title" TEXT NOT NULL
);

CREATE TABLE "Students" (
    "StudentId" INTEGER NOT NULL CONSTRAINT "PK_Students" PRIMARY KEY
AUTOINCREMENT,
    "FirstName" TEXT NULL,
    "LastName" TEXT NOT NULL
);

CREATE TABLE "CourseStudent" (
    "CoursesCourseId" INTEGER NOT NULL,
    "StudentsStudentId" INTEGER NOT NULL,
    CONSTRAINT "PK_CourseStudent" PRIMARY KEY ("CoursesCourseId",
"StudentsStudentId"),
    CONSTRAINT "FK_CourseStudent_Courses_CoursesCourseId" FOREIGN KEY
("CoursesCourseId") REFERENCES "Courses" ("CourseId") ON DELETE CASCADE,
    CONSTRAINT "FK_CourseStudent_Students_StudentsStudentId" FOREIGN
KEY ("StudentsStudentId") REFERENCES "Students" ("StudentId") ON DELETE
CASCADE
);

INSERT INTO "Courses" ("CourseId", "Title")
VALUES (1, 'C# 10 and .NET 6');

INSERT INTO "Courses" ("CourseId", "Title")
VALUES (2, 'Web Development');

INSERT INTO "Courses" ("CourseId", "Title")
VALUES (3, 'Python for Beginners');

INSERT INTO "Students" ("StudentId", "FirstName", "LastName")
VALUES (1, 'Alice', 'Jones');

INSERT INTO "Students" ("StudentId", "FirstName", "LastName")
VALUES (2, 'Bob', 'Smith');

INSERT INTO "Students" ("StudentId", "FirstName", "LastName")
VALUES (3, 'Cecilia', 'Ramirez');
```

```
INSERT INTO "CourseStudent" ("CoursesCourseId", "StudentsStudentId")
VALUES (1, 1);

INSERT INTO "CourseStudent" ("CoursesCourseId", "StudentsStudentId")
VALUES (1, 2);

INSERT INTO "CourseStudent" ("CoursesCourseId", "StudentsStudentId")
VALUES (2, 2);

INSERT INTO "CourseStudent" ("CoursesCourseId", "StudentsStudentId")
VALUES (1, 3);

INSERT INTO "CourseStudent" ("CoursesCourseId", "StudentsStudentId")
VALUES (3, 3);

CREATE INDEX "IX_CourseStudent_StudentsStudentId" ON "CourseStudent"
("StudentsStudentId");

Alice Jones attends the following 1 course(s):
  C# 10 and .NET 6
Bob Smith attends the following 2 course(s):
  C# 10 and .NET 6
  Web Development
Cecilia Ramirez attends the following 2 course(s):
  C# 10 and .NET 6
  Python for Beginners
```

Note the following:

- The Title column is NOT NULL because the model was decorated with [Required].
- The LastName column is NOT NULL because the model used IsRequired().
- An intermediate table named CourseStudent was created to hold information about which students attend which courses.

13. Use Visual Studio Server Explorer or SQLiteStudio to connect to the `Academy` database and view the tables, as shown in *Figure 10.6*:

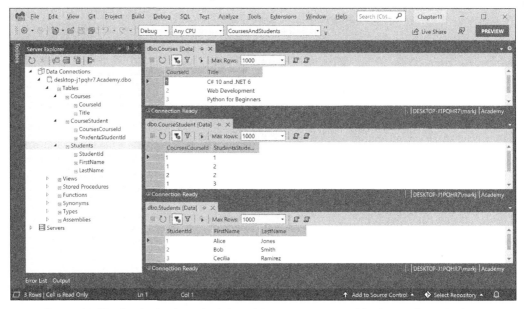

Figure 10.6: Viewing the Academy database in SQL Server using Visual Studio 2022 Server Explorer

Understanding migrations

After publishing a project that uses a database, it is likely that you will later need to change your entity data model and therefore the database structure. At that point, you should not use the `Ensure` methods. Instead, you need to use a system that allows you to incrementally update the database schema while preserving any existing data in the database. EF Core migrations are that system.

Migrations get complex fast, so are beyond the scope of this book. You can read about them at the following link: `https://docs.microsoft.com/en-us/ef/core/managing-schemas/migrations/`

Practicing and exploring

Test your knowledge and understanding by answering some questions, get some hands-on practice, and explore this chapter's topics with deeper research.

Exercise 10.1 – Test your knowledge

Answer the following questions:

1. What type would you use for the property that represents a table, for example, the Products property of a database context?
2. What type would you use for the property that represents a one-to-many relationship, for example, the Products property of a Category entity?
3. What is the EF Core convention for primary keys?
4. When might you use an annotation attribute in an entity class?
5. Why might you choose the Fluent API in preference to annotation attributes?
6. What does a transaction isolation level of Serializable mean?
7. What does the DbContext.SaveChanges() method return?
8. What is the difference between eager loading and explicit loading?
9. How should you define an EF Core entity class to match the following table?

    ```
    CREATE TABLE Employees(
        EmpId INT IDENTITY,
        FirstName NVARCHAR(40) NOT NULL,
        Salary MONEY
    )
    ```

10. What benefit do you get from declaring entity navigation properties as virtual?

Exercise 10.2 – Practice exporting data using different serialization formats

In the Chapter10 solution/workspace, create a console application named Exercise02 that queries the Northwind database for all the categories and products, and then serializes the data using at least three formats of serialization available to .NET. Which format of serialization uses the least number of bytes?

Exercise 10.3 – Explore topics

Use the links on the following page to learn more detail about the topics covered in this chapter:

```
https://github.com/markjprice/cs10dotnet6/blob/main/book-links.md#chapter-10---
working-with-data-using-entity-framework-core
```

Exercise 10.4 – Explore NoSQL databases

This chapter focused on RDBMSs such as SQL Server and SQLite. If you wish to learn more about NoSQL databases, such as Cosmos DB and MongoDB, and how to use them with EF Core, then I recommend the following links:

- **Welcome to Azure Cosmos DB**: `https://docs.microsoft.com/en-us/azure/cosmos-db/introduction`

- **Use NoSQL databases as a persistence infrastructure**: `https://docs.microsoft.com/en-us/dotnet/standard/microservices-architecture/microservice-ddd-cqrs-patterns/nosql-database-persistence-infrastructure`

- **Document Database Providers for Entity Framework Core**: `https://github.com/BlueshiftSoftware/EntityFrameworkCore`

Summary

In this chapter, you learned how to connect to an existing database, how to execute a simple LINQ query and process the results, how to use filtered includes, how to add, modify, and delete data, and how to build entity data models for an existing database, such as Northwind. You also learned how to define a Code First model and use it to create a new database and populate it with data.

In the next chapter, you will learn how to write more advanced LINQ queries to select, filter, sort, join, and group.

11

Querying and Manipulating Data Using LINQ

This chapter is about **Language INtegrated Query (LINQ)** expressions. LINQ is a set of language extensions that add the ability to work with sequences of items and then filter, sort, and project them into different outputs.

This chapter will cover the following topics:

- Writing LINQ expressions
- Working with sets using LINQ
- Using LINQ with EF Core
- Sweetening LINQ syntax with syntactic sugar
- Using multiple threads with parallel LINQ
- Creating your own LINQ extension methods
- Working with LINQ to XML

Writing LINQ expressions

Although we wrote a few LINQ expressions in *Chapter 10, Working with Data Using Entity Framework Core*, they weren't the focus, and so I didn't properly explain how LINQ works, so let's now take time to properly understand them.

What makes LINQ?

LINQ has several parts; some are required, and some are optional:

- **Extension methods (required)**: These include examples such as Where, OrderBy, and Select. These are what provide the functionality of LINQ.

- **LINQ providers (required)**: These include LINQ to Objects for processing in-memory objects, LINQ to Entities for processing data stored in external databases and modeled with EF Core, and LINQ to XML for processing data stored as XML. These providers are what execute LINQ expressions in a way specific to different types of data.

- **Lambda expressions (optional)**: These can be used instead of named methods to simplify LINQ queries, for example, for the conditional logic of the Where method for filtering.

- **LINQ query comprehension syntax (optional)**: These include C# keywords like from, in, where, orderby, descending, and select. These are aliases for some of the LINQ extension methods, and their use can simplify the queries you write, especially if you already have experience with other query languages, such as **Structured Query Language (SQL)**.

When programmers are first introduced to LINQ, they often believe that LINQ query comprehension syntax is LINQ, but ironically, that is one of the parts of LINQ that is optional!

Building LINQ expressions with the Enumerable class

The LINQ extension methods, such as Where and Select, are appended by the Enumerable static class to any type, known as a **sequence**, that implements IEnumerable<T>.

For example, an array of any type implements the IEnumerable<T> class, where T is the type of item in the array. This means that all arrays support LINQ to query and manipulate them.

All generic collections, such as List<T>, Dictionary<TKey, TValue>, Stack<T>, and Queue<T>, implement IEnumerable<T>, so they can be queried and manipulated with LINQ too.

Enumerable defines more than 50 extension methods, as summarized in the following table:

Method(s)	Description
First, FirstOrDefault, Last, LastOrDefault	Get the first or last item in the sequence or throw an exception, or return the default value for the type, for example, 0 for an int and null for a reference type, if there is not a first or last item.
Where	Return a sequence of items that match a specified filter.
Single, SingleOrDefault	Return an item that matches a specific filter or throw an exception, or return the default value for the type if there is not exactly one match.
ElementAt, ElementAtOrDefault	Return an item at a specified index position or throw an exception, or return the default value for the type if there is not an item at that position. New in .NET 6 are overloads that can be passed an Index instead of an int, which is more efficient when working with Span<T> sequences.
Select, SelectMany	Project items into a different shape, that is, a different type, and flatten a nested hierarchy of items.

OrderBy, OrderByDescending, ThenBy, ThenByDescending	Sort items by a specified field or property.
Reverse	Reverse the order of the items.
GroupBy, GroupJoin, Join	Group and/or join two sequences.
Skip, SkipWhile	Skip a number of items; or skip while an expression is true.
Take, TakeWhile	Take a number of items; or take while an expression is true. New in .NET 6 is a Take overload that can be passed a Range, for example, Take(range: 3..^5) meaning take a subset starting 3 items in from the start and ending 5 items in from the end, or instead of Skip(4) you could use Take(4..).
Aggregate, Average, Count, LongCount, Max, Min, Sum	Calculate aggregate values.
TryGetNonEnumeratedCount	Count() checks if a Count property is implemented on the sequence and returns its value, or it enumerates the entire sequence to count its items. New in .NET 6 is this method that only checks for Count and if it is missing it returns false and sets the out parameter to 0 to avoid a potentially poor-performing operation.
All, Any, Contains	Return true if all or any of the items match the filter, or if the sequence contains a specified item.
Cast	Cast items into a specified type. It is useful to convert non-generic objects to a generic type in scenarios where the compiler would otherwise complain.
OfType	Remove items that do not match a specified type.
Distinct	Remove duplicate items.
Except, Intersect, Union	Perform operations that return sets. Sets cannot have duplicate items. Although the inputs can be any sequence and so the inputs can have duplicates, the result is always a set.
Chunk	Divide a sequence into sized batches.
Append, Concat, Prepend	Perform sequence-combining operations.
Zip	Perform a match operation on two sequences based on the position of items, for example, the item at position 1 in the first sequence matches the item at position 1 in the second sequence. New in .NET 6 is a match operation on three sequences. Previously you would have had to run the two sequences overload twice to achieve the same goal.
ToArray, ToList, ToDictionary, ToHashSet, ToLookup	Convert the sequence into an array or collection. These are the only extension methods that execute the LINQ expression.
DistinctBy, ExceptBy, IntersectBy, UnionBy, MinBy, MaxBy	New in .NET 6 are the By extension methods. They allow the comparison to be performed on a subset of the item rather than the entire item. For example, instead of removing duplicates by comparing an entire Person object, you could remove duplicates by comparing just their LastName and DateOfBirth.

The `Enumerable` class also has some methods that are not extension methods, as shown in the following table:

Method	Description
Empty<T>	Returns an empty sequence of the specified type T. It is useful for passing an empty sequence to a method that requires an IEnumerable<T>.
Range	Returns a sequence of integers from the start value with count items. For example, Enumerable.Range(start: 5, count: 3) would contain the integers 5, 6, and 7.
Repeat	Returns a sequence that contains the same element repeated count times. For example, Enumerable.Repeat(element: "5", count: 3) would contain the string values "5", "5", and "5".

Understanding deferred execution

LINQ uses **deferred execution**. It is important to understand that calling most of these extension methods does not execute the query and get the results. Most of these extension methods return a LINQ expression that represents a *question*, not an *answer*. Let's explore:

1. Use your preferred code editor to create a new solution/workspace named Chapter11.

2. Add a console app project, as defined in the following list:

    1. Project template: **Console Application** / console

    2. Workspace/solution file and folder: Chapter11

    3. Project file and folder: LinqWithObjects

3. In Program.cs, delete the existing code and statically import Console.

4. Add statements to define a sequence of string values for people who work in an office, as shown in the following code:

    ```
    // a string array is a sequence that implements IEnumerable<string>
    string[] names = new[] { "Michael", "Pam", "Jim", "Dwight",
      "Angela", "Kevin", "Toby", "Creed" };

    WriteLine("Deferred execution");

    // Question: Which names end with an M?
    // (written using a LINQ extension method)
    var query1 = names.Where(name => name.EndsWith("m"));

    // Question: Which names end with an M?
    // (written using LINQ query comprehension syntax)
    var query2 = from name in names where name.EndsWith("m") select name;
    ```

5. To ask the question and get the answer, i.e. execute the query, you must **materialize** it by either calling one of the "To" methods like ToArray or ToLookup or by enumerating the query, as shown in the following code:

```
// Answer returned as an array of strings containing Pam and Jim
string[] result1 = query1.ToArray();

// Answer returned as a list of strings containing Pam and Jim
List<string> result2 = query2.ToList();

// Answer returned as we enumerate over the results
foreach (string name in query1)
{
  WriteLine(name); // outputs Pam
  names[2] = "Jimmy"; // change Jim to Jimmy
  // on the second iteration Jimmy does not end with an M
}
```

6. Run the console app and note the result, as shown in the following output:

```
Deferred execution
Pam
```

Due to deferred execution, after outputting the first result, Pam, if the original array values change, then by the time we loop back around, there are no more matches because Jim has become Jimmy and does not end with an M, so only Pam is outputted.

Before we get too deep into the weeds, let's slow down and look at some common LINQ extension methods and how to use them, one at a time.

Filtering entities with Where

The most common reason for using LINQ is to filter items in a sequence using the Where extension method. Let's explore filtering by defining a sequence of names and then applying LINQ operations to it:

1. In the project file, comment out the element that enables implicit usings, as shown highlighted in the following markup:

```
<Project Sdk="Microsoft.NET.Sdk">

  <PropertyGroup>
    <OutputType>Exe</OutputType>
    <TargetFramework>net6.0</TargetFramework>
    <Nullable>enable</Nullable>
    <!--<ImplicitUsings>enable</ImplicitUsings>-->
  </PropertyGroup>

</Project>
```

2. In `Program.cs`, attempt to call the `Where` extension method on the array of names, as shown in the following code:

```
WriteLine("Writing queries");

var query = names.W
```

3. As you try to type the `Where` method, note that it is missing from the IntelliSense list of members of a string array, as shown in *Figure 11.1*:

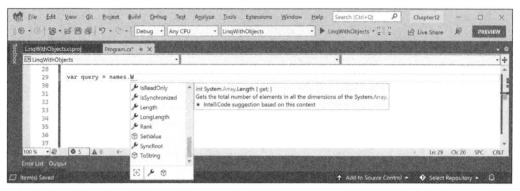

Figure 11.1: IntelliSense with the Where extension method missing

This is because `Where` is an extension method. It does not exist on the array type. To make the `Where` extension method available, we must import the `System.Linq` namespace. This is implicitly imported by default in new .NET 6 projects, but we disabled it.

4. In the project file, uncomment out the element that enables implicit usings.

5. Retype the `Where` method and note that the IntelliSense list now includes the extension methods added by the `Enumerable` class, as shown in *Figure 11.2*:

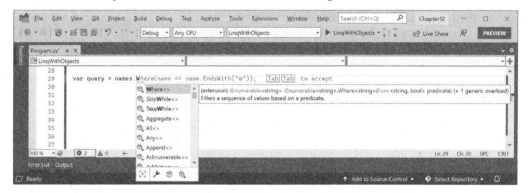

Figure 11.2: IntelliSense showing LINQ Enumerable extension methods now

6. As you type the parentheses for the `Where` method, IntelliSense tells us that to call `Where`, we must pass in an instance of a `Func<string, bool>` delegate.

7. Enter an expression to create a new instance of a Func<string, bool> delegate, and for now note that we have not yet supplied a method name because we will define it in the next step, as shown in the following code:

```
var query = names.Where(new Func<string, bool>( ))
```

The Func<string, bool> delegate tells us that for each string variable passed to the method, the method must return a bool value. If the method returns true, it indicates that we should include the string in the results, and if the method returns false, it indicates that we should exclude it.

Targeting a named method

Let's define a method that only includes names that are longer than four characters:

1. At the bottom of Program.cs, define a method that will include only names longer than four characters, as shown in the following code:

```
static bool NameLongerThanFour(string name)
{
    return name.Length > 4;
}
```

2. Above the NameLongerThanFour method, pass the method's name into the Func<string, bool> delegate, and then loop through the query items, as shown highlighted in the following code:

```
var query = names.Where(
    new Func<string, bool>(NameLongerThanFour));

foreach (string item in query)
{
    WriteLine(item);
}
```

3. Run the code and view the results, noting that only names longer than four letters are listed, as shown in the following output:

```
Writing queries
Michael
Dwight
Angela
Kevin
Creed
```

Simplifying the code by removing the explicit delegate instantiation

We can simplify the code by deleting the explicit instantiation of the `Func<string, bool>` delegate because the C# compiler can instantiate the delegate for us:

1. To help you learn by seeing progressively improved code, copy and paste the query

2. Comment out the first example, as shown in the following code:

```
// var query = names.Where(
//    new Func<string, bool>(NameLongerThanFour));
```

3. Modify the copy to remove the explicit instantiation of the delegate, as shown in the following code:

```
var query = names.Where(NameLongerThanFour);
```

4. Run the code and note that it has the same behavior.

Targeting a lambda expression

We can simplify our code even further using a **lambda expression** in place of a named method.

Although it can look complicated at first, a lambda expression is simply a *nameless function*. It uses the `=>` (read as "goes to") symbol to indicate the return value:

1. Copy and paste the query, comment the second example, and modify the query, as shown in the following code:

```
var query = names.Where(name => name.Length > 4);
```

Note that the syntax for a lambda expression includes all the important parts of the `NameLongerThanFour` method, but nothing more. A lambda expression only needs to define the following:

- The names of input parameters: `name`
- A return value expression: `name.Length > 4`

The type of the `name` input parameter is inferred from the fact that the sequence contains `string` values, and the return type must be a `bool` value as defined by the delegate for `Where` to work, so the expression after the `=>` symbol must return a `bool` value.

The compiler does most of the work for us, so our code can be as concise as possible.

2. Run the code and note that it has the same behavior.

Sorting entities

Other commonly used extension methods are `OrderBy` and `ThenBy`, used for sorting a sequence.

Extension methods can be chained if the previous method returns another sequence, that is, a type that implements the `IEnumerable<T>` interface.

Sorting by a single property using OrderBy

Let's continue working with the current project to explore sorting:

1. Append a call to `OrderBy` to the end of the existing query, as shown in the following code:

```
var query = names
  .Where(name => name.Length > 4)
  .OrderBy(name => name.Length);
```

 Good Practice: Format the LINQ statement so that each extension method call happens on its own line to make them easier to read.

2. Run the code and note that the names are now sorted by shortest first, as shown in the following output:

```
Kevin
Creed
Dwight
Angela
Michael
```

To put the longest name first, you would use `OrderByDescending`.

Sorting by a subsequent property using ThenBy

We might want to sort by more than one property, for example, to sort names of the same length in alphabetical order:

1. Add a call to the `ThenBy` method at the end of the existing query, as shown highlighted in the following code:

```
var query = names
  .Where(name => name.Length > 4)
  .OrderBy(name => name.Length)
  .ThenBy(name => name);
```

2. Run the code and note the slight difference in the following sort order. Within a group of names of the same length, the names are sorted alphabetically by the full value of the string, so Creed comes before Kevin, and Angela comes before Dwight, as shown in the following output:

```
Creed
Kevin
Angela
Dwight
Michael
```

Declaring a query using var or a specified type

While writing a LINQ expression it is convenient to use var to declare the query object. This is because the type frequently changes as you work on the LINQ expression. For example, our query started as an IEnumerable<string> and is currently an IOrderedEnumerable<string>:

1. Hover your mouse over the var keyword and note that its type is IOrderedEnumerable<string>

2. Replace var with the actual type, as shown highlighted in the following code:

```
IOrderedEnumerable<string> query = names
    .Where(name => name.Length > 4)
    .OrderBy(name => name.Length)
    .ThenBy(name => name);
```

 Good Practice: Once you have finished working on a query, you could change the declared type from var to the actual type to make it clearer what the type is. This is easy because your code editor can tell you what it is.

Filtering by type

The Where extension method is great for filtering by values, such as text and numbers. But what if the sequence contains multiple types, and you want to filter by a specific type and respect any inheritance hierarchy?

Imagine that you have a sequence of exceptions. There are hundreds of exception types that form a complex hierarchy, as partially shown in *Figure 11.3*:

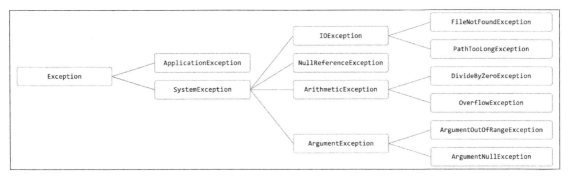

Figure 11.3: A partial exception inheritance hierarchy

Let's explore filtering by type:

1. In `Program.cs`, define a list of exception-derived objects, as shown in the following code:

```
WriteLine("Filtering by type");

List<Exception> exceptions = new()
{
  new ArgumentException(),
  new SystemException(),
  new IndexOutOfRangeException(),
  new InvalidOperationException(),
  new NullReferenceException(),
  new InvalidCastException(),
  new OverflowException(),
  new DivideByZeroException(),
  new ApplicationException()
};
```

2. Write statements using the `OfType<T>` extension method to remove exceptions that are not arithmetic exceptions and write only the arithmetic exceptions to the console, as shown in the following code:

```
IEnumerable<ArithmeticException> arithmeticExceptionsQuery =
  exceptions.OfType<ArithmeticException>();

foreach (ArithmeticException exception in arithmeticExceptionsQuery)
{
  WriteLine(exception);
}
```

3. Run the code and note that the results only include exceptions of the `ArithmeticException` type, or the `ArithmeticException`-derived types, as shown in the following output:

```
System.OverflowException: Arithmetic operation resulted in an overflow.
System.DivideByZeroException: Attempted to divide by zero.
```

Working with sets and bags using LINQ

Sets are one of the most fundamental concepts in mathematics. A **set** is a collection of one or more unique objects. A **multiset**, aka **bag**, is a collection of one or more objects that can have duplicates.

You might remember being taught about Venn diagrams in school. Common set operations include the **intersect** or **union** between sets.

Let's create a console application that will define three arrays of `string` values for cohorts of apprentices and then perform some common set and multiset operations on them:

1. Use your preferred code editor to add a new console app named `LinqWithSets` to the `Chapter11` solution/workspace:

    1. In Visual Studio, set the startup project for the solution to the current selection.

    2. In Visual Studio Code, select `LinqWithSets` as the active OmniSharp project.

2. In `Program.cs`, delete the existing code and statically import the `Console` type, as shown in the following code:

    ```
    using static System.Console;
    ```

3. At the bottom of `Program.cs`, add the following method that outputs any sequence of string variables as a comma-separated single `string` to the console output, along with an optional description, as shown in the following code:

    ```
    static void Output(IEnumerable<string> cohort, string description = "")
    {
      if (!string.IsNullOrEmpty(description))
      {
        WriteLine(description);
      }
      Write(" ");
      WriteLine(string.Join(", ", cohort.ToArray()));
      WriteLine();
    }
    ```

4. Above the `Output` method, add statements to define three arrays of names, output them, and then perform various set operations on them, as shown in the following code:

    ```
    string[] cohort1 = new[]
      { "Rachel", "Gareth", "Jonathan", "George" };
    ```

```
string[] cohort2 = new[]
  { "Jack", "Stephen", "Daniel", "Jack", "Jared" };

string[] cohort3 = new[]
  { "Declan", "Jack", "Jack", "Jasmine", "Conor" };

Output(cohort1, "Cohort 1");
Output(cohort2, "Cohort 2");
Output(cohort3, "Cohort 3");

Output(cohort2.Distinct(), "cohort2.Distinct()");
Output(cohort2.DistinctBy(name => name.Substring(0, 2)),
  "cohort2.DistinctBy(name => name.Substring(0, 2)):");
Output(cohort2.Union(cohort3), "cohort2.Union(cohort3)");
Output(cohort2.Concat(cohort3), "cohort2.Concat(cohort3)");
Output(cohort2.Intersect(cohort3), "cohort2.Intersect(cohort3)");
Output(cohort2.Except(cohort3), "cohort2.Except(cohort3)");
Output(cohort1.Zip(cohort2,(c1, c2) => $"{c1} matched with {c2}"),
  "cohort1.Zip(cohort2)");
```

5. Run the code and view the results, as shown in the following output:

```
Cohort 1
  Rachel, Gareth, Jonathan, George

Cohort 2
  Jack, Stephen, Daniel, Jack, Jared

Cohort 3
  Declan, Jack, Jack, Jasmine, Conor

cohort2.Distinct()
  Jack, Stephen, Daniel, Jared

cohort2.DistinctBy(name => name.Substring(0, 2)):
  Jack, Stephen, Daniel

cohort2.Union(cohort3)
  Jack, Stephen, Daniel, Jared, Declan, Jasmine, Conor

cohort2.Concat(cohort3)
  Jack, Stephen, Daniel, Jack, Jared, Declan, Jack, Jack, Jasmine, Conor

cohort2.Intersect(cohort3)
  Jack
```

```
cohort2.Except(cohort3)
  Stephen, Daniel, Jared

cohort1.Zip(cohort2)
  Rachel matched with Jack, Gareth matched with Stephen, Jonathan matched
with Daniel, George matched with Jack
```

With `Zip`, if there are unequal numbers of items in the two sequences, then some items will not have a matching partner. Those without a partner, like `Jared`, will not be included in the result.

For the `DistinctBy` example, instead of removing duplicates by comparing the whole name, we define a lambda key selector to remove duplicates by comparing the first two characters, so `Jared` is removed because `Jack` already is a name that starts with `Ja`.

So far, we have used the LINQ to Objects provider to work with in-memory objects. Next, we will use the LINQ to Entities provider to work with entities stored in a database.

Using LINQ with EF Core

We have looked at LINQ queries that filter and sort, but none that change the shape of the items in the sequence. This is called **projection** because it's about projecting items of one shape into another shape. To learn about projection, it is best to have some more complex types to work with, so in the next project, instead of using `string` sequences, we will use sequences of entities from the Northwind sample database.

 I will give instructions to use SQLite because it is cross-platform but if you prefer to use SQL Server then feel free to do so. I have included some commented code to enable SQL Server if you choose.

Building an EF Core model

We must define an EF Core model to represent the database and tables that we will work with. We will define the model manually to take complete control and to prevent a relationship from being automatically defined between the `Categories` and `Products` tables. Later, you will use LINQ to join the two entity sets:

1. Use your preferred code editor to add a new console app named `LinqWithEFCore` to the `Chapter11` solution/workspace.

2. In Visual Studio Code, select `LinqWithEFCore` as the active OmniSharp project.

3. In the `LinqWithEFCore` project, add a package reference to the EF Core provider for SQLite and/or SQL Server, as shown in the following markup:

   ```
   <ItemGroup>
   ```

```
<PackageReference
  Include="Microsoft.EntityFrameworkCore.Sqlite"
  Version="6.0.0" />
<PackageReference
  Include="Microsoft.EntityFrameworkCore.SqlServer"
  Version="6.0.0" />
</ItemGroup>
```

4. Build the project to restore packages.

5. Copy the `Northwind4Sqlite.sql` file into the `LinqWithEFCore` folder.

6. At a command prompt or terminal, create the Northwind database by executing the following command:

```
sqlite3 Northwind.db -init Northwind4Sqlite.sql
```

7. Be patient because this command might take a while to create the database structure. Eventually you will see the SQLite command prompt, as shown in the following output:

```
-- Loading resources from Northwind.sql
SQLite version 3.36.0 2021-08-02 15:20:15
Enter ".help" for usage hints.
sqlite>
```

8. Press *cmd + D* on macOS or *Ctrl + C* on Windows to exit SQLite command mode.

9. Add three class files to the project, named `Northwind.cs`, `Category.cs`, and `Product.cs`.

10. Modify the class file named `Northwind.cs`, as shown in the following code:

```
using Microsoft.EntityFrameworkCore; // DbContext, DbSet<T>

namespace Packt.Shared;

// this manages the connection to the database
public class Northwind : DbContext
{
  // these properties map to tables in the database
  public DbSet<Category>? Categories { get; set; }
  public DbSet<Product>? Products { get; set; }

  protected override void OnConfiguring(
    DbContextOptionsBuilder optionsBuilder)
  {
    string path = Path.Combine(
      Environment.CurrentDirectory, "Northwind.db");

    optionsBuilder.UseSqlite($"Filename={path}");
```

```
    /*
    string connection = "Data Source=.;" +
        "Initial Catalog=Northwind;" +
        "Integrated Security=true;" +
        "MultipleActiveResultSets=true;";

    optionsBuilder.UseSqlServer(connection);
    */
}

protected override void OnModelCreating(
    ModelBuilder modelBuilder)
{
    modelBuilder.Entity<Product>()
        .Property(product => product.UnitPrice)
        .HasConversion<double>();
}
}
```

11. Modify the class file named Category.cs, as shown in the following code:

```
using System.ComponentModel.DataAnnotations;

namespace Packt.Shared;

public class Category
{
    public int CategoryId { get; set; }

    [Required]
    [StringLength(15)]
    public string CategoryName { get; set; } = null!;

    public string? Description { get; set; }
}
```

12. Modify the class file named Product.cs, as shown in the following code:

```
using System.ComponentModel.DataAnnotations;
using System.ComponentModel.DataAnnotations.Schema;

namespace Packt.Shared;

public class Product
{
    public int ProductId { get; set; }
```

```
    [Required]
    [StringLength(40)]
    public string ProductName { get; set; } = null!;

    public int? SupplierId { get; set; }
    public int? CategoryId { get; set; }

    [StringLength(20)]
    public string? QuantityPerUnit { get; set; }

    [Column(TypeName = "money")] // required for SQL Server provider
    public decimal? UnitPrice { get; set; }
    public short? UnitsInStock { get; set; }
    public short? UnitsOnOrder { get; set; }
    public short? ReorderLevel { get; set; }
    public bool Discontinued { get; set; }
}
```

13. Build the project and fix any compiler errors.

    If you are using Visual Studio 2022 for Windows, then the compiled application
    executes in the LinqWithEFCore\bin\Debug\net6.0 folder so it will not find the database
    file unless we indicate that it should always be copied to the output directory.

14. In **Solution Explorer**, right-click the Northwind.db file and select **Properties**.

15. In **Properties**, set **Copy to Output Directory** to **Copy always**.

Filtering and sorting sequences

Now let's write statements to filter and sort sequences of rows from the tables:

1. In Program.cs, statically import the Console type and namespaces for working with EF
    Core and your entity model using LINQ, as shown in the following code:

    ```
    using Packt.Shared; // Northwind, Category, Product
    using Microsoft.EntityFrameworkCore; // DbSet<T>

    using static System.Console;
    ```

2. At the bottom of Program.cs, write a method to filter and sort products, as shown in the
    following code:

    ```
    static void FilterAndSort()
    {
      using (Northwind db = new())
      {
        DbSet<Product> allProducts = db.Products;

        IQueryable<Product> filteredProducts =
    ```

```
      allProducts.Where(product => product.UnitPrice < 10M);

    IOrderedQueryable<Product> sortedAndFilteredProducts =
      filteredProducts.OrderByDescending(product => product.UnitPrice);

    WriteLine("Products that cost less than $10:");
    foreach (Product p in sortedAndFilteredProducts)
    {
      WriteLine("{0}: {1} costs {2:$#,##0.00}",
        p.ProductId, p.ProductName, p.UnitPrice);
    }
    WriteLine();
  }
}
```

DbSet<T> implements IEnumerable<T>, so LINQ can be used to query and manipulate collections of entities in models built for EF Core. (Actually, I should say TEntity instead of T but the name of this generic type has no functional effect. The only requirement is that the type is a class. The name just indicates the class is expected to be an entity model.)

You might have also noticed that the sequences implement IQueryable<T> (or IOrderedQueryable<T> after a call to an ordering LINQ method) instead of IEnumerable<T> or IOrderedEnumerable<T>.

This is an indication that we are using a LINQ provider that builds the query in memory using expression trees. They represent code in a tree-like data structure and enable the creation of dynamic queries, which is useful for building LINQ queries for external data providers like SQLite.

The LINQ expression will be converted into another query language, such as SQL. Enumerating the query with foreach or calling a method such as ToArray will force the execution of the query and materialize the results.

3. After the namespace imports in Program.cs, call the FilterAndSort method.

4. Run the code and view the result, as shown in the following output:

```
Products that cost less than $10:
41: Jack's New England Clam Chowder costs $9.65
45: Rogede sild costs $9.50
47: Zaanse koeken costs $9.50
19: Teatime Chocolate Biscuits costs $9.20
23: Tunnbröd costs $9.00
75: Rhönbräu Klosterbier costs $7.75
54: Tourtière costs $7.45
52: Filo Mix costs $7.00
13: Konbu costs $6.00
24: Guaraná Fantástica costs $4.50
33: Geitost costs $2.50
```

Although this query outputs the information we want, it does so inefficiently because it gets all columns from the `Products` table instead of just the three columns we need, which is the equivalent of the following SQL statement:

```
SELECT * FROM Products;
```

In *Chapter 10, Working with Data Using Entity Framework Core,* you learned how to log the SQL commands executed against SQLite so that you could see this for yourself.

Projecting sequences into new types

Before we look at projection, we need to review object initialization syntax. If you have a class defined, then you can instantiate an object using the class name, `new()`, and curly braces to set initial values for fields and properties, as shown in the following code:

```
public class Person
{
  public string Name { get; set; }
  public DateTime DateOfBirth { get; set; }
}

Person knownTypeObject = new()
{
  Name = "Boris Johnson",
  DateOfBirth = new(year: 1964, month: 6, day: 19)
};
```

C# 3.0 and later allow instances of **anonymous types** to be instantiated using the var keyword, as shown in the following code:

```
var anonymouslyTypedObject = new
{
  Name = "Boris Johnson",
  DateOfBirth = new DateTime(year: 1964, month: 6, day: 19)
};
```

Although we did not specify a type, the compiler can infer an anonymous type from the setting of two properties named `Name` and `DateOfBirth`. The compiler can infer the types of the two properties from the values assigned: a literal `string` and a new instance of a date/time value.

This capability is especially useful when writing LINQ queries to project an existing type into a new type without having to explicitly define the new type. Since the type is anonymous, this can only work with var-declared local variables.

Let's make the SQL command executed against the database table more efficient by adding a call to the `Select` method to project instances of the `Product` class into instances of a new anonymous type with only three properties:

1. In `FilterAndSort`, add a statement to extend the LINQ query to use the `Select` method to return only the three properties (that is, table columns) that we need, and modify the `foreach` statement to use the `var` keyword and the projection LINQ expression, as shown highlighted in the following code:

```
IOrderedQueryable<Product> sortedAndFilteredProducts =
    filteredProducts.OrderByDescending(product => product.UnitPrice);

var projectedProducts = sortedAndFilteredProducts
  .Select(product => new // anonymous type
  {
    product.ProductId,
    product.ProductName,
    product.UnitPrice
  });

WriteLine("Products that cost less than $10:");
foreach (var p in projectedProducts)
{
```

2. Hover your mouse over the `new` keyword in the `Select` method call and the `var` keyword in the `foreach` statement and note that it is an anonymous type, as shown in *Figure 11.4*:

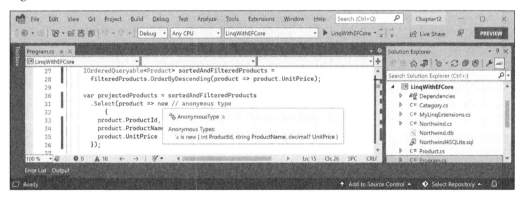

Figure 11.4: An anonymous type used during LINQ projection

3. Run the code and confirm that the output is the same as before.

Joining and grouping sequences

There are two extension methods for joining and grouping:

- **Join**: This method has four parameters: the sequence that you want to join with, the property or properties on the *left* sequence to match on, the property or properties on the *right* sequence to match on, and a projection.

- **GroupJoin**: This method has the same parameters, but it combines the matches into a group object with a Key property for the matching value and an IEnumerable<T> type for the multiple matches.

Joining sequences

Let's explore these methods when working with two tables: Categories and Products:

1. At the bottom of Program.cs, create a method to select categories and products, join them, and output them, as shown in the following code:

```
static void JoinCategoriesAndProducts()
{
  using (Northwind db = new())
  {
    // join every product to its category to return 77 matches
    var queryJoin = db.Categories.Join(
      inner: db.Products,
      outerKeySelector: category => category.CategoryId,
      innerKeySelector: product => product.CategoryId,
      resultSelector: (c, p) =>
        new { c.CategoryName, p.ProductName, p.ProductId });

    foreach (var item in queryJoin)
    {
      WriteLine("{0}: {1} is in {2}.",
        arg0: item.ProductId,
        arg1: item.ProductName,
        arg2: item.CategoryName);
    }
  }
}
```

In a join, there are two sequences, *outer* and *inner*. In the previous example, categories is the outer sequence and products is the inner sequence.

2. At the top of Program.cs, comment out the call to FilterAndSort and call JoinCategoriesAndProducts.

3. Run the code and view the results. Note that there is a single line of output for each of the 77 products, as shown in the following output (edited to only include the first 10 items):

```
1: Chai is in Beverages.
2: Chang is in Beverages.
3: Aniseed Syrup is in Condiments.
4: Chef Anton's Cajun Seasoning is in Condiments.
5: Chef Anton's Gumbo Mix is in Condiments.
6: Grandma's Boysenberry Spread is in Condiments.
```

```
7: Uncle Bob's Organic Dried Pears is in Produce.
8: Northwoods Cranberry Sauce is in Condiments.
9: Mishi Kobe Niku is in Meat/Poultry.
10: Ikura is in Seafood.
...
```

4. At the end of the existing query, call the `OrderBy` method to sort by `CategoryName`, as shown in the following code:

```
.OrderBy(cp => cp.CategoryName);
```

5. Run the code and view the results. Note that there is a single line of output for each of the 77 products, and the results show all products in the `Beverages` category first, then the `Condiments` category, and so on, as shown in the following partial output:

```
1: Chai is in Beverages.
2: Chang is in Beverages.
24: Guaraná Fantástica is in Beverages.
34: Sasquatch Ale is in Beverages.
35: Steeleye Stout is in Beverages.
38: Côte de Blaye is in Beverages.
39: Chartreuse verte is in Beverages.
43: Ipoh Coffee is in Beverages.
67: Laughing Lumberjack Lager is in Beverages.
70: Outback Lager is in Beverages.
75: Rhönbräu Klosterbier is in Beverages.
76: Lakkalikööri is in Beverages.
3: Aniseed Syrup is in Condiments.
4: Chef Anton's Cajun Seasoning is in Condiments.
...
```

Group-joining sequences

1. At the bottom of `Program.cs`, create a method to group and join, show the group name, and then show all the items within each group, as shown in the following code:

```
static void GroupJoinCategoriesAndProducts()
{
  using (Northwind db = new())
  {
    // group all products by their category to return 8 matches
    var queryGroup = db.Categories.AsEnumerable().GroupJoin(
      inner: db.Products,
      outerKeySelector: category => category.CategoryId,
      innerKeySelector: product => product.CategoryId,
      resultSelector: (c, matchingProducts) => new
      {
        c.CategoryName,
        Products = matchingProducts.OrderBy(p => p.ProductName)
```

```
      });

    foreach (var category in queryGroup)
    {
      WriteLine("{0} has {1} products.",
        arg0: category.CategoryName,
        arg1: category.Products.Count());

      foreach (var product in category.Products)
      {
        WriteLine($" {product.ProductName}");
      }
    }
  }
}
```

If we had not called the AsEnumerable method, then a runtime exception would have been thrown, as shown in the following output:

```
Unhandled exception. System.ArgumentException:  Argument type 'System.
Linq.IOrderedQueryable`1[Packt.Shared.Product]' does not match the
corresponding member type 'System.Linq.IOrderedEnumerable`1[Packt.Shared.
Product]' (Parameter 'arguments[1]')
```

This is because not all LINQ extension methods can be converted from expression trees into some other query syntax like SQL. In these cases, we can convert from IQueryable<T> to IEnumerable<T> by calling the AsEnumerable method, which forces query processing to use LINQ to EF Core only to bring the data into the application and then use LINQ to Objects to execute more complex processing in memory. But, often, this is less efficient.

2. At the top of Program.cs, comment out the previous method call and call GroupJoinCategoriesAndProducts.

3. Run the code, view the results, and note that the products inside each category have been sorted by their name, as defined in the query and as shown in the following partial output:

```
Beverages has 12 products.
  Chai
  Chang
  Chartreuse verte
  Côte de Blaye
  Guaraná Fantástica
  Ipoh Coffee
  Lakkalikööri
  Laughing Lumberjack Lager
  Outback Lager
  Rhönbräu Klosterbier
  Sasquatch Ale
```

```
    Steeleye Stout
Condiments has 12 products.
    Aniseed Syrup
    Chef Anton's Cajun Seasoning
    Chef Anton's Gumbo Mix
...
```

Aggregating sequences

There are LINQ extension methods to perform aggregation functions, such as Average and Sum. Let's write some code to see some of these methods in action aggregating information from the Products table:

1. At the bottom of Program.cs, create a method to show the use of the aggregation extension methods, as shown in the following code:

```
static void AggregateProducts()
{
  using (Northwind db = new())
  {
    WriteLine("{0,-25} {1,10}",
      arg0: "Product count:",
      arg1: db.Products.Count());

    WriteLine("{0,-25} {1,10:$#,##0.00}",
      arg0: "Highest product price:",
      arg1: db.Products.Max(p => p.UnitPrice));

    WriteLine("{0,-25} {1,10:N0}",
      arg0: "Sum of units in stock:",
      arg1: db.Products.Sum(p => p.UnitsInStock));

    WriteLine("{0,-25} {1,10:N0}",
      arg0: "Sum of units on order:",
      arg1: db.Products.Sum(p => p.UnitsOnOrder));

    WriteLine("{0,-25} {1,10:$#,##0.00}",
      arg0: "Average unit price:",
      arg1: db.Products.Average(p => p.UnitPrice));

    WriteLine("{0,-25} {1,10:$#,##0.00}",
      arg0: "Value of units in stock:",
      arg1: db.Products
        .Sum(p => p.UnitPrice * p.UnitsInStock));
  }
}
```

2. At the top of `Program.cs`, comment out the previous method and call `AggregateProducts`

3. Run the code and view the result, as shown in the following output:

```
Product count:                     77
Highest product price:        $263.50
Sum of units in stock:          3,119
Sum of units on order:            780
Average unit price:            $28.87
Value of units in stock:   $74,050.85
```

Sweetening LINQ syntax with syntactic sugar

C# 3.0 introduced some new language keywords in 2008 to make it easier for programmers with experience with SQL to write LINQ queries. This syntactic sugar is sometimes called the **LINQ query comprehension syntax**.

Consider the following array of `string` values:

```
string[] names = new[] { "Michael", "Pam", "Jim", "Dwight",
  "Angela", "Kevin", "Toby", "Creed" };
```

To filter and sort the names, you could use extension methods and lambda expressions, as shown in the following code:

```
var query = names
  .Where(name => name.Length > 4)
  .OrderBy(name => name.Length)
  .ThenBy(name => name);
```

Or you could achieve the same results by using query comprehension syntax, as shown in the following code:

```
var query = from name in names
  where name.Length > 4
  orderby name.Length, name
  select name;
```

The compiler changes the query comprehension syntax to the equivalent extension methods and lambda expressions for you.

The select keyword is always required for LINQ query comprehension syntax. The `Select` extension method is optional when using extension methods and lambda expressions because if you do not call `Select`, then the whole item is implicitly selected.

Not all extension methods have a C# keyword equivalent, for example, the `Skip` and `Take` extension methods, which are commonly used to implement paging for lots of data.

A query that skips and takes cannot be written using only the query comprehension syntax, so we could write the query using all extension methods, as shown in the following code:

```
var query = names
  .Where(name => name.Length > 4)
  .Skip(80)
  .Take(10);
```

Or you can wrap query comprehension syntax in parentheses and then switch to using extension methods, as shown in the following code:

```
var query = (from name in names
  where name.Length > 4
  select name)
  .Skip(80)
  .Take(10);
```

 Good Practice: Learn both extension methods with lambda expressions and the query comprehension syntax ways of writing LINQ queries, because you are likely to have to maintain code that uses both.

Using multiple threads with parallel LINQ

By default, only one thread is used to execute a LINQ query. **Parallel LINQ (PLINQ)** is an easy way to enable multiple threads to execute a LINQ query.

 Good Practice: Do not assume that using parallel threads will improve the performance of your applications. Always measure real-world timings and resource usage.

Creating an app that benefits from multiple threads

To see it in action, we will start with some code that only uses a single thread to calculate Fibonacci numbers for 45 integers. We will use the StopWatch type to measure the change in performance.

We will use operating system tools to monitor the CPU and CPU core usage. If you do not have multiple CPUs or at least multiple cores, then this exercise won't show much!

1. Use your preferred code editor to add a new console app named LinqInParallel to the Chapter11 solution/workspace.

2. In Visual Studio Code, select `LinqInParallel` as the active OmniSharp project.

3. In `Program.cs`, delete the existing statements and then import the `System.Diagnostics` namespace so that we can use the `StopWatch` type, and statically import the `System.Console` type.

4. Add statements to create a stopwatch to record timings, wait for a keypress before starting the timer, create 45 integers, calculate the last Fibonacci number for each of them, stop the timer, and display the elapsed milliseconds, as shown in the following code:

```
Stopwatch watch = new();
Write("Press ENTER to start. ");
ReadLine();
watch.Start();

int max = 45;

IEnumerable<int> numbers = Enumerable.Range(start: 1, count: max);

WriteLine($"Calculating Fibonacci sequence up to {max}. Please wait...");

int[] fibonacciNumbers = numbers
  .Select(number => Fibonacci(number)).ToArray();

watch.Stop();
WriteLine("{0:#,##0} elapsed milliseconds.",
  arg0: watch.ElapsedMilliseconds);

Write("Results:");
foreach (int number in fibonacciNumbers)
{
  Write($" {number}");
}

static int Fibonacci(int term) =>
  term switch
  {
    1 => 0,
    2 => 1,
    _ => Fibonacci(term - 1) + Fibonacci(term - 2)
  };
```

5. Run the code, but do not press *Enter* to start the stopwatch yet because we need to make sure a monitoring tool is showing processor activity.

Using Windows

1. If you are using Windows, then right-click on the Windows **Start** button or press *Ctrl + Alt + Delete*, and then click on **Task Manager**.

2. At the bottom of the **Task Manager** window, click **More details**.

3. At the top of the **Task Manager** window, click on the **Performance** tab.

4. Right-click on the **CPU Utilization** graph, select **Change graph to**, and then select **Logical processors**.

Using macOS

1. If you are using macOS, then launch **Activity Monitor**.

2. Navigate to **View | Update Frequency Very often (1 sec)**.

3. To see the CPU graphs, navigate to **Window | CPU History**.

For all operating systems

1. Rearrange your monitoring tool and your code editor so that they are side by side.

2. Wait for the CPUs to settle and then press *Enter* to start the stopwatch and run the query. The result should be a number of elapsed milliseconds, as shown in the following output:

```
Press ENTER to start.
Calculating Fibonacci sequence up to 45. Please wait...
17,624 elapsed milliseconds.
Results: 0 1 1 2 3 5 8 13 21 34 55 89 144 233 377 610 987 1597 2584 4181
6765 10946 17711 28657 46368 75025 121393 196418 317811 514229 832040
1346269 2178309 3524578 5702887 9227465 14930352 24157817 39088169
63245986 102334155 165580141 267914296 433494437 701408733
```

The monitoring tool will probably show that one or two CPUs were used the most, alternating over time. Others may execute background tasks at the same time, such as the garbage collector, so the other CPUs or cores won't be completely flat, but the work is certainly not being evenly spread among all the possible CPUs or cores. Also, note that some of the logical processors are maxing out at 100%.

3. In `Program.cs`, modify the query to make a call to the `AsParallel` extension method and to sort the resulting sequence because when processing in parallel the results can become misordered, as shown highlighted in the following code:

```
int[] fibonacciNumbers = numbers.AsParallel()
  .Select(number => Fibonacci(number))
  .OrderBy(number => number)
  .ToArray();
```

Good Practice: Never call `AsParallel` at the end of a query. This does nothing. You must perform at least one operation after the call to `AsParallel` for that operation to be parallelized. .NET 6 introduces a code analyzer that will warn about this type of misuse.

4. Run the code, wait for CPU charts in your monitoring tool to settle, and then press *Enter* to start the stopwatch and run the query. This time, the application should complete in less time (although it might not be as less as you might hope for — managing those multiple threads takes extra effort!):

```
Press ENTER to start.
Calculating Fibonacci sequence up to 45. Please wait...
9,028 elapsed milliseconds.
Results: 0 1 1 2 3 5 8 13 21 34 55 89 144 233 377 610 987 1597 2584 4181
6765 10946 17711 28657 46368 75025 121393 196418 317811 514229 832040
1346269 2178309 3524578 5702887 9227465 14930352 24157817 39088169
63245986 102334155 165580141 267914296 433494437 701408733
```

5. The monitoring tool should show that all CPUs were used equally to execute the LINQ query, and note that none of the logical processors max out at 100% because the work is more evenly spread.

You will learn more about managing multiple threads in *Chapter 12, Improving Performance and Scalability Using Multitasking*.

Creating your own LINQ extension methods

In *Chapter 6, Implementing Interfaces and Inheriting Classes*, you learned how to create your own extension methods. To create LINQ extension methods, all you must do is extend the `IEnumerable<T>` type.

Good Practice: Put your own extension methods in a separate class library so that they can be easily deployed as their own assembly or NuGet package.

We will improve the `Average` extension method as an example. A well-educated school child will tell you that *average* can mean one of three things:

- **Mean**: Sum the numbers and divide by the count.
- **Mode**: The most common number.
- **Median**: The number in the middle of the numbers when ordered.

Microsoft's implementation of the Average extension method calculates the *mean*. We might want to define our own extension methods for Mode and Median:

1. In the LinqWithEFCore project, add a new class file named MyLinqExtensions.cs.
2. Modify the class, as shown in the following code:

```
namespace System.Linq; // extend Microsoft's namespace

public static class MyLinqExtensions
{
  // this is a chainable LINQ extension method
  public static IEnumerable<T> ProcessSequence<T>(
    this IEnumerable<T> sequence)
  {
    // you could do some processing here
    return sequence;
  }

  public static IQueryable<T> ProcessSequence<T>(
    this IQueryable<T> sequence)
  {
    // you could do some processing here
    return sequence;
  }

  // these are scalar LINQ extension methods
  public static int? Median(
    this IEnumerable<int?> sequence)
  {
    var ordered = sequence.OrderBy(item => item);
    int middlePosition = ordered.Count() / 2;
    return ordered.ElementAt(middlePosition);
  }

  public static int? Median<T>(
    this IEnumerable<T> sequence, Func<T, int?> selector)
  {
    return sequence.Select(selector).Median();
  }

  public static decimal? Median(
    this IEnumerable<decimal?> sequence)
  {
    var ordered = sequence.OrderBy(item => item);
    int middlePosition = ordered.Count() / 2;
    return ordered.ElementAt(middlePosition);
  }
```

```
public static decimal? Median<T>(
  this IEnumerable<T> sequence, Func<T, decimal?> selector)
{
  return sequence.Select(selector).Median();
}

public static int? Mode(
  this IEnumerable<int?> sequence)
{
  var grouped = sequence.GroupBy(item => item);
  var orderedGroups = grouped.OrderByDescending(
    group => group.Count());
  return orderedGroups.FirstOrDefault()?.Key;
}

public static int? Mode<T>(
  this IEnumerable<T> sequence, Func<T, int?> selector)
{
  return sequence.Select(selector)?.Mode();
}

public static decimal? Mode(
  this IEnumerable<decimal?> sequence)
{
  var grouped = sequence.GroupBy(item => item);
  var orderedGroups = grouped.OrderByDescending(
    group => group.Count());
  return orderedGroups.FirstOrDefault()?.Key;
}

public static decimal? Mode<T>(
  this IEnumerable<T> sequence, Func<T, decimal?> selector)
{
  return sequence.Select(selector).Mode();
}
}
```

If this class was in a separate class library, to use your LINQ extension methods, you simply need to reference the class library assembly because the System.Linq namespace is already implicitly imported.

Warning! All but one of the above extension methods cannot be used with IQueryable sequences like those used by LINQ to SQLite or LINQ to SQL Server because we have not implemented a way to translate our code into the underlying query language like SQL.

Trying the chainable extension method

First, we will try chaining the ProcessSequence method with other extension methods:

1. In Program.cs, in the FilterAndSort method, modify the LINQ query for Products to call your custom chainable extension method, as shown highlighted in the following code:

    ```
    DbSet<Product>? allProducts = db.Products;

    if (allProducts is null)
    {
      WriteLine("No products found.");
      return;
    }

    IQueryable<Product> processedProducts = allProducts.ProcessSequence();

    IQueryable<Product> filteredProducts = processedProducts
      .Where(product => product.UnitPrice < 10M);
    ```

2. In Program.cs, uncomment the FilterAndSort method and comment out any calls to other methods.

3. Run the code and note that you see the same output as before because your method doesn't modify the sequence. But you now know how to extend a LINQ expression with your own functionality.

Trying the mode and median methods

Second, we will try using the Mode and Median methods to calculate other kinds of average:

1. At the bottom of Program.cs, create a method to output the mean, median, and mode, for UnitsInStock and UnitPrice for products, using your custom extension methods and the built-in Average extension method, as shown in the following code:

    ```
    static void CustomExtensionMethods()
    {
      using (Northwind db = new())
      {
        WriteLine("Mean units in stock: {0:N0}",
          db.Products.Average(p => p.UnitsInStock));

        WriteLine("Mean unit price: {0:$#,##0.00}",
          db.Products.Average(p => p.UnitPrice));

        WriteLine("Median units in stock: {0:N0}",
          db.Products.Median(p => p.UnitsInStock));
    ```

```
WriteLine("Median unit price: {0:$#,##0.00}",
    db.Products.Median(p => p.UnitPrice));

WriteLine("Mode units in stock: {0:N0}",
    db.Products.Mode(p => p.UnitsInStock));

WriteLine("Mode unit price: {0:$#,##0.00}",
    db.Products.Mode(p => p.UnitPrice));
  }
}
```

2. In `Program.cs`, comment any previous method calls and call `CustomExtensionMethods`.

3. Run the code and view the result, as shown in the following output:

```
Mean units in stock: 41
Mean unit price: $28.87
Median units in stock: 26
Median unit price: $19.50
Mode units in stock: 0
Mode unit price: $18.00
```

There are four products with a unit price of $18.00. There are five products with 0 units in stock.

Working with LINQ to XML

LINQ to XML is a LINQ provider that allows you to query and manipulate XML.

Generating XML using LINQ to XML

Let's create a method to convert the `Products` table into XML:

1. In the `LinqWithEFCore` project, at the top of `Program.cs`, import the `System.Xml.Linq` namespace.

2. At the bottom of `Program.cs`, create a method to output the products in XML format, as shown in the following code:

```
static void OutputProductsAsXml()
{
  using (Northwind db = new())
  {
    Product[] productsArray = db.Products.ToArray();

    XElement xml = new("products",
```

```
from p in productsArray
select new XElement("product",
  new XAttribute("id",  p.ProductId),
  new XAttribute("price", p.UnitPrice),
  new XElement("name", p.ProductName)));

    WriteLine(xml.ToString());
  }
}
```

3. In `Program.cs`, comment the previous method call and call `OutputProductsAsXml`.

4. Run the code, view the result, and note that the structure of the XML generated matches the elements and attributes that the LINQ to XML statement declaratively described in the preceding code, as shown in the following partial output:

```
<products>
  <product id="1" price="18">
    <name>Chai</name>
  </product>
  <product id="2" price="19">
    <name>Chang</name>
  </product>
...
```

Reading XML using LINQ to XML

You might want to use LINQ to XML to easily query or process XML files:

1. In the `LinqWithEFCore` project, add a file named `settings.xml`.

2. Modify its contents, as shown in the following markup:

```
<?xml version="1.0" encoding="utf-8" ?>
<appSettings>
  <add key="color" value="red" />
  <add key="size" value="large" />
  <add key="price" value="23.99" />
</appSettings>
```

If you are using Visual Studio 2022 for Windows, then the compiled application executes in the `LinqWithEFCore\bin\Debug\net6.0` folder so it will not find the `settings.xml` file unless we indicate that it should always be copied to the output directory.

3. In **Solution Explorer**, right-click the `settings.xml` file and select **Properties**.

4. In **Properties**, set **Copy to Output Directory** to **Copy always**.

5. At the bottom of `Program.cs`, create a method to complete these tasks, as shown in the following code:

    - Load the XML file.

    - Use LINQ to XML to search for an element named `appSettings` and its descendants named `add`.

    - Project the XML into an array of an anonymous type with `Key` and `Value` properties.

    - Enumerate through the array to show the results:

```
static void ProcessSettings()
{
  XDocument doc = XDocument.Load("settings.xml");

  var appSettings = doc.Descendants("appSettings")
    .Descendants("add")
    .Select(node => new
    {
      Key = node.Attribute("key")?.Value,
      Value = node.Attribute("value")?.Value
    }).ToArray();

  foreach (var item in appSettings)
  {
    WriteLine($"{item.Key}: {item.Value}");
  }
}
```

6. In `Program.cs`, comment the previous method call and call `ProcessSettings`.

7. Run the code and view the result, as shown in the following output:

```
color: red
size: large
price: 23.99
```

Practicing and exploring

Test your knowledge and understanding by answering some questions, get some hands-on practice, and explore with deeper research into the topics covered in this chapter.

Exercise 11.1 – Test your knowledge

Answer the following questions:

1. What are the two required parts of LINQ?

2. Which LINQ extension method would you use to return a subset of properties from a type?

3. Which LINQ extension method would you use to filter a sequence?

4. List five LINQ extension methods that perform aggregation.

5. What is the difference between the `Select` and `SelectMany` extension methods?

6. What is the difference between `IEnumerable<T>` and `IQueryable<T>`? And how do you switch between them?

7. What does the last type parameter `T` in generic `Func` delegates like `Func<T1, T2, T>` represent?

8. What is the benefit of a LINQ extension method that ends with `OrDefault`?

9. Why is query comprehension syntax optional?

10. How can you create your own LINQ extension methods?

Exercise 11.2 – Practice querying with LINQ

In the `Chapter11` solution/workspace, create a console application, named `Exercise02`, that prompts the user for a city and then lists the company names for Northwind customers in that city, as shown in the following output:

```
Enter the name of a city: London
There are 6 customers in London:
Around the Horn
B's Beverages
Consolidated Holdings
Eastern Connection
North/South
Seven Seas Imports
```

Then, enhance the application by displaying a list of all unique cities that customers already reside in as a prompt to the user before they enter their preferred city, as shown in the following output:

```
Aachen, Albuquerque, Anchorage, Århus, Barcelona, Barquisimeto, Bergamo, Berlin,
Bern, Boise, Bräcke, Brandenburg, Bruxelles, Buenos Aires, Butte, Campinas,
Caracas, Charleroi, Cork, Cowes, Cunewalde, Elgin, Eugene, Frankfurt a.M.,
Genève, Graz, Helsinki, I. de Margarita, Kirkland, Kobenhavn, Köln, Lander,
Leipzig, Lille, Lisboa, London, Luleå, Lyon, Madrid, Mannheim, Marseille,
México D.F., Montréal, München, Münster, Nantes, Oulu, Paris, Portland, Reggio
Emilia, Reims, Resende, Rio de Janeiro, Salzburg, San Cristóbal, San Francisco,
Sao Paulo, Seattle, Sevilla, Stavern, Strasbourg, Stuttgart, Torino, Toulouse,
Tsawassen, Vancouver, Versailles, Walla Walla, Warszawa
```

Exercise 11.3 – Explore topics

Use the links on the following page to learn more details about the topics covered in this chapter:

```
https://github.com/markjprice/cs10dotnet6/blob/main/book-links.md#chapter-11---
querying-and-manipulating-data-using-linq
```

Summary

In this chapter, you learned how to write LINQ queries to select, project, filter, sort, join, and group data in many different formats, including XML, which are tasks you will perform every day.

In the next chapter, you will use the Task type to improve the performance of your applications.

12

Improving Performance and Scalability Using Multitasking

This chapter is about allowing multiple actions to occur at the same time to improve performance, scalability, and user productivity for the applications that you build.

In this chapter, we will cover the following topics:

- Understanding processes, threads, and tasks
- Monitoring performance and resource usage
- Running tasks asynchronously
- Synchronizing access to shared resources
- Understanding async and await

Understanding processes, threads, and tasks

A **process**, with one example being each of the console applications we have created, has resources like memory and threads allocated to it.

A **thread** executes your code, statement by statement. By default, each process only has one thread, and this can cause problems when we need to do more than one task at the same time. Threads are also responsible for keeping track of things like the currently authenticated user and any internationalization rules that should be followed for the current language and region.

Windows and most other modern operating systems use **preemptive multitasking**, which simulates the parallel execution of tasks. It divides the processor time among the threads, allocating a **time slice** to each thread one after another. The current thread is suspended when its time slice finishes. The processor then allows another thread to run for a time slice.

When Windows switches from one thread to another, it saves the context of the thread and reloads the previously saved context of the next thread in the thread queue. This takes both time and resources to complete.

As a developer, if you have a small number of complex pieces of work and you want complete control over them, then you could create and manage individual Thread instances. If you have one main thread and multiple small pieces of work that can be executed in the background, then you can use the ThreadPool class to add delegate instances that point to those pieces of work implemented as methods to a queue, and they will be automatically allocated to threads in the thread pool.

In this chapter, we will use the Task type to manage threads at a higher abstraction level.

Threads may have to compete for and also wait for access to shared resources, such as variables, files, and database objects. There are types for managing this that you will see in action later in this chapter.

Depending on the task, doubling the number of threads (workers) to perform a task does not halve the number of seconds that it will take to complete that task. In fact, it can increase the duration of the task.

 Good Practice: Never assume that more threads will improve performance! Run performance tests on a baseline code implementation without multiple threads, and then again on a code implementation with multiple threads. You should also perform performance tests in a staging environment that is as close as possible to the production environment.

Monitoring performance and resource usage

Before we can improve the performance of any code, we need to be able to monitor its speed and efficiency to record a baseline that we can then measure improvements against.

Evaluating the efficiency of types

What is the best type to use for a scenario? To answer this question, we need to carefully consider what we mean by "best", and through this, we should consider the following factors:

- **Functionality**: This can be decided by checking whether the type provides the features you need.
- **Memory size**: This can be decided by the number of bytes of memory the type takes up.
- **Performance**: This can be decided by how fast the type is.
- **Future needs**: This depends on the changes in requirements and maintainability.

There will be scenarios, such as when storing numbers, where multiple types have the same functionality, so we will need to consider memory and performance to make a choice.

If we need to store millions of numbers, then the best type to use would be the one that requires the fewest bytes of memory. But if we only need to store a few numbers, yet we need to perform lots of calculations on them, then the best type to use would be the one that runs fastest on a specific CPU.

You have seen the use of the sizeof() function, which shows the number of bytes a single instance of a type uses in memory. When we are storing a large number of values in more complex data structures, such as arrays and lists, then we need a better way of measuring memory usage.

You can read lots of advice online and in books, but the only way to know for sure what the best type would be for your code is to compare the types yourself.

In the next section, you will learn how to write code to monitor the actual memory requirements and performance when using different types.

Today a short variable might be the best choice, but it might be an even better choice to use an int variable, even though it takes twice as much space in the memory. This is because we might need a wider range of values to be stored in the future.

There is an important metric that developers often forget: maintenance. This is a measure of how much effort another programmer would have to put in to understand and modify your code. If you make a nonobvious choice of type without explaining that choice with a helpful comment, then it might confuse the programmer who comes along later and needs to fix a bug or add a feature.

Monitoring performance and memory using diagnostics

The System.Diagnostics namespace has lots of useful types for monitoring your code. The first useful type that we will look at is the Stopwatch type:

1. Use your preferred coding tool to create a new workspace/solution named Chapter12.
2. Add a class library project, as defined in the following list:
    1. Project template: **Class Library** / classlib
    2. Workspace/solution file and folder: Chapter12
    3. Project file and folder: MonitoringLib
3. Add a console app project, as defined in the following list:
    1. Project template: **Console Application** / console
    2. Workspace/solution file and folder: Chapter12
    3. Project file and folder: MonitoringApp
    4. In Visual Studio, set the startup project for the solution to the current selection.
    5. In Visual Studio Code, select MonitoringApp as the active OmniSharp project.

6. In the `MonitoringLib` project, rename the `Class1.cs` file to `Recorder.cs`.

7. In the `MonitoringApp` project, add a project reference to the `MonitoringLib` class library, as shown in the following markup:

```
<ItemGroup>
  <ProjectReference
    Include="..\MonitoringLib\MonitoringLib.csproj" />
</ItemGroup>
```

8. Build the `MonitoringApp` project.

Useful members of the Stopwatch and Process types

The `Stopwatch` type has some useful members, as shown in the following table:

Member	Description
`Restart` method	This resets the elapsed time to zero and then starts the timer.
`Stop` method	This stops the timer.
`Elapsed` property	This is the elapsed time stored as a `TimeSpan` format (for example, hours:minutes:seconds)
`ElapsedMilliseconds` property	This is the elapsed time in milliseconds stored as an `Int64` value.

The `Process` type has some useful members, as shown in the following table:

Member	Description
`VirtualMemorySize64`	This displays the amount of virtual memory, in bytes, allocated for the process.
`WorkingSet64`	This displays the amount of physical memory, in bytes, allocated for the process.

Implementing a Recorder class

We will create a `Recorder` class that makes it easy to monitor time and memory resource usage. To implement our `Recorder` class, we will use the `Stopwatch` and `Process` classes:

1. In `Recorder.cs`, change its contents to use a `Stopwatch` instance to record timings and the current `Process` instance to record memory usage, as shown in the following code:

```
using System.Diagnostics; // Stopwatch

using static System.Console;
using static System.Diagnostics.Process; // GetCurrentProcess()

namespace Packt.Shared;
```

```
public static class Recorder
{
  private static Stopwatch timer = new();

  private static long bytesPhysicalBefore = 0;
  private static long bytesVirtualBefore = 0;

  public static void Start()
  {
    // force two garbage collections to release memory that is
    // no longer referenced but has not been released yet
    GC.Collect();
    GC.WaitForPendingFinalizers();
    GC.Collect();

    // store the current physical and virtual memory use
    bytesPhysicalBefore = GetCurrentProcess().WorkingSet64;
    bytesVirtualBefore = GetCurrentProcess().VirtualMemorySize64;
    timer.Restart();
  }

  public static void Stop()
  {
    timer.Stop();
    long bytesPhysicalAfter =
      GetCurrentProcess().WorkingSet64;

    long bytesVirtualAfter =
      GetCurrentProcess().VirtualMemorySize64;

    WriteLine("{0:N0} physical bytes used.",
      bytesPhysicalAfter - bytesPhysicalBefore);

    WriteLine("{0:N0} virtual bytes used.",
      bytesVirtualAfter - bytesVirtualBefore);

    WriteLine("{0} time span ellapsed.", timer.Elapsed);

    WriteLine("{0:N0} total milliseconds ellapsed.",
      timer.ElapsedMilliseconds);
  }
}
```

The Start method of the Recorder class uses the GC type (garbage collector) to ensure that any currently allocated but not referenced memory is collected before recording the amount of used memory. This is an advanced technique that you should almost never use in application code.

2. In `Program.cs`, write statements to start and stop the `Recorder` while generating an array of 10,000 integers, as shown in the following code:

```
using Packt.Shared; // Recorder

using static System.Console;

WriteLine("Processing. Please wait...");
Recorder.Start();

// simulate a process that requires some memory resources...
int[] largeArrayOfInts = Enumerable.Range(
  start: 1, count: 10_000).ToArray();

// ...and takes some time to complete
Thread.Sleep(new Random().Next(5, 10) * 1000);

Recorder.Stop();
```

3. Run the code and view the result, as shown in the following output:

```
Processing. Please wait...
655,360 physical bytes used.
536,576 virtual bytes used.
00:00:09.0038702 time span ellapsed.
9,003 total milliseconds ellapsed.
```

Remember that the time elapsed is randomly between 5 and 10 seconds. Your results will vary. For example, when run on my Mac mini M1, less physical memory but more virtual memory was used, as shown in the following output:

```
Processing. Please wait...
294,912 physical bytes used.
10,485,760 virtual bytes used.
00:00:06.0074221 time span ellapsed.
6,007 total milliseconds ellapsed.
```

Measuring the efficiency of processing strings

Now that you've seen how the `Stopwatch` and `Process` types can be used to monitor your code, we will use them to evaluate the best way to process `string` variables.

1. In `Program.cs`, comment out the previous statements by wrapping them in multi-line comment characters: `/* */`.

2. Write statements to create an array of 50,000 `int` variables and then concatenate them with commas as separators using a `string` and `StringBuilder` class, as shown in the following code:

```
int[] numbers = Enumerable.Range(
  start: 1, count: 50_000).ToArray();

WriteLine("Using string with +");
Recorder.Start();
string s = string.Empty; // i.e. ""
for (int i = 0; i < numbers.Length; i++)
{
  s += numbers[i] + ", ";
}
Recorder.Stop();

WriteLine("Using StringBuilder");
Recorder.Start();
System.Text.StringBuilder builder = new();
for (int i = 0; i < numbers.Length; i++)
{
  builder.Append(numbers[i]);
  builder.Append(", ");
}
Recorder.Stop();
```

3. Run the code and view the result, as shown in the following output:

```
Using string with +
14,883,072 physical bytes used.
3,609,728 virtual bytes used.
00:00:01.6220879 time span ellapsed.
1,622 total milliseconds ellapsed.
Using StringBuilder
12,288 physical bytes used.
0 virtual bytes used.
00:00:00.0006038 time span ellapsed.
0 total milliseconds ellapsed.
```

We can summarize the results as follows:

* The string class with the + operator used about 14 MB of physical memory, 1.5 MB of virtual memory, and took 1.5 seconds.

* The StringBuilder class used 12 KB of physical memory, zero virtual memory, and took less than 1 millisecond.

In this scenario, StringBuilder is more than 1,000 times faster and about 10,000 times more memory efficient when concatenating text! This is because string concatenation creates a new string each time you use it because string values are immutable so they can be safely pooled for reuse. StringBuilder creates a single buffer while it appends more characters.

Good Practice: Avoid using the String.Concat method or the + operator inside loops. Use StringBuilder instead.

Now that you've learned how to measure the performance and resource efficiency of your code using types built into .NET, let's learn about a NuGet package that provides more sophisticated performance measurements.

Monitoring performance and memory using Benchmark.NET

There is a popular benchmarking NuGet package for .NET that Microsoft uses in its blog posts about performance improvements, so it is good for .NET developers to know how it works and use it for their own performance testing. Let's see how we could use it to compare performance between string concatenation and StringBuilder:

1. Use your preferred code editor to add a new console app to the Chapter12 solution/ workspace named Benchmarking.

2. In Visual Studio Code, select Benchmarking as the active OmniSharp project.

3. Add a package reference to Benchmark.NET, remembering that you can find out the latest version and use that instead of the version I used, as shown in the following markup:

    ```
    <ItemGroup>
      <PackageReference Include="BenchmarkDotNet" Version="0.13.1" />
    </ItemGroup>
    ```

4. Build the project to restore packages.

5. In Program.cs, delete the existing statements and then import the namespace for running benchmarks, as shown in the following code:

    ```
    using BenchmarkDotNet.Running;
    ```

6. Add a new class file named StringBenchmarks.cs.

7. In StringBenchmarks.cs, add statements to define a class with methods for each benchmark you want to run, in this case, two methods that both combine twenty numbers comma-separated using either string concatenation or StringBuilder, as shown in the following code:

    ```
    using BenchmarkDotNet.Attributes; // [Benchmark]

    public class StringBenchmarks
    {
      int[] numbers;

      public StringBenchmarks()
    ```

```
  {
    numbers = Enumerable.Range(
      start: 1, count: 20).ToArray();
  }

  [Benchmark(Baseline = true)]
  public string StringConcatenationTest()
  {
    string s = string.Empty; // e.g. ""
    for (int i = 0; i < numbers.Length; i++)
    {
      s += numbers[i] + ", ";
    }
    return s;
  }

  [Benchmark]
  public string StringBuilderTest()
  {
    System.Text.StringBuilder builder = new();
    for (int i = 0; i < numbers.Length; i++)
    {
      builder.Append(numbers[i]);
      builder.Append(", ");
    }
    return builder.ToString();
  }
}
```

8. In `Program.cs`, add a statement to run the benchmarks, as shown in the following code:

   ```
   BenchmarkRunner.Run<StringBenchmarks>();
   ```

9. In Visual Studio 2022, in the toolbar, set **Solution Configurations** to **Release**.

10. In Visual Studio Code, in a terminal, use the `dotnet run --configuration Release` command.

11. Run the console app and note the results, including some artifacts like report files, and the most important, a summary table that shows that `string` concatenation took a mean of 412.990 ns and `StringBuilder` took a mean of 275.082 ns, as shown in the following partial output and in *Figure 12.1*:

```
// ***** BenchmarkRunner: Finish  *****

// * Export *
  BenchmarkDotNet.Artifacts\results\StringBenchmarks-report.csv
  BenchmarkDotNet.Artifacts\results\StringBenchmarks-report-github.md
```

```
   BenchmarkDotNet.Artifacts\results\StringBenchmarks-report.html

// * Detailed results *
StringBenchmarks.StringConcatenationTest: DefaultJob
Runtime = .NET 6.0.0 (6.0.21.37719), X64 RyuJIT; GC = Concurrent
Workstation
Mean = 412.990 ns, StdErr = 2.353 ns (0.57%), N = 46, StdDev = 15.957 ns
Min = 373.636 ns, Q1 = 413.341 ns, Median = 417.665 ns, Q3 = 420.775 ns,
Max = 434.504 ns
IQR = 7.433 ns, LowerFence = 402.191 ns, UpperFence = 431.925 ns
ConfidenceInterval = [404.708 ns; 421.273 ns] (CI 99.9%), Margin = 8.282
ns (2.01% of Mean)
Skewness = -1.51, Kurtosis = 4.09, MValue = 2
------------------- Histogram --------------------
[370.520 ns ; 382.211 ns) | @@@@@
[382.211 ns ; 394.583 ns) | @
[394.583 ns ; 411.300 ns) | @@
[411.300 ns ; 422.990 ns) | @@@@@@@@@@@@@@@@@@@@@@@@@@@@@@@@@@@
[422.990 ns ; 436.095 ns) | @@@@@
--------------------------------------------------------


StringBenchmarks.StringBuilderTest: DefaultJob
Runtime = .NET 6.0.0 (6.0.21.37719), X64 RyuJIT; GC = Concurrent
Workstation
Mean = 275.082 ns, StdErr = 0.558 ns (0.20%), N = 15, StdDev = 2.163 ns
Min = 271.059 ns, Q1 = 274.495 ns, Median = 275.403 ns, Q3 = 276.553 ns,
Max = 278.030 ns
IQR = 2.058 ns, LowerFence = 271.409 ns, UpperFence = 279.639 ns
ConfidenceInterval = [272.770 ns; 277.394 ns] (CI 99.9%), Margin = 2.312
ns (0.84% of Mean)
Skewness = -0.69, Kurtosis = 2.2, MValue = 2
------------------- Histogram --------------------
[269.908 ns ; 278.682 ns) | @@@@@@@@@@@@@@@
--------------------------------------------------------


// * Summary *

BenchmarkDotNet=v0.13.1, OS=Windows 10.0.19043.1165 (21H1/May2021Update)
11th Gen Intel Core i7-1165G7 2.80GHz, 1 CPU, 8 logical and 4 physical
cores
.NET SDK=6.0.100
  [Host]    : .NET 6.0.0 (6.0.21.37719), X64 RyuJIT
  DefaultJob : .NET 6.0.0 (6.0.21.37719), X64 RyuJIT


|                 Method |    Mean |   Error |  StdDev | Ratio |
RatioSD |
```

```
|--------------------- |---------:|--------:|--------:|------:|------
--:|
| StringConcatenationTest | 413.0 ns | 8.28 ns | 15.96 ns |  1.00 |
0.00 |
|        StringBuilderTest | 275.1 ns | 2.31 ns |  2.16 ns |  0.69 |
0.04 |

// * Hints *
Outliers
  StringBenchmarks.StringConcatenationTest: Default -> 7 outliers
were removed, 14 outliers were detected (376.78 ns..391.88 ns, 440.79
ns..506.41 ns)
  StringBenchmarks.StringBuilderTest: Default        -> 2 outliers were
detected (274.68 ns, 274.69 ns)

// * Legends *
  Mean     : Arithmetic mean of all measurements
  Error    : Half of 99.9% confidence interval
  StdDev   : Standard deviation of all measurements
  Ratio    : Mean of the ratio distribution ([Current]/[Baseline])
  RatioSD  : Standard deviation of the ratio distribution ([Current]/
[Baseline])
  1 ns     : 1 Nanosecond (0.000000001 sec)

// ***** BenchmarkRunner: End *****
// ** Remained 0 benchmark(s) to run **
Run time: 00:01:13 (73.35 sec), executed benchmarks: 2

Global total time: 00:01:29 (89.71 sec), executed benchmarks: 2
// * Artifacts cleanup *
```

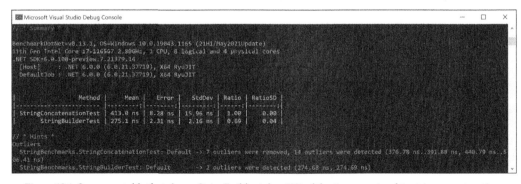

Figure 12.1: Summary table that shows StringBuilder takes 69% of the time compared to string concatenation

The Outliers section is especially interesting because it shows that not only is string concatenation slower than StringBuilder, but it is also more inconsistent in how long it takes. Your results will vary, of course.

You have now seen two ways to measure performance. Now let's see how we can run tasks asynchronously to potentially improve performance.

Running tasks asynchronously

To understand how multiple tasks can be run simultaneously (at the same time), we will create a console application that needs to execute three methods.

There will be three methods that need to be executed: the first takes 3 seconds, the second takes 2 seconds, and the third takes 1 second. To simulate that work, we can use the Thread class to tell the current thread to go to sleep for a specified number of milliseconds.

Running multiple actions synchronously

Before we make the tasks run simultaneously, we will run them synchronously, that is, one after the other.

1. Use your preferred code editor to add a new console app to the Chapter12 solution/workspace named WorkingWithTasks.

2. In Visual Studio Code, select WorkingWithTasks as the active OmniSharp project.

3. In Program.cs, import the namespace to work with a stopwatch (namespaces for working with threading and tasks are implicitly imported), and statically import Console, as shown in the following code:

    ```
    using System.Diagnostics; // Stopwatch

    using static System.Console;
    ```

4. At the bottom of Program.cs, create a method to output information about the current thread, as shown in the following code:

    ```
    static void OutputThreadInfo()
    {
      Thread t = Thread.CurrentThread;

      WriteLine(
        "Thread Id: {0}, Priority: {1}, Background: {2}, Name: {3}",
        t.ManagedThreadId, t.Priority,
        t.IsBackground, t.Name ?? "null");
    }
    ```

5. At the bottom of Program.cs, add three methods that simulate work, as shown in the following code:

    ```
    static void MethodA()
    {
      WriteLine("Starting Method A...");
    ```

```
    OutputThreadInfo();
    Thread.Sleep(3000); // simulate three seconds of work
    WriteLine("Finished Method A.");
}

static void MethodB()
{
    WriteLine("Starting Method B...");
    OutputThreadInfo();
    Thread.Sleep(2000); // simulate two seconds of work
    WriteLine("Finished Method B.");
}

static void MethodC()
{
    WriteLine("Starting Method C...");
    OutputThreadInfo();
    Thread.Sleep(1000); // simulate one second of work
    WriteLine("Finished Method C.");
}
```

6. At the top of `Program.cs`, add statements to call the method to output information about the thread, define and start a stopwatch, call the three simulated work methods, and then output the milliseconds elapsed, as shown in the following code:

```
OutputThreadInfo();
Stopwatch timer = Stopwatch.StartNew();

WriteLine("Running methods synchronously on one thread.");
MethodA();
MethodB();
MethodC();

WriteLine($"{timer.ElapsedMilliseconds:#,##0}ms elapsed.");
```

7. Run the code, view the result, and note that when there is only one unnamed foreground thread doing the work, the total time required is just over 6 seconds, as shown in the following output:

```
Thread Id: 1, Priority: Normal, Background: False, Name: null
Running methods synchronously on one thread.
Starting Method A...
Thread Id: 1, Priority: Normal, Background: False, Name: null
Finished Method A.
Starting Method B...
Thread Id: 1, Priority: Normal, Background: False, Name: null
Finished Method B.
```

```
Starting Method C...
Thread Id: 1, Priority: Normal, Background: False, Name: null
Finished Method C.
6,017ms elapsed.
```

Running multiple actions asynchronously using tasks

The Thread class has been available since the first version of .NET and can be used to create new threads and manage them, but it can be tricky to work with directly.

.NET Framework 4.0 introduced the Task class in 2010, which is a wrapper around a thread that enables easier creation and management. Managing multiple threads wrapped in tasks will allow our code to execute at the same time, aka asynchronously.

Each Task has a Status property and a CreationOptions property. A Task has a ContinueWith method that can be customized with the TaskContinuationOptions enum, and can be managed with the TaskFactory class.

Starting tasks

We will look at three ways to start the methods using Task instances. There are links in the GitHub repository to articles that discuss the pros and cons. Each has a slightly different syntax, but they all define a Task and start it:

1. Comment out the calls to the three methods and their associated console message, and add statements to create and start three tasks, one for each method, as shown highlighted in the following code:

    ```
    OutputThreadInfo();
    Stopwatch timer = Stopwatch.StartNew();

    /*
    WriteLine("Running methods synchronously on one thread.");
    MethodA();
    MethodB();
    MethodC();
    */

    WriteLine("Running methods asynchronously on multiple threads.");

    Task taskA = new(MethodA);
    taskA.Start();

    Task taskB = Task.Factory.StartNew(MethodB);

    Task taskC = Task.Run(MethodC);
    ```

```
WriteLine($"{timer.ElapsedMilliseconds:#,##0}ms elapsed.");
```

2. Run the code, view the result, and note that the elapsed milliseconds appear almost immediately. This is because each of the three methods is now being executed by three new background worker threads allocated from the thread pool, as shown in the following output:

```
Thread Id: 1, Priority: Normal, Background: False, Name: null
Running methods asynchronously on multiple threads.
Starting Method A...
Thread Id: 4, Priority: Normal, Background: True, Name: .NET ThreadPool
Worker
Starting Method C...
Thread Id: 7, Priority: Normal, Background: True, Name: .NET ThreadPool
Worker
Starting Method B...
Thread Id: 6, Priority: Normal, Background: True, Name: .NET ThreadPool
Worker
6ms elapsed.
```

It is even possible that the console app will end before one or more of the tasks have a chance to start and write to the console!

Waiting for tasks

Sometimes, you need to wait for a task to complete before continuing. To do this, you can use the `Wait` method on a `Task` instance, or the `WaitAll` or `WaitAny` static methods on an array of tasks, as described in the following table:

Method	Description
`t.Wait()`	This waits for the task instance named `t` to complete execution.
`Task.WaitAny(Task[])`	This waits for any of the tasks in the array to complete execution.
`Task.WaitAll(Task[])`	This waits for all the tasks in the array to complete execution.

Using wait methods with tasks

Let's see how we can use these wait methods to fix the problem with our console app.

1. In `Program.cs`, add statements after creating the three tasks and before outputting the elapsed time to combine references to the three tasks into an array and pass them to the `WaitAll` method, as shown in the following code:

```
Task[] tasks = { taskA, taskB, taskC };
Task.WaitAll(tasks);
```

2. Run the code and view the result, and note the original thread will pause on the call to WaitAll, waiting for all three tasks to finish before outputting the elapsed time, which is a little over 3 seconds, as shown in the following output:

```
Id: 1, Priority: Normal, Background: False, Name: null
Running methods asynchronously on multiple threads.
Starting Method A...
Id: 6, Priority: Normal, Background: True, Name: .NET ThreadPool Worker
Starting Method B...
Id: 7, Priority: Normal, Background: True, Name: .NET ThreadPool Worker
Starting Method C...
Id: 4, Priority: Normal, Background: True, Name: .NET ThreadPool Worker
Finished Method C.
Finished Method B.
Finished Method A.
3,013ms elapsed.
```

The three new threads execute their code simultaneously, and they can potentially start in any order. MethodC should finish first because it takes only 1 second, then MethodB, which takes 2 seconds, and finally MethodA, because it takes 3 seconds.

However, the actual CPU used has a big effect on the results. It is the CPU that allocates time slices to each process to allow them to execute their threads. You have no control over when the methods run.

Continuing with another task

If all three tasks can be performed at the same time, then waiting for all tasks to finish will be all we need to do. However, often a task is dependent on the output from another task. To handle this scenario, we need to define **continuation tasks**.

We will create some methods to simulate a call to a web service that returns a monetary amount that then needs to be used to retrieve how many products cost more than that amount in a database. The result returned from the first method needs to be fed into the input of the second method. This time, instead of waiting for fixed amounts of time, we will use the Random class to wait for a random interval between 2 and 4 seconds for each method call to simulate the work.

1. At the bottom of Program.cs, add two methods that simulate calling a web service and a database-stored procedure, as shown in the following code:

```
static decimal CallWebService()
{
  WriteLine("Starting call to web service...");
  OutputThreadInfo();
  Thread.Sleep((new Random()).Next(2000, 4000));
```

```
    WriteLine("Finished call to web service.");
    return 89.99M;
  }

  static string CallStoredProcedure(decimal amount)
  {
    WriteLine("Starting call to stored procedure...");
    OutputThreadInfo();
    Thread.Sleep((new Random()).Next(2000, 4000));
    WriteLine("Finished call to stored procedure.");
    return $"12 products cost more than {amount:C}.";
  }
```

2. Comment out the calls to the previous three tasks by wrapping them in multiline comment characters, /* */. Leave the statement that outputs the elapsed milliseconds.

3. Add statements before the existing statement to output the total time, as shown in the following code:

```
WriteLine("Passing the result of one task as an input into another.");

Task<string> taskServiceThenSProc = Task.Factory
  .StartNew(CallWebService) // returns Task<decimal>
  .ContinueWith(previousTask => // returns Task<string>
    CallStoredProcedure(previousTask.Result));

WriteLine($"Result: {taskServiceThenSProc.Result}");
```

4. Run the code and view the result, as shown in the following output:

```
Thread Id: 1, Priority: Normal, Background: False, Name: null
Passing the result of one task as an input into another.
Starting call to web service...
Thread Id: 4, Priority: Normal, Background: True, Name: .NET ThreadPool
Worker
Finished call to web service.
Starting call to stored procedure...
Thread Id: 6, Priority: Normal, Background: True, Name: .NET ThreadPool
Worker
Finished call to stored procedure.
Result: 12 products cost more than £89.99.
5,463ms elapsed.
```

You might see different threads running the web service and stored procedure calls as in the output above (threads 4 and 6), or the same thread might be reused since it is no longer busy.

Nested and child tasks

As well as defining dependencies between tasks, you can define nested and child tasks. A **nested task** is a task that is created inside another task. A **child task** is a nested task that must finish before its parent task is allowed to finish.

Let's explore how these types of tasks work:

1. Use your preferred code editor to add a new console app to the Chapter12 solution/ workspace named NestedAndChildTasks.

2. In Visual Studio Code, select NestedAndChildTasks as the active OmniSharp project.

3. In Program.cs, delete the existing statements, statically import Console, and then add two methods, one of which starts a task to run the other, as shown in the following code:

```
static void OuterMethod()
{
  WriteLine("Outer method starting...");
  Task innerTask = Task.Factory.StartNew(InnerMethod);
  WriteLine("Outer method finished.");
}

static void InnerMethod()
{
  WriteLine("Inner method starting...");
  Thread.Sleep(2000);
  WriteLine("Inner method finished.");
}
```

4. Above the methods, add statements to start a task to run the outer method and wait for it to finish before stopping, as shown in the following code:

```
Task outerTask = Task.Factory.StartNew(OuterMethod);
outerTask.Wait();
WriteLine("Console app is stopping.");
```

5. Run the code and view the result, as shown in the following output:

```
Outer method starting...
Inner method starting...
Outer method finished.
Console app is stopping.
```

Note that, although we wait for the outer task to finish, its inner task does not have to finish as well. In fact, the outer task might finish, and the console app could end, before the inner task even starts!

To link these nested tasks as parent and child, we must use a special option.

6. Modify the existing code that defines the inner task to add a `TaskCreationOption` value of `AttachedToParent`, as shown highlighted in the following code:

```
Task innerTask = Task.Factory.StartNew(InnerMethod,
  TaskCreationOptions.AttachedToParent);
```

7. Run the code, view the result, and note that the inner task must finish before the outer task can, as shown in the following output:

```
Outer method starting...
Inner method starting...
Outer method finished.
Inner method finished.
Console app is stopping.
```

The `OuterMethod` can finish before the `InnerMethod`, as shown by its writing to the console, but its task must wait, as shown by the console not stopping until both the outer and inner tasks finish.

Wrapping tasks around other objects

Sometimes you might have a method that you want to be asynchronous, but the result to be returned is not itself a task. You can wrap the return value in a successfully completed task, return an exception, or indicate that the task was canceled by using one of the methods shown in the following table:

Method	Description
`FromResult<TResult>(TResult)`	Creates a `Task<TResult>` object whose `Result` property is the non-task result and whose `Status` property is `RanToCompletion`.
`FromException<TResult>(Exception)`	Creates a `Task<TResult>` that's completed with a specified exception.
`FromCanceled<TResult>(CancellationToken)`	Creates a `Task<TResult>` that's completed due to cancellation with a specified cancellation token.

These methods are useful when you need to:

- Implement an interface that has async methods, but your implementation is synchronous. This is common for websites and services.

- Mock asynchronous implementations during unit testing.

In *Chapter 7, Packaging and Distributing .NET Types*, we created a class library with functions to check valid XML, passwords, and hex codes.

If we had wanted to make those methods conform to an interface that requires a Task<T> to be returned, we could use these helpful methods, as shown in the following code:

```
using System.Text.RegularExpressions;

namespace Packt.Shared;

public static class StringExtensions
{
  public static Task<bool> IsValidXmlTagAsync(this string input)
  {
    if (input == null)
    {
      return Task.FromException<bool>(
        new ArgumentNullException("Missing input parameter"));
    }
    if (input.Length == 0)
    {
      return Task.FromException<bool>(
        new ArgumentException("input parameter is empty."));
    }
    return Task.FromResult(Regex.IsMatch(input,
      @"^<([a-z]+)([^<]+)*(?:>(.*)<\/\1>|\s+\/>)$"));
  }

  // other methods
}
```

If the method you need to implement returns a Task (equivalent to void in a synchronous method) then you can return a predefined completed Task object, as shown in the following code:

```
public Task DeleteCustomerAsync()
{
  // ...
  return Task.CompletedTask;
}
```

Synchronizing access to shared resources

When you have multiple threads executing at the same time, there is a possibility that two or more of the threads may access the same variable or another resource at the same time, and as a result, may cause a problem. For this reason, you should carefully consider how to make your code **thread-safe**.

The simplest mechanism for implementing thread safety is to use an object variable as a flag or traffic light to indicate when a shared resource has an exclusive lock applied.

In William Golding's *Lord of the Flies*, Piggy and Ralph spot a conch shell and use it to call a meeting. The boys impose a "rule of the conch" on themselves, deciding that no one can speak unless they're holding the conch.

I like to name the object variable I use for implementing thread-safe code the "conch." When a thread has the conch, no other thread should access the shared resource(s) represented by that conch. Note that I say, *should*. Only code that respects the conch enables synchronized access. A conch is not a lock.

We will explore a couple of types that can be used to synchronize access to shared resources:

- `Monitor`: An object that can be used by multiple threads to check if they should access a shared resource within the same process.

- `Interlocked`: An object for manipulating simple numeric types at the CPU level.

Accessing a resource from multiple threads

1. Use your preferred code editor to add a new console app to the `Chapter12` solution/ workspace named `SynchronizingResourceAccess`.

2. In Visual Studio Code, select `SynchronizingResourceAccess` as the active OmniSharp project.

3. In `Program.cs`, delete the existing statements and then add statements to do the following:

   - Import the namespace for diagnostic types like `Stopwatch`.

   - Statically import the `Console` type.

   - At the bottom of `Program.cs`, create a static class with two fields:

     - A field to generate random wait times.

     - A `string` field to store a message (this is a shared resource).

   - Above the class, create two static methods that add a letter, A or B, to the shared string five times in a loop, and wait for a random interval of up to 2 seconds for each iteration:

```
static void MethodA()
{
  for (int i = 0; i < 5; i++)
  {
    Thread.Sleep(SharedObjects.Random.Next(2000));
    SharedObjects.Message += "A";
    Write(".");
  }
}

static void MethodB()
{
```

```
        for (int i = 0; i < 5; i++)
        {
          Thread.Sleep(SharedObjects.Random.Next(2000));
          SharedObjects.Message += "B";
          Write(".");
        }
      }

      static class SharedObjects
      {
        public static Random Random = new();
        public static string? Message; // a shared resource
      }
```

4. After the namespace imports, write statements to execute both methods on separate threads using a pair of tasks and wait for them to complete before outputting the elapsed milliseconds, as shown in the following code:

```
WriteLine("Please wait for the tasks to complete.");
Stopwatch watch = Stopwatch.StartNew();

Task a = Task.Factory.StartNew(MethodA);
Task b = Task.Factory.StartNew(MethodB);

Task.WaitAll(new Task[] { a, b });

WriteLine();
WriteLine($"Results: {SharedObjects.Message}.");
WriteLine($"{watch.ElapsedMilliseconds:N0} elapsed milliseconds.");
```

5. Run the code and view the result, as shown in the following output:

```
Please wait for the tasks to complete.
..........
Results: BABABAABBA.
5,753 elapsed milliseconds.
```

This shows that both threads were modifying the message concurrently. In an actual application, this could be a problem. But we can prevent concurrent access by applying a mutually exclusive lock to a conch object and code to the two methods to voluntarily check the conch before modifying the shared resource, which we will do in the following section.

Applying a mutually exclusive lock to a conch

Now, let's use a conch to ensure that only one thread accesses the shared resource at a time.

1. In `SharedObjects`, declare and instantiate an `object` variable to act as a conch, as shown in the following code:

   ```
   public static object Conch = new();
   ```

2. In both `MethodA` and `MethodB`, add a `lock` statement for the conch around the `for` statements, as shown highlighted in the following code:

   ```
   lock (SharedObjects.Conch)
   {
     for (int i = 0; i < 5; i++)
     {
       Thread.Sleep(SharedObjects.Random.Next(2000));
       SharedObjects.Message += "A";
       Write(".");
     }
   }
   ```

> **Good Practice**: Note that since checking the conch is voluntary, if you only use the `lock` statement in one of the two methods, the shared resource will continue to be accessed by both methods. Make sure that all methods that access a shared resource respect the conch.

3. Run the code and view the result, as shown in the following output:

   ```
   Please wait for the tasks to complete.
   . . . . . . . . . .
   Results: BBBBBAAAAA.
   10,345 elapsed milliseconds.
   ```

Although the time elapsed was longer, only one method at a time could access the shared resource. Either `MethodA` or `MethodB` can start first. Once a method has finished its work on the shared resource, then the conch gets released, and the other method has the chance to do its work.

Understanding the lock statement

You might wonder what the `lock` statement does when it "locks" an object variable (hint: it does not lock the object!), as shown in the following code:

```
lock (SharedObjects.Conch)
{
  // work with shared resource
}
```

The C# compiler changes the `lock` statement into a `try-finally` statement that uses the `Monitor` class to *enter* and *exit* the conch object (I like to think of it as *take* and *release* the conch object), as shown in the following code:

```
try
{
  Monitor.Enter(SharedObjects.Conch);

  // work with shared resource
}
finally
{
  Monitor.Exit(SharedObjects.Conch);
}
```

When a thread calls `Monitor.Enter` on any object, aka reference type, it checks to see if some other thread has already taken the conch. If it has, the thread waits. If it has not, the thread takes the conch and gets on with its work on the shared resource. Once the thread has finished its work, it calls `Monitor.Exit`, releasing the conch. If another thread was waiting, it can now take the conch and do its work. This requires all threads to respect the conch by calling `Monitor.Enter` and `Monitor.Exit` appropriately.

Avoiding deadlocks

Knowing how the `lock` statement is translated by the compiler to method calls on the `Monitor` class is also important because using the `lock` statement can cause a deadlock.

Deadlocks can occur when there are two or more shared resources (each with a conch to monitor which thread is currently doing work on each shared resource), and the following sequence of events happens:

- Thread X "locks" conch A and starts working on shared resource A.
- Thread Y "locks" conch B and starts working on shared resource B.
- While still working on resource A, thread X needs to also work with resource B, and so it attempts to "lock" conch B but is blocked because thread Y already has conch B.
- While still working on resource B, thread Y needs to also work with resource A, and so it attempts to "lock" conch A but is blocked because thread X already has conch A.

One way to prevent deadlocks is to specify a timeout when attempting to get a lock. To do this, you must manually use the `Monitor` class instead of using the `lock` statement.

1. Modify your code to replace the `lock` statements with code that tries to enter the conch with a timeout and outputs an error and then exits the monitor, allowing other threads to enter the monitor, as shown highlighted in the following code:

   ```
   try
   {
   ```

```
if (Monitor.TryEnter(SharedObjects.Conch, TimeSpan.FromSeconds(15)))
{
  for (int i = 0; i < 5; i++)
  {
    Thread.Sleep(SharedObjects.Random.Next(2000));
    SharedObjects.Message += "A";
    Write(".");
  }
}
else
{
  WriteLine("Method A timed out when entering a monitor on conch.");
}
}
finally
{
  Monitor.Exit(SharedObjects.Conch);
}
```

2. Run the code and view the result, which should return the same results as before (although either A or B could grab the conch first) but is better code because it will prevent potential deadlocks.

 Good Practice: Only use the `lock` keyword if you can write your code such that it avoids potential deadlocks. If you cannot avoid potential deadlocks, then always use the `Monitor.TryEnter` method instead of `lock`, in combination with a `try-finally` statement, so that you can supply a timeout and one of the threads will back out of a deadlock if it occurs. You can read more about good threading practices at the following link: https://docs.microsoft.com/en-us/dotnet/standard/threading/managed-threading-best-practices

Synchronizing events

In *Chapter 6, Implementing Interfaces and Inheriting Classes*, you learned how to raise and handle events. But .NET events are not thread-safe, so you should avoid using them in multithreaded scenarios and follow the standard event raising code I showed you earlier.

After learning that .NET events are not thread-safe, some developers attempt to use exclusive locks when adding and removing event handlers or when raising an event, as shown in the following code:

```
// event delegate field
public event EventHandler Shout;

// conch
```

```
private object eventLock = new();

// method
public void Poke()
{
  lock (eventLock) // bad idea
  {
    // if something is listening...
    if (Shout != null)
    {
      // ...then call the delegate to raise the event
      Shout(this, EventArgs.Empty);
    }
  }
}
```

Good Practice: You can read more about events and thread-safety at the following link: `https://docs.microsoft.com/en-us/archive/blogs/cburrows/field-like-events-considered-harmful`

But it is complicated, as explained by Stephen Cleary in the following blog post: `https://blog.stephencleary.com/2009/06/threadsafe-events.html`

Making CPU operations atomic

Atomic is from the Greek word **atomos**, which means *undividable*. It is important to understand which operations are atomic in multithreading because if they are not atomic, then they could be interrupted by another thread partway through their operation. Is the C# increment operator atomic, as shown in the following code?

```
int x = 3;
x++; // is this an atomic CPU operation?
```

It is not atomic! Incrementing an integer requires the following three CPU operations:

1. Load a value from an instance variable into a register.
2. Increment the value.
3. Store the value in the instance variable.

A thread could be interrupted after executing the first two steps. A second thread could then execute all three steps. When the first thread resumes execution, it will overwrite the value in the variable, and the effect of the increment or decrement performed by the second thread will be lost!

There is a type named `Interlocked` that can perform atomic actions on value types, such as integers and floats. Let's see it in action:

1. Declare another field in the `SharedObjects` class that will count how many operations have occurred, as shown in the following code:

   ```
   public static int Counter; // another shared resource
   ```

2. In both methods A and B, inside the `for` statement and after modifying the `string` value, add a statement to safely increment the counter, as shown in the following code:

   ```
   Interlocked.Increment(ref SharedObjects.Counter);
   ```

3. After outputting the elapsed time, write the current value of the counter to the console, as shown in the following code:

   ```
   WriteLine($"{SharedObjects.Counter} string modifications.");
   ```

4. Run the code and view the result, as shown highlighted in the following output:

   ```
   Please wait for the tasks to complete.
   ..........
   Results: BBBBBAAAAA.
   13,531 elapsed milliseconds.
   10 string modifications.
   ```

Observant readers will realize that the existing conch object protects all shared resources accessed within a block of code locked by the conch, and therefore it is actually unnecessary to use `Interlocked` in this specific example. But if we had not already been protecting another shared resource like `Message` then using `Interlocked` would be necessary.

Applying other types of synchronization

`Monitor` and `Interlocked` are mutually exclusive locks that are simple and effective, but sometimes, you need more advanced options to synchronize access to shared resources, as shown in the following table:

Type	Description
`ReaderWriterLock` and `ReaderWriterLockSlim`	These allow multiple threads to be in **read mode**, one thread to be in **write mode** with exclusive ownership of the write lock, and one thread that has read access to be in **upgradeable read mode**, from which the thread can upgrade to write mode without having to relinquish its read access to the resource.
`Mutex`	Like `Monitor`, this provides exclusive access to a shared resource, except it is used for inter-process synchronization.
`Semaphore` and `SemaphoreSlim`	These limit the number of threads that can access a resource or pool of resources concurrently by defining slots. This is known as resource throttling rather than resource locking.
`AutoResetEvent` and `ManualResetEvent`	Event wait handles allow threads to synchronize activities by signaling each other and by waiting for each other's signals.

Understanding async and await

C# 5 introduced two C# keywords when working with the `Task` type. They are especially useful for the following:

- Implementing multitasking for a **graphical user interface (GUI)**.
- Improving the scalability of web applications and web services.

In *Chapter 15, Building Websites Using the Model-View-Controller Pattern*, we will see how the async and await keywords can improve scalability for websites.

In *Chapter 19, Building Mobile and Desktop Apps Using .NET MAUI*, we will see how the async and await keywords can implement multitasking for a GUI.

But for now, let's learn the theory of why these two C# keywords were introduced, and then later you will see them used in practice.

Improving responsiveness for console apps

One of the limitations with console applications is that you can only use the await keyword inside methods that are marked as async but C# 7 and earlier do not allow the Main method to be marked as async! Luckily, a new feature introduced in C# 7.1 was support for async in Main:

1. Use your preferred code editor to add a new console app to the `Chapter12` solution/workspace named `AsyncConsole`.

2. In Visual Studio Code, select `AsyncConsole` as the active OmniSharp project.

3. In `Program.cs`, delete the existing statements and statically import `Console`, as shown in the following code:

   ```
   using static System.Console;
   ```

4. Add statements to create an `HttpClient` instance, make a request for Apple's home page, and output how many bytes it has, as shown in the following code:

   ```
   HttpClient client = new();

   HttpResponseMessage response =
     await client.GetAsync("http://www.apple.com/");

   WriteLine("Apple's home page has {0:N0} bytes.",
     response.Content.Headers.ContentLength);
   ```

5. Build the project and note that it builds successfully. In .NET 5 and earlier, you would have seen an error message, as shown in the following output:

   ```
   Program.cs(14,9): error CS4033: The 'await' operator can only be used
   within an async method. Consider marking this method with the 'async'
   modifier and changing its return type to 'Task'. [/Users/markjprice/Code/
   Chapter12/AsyncConsole/AsyncConsole.csproj]
   ```

6. You would have had to add the `async` keyword to the `Main` method and change its return type to `Task`. With .NET 6 and later, the console app project template uses the top-level program feature to automatically define the `Program` class with an asynchronous `Main` method for you.

7. Run the code and view the result, which is likely to have a different number of bytes since Apple changes its home page frequently, as shown in the following output:

```
Apple's home page has 40,252 bytes.
```

Improving responsiveness for GUI apps

So far in this book, we have only built console applications. Life for a programmer gets more complicated when building web applications, web services, and apps with GUIs such as Windows desktop and mobile apps.

One reason for this is that for a GUI app, there is a special thread: the **user interface** (**UI**) thread.

There are two rules for working in GUIs:

- Do not perform long-running tasks on the UI thread.
- Do not access UI elements on any thread except the UI thread.

To handle these rules, programmers used to have to write complex code to ensure that long-running tasks were executed by a non-UI thread, but once complete, the results of the task were safely passed to the UI thread to present to the user. It could quickly get messy!

Luckily, with C# 5 and later, you have the use of `async` and `await`. They allow you to continue to write your code as if it is synchronous, which keeps your code clean and easy to understand, but underneath, the C# compiler creates a complex state machine and keeps track of running threads. It's kind of magical!

Let's see an example. We will build a Windows desktop app using WPF that gets employees from the Northwind database in an SQL Server database using low-level types like `SqlConnection`, `SqlCommand`, and `SqlDataReader`. You will only be able to complete this task if you have Windows and the Northwind database stored in SQL Server. This is the only section in this book that is not cross-platform and modern (WPF is 16 years old!).

At this point, we are focusing on making a GUI app responsive. You will learn about XAML and building cross-platform GUI apps in *Chapter 19, Building Mobile and Desktop Apps Using .NET MAUI*. Since this book does not cover WPF elsewhere, I thought this task would be a good opportunity to at least see an example app built using WPF even if we do not look at it in detail.

Let's go!

1. If you are using Visual Studio 2022 for Windows, add a new **WPF Application [C#]** project named `WpfResponsive` to the `Chapter12` solution. If you are using Visual Studio Code, use the following command: `dotnet new wpf`.

2. In the project file, note the output type is a Windows EXE, the target framework is .NET 6 for Windows (it will not run on other platforms like macOS and Linux), and the project uses WPF.

3. Add a package reference for `Microsoft.Data.SqlClient` to the project, as shown highlighted in the following markup:

```
<Project Sdk="Microsoft.NET.Sdk">

  <PropertyGroup>
    <OutputType>WinExe</OutputType>
    <TargetFramework>net6.0-windows</TargetFramework>
    <Nullable>enable</Nullable>
    <UseWPF>true</UseWPF>
  </PropertyGroup>

  <ItemGroup>
    <PackageReference Include="Microsoft.Data.SqlClient" Version="3.0.0"
/>
  </ItemGroup>

</Project>
```

4. Build the project to restore packages.

5. In `MainWindow.xaml`, in the `<Grid>` element, add elements to define two buttons, a text box and a list box, laid out vertically in a stack panel, as shown highlighted in the following markup:

```
<Grid>
  <StackPanel>
    <Button Name="GetEmployeesSyncButton"
            Click="GetEmployeesSyncButton_Click">
      Get Employees Synchronously</Button>
    <Button Name="GetEmployeesAsyncButton"
            Click="GetEmployeesAsyncButton_Click">
      Get Employees Asynchronously</Button>
    <TextBox HorizontalAlignment="Stretch" Text="Type in here" />
    <ListBox Name="EmployeesListBox" Height="400" />
  </StackPanel>
</Grid>
```

 Visual Studio 2022 for Windows has good support for building WPF apps and will provide IntelliSense as you edit code and XAML markup. Visual Studio Code does not.

6. In `MainWindow.xaml.cs`, in the `MainWindow` class, import the `System.Diagnostics` and `Microsoft.Data.SqlClient` namespaces, then create two `string` constants for the database connection string and SQL statement and create event handlers for clicking on the two buttons that use those `string` constants to open a connection to the Northwind database and populate the list box with the ids and names of all employees, as shown in the following code:

```
private const string connectionString =
  "Data Source=.;" +
  "Initial Catalog=Northwind;" +
  "Integrated Security=true;" +
  "MultipleActiveResultSets=true;";

private const string sql =
  "WAITFOR DELAY '00:00:05';" +
  "SELECT EmployeeId, FirstName, LastName FROM Employees";

private void GetEmployeesSyncButton_Click(object sender, RoutedEventArgs e)
{
  Stopwatch timer = Stopwatch.StartNew();
  using (SqlConnection connection = new(connectionString))
  {
    connection.Open();
    SqlCommand command = new(sql, connection);
    SqlDataReader reader = command.ExecuteReader();

    while (reader.Read())
    {
      string employee = string.Format("{0}: {1} {2}",
        reader.GetInt32(0), reader.GetString(1), reader.GetString(2));

      EmployeesListBox.Items.Add(employee);
    }
    reader.Close();
    connection.Close();
  }
  EmployeesListBox.Items.Add($"Sync: {timer.ElapsedMilliseconds:N0}ms");
}

private async void GetEmployeesAsyncButton_Click(
  object sender, RoutedEventArgs e)
{
  Stopwatch timer = Stopwatch.StartNew();
  using (SqlConnection connection = new(connectionString))
  {
```

```
        await connection.OpenAsync();
        SqlCommand command = new(sql, connection);
        SqlDataReader reader = await command.ExecuteReaderAsync();

        while (await reader.ReadAsync())
        {
          string employee = string.Format("{0}: {1} {2}",
            await reader.GetFieldValueAsync<int>(0),
            await reader.GetFieldValueAsync<string>(1),
            await reader.GetFieldValueAsync<string>(2));

          EmployeesListBox.Items.Add(employee);
        }
        await reader.CloseAsync();
        await connection.CloseAsync();
      }
      EmployeesListBox.Items.Add($"Async: {timer.ElapsedMilliseconds:N0}ms");
    }
```

Note the following:

- The SQL statement uses the SQL Server command WAITFOR DELAY to simulate processing that takes five seconds. It then selects three columns from the Employees table.

- The GetEmployeesSyncButton_Click event handler uses synchronous methods to open a connection and fetch the employee rows.

- The GetEmployeesAsyncButton_Click event handler is marked as async and uses asynchronous methods with the await keyword to open a connection and fetch the employee rows.

- Both event handlers use a stopwatch to record the number of milliseconds the operation takes and add it to the list box.

7. Start the WPF app without debugging.

8. Click in the text box, enter some text, and note the GUI is responsive.

9. Click the **Get Employees Synchronously** button.

10. Try to click in the text box, and note the GUI is not responsive.

11. Wait for at least five seconds until the list box is filled with employees.

12. Click in the text box, enter some text, and note the GUI is responsive again.

13. Click the **Get Employees Asynchronously** button.

14. Click in the text box, enter some text, and note the GUI is still responsive while it performs the operation. Continue typing until the list box is filled with the employees.

15. Note the difference in timings for the two operations. The UI is blocked when fetching data synchronously, while the UI remains responsive when fetching data asynchronously.

16. Close the WPF app.

Improving scalability for web applications and web services

The `async` and `await` keywords can also be applied on the server side when building websites, applications, and services. From the client application's point of view, nothing changes (or they might even notice a small increase in the time taken for a request to return). So, from a single client's point of view, the use of `async` and `await` to implement multitasking on the server side makes their experience worse!

On the server side, additional, cheaper worker threads are created to wait for long-running tasks to finish so that expensive I/O threads can handle other client requests instead of being blocked. This improves the overall scalability of a web application or service. More clients can be supported simultaneously.

Common types that support multitasking

There are many common types that have asynchronous methods that you can await, as shown in the following table:

Type	Methods
DbContext<T>	AddAsync, AddRangeAsync, FindAsync, and SaveChangesAsync
DbSet<T>	AddAsync, AddRangeAsync, ForEachAsync, SumAsync, ToListAsync, ToDictionaryAsync, AverageAsync, and CountAsync
HttpClient	GetAsync, PostAsync, PutAsync, DeleteAsync, and SendAsync
StreamReader	ReadAsync, ReadLineAsync, and ReadToEndAsync
StreamWriter	WriteAsync, WriteLineAsync, and FlushAsync

> **Good Practice**: Any time you see a method that ends in the suffix Async, check to see whether it returns Task or Task<T>. If it does, then you could use it instead of the synchronous non-Async suffixed method. Remember to call it using await and decorate your method with async.

Using await in catch blocks

When async and await were first introduced in C# 5, it was only possible to use the `await` keyword in a `try` block, but not in a `catch` block. In C# 6 and later, it is now possible to use await in both try and catch blocks.

Working with async streams

With .NET Core 3.0, Microsoft introduced the asynchronous processing of streams.

You can complete a tutorial about async streams at the following link: `https://docs.` `microsoft.com/en-us/dotnet/csharp/tutorials/generate-consume-asynchronous-stream`

Before C# 8.0 and .NET Core 3.0, the `await` keyword only worked with tasks that return scalar values. Async stream support in .NET Standard 2.1 allows an async method to return a sequence of values.

Let's see a simulated example that returns three random integers as an async stream.

1. Use your preferred code editor to add a new console app to the `Chapter12` solution/ workspace named `AsyncEnumerable`.

2. In Visual Studio Code, select `AsyncEnumerable` as the active OmniSharp project.

3. In `Program.cs`, delete the existing statements and statically import `Console`, as shown in the following code:

   ```
   using static System.Console; // WriteLine()
   ```

4. At the bottom of `Program.cs`, create a method that uses the `yield` keyword to return a random sequence of three numbers asynchronously, as shown in the following code:

   ```
   async static IAsyncEnumerable<int> GetNumbersAsync()
   {
     Random r = new();

     // simulate work
     await Task.Delay(r.Next(1500, 3000));
     yield return r.Next(0, 1001);

     await Task.Delay(r.Next(1500, 3000));
     yield return r.Next(0, 1001);

     await Task.Delay(r.Next(1500, 3000));
     yield return r.Next(0, 1001);
   }
   ```

5. Above `GetNumbersAsync`, add statements to enumerate the sequence of numbers, as shown in the following code:

   ```
   await foreach (int number in GetNumbersAsync())
   {
     WriteLine($"Number: {number}");
   }
   ```

6. Run the code and view the result, as shown in the following output:

```
Number: 509
Number: 813
Number: 307
```

Practicing and exploring

Test your knowledge and understanding by answering some questions, get some hands-on practice, and explore this chapter's topics with deeper research.

Exercise 12.1 – Test your knowledge

Answer the following questions:

1. What information can you find out about a process?
2. How accurate is the Stopwatch class?
3. By convention, what suffix should be applied to a method that returns Task or Task<T>?
4. To use the await keyword inside a method, what keyword must be applied to the method declaration?
5. How do you create a child task?
6. Why should you avoid the lock keyword?
7. When should you use the Interlocked class?
8. When should you use the Mutex class instead of the Monitor class?
9. What is the benefit of using async and await in a website or web service?
10. Can you cancel a task? If so, how?

Exercise 12.2 – Explore topics

Use the links on the following webpage to learn more detail about the topics covered in this chapter:

https://github.com/markjprice/cs10dotnet6/blob/main/book-links.md#chapter-12---improving-performance-and-scalability-using-multitasking

Summary

In this chapter, you learned not only how to define and start a task but also how to wait for one or more tasks to finish and how to control task completion order. You've also learned how to synchronize access to shared resources and the magic behind async and await.

In the seven chapters that follow, you will learn how to create applications for the **app models**, aka **workloads** supported by .NET, such as websites and services, and cross-platform desktop and mobile apps.

13

Introducing Practical Applications of C# and .NET

The third and final part of this book is about practical applications of C# and .NET. You will learn how to build cross-platform projects such as websites, services, and mobile and desktop apps.

Microsoft calls platforms for building applications **app models** or **workloads**.

In *Chapters 1* to *18* and *20*, you can use OS-specific Visual Studio or cross-platform Visual Studio Code and JetBrains Rider to build all the apps. In *Chapter 19, Building Mobile and Desktop Apps Using .NET MAUI*, although you could use Visual Studio Code to build the mobile and desktop app, it is not easy. Visual Studio 2022 for Windows has better support for .NET MAUI than Visual Studio Code does (for now).

I recommend that you work through this and subsequent chapters sequentially because later chapters will reference projects in earlier chapters, and you will build up sufficient knowledge and skills to tackle the trickier problems in later chapters.

In this chapter, we will cover the following topics:

- Understanding app models for C# and .NET
- New features in ASP.NET Core
- Structuring projects
- Using other project templates
- Building an entity data model for Northwind

Understanding app models for C# and .NET

Since this book is about C# 10 and .NET 6, we will learn about app models that use them to build the practical applications that we will encounter in the remaining chapters of this book.

Learn More: Microsoft has extensive guidance for implementing app models in its .NET Application Architecture Guidance documentation, which you can read at the following link: `https://www.microsoft.com/net/learn/architecture`

Building websites using ASP.NET Core

Websites are made up of multiple web pages loaded statically from the filesystem or generated dynamically by a server-side technology such as ASP.NET Core. A web browser makes GET requests using **Unique Resource Locators** (**URLs**) that identify each page and can manipulate data stored on the server using POST, PUT, and DELETE requests.

With many websites, the web browser is treated as a presentation layer, with almost all the processing performed on the server side. Some JavaScript might be used on the client side to implement some presentation features, such as carousels.

ASP.NET Core provides multiple technologies for building websites:

- **ASP.NET Core Razor Pages** and **Razor class libraries** are ways to dynamically generate HTML for simple websites. You will learn about them in detail in *Chapter 14, Building Websites Using ASP.NET Core Razor Pages*.

- **ASP.NET Core MVC** is an implementation of the **Model-View-Controller** (**MVC**) design pattern that is popular for developing complex websites. You will learn about it in detail in *Chapter 15, Building Websites Using the Model-View-Controller Pattern*.

- **Blazor** lets you build user interface components using C# and .NET instead of a JavaScript-based UI framework like Angular, React, and Vue. **Blazor WebAssembly** runs your code in the browser like a JavaScript-based framework would. **Blazor Server** runs your code on the server and updates the web page dynamically. You will learn about Blazor in detail in *Chapter 17, Building User Interfaces Using Blazor*. Blazor is not just for building websites; it can also be used to create hybrid mobile and desktop apps.

Building websites using a content management system

Most websites have a lot of content, and if developers had to be involved every time some content needed to be changed, that would not scale well. A **Content Management System** (**CMS**) enables developers to define content structure and templates to provide consistency and good design while making it easy for a non-technical content owner to manage the actual content. They can create new pages or blocks of content, and update existing content, knowing it will look great for visitors with minimal effort.

There is a multitude of CMSs available for all web platforms, like WordPress for PHP or Django CMS for Python. CMSs that support modern .NET include Optimizely Content Cloud, Piranha CMS, and Orchard Core.

The key benefit of using a CMS is that it provides a friendly content management user interface. Content owners log in to the website and manage the content themselves. The content is then rendered and returned to visitors using ASP.NET Core MVC controllers and views, or via web service endpoints, known as a **headless CMS**, to provide that content to "heads" implemented as mobile or desktop apps, in-store touchpoints, or clients built with JavaScript frameworks or Blazor.

This book does not cover .NET CMSs, so I have included links where you can learn more about them in the GitHub repository:

```
https://github.com/markjprice/cs10dotnet6/blob/main/book-links.md#net-content-
management-systems
```

Building web applications using SPA frameworks

Web applications, also known as **Single-Page Applications** (**SPAs**), are made up of a single web page built with a frontend technology such as Blazor WebAssembly, Angular, React, Vue, or a proprietary JavaScript library that can make requests to a backend web service for getting more data when needed and posting updated data using common serialization formats such as XML and JSON. The canonical examples are Google web apps like Gmail, Maps, and Docs.

With a web application, the client side uses JavaScript frameworks or Blazor WebAssembly to implement sophisticated user interactions, but most of the important processing and data access still happens on the server side, because the web browser has limited access to local system resources.

JavaScript is loosely typed and is not designed for complex projects, so most JavaScript libraries these days use Microsoft TypeScript, which adds strong typing to JavaScript and is designed with many modern language features for handling complex implementations.

.NET SDK has project templates for JavaScript and TypeScript-based SPAs, but we will not spend any time learning how to build JavaScript- and TypeScript-based SPAs in this book, even though these are commonly used with ASP.NET Core as the backend, because this book is about C#, it is not about other languages.

In summary, C# and .NET can be used on both the server side and the client side to build websites, as shown in *Figure 13.1*:

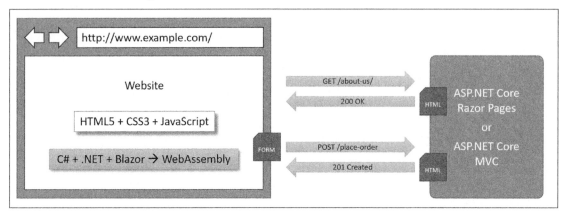

Figure 13.1: The use of C# and .NET to build websites on both the server side and the client side

Building web and other services

Although we will not learn about JavaScript- and TypeScript-based SPAs, we will learn how to build a web service using the **ASP.NET Core Web API**, and then call that web service from the server-side code in our ASP.NET Core websites, and then later, we will call that web service from Blazor WebAssembly components and cross-platform mobile and desktop apps.

There are no formal definitions, but services are sometimes described based on their complexity:

- **Service**: all functionality needed by a client app in one monolithic service.
- **Microservice**: multiple services that each focus on a smaller set of functionalities.
- **Nanoservice**: a single function provided as a service. Unlike services and microservices that are hosted 24/7/365, nanoservices are often inactive until called upon to reduce resources and costs.

As well as web services that use HTTP as the underlying communication technology and the design principles of the API, we will learn how to build services using other technologies and design philosophies, including:

- **gRPC** for building highly efficient and performant services with support for almost any platform.
- **SignalR** for building real-time communications between components.
- **OData** for wrapping Entity Framework Core and other data models with a web API.
- **GraphQL** for letting the client control what data is retrieved across multiple data sources.
- **Azure Functions** for hosting serverless nanoservices in the cloud.

Building mobile and desktop apps

There are two major mobile platforms: Apple's iOS and Google's Android, each with its own programming languages and platform APIs. There are also two major desktop platforms: Apple's macOS and Microsoft's Windows, each with its own programming languages and platform APIs, as shown in the following list:

- **iOS**: Objective C or Swift and UIkit.
- **Android**: Java or Kotlin and the Android API.
- **macOS**: Objective C or Swift and AppKit or Catalyst.
- **Windows**: C, C++, or many other languages and the Win32 API or Windows App SDK.

Since this book is about modern cross-platform development using C# and .NET it does not include coverage of building desktop apps using **Windows Forms**, **Windows Presentation Foundation** (**WPF**), or **Universal Windows Platform** (**UWP**) apps because they are Windows-only.

Cross-platform mobile and desktop apps can be built once for the **.NET Multi-platform App User Interfaces** (**MAUI**) platform, and then can run on many mobile and desktop platforms.

.NET MAUI makes it easy to develop those apps by sharing user interface components as well as business logic. They can target the same .NET APIs as used by console apps, websites, and web services. The app will be executed by the Mono runtime on mobile devices and the CoreCLR runtime on desktop devices. The Mono runtime is better optimized for mobile devices compared to the normal .NET CoreCLR runtime. Blazor WebAssembly also uses the Mono runtime because like a mobile app, it is resource constrained.

The apps can exist on their own, but they usually call services to provide an experience that spans across all your computing devices, from servers and laptops to phones and gaming systems.

Future updates to .NET MAUI will support existing MVVM and XAML patterns as well as ones like **Model-View-Update** (**MVU**) with C#, which is like Apple's Swift UI.

The penultimate chapter in this sixth edition is *Chapter 19, Building Mobile and Desktop Apps Using .NET MAUI*, and covers using .NET MAUI to build cross-platform mobile and desktop apps.

Alternatives to .NET MAUI

Before Microsoft created .NET MAUI, third parties created open-source initiatives to enable .NET developers to build cross-platform apps using XAML named **Uno** and **Avalonia**.

Understanding Uno Platform

As Uno state on their website, it is "the first and only UI Platform for single-codebase applications for Windows, WebAssembly, iOS, macOS, Android, and Linux."

Developers can reuse 99% of the business logic and UI layer across native mobile, web, and desktop.

Uno Platform uses the Xamarin native platform but not Xamarin.Forms. For WebAssembly, Uno uses the Mono-WASM runtime just like Blazor WebAssembly. For Linux, Uno uses Skia to draw the user interface on the canvas.

Understanding Avalonia

As stated on .NET Foundation's website, Avalonia "is a cross-platform XAML-based UI framework providing a flexible styling system and supporting a wide range of Operating Systems such as Windows, Linux via Xorg, macOS. Avalonia is ready for General-Purpose Desktop App Development."

You can think of Avalonia as a spiritual successor to WPF. WPF, Silverlight, and UWP developers familiar with WPF can continue to benefit from their years of pre-existing knowledge and skills.

It was used by JetBrains to modernize their WPF-based tools and take them cross-platform.

The Avalonia extension for Visual Studio and deep integration with JetBrains Rider makes development easier and more productive.

New features in ASP.NET Core

Over the past few years, Microsoft has rapidly expanded the capabilities of ASP.NET Core. You should note which .NET platforms are supported, as shown in the following list:

- ASP.NET Core 1.0 to 2.2 runs on either .NET Core or .NET Framework.
- ASP.NET Core 3.0 or later only runs on .NET Core 3.0 or later.

ASP.NET Core 1.0

ASP.NET Core 1.0 was released in June 2016 and focused on implementing a minimum API suitable for building modern cross-platform web apps and services for Windows, macOS, and Linux.

ASP.NET Core 1.1

ASP.NET Core 1.1 was released in November 2016 and focused on bug fixes and general improvements to features and performance.

ASP.NET Core 2.0

ASP.NET Core 2.0 was released in August 2017 and focused on adding new features such as Razor Pages, bundling assemblies into a `Microsoft.AspNetCore.All` metapackage, targeting .NET Standard 2.0, providing a new authentication model, and performance improvements.

The biggest new features introduced with ASP.NET Core 2.0 are ASP.NET Core Razor Pages, which is covered in *Chapter 14, Building Websites Using ASP.NET Core Razor Pages*, and ASP.NET Core OData support, which is covered in *Chapter 18, Building and Consuming Specialized Services*.

ASP.NET Core 2.1

ASP.NET Core 2.1 was released in May 2018 and was a **Long Term Support (LTS)** release, meaning it was supported for three years until August 21, 2021 (LTS designation was not officially assigned to it until August 2018 with version 2.1.3).

It focused on adding new features such as **SignalR** for real-time communication, **Razor class libraries** for reusing web components, **ASP.NET Core Identity** for authentication, and better support for HTTPS and the European Union's **General Data Protection Regulation (GDPR)**, including the topics listed in the following table:

Feature	Chapter	Topic
Razor class libraries	14	Using Razor class libraries
GDPR support	15	Creating and exploring an ASP.NET Core MVC website
Identity UI library and scaffolding	15	Exploring an ASP.NET Core MVC website
Integration tests	15	Testing an ASP.NET Core MVC website
[ApiController], ActionResult<T>	16	Creating an ASP.NET Core Web API project
Problem details	16	Implementing a Web API controller
IHttpClientFactory	16	Configuring HTTP clients using HttpClientFactory
ASP.NET Core SignalR	18	Implementing Real-time communication using SignalR

ASP.NET Core 2.2

ASP.NET Core 2.2 was released in December 2018 and focused on improving the building of RESTful HTTP APIs, updating the project templates to Bootstrap 4 and Angular 6, an optimized configuration for hosting in Azure, and performance improvements, including the topics listed in the following table:

Feature	Chapter	Topic
HTTP/2 in Kestrel	14	Classic ASP.NET versus modern ASP.NET Core
In-process hosting model	14	Creating an ASP.NET Core project
Endpoint routing	14	Understanding endpoint routing
Health Check API	16	Implementing a health check API
Open API analyzers	16	Implementing Open API analyzers and conventions

ASP.NET Core 3.0

ASP.NET Core 3.0 was released in September 2019 and focused on fully leveraging .NET Core 3.0 and .NET Standard 2.1, which meant it could not support .NET Framework, and it added useful refinements, including the topics listed in the following table:

Feature	Chapter	Topic
Static assets in Razor class libraries	14	Using Razor class libraries
New options for MVC service registration	15	Understanding ASP.NET Core MVC startup
ASP.NET Core gRPC	18	Building services using ASP.NET Core gRPC
Blazor Server	17	Building components using Blazor Server

ASP.NET Core 3.1

ASP.NET Core 3.1 was released in December 2019 and is an LTS release, meaning it will be supported until December 3, 2022. It focused on refinements like partial class support for Razor components and a new `<component>` tag helper.

Blazor WebAssembly 3.2

Blazor WebAssembly 3.2 was released in May 2020. It was a Current release, meaning that projects had to be upgraded to the .NET 5 version within three months of the .NET 5 release, that is, by February 10, 2021. Microsoft finally delivered on the promise of full-stack web development with .NET, and both Blazor Server and Blazor WebAssembly are covered in *Chapter 17, Building User Interfaces Using Blazor*.

ASP.NET Core 5.0

ASP.NET Core 5.0 was released in November 2020 and focused on bug fixes, performance improvements using caching for certificate authentication, HPACK dynamic compression of HTTP/2 response headers in Kestrel, nullable annotations for ASP.NET Core assemblies, and a reduction in container image sizes, including the topics listed in the following table:

Feature	Chapter	Topic
Extension method to allow anonymous access to an endpoint	16	Securing web services
JSON extension methods for `HttpRequest` and `HttpResponse`	16	Getting customers as JSON in the controller

ASP.NET Core 6.0

ASP.NET Core 6.0 was released in November 2021 and focused on productivity improvements like minimizing code to implement basic websites and services, .NET Hot Reload, and new hosting options for Blazor, like hybrid apps using .NET MAUI, including the topics listed in the following table:

Feature	Chapter	Topic
New empty web project template	14	Understanding the empty web template
HTTP logging middleware	16	Enabling HTTP logging
Minimal APIs	16	Implementing minimal Web APIs
Blazor error boundaries	17	Defining Blazor error boundaries
Blazor WebAssembly AOT	17	Enabling Blazor WebAssembly ahead-of-time compilation
.NET Hot Reload	17	Fixing code using .NET Hot Reload
.NET MAUI Blazor apps	19	Hosting Blazor components in .NET MAUI apps

Building Windows-only desktop apps

Technologies for building Windows-only desktop apps include:

- **Windows Forms**, 2002.
- **Windows Presentation Foundation (WPF)**, 2006.
- **Windows Store** apps, 2012.
- **Universal Windows Platform (UWP)** apps, 2015.
- **Windows App SDK** (formerly **WinUI 3** and **Project Reunion**) apps, 2021.

Understanding legacy Windows application platforms

With the Microsoft Windows 1.0 release in 1985, the only way to create Windows applications was to use the C language and call functions in three core DLLs named kernel, user, and GDI. Once Windows became 32-bit with Windows 95, the DLLs were suffixed with 32 and became known as **Win32 API**.

In 1991, Microsoft introduced Visual Basic, which provided developers with a visual, drag-and-drop-from-a-toolbox-of-controls way to build the user interface for Windows applications. It was immensely popular, and the Visual Basic runtime is still distributed as part of Windows 10 today.

With the first version of C# and .NET Framework released in 2002, Microsoft provided technology for building Windows desktop applications named **Windows Forms**. The equivalent at the time for web development was named **Web Forms**, hence the complimentary names. The code could be written in either Visual Basic or C# languages. Windows Forms had a similar drag-and-drop visual designer, although it generated C# or Visual Basic code to define the user interface, which can be difficult for humans to understand and edit directly.

In 2006, Microsoft released a more powerful technology for building Windows desktop applications, named **Windows Presentation Foundation (WPF)**, as a key component of .NET Framework 3.0 alongside **Windows Communication Foundation (WCF)** and **Windows Workflow (WF)**.

Although a WPF app can be created by writing only C# statements, it can also use **eXtensible Application Markup Language (XAML)** to specify its user interface, which is easy for both humans and code to understand. Visual Studio for Windows is partially built with WPF.

In 2012, Microsoft released Windows 8 with its Windows Store apps that run in a protected sandbox.

In 2015, Microsoft released Windows 10 with an updated Windows Store app concept named **Universal Windows Platform (UWP)**. UWP apps can be built using C++ and the DirectX UI, or JavaScript and HTML, or C# using a custom fork of modern .NET that is not cross-platform but provides full access to the underlying WinRT APIs.

UWP apps can only execute on the Windows 10 platform, not earlier versions of Windows, but UWP apps can run on Xbox and Windows Mixed Reality headsets with motion controllers.

Many Windows developers rejected Windows Store and UWP apps because they have limited access to the underlying system. Microsoft recently created **Project Reunion** and **WinUI 3**, which work together to allow Windows developers to bring some of the benefits of modern Windows development to their existing WPF apps and allow them to have the same benefits and system integrations that UWP apps have. This initiative is now known as **Windows App SDK**.

Understanding modern .NET support for legacy Windows platforms

The on-disk size of the .NET SDKs for Linux and macOS is about 330 MB. The on-disk size of the .NET SDK for Windows is about 440 MB. This is because it includes the Windows Desktop Runtime, which allows the legacy Windows application platforms Windows Forms and WPF to be run on modern .NET.

There are many enterprise applications built using Windows Forms and WPF that need to be maintained or enhanced with new features, but until recently they were stuck on .NET Framework, which is now a legacy platform. With modern .NET and its Windows Desktop Pack, these apps can now use the full modern capabilities of .NET.

Structuring projects

How should you structure your projects? So far, we have built small individual console apps to illustrate language or library features. In the rest of this book, we will build multiple projects using different technologies that work together to provide a single solution.

With large, complex solutions, it can be difficult to navigate amongst all the code. So, the primary reason to structure your projects is to make it easier to find components. It is good to have an overall name for your solution or workspace that reflects the application or solution.

We will build multiple projects for a fictional company named **Northwind**. We will name the solution or workspace `PracticalApps` and use the name `Northwind` as a prefix for all the project names.

There are many ways to structure and name projects and solutions, for example, using a folder hierarchy as well as a naming convention. If you work in a team, make sure you know how your team does it.

Structuring projects in a solution or workspace

It is good to have a naming convention for your projects in a solution or workspace so that any developer can tell what each one does instantly. A common choice is to use the type of project, for example, class library, console app, website, and so on, as shown in the following table:

Name	Description
Northwind.Common	A class library project for common types like interfaces, enums, classes, records, and structs, used across multiple projects.
Northwind.Common.EntityModels	A class library project for common EF Core entity models. Entity models are often used on both the server and client side, so it is best to separate dependencies on specific database providers.
Northwind.Common.DataContext	A class library project for the EF Core database context with dependencies on specific database providers.
Northwind.Web	An ASP.NET Core project for a simple website that uses a mixture of static HTML files and dynamic Razor Pages.
Northwind.Razor.Component	A class library project for Razor Pages used in multiple projects.
Northwind.Mvc	An ASP.NET Core project for a complex website that uses the MVC pattern and can be more easily unit tested.
Northwind.WebApi	An ASP.NET Core project for an HTTP API service. A good choice for integrating with websites because they can use any JavaScript library or Blazor to interact with the service.
Northwind.OData	An ASP.NET Core project for an HTTP API service that implements the OData standard to enable a client to control queries.
Northwind.GraphQL	An ASP.NET Core project for an HTTP API service that implements the GraphQL standard to enable a client to control queries.
Northwind.gRPC	An ASP.NET Core project for a gRPC service. A good choice for integrating with apps built with any language and platform since gRPC has wide support and is highly efficient and performant.
Northwind.SignalR	An ASP.NET Core project for real-time communication.
Northwind.AzureFuncs	An ASP.NET Core project for implementing a serverless nanoservice for hosting in Azure Functions.
Northwind.BlazorServer	An ASP.NET Core Blazor Server project.
Northwind.BlazorWasm.Client	An ASP.NET Core Blazor WebAssembly client-side project.
Northwind.BlazorWasm.Server	An ASP.NET Core Blazor WebAssembly server-side project.
Northwind.Maui	A .NET MAUI project for a cross-platform desktop/mobile app.
Northwind.MauiBlazor	A .NET MAUI project for hosting Blazor components with native integrations with the OS.

Using other project templates

When you install the .NET SDK, there are many project templates included:

1. At a command prompt or terminal, enter the following command:

```
dotnet new --list
```

2. You will see a list of currently installed templates, including templates for Windows desktop development if you are running on Windows, as shown in *Figure 13.2*:

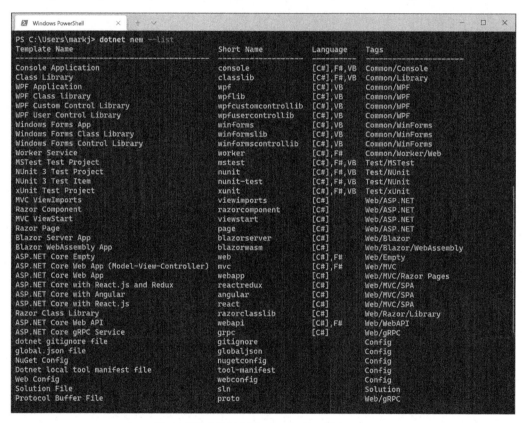

Figure 13.2: A list of dotnet project templates

3. Note the web-related project templates, including ones for creating SPAs using Blazor, Angular, and React. But another common JavaScript SPA library is missing: Vue.

Installing additional template packs

Developers can install lots of additional template packs:

1. Start a browser and navigate to http://dotnetnew.azurewebsites.net/.

2. Enter vue in the textbox and note the list of available templates for Vue.js, including one published by Microsoft, as shown in *Figure 13.3*:

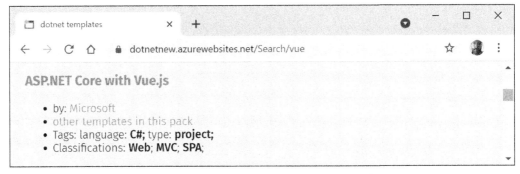

Figure 13.3: A project template for Vue.js by Microsoft

3. Click on **ASP.NET Core with Vue.js** by Microsoft, and note the instructions for installing and using this template, as shown in the following commands:

```
dotnet new --install "Microsoft.AspNetCore.SpaTemplates"
dotnet new vue
```

4. Click **View other templates in this package**, and note that as well as a project template for Vue.js, it also has project templates for Aurelia and Knockout.js.

Building an entity data model for the Northwind database

Practical applications usually need to work with data in a relational database or another data store. In this chapter, we will define an entity data model for the Northwind database stored in SQL Server or SQLite. It will be used in most of the apps that we create in subsequent chapters.

> The Northwind4SQLServer.sql and Northwind4SQLite.sql script files are different. The script for SQL Server creates 13 tables as well as related views and stored procedures. The script for SQLite is a simplified version that only creates 10 tables because SQLite does not support as many features. The main projects in this book only need those 10 tables so you can complete every task in this book with either database.

Instructions to install SQL Server and SQLite can be found in *Chapter 10, Working with Data Using Entity Framework Core*. In that chapter, you will also find instructions for installing the dotnet-ef tool, which you will use to scaffold an entity model from an existing database.

> **Good Practice:** You should create a separate class library project for your entity data models. This allows easier sharing between backend web servers and frontend desktop, mobile, and Blazor WebAssembly clients.

Creating a class library for entity models using SQLite

You will now define entity data models in a class library so that they can be reused in other types of projects including client-side app models. If you are not using SQL Server, you will need to create this class library for SQLite. If you are using SQL Server, then you can create both a class library for SQLite and one for SQL Server and then switch between them as you choose.

We will automatically generate some entity models using the EF Core command-line tool:

1. Use your preferred code editor to create a new solution/workspace named `PracticalApps`.

2. Add a class library project, as defined in the following list:

    1. Project template: **Class Library** / `classlib`
    2. Workspace/solution file and folder: `PracticalApps`
    3. Project file and folder: `Northwind.Common.EntityModels.Sqlite`

3. In the `Northwind.Common.EntityModels.Sqlite` project, add package references for the SQLite database provider and EF Core design-time support, as shown in the following markup:

```
<ItemGroup>
  <PackageReference
    Include="Microsoft.EntityFrameworkCore.Sqlite"
    Version="6.0.0" />
  <PackageReference
    Include="Microsoft.EntityFrameworkCore.Design"
    Version="6.0.0">
    <PrivateAssets>all</PrivateAssets>
    <IncludeAssets>runtime; build; native; contentfiles; analyzers;
buildtransitive</IncludeAssets>
  </PackageReference>
</ItemGroup>
```

4. Delete the `Class1.cs` file.

5. Build the project.

6. Create the `Northwind.db` file for SQLite by copying the `Northwind4SQLite.sql` file into the `PracticalApps` folder, and then enter the following command at a command prompt or terminal:

```
sqlite3 Northwind.db -init Northwind4SQLite.sql
```

7. Be patient because this command might take a while to create the database structure, as shown in the following output:

```
-- Loading resources from Northwind4SQLite.sql
SQLite version 3.35.5 2021-04-19 14:49:49
Enter ".help" for usage hints.
sqlite>
```

8. Press *Ctrl + C* on Windows or *Cmd + D* on macOS to exit SQLite command mode.

9. Open a command prompt or terminal for the `Northwind.Common.EntityModels.Sqlite` folder.

10. At the command line, generate entity class models for all tables, as shown in the following commands:

```
dotnet ef dbcontext scaffold "Filename=../Northwind.db" Microsoft.
EntityFrameworkCore.Sqlite --namespace Packt.Shared --data-annotations
```

Note the following:

- The command to perform: `dbcontext scaffold`
- The connection strings. `"Filename=../Northwind.db"`
- The database provider: `Microsoft.EntityFrameworkCore.Sqlite`
- The namespace: `--namespace Packt.Shared`
- To use data annotations as well as the Fluent API: `--data-annotations`

11. Note the build messages and warnings, as shown in the following output:

```
Build started...
Build succeeded.
To protect potentially sensitive information in your connection string,
you should move it out of source code. You can avoid scaffolding the
connection string by using the Name= syntax to read it from configuration
- see https://go.microsoft.com/fwlink/?linkid=2131148. For more
guidance on storing connection strings, see http://go.microsoft.com/
fwlink/?LinkId=723263.
```

Improving the class-to-table mapping

The `dotnet-ef` command-line tool generates different code for SQL Server and SQLite because they support different levels of functionality.

For example, SQL Server text columns can have limits to the number of characters. SQLite does not support this. So, `dotnet-ef` will generate validation attributes to ensure `string` properties are limited to a specified number of characters for SQL Server but not for SQLite, as shown in the following code:

```
// SQLite database provider-generated code
[Column(TypeName = "nvarchar (15)")]
public string CategoryName { get; set; } = null!;
```

```
// SQL Server database provider-generated code
[StringLength(15)]
public string CategoryName { get; set; } = null!;
```

Neither database provider will mark non-nullable string properties as required:

```
// no runtime validation of non-nullable property
public string CategoryName { get; set; } = null!;
// nullable property
public string? Description { get; set; }

// decorate with attribute to perform runtime validation
[Required]
public string CategoryName { get; set; } = null!;
```

We will make some small changes to improve the entity model mapping and validation rules for SQLite:

1. Open the Customer.cs file and add a regular expression to validate its primary key value to only allow uppercase Western characters, as shown highlighted in the following code:

   ```
   [Key]
   [Column(TypeName = "nchar (5)")]
   [RegularExpression("[A-Z]{5}")]
   public string CustomerId { get; set; }
   ```

2. Activate your code editor's find and replace feature (in Visual Studio 2022, navigate to **Edit | Find and Replace | Quick Replace**), toggle on **Use Regular Expressions**, and then type a regular expression in the search box, as shown in the following expression:

   ```
   \[Column\(TypeName = "(nchar|nvarchar) \((.*)\)"\)\]
   ```

3. In the replace box, type a replacement regular expression, as shown in the following expression:

   ```
   $&\n    [StringLength($2)]
   ```

    After the newline character, \n, I have included four space characters to indent correctly on my system, which uses two space characters per indentation level. You can insert as many as you wish.

4. Set the find and replace to search files in the current project.
5. Execute the search and replace to replace all, as shown in *Figure 13.4*:

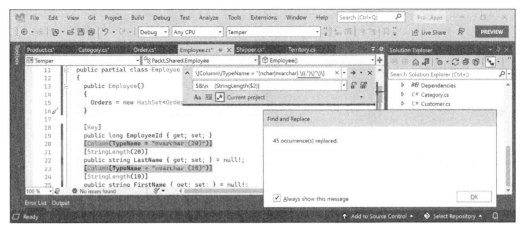

Figure 13.4: Search and replace all matches using regular expressions in Visual Studio 2022

6. Change any date/time properties, for example, in `Employee.cs`, to use a nullable `DateTime` instead of an array of bytes, as shown in the following code:

```
// before
[Column(TypeName = "datetime")]
public byte[] BirthDate { get; set; }

// after
[Column(TypeName = "datetime")]
public DateTime? BirthDate { get; set; }
```

Use your code editor's find feature to search for `"datetime"` to find all the properties that need changing.

7. Change any money properties, for example, in `Order.cs`, to use a nullable `decimal` instead of an array of bytes, as shown in the following code:

```
// before
[Column(TypeName =  "money")]
public byte[] Freight { get; set; }

// after
[Column(TypeName = "money")]
public decimal? Freight { get; set; }
```

Use your code editor's find feature to search for `"money"` to find all the properties that need changing.

8. Change any `bit` properties, for example, in `Product.cs`, to use a `bool` instead of an array of bytes, as shown in the following code:

```
// before
[Column(TypeName = "bit")]
public byte[] Discontinued { get; set; } = null!;

// after
[Column(TypeName = "bit")]
public bool Discontinued { get; set; }
```

 Use your code editor's find feature to search for "bit" to find all the properties that need changing.

9. In `Category.cs`, make the `CategoryId` property an `int`, as shown highlighted in the following code:

```
[Key]
public int CategoryId { get; set; }
```

10. In `Category.cs`, make the `CategoryName` property required, as shown highlighted in the following code:

```
[Required]
[Column(TypeName = "nvarchar (15)")]
[StringLength(15)]
public string CategoryName { get; set; }
```

11. In `Customer.cs`, make the `CompanyName` property required, as shown highlighted in the following code:

```
[Required]
[Column(TypeName = "nvarchar (40)")]
[StringLength(40)]
public string CompanyName { get; set; }
```

12. In `Employee.cs`, make the `EmployeeId` property an `int` instead of a `long`.

13. In `Employee.cs`, make the `FirstName` and `LastName` properties required.

14. In `Employee.cs`, make the `ReportsTo` property an `int?` instead of a `long?`.

15. In `EmployeeTerritory.cs`, make the `EmployeeId` property an `int` instead of a `long`.

16. In `EmployeeTerritory.cs`, make the `TerritoryId` property required.

17. In `Order.cs`, make the `OrderId` property an `int` instead of a `long`.

18. In `Order.cs`, decorate the `CustomerId` property with a regular expression to enforce five uppercase characters.

19. In `Order.cs`, make the `EmployeeId` property an `int?` instead of a `long?`.

20. In `Order.cs`, make the `ShipVia` property an `int?` instead of a `long?`.

21. In `OrderDetail.cs`, make the `OrderId` property an `int` instead of a `long`.

22. In `OrderDetail.cs`, make the `ProductId` property an `int` instead of a `long`.

23. In `OrderDetail.cs`, make the `Quantity` property a `short` instead of a `long`.

24. In `Product.cs`, make the `ProductId` property an `int` instead of a `long`.

25. In `Product.cs`, make the `ProductName` property required.

26. In `Product.cs`, make the `SupplierId` and `CategoryId` properties an `int?` instead of a `long?`.

27. In `Product.cs`, make the `UnitsInStock`, `UnitsOnOrder`, and `ReorderLevel` properties a `short?` instead of a `long?`.

28. In `Shipper.cs`, make the `ShipperId` property an `int` instead of a `long`.

29. In `Shipper.cs`, make the `CompanyName` property required.

30. In `Supplier.cs`, make the `SupplierId` property an `int` instead of a `long`.

31. In `Supplier.cs`, make the `CompanyName` property required.

32. In `Territory.cs`, make the `RegionId` property an `int` instead of a `long`.

33. In `Territory.cs`, make the `TerritoryId` and `TerritoryDescription` properties required.

Now that we have a class library for the entity classes, we can create a class library for the database context.

Creating a class library for a Northwind database context

You will now define a database context class library:

1. Add a class library project to the solution/workspace, as defined in the following list:

    1. Project template: **Class Library** / `classlib`

    2. Workspace/solution file and folder: `PracticalApps`

    3. Project file and folder: `Northwind.Common.DataContext.Sqlite`

2. In Visual Studio, set the startup project for the solution to the current selection.

3. In Visual Studio Code, select `Northwind.Common.DataContext.Sqlite` as the active OmniSharp project.

4. In the `Northwind.Common.DataContext.Sqlite` project, add a project reference to the `Northwind.Common.EntityModels.Sqlite` project and add a package reference to the EF Core data provider for SQLite, as shown in the following markup:

```
<ItemGroup>
  <PackageReference
    Include="Microsoft.EntityFrameworkCore.SQLite"
    Version="6.0.0" />
</ItemGroup>
<ItemGroup>
```

```
<ProjectReference Include=
  "..\Northwind.Common.EntityModels.Sqlite\Northwind.Common
.EntityModels.Sqlite.csproj" />
</ItemGroup>
```

 The path to the project reference should not have a line break in your project file.

5. In the `Northwind.Common.DataContext.Sqlite` project, delete the `Class1.cs` class file.

6. Build the `Northwind.Common.DataContext.Sqlite` project.

7. Move the `NorthwindContext.cs` file from the `Northwind.Common.EntityModels.Sqlite` project/folder to the `Northwind.Common.DataContext.Sqlite` project/folder.

 In Visual Studio **Solution Explorer**, if you drag and drop a file between projects it will be copied. If you hold down *Shift* while dragging and dropping, it will be moved. In Visual Studio Code **EXPLORER**, if you drag and drop a file between projects it will be moved. If you hold down *Ctrl* while dragging and dropping, it will be copied.

8. In `NorthwindContext.cs`, in the `OnConfiguring` method, remove the compiler `#warning` about the connection string.

 Good Practice: We will override the default database connection string in any projects such as websites that need to work with the Northwind database, so the class derived from `DbContext` must have a constructor with a `DbContextOptions` parameter for this to work, as shown in the following code:

```
public NorthwindContext(DbContextOptions<NorthwindConte
xt> options)
  : base(options)
{
}
```

9. In the `OnModelCreating` method, remove all Fluent API statements that call the `ValueGeneratedNever` method to configure primary key properties like `SupplierId` to never generate a value automatically or call the `HasDefaultValueSql` method, as shown in the following code:

```
modelBuilder.Entity<Supplier>(entity =>
{
  entity.Property(e => e.SupplierId).ValueGeneratedNever();
});
```

If we do not remove the configuration like the statements above, then when we add new suppliers, the `SupplierId` value would always be 0 and we would only be able to add one supplier with that value and then all other attempts would throw an exception.

10. For the `Product` entity, tell SQLite that the `UnitPrice` can be converted from `decimal` to `double`. The `OnModelCreating` method should now be much simplified, as shown in the following code:

```
protected override void OnModelCreating(ModelBuilder modelBuilder)
{
  modelBuilder.Entity<OrderDetail>(entity =>
  {
    entity.HasKey(e => new { e.OrderId, e.ProductId });

    entity.HasOne(d => d.Order)
      .WithMany(p => p.OrderDetails)
      .HasForeignKey(d => d.OrderId)
      .OnDelete(DeleteBehavior.ClientSetNull);

    entity.HasOne(d => d.Product)
      .WithMany(p => p.OrderDetails)
      .HasForeignKey(d => d.ProductId)
      .OnDelete(DeleteBehavior.ClientSetNull);
  });

  modelBuilder.Entity<Product>()
    .Property(product => product.UnitPrice)
    .HasConversion<double>();

  OnModelCreatingPartial(modelBuilder);
}
```

11. Add a class named `NorthwindContextExtensions.cs` and modify its contents to define an extension method that adds the Northwind database context to a collection of dependency services, as shown in the following code:

```
using Microsoft.EntityFrameworkCore; // UseSqlite
using Microsoft.Extensions.DependencyInjection; // IServiceCollection

namespace Packt.Shared;

public static class NorthwindContextExtensions
{
  /// <summary>
  /// Adds NorthwindContext to the specified IServiceCollection. Uses the
  Sqlite database provider.
```

```
/// </summary>
/// <param name="services"></param>
/// <param name="relativePath">Set to override the default of ".."</
param>
/// <returns>An IServiceCollection that can be used to add more
services.</returns>
public static IServiceCollection AddNorthwindContext(
  this IServiceCollection services, string relativePath = "..")
{
  string databasePath = Path.Combine(relativePath, "Northwind.db");

  services.AddDbContext<NorthwindContext>(options =>
    options.UseSqlite($"Data Source={databasePath}")
  );

  return services;
}
}
```

12. Build the two class libraries and fix any compiler errors.

Creating a class library for entity models using SQL Server

To use SQL Server, you will not need to do anything if you already set up the Northwind database in *Chapter 10, Working with Data Using Entity Framework Core*. But you will now create the entity models using the dotnet-ef tool:

1. Use your preferred code editor to create a new solution/workspace named PracticalApps.

2. Add a class library project, as defined in the following list:

    1. Project template: **Class Library** / classlib

    2. Workspace/solution file and folder: PracticalApps

    3. Project file and folder: Northwind.Common.EntityModels.SqlServer

3. In the Northwind.Common.EntityModels.SqlServer project, add package references for the SQL Server database provider and EF Core design-time support, as shown in the following markup:

```
<ItemGroup>
  <PackageReference
    Include="Microsoft.EntityFrameworkCore.SqlServer"
    Version="6.0.0" />
  <PackageReference
    Include="Microsoft.EntityFrameworkCore.Design"
```

```
    Version="6.0.0">
    <PrivateAssets>all</PrivateAssets>
    <IncludeAssets>runtime; build; native; contentfiles; analyzers;
buildtransitive</IncludeAssets>
    </PackageReference>
</ItemGroup>
```

4. Delete the `Class1.cs` file.

5. Build the project.

6. Open a command prompt or terminal for the `Northwind.Common.EntityModels.SqlServer` folder.

7. At the command line, generate entity class models for all tables, as shown in the following commands:

```
dotnet ef dbcontext scaffold "Data Source=.;Initial
Catalog=Northwind;Integrated Security=true;" Microsoft.
EntityFrameworkCore.SqlServer --namespace Packt.Shared --data-annotations
```

Note the following:

-   The command to perform: `dbcontext scaffold`

-   The connection strings. `"Data Source=.;Initial Catalog=Northwind;Integrated Security=true;"`

-   The database provider: `Microsoft.EntityFrameworkCore.SqlServer`

-   The namespace: `--namespace Packt.Shared`

-   To use data annotations as well as the Fluent API: `--data-annotations`

8. In `Customer.cs`, add a regular expression to validate its primary key value to only allow uppercase Western characters, as shown highlighted in the following code:

```
[Key]
[StringLength(5)]
[RegularExpression("[A-Z]{5}")]
public string CustomerId { get; set; } = null!;
```

9. In `Customer.cs`, make the `CustomerId` and `CompanyName` properties required.

10. Add a class library project to the solution/workspace, as defined in the following list:

    1. Project template: **Class Library** / `classlib`

    2. Workspace/solution file and folder: `PracticalApps`

    3. Project file and folder: `Northwind.Common.DataContext.SqlServer`

11. In Visual Studio Code, select `Northwind.Common.DataContext.SqlServer` as the active OmniSharp project.

12. In the `Northwind.Common.DataContext.SqlServer` project, add a project reference to the `Northwind.Common.EntityModels.SqlServer` project and add a package reference to the EF Core data provider for SQL Server, as shown in the following markup:

```
<ItemGroup>
  <PackageReference
    Include="Microsoft.EntityFrameworkCore.SqlServer"
    Version="6.0.0" />
</ItemGroup>

<ItemGroup>
  <ProjectReference Include=
    "..\Northwind.Common.EntityModels.SqlServer\Northwind.Common
.EntityModels.SqlServer.csproj" />
</ItemGroup>
```

13. In the `Northwind.Common.DataContext.SqlServer` project, delete the `Class1.cs` class file.

14. Build the `Northwind.Common.DataContext.SqlServer` project.

15. Move the `NorthwindContext.cs` file from the `Northwind.Common.EntityModels.SqlServer` project/folder to the `Northwind.Common.DataContext.SqlServer` project/folder.

16. In `NorthwindContext.cs`, remove the compiler warning about the connection string.

17. Add a class named `NorthwindContextExtensions.cs`, and modify its contents to define an extension method that adds the Northwind database context to a collection of dependency services, as shown in the following code:

```
using Microsoft.EntityFrameworkCore; // UseSqlServer
using Microsoft.Extensions.DependencyInjection; // IServiceCollection

namespace Packt.Shared;

public static class NorthwindContextExtensions
{
  /// <summary>
  /// Adds NorthwindContext to the specified IServiceCollection. Uses the
SqlServer database provider.
  /// </summary>
  /// <param name="services"></param>
  /// <param name="connectionString">Set to override the default.</param>
  /// <returns>An IServiceCollection that can be used to add more
services.</returns>
  public static IServiceCollection AddNorthwindContext(
    this IServiceCollection services, string connectionString =
      "Data Source=.;Initial Catalog=Northwind;"
      + "Integrated Security=true;MultipleActiveResultsets=true;")
  {
```

```
        services.AddDbContext<NorthwindContext>(options =>
          options.UseSqlServer(connectionString));

        return services;
      }
    }
```

18. Build the two class libraries and fix any compiler errors.

 Good Practice: We have provided optional arguments for the
AddNorthwindContext method so that we can override the hardcoded
SQLite database filename path or the SQL Server database connection string.
This will allow us more flexibility, for example, to load these values from a
configuration file.

Practicing and exploring

Explore this chapter's topics with deeper research.

Exercise 13.1 – Test your knowledge

1. .NET 6 is cross-platform. Windows Forms and WPF apps can run on .NET 6. Can those apps therefore run on macOS and Linux?

2. How does a Windows Forms app define its user interface, and why is this a potential problem?

3. How can a WPF or UWP app define its user interface, and why is this good for developers?

Exercise 13.2 – Explore topics

Use the links on the following page to learn more detail about the topics covered in this chapter:

```
https://github.com/markjprice/cs10dotnet6/blob/main/book-links.md#chapter-13---
introducing-practical-applications-of-c-and-net
```

Summary

In this chapter, you have been introduced to some of the app models and workloads that you can use to build practical applications using C# and .NET.

You have created two to four class libraries to define an entity data model for working with the Northwind database using either SQLite or SQL Server or both.

In the following six chapters, you will learn the details about how to build the following:

- Simple websites using static HTML pages and dynamic Razor Pages.
- Complex websites using the Model-View-Controller (MVC) design pattern.
- Web services that can be called by any platform that can make an HTTP request and client websites that call those web services.
- Blazor user interface components that can be hosted on a web server, in the browser, or on hybrid web-native mobile and desktop apps.
- Services that implement remote procedure calls using gRPC.
- Services that implement real-time communication using SignalR.
- Services that provide easy and flexible access to an EF Core model.
- Serverless nano services hosted in Azure Functions.
- Cross-platform native mobile and desktop apps using .NET MAUI.

14

Building Websites Using ASP.NET Core Razor Pages

This chapter is about building websites with a modern HTTP architecture on the server side using Microsoft ASP.NET Core. You will learn about building simple websites using the ASP.NET Core Razor Pages feature introduced with ASP.NET Core 2.0 and the Razor class library feature introduced with ASP.NET Core 2.1.

This chapter will cover the following topics:

- Understanding web development
- Understanding ASP.NET Core
- Exploring ASP.NET Core Razor Pages
- Using Entity Framework Core with ASP.NET Core
- Using Razor class libraries
- Configuring services and the HTTP request pipeline

Understanding web development

Developing for the web means developing with **Hypertext Transfer Protocol (HTTP)**, so we will start by reviewing this important foundational technology.

Understanding HTTP

To communicate with a web server, the client, also known as the **user agent**, makes calls over the network using HTTP. As such, HTTP is the technical underpinning of the web. So, when we talk about websites and web services, we mean that they use HTTP to communicate between a client (often a web browser) and a server.

A client makes an HTTP request for a resource, such as a page, uniquely identified by a **Uniform Resource Locator (URL)**, and the server sends back an HTTP response, as shown in *Figure 14.1*:

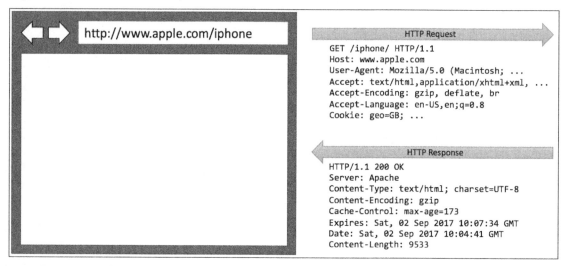

Figure 14.1: An HTTP request and response

You can use Google Chrome and other browsers to record requests and responses.

Good Practice: Google Chrome is available on more operating systems than any other browser, and it has powerful, built-in developer tools, so it is a good first choice of browser for testing your websites. Always test your web application with Chrome and at least two other browsers, for example, Firefox and Safari for macOS and iPhone. Microsoft Edge switched from using Microsoft's own rendering engine to using Chromium in 2019, so it is less important to test with it. If Microsoft's Internet Explorer is used at all, it tends to mostly be inside organizations for intranets.

Understanding the components of a URL

A URL is made up of several components:

- **Scheme**: http (clear text) or https (encrypted).
- **Domain**: For a production website or service, the **top-level domain (TLD)** might be example.com. You might have subdomains such as www, jobs, or extranet. During development, you typically use localhost for all websites and services.

- **Port number**: For a production website or service, 80 for http, 443 for https. These port numbers are usually inferred from the scheme. During development, other port numbers are commonly used, such as 5000, 5001, and so on, to differentiate between websites and services that all use the shared domain localhost.
- **Path**: A relative path to a resource, for example, /customers/germany.
- **Query string**: A way to pass parameter values, for example, ?country=Germany&searchtext=shoes.
- **Fragment**: A reference to an element on a web page using its id, for example, #toc.

Assigning port numbers for projects in this book

In this book, we will use the domain localhost for all websites and services, so we will use port numbers to differentiate projects when multiple need to execute at the same time, as shown in the following table:

Project	Description	Port numbers
Northwind.Web	ASP.NET Core Razor Pages website	5000 HTTP, 5001 HTTPS
Northwind.Mvc	ASP.NET Core MVC website	5000 HTTP, 5001 HTTPS
Northwind.WebApi	ASP.NET Core Web API service	5002 HTTPS, 5008 HTTP
Minimal.WebApi	ASP.NET Core Web API (minimal)	5003 HTTPS
Northwind.OData	ASP.NET Core OData service	5004 HTTPS
Northwind.GraphQL	ASP.NET Core GraphQL service	5005 HTTPS
Northwind.gRPC	ASP.NET Core gRPC service	5006 HTTPS
Northwind.AzureFuncs	Azure Functions nanoservice	7071 HTTP

Using Google Chrome to make HTTP requests

Let's explore how to use Google Chrome to make HTTP requests:

1. Start Google Chrome.
2. Navigate to **More tools | Developer tools**.

3. Click the **Network** tab, and Chrome should immediately start recording the network traffic between your browser and any web servers (note the red circle), as shown in *Figure 14.2*:

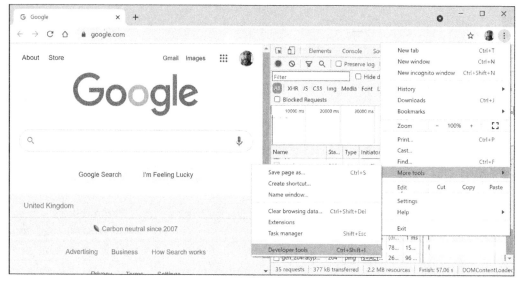

Figure 14.2: Chrome Developer Tools recording network traffic

4. In Chrome's address box, enter the address of Microsoft's website for learning ASP.NET, as shown in the following URL:

```
https://dotnet.microsoft.com/learn/aspnet
```

5. In Developer Tools, in the list of recorded requests, scroll to the top and click on the first entry, the row where the **Type** is **document**, as shown in *Figure 14.3*:

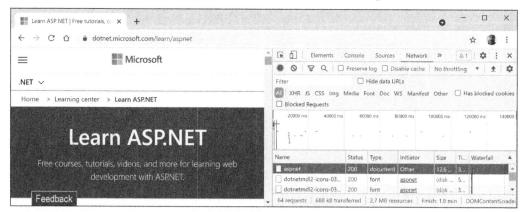

Figure 14.3: Recorded requests in Developer Tools

6. On the right-hand side, click on the **Headers** tab, and you will see details about **Request Headers** and **Response Headers**, as shown in *Figure 14.4*:

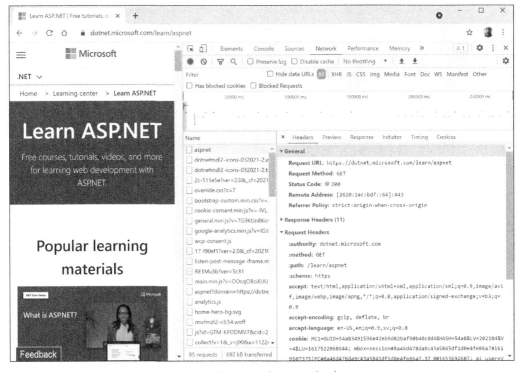

Figure 14.4: Request and response headers

Note the following aspects:

- **Request Method** is GET. Other HTTP methods that you could see here include POST, PUT, DELETE, HEAD, and PATCH.

- **Status Code** is 200 OK. This means that the server found the resource that the browser requested and has returned it in the body of the response. Other status codes that you might see in response to a GET request include 301 Moved Permanently, 400 Bad Request, 401 Unauthorized, and 404 Not Found.

- **Request Headers** sent by the browser to the web server include:

  - **accept**, which lists what formats the browser accepts. In this case, the browser is saying it understands HTML, XHTML, XML, and some image formats, but it will accept all other files (*/*). Default weightings, also known as quality values, are 1.0. XML is specified with a quality value of 0.9 so it is preferred less than HTML or XHTML. All other file types are given a quality value of 0.8 so are least preferred.

  - **accept-encoding**, which lists what compression algorithms the browser understands, in this case, GZIP, DEFLATE, and Brotli.

  - **accept-language**, which lists the human languages it would prefer the content to use. In this case, US English, which has a default quality value of 1.0, then any dialect of English that has an explicitly specified quality value of 0.9, and then any dialect of Swedish that has an explicitly specified quality value of 0.8.

- **Response Headers**, content-encoding tells me the server has sent back the HTML web page response compressed using the GZIP algorithm because it knows that the client can decompress that format. (This is not visible in *Figure 14.4* because there is not enough space to expand the **Response Headers** section.)

7. Close Chrome.

Understanding client-side web development technologies

When building websites, a developer needs to know more than just C# and .NET. On the client (that is, in the web browser), you will use a combination of the following technologies:

- **HTML5**: This is used for the content and structure of a web page.
- **CSS3**: This is used for the styles applied to elements on the web page.
- **JavaScript**: This is used to code any business logic needed on the web page, for example, validating form input or making calls to a web service to fetch more data needed by the web page.

Although HTML5, CSS3, and JavaScript are the fundamental components of frontend web development, there are many additional technologies that can make frontend web development more productive, including Bootstrap, the world's most popular frontend open-source toolkit, and CSS preprocessors such as SASS and LESS for styling, Microsoft's TypeScript language for writing more robust code, and JavaScript libraries such as jQuery, Angular, React, and Vue. All these higher-level technologies ultimately translate or compile to the underlying three core technologies, so they work across all modern browsers.

As part of the build and deploy process, you will likely use technologies such as Node.js; Node Package Manager (npm) and Yarn, which are both client-side package managers; and webpack, which is a popular module bundler, a tool for compiling, transforming, and bundling website source files.

Understanding ASP.NET Core

Microsoft ASP.NET Core is part of a history of Microsoft technologies used to build websites and services that have evolved over the years:

- **Active Server Pages (ASP)** was released in 1996 and was Microsoft's first attempt at a platform for dynamic server-side execution of website code. ASP files contain a mix of HTML and code that executes on the server written in the VBScript language.
- **ASP.NET Web Forms** was released in 2002 with the .NET Framework and was designed to enable non-web developers, such as those familiar with Visual Basic, to quickly create websites by dragging and dropping visual components and writing event-driven code in Visual Basic or C#. Web Forms should be avoided for new .NET Framework web projects in favor of ASP.NET MVC.

- **Windows Communication Foundation (WCF)** was released in 2006 and enables developers to build SOAP and REST services. SOAP is powerful but complex, so it should be avoided unless you need advanced features, such as distributed transactions and complex messaging topologies.

- **ASP.NET MVC** was released in 2009 to cleanly separate the concerns of web developers between the **models**, which temporarily store the data; the **views**, which present the data using various formats in the UI; and the **controllers**, which fetch the model and pass it to a view. This separation enables improved reuse and unit testing.

- **ASP.NET Web API** was released in 2012 and enables developers to create HTTP services (aka REST services) that are simpler and more scalable than SOAP services.

- **ASP.NET SignalR** was released in 2013 and enables real-time communication in websites by abstracting underlying technologies and techniques, such as WebSockets and Long Polling. This enables website features such as live chat or updates to time-sensitive data such as stock prices across a wide variety of web browsers, even when they do not support an underlying technology such as WebSockets.

- **ASP.NET Core** was released in 2016 and combines modern implementations of .NET Framework technologies such as MVC, Web API, and SignalR, with newer technologies such as Razor Pages, gRPC, and Blazor, all running on modern .NET. Therefore, it can execute cross-platform. ASP.NET Core has many project templates to get you started with its supported technologies.

 Good Practice: Choose ASP.NET Core to develop websites and services because it includes web-related technologies that are modern and cross-platform.

ASP.NET Core 2.0 to 2.2 can run on .NET Framework 4.6.1 or later (Windows only) as well as .NET Core 2.0 or later (cross-platform). ASP.NET Core 3.0 only supports .NET Core 3.0. ASP.NET Core 6.0 only supports .NET 6.0.

Classic ASP.NET versus modern ASP.NET Core

Until now, ASP.NET has been built on top of a large assembly in the .NET Framework named System.Web.dll and it is tightly coupled to Microsoft's Windows-only web server named **Internet Information Services (IIS)**. Over the years, this assembly has accumulated a lot of features, many of which are not suitable for modern cross-platform development.

ASP.NET Core is a major redesign of ASP.NET. It removes the dependency on the System.Web.dll assembly and IIS and is composed of modular lightweight packages, just like the rest of modern .NET. Using IIS as the web server is still supported by ASP.NET Core but there is a better option.

You can develop and run ASP.NET Core applications cross-platform on Windows, macOS, and Linux. Microsoft has even created a cross-platform, super-performant web server named **Kestrel**, and the entire stack is open source.

ASP.NET Core 2.2 or later projects default to the new in-process hosting model. This gives a 400% performance improvement when hosting in Microsoft IIS, but Microsoft still recommends using Kestrel for even better performance.

Creating an empty ASP.NET Core project

We will create an ASP.NET Core project that will show a list of suppliers from the Northwind database.

The dotnet tool has many project templates that do a lot of work for you, but it can be difficult to know which works best for a given situation, so we will start with the empty website project template and then add features step by step so that you can understand all the pieces:

1. Use your preferred code editor to add a new project, as defined in the following list:

    1. Project template: **ASP.NET Core Empty** / web
    2. Language: C#
    3. Workspace/solution file and folder: PracticalApps
    4. Project file and folder: Northwind.Web
    5. For Visual Studio 2022, leave all other options as their defaults, for example, **Configure for HTTPS** selected, and **Enable Docker** cleared

2. In Visual Studio Code, select Northwind.Web as the active OmniSharp project.

3. Build the Northwind.Web project.

4. Open the Northwind.Web.csproj file and note that the project is like a class library except that the SDK is Microsoft.NET.Sdk.Web, as shown highlighted in the following markup:

```
<Project Sdk="Microsoft.NET.Sdk.Web">

  <PropertyGroup>
    <TargetFramework>net6.0</TargetFramework>
    <Nullable>enable</Nullable>
    <ImplicitUsings>enable</ImplicitUsings>
  </PropertyGroup>

</Project>
```

5. If you are using Visual Studio 2022, in **Solution Explorer**, toggle **Show All Files**.

6. Expand the obj folder, expand the Debug folder, expand the net6.0 folder, select the Northwind.Web.GlobalUsings.g.cs file, and note the implicitly imported namespaces include all the ones for a console app or class library, as well as some ASP.NET Core ones, such as Microsoft.AspNetCore.Builder, as shown in the following code:

```
// <autogenerated />
global using global::Microsoft.AspNetCore.Builder;
```

```
global using global::Microsoft.AspNetCore.Hosting;
global using global::Microsoft.AspNetCore.Http;
global using global::Microsoft.AspNetCore.Routing;
global using global::Microsoft.Extensions.Configuration;
global using global::Microsoft.Extensions.DependencyInjection;
global using global::Microsoft.Extensions.Hosting;
global using global::Microsoft.Extensions.Logging;
global using global::System;
global using global::System.Collections.Generic;
global using global::System.IO;
global using global::System.Linq;
global using global::System.Net.Http;
global using global::System.Net.Http.Json;
global using global::System.Threading;
global using global::System.Threading.Tasks;
```

7. Collapse the obj folder.

8. Open Program.cs, and note the following:

   - An ASP.NET Core project is like a top-level console application, with a hidden Main method as its entry point that has an argument passed using the name args.

   - It calls WebApplication.CreateBuilder, which creates a host for the website using defaults for a web host that is then built.

   - The website will respond to all HTTP GET requests with plain text: Hello World!.

   - The call to the Run method is a blocking call, so the hidden Main method does not return until the web server stops running, as shown in the following code:

```
var builder = WebApplication.CreateBuilder(args);
var app = builder.Build();

app.MapGet("/", () => "Hello World!");

app.Run();
```

9. At the bottom of the file, add a statement to write a message to the console after the call to the Run method and therefore after the web server has stopped, as shown highlighted in the following code:

```
app.Run();

Console.WriteLine("This executes after the web server has stopped!");
```

Testing and securing the website

We will now test the functionality of the ASP.NET Core Empty website project. We will also enable encryption of all traffic between the browser and web server for privacy by switching from HTTP to HTTPS. HTTPS is the secure encrypted version of HTTP.

1. For Visual Studio:

   1. In the toolbar, make sure that **Northwind.Web** is selected rather than **IIS Express** or **WSL**, and switch the **Web Browser (Microsoft Edge)** to **Google Chrome**, as shown in *Figure 14.5*:

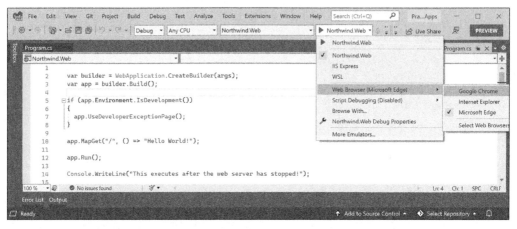

Figure 14.5: Selecting the Northwind.Web profile with its Kestrel web server in Visual Studio

   2. Navigate to **Debug | Start Without Debugging...**.

   3. The first time you start a secure website, you will be prompted that your project is configured to use SSL, and to avoid warnings in the browser you can choose to trust the self-signed certificate that ASP.NET Core has generated. Click **Yes**.

   4. When you see the **Security Warning** dialog box, click **Yes** again.

2. For Visual Studio Code, in **TERMINAL**, enter the dotnet run command.

3. In either Visual Studio's command prompt window or Visual Studio Code's terminal, note the Kestrel web server has started listening on random ports for HTTP and HTTPS, that you can press *Ctrl + C* to shut down the Kestrel web server, and the hosting environment is Development, as shown in the following output:

```
info: Microsoft.Hosting.Lifetime[14]
      Now listening on: https://localhost:5001
info: Microsoft.Hosting.Lifetime[14]
      Now listening on: http://localhost:5000
info: Microsoft.Hosting.Lifetime[0]
```

```
    Application started. Press Ctrl+C to shut down.
info: Microsoft.Hosting.Lifetime[0]
    Hosting environment: Development
info: Microsoft.Hosting.Lifetime[0]
    Content root path: C:\Code\PracticalApps\Northwind.Web
```

 Visual Studio will also start your chosen browser automatically. If you are using Visual Studio Code, you will have to start Chrome manually.

4. Leave the web server running.

5. In Chrome, show **Developer Tools**, and click the **Network** tab.

6. Enter the address `http://localhost:5000/`, or whatever port number was assigned to HTTP, and note the response is `Hello World!` in plain text, from the cross-platform Kestrel web server, as shown in *Figure 14.6*:

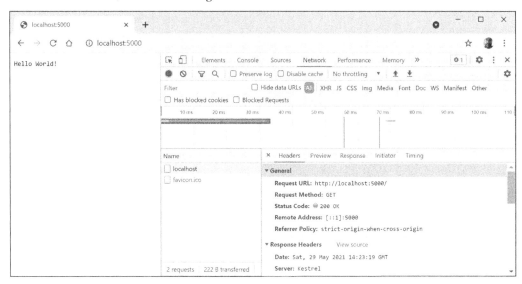

Figure 14.6: Plain text response from http://localhost:5000/

 Chrome also requests a `favicon.ico` file automatically to show in the browser tab but this is missing so it shows as a `404 Not Found` error.

7. Enter the address `https://localhost:5001/`, or whatever port number was assigned to HTTPS, and note if you are not using Visual Studio or if you clicked **No** when prompted to trust the SSL certificate, then the response is a privacy error, as shown in *Figure 14.7*:

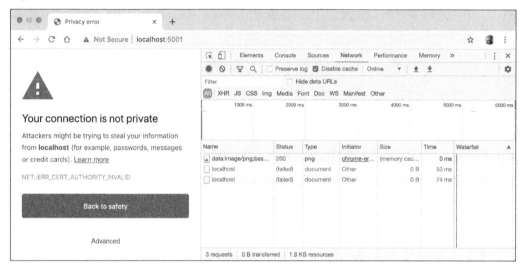

Figure 14.7: Privacy error showing SSL encryption has not been enabled with a certificate

You will see this error when you have not configured a certificate that the browser can trust to encrypt and decrypt HTTPS traffic (and so if you do not see this error, it is because you have already configured a certificate).

In a production environment, you would want to pay a company such as Verisign for an SSL certificate because they provide liability protection and technical support.

 For Linux Developers: If you use a Linux variant that cannot create self-signed certificates or you do not mind reapplying for a new certificate every 90 days, then you can get a free certificate from the following link: `https://letsencrypt.org`

During development, you can tell your OS to trust a temporary development certificate provided by ASP.NET Core.

8. At the command line or in **TERMINAL**, press *Ctrl + C* to shut down the web server, and note the message that is written, as shown highlighted in the following output:

```
info: Microsoft.Hosting.Lifetime[0]
      Application is shutting down...
This executes after the web server has stopped!

C:\Code\PracticalApps\Northwind.Web\bin\Debug\net6.0\Northwind.Web.exe
(process 19888) exited with code 0.
```

9. If you need to trust a local self-signed SSL certificate, then at the command line or in **TERMINAL**, enter the `dotnet dev-certs https --trust` command, and note the message, **Trusting the HTTPS development certificate was requested**. You might be prompted to enter your password and a valid HTTPS certificate may already be present.

Enabling stronger security and redirect to a secure connection

It is good practice to enable stricter security and automatically redirect requests for HTTP to HTTPS.

 Good Practice: HTTP Strict Transport Security (HSTS) is an opt-in security enhancement that you should always enable. If a website specifies it and a browser supports it, then it forces all communication over HTTPS and prevents the visitor from using untrusted or invalid certificates.

Let's do that now:

1. In `Program.cs`, add an `if` statement to enable HSTS when not in development, as shown in the following code:

    ```
    if (!app.Environment.IsDevelopment())
    {
      app.UseHsts();
    }
    ```

2. Add a statement before the call to `app.MapGet` to redirect HTTP requests to HTTPS, as shown in the following code:

    ```
    app.UseHttpsRedirection();
    ```

3. Start the **Northwind.Web** website project.

4. If Chrome is still running, close and restart it.

5. In Chrome, show **Developer Tools**, and click the **Network** tab.

6. Enter the address `http://localhost:5000/`, or whatever port number was assigned to HTTP, and note how the server responds with a `307 Temporary Redirect` to port `5001` and that the certificate is now valid and trusted, as shown in *Figure 14.8*:

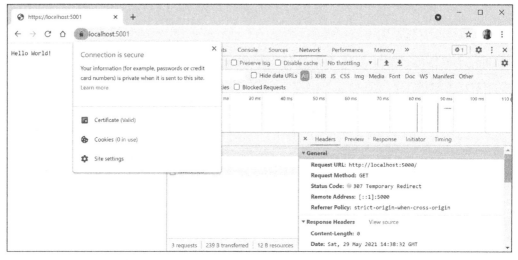

Figure 14.8: The connection is now secured using a valid certificate and a 307 redirect

7. Close Chrome.

8. Shut down the web server.

Good Practice: Remember to shut down the Kestrel web server whenever you have finished testing a website.

Controlling the hosting environment

In earlier versions of ASP.NET Core, the project template set a rule to say that while in development mode, any unhandled exceptions will be shown in the browser window for the developer to see the details of the exception, as shown in the following code:

```
if (app.Environment.IsDevelopment())
{
  app.UseDeveloperExceptionPage();
}
```

With ASP.NET Core 6 and later, this code is executed automatically by default so it is not included in the project template.

How does ASP.NET Core know when we are running in development mode so that the `IsDevelopment` method returns `true`? Let's find out.

ASP.NET Core can read from environment variables to determine what hosting environment to use, for example, DOTNET_ENVIRONMENT or ASPNETCORE_ENVIRONMENT.

You can override these settings during local development:

1. In the Northwind.Web folder, expand the folder named Properties, open the file named launchSettings.json, and note the profile named Northwind.Web that sets the hosting environment to Development, as shown highlighted in the following configuration:

```
{
  "iisSettings": {
    "windowsAuthentication": false,
    "anonymousAuthentication": true,
    "iisExpress": {
      "applicationUrl": "http://localhost:56111",
      "sslPort": 44329
    }
  },
  "profiles": {
    "Northwind.Web": {
      "commandName": "Project",
      "dotnetRunMessages": "true",
      "launchBrowser": true,
      "applicationUrl": "https://localhost:5001;http://localhost:5000",
      "environmentVariables": {
        "ASPNETCORE_ENVIRONMENT": "Development"
      }
    },
    "IIS Express": {
      "commandName": "IISExpress",
      "launchBrowser": true,
      "environmentVariables": {
        "ASPNETCORE_ENVIRONMENT": "Development"
      }
    }
  }
}
```

2. Change the randomly assigned port numbers for HTTP to 5000 and HTTPS to 5001.

3. Change the environment to Production. Optionally, change launchBrowser to false to prevent Visual Studio from automatically launching a browser.

4. Start the website and note the hosting environment is Production, as shown in the following output:

```
info: Microsoft.Hosting.Lifetime[0]
  Hosting environment: Production
```

5. Shut down the web server.

6. In `launchSettings.json`, change the environment back to `Development`.

 The `launchSettings.json` file also has a configuration for using IIS as the web server using random port numbers. In this book, we will only be using Kestrel as the web server since it is cross-platform.

Separating configuration for services and pipeline

Putting all code to initialize a simple web project in `Program.cs` can be a good idea, especially for web services, so we will see this style again in *Chapter 16, Building and Consuming Web Services*.

However, for anything more than the most basic web project, you might prefer to separate configuration into a separate `Startup` class with two methods:

- `ConfigureServices(IServiceCollection services)`: to add dependency services to a dependency injection container, such as Razor Pages support, **Cross-Origin Resource Sharing (CORS)** support, or a database context for working with the Northwind database.

- `Configure(IApplicationBuilder app, IWebHostEnvironment env)`: to set up the HTTP pipeline through which requests and responses flow. Call various `Use` methods on the app parameter to construct the pipeline in the order the features should be processed.

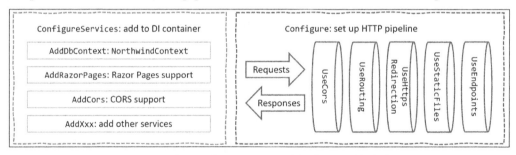

Figure 14.9: Startup class ConfigureServices and Configure methods diagram

Both methods will get called automatically by the runtime.

Let's create a `Startup` class now:

1. Add a new class file to the `Northwind.Web` project named `Startup.cs`.

2. Modify `Startup.cs`, as shown in the following code:

```
namespace Northwind.Web;

public class Startup
```

```
{
  public void ConfigureServices(IServiceCollection services)
  {
  }

  public void Configure(
    IApplicationBuilder app, IWebHostEnvironment env)
  {
    if (!env.IsDevelopment())
    {
      app.UseHsts();
    }

    app.UseRouting(); // start endpoint routing

    app.UseHttpsRedirection();

    app.UseEndpoints(endpoints =>
    {
      endpoints.MapGet("/", () => "Hello World!");
    });
  }
}
```

Note the following about the code:

- The ConfigureServices method is currently empty because we do not yet need any dependency services added.
- The Configure method sets up the HTTP request pipeline and enables the use of endpoint routing. It configures a routed endpoint to wait for requests using the same map for each HTTP GET request for the root path / that responds to those requests by returning the plain text "Hello World!". We will learn about routed endpoints and their benefits at the end of this chapter.

Now we must specify that we want to use the Startup class in the application entry point.

3. Modify Program.cs, as shown in the following code:

```
using Northwind.Web; // Startup

Host.CreateDefaultBuilder(args)
  .ConfigureWebHostDefaults(webBuilder =>
  {
    webBuilder.UseStartup<Startup>();
  }).Build().Run();

Console.WriteLine("This executes after the web server has stopped!");
```

4. Start the website and note that it has the same behavior as before.

5. Shut down the web server.

 In all the other website and service projects that we create in this book, we will use the single `Program.cs` file created by .NET 6 project templates. If you like the `Startup.cs` way of doing things, then you will see in this chapter how to use it.

Enabling a website to serve static content

A website that only ever returns a single plain text message isn't very useful!

At a minimum, it ought to return static HTML pages, CSS that the web pages will use for styling, and any other static resources, such as images and videos.

By convention, these files should be stored in a directory named `wwwroot` to keep them separate from the dynamically executing parts of your website project.

Creating a folder for static files and a web page

You will now create a folder for your static website resources and a basic index page that uses Bootstrap for styling:

1. In the `Northwind.Web` project/folder, create a folder named `wwwroot`.

2. Add a new HTML page file to the `wwwroot` folder named `index.html`.

3. Modify its content to link to CDN-hosted Bootstrap for styling, and use modern good practices such as setting the viewport, as shown in the following markup:

```html
<!doctype html>
<html lang="en">

<head>
  <!-- Required meta tags -->
  <meta charset="utf-8" />
  <meta name="viewport" content=
    "width=device-width, initial-scale=1 " />

  <!-- Bootstrap CSS -->
  <link href=
"https://cdn.jsdelivr.net/npm/bootstrap@5.1.0/dist/css/bootstrap.min.css"
rel="stylesheet" integrity="sha384-KyZXEAg3QhqLMpG8r+8fhAXLRk2vvoC2f3B09zV
Xn8CA5QIVfZOJ3BCsw2P0p/We" crossorigin="anonymous">

  <title>Welcome ASP.NET Core!</title>
</head>
```

```html
<body>
  <div class="container">
    <div class="jumbotron">
      <h1 class="display-3">Welcome to Northwind B2B</h1>
      <p class="lead">We supply products to our customers.</p>
      <hr />
      <h2>This is a static HTML page.</h2>
      <p>Our customers include restaurants, hotels, and cruise lines.</p>
      <p>
        <a class="btn btn-primary"
          href="https://www.asp.net/">Learn more</a>
      </p>
    </div>
  </div>
</body>

</html>
```

 Good Practice: To get the latest `<link>` element for Bootstrap, copy and paste it from the documentation at the following link: `https://getbootstrap.com/docs/5.0/getting-started/introduction/#starter-template`.

Enabling static and default files

If you were to start the website now and enter `http://localhost:5000/index.html` in the address box, the website would return a `404 Not Found` error saying no web page was found. To enable the website to return static files such as `index.html`, we must explicitly configure that feature.

Even if we enable static files, if you were to start the website and enter `http://localhost:5000/` in the address box, the website will return a `404 Not Found` error because the web server does not know what to return by default if no named file is requested.

You will now enable static files, explicitly configure default files, and change the URL path registered that returns the plain text `Hello World!` response:

1. In `Startup.cs`, in the `Configure` method, add statements after enabling HTTPS redirection to enable static files and default files, and modify the statement that maps a `GET` request to return the `Hello World!` plain text response to only respond to the URL path `/hello`, as shown highlighted in the following code:

    ```
    app.UseHttpsRedirection();

    app.UseDefaultFiles(); // index.html, default.html, and so on
    ```

```
app.UseStaticFiles();

app.UseEndpoints(endpoints =>
{
  endpoints.MapGet("/hello", () => "Hello World!");
});
```

 The call to UseDefaultFiles must come before the call to UseStaticFiles, or it will not work! You will learn more about the ordering of middleware and endpoint routing at the end of this chapter.

2. Start the website.

3. Start **Chrome** and show **Developer Tools**.

4. In Chrome, enter http://localhost:5000/ and note that you are redirected to the HTTPS address on port 5001, and the index.html file is now returned over that secure connection because it is one of the possible default files for this website.

5. In **Developer Tools**, note the request for the Bootstrap stylesheet.

6. In Chrome, enter http://localhost:5000/hello and note that it returns the plain text Hello World! as before.

7. Close Chrome and shut down the web server.

If all web pages are static, that is, they only get changed manually by a web editor, then our website programming work is complete. But almost all websites need dynamic content, which means a web page that is generated at runtime by executing code.

The easiest way to do that is to use a feature of ASP.NET Core named **Razor Pages**.

Exploring ASP.NET Core Razor Pages

ASP.NET Core Razor Pages allow a developer to easily mix C# code statements with HTML markup to make the generated web page dynamic. That is why they use the .cshtml file extension.

By convention, ASP.NET Core looks for Razor Pages in a folder named Pages.

Enabling Razor Pages

You will now copy and change the static HTML page into a dynamic Razor Page, and then add and enable the Razor Pages service:

1. In the Northwind.Web project folder, create a folder named Pages.

2. Copy the index.html file into the Pages folder.

3. For the file in the Pages folder, rename the file extension from .html to .cshtml.

4. Remove the <h2> element that says that this is a static HTML page.

5. In Startup.cs, in the ConfigureServices method, add a statement to add ASP.NET Core Razor Pages and its related services, such as model binding, authorization, anti-forgery, views, and tag helpers, to the builder, as shown in the following code:

```
services.AddRazorPages();
```

6. In Startup.cs, in the Configure method, in the configuration to use endpoints, add a statement to call the MapRazorPages method, as shown highlighted in the following code:

```
app.UseEndpoints(endpoints =>
{
    endpoints.MapRazorPages();

    endpoints.MapGet("/hello",  () => "Hello World!");
});
```

Adding code to a Razor Page

In the HTML markup of a web page, Razor syntax is indicated by the @ symbol. Razor Pages can be described as follows:

- They require the @page directive at the top of the file.
- They can optionally have an @functions section that defines any of the following:
    - Properties for storing data values, like in a class definition. An instance of that class is automatically instantiated named Model that can have its properties set in special methods and you can get the property values in the HTML.
    - Methods named OnGet, OnPost, OnDelete, and so on that execute when HTTP requests are made, such as GET, POST, and DELETE.

Let's now convert the static HTML page into a Razor Page:

1. In the Pages folder, open index.cshtml.

2. Add the @page statement to the top of the file.

3. After the @page statement, add an @functions statement block.

4. Define a property to store the name of the current day as a string value.

5. Define a method to set DayName that executes when an HTTP GET request is made for the page, as shown in the following code:

```
@page

@functions
{
```

```
public string? DayName { get; set; }

public void OnGet()
{
  Model.DayName = DateTime.Now.ToString("dddd");
}
}
```

6. Output the day name inside the second HTML paragraph, as shown highlighted in the following markup:

```
<p>It's @Model.DayName! Our customers include restaurants, hotels, and
cruise lines.</p>
```

7. Start the website.

8. In Chrome, enter `https://localhost:5001/` and note the current day name is output on the page, as shown in *Figure 14.10*:

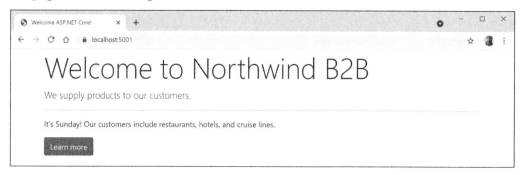

Figure 14.10: Welcome to Northwind page showing the current day

9. In Chrome, enter `https://localhost:5001/index.html`, which exactly matches the static filename, and note that it returns the static HTML page as before.

10. In Chrome, enter `https://localhost:5001/hello`, which exactly matches the endpoint route that returns plain text, and note that it returns `Hello World!` as before.

11. Close Chrome and shut down the web server.

Using shared layouts with Razor Pages

Most websites have more than one page. If every page had to contain all of the boilerplate markup that is currently in `index.cshtml`, that would become a pain to manage. So, ASP.NET Core has a feature named **layouts**.

To use layouts, we must create a Razor file to define the default layout for all Razor Pages (and all MVC views) and store it in a `Shared` folder so that it can be easily found by convention. The name of this file can be anything, because we will specify it, but `_Layout.cshtml` is good practice.

We must also create a specially named file to set the default layout file for all Razor Pages (and all MVC views). This file must be named _ViewStart.cshtml.

Let's see layouts in action:

1. In the Pages folder, add a file named _ViewStart.cshtml. (The Visual Studio item template is named **Razor View Start**.)

2. Modify its content, as shown in the following markup:

```
@{
    Layout = "_Layout";
}
```

3. In the Pages folder, create a folder named Shared.

4. In the Shared folder, create a file named _Layout.cshtml. (The Visual Studio item template is named **Razor Layout**.)

5. Modify the content of _Layout.cshtml (it is similar to index.cshtml so you can copy and paste the HTML markup from there), as shown in the following markup:

```
<!doctype html>
<html lang="en">

<head>
  <!-- Required meta tags -->
  <meta charset="utf-8" />
  <meta name="viewport" content=
    "width=device-width, initial-scale=1, shrink-to-fit=no" />

  <!-- Bootstrap CSS -->
  <link href=
"https://cdn.jsdelivr.net/npm/bootstrap@5.1.0/dist/css/bootstrap.min.css"
rel="stylesheet" integrity="sha384-KyZXEAg3QhqLMpG8r+8fhAXLRk2vvoC2f3B09zV
Xn8CA5QIVfZOJ3BCsw2P0p/We" crossorigin="anonymous">

  <title>@ViewData["Title"]</title>
</head>

<body>
  <div class="container">
    @RenderBody()
    <hr />
    <footer>
      <p>Copyright &copy; 2021 - @ViewData["Title"]</p>
    </footer>
  </div>

  <!-- JavaScript to enable features like carousel -->
```

```
<script src="https://cdn.jsdelivr.net/npm/bootstrap@5.1.0/
dist/js/bootstrap.bundle.min.js" integrity="sha384-
U1DAWAznBHeqEIlVSCgzq+c9gqGAJn5c/t99JyeKa9xxaYpSvHU5awsuZVVFIhvj"
crossorigin="anonymous"></script>

@RenderSection("Scripts", required: false)

</body>
</html>
```

While reviewing the preceding markup, note the following:

- `<title>` is set dynamically using server-side code from a dictionary named `ViewData`. This is a simple way to pass data between different parts of an ASP.NET Core website. In this case, the data will be set in a Razor Page class file and then output in the shared layout.

- `@RenderBody()` marks the insertion point for the view being requested.

- A horizontal rule and footer will appear at the bottom of each page.

- At the bottom of the layout is a script to implement some cool features of Bootstrap that we can use later, such as a carousel of images.

- After the `<script>` elements for Bootstrap, we have defined a section named `Scripts` so that a Razor Page can optionally inject additional scripts that it needs.

6. Modify `index.cshtml` to remove all HTML markup except `<div class="jumbotron">` and its contents, and leave the C# code in the `@functions` block that you added earlier.

7. Add a statement to the `OnGet` method to store a page title in the `ViewData` dictionary, and modify the button to navigate to a suppliers page (which we will create in the next section), as shown highlighted in the following markup:

```
@page

@functions
{
  public string? DayName { get; set; }

  public void OnGet()
  {
    ViewData["Title"] = "Northwind B2B";

    Model.DayName = DateTime.Now.ToString("dddd");
  }
}
<div class="jumbotron">
  <h1 class="display-3">Welcome to Northwind B2B</h1>
  <p class="lead">We supply products to our customers.</p>
```

```
<hr />
<p>It's @Model.DayName! Our customers include restaurants, hotels, and
cruise lines.</p>
<p>
    <a class="btn btn-primary" href="suppliers">
      Learn more about our suppliers</a>
</p>
</div>
```

8. Start the website, visit it with Chrome, and note that it has similar behavior as before, although clicking the button for suppliers will give a 404 Not Found error because we have not created that page yet.

Using code-behind files with Razor Pages

Sometimes, it is better to separate the HTML markup from the data and executable code, so Razor Pages allows you to do this by putting the C# code in **code-behind** class files. They have the same name as the .cshtml file but end with .cshtml.cs.

You will now create a page that shows a list of suppliers. In this example, we are focusing on learning about code-behind files. In the next topic, we will load the list of suppliers from a database, but for now, we will simulate that with a hardcoded array of string values:

1. In the Pages folder, add two new files named Suppliers.cshtml and Suppliers.cshtml.cs. (The Visual Studio item template is named **Razor Page - Empty** and it creates both files.)

2. Add statements to the code-behind file named Suppliers.cshtml.cs, as shown in the following code:

```
using Microsoft.AspNetCore.Mvc.RazorPages; // PageModel

namespace Northwind.Web.Pages;

public class SuppliersModel : PageModel
{
  public IEnumerable<string>? Suppliers { get; set; }

  public void OnGet()
  {
    ViewData["Title"] = "Northwind B2B - Suppliers";

    Suppliers = new[]
    {
      "Alpha Co", "Beta Limited", "Gamma Corp"
    };
  }
}
```

While reviewing the preceding markup, note the following:

- `SuppliersModel` inherits from `PageModel`, so it has members such as the `ViewData` dictionary for sharing data. You can right-click on `PageModel` and select **Go To Definition** to see that it has lots more useful features, such as the entire `HttpContext` of the current request.

- `SuppliersModel` defines a property for storing a collection of `string` values named `Suppliers`.

- When an HTTP `GET` request is made for this Razor Page, the `Suppliers` property is populated with some example supplier names from an array of `string` values. Later, we will populate this from the Northwind database.

3. Modify the contents of `Suppliers.cshtml`, as shown in the following markup:

```
@page
@model Northwind.Web.Pages.SuppliersModel
<div class="row">
  <h1 class="display-2">Suppliers</h1>
  <table class="table">
    <thead class="thead-inverse">
      <tr><th>Company Name</th></tr>
    </thead>
    <tbody>
    @if (Model.Suppliers is not null)
    {
      @foreach(string name in Model.Suppliers)
      {
        <tr><td>@name</td></tr>
      }
    }
    </tbody>
  </table>
</div>
```

While reviewing the preceding markup, note the following:

- The model type for this Razor Page is set to `SuppliersModel`.
- The page outputs an HTML table with Bootstrap styles.
- The data rows in the table are generated by looping through the `Suppliers` property of `Model` if it is not `null`.

4. Start the website and visit it using Chrome.

5. Click on the button to learn more about suppliers, and note the table of suppliers, as shown in *Figure 14.11*:

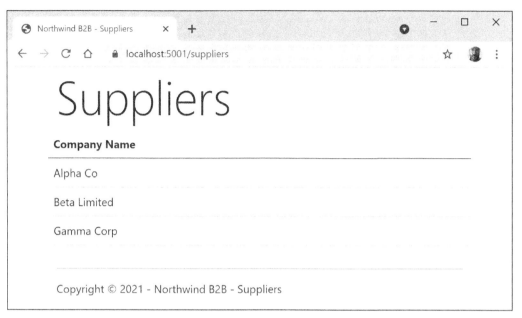

Figure 14.11: The table of suppliers loaded from an array of strings

Using Entity Framework Core with ASP.NET Core

Entity Framework Core is a natural way to get real data into a website. In *Chapter 13, Introducing Practical Applications of C# and .NET*, you created two pairs of class libraries: one for the entity models and one for the Northwind database context, for either SQL Server or SQLite or both. You will now use them in your website project.

Configure Entity Framework Core as a service

Functionality such as Entity Framework Core database contexts that are needed by ASP.NET Core must be registered as a service during website startup. The code in the GitHub repository solution and below uses SQLite, but you can easily use SQL Server if you prefer.

Let's see how:

1. In the Northwind.Web project, add a project reference to the Northwind.Common. DataContext project for either SQLite or SQL Server, as shown in the following markup:

    ```
    <!-- change Sqlite to SqlServer if you prefer -->
    <ItemGroup>
      <ProjectReference Include="..\Northwind.Common.DataContext.Sqlite\
    Northwind.Common.DataContext.Sqlite.csproj" />
    </ItemGroup>
    ```

The project reference must go all on one line with no line break.

2. Build the `Northwind.Web` project.

3. In `Startup.cs`, import namespaces to work with your entity model types, as shown in the following code:

   ```
   using Packt.Shared; // AddNorthwindContext extension method
   ```

4. Add a statement to the `ConfigureServices` method to register the `Northwind` database context class, as shown in the following code:

   ```
   services.AddNorthwindContext();
   ```

5. In the `Northwind.Web` project, in the `Pages` folder, open `Suppliers.cshtml.cs`, and import the namespace for our database context, as shown in the following code:

   ```
   using Packt.Shared; // NorthwindContext
   ```

6. In the `SuppliersModel` class, add a private field to store the `Northwind` database context and a constructor to set it, as shown in the following code:

   ```
   private NorthwindContext db;

   public SuppliersModel(NorthwindContext injectedContext)
   {
       db = injectedContext;
   }
   ```

7. Change the `Suppliers` property to contain `Supplier` objects instead of `string` values.

8. In the `OnGet` method, modify the statements to set the `Suppliers` property from the `Suppliers` property of the database context, sorted by country and then company name, as shown highlighted in the following code:

   ```
   public void OnGet()
   {
       ViewData["Title"] = "Northwind B2B - Suppliers";

       Suppliers = db.Suppliers
           .OrderBy(c => c.Country).ThenBy(c => c.CompanyName);
   }
   ```

9. Modify the contents of `Suppliers.cshtml` to import the `Packt.Shared` namespace and render multiple columns for each supplier, as shown highlighted in the following markup:

   ```
   @page
   @using Packt.Shared
   ```

```
@model Northwind.Web.Pages.SuppliersModel
<div class="row">
  <h1 class="display-2">Suppliers</h1>
  <table class="table">
    <thead class="thead-inverse">
      <tr>
        <th>Company Name</th>
        <th>Country</th>
        <th>Phone</th>
      </tr>
    </thead>
    <tbody>
    @if (Model.Suppliers is not null)
    {
      @foreach(Supplier s in Model.Suppliers)
      {
        <tr>
          <td>@s.CompanyName</td>
          <td>@s.Country</td>
          <td>@s.Phone</td>
        </tr>
      }
    }
    </tbody>
  </table>
</div>
```

10. Start the website.

11. In Chrome, enter `https://localhost:5001/`.

12. Click **Learn more about our suppliers** and note that the supplier table now loads from the database, as shown in *Figure 14.12*:

Figure 14.12: The suppliers table loaded from the Northwind database

Manipulating data using Razor Pages

You will now add functionality to insert a new supplier.

Enabling a model to insert entities

First, you will modify the supplier model so that it responds to HTTP POST requests when a visitor submits a form to insert a new supplier:

1. In the Northwind.Web project, in the Pages folder, open Suppliers.cshtml.cs and import the following namespace:

   ```
   using Microsoft.AspNetCore.Mvc; // [BindProperty], IActionResult
   ```

2. In the SuppliersModel class, add a property to store a single supplier and a method named OnPost that adds the supplier to the Suppliers table in the Northwind database if its model is valid, as shown in the following code:

   ```
   [BindProperty]
   public Supplier? Supplier { get; set; }

   public IActionResult OnPost()
   {
     if ((Supplier is not null) && ModelState.IsValid)
     {
       db.Suppliers.Add(Supplier);
       db.SaveChanges();
       return RedirectToPage("/suppliers");
     }
     else
     {
       return Page(); // return to original page
     }
   }
   ```

While reviewing the preceding code, note the following:

- We added a property named Supplier that is decorated with the [BindProperty] attribute so that we can easily connect HTML elements on the web page to properties in the Supplier class.

- We added a method that responds to HTTP POST requests. It checks that all property values conform to validation rules on the Supplier class entity model (such as [Required] and [StringLength]) and then adds the supplier to the existing table and saves changes to the database context. This will generate a SQL statement to perform the insert into the database. Then it redirects to the Suppliers page so that the visitor sees the newly added supplier.

Defining a form to insert a new supplier

Next, you will modify the Razor Page to define a form that a visitor can fill in and submit to insert a new supplier:

1. In `Suppliers.cshtml`, add tag helpers after the `@model` declaration so that we can use tag helpers such as `asp-for` on this Razor Page, as shown in the following markup:

   ```
   @addTagHelper *, Microsoft.AspNetCore.Mvc.TagHelpers
   ```

2. At the bottom of the file, add a form to insert a new supplier, and use the `asp-for` tag helper to bind the `CompanyName`, `Country`, and `Phone` properties of the `Supplier` class to the input box, as shown in the following markup:

   ```
   <div class="row">
     <p>Enter details for a new supplier:</p>
     <form method="POST">
       <div><input asp-for="Supplier.CompanyName"
                   placeholder="Company Name" /></div>
       <div><input asp-for="Supplier.Country"
                   placeholder="Country" /></div>
       <div><input asp-for="Supplier.Phone"
                   placeholder="Phone" /></div>
       <input type="submit" />
     </form>
   </div>
   ```

   While reviewing the preceding markup, note the following:

   - The `<form>` element with a `POST` method is normal HTML, so an `<input type="submit" />` element inside it will make an HTTP `POST` request back to the current page with values of any other elements inside that form.

   - An `<input>` element with a tag helper named `asp-for` enables data binding to the model behind the Razor Page.

3. Start the website.

4. Click **Learn more about our suppliers**, scroll down to the bottom of the page, enter `Bob's Burgers`, `USA`, and `(603) 555-4567`, and click **Submit**.

5. Note that you see a refreshed suppliers table with the new supplier added.

6. Close Chrome and shut down the web server.

Injecting a dependency service into a Razor Page

If you have a `.cshtml` Razor Page that does not have a code-behind file, then you can inject a dependency service using the `@inject` directive instead of constructor parameter injection, and then directly reference the injected database context using Razor syntax in the middle of the markup.

Let's create a simple example:

1. In the Pages folder, add a new file named Orders.cshtml. (The Visual Studio item template is named **Razor Page - Empty** and it creates two files. Delete the .cs file.)

2. In Orders.cshtml, write code to output the number of orders in the Northwind database, as shown in the following markup:

```
@page
@using Packt.Shared
@inject NorthwindContext db
@{
  string title = "Orders";
  ViewData["Title"] = $"Northwind B2B - {title}";
}
<div class="row">
  <h1 class="display-2">@title</h1>
  <p>
    There are @db.Orders.Count() orders in the Northwind database.
  </p>
</div>
```

3. Start the website.

4. Navigate to /orders and note that you see that there are 830 orders in the Northwind database.

5. Close Chrome and shut down the web server.

Using Razor class libraries

Everything related to a Razor Page can be compiled into a class library for easier reuse in multiple projects. With ASP.NET Core 3.0 and later, this can include static files such as HTML, CSS, JavaScript libraries, and media assets such as image files. A website can either use the Razor Page's view as defined in the class library or override it.

Creating a Razor class library

Let's create a new Razor class library:

Use your preferred code editor to add a new project, as defined in the following list:

1. Project template: **Razor Class Library** / razorclasslib

2. Checkbox/switch: **Support pages and views** / -s

3. Workspace/solution file and folder: PracticalApps

4. Project file and folder: Northwind.Razor.Employees

-s is short for the --support-pages-and-views switch that enables the class library to use Razor Pages and .cshtml file views.

Disabling compact folders for Visual Studio Code

Before we implement our Razor class library, I want to explain a Visual Studio Code feature that confused some readers of a previous edition because the feature was added after publishing.

The compact folders feature means that nested folders such as /Areas/MyFeature/Pages/ are shown in a compact form if the intermediate folders in the hierarchy do not contain files, as shown in *Figure 14.13*:

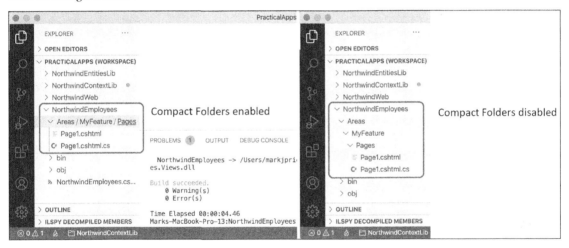

Figure 14.13: Compact folders enabled or disabled

If you would like to disable the Visual Studio Code compact folders feature, complete the following steps:

1. On Windows, navigate to **File | Preferences | Settings**. On macOS, navigate to **Code | Preferences | Settings**.
2. In the **Search** settings box, enter compact.

3. Clear the **Explorer: Compact Folders** checkbox, as shown in *Figure 14.14*:

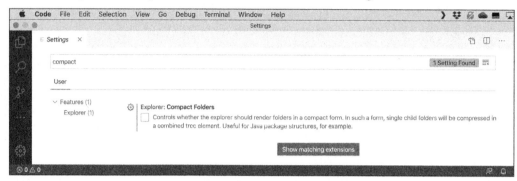

Figure 14.14: Disabling compact folders for Visual Studio Code

4. Close the **Settings** tab.

Implementing the employees feature using EF Core

Now we can add a reference to our entity models to get the employees to show in the Razor class library:

1. In the `Northwind.Razor.Employees` project, add a project reference to the `Northwind.Common.DataContext` project for either SQLite or SQL Server and note the SDK is `Microsoft.NET.Sdk.Razor`, as shown highlighted in the following markup:

```
<Project Sdk="Microsoft.NET.Sdk.Razor">

  <PropertyGroup>
    <TargetFramework>net6.0</TargetFramework>
    <Nullable>enable</Nullable>
    <ImplicitUsings>enable</ImplicitUsings>
    <AddRazorSupportForMvc>true</AddRazorSupportForMvc>
  </PropertyGroup>

  <ItemGroup>
    <FrameworkReference Include="Microsoft.AspNetCore.App" />
  </ItemGroup>

  <!-- change Sqlite to SqlServer if you prefer -->
  <ItemGroup>
    <ProjectReference Include="..\Northwind.Common.DataContext.Sqlite
\Northwind.Common.DataContext.Sqlite.csproj" />
  </ItemGroup>

</Project>
```

The project reference must go all on one line with no line break. Also, do not mix our SQLite and SQL Server projects or you will see compiler errors. If you used SQL Server in the Northwind.Web project, then you must use SQL Server in the Northwind.Razor.Employees project as well.

2. Build the Northwind.Razor.Employees project.

3. In the Areas folder, right-click the MyFeature folder, select **Rename**, enter the new name PacktFeatures, and press *Enter*.

4. In the PacktFeatures folder, in the Pages subfolder, add a new file named _ViewStart.cshtml. (The Visual Studio item template is named **Razor View Start**. Or just copy it from the Northwind.Web project.)

5. Modify its content to inform this class library that any Razor Pages should look for a layout with the same name as used in the Northwind.Web project, as shown in the following markup:

```
@{
    Layout = "_Layout";
}
```

 We do not need to create the _Layout.cshtml file in this project. It will use the one in its host project, for example, the one in the Northwind.Web project.

6. In the Pages subfolder, rename Page1.cshtml to Employees.cshtml, and rename Page1.cshtml.cs to Employees.cshtml.cs.

7. Modify Employees.cshtml.cs to define a page model with an array of Employee entity instances loaded from the Northwind database, as shown in the following code:

```
using Microsoft.AspNetCore.Mvc.RazorPages; // PageModel
using Packt.Shared; // Employee, NorthwindContext

namespace PacktFeatures.Pages;

public class EmployeesPageModel : PageModel
{
    private NorthwindContext db;

    public EmployeesPageModel(NorthwindContext injectedContext)
    {
        db = injectedContext;
    }
```

```
    public Employee[] Employees { get; set; } = null!;

    public void OnGet()
    {
      ViewData["Title"] = "Northwind B2B - Employees";
      Employees = db.Employees.OrderBy(e => e.LastName)
        .ThenBy(e => e.FirstName).ToArray();
    }
  }
```

8. Modify `Employees.cshtml`, as shown in the following markup:

```
@page
@using Packt.Shared
@addTagHelper *, Microsoft.AspNetCore.Mvc.TagHelpers
@model PacktFeatures.Pages.EmployeesPageModel
<div class="row">
  <h1 class="display-2">Employees</h1>
</div>
<div class="row">
@foreach(Employee employee in Model.Employees)
{
  <div class="col-sm-3">
    <partial name="_Employee" model="employee" />
  </div>
}
</div>
```

While reviewing the preceding markup, note the following:

- We import the `Packt.Shared` namespace so that we can use classes in it such as `Employee`.

- We add support for tag helpers so that we can use the `<partial>` element.

- We declare the `@model` type for this Razor Page to use the page model class that you just defined.

- We enumerate through the `Employees` in the model, outputting each one using a partial view.

Implementing a partial view to show a single employee

The `<partial>` tag helper was introduced in ASP.NET Core 2.1. A partial view is like a piece of a Razor Page. You will create one in the next few steps to render a single employee:

1. In the `Northwind.Razor.Employees` project, in the `Pages` folder, create a `Shared` folder.

2. In the `Shared` folder, create a file named `_Employee.cshtml`. (The Visual Studio item template is named **Razor View - Empty**.)

3. Modify `_Employee.cshtml`, as shown in the following markup:

```
@model Packt.Shared.Employee
<div class="card border-dark mb-3" style="max-width: 18rem;">
  <div class="card-header">@Model?.LastName, @Model?.FirstName</div>
  <div class="card-body text-dark">
    <h5 class="card-title">@Model?.Country</h5>
    <p class="card-text">@Model?.Notes</p>
  </div>
</div>
```

While reviewing the preceding markup, note the following:

- By convention, the names of partial views start with an underscore.
- If you put a partial view in the `Shared` folder, then it can be found automatically.
- The model type for this partial view is a single `Employee` entity.
- We use Bootstrap card styles to output information about each employee.

Using and testing a Razor class library

You will now reference and use the Razor class library in the website project:

1. In the `Northwind.Web` project, add a project reference to the `Northwind.Razor.Employees` project, as shown in the following markup:

```
<ProjectReference Include=
  "..\Northwind.Razor.Employees\Northwind.Razor.Employees.csproj" />
```

2. Modify `Pages\index.cshtml` to add a paragraph with a link to the Packt feature employees page after the link to the suppliers page, as shown in the following markup:

```
<p>
  <a class="btn btn-primary" href="packtfeatures/employees">
    Contact our employees
  </a>
</p>
```

3. Start the website, visit the website using Chrome, and click the **Contact our employees** button to see the cards of employees, as shown in *Figure 14.15*:

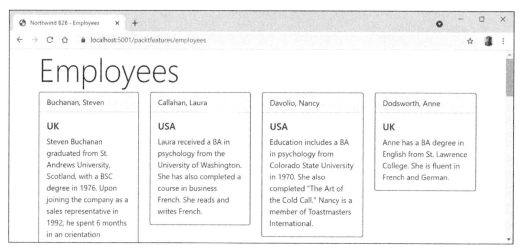

Figure 14.15: A list of employees from a Razor class library feature

Configuring services and the HTTP request pipeline

Now that we have built a website, we can return to the Startup configuration and review how services and the HTTP request pipeline work in more detail.

Understanding endpoint routing

In earlier versions of ASP.NET Core, the routing system and the extendable middleware system did not always work easily together; for example, if you wanted to implement a policy such as CORS in both middleware and MVC. Microsoft has invested in improving routing with a system named **endpoint routing** introduced with ASP.NET Core 2.2.

 Good Practice: Endpoint routing replaces the IRouter-based routing used in ASP.NET Core 2.1 and earlier. Microsoft recommends every older ASP.NET Core project migrates to endpoint routing if possible.

Endpoint routing is designed to enable better interoperability between frameworks that need routing, such as Razor Pages, MVC, or Web APIs, and middleware that needs to understand how routing affects them, such as localization, authorization, CORS, and so on.

Endpoint routing gets its name because it represents the route table as a compiled tree of endpoints that can be walked efficiently by the routing system. One of the biggest improvements is the performance of routing and action method selection.

It is on by default with ASP.NET Core 2.2 or later if compatibility is set to 2.2 or later. Traditional routes registered using the MapRoute method or with attributes are mapped to the new system.

The new routing system includes a link generation service registered as a dependency service that does not need an HttpContext.

Configuring endpoint routing

Endpoint routing requires a pair of calls to the UseRouting and UseEndpoints methods:

- UseRouting marks the pipeline position where a routing decision is made.
- UseEndpoints marks the pipeline position where the selected endpoint is executed.

Middleware such as localization that runs in between these methods can see the selected endpoint and can switch to a different endpoint if necessary.

Endpoint routing uses the same route template syntax that has been used in ASP.NET MVC since 2010 and the [Route] attribute introduced with ASP.NET MVC 5 in 2013. Migration often only requires changes to the Startup configuration.

MVC controllers, Razor Pages, and frameworks such as SignalR used to be enabled by a call to UseMvc or similar methods, but they are now added inside the UseEndpoints method call because they are all integrated into the same routing system along with middleware.

Reviewing the endpoint routing configuration in our project

Review the Startup.cs class file, as shown in the following code:

```
using Packt.Shared; // AddNorthwindContext extension method

namespace Northwind.Web;

public class Startup
{
  public void ConfigureServices(IServiceCollection services)
  {
    services.AddRazorPages();

    services.AddNorthwindContext();
  }

  public void Configure(
    IApplicationBuilder app, IWebHostEnvironment env)
  {
```

```
        if (!env.IsDevelopment())
        {
          app.UseHsts();
        }

        app.UseRouting();

        app.UseHttpsRedirection();

        app.UseDefaultFiles(); // index.html, default.html, and so on
        app.UseStaticFiles();

        app.UseEndpoints(endpoints =>
        {
          endpoints.MapRazorPages();

          endpoints.MapGet("/hello", () => "Hello World!");
        });
      }
  }
```

The Startup class has two methods that are called automatically by the host to configure the website.

The ConfigureServices method registers services that can then be retrieved when the functionality they provide is needed using dependency injection. Our code registers two services: Razor Pages and an EF Core database context.

Registering services in the ConfigureServices method

Common methods that register dependency services, including services that combine other method calls that register services, are shown in the following table:

Method	Services that it registers
AddMvcCore	Minimum set of services necessary to route requests and invoke controllers. Most websites will need more configuration than this.
AddAuthorization	Authentication and authorization services.
AddDataAnnotations	MVC data annotations service.
AddCacheTagHelper	MVC cache tag helper service.

AddRazorPages	Razor Pages service including the Razor view engine. Commonly used in simple website projects. It calls the following additional methods:
	AddMvcCore
	AddAuthorization
	AddDataAnnotations
	AddCacheTagHelper
AddApiExplorer	Web API explorer service.
AddCors	CORS support for enhanced security.
AddFormatterMappings	Mappings between a URL format and its corresponding media type.
AddControllers	Controller services but not services for views or pages. Commonly used in ASP.NET Core Web API projects. It calls the following additional methods:
	AddMvcCore
	AddAuthorization
	AddDataAnnotations
	AddCacheTagHelper
	AddApiExplorer
	AddCors
	AddFormatterMappings
AddViews	Support for .cshtml views including default conventions.
AddRazorViewEngine	Support for Razor view engine including processing the @ symbol.

AddControllersWithViews	Controller, views, and pages services. Commonly used in ASP. NET Core MVC website projects. It calls the following additional methods:
	AddMvcCore
	AddAuthorization
	AddDataAnnotations
	AddCacheTagHelper
	AddApiExplorer
	AddCors
	AddFormatterMappings
	AddViews
	AddRazorViewEngine
AddMvc	Similar to AddControllersWithViews, but you should only use it for backward compatibility.
AddDbContext<T>	Your DbContext type and its optional DbContextOptions<TContext>.
AddNorthwindContext	A custom extension method we created to make it easier to register the NorthwindContext class for either SQLite or SQL Server based on the project referenced.

You will see more examples of using these extension methods for registering services in the next few chapters when working with MVC and Web API services.

Setting up the HTTP request pipeline in the Configure method

The Configure method configures the HTTP request pipeline, which is made up of a connected sequence of delegates that can perform processing and then decide to either return a response themselves or pass processing on to the next delegate in the pipeline. Responses that come back can also be manipulated.

Remember that delegates define a method signature that a delegate implementation can plug into. The delegate for the HTTP request pipeline is simple, as shown in the following code:

```
public delegate Task RequestDelegate(HttpContext context);
```

You can see that the input parameter is an HttpContext. This provides access to everything you might need to process the incoming HTTP request, including the URL path, query string parameters, cookies, and user agent.

These delegates are often called middleware because they sit in between the browser client and the website or service.

Middleware delegates are configured using one of the following methods or a custom method that calls them itself:

- Run: Adds a middleware delegate that terminates the pipeline by immediately returning a response instead of calling the next middleware delegate.
- Map: Adds a middleware delegate that creates a branch in the pipeline when there is a matching request usually based on a URL path like /hello.
- Use: Adds a middleware delegate that forms part of the pipeline so it can decide if it wants to pass the request to the next delegate in the pipeline and it can modify the request and response before and after the next delegate.

For convenience, there are many extension methods that make it easier to build the pipeline, for example, UseMiddleware<T>, where T is a class that has:

1. A constructor with a RequestDelegate parameter that will be passed the next pipeline component
2. An Invoke method with a HttpContext parameter and returns a Task

Summarizing key middleware extension methods

Key middleware extension methods used in our code include the following:

- UseDeveloperExceptionPage: Captures synchronous and asynchronous System. Exception instances from the pipeline and generates HTML error responses.
- UseHsts: Adds middleware for using HSTS, which adds the Strict-Transport-Security header.
- UseRouting: Adds middleware that defines a point in the pipeline where routing decisions are made and must be combined with a call to UseEndpoints where the processing is then executed. This means that for our code, any URL paths that match / or /index or /suppliers will be mapped to Razor Pages and a match on /hello will be mapped to the anonymous delegate. Any other URL paths will be passed on to the next delegate for matching, for example, static files. This is why, although it looks like the mapping for Razor Pages and /hello happen after static files in the pipeline, they actually take priority because the call to UseRouting happens before UseStaticFiles.
- UseHttpsRedirection: Adds middleware for redirecting HTTP requests to HTTPS, so in our code a request for http://localhost:5000 would be modified to https://localhost:5001.
- UseDefaultFiles: Adds middleware that enables default file mapping on the current path, so in our code it would identify files such as index.html.
- UseStaticFiles: Adds middleware that looks in wwwroot for static files to return in the HTTP response.

- **UseEndpoints**: Adds middleware to execute to generate responses from decisions made earlier in the pipeline. Two endpoints are added, as shown in the following sub-list:

  - **MapRazorPages**: Adds middleware that will map URL paths such as /suppliers to a Razor Page file in the /Pages folder named suppliers.cshtml and return the results as the HTTP response.

  - **MapGet**: Adds middleware that will map URL paths such as /hello to an inline delegate that writes plain text directly to the HTTP response.

Visualizing the HTTP pipeline

The HTTP request and response pipeline can be visualized as a sequence of request delegates, called one after the other, as shown in the following simplified diagram, which excludes some middleware delegates, such as UseHsts:

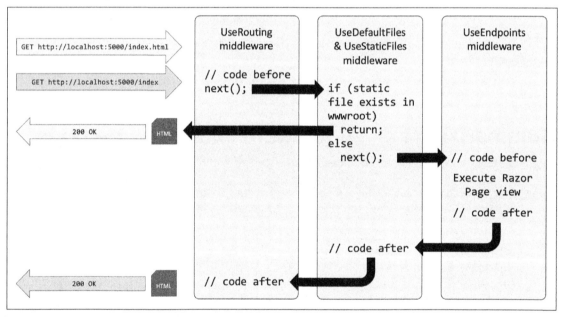

Figure 14.16: The HTTP request and response pipeline

As mentioned before, the UseRouting and UseEndpoints methods must be used together. Although the code to define the mapped routes such as /hello are written in UseEndpoints, the decision about whether an incoming HTTP request URL path matches and therefore which endpoint to execute is made at the UseRouting point in the pipeline.

Implementing an anonymous inline delegate as middleware

A delegate can be specified as an inline anonymous method. We will register one that plugs into the pipeline after routing decisions for endpoints have been made.

It will output which endpoint was chosen, as well as handling one specific route: /bonjour. If that route is matched, it will respond with plain text, without calling any further into the pipeline:

1. In Startup.cs, statically import Console, as shown in the following code:

    ```
    using static System.Console;
    ```

2. Add statements after the call to UseRouting and before the call to UseHttpsRedirection to use an anonymous method as a middleware delegate, as shown in the following code:

    ```
    app.Use(async (HttpContexl context, Func<Task> next) =>
    {
      RouteEndpoint? rep = context.GetEndpoint() as RouteEndpoint;
      if (rep is not null)
      {
        WriteLine($"Endpoint name: {rep.DisplayName}");
        WriteLine($"Endpoint route pattern: {rep.RoutePattern.RawText}");
      }

      if (context.Request.Path == "/bonjour")
      {
        // in the case of a match on URL path, this becomes a terminating
        // delegate that returns so does not call the next delegate
        await context.Response.WriteAsync("Bonjour Monde!");
        return;
      }

      // we could modify the request before calling the next delegate
      await next();
      // we could modify the response after calling the next delegate
    });
    ```

3. Start the website.

4. In Chrome, navigate to https://localhost:5001/, look at the console output and note that there was a match on an endpoint route /, it was processed as /index, and the Index.cshtml Razor Page was executed to return the response, as shown in the following output:

    ```
    Endpoint name: /index
    Endpoint route pattern:
    ```

5. Navigate to https://localhost:5001/suppliers and note that you can see that there was a match on an endpoint route /Suppliers and the Suppliers.cshtml Razor Page was executed to return the response, as shown in the following output:

    ```
    Endpoint name: /Suppliers
    Endpoint route pattern: Suppliers
    ```

6. Navigate to `https://localhost:5001/index` and note that there was a match on an endpoint route /index and the `Index.cshtml` Razor Page was executed to return the response, as shown in the following output:

```
Endpoint name: /index
Endpoint route pattern: index
```

7. Navigate to `https://localhost:5001/index.html` and note that there is no output written to the console because there was no match on an endpoint route but there was a match for a static file, so it was returned as the response.

8. Navigate to `https://localhost:5001/bonjour` and note that there is no output written to the console because there was no match on an endpoint route. Instead, our delegate matched on /bonjour, wrote directly to the response stream, and returned with no further processing.

9. Close Chrome and shut down the web server.

Practicing and exploring

Test your knowledge and understanding by answering some questions, get some hands-on practice, and explore this chapter's topics with deeper research.

Exercise 14.1 – Test your knowledge

Answer the following questions:

1. List six method names that can be specific in an HTTP request.
2. List six status codes and their descriptions that can be returned in an HTTP response.
3. In ASP.NET Core, what is the `Startup` class used for?
4. What does the acronym HSTS stand for and what does it do?
5. How do you enable static HTML pages for a website?
6. How do you mix C# code into the middle of HTML to create a dynamic page?
7. How can you define shared layouts for Razor Pages?
8. How can you separate the markup from the code-behind in a Razor Page?
9. How do you configure an Entity Framework Core data context for use with an ASP.NET Core website?
10. How can you reuse Razor Pages with ASP.NET Core 2.2 or later?

Exercise 14.2 – Practice building a data-driven web page

Add a Razor Page to the Northwind.Web website that enables the user to see a list of customers grouped by country. When the user clicks on a customer record, they then see a page showing the full contact details of that customer, and a list of their orders.

Exercise 14.3 – Practice building web pages for console apps

Reimplement some of the console apps from earlier chapters as Razor Pages, for example, from *Chapter 4, Writing, Debugging, and Testing Functions*, provide a web user interface to output times tables, calculate tax, and generate factorials and the Fibonacci sequence.

Exercise 14.4 – Explore topics

Use the links on the following page to learn more about the topics covered in this chapter:

```
https://github.com/markjprice/cs10dotnet6/blob/main/book-links.md#chapter-14---
building-websites-using-aspnet-core-razor-pages
```

Summary

In this chapter, you learned about the foundations of web development using HTTP, how to build a simple website that returns static files, and you used ASP.NET Core Razor Pages with Entity Framework Core to create web pages that were dynamically generated from information in a database.

We reviewed the HTTP request and response pipeline, what the helper extension methods do, and how you can add your own middleware that affects processing.

In the next chapter, you will learn how to build more complex websites using ASP.NET Core MVC, which separates the technical concerns of building a website into models, views, and controllers to make them easier to manage.

15

Building Websites Using the Model-View-Controller Pattern

This chapter is about building websites with a modern HTTP architecture on the server side using Microsoft ASP.NET Core MVC, including the startup configuration, authentication, authorization, routes, request and response pipeline, models, views, and controllers that make up an ASP.NET Core MVC project.

This chapter will cover the following topics:

- Setting up an ASP.NET Core MVC website
- Exploring an ASP.NET Core MVC website
- Customizing an ASP.NET Core MVC website
- Querying a database and using display templates
- Improving scalability using asynchronous tasks

Setting up an ASP.NET Core MVC website

ASP.NET Core Razor Pages are great for simple websites. For more complex websites, it would be better to have a more formal structure to manage that complexity.

This is where the **Model-View-Controller** (**MVC**) design pattern is useful. It uses technologies like Razor Pages, but allows a cleaner separation between technical concerns, as shown in the following list:

- **Models**: Classes that represent the data entities and view models used on the website.
- **Views**: Razor files, that is, .cshtml files, that render data in view models into HTML web pages. Blazor uses the .razor file extension, but do not confuse them with Razor files!

- **Controllers**: Classes that execute code when an HTTP request arrives at the web server. The controller methods usually create a view model that may contain entity models and passes it to a view to generate an HTTP response to send back to the web browser or other client.

The best way to understand using the MVC design pattern for web development is to see a working example.

Creating an ASP.NET Core MVC website

You will use a project template to create an ASP.NET Core MVC website project that has a database for authenticating and authorizing users. Visual Studio 2022 defaults to using SQL Server LocalDB for the accounts database. Visual Studio Code (or more accurately the `dotnet` tool) uses SQLite by default and you can specify a switch to use SQL Server LocalDB instead.

Let's see it in action:

1. Use your preferred code editor to add a MVC website project with authentication accounts stored in a database, as defined in the following list:

    1. Project template: **ASP.NET Core Web App (Model-View-Controller)** / `mvc`
    2. Language: C#
    3. Workspace/solution file and folder: `PracticalApps`
    4. Project file and folder: `Northwind.Mvc`
    5. Options: **Authentication Type: Individual Accounts** / `--auth Individual`
    6. For Visual Studio, leave all other options as their defaults

2. In Visual Studio Code, select `Northwind.Mvc` as the active OmniSharp project.

3. Build the `Northwind.Mvc` project.

4. At the command line or terminal, use the `help` switch to see other options for this project template, as shown in the following command:

```
dotnet new mvc --help
```

5. Note the results, as shown in the following partial output:

```
ASP.NET Core Web App (Model-View-Controller) (C#)
Author: Microsoft
Description: A project template for creating an ASP.NET Core application
with example ASP.NET Core MVC Views and Controllers. This template can
also be used for RESTful HTTP services.
This template contains technologies from parties other than Microsoft, see
https://aka.ms/aspnetcore/6.0-third-party-notices for details.
```

There are many options, especially related to authentication, as shown in the following table:

Switches	Description
-au|--auth	The type of authentication to use: None (default): This choice also allows you to disable HTTPS. Individual: Individual authentication that stores registered users and their passwords in a database (SQLite by default). We will use this in the project we create for this chapter. IndividualB2C: Individual authentication with Azure AD B2C. SingleOrg: Organizational authentication for a single tenant. MultiOrg: Organizational authentication for multiple tenants. Windows: Windows authentication. Mostly useful for intranets.
-uld|--use-local-db	Whether to use SQL Server LocalDB instead of SQLite. This option only applies if --auth Individual or --auth IndividualB2C is specified. The value is an optional bool with a default of false.
-rrc|--razor-runtime-compilation	Determines if the project is configured to use Razor runtime compilation in Debug builds. This can improve the performance of startup during debugging because it can defer the compilation of Razor views. The value is an optional bool with a default of false.
-f|--framework	The target framework for the project. Values can be: net6.0 (default), net5.0, or netcoreapp3.1

Creating the authentication database for SQL Server LocalDB

If you created the MVC project using Visual Studio 2022, or you used dotnet new mvc with the -uld or --use-local-db switch, then the database for authentication and authorization will be stored in SQL Server LocalDB. But the database does not yet exist. Let's create it now.

At a command prompt or terminal, in the Northwind.Mvc folder, enter the command to run database migrations so that the database used to store credentials for authentication is created, as shown in the following command:

```
dotnet ef database update
```

If you created the MVC project using dotnet new, then the database for authentication and authorization will be stored in SQLite and the file has already been created named app.db.

The connection string for the authentication database is named DefaultConnection and it is stored in the appsettings.json file in the root folder for the MVC website project.

For SQL Server LocalDB (with a truncated connection string), see the following markup:

```
{
  "ConnectionStrings": {
    "DefaultConnection": "Server=(localdb)\\mssqllocaldb;Database=aspnet-
Northwind.Mvc-...;Trusted_Connection=True;MultipleActiveResultSets=true"
  },
```

For SQLite, see the following markup:

```
{
  "ConnectionStrings": {
    "DefaultConnection": "DataSource=app.db;Cache=Shared"
  },
```

Exploring the default ASP.NET Core MVC website

Let's review the behavior of the default ASP.NET Core MVC website project template:

1. In the `Northwind.Mvc` project, expand the `Properties` folder, open the `launchSettings.json` file, and note the random port numbers (yours will be different) configured for the project for `HTTPS` and `HTTP`, as shown in the following markup:

   ```
   "profiles": {
     "Northwind.Mvc": {
       "commandName": "Project",
       "dotnetRunMessages": true,
       "launchBrowser": true,
       "applicationUrl": "https://localhost:7274;http://localhost:5274",
       "environmentVariables": {
         "ASPNETCORE_ENVIRONMENT": "Development"
       }
     },
   ```

2. Change the port numbers to `5001` for `HTTPS` and `5000` for `HTTP`, as shown in the following markup:

   ```
   "applicationUrl": "https://localhost:5001;http://localhost:5000",
   ```

3. Save the changes to the `launchSettings.json` file.

4. Start the website.

5. Start Chrome and open **Developer Tools**.

6. Navigate to `http://localhost:5000/` and note the following, as shown in *Figure 15.1*:

   - Requests for HTTP are automatically redirected to HTTPS on port `5001`.

- The top navigation menu with links to **Home**, **Privacy**, **Register**, and **Login**. If the viewport width is 575 pixels or less, then the navigation collapses into a hamburger menu.

- The title of the website, **Northwind.Mvc**, shown in the header and footer.

Figure 15.1: The ASP.NET Core MVC project template website home page

Understanding visitor registration

By default, passwords must have at least one non-alphanumeric character, they must have at least one digit (0-9), and they must have at least one uppercase letter (A-Z). I use Pa$$w0rd in scenarios like this when I am just exploring.

The MVC project template follows best practice for **double-opt-in (DOI)**, meaning that after filling in an email and password to register, an email is sent to the email address, and the visitor must click a link in that email to confirm that they want to register.

We have not yet configured an email provider to send that email, so we must simulate that step:

1. In the top navigation menu, click **Register**.
2. Enter an email and password, and then click the **Register** button. (I used test@example.com and Pa$$w0rd.)
3. Click the link with the text **Click here to confirm your account** and note that you are redirected to a **Confirm email** web page that you could customize.
4. In the top navigation menu, click **Login**, enter your email and password (note that there is an optional checkbox to remember you, and there are links if the visitor has forgotten their password or they want to register as a new visitor), and then click the **Log in** button.

5. Click your email address in the top navigation menu. This will navigate to an account management page. Note that you can set a phone number, change your email address, change your password, enable two-factor authentication (if you add an authenticator app), and download and delete your personal data.

6. Close Chrome and shut down the web server.

Reviewing an MVC website project structure

In your code editor, in Visual Studio **Solution Explorer** (toggle on **Show All Files**) or in Visual Studio Code **EXPLORER**, review the structure of an MVC website project, as shown in *Figure 15.2*:

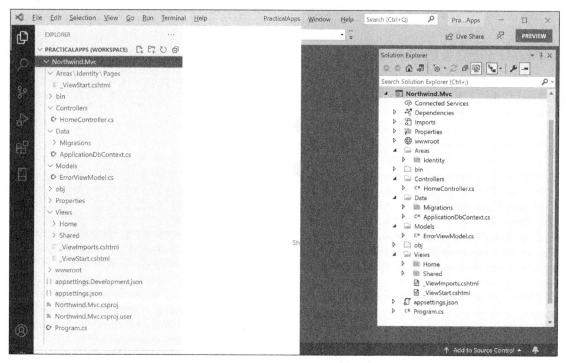

Figure 15.2: The default folder structure of an ASP.NET Core MVC project

We will look in more detail at some of these parts later, but for now, note the following:

- Areas: This folder contains nested folders and a file needed to integrate your website project with **ASP.NET Core Identity**, which is used for authentication.

- bin, obj: These folders contain temporary files needed during the build process and the compiled assemblies for the project.

- Controllers: This folder contains C# classes that have methods (known as actions) that fetch a model and pass it to a view, for example, HomeController.cs.

- `Data`: This folder contains Entity Framework Core migration classes used by the ASP.NET Core Identity system to provide data storage for authentication and authorization, for example, `ApplicationDbContext.cs`.

- `Models`: This folder contains C# classes that represent all of the data gathered together by a controller and passed to a view, for example, `ErrorViewModel.cs`.

- `Properties`: This folder contains a configuration file for IIS or IIS Express on Windows and for launching the website during development named `launchSettings.json`. This file is only used on the local development machine and is not deployed to your production website.

- `Views`: This folder contains the `.cshtml` Razor files that combine HTML and C# code to dynamically generate HTML responses. The `_ViewStart` file sets the default layout and `_ViewImports` imports common namespaces used in all views like tag helpers:

  - `Home`: This subfolder contains Razor files for the home and privacy pages.

  - `Shared`: This subfolder contains Razor files for the shared layout, an error page, and two partial views for logging in and validation scripts.

- `wwwroot`: This folder contains static content used by the website, such as CSS for styling, libraries of JavaScript, JavaScript for this website project, and a `favicon.ico` file. You also put images and other static file resources like PDF documents in here. The project template includes Bootstrap and jQuery libraries.

- `app.db`: This is the SQLite database that stores registered visitors. (If you used SQL Server LocalDB, then it will not be needed.)

- `appsettings.json` and `appsettings.Development.json`: These files contain settings that your website can load at runtime, for example, the database connection string for the ASP.NET Core Identity system and logging levels.

- `Northwind.Mvc.csproj`: This file contains project settings like the use of the Web .NET SDK, an entry for SQLite to ensure that the `app.db` file is copied to the website's output folder, and a list of NuGet packages that your project requires, including:

  - `Microsoft.AspNetCore.Diagnostics.EntityFrameworkCore`

  - `Microsoft.AspNetCore.Identity.EntityFrameworkCore`

  - `Microsoft.AspNetCore.Identity.UI`

  - `Microsoft.EntityFrameworkCore.Sqlite` or `Microsoft.EntityFrameworkCore.SqlServer`

  - `Microsoft.EntityFrameworkCore.Tools`

- `Program.cs`: This file defines a hidden `Program` class that contains the `Main` entry point. It builds a pipeline for processing incoming HTTP requests and hosts the website using default options like configuring the Kestrel web server and loading `appsettings`. It adds and configures services that your website needs, for example, ASP.NET Core Identity for authentication, SQLite or SQL Server for identity data storage, and so on, and routes for your application.

Reviewing the ASP.NET Core Identity database

Open `appsettings.json` to find the connection string used for the ASP.NET Core Identity database, as shown highlighted for SQL Server LocalDB in the following markup:

```
{
  "ConnectionStrings": {
    "DefaultConnection": "Server=(localdb)\\mssqllocaldb;Database=aspnet-
Northwind.Mvc-2F6A1E12-F9CF-480C-987D-FEFB4827DE22;Trusted_Connection=True;Multi
pleActiveResultSets=true"
  },
  "Logging": {
    "LogLevel": {
      "Default": "Information",
      "Microsoft": "Warning",
      "Microsoft.Hosting.Lifetime": "Information"
    }
  },
  "AllowedHosts": "*"
}
```

If you used SQL Server LocalDB for the identity data store, then you can use **Server Explorer** to connect to the database. You can copy and paste the connection string from the `appsettings.json` file (but remove the second backslash between (`localdb`) and `mssqllocaldb`).

If you installed an SQLite tool such as SQLiteStudio, then you can open the SQLite `app.db` database file.

You can then see the tables that the ASP.NET Core Identity system uses to register users and roles, including the `AspNetUsers` table used to store the registered visitor.

 Good Practice: The ASP.NET Core MVC project template follows good practice by storing a hash of the password instead of the password itself, which you will learn more about in *Chapter 20, Protecting Your Data and Applications*.

Exploring an ASP.NET Core MVC website

Let's walk through the parts that make up a modern ASP.NET Core MVC website.

Understanding ASP.NET Core MVC initialization

Appropriately enough, we will start by exploring the MVC website's default initialization and configuration:

1. Open the `Program.cs` file and note that it uses the top-level program feature (so there is a hidden `Program` class with a `Main` method). This file can be considered to be divided into four important sections from top to bottom.

> .NET 5 and earlier ASP.NET Core project templates used a `Startup` class to separate these parts into separate methods but with .NET 6, Microsoft encourages putting everything in a single `Program.cs` file.

2. The first section imports some namespaces, as shown in the following code:

```
using Microsoft.AspNetCore.Identity; // IdentityUser
using Microsoft.EntityFrameworkCore; // UseSqlServer, UseSqlite
using Northwind.Mvc.Data; // ApplicationDbContext
```

> Remember that by default, many other namespaces are imported using the implicit usings feature of .NET 6 and later. Build the project and then the globally imported namespaces can be found in the following path: `obj\Debug\net6.0\Northwind.Mvc.GlobalUsings.g.cs`.

3. The second section creates and configures a web host builder. It registers an application database context using SQL Server or SQLite with its database connection string loaded from the `appsettings.json` file for its data storage, adds ASP.NET Core Identity for authentication and configures it to use the application database, and adds support for MVC controllers with views, as shown in the following code:

```
var builder = WebApplication.CreateBuilder(args);

// Add services to the container.
var connectionString = builder.Configuration
  .GetConnectionString("DefaultConnection");

builder.Services.AddDbContext<ApplicationDbContext>(options =>
  options.UseSqlServer(connectionString)); // or UseSqlite

builder.Services.AddDatabaseDeveloperPageExceptionFilter();

builder.Services.AddDefaultIdentity<IdentityUser>(options =>
  options.SignIn.RequireConfirmedAccount = true)
  .AddEntityFrameworkStores<ApplicationDbContext>();

builder.Services.AddControllersWithViews();
```

The `builder` object has two commonly used objects: `Configuration` and `Services`:

- `Configuration` contains merged values from all the places you could set configuration: `appsettings.json`, environment variables, command-line arguments, and so on

- `Services` is a collection of registered dependency services

The call to `AddDbContext` is an example of registering a dependency service. ASP.NET Core implements the **dependency injection (DI)** design pattern so that other components like controllers can request needed services through their constructors. Developers register those services in this section of `Program.cs` (or if using a `Startup` class then in its `ConfigureServices` method.)

4. The third section configures the HTTP request pipeline. It configures a relative URL path to run database migrations if the website runs in development, or a friendlier error page and HSTS for production. HTTPS redirection, static files, routing, and ASP.NET Identity are enabled, and an MVC default route and Razor Pages are configured, as shown in the following code:

```
// Configure the HTTP request pipeline.
if (app.Environment.IsDevelopment())
{
    app.UseMigrationsEndPoint();
}
else
{
    app.UseExceptionHandler("/Home/Error");
    // The default HSTS value is 30 days. You may want to change this for
production scenarios, see https://aka.ms/aspnetcore-hsts.
    app.UseHsts();
}

app.UseHttpsRedirection();
app.UseStaticFiles();

app.UseRouting();

app.UseAuthentication();
app.UseAuthorization();

app.MapControllerRoute(
    name: "default",
    pattern: "{controller=Home}/{action=Index}/{id?}");

app.MapRazorPages();
```

We learned about most of these methods and features in *Chapter 14, Building Websites Using ASP.NET Core Razor Pages.*

Good Practice: What does the extension method
`UseMigrationsEndPoint` do? You could read the official
documentation, but it does not help much. For example, it does
not tell us what relative URL path it defines by default: `https://`
`docs.microsoft.com/en-us/dotnet/api/microsoft.`
`aspnetcore.builder.migrationsendpointextensions.`
`usemigrationsendpoint`. Luckily, ASP.NET Core is open source,
so we can read the source code and discover what it does, at the
following link: `https://github.com/dotnet/aspnetcore/blob/`
`main/src/Middleware/Diagnostics.EntityFrameworkCore/`
`src/MigrationsEndPointOptions.cs#L18`. Get into the habit of
exploring the source code for ASP.NET Core to understand how it
works.

Apart from the `UseAuthentication` and `UseAuthorization` methods, the most important
new method in this section of `Program.cs` is `MapControllerRoute`, which maps a default
route for use by MVC. This route is very flexible because it will map to almost any
incoming URL, as you will see in the next topic.

Although we will not create any Razor Pages in this chapter, we need to leave the
method call that maps Razor Page support because our MVC website uses ASP.NET
Core Identity for authentication and authorization, and it uses a Razor Class Library for
its user interface components, like visitor registration and login.

5. The fourth and final section has a thread-blocking method call that runs the website
    and waits for incoming HTTP requests to respond to, as shown in the following code:

    ```
    app.Run(); // blocking call
    ```

Understanding the default MVC route

The responsibility of a route is to discover the name of a controller class to instantiate and
an action method to execute with an optional `id` parameter to pass into the method that will
generate an HTTP response.

A default route is configured for MVC, as shown in the following code:

```
endpoints.MapControllerRoute(
  name: "default",
  pattern: "{controller=Home}/{action=Index}/{id?}");
```

The route pattern has parts in curly brackets {} called **segments**, and they are like named
parameters of a method. The value of these segments can be any `string`. Segments in URLs are
not case-sensitive.

The route pattern looks at any URL path requested by the browser and matches it to extract the
name of a `controller`, the name of an `action`, and an optional `id` value (the `?` symbol makes it
optional).

If the user hasn't entered these names, it uses defaults of Home for the controller and Index for the action (the = assignment sets a default for a named segment).

The following table contains example URLs and how the default route would work out the names of a controller and action:

URL	Controller	Action	ID
/	Home	Index	
/Muppet	Muppet	Index	
/Muppet/Kermit	Muppet	Kermit	
/Muppet/Kermit/Green	Muppet	Kermit	Green
/Products	Products	Index	
/Products/Detail	Products	Detail	
/Products/Detail/3	Products	Detail	3

Understanding controllers and actions

In MVC, the C stands for *controller*. From the route and an incoming URL, ASP.NET Core knows the name of the controller, so it will then look for a class that is decorated with the [Controller] attribute or derives from a class decorated with that attribute, for example, the Microsoft-provided class named ControllerBase, as shown in the following code:

```
namespace Microsoft.AspNetCore.Mvc
{
  //
  // Summary:
  // A base class for an MVC controller without view support.
  [Controller]
  public abstract class ControllerBase
  {
...
```

Understanding the ControllerBase class

As you can see in the XML comment, ControllerBase does not support views. It is used for creating web services, as you will see in *Chapter 16, Building and Consuming Web Services*.

ControllerBase has many useful properties for working with the current HTTP context, as shown in the following table:

Property	Description
Request	Just the HTTP request. For example, headers, query string parameters, the body of the request as a stream that you can read from, the content type and length, and cookies.
Response	Just the HTTP response. For example, headers, the body of the response as a stream that you can write to, the content type and length, status code, and cookies. There are also delegates like OnStarting and OnCompleted that you can hook a method up to.
HttpContext	Everything about the current HTTP context including the request and response, information about the connection, a collection of features that have been enabled on the server with middleware, and a User object for authentication and authorization.

Understanding the Controller class

Microsoft provides another class named Controller that your classes can inherit from if they do need view support, as shown in the following code:

```
namespace Microsoft.AspNetCore.Mvc
{
  //
  // Summary:
  // A base class for an MVC controller with view support.
  public abstract class Controller : ControllerBase,
    IActionFilter, IFilterMetadata, IAsyncActionFilter, IDisposable
  {
...
```

Controller has many useful properties for working with views, as shown in the following table:

Property	Description
ViewData	A dictionary that the controller can store key/value pairs in that is accessible in a view. The dictionary's lifetime is only for the current request/response.
ViewBag	A dynamic object that wraps the ViewData to provide a friendlier syntax for setting and getting dictionary values.
TempData	A dictionary that the controller can store key/value pairs in that is accessible in a view. The dictionary's lifetime is for the current request/response and the next request/response for the same visitor session. This is useful for storing a value during an initial request, responding with a redirect, and then reading the stored value in the subsequent request.

`Controller` has many useful methods for working with views, as shown in the following table:

Property	Description
`View`	Returns a `ViewResult` after executing a view that renders a full response, for example, a dynamically generated web page. The view can be selected using a convention or be specified with a string name. A model can be passed to the view.
`PartialView`	Returns a `PartialViewResult` after executing a view that is part of a full response, for example, a dynamically generated chunk of HTML. The view can be selected using a convention or be specified with a string name. A model can be passed to the view.
`ViewComponent`	Returns a `ViewComponentResult` after executing a component that dynamically generates HTML. The component must be selected by specifying its type or its name. An object can be passed as an argument.
`Json`	Returns a `JsonResult` containing a JSON-serialized object. This can be useful for implementing a simple Web API as part of an MVC controller that primarily returns HTML for a human to view.

Understanding the responsibilities of a controller

The responsibilities of a controller are as follows:

- Identify the services that the controller needs to be in a valid state and to function properly in their class constructor(s).

- Use the action name to identify a method to execute.

- Extract parameters from the HTTP request.

- Use the parameters to fetch any additional data needed to construct a view model and pass it to the appropriate view for the client. For example, if the client is a web browser, then a view that renders HTML would be most appropriate. Other clients might prefer alternative renderings, like document formats such as a PDF file or an Excel file, or data formats, like JSON or XML.

- Return the results from the view to the client as an HTTP response with an appropriate status code.

Let's review the controller used to generate the home, privacy, and error pages:

1. Expand the `Controllers` folder

2. Open the file named `HomeController.cs`

3. Note, as shown in the following code, that:

    - Extra namespaces are imported, which I have added comments for to show which types they are needed for.

    - A private read-only field is declared to store a reference to a logger for the `HomeController` that is set in a constructor.

    - All three action methods call a method named `View` and return the results as an `IActionResult` interface to the client.

- The `Error` action method passes a view model into its view with a request ID used for tracing. The error response will not be cached:

```
using Microsoft.AspNetCore.Mvc; // Controller, IActionResult
using Northwind.Mvc.Models; // ErrorViewModel
using System.Diagnostics; // Activity

namespace Northwind.Mvc.Controllers;
public class HomeController : Controller
{
  private readonly ILogger<HomeController> _logger;

  public HomeController(ILogger<HomeController> logger)
  {
    _logger = logger;
  }

  public IActionResult Index()
  {
    return View();
  }

  public IActionResult Privacy()
  {
    return View();
  }

  [ResponseCache(Duration = 0,
    Location = ResponseCacheLocation.None, NoStore = true)]
  public IActionResult Error()
  {
    return View(new ErrorViewModel { RequestId =
      Activity.Current?.Id ?? HttpContext.TraceIdentifier });
  }
}
```

If the visitor navigates to a path of / or /Home, then it is the equivalent of /Home/Index because those were the default names for controller and action in the default route.

Understanding the view search path convention

The `Index` and `Privacy` methods are identical in implementation, yet they return different web pages. This is because of **conventions**. The call to the `View` method looks in different paths for the Razor file to generate the web page.

Let's deliberately break one of the page names so that we can see the paths searched by default:

1. In the `Northwind.Mvc` project, expand the `Views` folder and then the `Home` folder.

2. Rename the `Privacy.cshtml` file to `Privacy2.cshtml`.

3. Start the website.

4. Start Chrome, navigate to `https://localhost:5001/`, click **Privacy**, and note the paths that are searched for a view to render the web page (including in `Shared` folders for MVC views and Razor Pages), as shown in *Figure 15.3*:

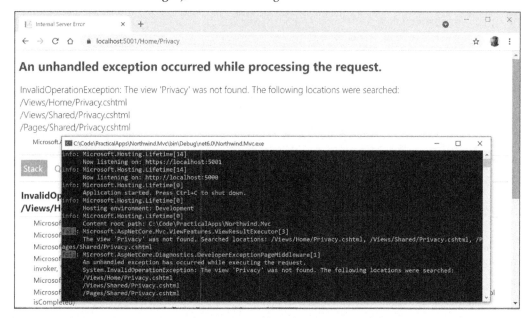

Figure 15.3: An exception showing the default search path for views

5. Close Chrome and shut down the web server.

6. Rename the `Privacy2.cshtml` file back to `Privacy.cshtml`.

You have now seen the view search path convention, as shown in the following list:

- Specific Razor view: `/Views/{controller}/{action}.cshtml`

- Shared Razor view: `/Views/Shared/{action}.cshtml`

- Shared Razor Page: `/Pages/Shared/{action}.cshtml`

Understanding logging

You have just seen that some errors are caught and written to the console. You can write messages to the console in the same way by using the logger.

1. In the `Controllers` folder, in `HomeController.cs`, in the `Index` method, add statements to use the logger to write some messages of various levels to the console, as shown in the following code:

```
_logger.LogError("This is a serious error (not really!)");
_logger.LogWarning("This is your first warning!");
```

```
_logger.LogWarning("Second warning!");
_logger.LogInformation("I am in the Index method of the HomeController.");
```

2. Start the `Northwind.Mvc` website project.

3. Start a web browser and navigate to the home page for the website.

4. At the command prompt or terminal, note the messages, as shown in the following output:

```
fail: Northwind.Mvc.Controllers.HomeController[0]
      This is a serious error (not really!)
warn: Northwind.Mvc.Controllers.HomeController[0]
      This is your first warning!
warn: Northwind.Mvc.Controllers.HomeController[0]
      Second warning!
info: Northwind.Mvc.Controllers.HomeController[0]
      I am in the Index method of the HomeController.
```

5. Close Chrome and shut down the web server.

Understanding filters

When you need to add some functionality to multiple controllers and actions, you can use or define your own filters that are implemented as an attribute class.

Filters can be applied at the following levels:

- At the action level by decorating an action method with the attribute. This will only affect the one action method.

- At the controller level by decorating the controller class with the attribute. This will affect all methods of the controller.

- At the global level by adding the attribute type to the `Filters` collection of the `MvcOptions` instance that can be used to configure MVC when calling the `AddControllersWithViews` method, as shown in the following code:

```
builder.Services.AddControllersWithViews(options =>
  {
    options.Filters.Add(typeof(MyCustomFilter));
  });
```

Using a filter to secure an action method

You might want to ensure that one particular action method of a controller class can only be called by members of certain security roles. You do this by decorating the method with the `[Authorize]` attribute, as described in the following list:

- `[Authorize]`: Only allow authenticated (non-anonymous, logged-in) visitors to access this action method.

- [Authorize(Roles = "Sales,Marketing")]: Only allow visitors who are members of the specified role(s) to access this action method.

Let's see an example:

1. In HomeController.cs, import the Microsoft.AspNetCore.Authorization namespace.

2. Add an attribute to the Privacy method to only allow access to logged-in users who are members of a group/role named Administrators, as shown highlighted in the following code:

```
[Authorize(Roles = "Administrators")]
public IActionResult Privacy()
```

3. Start the website.

4. Click **Privacy** and note that you are redirected to the log in page.

5. Enter your email and password.

6. Click **Log in** and note that you are denied access.

7. Close Chrome and shut down the web server.

Enabling role management and creating a role programmatically

By default, role management is not enabled in an ASP.NET Core MVC project, so we must first enable it before creating roles, and then we will create a controller that will programmatically create an Administrators role (if it does not already exist) and assign a test user to that role:

1. In Program.cs, in the setup of ASP.NET Core Identity and its database, add a call to AddRoles to enable role management, as shown highlighted in the following code:

```
services.AddDefaultIdentity<IdentityUser>(
  options => options.SignIn.RequireConfirmedAccount = true)
  .AddRoles<IdentityRole>() // enable role management
  .AddEntityFrameworkStores<ApplicationDbContext>();
```

2. In Controllers, add an empty controller class named RolesController.cs and modify its contents, as shown in the following code:

```
using Microsoft.AspNetCore.Identity; // RoleManager, UserManager
using Microsoft.AspNetCore.Mvc; // Controller, IActionResult

using static System.Console;

namespace Northwind.Mvc.Controllers;

public class RolesController : Controller
{
  private string AdminRole = "Administrators";
```

```
private string UserEmail = "test@example.com";

private readonly RoleManager<IdentityRole> roleManager;
private readonly UserManager<IdentityUser> userManager;

public RolesController(RoleManager<IdentityRole> roleManager,
  UserManager<IdentityUser> userManager)
{
  this.roleManager = roleManager;
  this.userManager = userManager;
}

public async Task<IActionResult> Index()
{
  if (!(await roleManager.RoleExistsAsync(AdminRole)))
  {
    await roleManager.CreateAsync(new IdentityRole(AdminRole));
  }

  IdentityUser user = await userManager.FindByEmailAsync(UserEmail);

  if (user == null)
  {
    user = new();
    user.UserName = UserEmail;
    user.Email = UserEmail;
    IdentityResult result = await userManager.CreateAsync(
      user, "Pa$$w0rd");

    if (result.Succeeded)
    {
      WriteLine($"User {user.UserName} created successfully.");
    }
    else
    {
      foreach (IdentityError error in result.Errors)
      {
        WriteLine(error.Description);
      }
    }
  }

  if (!user.EmailConfirmed)
  {
    string token = await userManager
```

```
       .GenerateEmailConfirmationTokenAsync(user);
    IdentityResult result = await userManager
       .ConfirmEmailAsync(user, token);

    if (result.Succeeded)
    {
      WriteLine($"User {user.UserName} email confirmed successfully.");
    }
    else
    {
      foreach (IdentityError error in result.Errors)
      {
        WriteLine(error.Description);
      }
    }
  }

  if (!(await userManager.IsInRoleAsync(user, AdminRole)))
  {
    IdentityResult result = await userManager
       .AddToRoleAsync(user, AdminRole);

    if (result.Succeeded)
    {
      WriteLine($"User {user.UserName} added to {AdminRole}
successfully.");
    }
    else
    {
      foreach (IdentityError error in result.Errors)
      {
        WriteLine(error.Description);
      }
    }
  }

  return Redirect("/");
  }
}
```

Note the following:

- Two fields for the name of the role and email of the user.
- The constructor gets and stores the registered user and role manager dependency services.
- If the Administrators role does not exist, we use the role manager to create it.

- We try to find a test user by its email, create it if it does not exist, and then assign the user to the `Administrators` role.

- Since the website uses DOI, we must generate an email confirmation token and use it to confirm the new users email address.

- Success messages and any errors are written out to the console.

- You will be automatically redirected to the home page.

3. Start the website.

4. Click **Privacy** and note that you are redirected to the login page.

5. Enter your email and password. (I used `mark@example.com`.)

6. Click **Log in** and note that you are denied access as before.

7. Click **Home**.

8. In the address bar, manually enter `roles` as a relative URL path, as shown in the following link: `https://localhost:5001/roles`.

9. View the success messages written to the console, as shown in the following output:

```
User test@example.com created successfully.
User test@example.com email confirmed successfully.
User test@example.com added to Administrators successfully.
```

10. Click **Logout**, because you must log out and log back in to load your role memberships when they are created after you have already logged in.

11. Try accessing the **Privacy** page again, enter the email for the new user that was programmatically created, for example, `test@example.com`, and their password, and then click **Log in**, and you should now have access.

12. Close Chrome and shut down the web server.

Using a filter to cache a response

To improve response times and scalability, you might want to cache the HTTP response that is generated by an action method by decorating the method with the `[ResponseCache]` attribute.

You control where the response is cached and for how long by setting parameters, as shown in the following list:

- `Duration`: In seconds. This sets the `max-age` HTTP response header measured in seconds. Common choices are one hour (3600 seconds) and one day (86400 seconds).

- `Location`: One of the `ResponseCacheLocation` values, `Any`, `Client`, or `None`. This sets the `cache-control` HTTP response header.

- `NoStore`: If true, this ignores `Duration` and `Location` and sets the cache-control HTTP response header to `no-store`.

Let's see an example:

1. In `HomeController.cs`, add an attribute to the `Index` method to cache the response for 10 seconds on the browser or any proxies between the server and browser, as shown highlighted in the following code:

```
[ResponseCache(Duration = 10, Location = ResponseCacheLocation.Any)]
public IActionResult Index()
```

2. In `Views`, in `Home`, open `Index.cshtml`, and add a paragraph to output the current time in long format to include seconds, as shown in the following markup:

```
<p class="alert alert-primary">@DateTime.Now.ToLongTimeString()</p>
```

3. Start the website.

4. Note the time on the home page.

5. Click **Register**.

6. Click **Home** and note the time on the home page is the same because a cached version of the page is used.

7. Click **Register**. Wait at least ten seconds.

8. Click **Home** and note the time has now updated.

9. Click **Log in**, enter your email and password, and then click **Log in**.

10. Note the time on the home page.

11. Click **Privacy**.

12. Click **Home** and note the page is not cached.

13. View the console and note the warning message explaining that your caching has been overridden because the visitor is logged in and, in this scenario, ASP.NET Core uses anti-forgery tokens and they should not be cached, as shown in the following output:

```
warn: Microsoft.AspNetCore.Antiforgery.DefaultAntiforgery[8]
      The 'Cache-Control' and 'Pragma' headers have been overridden and
set to 'no-cache, no-store' and 'no-cache' respectively to prevent caching
of this response. Any response that uses antiforgery should not be cached.
```

14. Close Chrome and shut down the web server.

Using a filter to define a custom route

You might want to define a simplified route for an action method instead of using the default route.

For example, to show the privacy page currently requires the following URL path, which specifies both the controller and action:

```
https://localhost:5001/home/privacy
```

We could make the route simpler, as shown in the following link:

```
https://localhost:5001/private
```

Let's see how to do that:

1. In `HomeController.cs`, add an attribute to the `Privacy` method to define a simplified route, as shown highlighted in the following code:

    ```
    [Route("private")]
    [Authorize(Roles = "Administrators")]
    public IActionResult Privacy()
    ```

2. Start the website.

3. In the address bar, enter the following URL path:

    ```
    https://localhost:5001/private
    ```

4. Enter your email and password, click **Log in**, and note that the simplified path shows the **Privacy** page.

5. Close Chrome and shut down the web server.

Understanding entity and view models

In MVC, the M stands for *model*. Models represent the data required to respond to a request. There are two types of models commonly used: entity models and view models.

Entity models represent entities in a database like SQL Server or SQLite. Based on the request, one or more entities might need to be retrieved from data storage. Entity models are defined using classes since they might need to change and then be used to update the underlying data store.

All the data that we want to show in response to a request is the **MVC model**, sometimes called a **view model**, because it is a model that is passed into a view for rendering into a response format like HTML or JSON. View models should be immutable, so they are commonly defined using records.

For example, the following HTTP GET request might mean that the browser is asking for the product details page for product number 3:

```
http://www.example.com/products/details/3
```

The controller would need to use the ID route value 3 to retrieve the entity for that product and pass it to a view that can then turn the model into HTML for display in a browser.

Imagine that when a user comes to our website, we want to show them a carousel of categories, a list of products, and a count of the number of visitors we have had this month.

We will reference the Entity Framework Core entity data model for the Northwind database that you created in *Chapter 13, Introducing Practical Applications of C# and .NET*:

1. In the `Northwind.Mvc` project, add a project reference to `Northwind.Common.DataContext` for either SQLite or SQL Server, as shown in the following markup:

    ```
    <ItemGroup>
      <!-- change Sqlite to SqlServer if you prefer -->
      <ProjectReference Include=
    "..\Northwind.Common.DataContext.Sqlite\Northwind.Common.DataContext.
    Sqlite.csproj" />
    </ItemGroup>
    ```

2. Build the `Northwind.Mvc` project to compile its dependencies.

3. If you are using SQL Server, or might want to switch between SQL Server and SQLite, then in `appsettings.json`, add a connection string for the Northwind database using SQL Server, as shown highlighted in the following markup:

    ```
    {
      "ConnectionStrings": {
        "DefaultConnection": "Server=(localdb)\\mssqllocaldb;Database=aspnet-
    Northwind.Mvc-DC9C4FAF-DD84-4FC9-B925-69A61240EDA7;Trusted_Connection=True
    ;MultipleActiveResultSets=true",
        "NorthwindConnection": "Server=.;Database=Northwind;Trusted_Connection
    =True;MultipleActiveResultSets=true"
      },
    ```

4. In `Program.cs`, import the namespace to work with your entity model types, as shown in the following code:

    ```
    using Packt.Shared; // AddNorthwindContext extension method
    ```

5. Before the `builder.Build` method call, add statements to load the appropriate connection string and then to register the Northwind database context, as shown in the following code:

    ```
    // if you are using SQL Server
    string sqlServerConnection = builder.Configuration
      .GetConnectionString("NorthwindConnection");
    builder.Services.AddNorthwindContext(sqlServerConnection);

    // if you are using SQLite default is ..\Northwind.db
    builder.Services.AddNorthwindContext();
    ```

6. Add a class file to the `Models` folder and name it `HomeIndexViewModel.cs`.

> **Good Practice**: Although the `ErrorViewModel` class created by the MVC project template does not follow this convention, I recommend that you use the naming convention {Controller}{Action} ViewModel for your view model classes.

7. Modify the statements to define a record that has three properties for a count of the number of visitors, and lists of categories and products, as shown in the following code:

```
using Packt.Shared; // Category, Product

namespace Northwind.Mvc.Models;

public record HomeIndexViewModel
(
  int VisitorCount,
  IList<Category> Categories,
  IList<Product> Products
);
```

8. In `HomeController.cs`, import the `Packt.Shared` namespace, as shown in the following code:

```
using Packt.Shared; // NorthwindContext
```

9. Add a field to store a reference to a `Northwind` instance, and initialize it in the constructor, as shown highlighted in the following code:

```
public class HomeController : Controller
{
  private readonly ILogger<HomeController> _logger;
  private readonly NorthwindContext db;

  public HomeController(ILogger<HomeController> logger,
    NorthwindContext injectedContext)
  {
    _logger = logger;
    db = injectedContext;
  }
...
```

ASP.NET Core will use constructor parameter injection to pass an instance of the `NorthwindContext` database context using the connection string you specified in `Program.cs`.

10. Modify the statements in the `Index` action method to create an instance of the view model for this method, simulating a visitor count using the `Random` class to generate a number between 1 and 1000, and using the `Northwind` database to get lists of categories and products, and then pass the model to the view, as shown highlighted in the following code:

```
[ResponseCache(Duration = 10, Location = ResponseCacheLocation.Any)]
public IActionResult Index()
{
  _logger.LogError("This is a serious error (not really!)");
  _logger.LogWarning("This is your first warning!");
```

```
    _logger.LogWarning("Second warning!");
    _logger.LogInformation("I am in the Index method of the
HomeController.");

    HomeIndexViewModel model = new
    (
      VisitorCount: (new Random()).Next(1, 1001),
      Categories: db.Categories.ToList(),
      Products: db.Products.ToList()
    );
    return View(model); // pass model to view
  }
```

Remember the view search convention: when the `View` method is called in a controller's action method, ASP.NET Core MVC looks in the `Views` folder for a subfolder with the same name as the current controller, that is, `Home`. It then looks for a file with the same name as the current action, that is, `Index.cshtml`. It will also search for views that match the action method name in the `Shared` folder and for Razor Pages in the `Pages` folder.

Understanding views

In MVC, the V stands for *view*. The responsibility of a view is to transform a model into HTML or other formats.

There are multiple **view engines** that could be used to do this. The default view engine is called **Razor**, and it uses the @ symbol to indicate server-side code execution. The Razor Pages feature introduced with ASP.NET Core 2.0 uses the same view engine and so can use the same Razor syntax.

Let's modify the home page view to render the lists of categories and products:

1. Expand the `Views` folder, and then expand the `Home` folder.

2. Open the `Index.cshtml` file and note the block of C# code wrapped in @{ }. This will execute first and can be used to store data that needs to be passed into a shared layout file like the title of the web page, as shown in the following code:

    ```
    @{
        ViewData["Title"] = "Home Page";
    }
    ```

3. Note the static HTML content in the `<div>` element that uses Bootstrap for styling.

> **Good Practice**: As well as defining your own styles, base your styles on a common library, such as Bootstrap, that implements responsive design.

Just as with Razor Pages, there is a file named `_ViewStart.cshtml` that gets executed by the `View` method. It is used to set defaults that apply to all views.

For example, it sets the `Layout` property of all views to a shared layout file, as shown in the following markup:

```
@{
    Layout = "_Layout";
}
```

4. In the `Views` folder, open the `_ViewImports.cshtml` file and note that it imports some namespaces and then adds the ASP.NET Core tag helpers, as shown in the following code:

```
@using Northwind.Mvc
@using Northwind.Mvc.Models
@addTagHelper *, Microsoft.AspNetCore.Mvc.TagHelpers
```

5. In the `Shared` folder, open the `_Layout.cshtml` file.

6. Note that the title is being read from the `ViewData` dictionary that was set earlier in the `Index.cshtml` view, as shown in the following markup:

```
<title>@ViewData["Title"] - Northwind.Mvc</title>
```

7. Note the rendering of links to support Bootstrap and a site stylesheet, where ~ means the `wwwroot` folder, as shown in the following markup:

```
<link rel="stylesheet"
    href="~/lib/bootstrap/dist/css/bootstrap.css" />
<link rel="stylesheet" href="~/css/site.css" />
```

8. Note the rendering of a navigation bar in the header, as shown in the following markup:

```
<body>
  <header>
    <nav class="navbar ...">
```

9. Note the rendering of a collapsible `<div>` containing a partial view for logging in and hyperlinks to allow users to navigate between pages using ASP.NET Core tag helpers with attributes like `asp-controller` and `asp-action`, as shown in the following markup:

```
<div class=
  "navbar-collapse collapse d-sm-inline-flex justify-content-between">
  <ul class="navbar-nav flex-grow-1">
    <li class="nav-item">
      <a class="nav-link text-dark" asp-area=""
        asp-controller="Home" asp-action="Index">Home</a>
    </li>
    <li class="nav-item">
      <a class="nav-link text-dark"
```

```
        asp-area="" asp-controller="Home"
        asp-action="Privacy">Privacy</a>
    </li>
    </ul>
    <partial name="_LoginPartial" />
</div>
```

The `<a>` elements use tag helper attributes named `asp-controller` and `asp-action` to specify the controller name and action name that will execute when the link is clicked on. If you want to navigate to a feature in a Razor Class Library, like the `employees` component that you created in the previous chapter, then you use `asp-area` to specify the feature name.

10. Note the rendering of the body inside the `<main>` element, as shown in the following markup:

```
<div class="container">
  <main role="main" class="pb-3">
    @RenderBody()
  </main>
</div>
```

The `RenderBody` method injects the contents of a specific Razor view for a page like the `Index.cshtml` file at that point in the shared layout.

11. Note the rendering of `<script>` elements at the bottom of the page so that it does not slow down the display of the page and that you can add your own script blocks into an optional defined section named `scripts`, as shown in the following markup:

```
<script src="~/lib/jquery/dist/jquery.min.js"></script>
<script src="~/lib/bootstrap/dist/js/bootstrap.bundle.min.js">
</script>
<script src="~/js/site.js" asp-append-version="true"></script>
@await RenderSectionAsync("scripts", required: false)
```

When `asp-append-version` is specified with a `true` value in any element like `<img>` or `<script>` along with a `src` attribute, the Image Tag Helper is invoked (this helper is poorly named because it does not only affect images!).

It works by automatically appending a query string value named v that is generated from a hash of the referenced source file, as shown in the following example generated output:

```
<script src="~/js/site.js? v=Kl_dqr9NVtnMdsM2MUg4qthUnWZm5T1fCEimBPWDNgM"></
script>
```

If even a single byte within the `site.js` file changes, then its hash value will be different, and therefore if a browser or CDN is caching the script file, then it will bust the cached copy and replace it with the new version.

Customizing an ASP.NET Core MVC website

Now that you've reviewed the structure of a basic MVC website, you will customize and extend it. You have already registered an EF Core model for the Northwind database, so the next task is to output some of that data on the home page.

Defining a custom style

The home page will show a list of the 77 products in the Northwind database. To make efficient use of space, we want to show the list in three columns. To do this, we need to customize the stylesheet for the website:

1. In the wwwroot\css folder, open the site.css file.

2. At the bottom of the file, add a new style that will apply to an element with the product-columns ID, as shown in the following code:

    ```
    #product-columns
    {
      column-count: 3;
    }
    ```

Setting up the category images

The Northwind database includes a table of eight categories, but they do not have images, and websites look better with some colorful pictures:

1. In the wwwroot folder, create a folder named images.

2. In the images folder, add eight image files named category1.jpeg, category2.jpeg, and so on, up to category8.jpeg.

 You can download images from the GitHub repository for this book at the following link: https://github.com/markjprice/cs10dotnet6/tree/master/Assets/Categories

Understanding Razor syntax

Before we customize the home page view, let's review an example Razor file that has an initial Razor code block that instantiates an order with price and quantity and then outputs information about the order on the web page, as shown in the following markup:

```
@{
  Order order = new()
  {
    OrderId = 123,
```

```
      Product = "Sushi",
      Price = 8.49M,
      Quantity = 3
    };
}
```

```
<div>Your order for @order.Quantity of @order.Product has a total cost of $@
order.Price * @order.Quantity</div>
```

The preceding Razor file would result in the following incorrect output:

```
Your order for 3 of Sushi has a total cost of $8.49 * 3
```

Although Razor markup can include the value of any single property using the @object. property syntax, you should wrap expressions in parentheses, as shown in the following markup:

```
<div>Your order for @order.Quantity of @order.Product has a total cost of $@
(order.Price * order.Quantity)</div>
```

The preceding Razor expression results in the following correct output:

```
Your order for 3 of Sushi has a total cost of $25.47
```

Defining a typed view

To improve the IntelliSense when writing a view, you can define what type the view can expect using an @model directive at the top:

1. In the Views\Home folder, open Index.cshtml.

2. At the top of the file, add a statement to set the model type to use the HomeIndexViewModel, as shown in the following code:

    ```
    @model HomeIndexViewModel
    ```

    Now, whenever we type Model in this view, your code editor will know the correct type for the model and will provide IntelliSense for it.

    While entering code in a view, remember the following:

    *   Declare the type for the model, use @model (with a lowercase m).
    *   Interact with the instance of the model, use @Model (with an uppercase M).

    Let's continue customizing the view for the home page.

3. In the initial Razor code block, add a statement to declare a string variable for the current item and under the existing <div> element add new markup to output categories in a carousel and products as an unordered list, as shown in the following markup:

```
@using Packt.Shared
@model HomeIndexViewModel
@{
  ViewData["Title"] = "Home Page";
  string currentItem = "";
}

<div class="text-center">
  <h1 class="display-4">Welcome</h1>
  <p>Learn about <a href="https://docs.microsoft.com/aspnet/core">building
Web apps with ASP.NET Core</a>.</p>
  <p class="alert alert-primary">@DateTime.Now.ToLongTimeString()</p>
</div>
@if (Model is not null)
{
<div id="categories" class="carousel slide" data-ride="carousel"
    data-interval="3000" data-keyboard="true">
  <ol class="carousel-indicators">
  @for (int c = 0; c < Model.Categories.Count; c++)
  {
    if (c == 0)
    {
      currentItem = "active";
    }
    else
    {
      currentItem = "";
    }
    <li data-target="#categories" data-slide-to="@c"
        class="@currentItem"></li>
  }
  </ol>
  <div class="carousel-inner">
  @for (int c = 0; c < Model.Categories.Count; c++)
  {
    if (c == 0)
    {
      currentItem = "active";
    }
    else
    {
      currentItem = "";
    }
    <div class="carousel-item @currentItem">
      <img class="d-block w-100" src=
```

```
          "~/images/category@(Model.Categories[c].CategoryId).jpeg"
          alt="@Model.Categories[c].CategoryName" />
        <div class="carousel-caption d-none d-md-block">
          <h2>@Model.Categories[c].CategoryName</h2>
          <h3>@Model.Categories[c].Description</h3>
          <p>
            <a class="btn btn-primary"
              href="/category/@Model.Categories[c].CategoryId">View</a>
          </p>
        </div>
      </div>
    }
    </div>
    <a class="carousel-control-prev" href="#categories"
      role="button" data-slide="prev">
      <span class="carousel-control-prev-icon"
        aria-hidden="true"></span>
      <span class="sr-only">Previous</span>
    </a>
    <a class="carousel-control-next" href="#categories"
      role="button" data-slide="next">
      <span class="carousel-control-next-icon" aria-hidden="true"></span>
      <span class="sr-only">Next</span>
    </a>
  </div>
}
<div class="row">
  <div class="col-md-12">
    <h1>Northwind</h1>
    <p class="lead">
      We have had @Model?.VisitorCount visitors this month.
    </p>
    @if (Model is not null)
    {
    <h2>Products</h2>
    <div id="product-columns">
      <ul>
      @foreach (Product p in @Model.Products)
      {
```

```
        <li>
          <a asp-controller="Home"
             asp-action="ProductDetail"
             asp-route-id="@p.ProductId">
            @p.ProductName costs
   @(p.UnitPrice is null ? "zero" : p.UnitPrice.Value.ToString("C"))
          </a>
        </li>
      }
      </ul>
    </div>
    }
  </div>
</div>
```

While reviewing the preceding Razor markup, note the following:

- It is easy to mix static HTML elements such as <ul> and <li> with C# code to output the carousel of categories and the list of product names.
- The <div> element with the id attribute of product-columns will use the custom style that we defined earlier, so all of the content in that element will display in three columns.
- The <img> element for each category uses parentheses around a Razor expression to ensure that the compiler does not include the .jpeg as part of the expression, as shown in the following markup: "~/images/category@(Model.Categories[c].CategoryID). jpeg"
- The <a> elements for the product links use tag helpers to generate URL paths. Clicks on these hyperlinks will be handled by the HomeController and its ProductDetail action method. This action method does not exist yet, but you will add it later in this chapter. The ID of the product is passed as a route segment named id, as shown in the following URL path for Ipoh Coffee: https://localhost:5001/Home/ProductDetail/43.

Reviewing the customized home page

Let's see the result of our customized home page:

1. Start the Northwind.Mvc website project.

2. Note the home page has a rotating carousel showing categories, a random number of visitors, and a list of products in three columns, as shown in *Figure 15.4*:

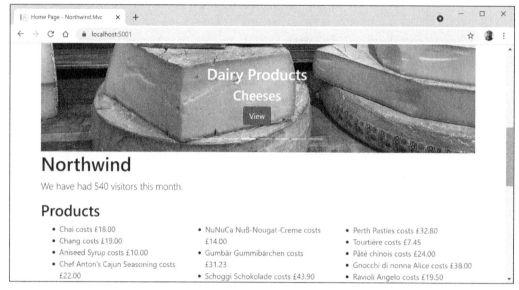

Figure 15.4: The updated Northwind MVC website home page

For now, clicking on any of the categories or product links gives **404 Not Found** errors, so let's see how we can implement pages that use the passed parameters to see the details of a product or category.

3. Close Chrome and shut down the web server.

Passing parameters using a route value

One way to pass a simple parameter is to use the id segment defined in the default route:

1. In the HomeController class, add an action method named ProductDetail, as shown in the following code:

```
public IActionResult ProductDetail(int? id)
{
  if (!id.HasValue)
  {
    return BadRequest("You must pass a product ID in the route, for
example, /Home/ProductDetail/21");
  }

  Product? model = db.Products
    .SingleOrDefault(p => p.ProductId == id);

  if (model == null)
  {
```

```
            return NotFound($"ProductId {id} not found.");
        }

        return View(model); // pass model to view and then return result
    }
```

Note the following:

- This method uses a feature of ASP.NET Core called **model binding** to automatically match the id passed in the route to the parameter named id in the method.

- Inside the method, we check to see whether id does not have a value, and if so, we call the BadRequest method to return a 400 status code with a custom message explaining the correct URL path format.

- Otherwise, we can connect to the database and try to retrieve a product using the id value.

- If we find a product, we pass it to a view; otherwise, we call the NotFound method to return a 404 status code and a custom message explaining that a product with that ID was not found in the database.

2. Inside the Views/Home folder, add a new file named ProductDetail.cshtml.

3. Modify the contents, as shown in the following markup:

```
@model Packt.Shared.Product
@{
    ViewData["Title"] = "Product Detail - " + Model.ProductName;
}
<h2>Product Detail</h2>
<hr />
<div>
    <dl class="dl-horizontal">
        <dt>Product Id</dt>
        <dd>@Model.ProductId</dd>
        <dt>Product Name</dt>
        <dd>@Model.ProductName</dd>
        <dt>Category Id</dt>
        <dd>@Model.CategoryId</dd>
        <dt>Unit Price</dt>
        <dd>@Model.UnitPrice.Value.ToString("C")</dd>
        <dt>Units In Stock</dt>
        <dd>@Model.UnitsInStock</dd>
    </dl>
</div>
```

4. Start the Northwind.Mvc project.

5. When the home page appears with the list of products, click on one of them, for example, the second product, **Chang**.

6. Note the URL path in the browser's address bar, the page title shown in the browser tab, and the product details page, as shown in *Figure 15.5*:

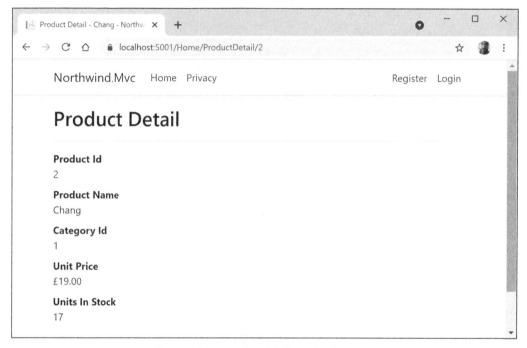

Figure 15.5: The product detail page for Chang

7. View **Developer tools**.

8. Edit the URL in the address box of Chrome to request a product ID that does not exist, like 99, and note the 404 Not Found status code and custom error response.

Understanding model binders in more detail

Model binders are powerful, and the default one does a lot for you. After the default route identifies a controller class to instantiate and an action method to call, if that method has parameters, then those parameters need to have values set.

Model binders do this by looking for parameter values passed in the HTTP request as any of the following types of parameters:

- **Route parameter**, like id as we did in the previous section, as shown in the following URL path: /Home/ProductDetail/2

- **Query string parameter**, as shown in the following URL path: /Home/ ProductDetail?id=2

- **Form parameter**, as shown in the following markup:

```
<form action="post" action="/Home/ProductDetail">
  <input type="text" name="id" value="2" />
  <input type="submit" />
</form>
```

Model binders can populate almost any type:

- Simple types, like int, string, DateTime, and bool.
- Complex types defined by class, record, or struct.
- Collection types, like arrays and lists.

Let's create a somewhat artificial example to illustrate what can be achieved using the default model binder:

1. In the Models folder, add a new file named Thing.cs.

2. Modify the contents to define a class with two properties for a nullable integer named Id and a string named Color, as shown in the following code:

    ```
    namespace Northwind.Mvc.Models;

    public class Thing
    {
      public int? Id { get; set; }
      public string? Color { get; set; }
    }
    ```

3. In HomeController, add two new action methods, one to show a page with a form and one to display a thing with a parameter using your new model type, as shown in the following code:

    ```
    public IActionResult ModelBinding()
    {
      return View(); // the page with a form to submit
    }

    public IActionResult ModelBinding(Thing thing)
    {
      return View(thing); // show the model bound thing
    }
    ```

4. In the Views\Home folder, add a new file named ModelBinding.cshtml.

5. Modify its contents, as shown in the following markup:

    ```
    @model Thing
    @{
      ViewData["Title"] = "Model Binding Demo";
    }
    <h1>@ViewData["Title"]</h1>
    ```

```
<div>
  Enter values for your thing in the following form:
</div>
<form method="POST" action="/home/modelbinding?id=3">
  <input name="color" value="Red" />
  <input type="submit" />
</form>
@if (Model != null)
{
<h2>Submitted Thing</h2>
<hr />
<div>
  <dl class="dl-horizontal">
    <dt>Model.Id</dt>
    <dd>@Model.Id</dd>
    <dt>Model.Color</dt>
    <dd>@Model.Color</dd>
  </dl>
</div>
}
```

6. In Views/Home, open Index.cshtml, and in the first <div>, add a new paragraph with a link to the model binding page, as shown in the following markup:

    ```
    <p><a asp-action="ModelBinding" asp-controller="Home">Binding</a></p>
    ```

7. Start the website.

8. On the home page, click **Binding**.

9. Note the unhandled exception about an ambiguous match, as shown in *Figure 15.6*:

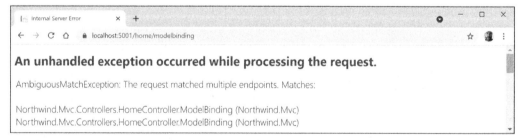

Figure 15.6: An unhandled ambiguous action method mismatch exception

10. Close Chrome and shut down the web server.

Disambiguating action methods

Although the C# compiler can differentiate between the two methods by noting that the signatures are different, from the routing of an HTTP request's point of view, both methods are potential matches. We need an HTTP-specific way to disambiguate the action methods.

We could do this by creating different names for the actions or by specifying that one method should be used for a specific HTTP verb, like GET, POST, or DELETE. That is how we will solve the problem:

1. In HomeController, decorate the second ModelBinding action method to indicate that it should be used for processing HTTP POST requests, that is, when a form is submitted, as shown highlighted in the following code:

```
[HttpPost]
public IActionResult ModelBinding(Thing thing)
```

 The other ModelBinding action method will implicitly be used for all other types of HTTP request, like GET, PUT, DELETE, and so on.

2. Start the website.

3. On the home page, click **Binding**.

4. Click the **Submit** button and note the value for the Id property is set from the query string parameter and the value for the color property is set from the form parameter, as shown in *Figure 15.7*:

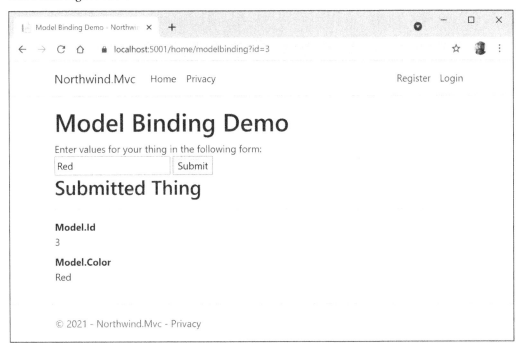

Figure 15.7: The Model Binding Demo page

5. Close Chrome and shut down the web server.

Passing a route parameter

Now we will set the property using a route parameter:

1. Modify the action for the form to pass the value 2 as a route parameter, as shown highlighted in the following markup:

   ```
   <form method="POST" action="/home/modelbinding/2?id=3">
   ```

2. Start the website.
3. On the home page, click **Binding**.
4. Click the **Submit** button and note the value for the Id property is set from the route parameter and the value for the Color property is set from the form parameter.
5. Close Chrome and shut down the web server.

Passing a form parameter

Now we will set the property using a form parameter:

1. Modify the action for the form to pass the value 1 as a form parameter, as shown highlighted in the following markup:

   ```
   <form method="POST" action="/home/modelbinding/2?id=3">
     <input name="id" value="1" />
     <input name="color" value="Red" />
     <input type="submit" />
   </form>
   ```

2. Start the website.
3. On the home page, click **Binding**.
4. Click the **Submit** button and note the values for the Id and Color properties are both set from the form parameters.

 Good Practice: If you have multiple parameters with the same name, then remember that form parameters have the highest priority and query string parameters have the lowest priority for automatic model binding.

Validating the model

The process of model binding can cause errors, for example, data type conversions or validation errors if the model has been decorated with validation rules. What data has been bound and any binding or validation errors are stored in ControllerBase.ModelState.

Let's explore what we can do with model state by applying some validation rules to the bound model and then showing invalid data messages in the view:

1. In the `Models` folder, open `Thing.cs`.

2. Import the `System.ComponentModel.DataAnnotations` namespace.

3. Decorate the `Id` property with a validation attribute to limit the range of allowed numbers to 1 to 10, and one to ensure that the visitor supplies a color, and add a new `Email` property with a regular expression for validation, as shown highlighted in the following code:

```
public class Thing
{
  [Range(1, 10)]
  public int? Id { get; set; }

  [Required]
  public string? Color { get; set; }

  [EmailAddress]
  public string? Email { get; set; }
}
```

4. In the `Models` folder, add a new file named `HomeModelBindingViewModel.cs`.

5. Modify its contents to define a record with properties to store the bound model, a flag to indicate that there are errors, and a sequence of error messages, as shown in the following code:

```
namespace Northwind.Mvc.Models;

public record HomeModelBindingViewModel
(
  Thing Thing,
  bool HasErrors,
  IEnumerable<string> ValidationErrors
);
```

6. In `HomeController`, in the `ModelBinding` method that handles HTTP POST, comment out the previous statement that passed the thing to the view, and instead add statements to create an instance of the view model. Validate the model and store an array of error messages, and then pass the view model to the view, as shown highlighted in the following code:

```
[HttpPost]
public IActionResult ModelBinding(Thing thing)
{
  HomeModelBindingViewModel model = new(
    thing,
    !ModelState.IsValid,
    ModelState.Values
      .SelectMany(state => state.Errors)
```

```
            .Select(error => error.ErrorMessage)
    );
    return View(model);
}
```

7. In Views\Home, open ModelBinding.cshtml.

8. Modify the model type declaration to use the view model class, as shown in the following markup:

   ```
   @model Northwind.Mvc.Models.HomeModelBindingViewModel
   ```

9. Add a <div> to show any model validation errors, and change the output of the thing's properties because the view model has changed, as shown highlighted in the following markup:

   ```
   <form method="POST" action="/home/modelbinding/2?id=3">
     <input name="id" value="1" />
     <input name="color" value="Red" />
     <input name="email" value="test@example.com" />
     <input type="submit" />
   </form>
   @if (Model != null)
   {
     <h2>Submitted Thing</h2>
     <hr />
     <div>
       <dl class="dl-horizontal">
         <dt>Model.Thing.Id</dt>
         <dd>@Model.Thing.Id</dd>
         <dt>Model.Thing.Color</dt>
         <dd>@Model.Thing.Color</dd>
         <dt>Model.Thing.Email</dt>
         <dd>@Model.Thing.Email</dd>
       </dl>
     </div>
     @if (Model.HasErrors)
     {
       <div>
         @foreach(string errorMessage in Model.ValidationErrors)
         {
           <div class="alert alert-danger" role="alert">@errorMessage</div>
         }
       </div>
     }
   }
   ```

10. Start the website.

11. On the home page, click **Binding**.

12. Click the **Submit** button and note that 1, Red, and test@example.com are valid values.

13. Enter an Id of 13, clear the color textbox, delete the @ from the email address, click the **Submit** button, and note the error messages, as shown in *Figure 15.8*:

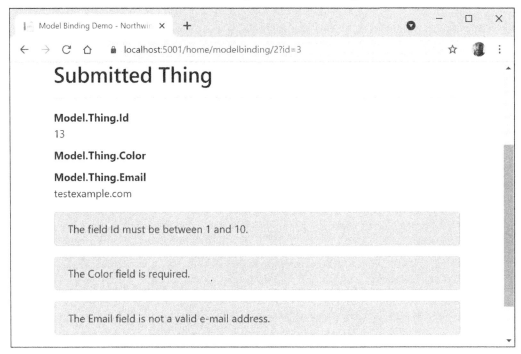

Figure 15.8: The Model Binding Demo page with field validations

14. Close Chrome and shut down the web server.

Good Practice: What regular expression does Microsoft use for the implementation of the EmailAddress validation attribute? Find out at the following link: https://github.com/microsoft/referencesource/blob/5697c29004a34d80acdaf5742d7e699022c64ecd/System.ComponentModel.DataAnnotations/DataAnnotations/EmailAddressAttribute.cs#L54

Understanding view helper methods

While creating a view for ASP.NET Core MVC, you can use the Html object and its methods to generate markup.

Some useful methods include the following:

- `ActionLink`: Use this to generate an anchor `<a>` element that contains a URL path to the specified controller and action. For example, `Html.ActionLink(linkText: "Binding", actionName: "ModelBinding", controllerName: "Home")` would generate `<a href="/home/modelbinding">Binding</a>`. You can achieve the same result using the anchor tag helper: `<a asp-action="ModelBinding" asp-controller="Home">Binding</a>`.

- `AntiForgeryToken`: Use this inside a `<form>` to insert a `<hidden>` element containing an anti-forgery token that will be validated when the form is submitted.

- `Display` and `DisplayFor`: Use this to generate HTML markup for the expression relative to the current model using a display template. There are built-in display templates for .NET types and custom templates can be created in the `DisplayTemplates` folder. The folder name is case-sensitive on case-sensitive filesystems.

- `DisplayForModel`: Use this to generate HTML markup for an entire model instead of a single expression.

- `Editor` and `EditorFor`: Use this to generate HTML markup for the expression relative to the current model using an editor template. There are built-in editor templates for .NET types that use `<label>` and `<input>` elements, and custom templates can be created in the `EditorTemplates` folder. The folder name is case-sensitive on case-sensitive filesystems.

- `EditorForModel`: Use this to generate HTML markup for an entire model instead of a single expression.

- `Encode`: Use this to safely encode an object or string into HTML. For example, the string value `"<script>"` would be encoded as `"&lt;script&gt;"`. This is not normally necessary since the Razor @ symbol encodes string values by default.

- `Raw`: Use this to render a string value *without* encoding as HTML.

- `PartialAsync` and `RenderPartialAsync`: Use these to generate HTML markup for a partial view. You can optionally pass a model and view data.

Let's see an example:

1. In `Views/Home`, open `ModelBinding.cshtml`.
2. Modify the rendering of the `Email` property to use `DisplayFor`, as shown in the following markup:

   ```
   <dd>@Html.DisplayFor(model => model.Thing.Email)</dd>
   ```

3. Start the website.
4. Click **Binding**.
5. Click **Submit**.
6. Note the email address is a clickable hyperlink instead of just text.
7. Close Chrome and shut down the web server.

8. In Models/Thing.cs, comment out the [EmailAddress] attribute above the Email property.

9. Start the website.

10. Click **Binding**.

11. Click **Submit**.

12. Note the email address is just text.

13. Close Chrome and shut down the web server.

14. In Models/Thing.cs, uncomment the [EmailAddress] attribute.

It is the combination of decorating the Email property with the [EmailAddress] validation attribute and rendering it using DisplayFor that notifies ASP.NET Core to treat the value as an email address and therefore render it as a clickable link.

Querying a database and using display templates

Let's create a new action method that can have a query string parameter passed to it and use that to query the Northwind database for products that cost more than a specified price.

In previous examples, we defined a view model that contained properties for every value that needed to be rendered in the view. In this example, there will be two values: a list of products and the price the visitor entered. To avoid having to define a class or record for the view model, we will pass the list of products as the model and store the maximum price in the ViewData collection.

Let's implement this feature:

1. In HomeController, import the Microsoft.EntityFrameworkCore namespace. We need this to add the Include extension method so that we can include related entities, as you learned in *Chapter 10, Working with Data Using Entity Framework Core*.

2. Add a new action method, as shown in the following code:

```
public IActionResult ProductsThatCostMoreThan(decimal? price)
{
  if (!price.HasValue)
  {
    return BadRequest("You must pass a product price in the query string,
for example, /Home/ProductsThatCostMoreThan?price=50");
  }

  IEnumerable<Product> model = db.Products
    .Include(p => p.Category)
    .Include(p => p.Supplier)
    .Where(p => p.UnitPrice > price);
```

```
    if (!model.Any())
    {
      return NotFound(
        $"No products cost more than {price:C}.");
    }

    ViewData["MaxPrice"] = price.Value.ToString("C");
    return View(model); // pass model to view
}
```

3. In the `Views/Home` folder, add a new file named `ProductsThatCostMoreThan.cshtml`.

4. Modify the contents, as shown in the following code:

```
@using Packt.Shared
@model IEnumerable<Product>
@{
  string title =
    "Products That Cost More Than " + ViewData["MaxPrice"];
  ViewData["Title"] = title;
}
<h2>@title</h2>
@if (Model is null)
{
  <div>No products found.</div>
}
else
{
  <table class="table">
    <thead>
      <tr>
        <th>Category Name</th>
        <th>Supplier's Company Name</th>
        <th>Product Name</th>
        <th>Unit Price</th>
        <th>Units In Stock</th>
      </tr>
    </thead>
    <tbody>
    @foreach (Product p in Model)
    {
      <tr>
        <td>
          @Html.DisplayFor(modelItem => p.Category.CategoryName)
        </td>
        <td>
          @Html.DisplayFor(modelItem => p.Supplier.CompanyName)
        </td>
```

```
            <td>
              @Html.DisplayFor(modelItem => p.ProductName)
            </td>
            <td>
              @Html.DisplayFor(modelItem => p.UnitPrice)
            </td>
            <td>
              @Html.DisplayFor(modelItem => p.UnitsInStock)
            </td>
          </tr>
        }
        <tbody>
      </table>
    }
```

5. In the `Views/Home` folder, open `Index.cshtml`.

6. Add the following form element below the visitor count and above the **Products** heading and its listing of products. This will provide a form for the user to enter a price. The user can then click **Submit** to call the action method that shows only products that cost more than the entered price:

```
<h3>Query products by price</h3>
<form asp-action="ProductsThatCostMoreThan" method="GET">
  <input name="price" placeholder="Enter a product price" />
  <input type="submit" />
</form>
```

7. Start the website.

8. On the home page, enter a price in the form, for example, 50, and then click on **Submit**.

9. Note the table of the products that cost more than the price that you entered, as shown in *Figure 15.9*:

Figure 15.9: A filtered list of products that cost more than £50

10. Close Chrome and shut down the web server.

Improving scalability using asynchronous tasks

When building a desktop or mobile app, multiple tasks (and their underlying threads) can be used to improve responsiveness, because while one thread is busy with the task, another can handle interactions with the user.

Tasks and their threads can be useful on the server side too, especially with websites that work with files, or request data from a store or a web service that could take a while to respond. But they are detrimental to complex calculations that are CPU-bound, so leave these to be processed synchronously as normal.

When an HTTP request arrives at the web server, a thread from its pool is allocated to handle the request. But if that thread must wait for a resource, then it is blocked from handling any more incoming requests. If a website receives more simultaneous requests than it has threads in its pool, then some of those requests will respond with a server timeout error, **503 Service Unavailable**.

The threads that are locked are not doing useful work. They *could* handle one of those other requests but only if we implement asynchronous code in our websites.

Whenever a thread is waiting for a resource it needs, it can return to the thread pool and handle a different incoming request, improving the scalability of the website, that is, increasing the number of simultaneous requests it can handle.

Why not just have a larger thread pool? In modern operating systems, every thread in the pool has a 1 MB stack. An asynchronous method uses a smaller amount of memory. It also removes the need to create new threads in the pool, which takes time. The rate at which new threads are added to the pool is typically one every two seconds, which is a looooooong time compared to switching between asynchronous threads.

 Good Practice: Make your controller action methods asynchronous.

Making controller action methods asynchronous

It is easy to make an existing action method asynchronous:

1. Modify the Index action method to be asynchronous, to return a task, and to await the calls to asynchronous methods to get the categories and products, as shown highlighted in the following code:

```
public async Task<IActionResult> Index()
{
```

```
HomeIndexViewModel model = new
(
  VisitorCount = (new Random()).Next(1, 1001),
  Categories = await db.Categories.ToListAsync(),
  Products = await db.Products.ToListAsync()
);
return View(model); // pass model to view
}
```

2. Modify the ProductDetail action method in a similar way, as shown highlighted in the following code:

```
public async Task<IActionResult> ProductDetail(int? id)
{
  if (!id.HasValue)
  {
    return BadRequest("You must pass a product ID in the route, for
example,
/Home/ProductDetail/21");
  }

  Product? model = await db.Products
    .SingleOrDefaultAsync(p => p.ProductId == id);

  if (model == null)
  {
    return NotFound($"ProductId {id} not found.");
  }
  return View(model); // pass model to view and then return result
}
```

3. Start the website and note that the functionality of the website is the same, but trust that it will now scale better.

4. Close Chrome and shut down the web server.

Practicing and exploring

Test your knowledge and understanding by answering some questions, get some hands-on practice, and explore this chapter's topics with deeper research.

Exercise 15.1 – Test your knowledge

Answer the following questions:

1. What do the files with the special names _ViewStart and _ViewImports do when created in the Views folder?

2. What are the names of the three segments defined in the default ASP.NET Core MVC route, what do they represent, and which are optional?

3. What does the default model binder do, and what data types can it handle?

4. In a shared layout file like _Layout.cshtml, how do you output the content of the current view?

5. In a shared layout file like _Layout.cshtml, how do you output a section that the current view can supply content for, and how does the view supply the contents for that section?

6. When calling the View method inside a controller's action method, what paths are searched for the view by convention?

7. How can you instruct the visitor's browser to cache the response for 24 hours?

8. Why might you enable Razor Pages even if you are not creating any yourself?

9. How does ASP.NET Core MVC identify classes that can act as controllers?

10. In what ways does ASP.NET Core MVC make it easier to test a website?

Exercise 15.2 – Practice implementing MVC by implementing a category detail page

The Northwind.Mvc project has a home page that shows categories, but when the View button is clicked, the website returns a 404 Not Found error, for example, for the following URL:

```
https://localhost:5001/category/1
```

Extend the Northwind.Mvc project by adding the ability to show a detail page for a category.

Exercise 15.3 – Practice improving scalability by understanding and implementing async action methods

A few years ago, Stephen Cleary wrote an excellent article for MSDN Magazine explaining the scalability benefits of implementing async action methods for ASP.NET. The same principles apply to ASP.NET Core, but even more so, because unlike the old ASP.NET as described in the article, ASP.NET Core supports asynchronous filters and other components.

Read the article at the following link:

```
https://docs.microsoft.com/en-us/archive/msdn-magazine/2014/october/async-
programming-introduction-to-async-await-on-asp-net
```

Exercise 15.4 – Practice unit testing MVC controllers

Controllers are where the business logic of your website runs, so it is important to test the correctness of that logic using unit tests, as you learned in *Chapter 4, Writing, Debugging, and Testing Functions*.

Write some unit tests for HomeController.

 Good Practice: You can read more about how to unit test controllers at the following link: https://docs.microsoft.com/en-us/aspnet/core/mvc/controllers/testing

Exercise 15.5 – Explore topics

Use the links on the following page to learn more about the topics covered in this chapter:

https://github.com/markjprice/cs10dotnet6/blob/main/book-links.md#chapter-15---building-websites-using-the-model-view-controller-pattern

Summary

In this chapter, you learned how to build large, complex websites in a way that is easy to unit test by registering and injecting dependency services like database contexts and loggers and is easier to manage with teams of programmers using ASP.NET Core MVC. You learned about configuration, authentication, routes, models, views, and controllers.

In the next chapter, you will learn how to build and consume services that use HTTP as the communication layer, aka web services.

16

Building and Consuming
Web Services

This chapter is about learning how to build web services (aka HTTP or REST services) using the ASP.NET Core Web API and consuming web services using HTTP clients that could be any other type of .NET app, including a website or a mobile or desktop app.

This chapter requires knowledge and skills that you learned in *Chapter 10, Working with Data Using Entity Framework Core*, and *Chapters 13* to *15*, about practical applications of C# and .NET and building websites using ASP.NET Core.

In this chapter, we will cover the following topics:

- Building web services using ASP.NET Core Web API
- Documenting and testing web services
- Consuming web services using HTTP clients
- Implementing advanced features for web services
- Building web services using minimal APIs

Building web services using ASP.NET Core Web API

Before we build a modern web service, we need to cover some background to set the context for this chapter.

Understanding web service acronyms

Although HTTP was designed originally to request and respond with HTML and other resources for humans to look at, it is also good for building services.

Roy Fielding stated in his doctoral dissertation, describing the **Representational State Transfer (REST)** architectural style, that the HTTP standard would be good for building services because it defines the following:

- URIs to uniquely identify resources, like `https://localhost:5001/api/products/23`.

- Methods to perform common tasks on those resources, like `GET`, `POST`, `PUT`, and `DELETE`.

- The ability to negotiate the media type of content exchanged in requests and responses, such as XML and JSON. Content negotiation happens when the client specifies a request header like `Accept: application/xml,*/*;q=0.8`. The default response format used by the ASP.NET Core Web API is JSON, which means one of the response headers would be `Content-Type: application/json; charset=utf-8`.

Web services use the HTTP communication standard, so they are sometimes called HTTP or RESTful services. HTTP or RESTful services are what this chapter is about.

Web services can also mean **Simple Object Access Protocol (SOAP)** services that implement some of the **WS-* standards**. These standards enable clients and services implemented on different systems to communicate with each other. The WS-* standards were originally defined by IBM with input from other companies like Microsoft.

Understanding Windows Communication Foundation (WCF)

.NET Framework 3.0 and later includes a **remote procedure call (RPC)** technology named **Windows Communication Foundation (WCF)**. RPC technologies enable code on one system to execute code on another over a network.

WCF makes it easy for developers to create services, including SOAP services that implement WS-* standards. It later also supported building Web/HTTP/REST-style services, but it was rather over-engineered if that was all you needed.

If you have existing WCF services and you would like to port them to modern .NET, then there is an open-source project that had its first **General Availability (GA)** release in February 2021. You can read about it at the following link:

`https://corewcf.github.io/blog/2021/02/19/corewcf-ga-release`

An alternative to WCF

The Microsoft recommended alternative to WCF is **gRPC**. gRPC is a modern cross-platform open-source RPC framework created by Google (unofficially the "g" in gRPC). You will learn more about gRPC in *Chapter 18, Building and Consuming Specialized Services*.

Understanding HTTP requests and responses for Web APIs

HTTP defines standard types of requests and standard codes to indicate a type of response. Most of them can be used to implement Web API services.

The most common type of request is GET, to retrieve a resource identified by a unique path, with additional options like what media type is acceptable, set as request headers, as shown in the following example:

```
GET /path/to/resource
Accept: application/json
```

Common responses include success and multiple types of failure, as shown in the following table:

Status code	Description
200 OK	The path was correctly formed, the resource was successfully found, serialized into an acceptable media type, and then returned in the response body. The response headers specify the Content-Type, Content-Length, and Content-Encoding, for example, GZIP.
301 Moved Permanently	Over time a web service may change its resource model including the path used to identify an existing resource. The web service can indicate the new path by returning this status code and a response header named Location that has the new path.
302 Found	Similar to 301.
304 Not Modified	If the request included the If-Modified-Since header, then the web service can respond with this status code. The response body is empty because the client should use its cached copy of the resource.
400 Bad Request	The request was invalid, for example, it used a path for a product using an integer ID where the ID value is missing.
401 Unauthorized	The request was valid, the resource was found, but the client did not supply credentials or is not authorized to access that resource. Re-authenticating may enable access, for example, by adding or changing the Authorization request header.
403 Forbidden	The request was valid, the resource was found, but the client is not authorized to access that resource. Re-authenticating will not fix the issue.
404 Not Found	The request was valid, but the resource was not found. The resource may be found if the request is repeated later. To indicate that a resource will never be found, return 410 Gone.
406 Not Acceptable	If the request has an Accept header that only lists media types that the web service does not support. For example, if the client requests JSON but the web service can only return XML.

451 Unavailable for Legal Reasons	A website hosted in the USA might return this for requests coming from Europe to avoid having to comply with the General Data Protection Regulation (GDPR). The number was chosen as a reference to the novel Fahrenheit 451 in which books are banned and burned.
500 Server Error	The request was valid, but something went wrong on the server side while processing the request. Retrying again later might work.
503 Service Unavailable	The web service is busy and cannot handle the request. Trying again later might work.

Other common types of HTTP requests include POST, PUT, PATCH, or DELETE that create, modify, or delete resources.

To create a new resource, you might make a POST request with a body that contains the new resource, as shown in the following code:

```
POST /path/to/resource
Content-Length: 123
Content-Type: application/json
```

To create a new resource or update an existing resource, you might make a PUT request with a body that contains a whole new version of the existing resource, and if the resource does not exist, it is created, or if it does exist, it is replaced (sometimes called an **upsert** operation), as shown in the following code:

```
PUT /path/to/resource
Content-Length: 123
Content-Type: application/json
```

To update an existing resource more efficiently, you might make a PATCH request with a body that contains an object with only the properties that need changing, as shown in the following code:

```
PATCH /path/to/resource
Content-Length: 123
Content-Type: application/json
```

To delete an existing resource, you might make a DELETE request, as shown in the following code:

```
DELETE /path/to/resource
```

As well as the responses shown in the table above for a GET request, all the types of requests that create, modify, or delete a resource have additional possible common responses, as shown in the following table:

Status code	Description
201 Created	The new resource was created successfully, the response header named Location contains its path, and the response body contains the newly created resource. Immediately GET-ing the resource should return 200.
202 Accepted	The new resource cannot be created immediately so the request is queued for later processing and immediately GET-ing the resource might return 404. The body can contain a resource that points to some form of status checker or an estimate of when the resource will become available.
204 No Content	Commonly used in response to a DELETE request since returning the resource in the body after deleting it does not usually make sense! Sometimes used in response to POST, PUT, or PATCH requests if the client does not need to confirm that the request was processed correctly.
405 Method Not Allowed	Returned when the request used a method that is not supported. For example, a web service designed to be read-only may explicitly disallow PUT, DELETE, and so on.
415 Unsupported Media Type	Returned when the resource in the request body uses a media type that the web service cannot handle. For example, if the body contains a resource in XML format but the web service can only process JSON.

Creating an ASP.NET Core Web API project

We will build a web service that provides a way to work with data in the Northwind database using ASP.NET Core so that the data can be used by any client application on any platform that can make HTTP requests and receive HTTP responses:

1. Use your preferred code editor to add a new project, as defined in the following list:
   1. Project template: **ASP.NET Core Web API** / webapi
   2. Workspace/solution file and folder: PracticalApps
   3. Project file and folder: Northwind.WebApi
   4. Other Visual Studio options: **Authentication Type**: None, **Configure for HTTPS**: selected, **Enable Docker**: cleared, **Enable OpenAPI support**: selected.

2. In Visual Studio Code, select Northwind.WebApi as the active OmniSharp project.

3. Build the Northwind.WebApi project.

4. In the Controllers folder, open and review WeatherForecastController.cs, as shown in the following code:

```
using Microsoft.AspNetCore.Mvc;

namespace Northwind.WebApi.Controllers;

[ApiController]
[Route("[controller]")]
```

```
public class WeatherForecastController : ControllerBase
{
  private static readonly string[] Summaries = new[]
  {
    "Freezing", "Bracing", "Chilly", "Cool", "Mild",
    "Warm", "Balmy", "Hot", "Sweltering", "Scorching"
  };

  private readonly ILogger<WeatherForecastController> _logger;

  public WeatherForecastController(
    ILogger<WeatherForecastController> logger)
  {
    _logger = logger;
  }

  [HttpGet]
  public IEnumerable<WeatherForecast> Get()
  {
    return Enumerable.Range(1, 5).Select(index =>
      new WeatherForecast
      {
        Date = DateTime.Now.AddDays(index),
        TemperatureC = Random.Shared.Next(-20, 55),
        Summary = Summaries[Random.Shared.Next(Summaries.Length)]
      })
      .ToArray();
  }
}
```

While reviewing the preceding code, note the following:

- The Controller class inherits from ControllerBase. This is simpler than the Controller class used in MVC because it does not have methods like View to generate HTML responses by passing a view model to a Razor file.

- The [Route] attribute registers the /weatherforecast relative URL for clients to use to make HTTP requests that will be handled by this controller. For example, an HTTP request for https://localhost:5001/weatherforecast/ would be handled by this controller. Some developers like to prefix the controller name with api/, which is a convention to differentiate between MVC and Web API in mixed projects. If you use [controller] as shown, it uses the characters before Controller in the class name, in this case, WeatherForecast, or you can simply enter a different name without the square brackets, for example, [Route("api/forecast")].

- The [ApiController] attribute was introduced with ASP.NET Core 2.1 and it enables REST-specific behavior for controllers, like automatic HTTP 400 responses for invalid models, as you will see later in this chapter.

- The [HttpGet] attribute registers the Get method in the Controller class to respond to HTTP GET requests, and its implementation uses the shared Random object to return an array of WeatherForecast objects with random temperatures and summaries like Bracing or Balmy for the next five days of weather.

5. Add a second Get method that allows the call to specify how many days ahead the forecast should be by implementing the following:

- Add a comment above the original method to show the action method and URL path that it responds to.

- Add a new method with an integer parameter named days.

- Cut and paste the original Get method implementation code statements into the new Get method.

- Modify the new method to create an IEnumerable of integers up to the number of days requested, and modify the original Get method to call the new Get method and pass the value 5.

Your methods should be as shown highlighted in the following code:

```
// GET /weatherforecast
[HttpGet]
public IEnumerable<WeatherForecast> Get() // original method
{
  return Get(5); // five day forecast
}

// GET /weatherforecast/7
[HttpGet("{days:int}")]
public IEnumerable<WeatherForecast> Get(int days) // new method
{
  return Enumerable.Range(1, days).Select(index =>
    new WeatherForecast
    {
      Date = DateTime.Now.AddDays(index),
      TemperatureC = Random.Shared.Next(-20, 55),
      Summary = Summaries[Random.Shared.Next(Summaries.Length)]
    })
    .ToArray();
}
```

In the [HttpGet] attribute, note the route format pattern {days:int} that constrains the days parameter to int values.

Reviewing the web service's functionality

Now, we will test the web service's functionality:

1. If you are using Visual Studio, in **Properties**, open the launchSettings.json file, and note that by default, it will launch the browser and navigate to the /swagger relative URL path, as shown highlighted in the following markup:

   ```
   "profiles": {
     "Northwind.WebApi": {
       "commandName": "Project",
       "dotnetRunMessages": "true",
       "launchBrowser": true,
       "launchUrl": "swagger",
       "applicationUrl": "https://localhost:5001;http://localhost:5000",
       "environmentVariables": {
         "ASPNETCORE_ENVIRONMENT": "Development"
       }
     },
   ```

2. Modify the profile named Northwind.WebApi to set launchBrowser to false.

3. For the applicationUrl, change the random port number for HTTP to 5000 and for HTTPS to 5001.

4. Start the web service project.

5. Start Chrome.

6. Navigate to https://localhost:5001/ and note you will get a 404 status code response because we have not enabled static files and there is not an index.html, nor is there an MVC controller with a route configured, either. Remember that this project is not designed for a human to view and interact with, so this is expected behavior for a web service.

    The solution on GitHub is configured to use port 5002 because we will change its configuration later in the book.

7. In Chrome, show **Developer tools**.

8. Navigate to https://localhost:5001/weatherforecast and note the Web API service should return a JSON document with five random weather forecast objects in an array, as shown in *Figure 16.1*:

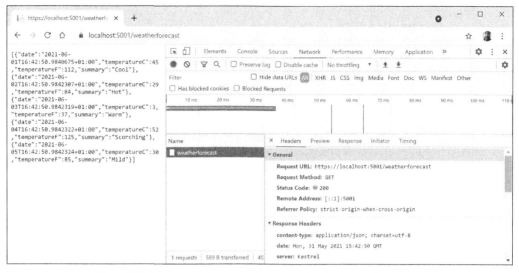

Figure 16.1: A request and response from a weather forecast web service

9. Close **Developer tools**.

10. Navigate to `https://localhost:5001/weatherforecast/14` and note the response when requesting a two-week weather forecast, as shown in *Figure 16.2*:

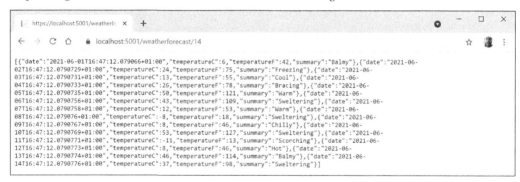

Figure 16.2: A two-week weather forecast as a JSON document

11. Close Chrome and shut down the web server.

Creating a web service for the Northwind database

Unlike MVC controllers, Web API controllers do not call Razor views to return HTML responses for website visitors to see in browsers. Instead, they use content negotiation with the client application that made the HTTP request to return data in formats such as XML, JSON, or X-WWW-FORM-URLENCODED in their HTTP response.

The client application must then deserialize the data from the negotiated format. The most commonly used format for modern web services is **JavaScript Object Notation (JSON)** because it is compact and works natively with JavaScript in a browser when building **Single-Page Applications (SPAs)** with client-side technologies like Angular, React, and Vue.

We will reference the Entity Framework Core entity data model for the Northwind database that you created in *Chapter 13, Introducing Practical Applications of C# and .NET*:

1. In the `Northwind.WebApi` project, add a project reference to `Northwind.Common.DataContext` for either SQLite or SQL Server, as shown in the following markup:

    ```
    <ItemGroup>
      <!-- change Sqlite to SqlServer if you prefer -->
      <ProjectReference Include=
    "..\Northwind.Common.DataContext.Sqlite\Northwind.Common.DataContext.
    Sqlite.csproj" />
    </ItemGroup>
    ```

2. Build the project and fix any compile errors in your code.

3. Open `Program.cs` and import namespaces for working with web media formatters and the shared Packt classes, as shown in the following code:

    ```
    using Microsoft.AspNetCore.Mvc.Formatters;
    using Packt.Shared; // AddNorthwindContext extension method

    using static System.Console;
    ```

4. Add a statement before the call to `AddControllers` to register the `Northwind` database context class (it will use either SQLite or SQL Server depending on which database provider you referenced in the project file), as shown in the following code:

    ```
    // Add services to the container.
    builder.Services.AddNorthwindContext();
    ```

5. In the call to `AddControllers`, add a lambda block with statements to write the names and supported media types of the default output formatters to the console, and then add XML serializer formatters, as shown in the following code:

    ```
    builder.Services.AddControllers(options =>
    {
      WriteLine("Default output formatters:");
      foreach (IOutputFormatter formatter in options.OutputFormatters)
      {
        OutputFormatter? mediaFormatter = formatter as OutputFormatter;
        if (mediaFormatter == null)
        {
          WriteLine($"  {formatter.GetType().Name}");
        }
        else // OutputFormatter class has SupportedMediaTypes
    ```

```
    {
      WriteLine("  {0}, Media types: {1}",
        arg0: mediaFormatter.GetType().Name,
        arg1: string.Join(", ",
          mediaFormatter.SupportedMediaTypes));
    }
  }
})
.AddXmlDataContractSerializerFormatters()
.AddXmlSerializerFormatters();
```

6. Start the web service.

7. In a command prompt or terminal, note that there are four default output formatters, including ones that convert null values into 204 No Content and ones to support responses that are plain text, byte streams, and JSON, as shown in the following output:

```
Default output formatters:
  HttpNoContentOutputFormatter
  StringOutputFormatter, Media types: text/plain
  StreamOutputFormatter
  SystemTextJsonOutputFormatter, Media types: application/json, text/json,
application/*+json
```

8. Shut down the web server.

Creating data repositories for entities

Defining and implementing a data repository to provide CRUD operations is good practice. The CRUD acronym includes the following operations:

- C for Create
- R for Retrieve (or Read)
- U for Update
- D for Delete

We will create a data repository for the Customers table in Northwind. There are only 91 customers in this table, so we will store a copy of the whole table in memory to improve scalability and performance when reading customer records.

 Good Practice: In a real web service, you should use a distributed cache like Redis, an open-source data structure store that can be used as a high-performance, high-availability database, cache, or message broker.

We will follow modern good practice and make the repository API asynchronous. It will be instantiated by a `Controller` class using constructor parameter injection, so a new instance is created to handle every HTTP request:

1. In the `Northwind.WebApi` project, create a folder named `Repositories`.

2. Add two class files to the `Repositories` folder named `ICustomerRepository.cs` and `CustomerRepository.cs`.

3. The `ICustomerRepository` interface will define five methods, as shown in the following code:

```
using Packt.Shared; // Customer

namespace Northwind.WebApi.Repositories;

public interface ICustomerRepository
{
  Task<Customer?> CreateAsync(Customer c);
  Task<IEnumerable<Customer>> RetrieveAllAsync();
  Task<Customer?> RetrieveAsync(string id);
  Task<Customer?> UpdateAsync(string id, Customer c);
  Task<bool?> DeleteAsync(string id);
}
```

4. The `CustomerRepository` class will implement the five methods, remembering that methods that use `await` inside them must be marked as `async`, as shown in the following code:

```
using Microsoft.EntityFrameworkCore.ChangeTracking; // EntityEntry<T>
using Packt.Shared; // Customer
using System.Collections.Concurrent; // ConcurrentDictionary

namespace Northwind.WebApi.Repositories;

public class CustomerRepository : ICustomerRepository
{
  // use a static thread-safe dictionary field to cache the customers
  private static ConcurrentDictionary
    <string, Customer>? customersCache;

  // use an instance data context field because it should not be
  // cached due to their internal caching
  private NorthwindContext db;

  public CustomerRepository(NorthwindContext injectedContext)
  {
    db = injectedContext;
```

```csharp
    // pre-load customers from database as a normal
    // Dictionary with CustomerId as the key,
    // then convert to a thread-safe ConcurrentDictionary
    if (customersCache is null)
    {
      customersCache = new ConcurrentDictionary<string, Customer>(
        db.Customers.ToDictionary(c => c.CustomerId));
    }
}

public async Task<Customer?> CreateAsync(Customer c)
{
  // normalize CustomerId into uppercase
  c.CustomerId = c.CustomerId.ToUpper();

  // add to database using EF Core
  EntityEntry<Customer> added = await db.Customers.AddAsync(c);
  int affected = await db.SaveChangesAsync();
  if (affected == 1)
  {
    if (customersCache is null) return c;
    // if the customer is new, add it to cache, else
    // call UpdateCache method
    return customersCache.AddOrUpdate(c.CustomerId, c, UpdateCache);
  }
  else
  {
    return null;
  }
}

public Task<IEnumerable<Customer>> RetrieveAllAsync()
{
  // for performance, get from cache
  return Task.FromResult(customersCache is null
      ? Enumerable.Empty<Customer>() : customersCache.Values);
}

public Task<Customer?> RetrieveAsync(string id)
{
  // for performance, get from cache
  id = id.ToUpper();
  if (customersCache is null) return null!;
  customersCache.TryGetValue(id, out Customer? c);
```

```
        return Task.FromResult(c);
    }

    private Customer UpdateCache(string id, Customer c)
    {
      Customer? old;
      if (customersCache is not null)
      {
        if (customersCache.TryGetValue(id, out old))
        {
          if (customersCache.TryUpdate(id, c, old))
          {
            return c;
          }
        }
      }
      return null!;
    }

    public async Task<Customer?> UpdateAsync(string id, Customer c)
    {
      // normalize customer Id
      id = id.ToUpper();
      c.CustomerId = c.CustomerId.ToUpper();

      // update in database
      db.Customers.Update(c);
      int affected = await db.SaveChangesAsync();
      if (affected == 1)
      {
        // update in cache
        return UpdateCache(id, c);
      }
      return null;
    }

    public async Task<bool?> DeleteAsync(string id)
    {
      id = id.ToUpper();

      // remove from database
      Customer? c = db.Customers.Find(id);
      if (c is null) return null;
      db.Customers.Remove(c);
      int affected = await db.SaveChangesAsync();
```

```
        if (affected == 1)
        {
          if (customersCache is null) return null;
          // remove from cache
          return customersCache.TryRemove(id, out c);
        }
        else
        {
          return null;
        }
      }
    }
```

Implementing a Web API controller

There are some useful attributes and methods for implementing a controller that returns data instead of HTML.

With MVC controllers, a route like /home/index tells us the controller class name and the action method name, for example, the HomeController class and the Index action method.

With Web API controllers, a route like /weatherforecast only tells us the controller class name, for example, WeatherForecastController. To determine the action method name to execute, we must map HTTP methods like GET and POST to methods in the controller class.

You should decorate controller methods with the following attributes to indicate the HTTP method that they will respond to:

- [HttpGet], [HttpHead]: These action methods respond to GET or HEAD requests to retrieve a resource and return either the resource and its response headers or just the response headers.

- [HttpPost]: This action method responds to POST requests to create a new resource or perform some other action defined by the service.

- [HttpPut], [HttpPatch]: These action methods respond to PUT or PATCH requests to update an existing resource either by replacing it or updating a subset of its properties.

- [HttpDelete]: This action method responds to DELETE requests to remove a resource.

- [HttpOptions]: This action method responds to OPTIONS requests.

Understanding action method return types

An action method can return .NET types like a single string value, complex objects defined by a class, record, or struct, or collections of complex objects. The ASP.NET Core Web API will serialize them into the requested data format set in the HTTP request Accept header, for example, JSON, if a suitable serializer has been registered.

For more control over the response, there are helper methods that return an `ActionResult` wrapper around the .NET type.

Declare the action method's return type to be `IActionResult` if it could return different return types based on inputs or other variables. Declare the action method's return type to be `ActionResult<T>` if it will only return a single type but with different status codes.

Good Practice: Decorate action methods with the [`ProducesResponseType`] attribute to indicate all the known types and HTTP status codes that the client should expect in a response. This information can then be publicly exposed to document how a client should interact with your web service. Think of it as part of your formal documentation. Later in this chapter, you will learn how you can install a code analyzer to give you warnings when you do not decorate your action methods like this.

For example, an action method that gets a product based on an id parameter would be decorated with three attributes – one to indicate that it responds to GET requests and has an id parameter, and two to indicate what happens when it succeeds and when the client has supplied an invalid product ID, as shown in the following code:

```
[HttpGet("{id}")]
[ProducesResponseType(200, Type = typeof(Product))]
[ProducesResponseType(404)]
public IActionResult Get(string id)
```

The `ControllerBase` class has methods to make it easy to return different responses, as shown in the following table:

Method	Description
Ok	Returns a 200 status code and a resource converted to the client's preferred format, like JSON or XML. Commonly used in response to a GET request.
CreatedAtRoute	Returns a 201 status code and the path to the new resource. Commonly used in response to a POST request to create a resource that can be performed quickly.
Accepted	Returns a 202 status code to indicate the request is being processed but has not completed. Commonly used in response to a POST, PUT, PATCH, or DELETE request that triggers a background process that takes a long time to complete.
NoContentResult	Returns a 204 status code and an empty response body. Commonly used in response to a PUT, PATCH, or DELETE request when the response does not need to contain the affected resource.
BadRequest	Returns a 400 status code and an optional message string with more details.
NotFound	Returns a 404 status code and an automatically populated `ProblemDetails` body (requires a compatibility version of 2.2 or later).

Configuring the customer repository and Web API controller

Now you will configure the repository so that it can be called from within a Web API controller.

You will register a scoped dependency service implementation for the repository when the web service starts up and then use constructor parameter injection to get it in a new Web API controller for working with customers.

To show an example of differentiating between MVC and Web API controllers using routes, we will use the common /api URL prefix convention for the customers controller:

1. Open `Program.cs` and import the `Northwind.WebApi.Repositories` namespace.

2. Add a statement before the call to the `Build` method, which will register the `CustomerRepository` for use at runtime as a scoped dependency, as shown highlighted in the following code:

```
builder.Services.AddScoped<ICustomerRepository, CustomerRepository>();

var app = builder.Build();
```

 Good Practice: Our repository uses a database context that is registered as a scoped dependency. You can only use scoped dependencies inside other scoped dependencies, so we cannot register the repository as a singleton. You can read more about this at the following link: https://docs.microsoft.com/en-us/dotnet/core/extensions/dependency-injection#scoped

3. In the `Controllers` folder, add a new class named `CustomersController.cs`.

4. In the `CustomersController` class file, add statements to define a Web API controller class to work with customers, as shown in the following code:

```
using Microsoft.AspNetCore.Mvc; // [Route], [ApiController],
ControllerBase
using Packt.Shared; // Customer
using Northwind.WebApi.Repositories; // ICustomerRepository

namespace Northwind.WebApi.Controllers;

// base address: api/customers
[Route("api/[controller]")]
[ApiController]
public class CustomersController : ControllerBase
{
```

```
    private readonly ICustomerRepository repo;

    // constructor injects repository registered in Startup
    public CustomersController(ICustomerRepository repo)
    {
      this.repo = repo;
    }

    // GET: api/customers
    // GET: api/customers/?country=[country]
    // this will always return a List of customers (but it might be empty)
    [HttpGet]
    [ProducesResponseType(200, Type = typeof(IEnumerable<Customer>)))]
    public async Task<IEnumerable<Customer>> GetCustomers(string? country)
    {
      if (string.IsNullOrWhiteSpace(country))
      {
        return await repo.RetrieveAllAsync();
      }
      else
      {
        return (await repo.RetrieveAllAsync())
          .Where(customer => customer.Country == country);
      }
    }

    // GET: api/customers/[id]
    [HttpGet("{id}", Name = nameof(GetCustomer))] // named route
    [ProducesResponseType(200, Type = typeof(Customer))]
    [ProducesResponseType(404)]
    public async Task<IActionResult> GetCustomer(string id)
    {
      Customer? c = await repo.RetrieveAsync(id);
      if (c == null)
      {
        return NotFound(); // 404 Resource not found
      }
      return Ok(c); // 200 OK with customer in body
    }

    // POST: api/customers
    // BODY: Customer (JSON, XML)
    [HttpPost]
    [ProducesResponseType(201, Type = typeof(Customer))]
    [ProducesResponseType(400)]
    public async Task<IActionResult> Create([FromBody] Customer c)
    {
      if (c == null)
```

```
  {
    return BadRequest(); // 400 Bad request
  }

  Customer? addedCustomer = await repo.CreateAsync(c);

  if (addedCustomer == null)
  {
    return BadRequest("Repository failed to create customer.");
  }
  else
  {
    return CreatedAtRoute( // 201 Created
      routeName: nameof(GetCustomer),
      routeValues: new { id = addedCustomer.CustomerId.ToLower() },
      value: addedCustomer);
  }
}

// PUT: api/customers/[id]
// BODY: Customer (JSON, XML)
[HttpPut("{id}")]
[ProducesResponseType(204)]
[ProducesResponseType(400)]
[ProducesResponseType(404)]
public async Task<IActionResult> Update(
  string id, [FromBody] Customer c)
{
  id = id.ToUpper();
  c.CustomerId = c.CustomerId.ToUpper();

  if (c == null || c.CustomerId != id)
  {
    return BadRequest(); // 400 Bad request
  }

  Customer? existing = await repo.RetrieveAsync(id);
  if (existing == null)
  {
    return NotFound(); // 404 Resource not found
  }

  await repo.UpdateAsync(id, c);

  return new NoContentResult(); // 204 No content
}

// DELETE: api/customers/[id]
```

```
[HttpDelete("{id}")]
[ProducesResponseType(204)]
[ProducesResponseType(400)]
[ProducesResponseType(404)]
public async Task<IActionResult> Delete(string id)
{
  Customer? existing = await repo.RetrieveAsync(id);
  if (existing == null)
  {
    return NotFound(); // 404 Resource not found
  }

  bool? deleted = await repo.DeleteAsync(id);

  if (deleted.HasValue && deleted.Value) // short circuit AND
  {
    return new NoContentResult(); // 204 No content
  }
  else
  {
    return BadRequest( // 400 Bad request
      $"Customer {id} was found but failed to delete.");
  }
}
}
}
```

While reviewing this Web API controller class, note the following:

- The Controller class registers a route that starts with api/ and includes the name of the controller, that is, api/customers.

- The constructor uses dependency injection to get the registered repository for working with customers.

- There are five action methods to perform CRUD operations on customers — two GET methods (for all customers or one customer), POST (create), PUT (update), and DELETE.

- The GetCustomers method can have a string parameter passed with a country name. If it is missing, all customers are returned. If it is present, it is used to filter customers by country.

- The GetCustomer method has a route explicitly named GetCustomer so that it can be used to generate a URL after inserting a new customer.

- The Create and Update methods both decorate the customer parameter with [FromBody] to tell the model binder to populate it with values from the body of the POST request.

- The Create method returns a response that uses the GetCustomer route so that the client knows how to get the newly created resource in the future. We are matching up two methods to create and then get a customer.

- The Create and Update methods do not need to check the model state of the customer passed in the body of the HTTP request and return a 400 Bad Request containing details of the model validation errors if it is not valid because the controller is decorated with [ApiController], which does this for you.

When an HTTP request is received by the service, then it will create an instance of the Controller class, call the appropriate action method, return the response in the format preferred by the client, and release the resources used by the controller, including the repository and its data context.

Specifying problem details

A feature added in ASP.NET Core 2.1 and later is an implementation of a web standard for specifying problem details.

In Web API controllers decorated with [ApiController] in a project with ASP.NET Core 2.2 or later compatibility enabled, action methods that return IActionResult and return a client error status code, that is, 4xx, will automatically include a serialized instance of the ProblemDetails class in the response body.

If you want to take control, then you can create a ProblemDetails instance yourself and include additional information.

Let's simulate a bad request that needs custom data returned to the client:

1. At the top of the implementation of the Delete method, add statements to check if the id matches the literal string value "bad", and if so, then return a custom problem details object, as shown in the following code:

```
// take control of problem details
if (id == "bad")
{
  ProblemDetails problemDetails = new()
  {
    Status = StatusCodes.Status400BadRequest,
    Type = "https://localhost:5001/customers/failed-to-delete",
    Title = $"Customer ID {id} found but failed to delete.",
    Detail = "More details like Company Name, Country and so on.",
    Instance = HttpContext.Request.Path
  };
  return BadRequest(problemDetails); // 400 Bad Request
}
```

2. You will test this functionality later.

Controlling XML serialization

In `Program.cs`, we added the `XmlSerializer` so that our Web API service can return XML as well as JSON if the client requests that.

However, the `XmlSerializer` cannot serialize interfaces, and our entity classes use `ICollection<T>` to define related child entities. This causes a warning at runtime, for example, for the `Customer` class and its `Orders` property, as shown in the following output:

```
warn: Microsoft.AspNetCore.Mvc.Formatters.XmlSerializerOutputFormatter[1]
An error occurred while trying to create an XmlSerializer for the type 'Packt.
Shared.Customer'.
System.InvalidOperationException: There was an error reflecting type 'Packt.
Shared.Customer'.
---> System.InvalidOperationException: Cannot serialize member 'Packt.
Shared.Customer.Orders' of type 'System.Collections.Generic.ICollection`1[[Packt.
Shared.Order, Northwind.Common.EntityModels, Version=1.0.0.0, Culture=neutral,
PublicKeyToken=null]]', see inner exception for more details.
```

We can prevent this warning by excluding the `Orders` property when serializing a `Customer` to XML:

1. In the `Northwind.Common.EntityModels.Sqlite` and the `Northwind.Common.EntityModels.SqlServer` projects, open `Customers.cs`.

2. Import the `System.Xml.Serialization` namespace so that we can use the `[XmlIgnore]` attribute.

3. Decorate the `Orders` property with an attribute to ignore it when serializing, as shown highlighted in the following code:

```
[InverseProperty(nameof(Order.Customer))]
[XmlIgnore]
public virtual ICollection<Order> Orders { get; set; }
```

4. In the `Northwind.Common.EntityModels.SqlServer` project, decorate the `CustomerCustomerDemos` property with `[XmlIgnore]` too.

Documenting and testing web services

You can easily test a web service by making HTTP GET requests using a browser. To test other HTTP methods, we need a more advanced tool.

Testing GET requests using a browser

You will use Chrome to test the three implementations of a GET request – for all customers, for customers in a specified country, and for a single customer using their unique customer ID:

1. Start the `Northwind.WebApi` web service.

2. Start Chrome.

3. Navigate to `https://localhost:5001/api/customers` and note the JSON document returned, containing all 91 customers in the Northwind database (unsorted), as shown in *Figure 16.3*:

Figure 16.3: Customers from the Northwind database as a JSON document

4. Navigate to `https://localhost:5001/api/customers/?country=Germany` and note the JSON document returned, containing only the customers in Germany, as shown in *Figure 16.4*:

Figure 16.4: A list of customers from Germany as a JSON document

 If you get an empty array returned, then make sure you have entered the country name using the correct casing because the database query is case-sensitive. For example, compare the results of uk and UK.

5. Navigate to `https://localhost:5001/api/customers/alfki` and note the JSON document returned containing only the customer named **Alfreds Futterkiste**, as shown in *Figure 16.5*:

Figure 16.5: Specific customer information as a JSON document

Unlike with country names, we do not need to worry about casing for the customer `id` value because inside the controller class, we normalized the `string` value to uppercase in code.

But how can we test the other HTTP methods, such as POST, PUT, and DELETE? And how can we document our web service so it's easy for anyone to understand how to interact with it?

To solve the first problem, we can install a Visual Studio Code extension named **REST Client**. To solve the second, we can use **Swagger**, the world's most popular technology for documenting and testing HTTP APIs. But first, let's see what is possible with the Visual Studio Code extension.

There are many tools for testing Web APIs, for example, **Postman**. Although Postman is popular, I prefer **REST Client** because it does not hide what is actually happening. I feel Postman is too GUI-y. But I encourage you to explore different tools and find the ones that fit your style. You can learn more about Postman at the following link: https://www.postman.com/

Testing HTTP requests with the REST Client extension

REST Client is an extension that allows you to send any type of HTTP request and view the response in Visual Studio Code. Even if you prefer to use Visual Studio as your code editor, it is useful to install Visual Studio Code to use an extension like REST Client.

Making GET requests using REST Client

We will start by creating a file for testing GET requests:

1. If you have not already installed REST Client by Huachao Mao (humao.rest-client), then install it in Visual Studio Code now.

2. In your preferred code editor, start the Northwind.WebApi project web service.

3. In Visual Studio Code, in the PracticalApps folder, create a RestClientTests folder, and then open the folder.

4. In the RestClientTests folder, create a file named get-customers.http, and modify its contents to contain an HTTP GET request to retrieve all customers, as shown in the following code:

    ```
    GET https://localhost:5001/api/customers/ HTTP/1.1
    ```

5. In Visual Studio Code, navigate to **View** | **Command Palette**, enter rest client, select the command **Rest Client: Send Request**, and press *Enter*, as shown in *Figure 16.6*:

Figure 16.6: Sending an HTTP GET request using REST Client

6. Note the **Response** is shown in a new tabbed window pane vertically and that you can rearrange the open tabs to a horizontal layout by dragging and dropping tabs.

7. Enter more GET requests, each separated by three hash symbols, to test getting customers in various countries and getting a single customer using their ID, as shown in the following code:

```
###
GET https://localhost:5001/api/customers/?country=Germany HTTP/1.1
###
GET https://localhost:5001/api/customers/?country=USA HTTP/1.1
Accept: application/xml
###
GET https://localhost:5001/api/customers/ALFKI HTTP/1.1
###
GET https://localhost:5001/api/customers/abcxy HTTP/1.1
```

8. Click the **Send Request** link above each request to send it; for example, the GET that has a request header to request customers in the USA as XML instead of JSON, as shown in *Figure 16.7*:

Figure 16.7: Sending a request for XML and getting a response using REST Client

Making other requests using REST Client

Next, we will create a file for testing other requests like POST:

1. In the RestClientTests folder, create a file named create-customer.http and modify its contents to define a POST request to create a new customer, noting that REST Client will provide IntelliSense while you type common HTTP requests, as shown in the following code:

```
POST https://localhost:5001/api/customers/ HTTP/1.1
Content-Type: application/json
Content-Length: 301

{
    "customerID": "ABCXY",
    "companyName": "ABC Corp",
    "contactName": "John Smith",
    "contactTitle": "Sir",
    "address": "Main Street",
    "city": "New York",
    "region": "NY",
    "postalCode": "90210",
    "country":   "USA",
    "phone": "(123) 555-1234",
    "fax": null,
    "orders": null
}
```

2. Due to different line endings in different operating systems, the value for the Content-Length header will be different on Windows and macOS or Linux. If the value is wrong, then the request will fail. To discover the correct content length, select the body of the request and then look in the status bar for the number of characters, as shown in *Figure 16.8*:

Figure 16.8: Checking the correct content length

3. Send the request and note the response is `201 Created`. Also note the location (that is, the URL) of the newly created customer is `https://localhost:5001/api/Customers/abcxy`, and includes the newly created customer in the response body, as shown in *Figure 16.9*:

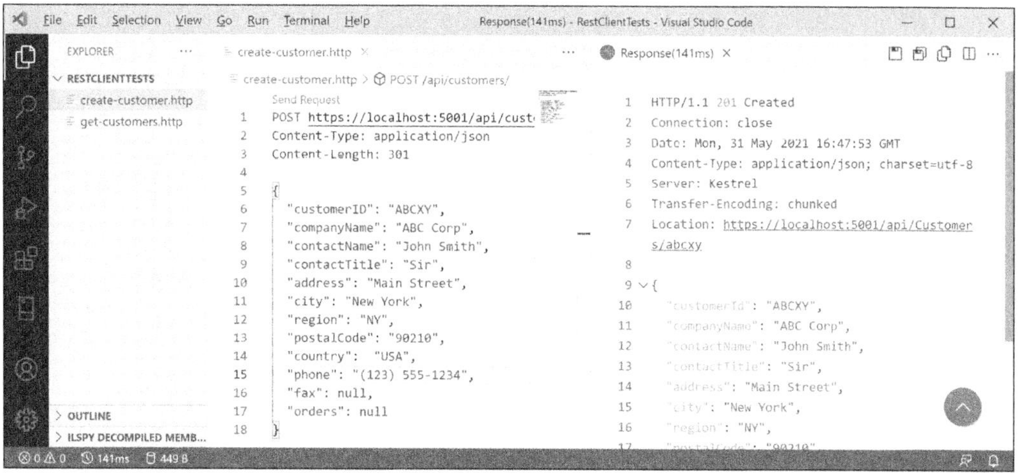

Figure 16.9: Adding a new customer

I will leave you an optional challenge to create REST Client files that test updating a customer (using `PUT`) and deleting a customer (using `DELETE`). Try them on customers that do exist as well as customers that do not. Solutions are in the GitHub repository for this book.

Now that we've seen a quick and easy way to test our service, which also happens to be a great way to learn HTTP, what about external developers? We want it to be as easy as possible for them to learn and then call our service. For that purpose, we will use Swagger.

Understanding Swagger

The most important part of Swagger is the **OpenAPI Specification**, which defines a REST-style contract for your API, detailing all its resources and operations in a human- and machine-readable format for easy development, discovery, and integration.

Developers can use the OpenAPI Specification for a Web API to automatically generate strongly-typed client-side code in their preferred language or library.

For us, another useful feature is **Swagger UI**, because it automatically generates documentation for your API with built-in visual testing capabilities.

Let's review how Swagger is enabled for our web service using the `Swashbuckle` package:

1. If the web service is running, shut down the web server.

2. Open `Northwind.WebApi.csproj` and note the package reference for `Swashbuckle.AspNetCore`, as shown in the following markup:

```
<ItemGroup>
  <PackageReference Include="Swashbuckle.AspNetCore" Version="6.1.5" />
</ItemGroup>
```

3. Update the version of the `Swashbuckle.AspNetCore` package to the latest, for example, at the time of writing in September 2021, it is `6.2.1`.

4. In `Program.cs`, note the import for Microsoft's OpenAPI models namespace, as shown in the following code:

```
using Microsoft.OpenApi.Models;
```

5. Import Swashbuckle's SwaggerUI namespace, as shown in the following code:

```
using Swashbuckle.AspNetCore.SwaggerUI; // SubmitMethod
```

6. About halfway down `Program.cs`, note the statement to add Swagger support including documentation for the Northwind service, indicating that this is the first version of your service, and change the title, as shown highlighted in the following code:

```
builder.Services.AddSwaggerGen(c =>
  {
    c.SwaggerDoc("v1", new()
      { Title = "Northwind Service API", Version = "v1" });
  });
```

7. In the section that configures the HTTP request pipeline, note the statements to use Swagger and Swagger UI when in development mode, and define an endpoint for the OpenAPI specification JSON document.

8. Add code to explicitly list the HTTP methods that we want to support in our web service and change the endpoint name, as shown highlighted in the following code:

```
var app = builder.Build();

// Configure the HTTP request pipeline.
if (builder.Environment.IsDevelopment())
{
  app.UseSwagger();
  app.UseSwaggerUI(c =>
  {
    c.SwaggerEndpoint("/swagger/v1/swagger.json",
      "Northwind Service API Version 1");

    c.SupportedSubmitMethods(new[] {
      SubmitMethod.Get, SubmitMethod.Post,
      SubmitMethod.Put, SubmitMethod.Delete });
  });
}
```

Testing requests with Swagger UI

You are now ready to test an HTTP request using Swagger:

1. Start the `Northwind.WebApi` web service.

2. In Chrome, navigate to `https://localhost:5001/swagger/` and note that both the **Customers** and **WeatherForecast** Web API controllers have been discovered and documented, as well as **Schemas** used by the API.

3. Click **GET /api/Customers/{id}** to expand that endpoint and note the required parameter for the **id** of a customer, as shown in *Figure 16.10*:

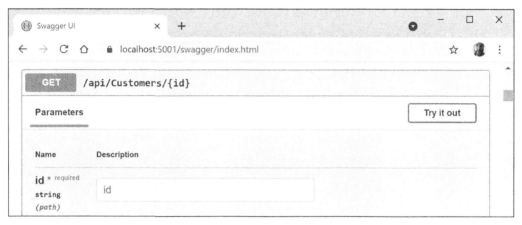

Figure 16.10: Checking the parameters for a GET request in Swagger

4. Click **Try it out**, enter an **id** of `ALFKI`, and then click the wide blue **Execute** button, as shown in *Figure 16.11*:

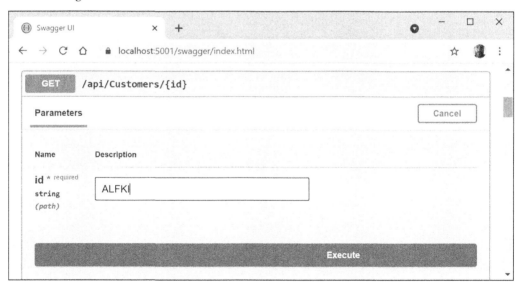

Figure 16.11: Inputting a customer id before clicking the Execute button

5. Scroll down and note the **Request URL**, **Server response** with **Code**, and **Details** including **Response body** and **Response headers**, as shown in *Figure 16.12*:

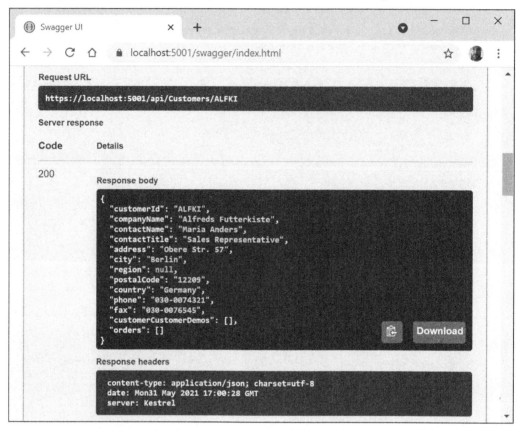

Figure 16.12: Information on ALFKI in a successful Swagger request

6. Scroll back up to the top of the page, click **POST /api/Customers** to expand that section, and then click **Try it out**.

7. Click inside the **Request body** box, and modify the JSON to define a new customer, as shown in the following JSON:

```
{
    "customerID": "SUPER",
    "companyName": "Super Company",
    "contactName": "Rasmus Ibensen",
    "contactTitle": "Sales Leader",
    "address": "Rotterslef 23",
    "city": "Billund",
    "region": null,
```

```
        "postalCode": "4371",
        "country": "Denmark",
        "phone": "31 21 43 21",
        "fax": "31 21 43 22"
    }
```

8. Click **Execute**, and note the **Request URL**, **Server response** with **Code**, and **Details** including **Response body** and **Response headers**, noting that a response code of 201 means the customer was successfully created, as shown in *Figure 16.13*:

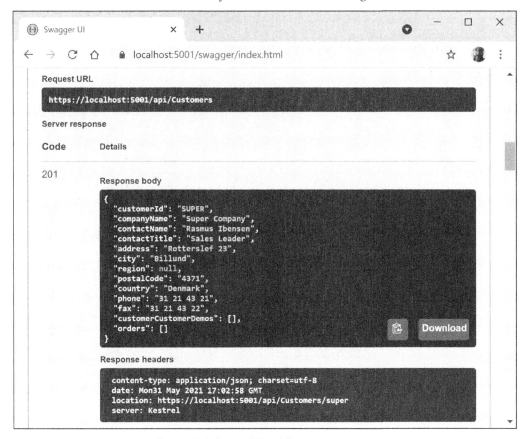

Figure 16.13: Successfully adding a new customer

9. Scroll back up to the top of the page, click **GET /api/Customers**, click **Try it out**, enter Denmark for the country parameter, and click **Execute**, to confirm that the new customer was added to the database, as shown in *Figure 16.14*:

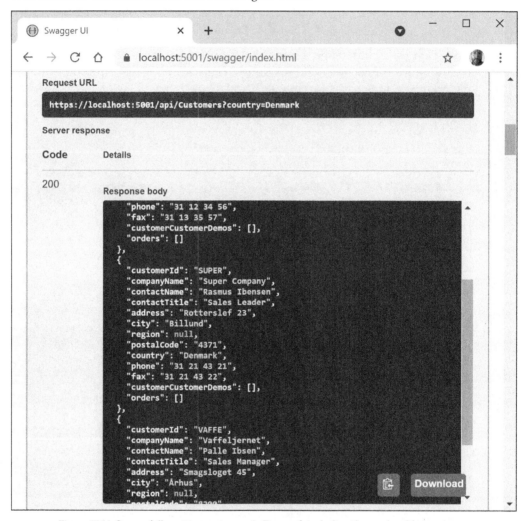

Figure 16.14: Successfully getting customers in Denmark including the newly added customer

10. Click **DELETE /api/Customers/{id}**, click **Try it out**, enter super for the **id**, click **Execute**, and note that the **Server response Code** is 204, indicating that it was successfully deleted, as shown in *Figure 16.15*:

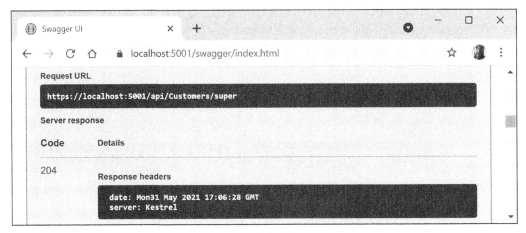

Figure 16.15: Successfully deleting a customer

11. Click **Execute** again, and note that the **Server response Code** is 404, indicating that the customer does not exist anymore, and the **Response body** contains a problem details JSON document, as shown in *Figure 16.16*:

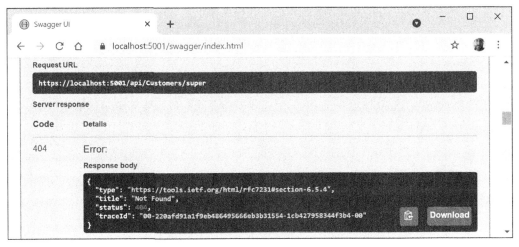

Figure 16.16: The deleted customer does not exist anymore

12. Enter bad for the **id**, click **Execute** again, and note that the **Server response Code** is 400, indicating that the customer did exist but failed to be deleted (in this case, because the web service is simulating this error), and the **Response body** contains a custom problem details JSON document, as shown in *Figure 16.17*:

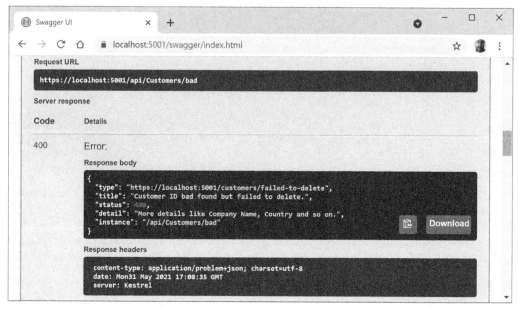

Figure 16.17: The customer did exist but failed to be deleted

13. Use the GET methods to confirm that the new customer has been deleted from the database (there were originally only two customers in Denmark).

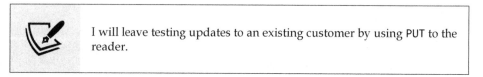

I will leave testing updates to an existing customer by using PUT to the reader.

14. Close Chrome and shut down the web server.

Enabling HTTP logging

HTTP logging is an optional middleware component that logs information about HTTP requests and HTTP responses including the following:

- Information about the HTTP request
- Headers
- Body
- Information about the HTTP response

This is valuable in web services for auditing and debugging scenarios but beware because it can negatively impact performance. You might also log **personally identifiable information (PII)** which can cause compliance issues in some jurisdictions.

Let's see HTTP logging in action:

1. In `Program.cs`, import the namespace for working with HTTP logging, as shown in the following code:

   ```
   using Microsoft.AspNetCore.HttpLogging; // HttpLoggingFields
   ```

2. In the services configuration section, add a statement to configure HTTP logging, as shown in the following code:

   ```
   builder.Services.AddHttpLogging(options =>
   {
     options.LoggingFields = HttpLoggingFields.All;
     options.RequestBodyLogLimit = 4096; // default is 32k
     options.ResponseBodyLogLimit = 4096; // default is 32k
   });
   ```

3. In the HTTP pipeline configuration section, add a statement to add HTTP logging before the call to use routing, as shown in the following code:

   ```
   app.UseHttpLogging();
   ```

4. Start the `Northwind.WebApi` web service.

5. Start Chrome.

6. Navigate to `https://localhost:5001/api/customers`.

7. In a command prompt or terminal, note the request and response have been logged, as shown in the following output:

   ```
   info: Microsoft.AspNetCore.HttpLogging.HttpLoggingMiddleware[1]
         Request:
         Protocol: HTTP/1.1
         Method: GET
         Scheme: https
         PathBase:
         Path: /api/customers
         QueryString:
         Connection: keep-alive
         Accept: */*
         Accept-Encoding: gzip, deflate, br
         Host: localhost:5001

   info: Microsoft.AspNetCore.HttpLogging.HttpLoggingMiddleware[2]
         Response:
   ```

```
StatusCode: 200
Content-Type: application/json; charset=utf-8
...
Transfer-Encoding: chunked
```

8. Close Chrome and shut down the web server.

You are now ready to build applications that consume your web service.

Consuming web services using HTTP clients

Now that we have built and tested our Northwind service, we will learn how to call it from any .NET app using the HttpClient class and its factory.

Understanding HttpClient

The easiest way to consume a web service is to use the HttpClient class. However, many people use it wrongly because it implements IDisposable and Microsoft's own documentation shows poor usage of it. See the book links in the GitHub repository for articles with more discussion of this.

Usually, when a type implements IDisposable, you should create it inside a using statement to ensure that it is disposed of as soon as possible. HttpClient is different because it is shared, reentrant, and partially thread-safe.

The problem has to do with how the underlying network sockets have to be managed. The bottom line is that you should use a single instance of it for each HTTP endpoint that you consume during the life of your application. This will allow each HttpClient instance to have defaults set that are appropriate for the endpoint it works with, while managing the underlying network sockets efficiently.

Configuring HTTP clients using HttpClientFactory

Microsoft is aware of the issue, and in ASP.NET Core 2.1 they introduced HttpClientFactory to encourage best practice; that is the technique we will use.

In the following example, we will use the Northwind MVC website as a client to the Northwind Web API service. Since both need to be hosted on a web server simultaneously, we first need to configure them to use different port numbers, as shown in the following list:

- The Northwind Web API service will listen on port 5002 using HTTPS.
- The Northwind MVC website will continue to listen on port 5000 using HTTP and port 5001 using HTTPS.

Let's configure those ports:

1. In the `Northwind.WebApi` project, in `Program.cs`, add an extension method call to `UseUrls` to specify port `5002` for HTTPS, as shown highlighted in the following code:

```
var builder = WebApplication.CreateBuilder(args);

builder.WebHost.UseUrls("https://localhost:5002/");
```

2. In the `Northwind.Mvc` project, open `Program.cs` and import the namespace for working with HTTP client factory, as shown in the following code:

```
using System.Net.Http.Headers; // MediaTypeWithQualityHeaderValue
```

3. Add a statement to enable `HttpClientFactory` with a named client to make calls to the Northwind Web API service using HTTPS on port `5002` and request JSON as the default response format, as shown in the following code:

```
builder.Services.AddHttpClient(name: "Northwind.WebApi",
  configureClient: options =>
  {
    options.BaseAddress = new Uri("https://localhost:5002/");
    options.DefaultRequestHeaders.Accept.Add(
      new MediaTypeWithQualityHeaderValue(
      "application/json", 1.0));
  });
```

Getting customers as JSON in the controller

We can now create an MVC controller action method that uses the factory to create an HTTP client, makes a GET request for customers, and deserializes the JSON response using convenience extension methods introduced with .NET 5 in the `System.Net.Http.Json` assembly and namespace:

1. Open `Controllers/HomeController.cs` and declare a field to store the HTTP client factory, as shown in the following code:

```
private readonly IHttpClientFactory clientFactory;
```

2. Set the field in the constructor, as shown highlighted in the following code:

```
public HomeController(
  ILogger<HomeController> logger,
  NorthwindContext injectedContext,
  IHttpClientFactory httpClientFactory)
{
  _logger = logger;
  db = injectedContext;
  clientFactory = httpClientFactory;
}
```

3. Create a new action method for calling the Northwind Web API service, fetching all customers, and passing them to a view, as shown in the following code:

```csharp
public async Task<IActionResult> Customers(string country)
{
  string uri;

  if (string.IsNullOrEmpty(country))
  {
    ViewData["Title"] = "All Customers Worldwide";
    uri = "api/customers/";
  }
  else
  {
    ViewData["Title"] = $"Customers in {country}";
    uri = $"api/customers/?country={country}";
  }

  HttpClient client = clientFactory.CreateClient(
    name: "Northwind.WebApi");

  HttpRequestMessage request = new(
    method: HttpMethod.Get, requestUri: uri);

  HttpResponseMessage response = await client.SendAsync(request);

  IEnumerable<Customer>? model = await response.Content
    .ReadFromJsonAsync<IEnumerable<Customer>>();

  return View(model);
}
```

4. In the `Views/Home` folder, create a Razor file named `Customers.cshtml`.

5. Modify the Razor file to render the customers, as shown in the following markup:

```razor
@using Packt.Shared
@model IEnumerable<Customer>
<h2>@ViewData["Title"]</h2>
<table class="table">
  <thead>
    <tr>
      <th>Company Name</th>
      <th>Contact Name</th>
      <th>Address</th>
      <th>Phone</th>
    </tr>
  </thead>
```

```
<tbody>
  @if (Model is not null)
  {
    @foreach (Customer c in Model)
    {
      <tr>
        <td>
          @Html.DisplayFor(modelItem => c.CompanyName)
        </td>
        <td>
          @Html.DisplayFor(modelItem => c.ContactName)
        </td>
        <td>
          @Html.DisplayFor(modelItem => c.Address)
          @Html.DisplayFor(modelItem => c.City)
          @Html.DisplayFor(modelItem => c.Region)
          @Html.DisplayFor(modelItem => c.Country)
          @Html.DisplayFor(modelItem => c.PostalCode)
        </td>
        <td>
          @Html.DisplayFor(modelItem => c.Phone)
        </td>
      </tr>
    }
  }
</tbody>
</table>
```

6. In `Views/Home/Index.cshtml`, add a form after rendering the visitor count to allow visitors to enter a country and see the customers, as shown in the following markup:

```
<h3>Query customers from a service</h3>
<form asp-action="Customers" method="get">
  <input name="country" placeholder="Enter a country" />
  <input type="submit" />
</form>
```

Enabling Cross-Origin Resource Sharing

Cross-Origin Resource Sharing (CORS) is an HTTP-header-based standard for protecting web resources when the client and server are on different domains (origins). It allows a server to indicate which origins (defined by a combination of domain, scheme, or port) other than its own it will permit the loading of resources from.

Since our web service is hosted on port 5002 and our MVC website is hosted on ports 5000 and 5001, they are considered different origins and so resources cannot be shared.

It would be useful to enable CORS on the server and configure our web service to only allow requests that originate from the MVC website:

1. In the `Northwind.WebApi` project, open `Program.cs`.

2. Add a statement in the services configuration section to add support for CORS, as shown in the following code:

   ```
   builder.Services.AddCors();
   ```

3. Add a statement in the HTTP pipeline configuration section, before calling `UseEndpoints`, to use CORS and allow `GET`, `POST`, `PUT`, and `DELETE` requests from any website like Northwind MVC that has an origin of `https://localhost:5001`, as shown in the following code:

   ```
   app.UseCors(configurePolicy: options =>
   {
     options.WithMethods("GET", "POST", "PUT", "DELETE");
     options.WithOrigins(
       "https://localhost:5001" // allow requests from the MVC client
     );
   });
   ```

4. Start the `Northwind.WebApi` project and confirm that the web service is listening only on port `5002`, as shown in the following output:

   ```
   info: Microsoft.Hosting.Lifetime[14]
         Now listening on: https://localhost:5002
   ```

5. Start the `Northwind.Mvc` project and confirm that the website is listening on ports `5000` and `5002`, as shown in the following output:

   ```
   info: Microsoft.Hosting.Lifetime[14]
         Now listening on: https://localhost:5001
   info: Microsoft.Hosting.Lifetime[14]
         Now listening on: http://localhost:5000
   ```

6. Start Chrome.

7. In the customer form, enter a country like Germany, UK, or USA, click **Submit**, and note the list of customers, as shown in *Figure 16.18*:

Figure 16.18: Customers in the UK

8. Click the **Back** button in your browser, clear the country textbox, click **Submit**, and note the worldwide list of customers.

9. In a command prompt or terminal, note the HttpClient writes each HTTP request that it makes and HTTP response that it receives, as shown in the following output:

```
info: System.Net.Http.HttpClient.Northwind.WebApi.ClientHandler[100]
      Sending HTTP request GET https://localhost:5002/api/
customers/?country=UK
info: System.Net.Http.HttpClient.Northwind.WebApi.ClientHandler[101]
      Received HTTP response headers after 931.864ms - 200
```

10. Close Chrome and shut down the web server.

You have successfully built a web service and called it from an MVC website.

Implementing advanced features for web services

Now that you have seen the fundamentals of building a web service and then calling it from a client, let's look at some more advanced features.

Implementing a Health Check API

There are many paid services that perform site availability tests that are basic pings, some with more advanced analysis of the HTTP response.

ASP.NET Core 2.2 and later makes it easy to implement more detailed website health checks. For example, your website might be live, but is it ready? Can it retrieve data from its database?

Let's add basic health check capabilities to our web service:

1. In the `Northwind.WebApi` project, add a project reference to enable Entity Framework Core database health checks, as shown in the following markup:

   ```
   <PackageReference Include=
     "Microsoft.Extensions.Diagnostics.HealthChecks.EntityFrameworkCore"
     Version="6.0.0" />
   ```

2. Build the project.

3. In `Program.cs`, at the bottom of the services configuration section, add a statement to add health checks, including to the Northwind database context, as shown in the following code:

   ```
   builder.Services.AddHealthChecks()
     .AddDbContextCheck<NorthwindContext>();
   ```

    By default, the database context check calls EF Core's `CanConnectAsync` method. You can customize what operation is run by calling the `AddDbContextCheck` method.

4. In the HTTP pipeline configuration section, before the call to `MapControllers`, add a statement to use basic health checks, as shown in the following code:

   ```
   app.UseHealthChecks(path: "/howdoyoufeel");
   ```

5. Start the web service.

6. Start Chrome.

7. Navigate to `https://localhost:5002/howdoyoufeel` and note that the web service responds with a plain text response: `Healthy`.

8. At the command prompt or terminal, note the SQL statement that was executed to test the health of the database, as shown in the following output:

   ```
   Level: Debug, Event Id: 20100, State: Executing DbCommand [Parameters=[],
   CommandType='Text', CommandTimeout='30']
   SELECT 1
   ```

9. Close Chrome and shut down the web server.

Implementing Open API analyzers and conventions

In this chapter, you learned how to enable Swagger to document a web service by manually decorating a controller class with attributes.

In ASP.NET Core 2.2 or later, there are API analyzers that reflect over controller classes that have been annotated with the `[ApiController]` attribute to document it automatically. The analyzer assumes some API conventions.

To use it, your project must enable the OpenAPI Analyzers, as shown highlighted in the following markup:

```
<PropertyGroup>
  <TargetFramework>net6.0</TargetFramework>
  <Nullable>enable</Nullable>
  <ImplicitUsings>enable</ImplicitUsings>
  <IncludeOpenAPIAnalyzers>true</IncludeOpenAPIAnalyzers>
</PropertyGroup>
```

After installing, controllers that have not been properly decorated should have warnings (green squiggles) and warnings when you compile the source code. For example, the `WeatherForecastController` class.

Automatic code fixes can then add the appropriate `[Produces]` and `[ProducesResponseType]` attributes, although this only currently works in Visual Studio. In Visual Studio Code, you will see warnings about where the analyzer thinks you should add attributes, but you must add them yourself.

Implementing transient fault handling

When a client app or website calls a web service, it could be from across the other side of the world. Network problems between the client and the server could cause issues that are nothing to do with your implementation code. If a client makes a call and it fails, the app should not just give up. If it tries again, the issue may now have been resolved. We need a way to handle these temporary faults.

To handle these transient faults, Microsoft recommends that you use the third-party library Polly to implement automatic retries with exponential backoff. You define a policy, and the library handles everything else.

 Good Practice: You can read more about how Polly can make your web services more reliable at the following link: https://docs.microsoft.com/en-us/dotnet/architecture/microservices/implement-resilient-applications/implement-http-call-retries-exponential-backoff-polly

Adding security HTTP headers

ASP.NET Core has built-in support for common security HTTP headers like HSTS. But there are many more HTTP headers that you should consider implementing.

The easiest way to add these headers is using a middleware class:

1. In the Northwind.WebApi project/folder, create a file named
    SecurityHeadersMiddleware.cs and modify its statements, as shown in the following
    code:

    ```
    using Microsoft.Extensions.Primitives; // StringValues

    public class SecurityHeaders
    {
      private readonly RequestDelegate next;

      public SecurityHeaders(RequestDelegate next)
      {
        this.next = next;
      }

      public Task Invoke(HttpContext context)
      {
        // add any HTTP response headers you want here
        context.Response.Headers.Add(
          "super-secure", new StringValues("enable"));

        return next(context);
      }
    }
    ```

2. In Program.cs, in the HTTP pipeline configuration section, add a statement to register
    the middleware before the call to UseEndpoints, as shown in the following code:

    ```
    app.UseMiddleware<SecurityHeaders>();
    ```

3. Start the web service.
4. Start Chrome.
5. Show **Developer tools** and its **Network** tab to record requests and responses.
6. Navigate to https://localhost:5002/weatherforecast.
7. Note the custom HTTP response header that we added named super-secure, as shown
    in *Figure 16.19*:

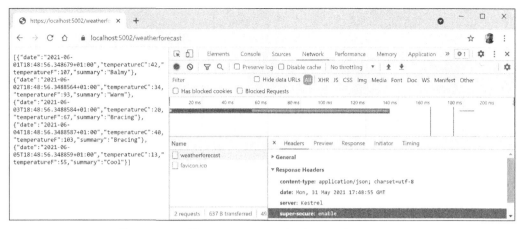

Figure 16.19: Adding a custom HTTP header named super-secure

Building web services using minimal APIs

For .NET 6, Microsoft put a lot of effort into adding new features to the C# 10 language and simplifying the ASP.NET Core libraries to enable the creation of web services using minimal APIs.

You might remember the weather forecast service that is provided in the Web API project template. It shows the use of a controller class to return a five-day weather forecast using faked data. We will now recreate that weather service using minimal APIs.

First, the weather service has a class to represent a single weather forecast. We will need to use this class in multiple projects, so let's create a class library for that:

1. Use your preferred code editor to add a new project, as defined in the following list:
    1. Project template: **Class Library** / classlib
    2. Workspace/solution file and folder: PracticalApps
    3. Project file and folder: Northwind.Common

2. Rename Class1.cs to WeatherForecast.cs.

3. Modify WeatherForecast.cs, as shown in the following code:

    ```
    namespace Northwind.Common
    {
      public class WeatherForecast
      {
        public static readonly string[] Summaries = new[]
        {
    ```

```
        "Freezing", "Bracing", "Chilly", "Cool", "Mild",
        "Warm", "Balmy", "Hot", "Sweltering", "Scorching"
    };

    public DateTime Date { get; set; }

    public int TemperatureC { get; set; }

    public int TemperatureF => 32 + (int)(TemperatureC / 0.5556);

    public string? Summary { get; set; }
    }
}
```

Building a weather service using minimal APIs

Now let's recreate that weather service using minimal APIs. It will listen on port 5003 and have CORS support enabled so that requests can only come from the MVC website and only GET requests are allowed:

1. Use your preferred code editor to add a new project, as defined in the following list:

   1. Project template: **ASP.NET Core Empty** / web
   2. Workspace/solution file and folder: PracticalApps
   3. Project file and folder: Minimal.WebApi
   4. Other Visual Studio options: **Authentication Type**: None, **Configure for HTTPS**: selected, **Enable Docker**: cleared, **Enable OpenAPI support**: selected.

2. In Visual Studio Code, select Minimal.WebApi as the active OmniSharp project.

3. In the Minimal.WebApi project, add a project reference to the Northwind.Common project, as shown in the following markup:

   ```
   <ItemGroup>
     <ProjectReference Include="..\Northwind.Common\Northwind.Common.csproj"
   />
   </ItemGroup>
   ```

4. Build the Minimal.WebApi project.

5. Modify Program.cs, as shown highlighted in the following code:

   ```
   using Northwind.Common; // WeatherForecast

   var builder = WebApplication.CreateBuilder(args);

   builder.WebHost.UseUrls("https://localhost:5003");
   ```

```
builder.Services.AddCors();

var app = builder.Build();

// only allow the MVC client and only GET requests
app.UseCors(configurePolicy: options =>
{
  options.WithMethods("GET");
  options.WithOrigins("https://localhost:5001");
});

app.MapGet("/api/weather", () =>
{
  return Enumerable.Range(1, 5).Select(index =>
    new WeatherForecast
    {
      Date = DateTime.Now.AddDays(index),
      TemperatureC = Random.Shared.Next(-20, 55),
      Summary = WeatherForecast.Summaries[
        Random.Shared.Next(WeatherForecast.Summaries.Length)]
    })
    .ToArray();
});

app.Run();
```

 Good Practice: For simple web services, avoid creating a controller class, and instead use minimal APIs to put all the configuration and implementation in one place, `Program.cs`.

6. In **Properties**, modify `launchSettings.json` to configure the `Minimal.WebApi` profile to launch the browser using port 5003 in the URL, as shown highlighted in the following markup:

```
"profiles": {
  "Minimal.WebApi": {
    "commandName": "Project",
    "dotnetRunMessages": "true",
    "launchBrowser": true,
    "applicationUrl": "https://localhost:5003/api/weather",
    "environmentVariables": {
      "ASPNETCORE_ENVIRONMENT": "Development"
    }
```

Testing the minimal weather service

Before creating a client to the service, let's test that it returns forecasts as JSON:

1. Start the web service project.
2. If you are not using Visual Studio 2022, start Chrome and navigate to `https://localhost:5003/api/weather`.
3. Note the Web API service should return a JSON document with five random weather forecast objects in an array.
4. Close Chrome and shut down the web server.

Adding weather forecasts to the Northwind website home page

Finally, let's add an HTTP client to the Northwind website so that it can call the weather service and show forecasts on the home page:

1. In the `Northwind.Mvc` project, add a project reference to `Northwind.Common`, as shown highlighted in the following markup:

   ```xml
   <ItemGroup>
     <!-- change Sqlite to SqlServer if you prefer -->
     <ProjectReference Include="..\Northwind.Common.DataContext.Sqlite\
   Northwind.Common.DataContext.Sqlite.csproj" />
     <ProjectReference Include="..\Northwind.Common\Northwind.Common.csproj"
   />
   </ItemGroup>
   ```

2. In `Program.cs`, add a statement to configure an HTTP client to call the minimal service on port `5003`, as shown in the following code:

   ```csharp
   builder.Services.AddHttpClient(name: "Minimal.WebApi",
     configureClient: options =>
     {
       options.BaseAddress = new Uri("https://localhost:5003/");
       options.DefaultRequestHeaders.Accept.Add(
         new MediaTypeWithQualityHeaderValue(
         "application/json", 1.0));
     });
   ```

3. In `HomeController.cs`, import the `Northwind.Common` namespace, and in the `Index` method, add statements to get and use an HTTP client to call the weather service to get forecasts and store them in `ViewData`, as shown in the following code:

   ```csharp
   try
   {
     HttpClient client = clientFactory.CreateClient(
   ```

```
    name: "Minimal.WebApi");

  HttpRequestMessage request = new(
    method: HttpMethod.Get, requestUri: "api/weather");

  HttpResponseMessage response = await client.SendAsync(request);

  ViewData["weather"] = await response.Content
    .ReadFromJsonAsync<WeatherForecast[]>();
}
catch (Exception ex)
{
  _logger.LogWarning($"The Minimal.WebApi service is not responding.
Exception: {ex.Message}");
  ViewData["weather"] = Enumerable.Empty<WeatherForecast>().ToArray();
}
```

4. In `Views/Home`, in `Index.cshtml`, import the `Northwind.Common` namespace and then in the top code block get the weather forecasts from the `ViewData` dictionary, as shown in the following markup:

```
@{
  ViewData["Title"] = "Home Page";
  string currentItem = "";
  WeatherForecast[]? weather = ViewData["weather"] as WeatherForecast[];
}
```

5. In the first `<div>`, after rendering the current time, add markup to enumerate the weather forecasts unless there aren't any, and render them in a table, as shown in the following markup:

```
<p>
  <h4>Five-Day Weather Forecast</h4>
  @if ((weather is null) || (!weather.Any()))
  {
    <p>No weather forecasts found.</p>
  }
  else
  {
  <table class="table table-info">
    <tr>
      @foreach (WeatherForecast w in weather)
      {
        <td>@w.Date.ToString("ddd d MMM") will be @w.Summary</td>
      }
    </tr>
  </table>
  }
</p>
```

6. Start the `Minimal.WebApi` service.

7. Start the `Northwind.Mvc` website.

8. Navigate to `https://localhost:5001/`, and note the weather forecast, as shown in *Figure 16.20*:

Figure 16.20: A five-day weather forecast on the home page of the Northwind website

9. View the command prompt or terminal for the MVC website and note the info messages that indicate a request was sent to the minimal API web service `api/weather` endpoint in about 83ms, as shown in the following output:

```
info: System.Net.Http.HttpClient.Minimal.WebApi.LogicalHandler[100]
      Start processing HTTP request GET https://localhost:5003/api/weather
info: System.Net.Http.HttpClient.Minimal.WebApi.ClientHandler[100]
      Sending HTTP request GET https://localhost:5003/api/weather
info: System.Net.Http.HttpClient.Minimal.WebApi.ClientHandler[101]
      Received HTTP response headers after 76.8963ms - 200
info: System.Net.Http.HttpClient.Minimal.WebApi.LogicalHandler[101]
      End processing HTTP request after 82.9515ms - 200
```

10. Stop the `Minimal.WebApi` service, refresh the browser, and note that after a few seconds the MVC website home page appears without weather forecasts.

11. Close Chrome and shut down the web server.

Practicing and exploring

Test your knowledge and understanding by answering some questions, get some hands-on practice, and explore this chapter's topics with deeper research.

Exercise 16.1 – Test your knowledge

Answer the following questions:

1. Which class should you inherit from to create a controller class for an ASP.NET Core Web API service?

2. If you decorate your controller class with the `[ApiController]` attribute to get default behavior like automatic 400 responses for invalid models, what else must you do?

3. What must you do to specify which controller action method will be executed in response to an HTTP request?

4. What must you do to specify what responses should be expected when calling an action method?

5. List three methods that can be called to return responses with different status codes.

6. List four ways that you can test a web service.

7. Why should you not wrap your use of `HttpClient` in a `using` statement to dispose of it when you are finished even though it implements the `IDisposable` interface, and what should you use instead?

8. What does the acronym CORS stand for and why is it important to enable it in a web service?

9. How can you enable clients to detect if your web service is healthy with ASP. NET Core 2.2 and later?

10. What benefits does endpoint routing provide?

Exercise 16.2 – Practice creating and deleting customers with HttpClient

Extend the `Northwind.Mvc` website project to have pages where a visitor can fill in a form to create a new customer, or search for a customer and then delete them. The MVC controller should make calls to the Northwind web service to create and delete customers.

Exercise 16.3 – Explore topics

Use the links on the following page to learn more detail about the topics covered in this chapter:

```
https://github.com/markjprice/cs10dotnet6/blob/main/book-links.md#chapter-16---
building-and-consuming-web-services
```

Summary

In this chapter, you learned how to build an ASP.NET Core Web API service that can be called by any app on any platform that can make an HTTP request and process an HTTP response.

You also learned how to test and document web service APIs with Swagger, as well as how to consume services efficiently.

In the next chapter, you will learn to build user interfaces using Blazor, Microsoft's cool new component technology that enables developers to build client-side, single-page applications (SPAs) for websites using C# instead of JavaScript, hybrid apps for desktop, and potentially mobile apps.

17

Building User Interfaces Using Blazor

This chapter is about using Blazor to build user interfaces. I will describe the different flavors of Blazor and their pros and cons.

You will learn how to build Blazor components that can execute their code on the web server or in the web browser. When hosted with Blazor Server, it uses SignalR to communicate needed updates to the user interface in the browser. When hosted with Blazor WebAssembly, the components execute their code in the client and must make HTTP calls to interact with the server.

In this chapter, we will cover the following topics:

- Understanding Blazor
- Comparing Blazor project templates
- Building components using Blazor Server
- Abstracting a service for a Blazor component
- Building components using Blazor WebAssembly
- Improving Blazor WebAssembly apps

Understanding Blazor

Blazor lets you build shared components and interactive web user interfaces using C# instead of JavaScript. In April 2019, Microsoft announced that Blazor "is no longer experimental and we are committing to ship it as a supported web UI framework, including support for running client side in the browser on WebAssembly." Blazor is supported on all modern browsers.

JavaScript and friends

Traditionally, any code that needs to execute in a web browser is written using the JavaScript programming language or a higher-level technology that **transpiles** (transforms or compiles) into JavaScript. This is because all browsers have supported JavaScript for about two decades, so it has become the lowest common denominator for implementing business logic on the client side.

JavaScript does have some issues, however. Although it has superficial similarities to C-style languages like C# and Java, it is actually very different once you dig beneath the surface. It is a dynamically typed pseudo-functional language that uses prototypes instead of class inheritance for object reuse. It might look human, but you will get a surprise when it's revealed to actually be a Skrull.

Wouldn't it be great if we could use the same language and libraries in a web browser as we do on the server side?

Silverlight – C# and .NET using a plugin

Microsoft made a previous attempt at achieving this goal with a technology named Silverlight. When Silverlight 2.0 was released in 2008, a C# and .NET developer could use their skills to build libraries and visual components that were executed in the web browser by the Silverlight plugin.

By 2011 and Silverlight 5.0, Apple's success with the iPhone and Steve Jobs' hatred of browser plugins like Flash eventually led to Microsoft abandoning Silverlight since, like Flash, Silverlight is banned from iPhones and iPads.

WebAssembly – a target for Blazor

A recent development in browsers has given Microsoft the opportunity to make another attempt. In 2017, the **WebAssembly Consensus** was completed, and all major browsers now support it: Chromium (Chrome, Edge, Opera, Brave), Firefox, and WebKit (Safari). Blazor is not supported by Microsoft's Internet Explorer because it is a legacy web browser.

WebAssembly (Wasm) is a binary instruction format for a virtual machine that provides a way to run code written in multiple languages on the web at near-native speed. Wasm is designed as a portable target for the compilation of high-level languages like C#.

Understanding Blazor hosting models

Blazor is a single programming or app model with multiple hosting models:

- **Blazor Server** runs on the server side, so the C# code that you write has full access to all resources that your business logic might need without needing to authenticate. It then uses SignalR to communicate user interface updates to the client side.

- The server must keep a live SignalR connection to each client and track the current state of every client, so Blazor Server does not scale well if you need to support lots of clients. It first shipped as part of ASP.NET Core 3.0 in September 2019 and is included with .NET 5.0 and later.

- **Blazor WebAssembly** runs on the client side, so the C# code that you write only has access to resources in the browser and it must make HTTP calls (that might require authentication) before it can access resources on the server. It first shipped as an extension to ASP.NET Core 3.1 in May 2020 and was versioned 3.2 because it is a Current release and therefore not covered by ASP.NET Core 3.1's Long Term Support. The Blazor WebAssembly 3.2 version used the Mono runtime and Mono libraries; .NET 5 and later versions use the Mono runtime and the .NET 5 libraries. *"Blazor WebAssembly runs on a .NET IL interpreter without any JIT so it's not going to win any speed competitions. We have made some significant speed improvements though in .NET 5, and we expect to improve things further for .NET 6."* — Daniel Roth

- **.NET MAUI Blazor App**, aka **Blazor Hybrid**, runs in the .NET process, renders its web UI to a web view control using a local interop channel, and is hosted in a .NET MAUI app. It is conceptually like Electron apps that use Node.js. We will see this hosting model in online chapter, *Chapter 19, Building Mobile and Desktop Apps Using .NET MAUI.*

This multi-host model means that, with careful planning, a developer can write Blazor components once, and then run them on the web server side, web client side, or within a desktop app.

Although Blazor Server is supported on Internet Explorer 11, Blazor WebAssembly is not.

Blazor WebAssembly has optional support for **Progressive Web Apps** (**PWAs**), meaning a website visitor can use a browser menu to add the app to their desktop and run the app offline.

Understanding Blazor components

It is important to understand that Blazor is used to create **user interface components**. Components define how to render the user interface, react to user events, and can be composed and nested, and compiled into a NuGet Razor class library for packaging and distribution.

For example, you might create a component named `Rating.razor`, as shown in the following markup:

```
<div>
@for (int i = 0; i < Maximum; i++)
{
  if (i < Value)
  {
    <span class="oi oi-star-filled" />
  }
  else
  {
    <span class="oi oi-star-empty" />
```

```
    }
  }
  </div>

  @code {
    [Parameter]
    public byte Maximum { get; set; }

    [Parameter]
    public byte Value { get; set; }
  }
```

 Instead of a single file with both markup and an @code block, the code can be stored in a separate code-behind file named Rating.razor.cs. The class in this file must be partial and have the same name as the component.

You could then use the component on a web page, as shown in the following markup:

```
<h1>Review</h1>
<Rating id="rating" Maximum="5" Value="3" />
<textarea id="comment" />
```

There are many built-in Blazor components, including ones to set elements like <title> in the <head> section of a web page, and plenty of third parties who will sell you components for common purposes.

In the future, Blazor might not be limited to only creating user interface components using web technologies. Microsoft has an experimental technology known as **Blazor Mobile Bindings** that allows developers to use Blazor to build mobile user interface components. Instead of using HTML and CSS to build a web user interface, it uses XAML and .NET MAUI to build a cross-platform graphical user interface.

What is the difference between Blazor and Razor?

You might wonder why Blazor components use .razor as their file extension. Razor is a template markup syntax that allows the mixing of HTML and C#. Older technologies that support Razor syntax use the .cshtml file extension to indicate the mix of C# and HTML.

Razor syntax is used for:

- ASP.NET Core MVC **views** and **partial views** that use the .cshtml file extension. The business logic is separated into a controller class that treats the view as a template to push the view model to, which then outputs it to a web page.

- **Razor Pages** that use the .cshtml file extension. The business logic can be embedded or separated into a file that uses the .cshtml.cs file extension. The output is a web page.

- **Blazor components** that use the .razor file extension. The output is not a web page, although layouts can be used to wrap a component so it outputs as a web page, and the @page directive can be used to assign a route that defines the URL path to retrieve the component as a page.

Comparing Blazor project templates

One way to understand the choice between the Blazor Server and Blazor WebAssembly hosting models is to review the differences in their default project templates.

Reviewing the Blazor Server project template

Let us look at the default template for a Blazor Server project. Mostly you will see that it is the same as an ASP.NET Core Razor Pages template, with a few key additions:

1. Use your preferred code editor to add a new project, as defined in the following list:

    1. Project template: **Blazor Server App** / blazorserver

    2. Workspace/solution file and folder: PracticalApps

    3. Project file and folder: Northwind.BlazorServer

    4. Other Visual Studio options: **Authentication Type: None**; **Configure for HTTPS**: selected; **Enable Docker**: cleared

2. In Visual Studio Code, select Northwind.BlazorServer as the active OmniSharp project.

3. Build the Northwind.BlazorServer project.

4. In the Northwind.BlazorServer project/folder, open Northwind.BlazorServer.csproj and note that it is identical to an ASP.NET Core project that uses the Web SDK and targets .NET 6.0.

5. Open Program.cs, and note it is almost identical to an ASP.NET Core project. Differences include the section that configures services, with its call to the AddServerSideBlazor method, as shown highlighted in the following code:

```
builder.Services.AddRazorPages();
builder.Services.AddServerSideBlazor();
builder.Services.AddSingleton<WeatherForecastService>();
```

6. Also note the section for configuring the HTTP pipeline, which adds the calls to the MapBlazorHub and MapFallbackToPage methods that configure the ASP.NET Core app to accept incoming SignalR connections for Blazor components, while other requests fall back to a Razor Page named _Host.cshtml, as shown highlighted in the following code:

```
app.UseRouting();

app.MapBlazorHub();
app.MapFallbackToPage("/_Host");

app.Run();
```

7. In the Pages folder, open _Host.cshtml and note that it sets a shared layout named _Layout and renders a Blazor component of type App that is prerendered on the server, as shown in the following markup:

```
@page "/"
@namespace  Northwind.BlazorServer.Pages
@addTagHelper *, Microsoft.AspNetCore.Mvc.TagHelpers
@{
    Layout = "_Layout";
}

<component type="typeof(App)" render-mode="ServerPrerendered" />
```

8. In the Pages folder, open the shared layout file named _Layout.cshtml, as shown in the following markup:

```
@using Microsoft.AspNetCore.Components.Web
@namespace Northwind.BlazorServer.Pages
@addTagHelper *, Microsoft.AspNetCore.Mvc.TagHelpers

<!DOCTYPE html>
<html lang="en">
<head>
    <meta charset="utf-8" />
    <meta name="viewport"
          content="width=device-width, initial-scale=1.0" />
    <base href="~/" />
    <link rel="stylesheet" href="css/bootstrap/bootstrap.min.css" />
    <link href="css/site.css" rel="stylesheet" />
    <link href="Northwind.BlazorServer.styles.css" rel="stylesheet" />
    <component type="typeof(HeadOutlet)" render-mode="ServerPrerendered" />
</head>
<body>
    @RenderBody()

    <div id="blazor-error-ui">
      <environment include="Staging,Production">
        An error has occurred. This application may no longer respond until
reloaded.
      </environment>
      <environment include="Development">
        An unhandled exception has occurred. See browser dev tools for
details.
      </environment>
      <a href="" class="reload">Reload</a>
      <a class="dismiss">✕</a>
    </div>
```

```
    <script src="_framework/blazor.server.js"></script>
  </body>
</html>
```

While reviewing the preceding markup, note the following:

- `<div id="blazor-error-ui">` for showing Blazor errors that will appear as a yellow bar at the bottom of the web page when an error occurs
- The script block for `blazor.server.js` manages the SignalR connection back to the server

9. In the `Northwind.BlazorServer` folder, open `App.razor` and note that it defines a `Router` for all components found in the current assembly, as shown in the following code:

```
<Router AppAssembly="@typeof(App).Assembly">
  <Found Context="routeData">
    <RouteView RouteData="@routeData"
               DefaultLayout="@typeof(MainLayout)" />
    <FocusOnNavigate RouteData="@routeData" Selector="h1" />
  </Found>
  <NotFound>
    <PageTitle>Not found</PageTitle>
    <LayoutView Layout="@typeof(MainLayout)">
      <p>Sorry, there's nothing at this address.</p>
    </LayoutView>
  </NotFound>
</Router>
```

While reviewing the preceding markup, note the following:

- If a matching route is found, then `RouteView` is executed that sets the default layout for the component to `MainLayout` and passes any route data parameters to the component.
- If a matching route is not found, then `LayoutView` is executed that renders the internal markup (in this case, a simple paragraph element with a message telling the visitor there is nothing at this address) inside `MainLayout`.

10. In the `Shared` folder, open `MainLayout.razor` and note that it defines `<div>` for a sidebar containing a navigation menu that is implemented by the `NavMenu.razor` component file in this project, and an HTML5 element such as `<main>` and `<article>` for the content, as shown in the following code:

```
@inherits LayoutComponentBase

<PageTitle>Northwind.BlazorServer</PageTitle>

<div class="page">
  <div class="sidebar">
```

```
    <NavMenu />
  </div>

  <main>
    <div class="top-row px-4">
      <a href="https://docs.microsoft.com/aspnet/"
         target="_blank">About</a>
    </div>
    <article class="content px-4">
      @Body
    </article>
  </main>
</div>
```

11. In the Shared folder, open MainLayout.razor.css and note that it contains isolated CSS styles for the component.

12. In the Shared folder, open NavMenu.razor and note that it has three menu items for **Home**, **Counter**, and **Fetch data**. These are created by using a Microsoft-provided Blazor component named NavLink, as shown in the following markup:

```
<div class="top-row ps-3 navbar navbar-dark">
  <div class="container-fluid">
    <a class="navbar-brand" href="">Northwind.BlazorServer</a>
    <button title="Navigation menu" class="navbar-toggler"
            @onclick="ToggleNavMenu">
      <span class="navbar-toggler-icon"></span>
    </button>
  </div>
</div>

<div class="@NavMenuCssClass" @onclick="ToggleNavMenu">
  <nav class="flex-column">
    <div class="nav-item px-3">
      <NavLink class="nav-link" href="" Match="NavLinkMatch.All">
        <span class="oi oi-home" aria-hidden="true"></span> Home
      </NavLink>
    </div>
    <div class="nav-item px-3">
      <NavLink class="nav-link" href="counter">
        <span class="oi oi-plus" aria-hidden="true"></span> Counter
      </NavLink>
    </div>
    <div class="nav-item px-3">
      <NavLink class="nav-link" href="fetchdata">
        <span class="oi oi-list-rich" aria-hidden="true"></span> Fetch
data
      </NavLink>
```

```
      </div>
    </nav>
  </div>

  @code {
    private bool collapseNavMenu = true;

    private string? NavMenuCssClass => collapseNavMenu ? "collapse" : null;

    private void ToggleNavMenu()
    {
      collapseNavMenu = !collapseNavMenu;
    }
  }
```

13. In the `Pages` folder, open `FetchData.razor` and note that it defines a component that fetches weather forecasts from an injected dependency weather service and then renders them in a table, as shown in the following code:

```
@page "/fetchdata"

<PageTitle>Weather forecast</PageTitle>

@using Northwind.BlazorServer.Data
@inject WeatherForecastService ForecastService

<h1>Weather forecast</h1>

<p>This component demonstrates fetching data from a service.</p>

@if (forecasts == null)
{
  <p><em>Loading...</em></p>
}
else
{
  <table class="table">
    <thead>
      <tr>
        <th>Date</th>
        <th>Temp. (C)</th>
        <th>Temp. (F)</th>
        <th>Summary</th>
      </tr>
    </thead>
    <tbody>
      @foreach (var forecast in forecasts)
```

```
    {
      <tr>
        <td>@forecast.Date.ToShortDateString()</td>
        <td>@forecast.TemperatureC</td>
        <td>@forecast.TemperatureF</td>
        <td>@forecast.Summary</td>
      </tr>
    }
    </tbody>
  </table>
}

@code {
  private WeatherForecast[]? forecasts;

  protected override async Task OnInitializedAsync()
  {
    forecasts = await ForecastService.GetForecastAsync(DateTime.Now);
  }
}
```

14. In the `Data` folder, open `WeatherForecastService.cs` and note that it is *not* a Web API controller class; it is just an ordinary class that returns random weather data, as shown in the following code:

```
namespace Northwind.BlazorServer.Data
{
  public class WeatherForecastService
  {
    private static readonly string[] Summaries = new[]
    {
      "Freezing", "Bracing", "Chilly", "Cool", "Mild", "Warm",
      "Balmy", "Hot", "Sweltering", "Scorching"
    };

    public Task<WeatherForecast[]> GetForecastAsync(DateTime startDate)
    {
      return Task.FromResult(Enumerable.Range(1, 5)
        .Select(index => new WeatherForecast
          {
            Date = startDate.AddDays(index),
            TemperatureC = Random.Shared.Next(-20, 55),
            Summary = Summaries[Random.Shared.Next(Summaries.Length)]
          }).ToArray());
    }
  }
}
```

Understanding CSS and JavaScript isolation

Blazor components often need to provide their own CSS to apply styling or JavaScript for activities that cannot be performed purely in C#, like access to browser APIs. To ensure this does not conflict with site-level CSS and JavaScript, Blazor supports CSS and JavaScript isolation. If you have a component named `Index.razor`, simply create a CSS file named `Index.razor.css`. The styles defined within this file will override any other styles in the project.

Understanding Blazor routing to page components

The `Router` component that we saw in the `App.razor` file enables routing to components. The markup for creating an instance of a component looks like an HTML tag where the name of the tag is the component type. Components can be embedded on a web page using an element, for example, `<Rating Stars="5" />`, or can be routed to like a Razor Page or MVC controller.

How to define a routable page component

To create a routable page component, add the `@page` directive to the top of a component's `.razor` file, as shown in the following markup:

```
@page "customers"
```

The preceding code is the equivalent of an MVC controller decorated with the `[Route]` attribute, as shown in the following code:

```
[Route("customers")]
public class CustomersController
{
```

The `Router` component scans the assembly specifically in its `AppAssembly` parameter for components decorated with the `[Route]` attribute and registers their URL paths.

Any single-page component can have multiple `@page` directives to register multiple routes.

At runtime, the page component is merged with any specific layout that you have specified, just like an MVC view or Razor Page would be. By default, the Blazor Server project template defines `MainLayout.razor` as the layout for page components.

 Good Practice: By convention, put routable page components in the `Pages` folder.

How to navigate Blazor routes

Microsoft provides a dependency service named `NavigationManager` that understands Blazor routing and the `NavLink` component.

The `NavigateTo` method is used to go to the specified URL.

How to pass route parameters

Blazor routes can include case-insensitive named parameters, and your code can most easily access the passed values by binding the parameter to a property in the code block using the `[Parameter]` attribute, as shown in the following markup:

```
@page "/customers/{country}"

<div>Country parameter as the value: @Country</div>

@code {
  [Parameter]
  public string Country { get; set; }
}
```

The recommended way to handle a parameter that should have a default value when it is missing is to suffix the parameter with ? and use the null coalescing operator in the `OnParametersSet` method, as shown in the following markup:

```
@page "/customers/{country?}"

<div>Country parameter as the value: @Country</div>

@code {
  [Parameter]
  public string Country { get; set; }

  protected override void OnParametersSet()
  {
    // if the automatically set property is null
    // set its value to USA
    Country = Country ?? "USA";
  }
}
```

Understanding base component classes

The `OnParametersSet` method is defined by the base class that components inherit from by default named `ComponentBase`, as shown in the following code:

```
using Microsoft.AspNetCore.Components;

public abstract class ComponentBase : IComponent, IHandleAfterRender,
IHandleEvent
{
```

```
    // members not shown
  }
```

ComponentBase has some useful methods that you can call and override, as shown in the
following table:

Method(s)	Description
InvokeAsync	Call this method to execute a function on the associated renderer's synchronization context.
OnAfterRender, OnAfterRenderAsync	Override these methods to invoke code after each time the component has been rendered.
OnInitialized, OnInitializedAsync	Override these methods to invoke code after the component has received its initial parameters from its parent in the render tree.
OnParametersSet, OnParametersSetAsync	Override these methods to invoke code after the component has received parameters and the values have been assigned to properties.
ShouldRender	Override this method to indicate if the component should render.
StateHasChanged	Call this method to cause the component to re-render.

Blazor components can have shared layouts in a similar way to MVC views and Razor Pages.

Create a .razor component file, but make it explicitly inherit from LayoutComponentBase, as
shown in the following markup:

```
@inherits LayoutComponentBase

<div>
  ...
  @Body
  ...
</div>
```

The base class has a property named Body that you can render in the markup at the correct
place within the layout.

Set a default layout for components in the App.razor file and its Router component. To
explicitly set a layout for a component, use the @layout directive, as shown in the following
markup:

```
@page "/customers"
@layout AlternativeLayout

<div>
  ...
</div>
```

How to use the navigation link component with routes

In HTML, you use the `<a>` element to define navigation links, as shown in the following markup:

```
<a href="/customers">Customers</a>
```

In Blazor, use the `<NavLink>` component, as shown in the following markup:

```
<NavLink href="/customers">Customers</NavLink>
```

The `NavLink` component is better than an anchor element because it automatically sets its class to `active` if its `href` is a match on the current location URL. If your CSS uses a different class name, then you can set the class name in the `NavLink.ActiveClass` property.

By default, in the matching algorithm, the `href` is a path *prefix*, so if `NavLink` has an `href` of `/customers`, as shown in the preceding code example, then it would match all the following paths and set them all to have the `active` class style:

```
/customers
/customers/USA
/customers/Germany/Berlin
```

To ensure that the matching algorithm only performs matches on *all* of the paths, set the `Match` parameter to `NavLinkMatch.All`, as shown in the following code:

```
<NavLink href="/customers" Match="NavLinkMatch.All">Customers</NavLink>
```

If you set other attributes such as `target`, they are passed through to the underlying `<a>` element that is generated.

Running the Blazor Server project template

Now that we have reviewed the project template and the important parts that are specific to Blazor Server, we can start the website and review its behavior:

1. In the `Properties` folder, open `launchSettings.json`.

2. Modify the `applicationUrl` to use port `5000` for HTTP and port `5001` for HTTPS, as shown highlighted in the following markup:

```
"profiles": {
  "Northwind.BlazorServer": {
    "commandName": "Project",
    "dotnetRunMessages": true,
    "launchBrowser": true,
    "applicationUrl": "https://localhost:5001;http://localhost:5000",
    "environmentVariables": {
      "ASPNETCORE_ENVIRONMENT": "Development"
    }
  },
```

3. Start the website.
4. Start Chrome.
5. Navigate to `https://localhost:5001/`.
6. In the left navigation menu, click **Fetch data**, as shown in *Figure 17.1*:

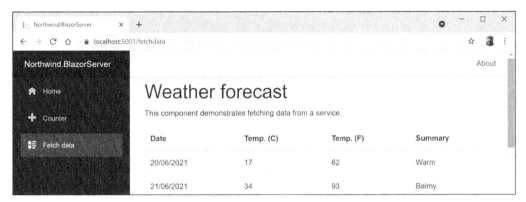

Figure 17.1: Fetching weather data into a Blazor Server app

7. In the browser address bar, change the route to `/apples` and note the missing message, as shown in *Figure 17.2*:

Figure 17.2: The missing component message

8. Close Chrome and shut down the web server.

Reviewing the Blazor WebAssembly project template

Now we will create a Blazor WebAssembly project. I will not show code in the book if the code is the same as in a Blazor Server project:

1. Use your preferred code editor to add a new project to the `PracticalApps` solution or workspace, as defined in the following list:

   1. Project template: **Blazor WebAssembly App** / `blazorwasm`
   2. Switches: `--pwa --hosted`
   3. Workspace/solution file and folder: `PracticalApps`

4. Project file and folder: `Northwind.BlazorWasm`

5. **Authentication Type: None**

6. **Configure for HTTPS**: checked

7. **ASP.NET Core hosted**: checked

8. **Progressive Web Application**: checked

While reviewing the generated folders and files, note that three projects are generated, as described in the following list:

- `Northwind.BlazorWasm.Client` is the Blazor WebAssembly project in the `Northwind.BlazorWasm\Client` folder.

- `Northwind.BlazorWasm.Server` is an ASP.NET Core project website in the `Northwind.BlazorWasm\Server` folder for hosting the weather service that has the same implementation for returning random weather forecasts as before, but is implemented as a proper Web API controller class. The project file has project references to `Shared` and `Client`, and a package reference to support Blazor WebAssembly on the server side.

- `Northwind.BlazorWasm.Shared` is a class library in the `Northwind.BlazorWasm\Shared` folder that contains models for the weather service.

The folder structure is simplified, as shown in *Figure 17.3*:

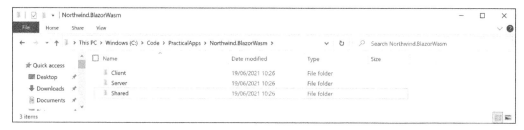

Figure 17.3: The folder structure for the Blazor WebAssembly project template

 There are two ways to deploy a Blazor WebAssembly app. You could deploy just the `Client` project by placing its published files in any static hosting web server. It could be configured to call the weather service that you created in *Chapter 16, Building and Consuming Web Services*, or you can deploy the `Server` project, which references the `Client` app and hosts both the weather service and the Blazor WebAssembly app. The app is placed in the server website `wwwroot` folder along with any other static assets. You can read more about these choices at the following link: `https://docs.microsoft.com/en-us/aspnet/core/blazor/host-and-deploy/webassembly`

2. In the `Client` folder, open `Northwind.BlazorWasm.Client.csproj` and note that it uses the Blazor WebAssembly SDK and references two WebAssembly packages and the `Shared` project, as well as the service worker required for PWA support, as shown in the following markup:

```xml
<Project Sdk="Microsoft.NET.Sdk.BlazorWebAssembly">

  <PropertyGroup>
    <TargetFramework>net6.0</TargetFramework>
    <Nullable>enable</Nullable>
    <ImplicitUsings>enable</ImplicitUsings>
    <ServiceWorkerAssetsManifest>service-worker-assets.js
      </ServiceWorkerAssetsManifest>
  </PropertyGroup>

  <ItemGroup>
    <PackageReference Include=
      "Microsoft.AspNetCore.Components.WebAssembly"
      Version="6.0.0" />
    <PackageReference Include=
      "Microsoft.AspNetCore.Components.WebAssembly.DevServer"
      Version="6.0.0" PrivateAssets="all" />
  </ItemGroup>

  <ItemGroup>
    <ProjectReference Include=
      "..\Shared\Northwind.BlazorWasm.Shared.csproj" />
  </ItemGroup>

  <ItemGroup>
    <ServiceWorker Include="wwwroot\service-worker.js"
      PublishedContent="wwwroot\service-worker.published.js" />
  </ItemGroup>

</Project>
```

3. In the `Client` folder, open `Program.cs` and note that the host builder is for `WebAssembly` instead of server-side ASP.NET Core, and that it registers a dependency service for making HTTP requests, which is an extremely common requirement for Blazor WebAssembly apps, as shown in the following code:

```csharp
using Microsoft.AspNetCore.Components.Web;
using Microsoft.AspNetCore.Components.WebAssembly.Hosting;
using Northwind.BlazorWasm.Client;

var builder = WebAssemblyHostBuilder.CreateDefault(args);
builder.RootComponents.Add<App>("#app");
builder.RootComponents.Add<HeadOutlet>("head::after");

builder.Services.AddScoped(sp => new HttpClient
  { BaseAddress = new Uri(builder.HostEnvironment.BaseAddress) });

await builder.Build().RunAsync();
```

4. In the wwwroot folder, open index.html and note the manifest.json and service-worker.js files supporting offline work, and the blazor.webassembly.js script that downloads all the NuGet packages for Blazor WebAssembly, as shown in the following markup:

```html
<!DOCTYPE html>
<html>

<head>
  <meta charset="utf-8" />
  <meta name="viewport" content="width=device-width, initial-scale=1.0, maximum-scale=1.0, user-scalable=no" />
  <title>Northwind.BlazorWasm</title>
  <base href="/" />
  <link href="css/bootstrap/bootstrap.min.css" rel="stylesheet" />
  <link href="css/app.css" rel="stylesheet" />
  <link href="Northwind.BlazorWasm.Client.styles.css" rel="stylesheet" />
  <link href="manifest.json" rel="manifest" />
  <link rel="apple-touch-icon" sizes="512x512" href="icon-512.png" />
  <link rel="apple-touch-icon" sizes="192x192" href="icon-192.png" />
</head>

<body>
  <div id="app">Loading...</div>

  <div id="blazor-error-ui">
    An unhandled error has occurred.
    <a href="" class="reload">Reload</a>
    <a class="dismiss">✖</a>
  </div>
  <script src="_framework/blazor.webassembly.js"></script>
  <script>navigator.serviceWorker.register('service-worker.js');</script>
</body>

</html>
```

5. Note that the following .razor files are identical to those in a Blazor Server project:

- App.razor
- Shared\MainLayout.razor
- Shared\NavMenu.razor
- Shared\SurveyPrompt.razor
- Pages\Counter.razor
- Pages\Index.razor

6. In the `Pages` folder, open `FetchData.razor` and note that the markup is like Blazor Server except for the injected dependency service for making HTTP requests, as shown highlighted in the following partial markup:

```
@page "/fetchdata"
@using Northwind.BlazorWasm.Shared
@inject HttpClient Http

<h1>Weather forecast</h1>

...

@code {
    private WeatherForecast[]? forecasts;

    protected override async Task OnInitializedAsync()
    {
        forecasts = await
          Http.GetFromJsonAsync<WeatherForecast[]>("WeatherForecast");
    }
}
```

7. Start the `Northwind.BlazorWasm.Server` project.

8. Note that the app has the same functionality as before. The Blazor component code is executing inside the browser instead of on the server. The weather service is running on the web server.

9. Close Chrome and shut down the web server.

Building components using Blazor Server

In this section, we will build a component to list, create, and edit customers in the Northwind database. We will build it first for Blazor Server naively, and then refactor it to work with both Blazor Server and Blazor WebAssembly.

Defining and testing a simple component

We will add the new component to the existing Blazor Server project:

1. In the `Northwind.BlazorServer` project (*not* the `Northwind.BlazorWasm.Server` project), in the `Pages` folder, add a new file named `Customers.razor`. In Visual Studio, the project item is named **Razor Component**.

 Good Practice: Component filenames must start with an uppercase letter, or you will have compile errors!

2. Add statements to output a heading for the Customers component and define a code block that defines a property to store the name of a country, as shown in the following markup:

```
<h3>Customers@(string.IsNullOrWhiteSpace(Country) ? " Worldwide" : " in "
+ Country)</h3>

@code {
  [Parameter]
  public string? Country { get; set; }
}
```

3. In the Pages folder, in the Index.razor component, add statements to the bottom of the file to instantiate the Customers component twice, once passing Germany as the country parameter, and once without setting the country, as shown in the following markup:

```
<Customers Country="Germany" />
<Customers />
```

4. Start the Northwind.BlazorServer website project.

5. Start Chrome.

6. Navigate to https://localhost:5001/ and note the Customers components, as shown in *Figure 17.4*:

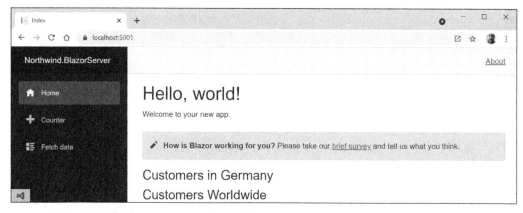

Figure 17.4: The Customers component with the Country parameter set to Germany and not set

7. Close Chrome and shut down the web server.

Making the component a routable page component

It is simple to turn this component into a routable page component with a route parameter for the country:

1. In the Pages folder, in the Customers.razor component, add a statement at the top of the file to register /customers as its route with an optional country route parameter, as shown in the following markup:

```
@page "/customers/{country?}"
```

2. In the Shared folder, open NavMenu.razor and add two list item elements for our routable page component to show customers worldwide and in Germany that both use an icon of people, as shown in the following markup:

```
<div class="nav-item px-3">
  <NavLink class="nav-link" href="customers" Match="NavLinkMatch.All">
    <span class="oi oi-people" aria-hidden="true"></span>
    Customers Worldwide
  </NavLink>
</div>
<div class="nav-item px-3">
  <NavLink class="nav-link" href="customers/Germany">
    <span class="oi oi-people" aria-hidden="true"></span>
    Customers in Germany
  </NavLink>
</div>
```

 We used an icon of people for the customers menu item. You can see the other available icons at the following link: https://iconify.design/icon-sets/oi/

3. Start the website project.

4. Start Chrome.

5. Navigate to https://localhost:5001/.

6. In the left navigation menu, click **Customers in Germany**, and note that the country name is correctly passed to the page component and that the component uses the same shared layout as the other page components, like Index.razor.

7. Close Chrome and shut down the web server.

Getting entities into a component

Now that you have seen the minimum implementation of a component, we can add some useful functionality to it. In this case, we will use the Northwind database context to fetch customers from the database:

1. In Northwind.BlazorServer.csproj, add a reference to the Northwind database context project for either SQL Server or SQLite, as shown in the following markup:

```
<ItemGroup>
  <!-- change Sqlite to SqlServer if you prefer -->
  <ProjectReference Include="..\Northwind.Common.DataContext.Sqlite
\Northwind.Common.DataContext.Sqlite.csproj" />
</ItemGroup>
```

2. Build the `Northwind.BlazorServer` project.

3. In `Program.cs`, import the namespace for working with the Northwind database context, as shown in the following code:

```
using Packt.Shared; // AddNorthwindContext extension method
```

4. In the section that configures services, add a statement to register the Northwind database context in the dependency services collection, as shown in the following code:

```
builder.Services.AddNorthwindContext();
```

5. Open `_Imports.razor` and import namespaces for working with the Northwind entities so that Blazor components that we build do not need to import the namespaces individually, as shown in the following markup:

```
@using Packt.Shared  @* Northwind entities *@
```

> The `_Imports.razor` file only applies to `.razor` files. If you use code-behind `.cs` files to implement component code, then they must have namespaces imported separately or use global usings to implicitly import the namespace.

6. In the `Pages` folder, in `Customers.razor`, add statements to inject the Northwind database context and then use it to output a table of all customers, as shown in the following code:

```
@using Microsoft.EntityFrameworkCore  @* ToListAsync extension method *@
@page "/customers/{country?}"
@inject NorthwindContext db

<h3>Customers @(string.IsNullOrWhiteSpace(Country)
        ? "Worldwide" : "in " + Country)</h3>

@if (customers == null)
{
<p><em>Loading...</em></p>
}
else
{
<table class="table">
  <thead>
    <tr>
      <th>Id</th>
      <th>Company Name</th>
      <th>Address</th>
      <th>Phone</th>
      <th></th>
    </tr>
```

```
      </thead>
      <tbody>
      @foreach (Customer c in customers)
      {
        <tr>
          <td>@c.CustomerId</td>
          <td>@c.CompanyName</td>
          <td>
            @c.Address<br/>
            @c.City<br/>
            @c.PostalCode<br/>
            @c.Country
          </td>
          <td>@c.Phone</td>
          <td>
            <a class="btn btn-info" href="editcustomer/@c.CustomerId">
              <i class="oi oi-pencil"></i></a>
            <a class="btn btn-danger"
               href="deletecustomer/@c.CustomerId">
              <i class="oi oi-trash"></i></a>
          </td>
        </tr>
      }
      </tbody>
    </table>
  }

  @code {
    [Parameter]
    public string? Country { get; set; }

    private IEnumerable<Customer>? customers;

    protected override async Task OnParametersSetAsync()
    {
      if (string.IsNullOrWhiteSpace(Country))
      {
        customers = await db.Customers.ToListAsync();
      }
      else
      {
        customers = await db.Customers
          .Where(c => c.Country == Country).ToListAsync();
      }
    }
  }
```

7. Start the `Northwind.BlazorServer` project website.

8. Start Chrome.

9. Navigate to `https://localhost:5001/`.

10. In the left navigation menu, click **Customers Worldwide**, and note that the table of customers loads from the database and renders in the web page, as shown in *Figure 17.5*:

Figure 17.5: The list of customers worldwide

11. In the left navigation menu, click **Customers in Germany**, and note that the table of customers is filtered to only show German customers.

12. In the browser address bar, change `Germany` to `UK`, and note that the table of customers is filtered to only show UK customers.

13. In the left navigation menu, click **Home**, and note that the customers component also works correctly when used as an embedded component on a page.

14. Click any of the edit or delete buttons and note that they return a message saying `Sorry, there's nothing at this address.` because we have not yet implemented that functionality.

15. Close the browser.

16. Shut down the web server.

Abstracting a service for a Blazor component

Currently, the Blazor component directly calls the Northwind database context to fetch the customers. This works fine in Blazor Server since the component executes on the server. But this component would not work when hosted in Blazor WebAssembly.

We will now create a local dependency service to enable better reuse of the components:

1. In the `Northwind.BlazorServer` project, in the `Data` folder, add a new file named `INorthwindService.cs`. (The Visual Studio project item template is named **Interface**.)

2. Modify its contents to define a contract for a local service that abstracts CRUD operations, as shown in the following code:

```
namespace Packt.Shared;

public interface INorthwindService
{
    Task<List<Customer>> GetCustomersAsync();
    Task<List<Customer>> GetCustomersAsync(string country);
    Task<Customer?> GetCustomerAsync(string id);
    Task<Customer> CreateCustomerAsync(Customer c);
    Task<Customer> UpdateCustomerAsync(Customer c);
    Task DeleteCustomerAsync(string id);
}
```

3. In the `Data` folder, add a new file named `NorthwindService.cs` and modify its contents to implement the `INorthwindService` interface by using the Northwind database context, as shown in the following code:

```
using Microsoft.EntityFrameworkCore;

namespace Packt.Shared;

public class NorthwindService : INorthwindService
{
    private readonly NorthwindContext db;

    public NorthwindService(NorthwindContext db)
    {
        this.db = db;
    }

    public Task<List<Customer>> GetCustomersAsync()
    {
        return db.Customers.ToListAsync();
    }

    public Task<List<Customer>> GetCustomersAsync(string country)
    {
        return db.Customers.Where(c => c.Country == country).ToListAsync();
    }
```

```csharp
        public Task<Customer?> GetCustomerAsync(string id)
        {
          return db.Customers.FirstOrDefaultAsync
            (c => c.CustomerId == id);
        }

        public Task<Customer> CreateCustomerAsync(Customer c)
        {
          db.Customers.Add(c);
          db.SaveChangesAsync();
          return Task.FromResult(c);
        }

        public Task<Customer> UpdateCustomerAsync(Customer c)
        {
          db.Entry(c).State = EntityState.Modified;
          db.SaveChangesAsync();
          return Task.FromResult(c);
        }

        public Task DeleteCustomerAsync(string id)
        {
          Customer? customer = db.Customers.FirstOrDefaultAsync
            (c => c.CustomerId == id).Result;

          if (customer == null)
          {
            return Task.CompletedTask;
          }
          else
          {
            db.Customers.Remove(customer);
            return db.SaveChangesAsync();
          }
        }
      }
    }
```

4. In `Program.cs`, in the section that configures services, add a statement to register `NorthwindService` as a transient service that implements the `INorthwindService` interface, as shown in the following code:

```csharp
    builder.Services.AddTransient<INorthwindService, NorthwindService>();
```

5. In the `Pages` folder, open `Customers.razor` and replace the directive to inject the Northwind database context with a directive to inject the registered Northwind service, as shown in the following code:

```csharp
    @inject INorthwindService service
```

6. Modify the `OnParametersSetAsync` method to call the service, as shown highlighted in the following code:

```
protected override async Task OnParametersSetAsync()
{
  if (string.IsNullOrWhiteSpace(Country))
  {
    customers = await service.GetCustomersAsync();
  }
  else
  {
    customers = await service.GetCustomersAsync(Country);
  }
}
```

7. Start the `Northwind.BlazorServer` website project and confirm that it retains the same functionality as before.

Defining forms using the EditForm component

Microsoft provides ready-made components for building forms. We will use them to provide, create, and edit functionality for customers.

Microsoft provides the `EditForm` component and several form elements such as `InputText` to make it easier to use forms with Blazor.

`EditForm` can have a model set to bind it to an object with properties and event handlers for custom validation, as well as recognizing standard Microsoft validation attributes on the model class, as shown in the following code:

```
<EditForm Model="@customer" OnSubmit="ExtraValidation">
  <DataAnnotationsValidator />
  <ValidationSummary />
  <InputText id="name" @bind-Value="customer.CompanyName" />
  <button type="submit">Submit</button>
</EditForm>

@code {
  private Customer customer = new();

  private void ExtraValidation()
  {
    // perform any extra validation
  }
}
```

As an alternative to a `ValidationSummary` component, you can use the `ValidationMessage` component to show a message next to an individual form element.

Building and using a customer form component

Now we can create a shared component to create or edit a customer:

1. In the Shared folder, create a new file named CustomerDetail.razor. (The Visual Studio project item template is named **Razor Component**.) This component will be reused on multiple page components.

2. Modify its contents to define a form to edit the properties of a customer, as shown in the following code:

```
<EditForm Model="@Customer" OnValidSubmit="@OnValidSubmit">
  <DataAnnotationsValidator />
  <div class="form-group">
    <div>
      <label>Customer Id</label>
      <div>
        <InputText @bind-Value="@Customer.CustomerId" />
        <ValidationMessage For="@(() => Customer.CustomerId)" />
      </div>
    </div>
  </div>
  <div class="form-group ">
    <div>
      <label>Company Name</label>
      <div>
        <InputText @bind-Value="@Customer.CompanyName" />
        <ValidationMessage For="@(() => Customer.CompanyName)" />
      </div>
    </div>
  </div>
  <div class="form-group ">
    <div>
      <label>Address</label>
      <div>
        <InputText @bind-Value="@Customer.Address" />
        <ValidationMessage For="@(() => Customer.Address)" />
      </div>
    </div>
  </div>
  <div class="form-group ">
    <div>
      <label>Country</label>
      <div>
        <InputText @bind-Value="@Customer.Country" />
        <ValidationMessage For="@(() => Customer.Country)" />
```

```
        </div>
      </div>
    </div>
    <button type="submit" class="btn btn-@ButtonStyle">
      @ButtonText
    </button>
  </EditForm>

  @code {
    [Parameter]
    public Customer Customer { get; set; } = null!;

    [Parameter]
    public string ButtonText { get; set; } = "Save Changes";

    [Parameter]
    public string ButtonStyle { get; set; } = "info";

    [Parameter]
    public EventCallback OnValidSubmit { get; set; }
  }
```

3. In the Pages folder, create a new file named CreateCustomer.razor. This will be a routable page component.

4. Modify its contents to use the customer detail component to create a new customer, as shown in the following code:

```
@page "/createcustomer"
@inject INorthwindService service
@inject NavigationManager navigation

<h3>Create Customer</h3>
<CustomerDetail ButtonText="Create Customer"
                Customer="@customer"
                OnValidSubmit="@Create" />

@code {
  private Customer customer = new();

  private async Task Create()
  {
    await service.CreateCustomerAsync(customer);
    navigation.NavigateTo("customers");
  }
}
```

5. In the Pages folder, open the file named `Customers.razor` and after the `<h3>` element, add a `<div>` element with a button to navigate to the `createcustomer` page component, as shown in the following markup:

```
<div class="form-group">
  <a class="btn btn-info" href="createcustomer">
  <i class="oi oi-plus"></i> Create New</a>
</div>
```

6. In the Pages folder, create a new file named `EditCustomer.razor` and modify its contents to use the customer detail component to edit and save changes to an existing customer, as shown in the following code:

```
@page "/editcustomer/{customerid}"
@inject INorthwindService service
@inject NavigationManager navigation

<h3>Edit Customer</h3>
<CustomerDetail ButtonText="Update"
                Customer="@customer"
                OnValidSubmit="@Update" />

@code {
  [Parameter]
  public string CustomerId { get; set; }

  private Customer? customer = new();

  protected async override Task OnParametersSetAsync()
  {
    customer = await service.GetCustomerAsync(CustomerId);
  }

  private async Task Update()
  {
    if (customer is not null)
    {
      await service.UpdateCustomerAsync(customer);
    }
    navigation.NavigateTo("customers");
  }
}
```

7. In the Pages folder, create a new file named `DeleteCustomer.razor` and modify its contents to use the customer detail component to show the customer that is about to be deleted, as shown in the following code:

```
@page "/deletecustomer/{customerid}"
@inject INorthwindService service
```

```
@inject NavigationManager navigation

<h3>Delete Customer</h3>
<div class="alert alert-danger">
  Warning! This action cannot be undone!
</div>
<CustomerDetail ButtonText="Delete Customer"
                ButtonStyle="danger"
                Customer="@customer"
                OnValidSubmit="@Delete" />

@code {
  [Parameter]
  public string CustomerId { get; set; }

  private Customer? customer = new();

  protected async override Task OnParametersSetAsync()
  {
    customer = await service.GetCustomerAsync(CustomerId);
  }

  private async Task Delete()
  {
    if (customer is not null)
    {
      await service.DeleteCustomerAsync(CustomerId);
    }
    navigation.NavigateTo("customers");
  }
}
```

Testing the customer form component

Now we can test the customer form component and how to use it to create, edit, and delete customers:

1. Start the Northwind.BlazorServer website project.
2. Start Chrome.
3. Navigate to https://localhost:5001/.
4. Navigate to **Customers Worldwide** and click the **+ Create New** button.

5. Enter an invalid **Customer Id** like ABCDEF, leave the textbox, and note the validation message, as shown in *Figure 17.6*:

Figure 17.6: Creating a new customer and entering an invalid customer ID

6. Change the **Customer Id** to ABCDE, enter values for the other textboxes, and click the **Create Customer** button.

7. When the list of customers appears, scroll down to the bottom of the page to see the new customer.

8. On the **ABCDE** customer row, click the **Edit** icon button, change the address, click the **Update** button, and note that the customer record has been updated.

9. On the **ABCDE** customer row, click the **Delete** icon button, note the warning, click the **Delete Customer** button, and note that the customer record has been deleted.

10. Close Chrome and shut down the web server.

Building components using Blazor WebAssembly

Now we will reuse the same functionality in the Blazor WebAssembly project so that you can clearly see the key differences.

Since we abstracted the local dependency service in the INorthwindService interface, we will be able to reuse all the components and that interface, as well as the entity model classes. The only part that will need to be rewritten is the implementation of the NorthwindService class. Instead of directly calling the NorthwindContext class, it will call a customer Web API controller on the server side, as shown in *Figure 17.7*:

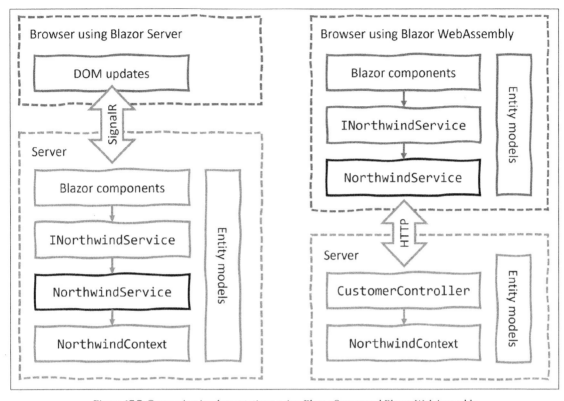

Figure 17.7: Comparing implementations using Blazor Server and Blazor WebAssembly

Configuring the server for Blazor WebAssembly

First, we need a web service that the client app can call to get and manage customers. If you completed *Chapter 16, Building and Consuming Web Services*, then you have a customer service in the Northwind.WebApi service project that you could use. However, to keep this chapter more self-contained, let's build a customer Web API controller in the Northwind.BlazorWasm.Server project:

 Warning! Unlike previous projects, relative path references for shared projects like the entity models and the database are two levels up, for example, "..\..".

1. In the Server project/folder, open Northwind.BlazorWasm.Server.csproj and add statements to reference the Northwind database context project for either SQL Server or SQLite, as shown in the following markup:

```
<ItemGroup>
  <!-- change Sqlite to SqlServer if you prefer -->
  <ProjectReference Include="..\..\Northwind.Common.DataContext.Sqlite
\Northwind.Common.DataContext.Sqlite.csproj" />
</ItemGroup>
```

2. Build the Northwind.BlazorWasm.Server project.

3. In the Server project/folder, open Program.cs and add a statement to import the namespace for working with the Northwind database context, as shown in the following code:

```
using Packt.Shared;
```

4. In the section that configures services, add a statement to register the Northwind database context for either SQL Server or SQLite, as shown in the following code:

```
// if using SQL Server
builder.Services.AddNorthwindContext();

// if using SQLite
builder.Services.AddNorthwindContext(
    relativePath: Path.Combine("..", ".."));
```

5. In the Server project, in the Controllers folder, create a file named CustomersController.cs and add statements to define a Web API controller class with similar CRUD methods as before, as shown in the following code:

```
using Microsoft.AspNetCore.Mvc; // [ApiController], [Route]
using Microsoft.EntityFrameworkCore; // ToListAsync, FirstOrDefaultAsync
using Packt.Shared; // NorthwindContext, Customer

namespace Northwind.BlazorWasm.Server.Controllers;

[ApiController]
[Route("api/[controller]")]
public class CustomersController : ControllerBase
{
    private readonly NorthwindContext db;

    public CustomersController(NorthwindContext db)
    {
        this.db = db;
    }

    [HttpGet]
```

```csharp
public async Task<List<Customer>> GetCustomersAsync()
{
  return await db.Customers.ToListAsync();
}

[HttpGet("in/{country}")] // different path to disambiguate
public async Task<List<Customer>> GetCustomersAsync(string country)
{
  return await db.Customers
    .Where(c => c.Country == country).ToListAsync();
}

[HttpGet("{id}")]
public async Task<Customer?> GetCustomerAsync(string id)
{
  return await db.Customers
    .FirstOrDefaultAsync(c => c.CustomerId == id);
}

[HttpPost]
public async Task<Customer?> CreateCustomerAsync
  (Customer customerToAdd)
{
  Customer? existing = await db.Customers.FirstOrDefaultAsync
    (c => c.CustomerId == customerToAdd.CustomerId);

  if (existing == null)
  {
    db.Customers.Add(customerToAdd);
    int affected = await db.SaveChangesAsync();
    if (affected == 1)
    {
      return customerToAdd;
    }
  }
  return existing;
}

[HttpPut]
public async Task<Customer?> UpdateCustomerAsync(Customer c)
{
  db.Entry(c).State = EntityState.Modified;
  int affected = await db.SaveChangesAsync();
  if (affected == 1)
  {
    return c;
```

```
      }
      return null;
    }


    [HttpDelete("{id}")]
    public async Task<int> DeleteCustomerAsync(string id)
    {
      Customer? c = await db.Customers.FirstOrDefaultAsync
        (c => c.CustomerId == id);

      if (c != null)
      {
        db.Customers.Remove(c);
        int affected = await db.SaveChangesAsync();
        return affected;
      }
      return 0;
    }
  }
}
```

Configuring the client for Blazor WebAssembly

Second, we can reuse the components from the Blazor Server project. Since the components will be identical, we can copy them and only need to make changes to the local implementation of the abstracted Northwind service:

1. In the Client project, open Northwind.BlazorWasm.Client.csproj and add statements to reference the Northwind entity models library project (not the database context project) for either SQL Server or SQLite, as shown in the following markup:

    ```
    <ItemGroup>
      <!-- change Sqlite to SqlServer if you prefer -->
      <ProjectReference Include="..\..\Northwind.Common.EntityModels.Sqlite\
    Northwind.Common.EntityModels.Sqlite.csproj" />
    </ItemGroup>
    ```

2. Build the Northwind.BlazorWasm.Client project.

3. In the Client project, open _Imports.razor and import the Packt.Shared namespace to make the Northwind entity model types available in all Blazor components, as shown in the following code:

    ```
    @using Packt.Shared
    ```

4. In the Client project, in the Shared folder, open NavMenu.razor and add a NavLink element for customers worldwide and in France, as shown in the following markup:

    ```
    <div class="nav-item px-3">
      <NavLink class="nav-link" href="customers" Match="NavLinkMatch.All">
    ```

```
      <span class="oi oi-people" aria-hidden="true"></span>
      Customers Worldwide
    </NavLink>
  </div>
  <div class="nav-item px-3">
    <NavLink class="nav-link" href="customers/France">
      <span class="oi oi-people" aria-hidden="true"></span>
      Customers in France
    </NavLink>
  </div>
```

5. Copy the `CustomerDetail.razor` component from the `Northwind.BlazorServer` project's `Shared` folder to the `Northwind.BlazorWasm Client` project's `Shared` folder.

6. Copy the following routable page components from the `Northwind.BlazorServer` project's `Pages` folder to the `Northwind.BlazorWasm Client` project's `Pages` folder:

   - `CreateCustomer.razor`

   - `Customers.razor`

   - `DeleteCustomer.razor`

   - `EditCustomer.razor`

7. In the `Client` project, create a `Data` folder.

8. Copy the `INorthwindService.cs` file from the `Northwind.BlazorServer` project's `Data` folder into the `Client` project's `Data` folder.

9. In the `Data` folder, add a new file named `NorthwindService.cs`.

10. Modify its contents to implement the `INorthwindService` interface by using an `HttpClient` to call the customers Web API service, as shown in the following code:

```
using System.Net.Http.Json; // GetFromJsonAsync, ReadFromJsonAsync
using Packt.Shared; // Customer

namespace Northwind.BlazorWasm.Client.Data
{
  public class NorthwindService : INorthwindService
  {
    private readonly HttpClient http;

    public NorthwindService(HttpClient http)
    {
      this.http = http;
    }

    public Task<List<Customer>> GetCustomersAsync()
    {
      return http.GetFromJsonAsync
        <List<Customer>>("api/customers");
```

```
        }

        public Task<List<Customer>> GetCustomersAsync(string country)
        {
          return http.GetFromJsonAsync
            <List<Customer>>($"api/customers/in/{country}");
        }

        public Task<Customer> GetCustomerAsync(string id)
        {
          return http.GetFromJsonAsync
            <Customer>($"api/customers/{id}");
        }

        public async Task<Customer>
          CreateCustomerAsync (Customer c)
        {
          HttpResponseMessage response = await
            http.PostAsJsonAsync("api/customers", c);

          return await response.Content
            .ReadFromJsonAsync<Customer>();
        }

        public async Task<Customer> UpdateCustomerAsync(Customer c)
        {
          HttpResponseMessage response = await
            http.PutAsJsonAsync("api/customers", c);

          return await response.Content
            .ReadFromJsonAsync<Customer>();
        }

        public async Task DeleteCustomerAsync(string id)
        {
          HttpResponseMessage response = await
            http.DeleteAsync($"api/customers/{id}");
        }
      }
    }
```

11. In `Program.cs`, import the `Packt.Shared` and `Northwind.BlazorWasm.Client.Data` namespaces.

12. In the section for configuring services, add a statement to register the Northwind dependency service, as shown in the following code:

```
builder.Services.AddTransient<INorthwindService, NorthwindService>();
```

Testing the Blazor WebAssembly components and service

Now we can start the Blazor WebAssembly server hosting project to test if the components work with the abstracted Northwind service that calls the customers Web API service:

1. In the `Server` project/folder, start the `Northwind.BlazorWasm.Server` website project.

2. Start Chrome, show **Developer Tools**, and select the **Network** tab.

3. Navigate to `https://localhost:5001/`. Your port number will be different since it is randomly assigned. View the console output to discover what it is.

4. Select the **Console** tab and note that Blazor WebAssembly has loaded .NET assemblies into the browser cache and that they take about 10 MB of space, as shown in *Figure 17.8*:

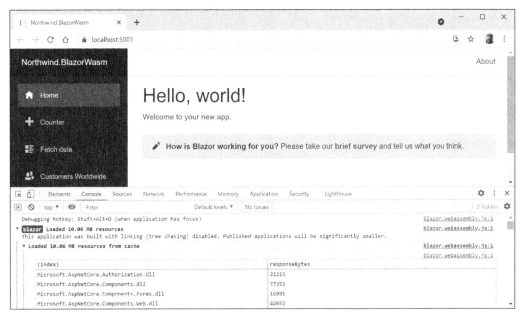

Figure 17.8: Blazor WebAssembly loading .NET assemblies into the browser cache

5. Select the **Network** tab.

6. In the left navigation menu, click **Customers Worldwide** and note the HTTP GET request with the JSON response containing all customers, as shown in *Figure 17.9*:

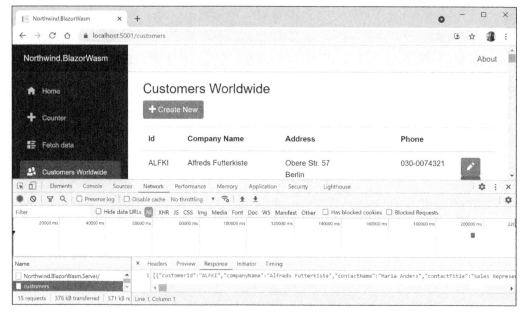

Figure 17.9: The HTTP GET request with the JSON response containing all customers

7. Click the **+ Create New** button, complete the form to add a new customer as before, and note the HTTP POST request made, as shown in *Figure 17.10*:

Figure 17.10: The HTTP POST request for creating a new customer

8. Repeat the steps as before to edit and then delete the newly created customer.

9. Close Chrome and shut down the web server.

Improving Blazor WebAssembly apps

There are common ways to improve Blazor WebAssembly apps. We'll look at some of the most popular ones now.

Enabling Blazor WebAssembly AOT

By default, the .NET runtime used by Blazor WebAssembly is doing IL interpretation using an interpreter written in WebAssembly. Unlike other .NET apps, it does not use a just-in-time (JIT) compiler, so the performance of CPU-intensive workloads is lower than you might hope for.

In .NET 6, Microsoft has added support for **ahead-of-time** (**AOT**) compilation, but you must explicitly opt-in because although it can dramatically improve runtime performance, AOT compilation can take several minutes on small projects like the ones in this book and potentially much longer for larger projects. The size of the compiled app is also larger than without AOT — typically twice the size. The decision to use AOT is therefore based on a balance of increased compile and browser download times, with potentially much faster runtimes.

AOT was the top requested feature in a Microsoft survey, and the lack of AOT was cited as a primary reason why some developers had not yet adopted .NET for developing **single-page applications** (**SPAs**).

Let's install the additional required workload for Blazor AOT named **.NET WebAssembly build tools** and then enable AOT for our Blazor WebAssembly project:

1. In the command prompt or terminal with admin rights, install the Blazor AOT workload, as shown in the following command:

    ```
    dotnet workload install wasm-tools
    ```

2. Note the messages, as shown in the following partial output:

    ```
    ...
    Installing pack Microsoft.NET.Runtime.MonoAOTCompiler.Task version
    6.0.0...
    Installing pack Microsoft.NETCore.App.Runtime.AOT.Cross.browser-wasm
    version 6.0.0...
    Successfully installed workload(s) wasm-tools.
    ```

3. Modify the Northwind.BlazorWasm.Client project file to enable AOT, as shown highlighted in the following markup:

    ```
    <PropertyGroup>
      <TargetFramework>net6.0</TargetFramework>
      <Nullable>enable</Nullable>
      <ImplicitUsings>enable</ImplicitUsings>
      <ServiceWorkerAssetsManifest>service-worker-assets.js
        </ServiceWorkerAssetsManifest>
      <RunAOTCompilation>true</RunAOTCompilation>
    </PropertyGroup>
    ```

4. Publish the Northwind.BlazorWasm.Client project, as shown in the following command:

    ```
    dotnet publish -c Release
    ```

5. Note that 75 assemblies have AOT applied, as shown in the following partial output:

```
    Northwind.BlazorWasm.Client -> C:\Code\PracticalApps\Northwind.
BlazorWasm\Client\bin\Release\net6.0\Northwind.BlazorWasm.Client.dll
    Northwind.BlazorWasm.Client (Blazor output) -> C:\Code\PracticalApps\
Northwind.BlazorWasm\Client\bin\Release\net6.0\wwwroot
    Optimizing assemblies for size, which may change the behavior of the
app. Be sure to test after publishing. See: https://aka.ms/dotnet-illink
    AOT'ing 75 assemblies
    [1/75] Microsoft.Extensions.Caching.Abstractions.dll -> Microsoft.
Extensions.Caching.Abstractions.dll.bc
    ...
    [75/75] Microsoft.EntityFrameworkCore.Sqlite.dll -> Microsoft.
EntityFrameworkCore.Sqlite.dll.bc
    Compiling native assets with emcc. This may take a while ...
    ...
    Linking with emcc. This may take a while ...
    ...
    Optimizing dotnet.wasm ...
    Compressing Blazor WebAssembly publish artifacts. This may take a
while...
```

6. Wait for the process to finish. The process can take around 20 minutes even on a modern multi-core CPU.

7. Navigate to the `Northwind.BlazorWasm\Client\bin\release\net6.0\publish` folder and note the increased size of the download from 10 MB to 112 MB.

Without AOT, the downloaded Blazor WebAssembly app took about 10 MB of space. With AOT, it took about 112 MB. This increase in size will affect a website visitor's experience.

The use of AOT is a balance between slower initial download and faster potential execution. Depending on the specifics of your app, AOT might not be worth it.

Exploring Progressive Web App support

Progressive Web App (PWA) support in Blazor WebAssembly projects means that the web app gains the following benefits:

- It acts as a normal web page until the visitor explicitly decides to progress to a full app experience.

- After the app is installed, launch it from the OS's start menu or desktop.

- It visually appears in its own app window instead of a browser tab.

- It works offline.

- It automatically updates.

Let us see PWA support in action:

1. Start the `Northwind.BlazorWasm.Server` web host project.

2. Navigate to `https://localhost:5001/` or whatever your port number is.

3. In Chrome, in the address bar on the right, click the icon with the tooltip **Install Northwind.BlazorWasm**, as shown in *Figure 17.11*:

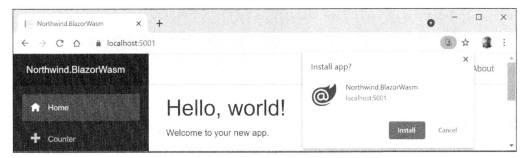

Figure 17.11: Installing Northwind.BlazorWasm as an app

4. Click the **Install** button.

5. Close Chrome. You might also need to close the app if it runs automatically.

6. Launch the **Northwind.BlazorWasm** app from your Windows Start menu or macOS Launchpad and note that it has a full app experience.

7. On the right of the title bar, click the three dots menu and note that you can uninstall the app, but do not do so yet.

8. Navigate to **Developer Tools**. On Windows, press *F12* or *Ctrl + Shift + I*. On macOS, press *Cmd + Shift + I*.

9. Select the **Network** tab and then, in the **Throttling** dropdown, select the **Offline** preset.

10. In the left navigation menu, click **Home** and then click **Customers Worldwide**, and note the failure to load any customers and the error message at the bottom of the app window, as shown in *Figure 17.12*:

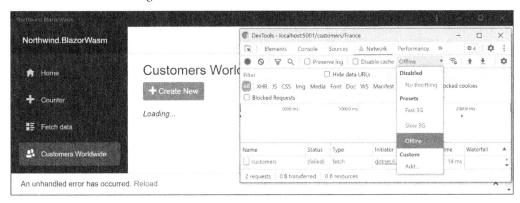

Figure 17.12: Failure to load any customers when the network is offline

11. In **Developer Tools**, set **Throttling** back to **Disabled: No throttling**.

12. Click the **Reload** link in the yellow error bar at the bottom of the app and note that functionality returns.

13. You could now uninstall the PWA app or just close it.

Implementing offline support for PWAs

We could improve the experience by caching HTTP GET responses from the Web API service locally, storing new, modified, or deleted customers locally, and then synchronizing with the server later by making the stored HTTP requests once network connectivity is restored. But that takes a lot of effort to implement well, so it is beyond the scope of this book.

Understanding the browser compatibility analyzer for Blazor WebAssembly

With .NET 6, Microsoft has unified the .NET library for all workloads. However, although in theory, this means that a Blazor WebAssembly app has full access to all .NET APIs, in practice, it runs inside a browser sandbox so there are limitations. If you call an unsupported API, this will throw a PlatformNotSupportedException.

To be forewarned about unsupported APIs, you can add a platform compatibility analyzer that will warn you when your code uses APIs that are not supported by browsers.

Blazor WebAssembly App and **Razor Class Library** project templates automatically enable browser compatibility checks.

To manually activate browser compatibility checks, for example, in a **Class Library** project, add an entry to the project file, as shown in the following markup:

```
<ItemGroup>
  <SupportedPlatform Include="browser" />
</ItemGroup>
```

Microsoft decorates unsupported APIs, as shown in the following code:

```
[UnsupportedOSPlatform("browser")]
public void DoSomethingOutsideTheBrowserSandbox()
{
  ...
}
```

 Good Practice: If you create libraries that should not be used in Blazor WebAssembly apps, then you should decorate your APIs in the same way.

Sharing Blazor components in a class library

We currently have components duplicated in a Blazor Server project and a Blazor WebAssembly project. It would be better to have them defined once in a class library project and reference them from the two other Blazor projects.

Let's create a new Razor class library:

1. Use your preferred code editor to add a new project, as defined in the following list:
    1. Project template: **Razor Class Library** / razorclasslib
    2. Workspace/solution file and folder: PracticalApps
    3. Project file and folder: Northwind.Blazor.Customers
    4. Support pages and views: checked

2. In the Northwind.Blazor.Customers project, add a project reference to the Northwind. Common.EntityModels.Sqlite or SqlServer project.

3. In the Northwind.Blazor.Customers project, add an entry to check browser compatibility, as shown highlighted in the following markup:

```
<Project Sdk="Microsoft.NET.Sdk.Razor">

  <PropertyGroup>
    <TargetFramework>net6.0</TargetFramework>
    <Nullable>enable</Nullable>
    <ImplicitUsings>enable</ImplicitUsings>
    <AddRazorSupportForMvc>true</AddRazorSupportForMvc>
  </PropertyGroup>

  <ItemGroup>
    <FrameworkReference Include="Microsoft.AspNetCore.App" />
  </ItemGroup>

  <ItemGroup>
    <ProjectReference Include="..\Northwind.Common.EntityModels.Sqlite
\Northwind.Common.EntityModels.Sqlite.csproj" />
  </ItemGroup>

  <ItemGroup>
    <SupportedPlatform Include="browser" />
  </ItemGroup>

</Project>
```

4. In the Northwind.BlazorServer project, add a project reference to the Northwind. Blazor.Customers project.

5. Build the Northwind.BlazorServer project.

6. In the `Northwind.Blazor.Customers` project, delete the `Areas` folder and all its contents.

7. Copy the `_Imports.razor` file from the root of the `Northwind.BlazorServer` project to the root of the `Northwind.Blazor.Customers` project.

8. In `_Imports.razor`, delete the two imports for the `Northwind.BlazorServer` namespace and add a statement to import the namespace that will contain our shared Blazor components, as shown in the following code:

   ```
   @using Northwind.Blazor.Customers.Shared
   ```

9. Create three folders named `Data`, `Pages`, and `Shared`.

10. Move `INorthwindService.cs` from the `Northwind.BlazorServer` project's `Data` folder to the `Northwind.Blazor.Customers` project's `Data` folder.

11. Move all the components from the `Northwind.BlazorServer` project's `Shared` folder to the `Northwind.Blazor.Customers` project's `Shared` folder.

12. Move the `CreateCustomer.razor`, `Customers.razor`, `EditCustomer.razor`, and `DeleteCustomer.razor` components from the `Northwind.BlazorServer` project's `Pages` folder to the `Northwind.Blazor.Customers` project's `Pages` folder.

 We will leave the other page components because they have dependencies on the weather service that has not been properly refactored.

13. In the `Northwind.BlazorServer` project, in `_Imports.razor`, remove the `using` statement for `Northwind.BlazorServer.Shared` and add statements to import the page and shared components in the class library, as shown in the following code:

    ```
    @using Northwind.Blazor.Customers.Pages
    @using Northwind.Blazor.Customers.Shared
    ```

14. In the `Northwind.BlazorServer` project, in `App.razor`, add a parameter to tell the `Router` component to scan the additional assembly to set up the routes for the page components in the class library, as shown highlighted in the following code:

    ```
    <Router AppAssembly="@typeof(App).Assembly"
        AdditionalAssemblies="new[] { typeof(Customers).Assembly }">
    ```

 Good Practice: It does not matter which class you specify as long as it is in the external assembly. I chose `Customers` since it is the most important and obvious component class.

15. Start the `Northwind.BlazorServer` project and note that it has the same behavior as before.

Good Practice: You can now reuse the Blazor components in other Blazor Server projects. However, you cannot use that class library in Blazor WebAssembly projects because it has a dependency on the full ASP.NET Core workload. Creating Blazor component libraries that work with both hosting models is beyond the scope of this book.

Interop with JavaScript

By default, Blazor components do not have access to browser capabilities like local storage, geolocation, and media capture, or any JavaScript libraries like React or Vue. If you need to interact with them, you can use JavaScript Interop.

Let's see an example that uses the browser window's alert box and local storage that can persist up to 5 MB of data per visitor indefinitely:

1. In the `Northwind.BlazorServer` project, in the `wwwroot` folder, add a folder named `scripts`.

2. In the `scripts` folder, add a file named `interop.js`.

3. Modify its contents, as shown in the following code:

```
function messageBox(message) {
  window.alert(message);
}

function setColorInStorage() {
  if (typeof (Storage) !== "undefined") {
    localStorage.setItem("color",
      document.getElementById("colorBox").value);
  }
}

function getColorFromStorage() {
  if (typeof (Storage) !== "undefined") {
    document.getElementById("colorBox").value =
      localStorage.getItem("color");
  }
}
```

4. In the `Pages` folder, in `_Layout.cshtml`, after the `script` element that adds Blazor Server support, add a `script` element that references the JavaScript file that you just created, as shown in the following code:

```
<script src="scripts/interop.js"></script>
```

5. In the Pages folder, in Index.razor, delete the two Customers component instances and then add a button and a code block that uses the Blazor JavaScript runtime dependency service to call a JavaScript function, as shown in the following code:

```
<button type="button" class="btn btn-info" @onclick="AlertBrowser">
  Poke the browser</button>

<hr />

<input id="colorBox" />

<button type="button" class="btn btn-info" @onclick="SetColor">
  Set Color</button>

<button type="button" class="btn btn-info" @onclick="GetColor">
  Get Color</button>

@code {
  [Inject]
  public IJSRuntime JSRuntime { get; set; } = null!;

  public async Task AlertBrowser()
  {
    await JSRuntime.InvokeVoidAsync(
      "messageBox", "Blazor poking the browser");
  }

  public async Task SetColor()
  {
    await JSRuntime.InvokeVoidAsync("setColorInStorage");
  }

  public async Task GetColor()
  {
    await JSRuntime.InvokeVoidAsync("getColorFromStorage");
  }
}
```

6. Start the Northwind.BlazorServer project.

7. Start Chrome and navigate to https://localhost:5001/.

8. On the home page, in the textbox, enter red and then click the **Set Color** button.

9. Show **Developer Tools**, select the **Application** tab, expand **Local Storage**, select `https://localhost:5001`, and note the key-value pair `color-red`, as shown in *Figure 17.13*:

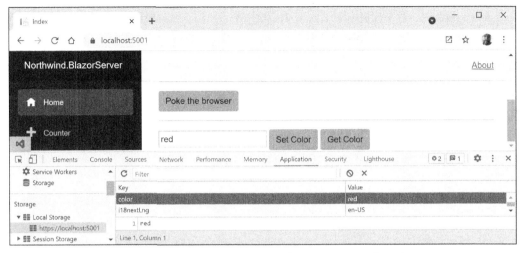

Figure 17.13: Storing a color in browser local storage using JavaScript Interop

10. Close Chrome and shut down the web server.

11. Start the `Northwind.BlazorServer` project.

12. Start Chrome and navigate to `https://localhost:5001/`.

13. On the home page, click the **Get Color** button and note that the value `red` is shown in the textbox, retrieved from local storage between visitor sessions.

14. Close Chrome and shut down the web server.

Libraries of Blazor components

There are many libraries of Blazor components. Paid component libraries are from companies like Telerik, DevExpress, and Syncfusion. Open source Blazor component libraries include the following:

- Radzen Blazor Components: `https://blazor.radzen.com/`
- Awesome Open Source Blazor Projects: `https://awesomeopensource.com/projects/blazor`

Practicing and exploring

Test your knowledge and understanding by answering some questions, get some hands-on practice, and explore this chapter's topics with deeper research.

Exercise 17.1 – Test your knowledge

Answer the following questions:

1. What are the two primary hosting models for Blazor, and how are they different?
2. In a Blazor Server website project, compared to an ASP.NET Core MVC website project, what extra configuration is required in the Startup class?
3. One of the benefits of Blazor is being able to implement client-side components using C# and .NET instead of JavaScript. Does a Blazor component need any JavaScript?
4. In a Blazor project, what does the App.razor file do?
5. What is a benefit of using the <NavLink> component?
6. How can you pass a value into a component?
7. What is a benefit of using the <EditForm> component?
8. How can you execute some statements when parameters are set?
9. How can you execute some statements when a component appears?
10. What are two key differences in the Program class between a Blazor Server and Blazor WebAssembly project?

Exercise 17.2 – Practice by creating a times table component

Create a component that renders a times table based on a parameter named Number and then test your component in two ways.

First, by adding an instance of your component to the Index.razor file, as shown in the following markup:

```
<timestable Number="6" />
```

Second, by entering a path in the browser address bar, as shown in the following link:

```
https://localhost:5001/timestable/6
```

Exercise 17.3 – Practice by creating a country navigation item

Add an action method to the CustomersController class to return a list of country names.

In the shared NavMenu component, call the customer's web service to get the list of country names and loop through them, creating a menu item for each country.

Exercise 17.4 – Explore topics

Use the links on the following page to learn more detail about the topics covered in this chapter:

```
https://github.com/markjprice/cs10dotnet6/blob/main/book-links.md#chapter-17---
building-user-interfaces-using-blazor
```

Summary

In this chapter, you learned how to build Blazor components hosted for both Server and WebAssembly. You saw some of the key differences between the two hosting models, like how data should be managed using dependency services.

Epilogue

I wanted this book to be different from the others on the market. I hope that you found it to be a brisk, fun read, packed with practical hands-on walkthroughs for each topic.

This epilogue contains the following short sections:

- Next steps on your C# and .NET learning journey
- .NET MAUI delayed
- Next edition coming November 2022
- Good luck!

Next steps on your C# and .NET learning journey

For topics that you wanted to learn more about than I had space to include in this book, I hope that the notes, good practice tips, and links in the GitHub repository pointed you in the right direction:

```
https://github.com/markjprice/cs10dotnet6/blob/main/book-links.md
```

Polishing your skills with design guidelines

Now that you have learned the fundamentals of developing using C# and .NET, you are ready to improve the quality of your code by learning more detailed design guidelines.

Back in the early .NET Framework era, Microsoft published a book of good practices in all areas of .NET development. Those recommendations are still very much applicable to modern .NET development.

The following topics are covered:

- Naming Guidelines
- Type Design Guidelines
- Member Design Guidelines
- Designing for Extensibility
- Design Guidelines for Exceptions
- Usage Guidelines
- Common Design Patterns

To make the guidance as easy to follow as possible, the recommendations are simply labeled with the terms **Do**, **Consider**, **Avoid**, and **Do not**.

Microsoft has made excerpts of the book available at the following link:

`https://docs.microsoft.com/en-us/dotnet/standard/design-guidelines/`

I strongly recommend that you review all the guidelines and apply them to your code.

Books to take your learning further

If you are looking for other books from my publisher that cover related subjects, there are many to choose from. I recommend Harrison Ferrone's *Learning C# by Developing Games with Unity 2021* as a fun complement to my book for learning C#.

And there are many books that take C# and .NET further, as shown in *Figure 18.1*:

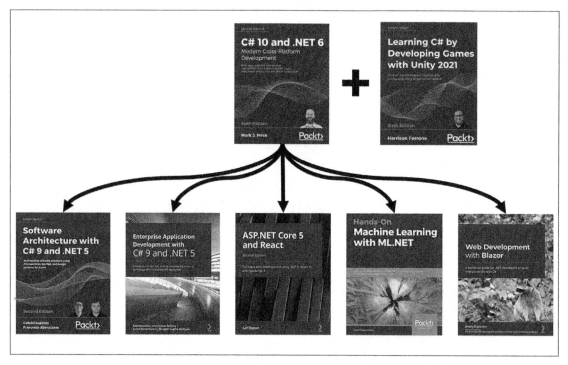

Figure 18.1: Packt books to take your C# and .NET learning further

.NET MAUI delayed

Microsoft planned to release .NET MAUI with .NET 6. But the team realized in September 2021 that they would not be able to meet that target. They need another six months to make sure it meets quality and performance expectations. You can read the official announcement about the .NET MAUI delay at the following link:

```
https://devblogs.microsoft.com/dotnet/update-on-dotnet-maui/
```

I expect that .NET MAUI will have a production release at the Microsoft Build conference in May 2022. Before then, the team will release monthly previews. Although I cannot make promises, I hope to post updates to the .NET MAUI chapter using those previews on the GitHub repository for this book, or at least an update using the final GA release.

Next edition coming November 2022

I have already started work on the seventh edition, which we plan to publish with the release of .NET 7.0 in November 2022. While I do not expect major new features at the level of Blazor or .NET MAUI, I do expect .NET 7.0 to make worthwhile improvements to all aspects of .NET.

If you have suggestions for topics that you would like to see covered or expanded upon, or you spot mistakes that need fixing in the text or code, then please let me know the details via the GitHub repository for this book, found at the following link:

```
https://github.com/markjprice/cs10dotnet6
```

Good luck!

I wish you the best of luck with all your C# and .NET projects!

Share your thoughts

Now you've finished *C# 10 and .NET 6 - Modern Cross-Platform Development, Sixth Edition*, we'd love to hear your thoughts! Scan the QR code below to go straight to the Amazon review page for this book and share your feedback or leave a review on the site that you purchased it from.

https://packt.link/r/1801077363

Your review is important to us and the tech community and will help us make sure we're delivering excellent quality content.

Index

cross-platform development
Visual Studio Code, using for 4
CSS isolation 729
C# standards 51
C# syntax
used, for modifying color scheme 57
culture 362
CultureInfo type
using, in System.Globalization namespace 363-365
custom attributes
creating 358, 359
customer repository
configuring 683, 686
customers
obtaining, as JSON in controller 703-705
C# vocabulary 53, 57, 63-65

D

database
querying 659-661
Data Definition Language (DDL) 421
data repositories
creating, for entities 677
data seeding
with Fluent API 423
data storing, within field
about 184
access modifiers 185
field, defining 184, 185
field values, outputting 186
field values, setting 186
multiple value, storing with enum type 188, 189
·value, storing with enum type 187, 188
data, with EF Core
database contexts, pooling 454
entities, deleting 453, 454
entities, inserting 450-452
entities, updating 452, 453
manipulating 450
date
working with 329
DateOnly 329
dates and times
globalization with 327, 328
types 325
values, specifying 325-327
working with 325
deadlocks
avoiding 528, 529

Debug
instrumenting with 154
debugging
breakpoints, customizing 151-153
code, creating with deliberate bug 144, 145
issues, at development time 144
stepping, through code 150, 151
windows 149
debugging toolbar
navigating with 148, 149
decimal number system 68
default trace listener
writing 154
deferred execution 348, 470, 471
delegates 226
defining 227-229
handling 227-229
used, for calling methods 226, 227
deliberate bug
code, creating with 144, 145
dependency injection (DI) 624
dependent assemblies 278
deserialization 394
desktop apps
building 545
destructor 244
development environment
setting up 2
dictionaries 338, 339
working with 342, 343
display templates
using 659-661
Dispose method
ensuring 246
DNS
working with 352, 353
Don't Repeat Yourself (DRY) 131
do statement
looping with 111
Dotfuscator tool 301
dotnet CLI
used, for compiling code 27
used, for running code 27
dotnet commands
about 289
project, creating 289
dotnet tool
help, obtaining for 39
double-opt-in (DOI) 619

generic collections 190
multiset 478
multi-targeting
  reference link 286
MVC model 637
MVC website project structure
  reviewing 620, 621

N

named method
  targeting 473
named parameter
  passing 201, 202
namespace 278
  class, defining 180
  globally, importing 59, 61
  implicitly, importing 59, 61
  importing 59
  importing, to type 182, 183
  importing, to use types 281
  in assemblies 279
namespace declaration
  simplifying 180
nanoservice 544
native-sized integers 283
nested function 225
nested task 522, 523
NetTopologySuite (NTS) library 275
network resources
  DNS, working with 352
  IP addresses, working with 352
  server, pinging 353, 354
  URIs, working with 352
  working with 351
Newtonsoft
  migrating, to JSON 404
non-generic types
  working with 230, 231
non-.NET Standard libraries
  using 312, 313
non-nullable parameter
  declaring 248-250
non-nullable reference type
  enabling 248
non-nullable variable
  declaring 248-250
non-null reference types 142
non-polymorphic inheritance 257

Northwind database 409
  context class, defining 418, 419, 420
  creating, for Microsoft SQL Server 412
  creating, for SQLite 415
  entity data model, building 553
  managing, with Server Explorer 413
  managing, with SQLiteStudio 415, 416
  web service, creating for 675, 677
Northwind database context
  class library, creating 559-562
  class table, adding to 426, 427
Northwind tables
  used, for building EF Core models 423
Northwind website home page
  weather forecasts, adding to 714-716
NoSQL database 407
NuGet distribution libraries
  packaging 302
NuGet library
  package, publishing to private NuGet feed 307
  package, publishing to public NuGet feed 306
  packaging 304-306
NuGet package 278, 280
  benefits 280
  fix dependencies 303
  referencing 302
NuGet Package Explorer
  about 307
  exploring 307, 308
null
  checking 250, 251
  checking, in method parameter 251
nullable reference type 247, 248
  enabling 248
nullable value type
  calling 246
null values
  working with 246
numbers
  big integers, working with 318, 319
  complex numbers, working with 319
  quaternions 320
  working with 318
numbers explicitly
  casting 114, 115
numbers implicitly
  casting 114, 115

O

object graphs
serializing 394
object-oriented programming (OOP) 177
object-relational mapping (ORM) 408
objects
defining 183
inheriting, from System.Object 184
OData 544
OmniSharp debugger
setting up 144
OOP concept
abstraction 178
aggregation 178
composition 178
encapsulation 178
inheritance 178
polymorphism 178
Open API analyzers
implementing 709
OpenAPI Specification 693
operands 95
operators 95
used, for implementing functionality 223, 224
optional parameter
passing 201, 202
ordered collections 337
ordinal numbers 136
overflow exceptions
throwing, with checked statement 125, 126

P

parallel LINQ (PLINQ)
multiple threads, using 492
parameters
defining, to methods 200
passing, to methods 200-204
simplifying 204
parameter values
naming, with method calling 203
Parse
using, errors 120
partial keyword
used, for splitting classes 205
pattern
matching, with if statement 105
matching, with switch statement 108, 109

pattern matching 142
enhancement, in C# 9 212
with objects 210
performance and memory
monitoring, with Benchmark.NET 512-515
monitoring, with diagnostics 507
personally identifiable information (PII) 701
polymorphic inheritance 257
polymorphism
preventing 257, 258
Portable Class Libraries (PCLs) 284
port numbers
assigning, for projects 569
positional data members
simplifying, in records language 215, 216
postfix operator 97
Postman 690
preemptive multitasking 505
prefix operator 97
preview features
enabling 314, 315
generic mathematics 315
requirement 314
working with 313
problem details
specifying 687
process 505, 506
process string
measuring 510, 511
Process type 508
program debug database file 294
program errors 167
programming language
versus human language 57
Progressive Web App (PWA) 721, 760
exploring 760-762
offline support, implementing 762
projection 480
Project Reunion 550
projects
structuring 550
structuring, in solution/workspace 551
project templates
using 552
properties 63
access control 206
requirement 209

Q

quaternions 320
query
  declaring, with specified type 476
  declaring, with var type 476
query tags
  logging with 443
queues 339
  working with 344, 345, 346

R

ranges
  using 350, 351
Range type
  used, for identifying ranges 350
Razor 640
  versus Blazor 722
Razor class libraries 542, 547
Razor class library
  compact folder, disabling for Visual Studio
    Code 599
  creating 598
  employees feature, implementing with
    EF Core 600-602
  partial view, implementing to single employee 602
  testing 603, 604
  using 598, 603, 604
read-only properties
  defining 206
real numbers
  code, writing to explore number sizes 70, 71
  double types, versus decimal types 71-73
  storing 70
Recorder class
  implementing 508-510
records language
  about 214, 215
  init-only properties 213
  positional data members 215
  working with 213
record struct type
  working with 243
recursion
  reference link 138
  used, for calculating factorials 137-140
reference type 78
  defining 239
  storing, in memory 240, 241

  used, for managing memory 239
reflection 354
  other activities 360
reflection technique 63
ref returns 205
regular expressions
  complex comma-separated string, splitting 333
  digits entered as text, checking 330, 331
  examples 332
  pattern matching 330
  performance improvements 331
  syntax 332
**Relational Database Management System
  (RDBMS) 407**
remote procedure call (RPC) 668
Representational State Transfer (REST) 668
resource
  accessing, from multiple threads 525, 526
resource usage
  monitoring 506
REST Client 690
  used, for making GET requests 690, 691
  used, for making other requests 692, 693
REST Client extension
  used, for testing HTTP requests 690
rounding rules 116
  control, taking of 117

S

sample relational database
  using 409, 410
scalability
  improving, with asynchronous tasks 662
scoped dependency
  reference link 683
Secure Sockets Layer (SSL) 105
security HTTP headers
  adding 710
segments 625
selection statements 103
sequence 468
serialization 394
server
  pinging 353, 354
Server Explorer
  used, for managing Northwind database 413
serve static content
  default files, enabling 585, 586
  folder, creating for static files 584

Printed in Great Britain
by Amazon